Dedication

All four volumes — To the families of all the Americans killed domestically and overseas in terrorist attacks, and U.S. government terrorism analysts, law enforcement agents, and intelligence and military operatives involved in the fight against terrorism at home and abroad over the past 50 years (1968–2018).

Volume I — To my parents, Andrew and Dorothy Pluchinsky.

Foreword

America's war on terrorism did not begin with the epochal September 11, 2001 attacks. As this four-volume analysis of the record and response of every U.S. presidential administration since Dwight D. Eisenhower shows, America has faced threats from — and been fighting — terrorists for more than 60 years. Indeed, since the 1960s, the most consistent feature of international terrorist trends and patterns was the frequency and intensity with which U.S. citizens and interests abroad were regularly targeted by terrorists.

The reasons for this, as Dennis Pluchinsky explains in *Anti-American Terrorism from Eisenhower to Trump: The Record and Response*, are not hard to discern. As the leader of the free world and a global superpower, the U.S. was often blamed for the inequities, injustices, and economic and political stasis afflicting many other places. Further, the vastness of the American diplomatic enterprise meant that there were a plethora of embassies and consulates along with associated cultural centers and information offices as well as a large numbers of diplomats, consular officers, and other U.S. government employees for terrorists to target. The extensive presence of U.S. military bases and personnel on foreign soil, whether the result of treaty obligations, alliance commitments, or for purposes of training and assisting host country armed forces, also presented a huge array of additional opportunities for terrorist attacks. The global reach of American businesses and the geographically diverse investments and operations of U.S.-owned multinational corporations with foreign offices, franchises, and manufacturing thus account for another target category that terrorists found immensely attractive. Ordinary tourists were not spared either, as U.S. citizens traveling on planes, trains, buses, or cars or sightseeing on foot found themselves to be the victims of terrorist attacks. Finally, terrorists understood the unrivaled power of the U.S. media — its extensive television, radio, and print news outlets — and the concomitant opportunity to focus unparalleled attention and publicity on even the most obscure organization and catapult it to prominence. Terrorists accordingly came to believe that an attack on any American target, anywhere — especially if it involved the death, injury, or captivity of citizens — was a proven means to attain fame and notoriety that would likely have otherwise eluded them.

As Mr. Pluchinsky reveals in this magisterial account of the history of anti-American terrorism from 1953 to the present, over 120 different terrorist organizations were responsible for more than 6,000 attacks that claimed the lives of 1,388 Americans. What is often forgotten now, given the paucity of contemporary terrorist attacks on U.S. embassies, consulates, and staff, is that from the late 1960s until the mid-1970s, American diplomats were the most frequent victims of politically motivated kidnappings — accounting for more than one-third of all victims during that period. Seizing embassies, for instance, was also a favored terrorist tactic throughout the 1970s. The most infamous incident, of course, was the 1979 seizure by Iranian students of the U.S. embassy in Tehran, Iran, and the subsequent hostage crisis when 52 American diplomats and citizens were held captive for 444 days.

A pattern had thus emerged in the terrorism incidents covered in volumes one and two of this collection, whereby terrorist takeovers of embassies flowed from the success that terrorists had experienced from the late 1960s onward in hijacking passenger aircraft. But, as airport security improved, passenger screening was introduced, and other protective and defensive measures were adopted, terrorists shifted their attention to this other manifestation of national power and prestige — diplomats and the facilities that they worked in. Then, once embassies and consulates were hardened and made more impervious to terrorist attack and seizure, embassy takeovers declined, but assassinations and kidnappings of individual diplomats went up and bombings of gathering places frequented by Americans overseas increased dramatically.

There are few persons better qualified to tell this story and analyze its many complex and variegated dimensions than Mr. Pluchinsky. For nearly 30 years, he was a senior terrorism analyst in the U.S. Department of State's Office of Intelligence and Threat Analysis. Among his responsibilities were the monitoring of terrorist activity and identification of threats to U.S. citizens and interests across Western Europe, in the former Soviet Union, the Middle East, and Asia. For his work on an inter-agency task force assembled when U.S. Army General James Dozier was kidnapped by terrorists belonging to Italy's Red Brigades in 1981, Mr. Pluchinsky received the Department of State's Meritorious Honor

Award. In 1992 and again 12 years later, he was selected for the prestigious Director of Central Intelligence's Exceptional Intelligence Analyst Program.

As the co-author of two leading books on European left-wing terrorist organizations, both of which were published at the height of their anti-American terrorist campaigns, and the sole author of hundreds of articles, commentaries, and official U.S. analytical products and threat assessments, Mr. Pluchinsky brings to this ambitious undertaking an expertise and pedigree few others possess. *Anti-American Terrorism from Eisenhower to Trump: The Record and Response* will likely stand as the seminal exegesis of how successive U.S. presidential administrations have coped with, responded to, and managed a threat that, as these volumes show, has frustrated and challenged policymakers for decades. Remarkably, Mr. Pluchinsky served in the government, occupying a key counter-terrorism position, for over half of the 17 presidential administrations covered in this collection. These four volumes represent a signal contribution to the literature on terrorism and counter-terrorism. Nothing else exists that is even close to this work in both scope and depth. Analysts of terrorism everywhere are therefore greatly in Mr. Pluchinsky's debt for completing this Herculean task and providing the myriad of fascinating insights, voluminous data, and penetrating analysis contained throughout this work.

Professor Bruce Hoffman
Director of the Center for Security Studies/Professor,
Edmund A. Walsh School of Foreign Service,
Georgetown University, Washington, D.C., USA

About the Author

 **Dennis Pluchinsky** received a BA in Sino-Soviet Studies from Madison College in 1973 and an MA in International Affairs (Russian studies concentration) from George Washington University in 1978. He is the co-author of *Europe's Red Terrorists: The Fighting Communist Organizations* (1992) and *European Terrorism: Today and Tomorrow* (1992).

He was professionally involved in monitoring and analyzing the terrorist threat to U.S. diplomatic and business interests overseas for five of the six decades discussed in these volumes. From January 1977 to January 2005, he was a terrorism analyst in the U.S. Department of State's Bureau of Diplomatic Security Threat Analysis Group/Division. His analytical portfolio involved, at various times, Africa, Western Europe, the Newly Independent States of the former Soviet Union, and al-Qaeda. He was also a supervisor for the Middle East and East Asian regions. He made 21 overseas trips to Western Europe, including Northern Ireland and the Basque region of Spain, the Soviet Union, Russia, Yugoslavia, Turkey, Syria, and the five "Stans" in Asia (Kazakhstan, Kyrgyzstan, Uzbekistan, Turkmenistan, and Tajikistan). All these trips were taken to exchange analytical assessments with the host country law enforcement, security, and intelligence services, and embassy officials.

In 1982, Dennis Pluchinsky received the State Department's Meritorious Honor Award for chairing the Intelligence Sub-Committee of the Dozier Working Group. U.S. Army General James Dozier was kidnapped by Red Brigade terrorists in Italy in 1981. In 1992, Pluchinsky was selected for the Director of Central

Intelligence's (DCI) Exceptional Intelligence Analyst Program. The subject of this one-year research sabbatical was ethnic conflict in Eastern Europe and the former Soviet Union. In 2004, he was again selected for the DCI Exceptional Intelligence Officer Program. The topic of this research project was terrorist surveillance methods, ruses, and disguises. From 1990 to 2016, he taught over 80 semesters of courses on terrorism and counter-terrorism at five universities in the Washington, D.C. area. From 1994 to the present, he has been a contributing editor to the journal, *Studies in Conflict and Terrorism.*

Author's Note

In January 1977, I joined a small, five-person unit in the State Department's Office of Security (SY). It was called the "Threat Analysis Group" or TAG. Its mission was to analyze the terrorist threat to U.S. diplomatic facilities and personnel overseas, U.S. business interests overseas, the Secretary of State, especially when he/she traveled overseas, and to foreign dignitaries below head of state level who visited the U.S. When a foreign dignitary who was not protected by the U.S. Secret Service visited the U.S., SY would provide a protective security detail. Over the years, SY protected members of the British royal family, the Dalai Lama, Nelson Mandela, Salman Rushdie, and foreign ministers from Turkey, Yugoslavia, Israel, and Great Britain. These last four countries faced a terrorist threat in the U.S. from Armenian, Croatian and Serbian, Palestinian, and Irish militants. When new ambassadors were going out to post, our group would brief them on the terrorist threat in that country. TAG analysts therefore had to monitor terrorism in the U.S. and overseas. At the time, TAG was the only specialized terrorism analytical unit in the State Department. Given the small number of analysts, each analyst had regional responsibilities overseas. Over the next 28 years in this unit, I was responsible for Africa, Western Europe, and later the newly independent states of the Soviet Union.

At the time I joined the State Department, terrorism analysis was still in its infancy, both in the U.S. government and academia. There were few courses on terrorism in the universities, and the government had no terrorism analysis training courses for intelligence analysts. There were less than 100 books written on terrorism at the time, and only a few that provided analytical insights. One learned how to analyze terrorism through on-the-job training. Analysts had to develop their personal analytical frameworks and typologies to help them understand this relatively new but growing field. The frameworks and typologies used in this multi-volume work were ones I developed in the late 1970s and have stood the test of time. I have made analytical mistakes where I have underestimated a group's operational capability and threat projection, and overestimated our protective security measures. As a result, I consider myself an expert on terrorism but with the following definition — "an expert is a man who has made all the mistakes which can be made, in a narrow field."[1]

I was also fortunate to work with knowledgeable and very cooperative foreign service officers in the State Department's Office for Combatting Terrorism, which played a leading role in developing coordinated strategies and approaches to counter-terrorism abroad and securing the counter-terrorism cooperation of other countries. The best and the brightest were Gene Bailey, Mike Kraft, and Joe Reap. In addition, I had the privilege of working with, in my opinion, the two most effective ambassadors-at-large for counter-terrorism: Ambassador Robert B. Oakley and Ambassador L. Paul Bremer III. As a result, for 28 years, I observed the anti-American terrorist threat evolve overseas and how the U.S. government responded and attempted to respond to it — the "record" and "response."

Starting in 1990 and continuing until 2016, I had the opportunity to become an adjunct professor at the George Washington University, the George Mason University, the University of Mary Washington, and the James Madison University, where I taught courses on terrorism and counter-terrorism for 80 semesters. In preparing for these courses, I discovered that there was no single work that addressed the threat and response in terms of terrorism in the U.S. and overseas in the post-World War II era. This was the genesis of this multi-volume work. This multi-volume work cannot be the definitive history of post-war, worldwide, anti-American terrorism. Histories are built on the works of others. The historian's ultimate objective is to produce an accurate, detailed, and definitive historical narrative. Each publication is a step taken to reach this goal. It is hoped that this current multi-volume work will advance in some way the understanding of the record and response of the U.S. to the domestic and overseas anti-American terrorist threat that prevailed in the post-World War II period. I express my appreciation and admiration to the following authors for the books they have written on America's experience with domestic and international terrorism at home and abroad. The value of the short histories noted below is that the authors had the opportunity to interview many U.S. government officials who were involved in the construction of U.S. counter-terrorism policy. Many of those officials have

---

[1]Danish Physicist Niels Bohr (1885–1962), http://www.quotationspage.com/quote/1102.html, accessed January 23, 2018.

died or are currently unavailable for interviews. Therefore, these books have a value as historical records as some of the interviews are the only recorded recollections of these participants.

Mark A. Celmer, *Terrorism, U.S. Strategy, and Reagan Policies* (1987); Bob Woodward, *Veil — The Secret Wars of the CIA 1981–1987* (1987); David C. Martin and John Walcott, *Best Laid Plans: The Inside Story of America's War Against Terrorism* (1988); David Tucker, *Skirmishes at the Edge of Empire: The U.S. and International Terrorism* (1997); Jeffrey D. Simon, *The Terrorist Trap: America's Experience with Terrorism* (2001); David C. Wills, *The First War on Terrorism: Counter-Terrorism Policy During the Reagan Administration* (2003); Timothy Naftali, *Blind Spot: The Secret History of American Counterterrorism* (2005); Bryan Burroughs, *Days of Rage: America's Underground, The FBI, and the Forgotten; Age of Revolutionary Violence* (2015); Mike Kraft and Ed Marks, *U.S. Government Counterterrorism: A Guide to Who Does What* (2011); Joseph Wheelan, *Jefferson's War — America's First War on Terrorism 1801–1805* (2003); Teresa Carpenter. *The Miss Stone Affair: America's First Modern Hostage Crisis!* (2003).

My aspirational goal is for this multi-volume work to become a standard reference for future scholars, intelligence analysts, and policymakers on anti-American terrorism at home and abroad in the post-World War II era. At a minimum, it would be viewed as another building block for future historians of terrorism. It is a descriptive and analytic overview and chronicle of anti-American terrorism at home and abroad from the Eisenhower to Trump administrations. It examines the individuals, groups, and states that carried out the attacks and the targets, tactics, and location of these attacks. It explains the motives/objectives for carrying out these attacks and discusses the events and developments that also triggered the attacks. It recounts the U.S. government's counter-terrorism response to the prevailing threat and assesses the success or failure of these measures.

Sources

The primary sources for these volumes are U.S. government documents released on various agencies' websites, such as the CIA's Freedom of Information Act (FOIA) electronic reading room at https://www.cia.gov/library/readingroom/home; the U.S. Department of State's FOIA virtual reading room at https://foia.state.gov/Search/Search.aspx; the FBI's vault at https://vault.fbi.gov/; the National Security Agency's FOIA reading room at https://www.nsa.gov/resources/everyone/foia/reading-room/; and the Defense Intelligence Agency's FOIA reading room at http://www.dia.mil/FOIA/FOIA-Electronic-Reading-Room/.

Future historians or chroniclers will have access to more declassified govern-ment documents and memoirs. I admit that I have not seen all the available rele-vant documents on this issue for each presidential administration. Terrorism was and remains a topic that is highly classified in the U.S. government. Another obstacle is that some government agencies, due to manpower and resource issues and the government's inherent tendency to be overcautious, have been slow in declassifying relevant documents. For example, as of January 2020, the State Department has 52 volumes for the Reagan administration (1981–1989) in its "Foreign Relations of the United States" series. Of those 52 volumes, 48 are being prepared, researched, or are under declassification review. The following key terrorism-relevant volumes for the Reagan administration are currently "under declassification review":

- 1981–1988, Volume XLVII, Part 1, Terrorism, January 1977–May 1985;
- 1981–1988, Volume XLVII, Part 2, Terrorism, June 1985–January 1989;
- 1981–1988, Volume XXIII, Iran-Contra Affair, 1985–1988.

In addition, the FOIA process in government agencies can be grueling and frus-trating. Other obstacles have been that not all key members of the administrations discussed in these volumes have written memoirs that comment on terrorism-related developments and issues; many key players have not yet written their memoirs, and most of them will never do so; and government agencies that have collected internal verbal or written histories have not allowed outside access to them. It is a reality that the longer historians wait to write the history of a subject immersed in classified information, the more accurate the history will be as the researcher would have had more access to declassified material, more recent memoirs, and earlier books on the subject.

Open source materials, especially the *New York Times*, *Chicago Tribune*, *Washington Post*, and *Los Angeles Times*, were used as they reported extensively and accurately on internal and international terrorism in the 1970s and 1980s. Terrorist communiques were also widely quoted as it is important to note the stated motivations for attacks.

It should also be noted that for statistics, presidential terms are defined as starting on January 20 of the inaugural year and ending December 31 of the fourth calendar year before a new administration takes over on the following January 20. Thus, the Carter administration is shown as being from 1977 (January 20)–1980 (December 31).

Unless re-elected for a second term, a first term president is generally a lame duck president for the first nineteen days of the inaugural January.

Acknowledgments

The following friends and colleagues provided comments, guidance, affirmation, and encouragement to me to various degrees and my appreciation extends to Ron Kelly (Former Director of Security for IBM), Dr. Bruce Hoffman, Noel Koch, Louis Andre, Steven Sloan, Mark Kauppi, Ed Mickolus, Aaron Danis, Gary Greco, Andrew Corsun, Lisbeth Renwick, Richard Holm, Magnus Ranstorp, Ariel Merari, Brian Jenkins, Jeff Simon, Ken Duncan, Robert Morris, and Jim Welsh. Aside from myself, only two other people read over 1,000 pages in Volumes I and II – Michael Kraft and my wife Catherine Pluchinsky.

Mike Kraft has been involved in terrorism issues from a variety of perspectives for nearly 40 years as a State Department official, Congressional national security specialist, author, consultant and researcher. He was a senior advisor in the State Department Counterterrorism office and worked on a number of government counterterrorism programs, often with other agencies. During his 19 years in the State Department (1985–2004), his activities included drafting and working with the Justice Department to enact counterterrorism legislation including the Material Support provisions that the Justice Department used to prosecute many cases against persons who provided funding or other forms of support for foreign terrorist groups. Mike also worked on sanctions and budget issues and the State Department's Anti-terrorism Training Assistance programs and inter-agency research and development and public diplomacy programs.

My wife Catherine, a French major and teacher and English minor, examined the manuscript with a jeweler's eye. Her patience, advice, and observations were invaluable. One of the obstacles for any retired government employee writing a book on a subject he/she had responsibility for while in government is the agency clearance process. While horror stories exist, I was very fortunate as the U.S. Department of State's Office of Information Programs and Services and, in particular, Anne Barbaro were expeditious and very cooperative during the clearance process for Volumes I and II.

I also owe a debt of gratitude to Peter Flemming at Vinyard Software. Peter provided many of the statistics used in volumes I and II. He was patient and responsive to my many, many queries for clarification. I was constantly comparing my statistics and those in the U.S. government publications with Vinyard Software.

The author would like to profoundly thank Jennifer Brough, Koe Shi Ying, and Aanand Jayaraman of World Scientific Publishing for their assistance and extreme effort in editing, composition, and art work for this multi-volume work. As a researcher, I am especially grateful to World Scientific for allowing footnotes, rather than endnotes in this multi-volume work.

The opinions and characterizations in these volumes are those of the author and do not necessarily represent those of the U.S. government or any of the above mentioned individuals. The appearance of U.S. government photos or schematic diagrams in these volumes do not imply or constitute U.S. government endorsement. U.S. government photos are in the pubic domain.

The author is solely responsible for the contents of this book.

Contents

Volume I — Acronyms

A6LM	April 6 Liberation Movement (Philippines)
AAA	Argentine Anticommunist Alliance
ALF	Arab Liberation Front
ANO	Abu Nidal Organization
ANYO	Arab Nationalist Youth Organization
ARA	Armenian Revolutionary Army (Turkey)
ASALA	Armenian Secret Army for the Liberation of Armenia (Turkey)
ATA	Anti-Terrorism Assistance (U.S. State Department)
ATC	Autonomous terrorist cell
ATF	Bureau of Alcohol, Tobacco, Firearms, and Explosives (U.S.)
BLA	Black Liberation Army (U.S.)
BPR	Popular Revolutionary Bloc (El Salvador)
BPP	Black Panther Party (U.S.)
BSO	Black September Organization
CAL	Armed Liberation Commandos (Puerto Rican)
CCPC	Critical Collection Problems Committee (CIA/IC)
CCCT	Cabinet Committee to Combat Terrorism (Nixon)
CIA	Central Intelligence Agency (U.S.)
CITD	Counterintelligence and Terrorism Division (U.S. Army)
CMUN	Cuban Mission to the United Nations (U.S.)

CNM	Cuban Nationalist Movement (Cuban exiles)
COINTELPRO	Counter-Intelligence Program (FBI)
CORU	Coordination of United Revolutionary Organizations (Cuban exiles)
CRB	Croatian Revolutionary Brotherhood (aka: OTPOR)
CRP	People's Revolutionary Commandos (Puerto Rican)
CTC	Counter Terrorism Center (CIA)
DA	Direct Action (France)
DCI	Director of Central Intelligence (CIA)
DCM	Deputy Chief of Mission (U.S.)
DDI	Directorate of Intelligence (CIA)
DEV YOL	Revolutionary Way (Turkey)
DEV GENC	Revolutionary Youth Federation (Turkey)
DEV SOL	Revolutionary Left (Turkey)
DFLP	Democratic Front for the Liberation of Palestine
DHKP/C	Revolutionary People's Liberation Party-Front (Turkey)
DINA	Chilean National Intelligence Directorate (as known in the 1970s)
DIA	Defense Intelligence Agency (DIA)
DOD	Department of Defense (U.S.)
DOJ	Department of Justice (U.S.)
DS	Bureau of Diplomatic Security (U.S. State Department)
DSS	Diplomatic Security Service (U.S. State Department)
EAA	Export Administration Act — 1979 (U.S.)
ECT	Executive Committee on Terrorism (Carter administration)
EGP	Guerrilla Army of the Poor (Guatemala)
ELA	Revolutionary Popular Struggle (Greece)
ELF	Eritrean Liberation Front (Ethiopia)
ENG	Electronic news gathering (cameras and video recorders)
EO	Executive Order (Office of the U.S. President)
EOKA	National Organization of Cypriot Fighters (Cyprus)
EPLF	Eritrean People's Liberation Front (Ethiopia)
EPS	Executive Protection Service (U.S. Secret Service)
ERDA	Energy Research and Development Administration

ERP	People's Revolutionary Army (Argentina)
ETA	Basque Homeland and Liberty (Spain)
FAA	Federal Aviation Administration (U.S.)
FAL	Armed Forces of Liberation (El Salvador)
FAR	Rebel Armed Forces (Colombia)
FAR	Rebel Armed Forces (Guatemala)
FALN	Armed Forces of National Liberation (Puerto Rican)
FALN	Armed Forces of National Liberation (Venezuela)
FARC	Revolutionary Armed Forces of Colombia
FARN	Armed Forces of National Resistance (El Salvador)
FARP	Armed Forces of Popular Resistance (Puerto Rican)
FBI	Federal Bureau of Investigation (U.S.)
FCO	Fighting Communist Organization
FER	Federation of Revolutionary Students (Mexico)
FISA	Foreign Intelligence Surveillance Act (U.S.)
FL	Front Line (Italy)
FLNC	National Liberation of the Congo (Congo)
FLNC	Cuban National Liberation Front
FLQ	Quebec Liberation Front (Canada)
FMLN	Farabundo Martí National Liberation Force (El Salvador)
FON	Freedom of Navigation naval exercises (U.S.)
FPMR	Manuel Rodríguez Patriotic Front (Chile)
FPL	Popular Liberation Front (El Salvador)
FRAP	Revolutionary Patriotic Anti-Fascist Front (Spain)
FRC	Fatah Revolutionary Council
FSLN	Sandinista National Liberation Front (Nicaragua)
GAM	Free Aceh Movement (Indonesia)
GARI	International Revolutionary Action Group (France, Spain, and Belgium)
GJB	George Jackson Brigade (U.S.)
GRAPO	First of October/Anti-Fascist Resistance Group (Spain)
HRT	Hostage Rescue Team (FBI)
HPSCI	House Permanent Select Committee on Intelligence

IATA	International Air Transport Association
IC	Intelligence Community (U.S.)
ICAO	International Civil Aviation Organization
ICC	Intelligence Coordination Committee (Carter administration)
IMRO	Internal Macedonian-Adrianople Revolutionary Organization (Macedonia 19th Century to early 20th Century)
INR	Bureau of Intelligence and Research (U.S.)
INSCOM	Intelligence and Security Command (U.S. Army)
IRA	Irish Republican Army (Northern Ireland)
IRT	Islamic Revolutionary Terrorism
ISIS	Islamic State in Iraq and Syria
ITAC	Intelligence and Threat Analysis Center (U.S. Army)
ITERATE	International Terrorism: Attributes of Terrorist Events (name of CIA database)
JCAG	Justice Commandos Against the Armenian Genocide (Turkey)
JCSS	Jaffee Center for Security Studies (Tel Aviv University)
JDL	Jewish Defense League (U.S.)
JRA	Japanese Red Army
JTTF	Joint Terrorism Task Force (U.S.)
KKK	Ku Klux Klan (U.S.)
LARF	Lebanese Armed Revolutionary Faction
LC-23	23rd of September Armed Communist League (Mexico)
LEAA	Law Enforcement Assistance Administration (U.S. Justice Department)
LPB	Libyan People's Bureau (Libyan embassy)
LTTE	Liberation Tigers of Tamil Eelam (Sri Lanka)
M-19	19th of April Movement (Colombia)
MAAG	Military Assistance Advisory Group (U.S.)
Macheteros	Boricua Popular Army (Puerto Rican)

MAP	Armed People's Movement (Puerto Rican)
MEK	People's Mujahedin of Iran (Iran)
MIRA	Armed Revolutionary Independence Movement (Puerto Rican)
M19CO	May 19 Communist Organization (U.S.)
MIR	Movement of the Revolutionary Left (Chile)
MLAPU	Marxist-Leninist Armed Propaganda Unit (Turkey)
MPL-Cinchoneros	People's Liberation Movement-Chinchoneros (Honduras)
MR-8	Movement of the 8th of October (Brazil)
MR-13	Revolutionary Movement 13th November (Guatemala)
MSG	Marine Security Guard (assigned to U.S. diplomatic facilities)
M2J	Movement 2 June (West Germany)
NAACP	National Association for the Advancement for Colored People (U.S.)
NEST	Nuclear Emergency Support Team
NFAC	National Foreign Assessment Center (CIA)
NPA	New People's Army (Philippines)
NSA	National Security Agency
NSC	National Security Council (U.S.)
NSD	National Security Directive (George H.W. Bush administration)
NSR	National Security Review (George H.W. Bush administration)
NSAM	National Security Action Memorandum (Johnson administration)
NSDM	National Security Decision Memorandum (Nixon administration)
NSDD	National Security Decision Directive (Reagan administration)
NSSD	National Security Study Directive (Reagan administration)
NSSM	National Security Study Memorandum (Nixon administration)
NYPD	New York Police Department
NWLF	New World Liberation Front (U.S.)

OAS	Organization of American States
OPR	Office of Political Research (CIA)
ONLF	Ogaden National Liberation Front (Ethiopia)
OPEC	Organization of the Petroleum Exporting Countries
ORPA	Revolutionary Organization of the People in Arms (Guatemala)
OVRP	Organization of Volunteers for the Puerto Rican Revolution
PFOC	Prairie Fire Organizing Committee (U.S.)
PCI	Communist Party of Italy
PD	Presidential Directives (Carter administration)
PL	Public Law
PFI	Popular Frontal Initiative (Greece)
PKK	Kurdistan Workers Party (Turkey)
PLO	Palestine Liberation Organization
PRM	Presidential Review Memorandum (Carter administration)
PSF	Popular Struggle Front
PFLP	Popular Front for the Liberation of Palestine
PFLP-GC	Popular Front for the Liberation of Palestine — General Command
PFLP-SC	Popular Front for the Liberation of Palestine — Special Command
PHOTINT	Photo intelligence
PRTC	Revolutionary Party of the Central American Workers (El Salvador)
PRTC-H	Revolutionary Party of Central American Workers (Honduras)
RAF	Red Army Faction (West Germany; aka: Baader-Meinhof Gang)
RAM	Revolutionary Action Movement (U.S.)
RB	Red Brigades (Italy)
RICO	Racketeer Influenced and Corrupt Organizations Act (U.S.)
RPG-7	Rocket propelled grenade (Soviet)
RNA	Republic of New Afrika (U.S.)

RSO	Regional Security Officer (in charge of security at U.S. diplomatic facilities)
RZ	Revolutionary Cells (West Germany)
RZ	Red Zora (West Germany — female unit of Revolutionary Cells)
SA-7	Surface to air missile (Soviet)
SAVAK	Organization of National Intelligence and Security of the Nation (Iran/Shah's regime)
17N	Revolutionary Organization 17 November (Greece)
SCC	Special Coordination Committee (NSC/Carter administration)
SCLC	Southern Christian Leadership Congress (U.S.)
SDS	Students for the Democratic Society (U.S.)
SEP	Security enhancement program (U.S. State Department)
SIGINT	Signals Intelligence
SLA	Symbionese Liberation Army (U.S.)
SNCC	Student Nonviolent Coordinating Committee (U.S.)
SNIE	Special National Intelligence Estimate
SSCI	Senate Select Committee on Intelligence
SOPO	Serbian Homeland Liberation Movement (U.S.)
SPLC	Southern Poverty Law Center (U.S.)
SY	Office of Security (State Department, pre-DS office)
TAG	Threat Analysis Group (State Department/Diplomatic Security)
TIKKO	Liberation Army of the Workers and Peasants of Turkey
TKP/ML	Communist Party of Turkey/Marxist-Leninist (TKP/ML)
TPLA	Turkish Peoples Liberation Army
TRAC	Terrorist Research and Analytical Center (FBI)
TR	Terrorism Review (CIA)
TSD	Technical Support Directorate (CIA)
UDBA	Yugoslav State Security Administration (name used in 1970s and 1980s)

UFF	United Freedom Front (U.S.)
UNABOM	FBI case designation for Unabomber, from FBI's six-letter naming convention — "UNiversity and Airline BOMber."
USAID	U.S. Agency for International Development
USIS	U.S. Information Service
USSID	United States Signals Intelligence Directives
USC	U.S. Code (official compilation and codification of the general and permanent federal statutes of the U.S.)
Ustashi	Croatian Revolutionary Movement
UVF	Ulster Volunteer Force (Northern Ireland)
VPR	People's Revolutionary Vanguard (Brazil)
WEO	Weather Underground Organization (U.S.)
WGT	Working Group on Terrorism (Nixon)
WGT	Working Group on Terrorism (Carter administration)
WHO	World Health Organization
WITS	Worldwide Incidents Tracking System (CIA database)
WSRIT	Weekly Situation Report on International Terrorism (CIA)
ZANLA	Zimbabwe African National Liberation Army (Rhodesia/now Zimbabwe)
ZIPRA	Zimbabwe People's Revolutionary Army (Rhodesia/now Zimbabwe)

Introduction to Volumes I–IV

If you would understand anything, observe its beginnings and its development.

— Aristotle[1]

In the post-World War II era, political terrorism, in various forms, has frequently posed a major security and political problem for the U.S. government at home and overseas, has caused fear and concern for the American people, and has attracted frequent and extensive media attention. It is important to understand the formation and evolution of this threat in order to more effectively address and mitigate the current and future iterations of this anti-American terrorist threat.

This multi-volume work, based on extensive research as well as the personal knowledge of the author and former colleagues, will chronicle and assess the evolution of anti-American terrorism at home and abroad during the Eisenhower, Kennedy, Johnson, Nixon, Ford, Carter, Reagan, George H.W. Bush, Clinton, George W. Bush, Obama, and Trump administrations. The prevailing terrorist threat during each administration as well as how each administration responded to the threat will be assessed. The bulk of this work will address the terrorist threat from 1968, the generally accepted start of the modern international terrorist threat, to the Trump administration.

In writing these four volumes, the author has two primary goals: (1) to provide a chronicle/reference describing anti-American terrorist activity at home and

---

[1] https://www.goodreads.com/quotes/366890-if-you-would-understand-anything-observe-its-beginning-and-its.

abroad in the post-World War II period; (2) to advance and expand the research repository on anti-American terrorism for future researchers and historians.

Why a Multi-volume Work on Anti-American Terrorism?

International terrorism emerged as a major national and global security development in the post-World War II era. Anti-American terrorism was a significant component in the evolution of this international terrorist threat. To understand the scope of the threat and the responses, the details of the terrorists' activities as well as the broad picture are important. Because there were so many incidents, terrorist groups, and resulting countermeasures, more than one volume is needed to describe the scope and details of the events.

Consider the following:

1. While U.S. interests overseas were periodically targeted by terrorists in the 1950s and early 1960s, it was not until the late 1960s that a more consistent, widespread, and lethal international terrorist threat emerged that would seriously affect the overseas security environment for the West, and especially the United States. No other country in the world has been subjected to the level, lethality, diversity, and geographic scope of international terrorist activity than the United States. Since the beginning of the modern era of international terrorism in 1968, one-third of all international terrorist attacks in the 1970s and 1980s were directed at U.S. interests.[2] Between 1968 and 2017, there have been over 6,000 anti-American attacks overseas. The countries with their overseas interests targeted the most behind America have been Great Britain (1,351), France (962), Israel (500–600), and Turkey (536).[3] The U.S. was targeted three times as much as Great Britain. This

---

[2] Of the 9,729 international terrorist attacks from 1968 to 1989 recorded by the State Department's Office for Combatting Terrorism, 3,455 (35.5%) were directed at U.S. targets. See the statistical section.

[3] Statistics from Vinyard Software's international terror database. Vinyard was founded by Dr. Ed Mickolus and Dr. Calvin Andrus in 1984. Dr. Peter Flemming and Dr. Todd Sandler have also been involved in the company's evolution. Mickolus was one of the first full-time terrorism analysts in the CIA's Office of Political Research. From 1975 to 1979, he developed one of the agency's first unclassified terrorism databases, named ITERATE (International Terrorism Attributes of Terrorist Events). Vinyard Software products include a version of ITERATE text and numeric datasets and Data on Terrorist Suspects (DOTS), at http://vinyardsoftware.com/home.html#1. Statistics on attacks on Israeli and Jewish targets from 1968 to 2016 from Michael Whine and Eran Benedek's research (email to author) which will update Michael Whine's article, "Terrorist Incidents against Jewish Communities

disproportionate gap between the United States and Great Britain underscored the severity of the overseas terrorist threat faced by the U.S.

It has been correctly pointed out that the U.S. was not the number one target of terrorist groups from 1970 to 2004 (Nixon through the George W. Bush administrations), but instead ranked 19th among all countries in terms of total attacks.[4] However, of the other 18 countries, only two — Israel and Turkey — had their overseas interests targeted. As noted above, neither of these countries came close to the number of overseas attacks faced by the U.S. This is a key point. Few experienced terrorism researchers would ever state that the U.S. has been targeted more often by terrorists than any other country. The concern has always been that the U.S. overseas interests were being targeted. There is a qualitative difference in the set of problems presented by an internal terrorist threat (like the ones those 18 countries faced) and those by an overseas terrorist threat (the primary U.S. concern). A country has more influence over its internal threats than overseas where a country has to rely on the will and capabilities of the host country to protect its diplomatic, military, and business interests, and its traveling citizens. An overseas terrorist threat also means that a country has to adhere more to international law and consider international public opinion. Given that a country's overseas interests (military, diplomatic, business, aviation, and government) are spread out over different regions, protecting them all from

---

and Israeli Citizens Abroad 1968–2010," Community Security Trust (U.K.), pp. 3–4, at https://cst.org. uk/docs/CST%20Terrorist%20Incidents%201968%20-%202010.pdf; and (1) "Terrorism Against Israel: Attacks Against Israeli Representatives Abroad (1969–Present)," Jewish virtual library, at https://www.jewishvirtuallibrary.org/attacks-against-israeli-representatives-abroad; (2) Israeli Ministry of Foreign Affairs, at http://www.mfa.gov.il/mfa/foreignpolicy/terrorism/palestinian/pages/ major%20terror%20attacks%20against%20israeli%20embassies%20and.aspx; (3) the Jaffe Center for Strategic Studies at Tel Aviv University 1986 publication "The International Dimension of Palestinian Terrorism," by Ariel Merari and Shlomi Elad; (4) Institute of Jewish Affairs, Research Report #8, Michael May, "Terrorism Against Jewish and Israeli Targets in Europe: 1980–1985," September 1986, 20 pages, in author's possession; and (5) "International Terror: July 1968-July 1986," chart on Terror Attacks Against Israeli and Jewish Targets Abroad, p. 3, Israeli Defense Forces press release June 1986 (mimeograph copy in author's possession). Even if attacks on "Jewish" targets are added to the official Israeli toll, it would not surpass that of the U.S., Great Britain, or France.

[4] Gary LeFree, Sue Ming Yang, and Martha Crenshaw, "Trajections of Terrorism: Attack Patterns of Foreign Groups That Have Targeted the United States, 1970–2004," *Criminology and Public Policy*, Vol. 8, Issue 3, 2009, p. 447. The other 18 countries ranking higher than the U.S. in terms of total terror attacks were: Colombia, Peru, El Salvador, India, Northern Ireland, Spain, Turkey, Pakistan, Sri Lanka, the Philippines, Chile, Guatemala, Israel (excluding the Palestinian territories), Nicaragua, Lebanon, Algeria, South Africa, and Italy.

terrorism is impossible and expensive. While the U.S. faced a serious internal terrorist threat in the 1970s, from the 1980s on, the major security concern and counter-terrorism resource deployment was overseas — to face an international terrorist threat.

2.   Of the two post-war superpowers, the U.S. was the only one that was consistently targeted by international terrorists. The Soviet Union was targeted in 277 attacks from 1968 to 1991(when it dissolved) and 175 attacks from 1992 to 2017 as the Russian Federation.[5]

3.   Anti-American terrorism in the post-World War II period has related to some of the most significant international events and developments of this era:

   • The Israeli–Palestinian Arab Conflict in the Middle East (1948 to the present).
   • Decolonization (1945–1962).
   • The Cold War (1946–1991).
   • The Vietnam War or the Second Indochina War (1955–1975).
   • The 1958 Cuban Revolution.
   • Qaddafi-led military coup in Libya (1969).
   • The Lebanese Civil War (1975–1990).
   • The Anti-Nuclear Movement (1977 to the present).
   • The 1979 Islamic Revolution in Iran.
   • The 1979 Soviet Invasion of Afghanistan.
   • The 1990 Iraqi Invasion of Kuwait.
   • The Emergence of the Internet (1991 to the present).
   • The U.S.'s post-9/11 military incursions into Afghanistan (2001) and Iraq (2003).

These events/developments directly or indirectly triggered anti-American terrorism overseas and terrorist attacks in the U.S. by domestic and foreign spillover terrorists. The latter are attacks by foreign terrorists sent into the U.S. or attacks by sympathetic Americans on U.S. soil to redress foreign grievances. Mostly, however, anti-American terrorism was a by-product of the Israeli–Palestinian Conflict, the Cold War, and the rise of Islamic fundamentalism.

---

[5]Data from Vinyard Software database of international terrorist attacks.

4. From 1968 to 2019, the U.S. has carried out military strikes and incursions against four countries: Libya, Iraq (twice), Afghanistan, and the Sudan. All these operations were carried out because of these countries' support for terrorism against the U.S. Only Israel has carried out more terrorism-provoked military strikes against other countries than the U.S.[6]

The U.S. was a prime target for international terrorists for two main reasons: (1) its political, economic, and cultural DNA and (2) its policies and actions. In other words, the U.S. was targeted due to what it represented and what it did. It supported Israel in its major Middle Eastern conflicts (1967, 1973) with many Arab countries and Palestinians. It backed some right-wing authoritarian regimes in Latin America, the Middle East, and Asia. It was entangled in the most contentious and divisive undeclared military conflict in U.S. history — Vietnam. It was also immersed in the most dangerous global political, economic, propaganda, and military chess game in history with the Soviet Union — the Cold War. Finally, the U.S. was identified by militant Islamic extremists as the primary enemy of Islam, and it engaged in prolonged military conflicts in Afghanistan and Iraq. All these factors combined to put a bull's-eye on U.S. interests overseas for over 120 terrorist groups and insurgent organizations, and the four most active state sponsors of terrorism. The attacks by these terrorism actors caused the deaths of 1,388 Americans from 1968 to 2018 in over 6,000 anti-American terrorist incidents in 64 countries.[7] No country has suffered more of its citizens killed overseas in terrorist-related incidents than the United States.

Most of the anti-American terrorist attacks overseas were carried out by small terrorist groups and larger insurgent organizations using terrorism as a tactic. However, few terrorist groups or insurgent organizations solely targeted U.S. interests. U.S. targets were usually part of a larger targeting effort that also hit other countries' interests. All of the over 6,000 international terrorist attacks against the U.S. interests overseas over the past six decades were carried out by five major terrorist threat strains that have been active worldwide: (1) state-sponsored terrorism, (2) left-wing terrorism (Marxist, Maoist, anarchist variations), (3) secular Palestinian terrorism (Marxist and non-Marxist variations), (4) Islamic revolutionary terrorism (domestic and global jihadist variations), and (5) ethnonational terrorism. The first four directly and consistently targeted U.S. military, diplomatic, government,

---

[6] See also, M.L. Malvesti, "Explaining the United States' Decision to Strike Back at Terrorists," *Terrorism and Political Violence,* Vol. 13, Issue 2, September 2010, pp. 85–106.

[7] Statistical data and data sources consulted for domestic and overseas terrorist incidents can be found in the final section.

aviation, and business interests overseas. It is these four strains that will be examined in detail in this multi-volume work.

During the post-World War II period, the U.S. at home was confronted internally by predominantly domestic left-wing, single-issue (anti-abortion, animal rights, the environment), and right-wing terrorism. The internal threat was compounded by foreign spillover terrorism. The U.S. was a spillover battlefield for Croatian, Serbian, Armenian, Jewish, Iranian, Palestinian, and Islamic terrorists. While the overseas terrorist threat was generated by terrorist groups, insurgent organizations, and states, the internal threat was precipitated by terrorist groups and, increasingly, lone terrorist actors, particularly in the post-9/11 attacks period. The threat from lone wolf terrorists appeared more often in the U.S. than any other country in the world. From 1969 to 2017, there were around 1,500 terrorist attacks in the U.S. and over 3,200 people killed, 3,000 alone killed in the four aerial attacks on September 11, 2001. Few countries in the world can match or exceed that internal terrorist-related death toll.[8]

Despite the larger internal death toll, the general focus of the public, media, Congress, and presidential administrations over the past six decades has been on the overseas terrorist threat. Mid-air bombings of aircraft occurred overseas. Kidnappings took place overseas. Vehicular suicide attacks were carried out overseas. Three U.S. embassies were attacked overseas. A total of 241 U.S. Marines and other servicemen were killed overseas in one attack. Except for the 1995 Oklahoma City bombing and the September 2001 aerial suicide attacks, which turned out to be aberrations but focused more attention on the internal terrorist threat, it has been the overseas terrorist threat that consumed the U.S. government's concern, attention and resources.

The real and perceived terrorist threat inside the U.S. and to U.S. interests overseas forced successive administrations to respond accordingly. The U.S. had no choice but to address these threats. However, it could choose where, when, and how to confront it. Each presidential administration encountered a different form, level, scope, and lethality of the terrorist threat. The development of U.S. counter-terrorism policy and programs from President Nixon through President Trump was an evolutionary not revolutionary process. It was measured, reactive, progressive, generally bipartisan, and usually event-driven.

The U.S. response consisted of a "whole of government approach" — a U.S. counter-terrorism package that was a thousand-piece mosaic composed of legislation, presidential directives, new military units, specialized training courses,

---

[8] Israel, Turkey, India, Sri Lanka, Pakistan, Great Britain (Northern Ireland), Lebanon, Colombia, and Egypt are the other countries with high internal terrorist-related death tolls.

treaties, sanctions, alliances, policies, programs, protective security measures, procedures, communication equipment, information technology software and hardware, personnel, analytical and operational units, research and development, offensive and preemptive counter-terrorism actions, committees, panels, meetings, budget supplementals, travel, contractors, naval maneuvers, drone strikes, bombing runs, cyber defense, counter-propaganda, special prisons, interrogation methods, and research projects. Most resources committed to combatting terrorism were incorporated into a variety of diplomatic, military, legal, and law enforcement programs. As a result, a precise identification and accounting of U.S. government manpower and financial resources devoted to counter-terrorism alone remains difficult to isolate.

In addition to the U.S. government's responses to the terrorist threat at home and abroad, non-government organizations such as universities, institutes, think tanks, and private sector firms also responded to this threat with increased attention, resources, and products. Universities developed courses on terrorism, and some of their academics became specialists on terrorism or corollary fields of study (strategic communications, psychology, sociology, Islam, national security, and country and regional studies, etc.). Institutes and think tanks conducted independent and government-contracted research on terrorism.

Tactically, risk assessment, protective intelligence, and defensive driving companies were formed to cater to the security concerns of the U.S. multinationals with a large and extensive footprint overseas. Armored cars, kidnapping insurance, crisis management, and bodyguard businesses emerged. By the end of the 1980s, terrorism became a "rice bowl" for government agencies, non-government organizations, and private security and risk assessment firms. The dictum "threat drives response" contributed to the development of this "terrorism industry."

The media covered the terrorist threat, and, as a result, shaped the perception of the threat for the American public. Print and broadcast reporters also developed a measure of expertise as they reported from attack sites, developed sources in and outside the U.S. government and in other countries, and acquired more access to terrorists and terrorist leaders for interviews.

Each incoming U.S. president has viewed the terrorism issue differently. Several factors influenced that view:

- Preconceptions of the threat.
- Promises or positions the president enunciated during the campaign as the contender.
- Counter-terrorism failures of the previous administration.
- Views of the president's national security advisor and cabinet members.

- The current threat as presented during initial intelligence briefings.
- Terrorist events that took place during the president's term.
- Congressional and public opinion attitudes, including those of victims' families.
- Other policy priorities.

It was also unusual to find 100% agreement in an administration on counter-terrorism policy, structure, or actions. Each cabinet official and directors of the National Security Council and CIA brought their own worldview, intellectual capability and political prejudices into the administration. Once on board, they also assumed an institutional turf they had to protect. Moreover, there were career government experts who had more experience and institutional memory than political appointees. There was always a churning process on policy priorities that occurred during the first year of an incoming administration. All administrations were compelled to act as a result of a traumatic terrorist-related development or event(s), that is, an incident that created extraordinary pressure on an administration by Congress, the media, or the public to address the incident or problem. For Nixon, it was the anti-Vietnam war protests and corollary domestic terrorism. For Carter, it was the Iran hostage dilemma that also signaled the birth of the Islamic revolutionary terrorist strain. For Reagan, it was the Islamic revolutionary terrorist threat in Lebanon, exemplified by the three suicide attacks against U.S. diplomatic and military interests, and the kidnapping of 18 Americans there, and the mercurial Qaddafi-led Libya. For George H.W. Bush, it was the Gulf War and the potential for retaliatory terrorism directed at the U.S. For Clinton, it was the Oklahoma City bombing, the al-Qaeda attacks on the U.S. embassies in Nairobi, Kenya and Dar-es-Salaam, Tanzania, and the USS Cole in the port of Aden, Yemen. For George W. Bush, it was the 9/11 attacks — the most seminal terrorist attack in U.S. history. President Obama faced an ISIS threat overseas and a series of lone wolf terrorist attacks in the U.S. inspired by the ISIS and al-Qaeda use of the Internet.

As of December 2019, the Trump administration has not been inflicted with a terrorist attack at home or abroad against U.S. interests that could be assessed as being traumatic as those that occurred in the past, although there were mass shootings in the U.S. Most were not politically inspired terrorism.

Organizational Structure of Each Volume

In retrospect, the U.S. faced four phases of the international terrorist threat. The first took place during the administration of Richard M. Nixon. This phase was marked by the commencement of international terrorism as a national security problem that required a government counter-terrorism structure, increased protective security measures overseas, and the development of a rudimentary policy to tackle this issue. The second and even more dangerous phase took place while Ronald Reagan was president. This phase was denoted by the introduction of two new anti-American threat strains: state-sponsored and Islamic revolutionary terrorism. The emergence of suicide as a tactical ingredient also occurred during this phase. The third phase emerged during Bill Clinton's presidency. This phase saw the advent of the first multinational terrorist group in history, al-Qaeda, which recruited globally; advocated the use of chemical, biological, radiological, and nuclear weapons; promoted suicide operations; and confronted the U.S. on a global battlefield. During the fourth phase when Barack Obama was president, the U.S. and the world coped with the Islamic State in Iraq and Syria (ISIS) — the first Islamic revolutionary terrorist organization to carve out a large territorial base in the Middle East. ISIS promoted and expanded suicide operations, beheadings, and an online inspirational and incitement program that fostered global jihadist leaderless terrorism in various countries.

Each volume will focus on one of these four phases of the international terrorist threat:

- Volume I will address the Eisenhower through Carter administrations and phase one of the international terrorist threat.
- Volume II will survey the Reagan and George H.W. Bush administrations and phase two of the international terrorist threat.
- Volume III will examine the Clinton and George W. Bush administrations and phase three of the threat.
- Volume IV will address the Obama and Trump administrations and phase four of the threat.

This multi-volume work utilizes the presidential administration as its primary unit of analysis because the character, mindset, worldview, and priorities of each president combined to significantly shape how the administration would respond to the perceived prevailing terrorist threat. The mindset and worldview of members of the national security team selected by each president also affected the construction of the U.S. government's assessment and reaction to the terrorist threat. However, it was the president who ultimately directed and influenced the final response either by his action or inaction.

In each volume, one or more chapters may be devoted to a presidential administration depending on the following: (1) the number of terms, (2) the level and scope of anti-American terrorist activity at home and abroad, (3) the quantity and extent of the administration's counter-terrorism response, and (4) the number and pace of developments in the field of terrorism in academia, the private sector, think tanks, media, and institutes. These four factors also apply to the number and length of sub-topics. Therefore, there will be an uneven, or eclectic topical approach to analyzing each administration.

The examination of each administration will contain three major sections: the record, the response, and the field of terrorism. The "Record" section will assess the internal and overseas terrorist threat for the U.S. The internal threat is composed of domestic and foreign spillover terrorist activity. The internal threat will be evaluated by applying an analytical framework that breaks down terrorist activity in the U.S. according to the type of group or terrorist entity: left-wing, right-wing, single-issue, ethnonational, secular Palestinian, state-sponsored, and Islamic revolutionary terrorism. The motivations, tactics, targets, locations, and the impact of terrorist attacks by these groups will be analyzed. The manifestation of lone wolf terrorism in the U.S. will also be addressed as it was unique to the U.S. and increased over the decades. The overseas terrorist threat to U.S. interests will be considered by identifying the most active regions and noting the motivations (quotes from terrorism communiques), tactics, targets, locations, impact, level, and scope of each of the four major anti-American terrorist strains overseas: left-wing, secular Palestinian, state-sponsored, and Islamic revolutionary. Right-wing and ethnonational terrorism will also be addressed when applicable.

The "Response" section will examine each administration's response to the perceived and real terrorist threats at home and abroad. Counter-terrorism policy, organizational structure, responsibilities, policies, legislation, executive orders, presidential directives and findings, counter-terrorism programs, resources, operations, and counter-terrorism successes and failures will be documented and assessed.

The final section will assess the development of the "field of terrorism" in the government, academia, think tanks and institutes, and the private sector. Political terrorism and counter-terrorism became, in effect, an industry that nourished government agencies, think tanks, universities, institutes, risk assessment companies, and private security firms with money, positions, notoriety, and influence.

Each volume will include appendices that will note by administration the number of international terrorist attacks, anti-American terrorist attacks, and Americans killed in overseas incidents. The number of internal terrorist attacks and people killed in these attacks in the U.S. will also be listed.

The goal of this multi-volume work is to advance the chronicling and understanding of how internal terrorism and anti-American terrorism overseas and the U.S. government responses evolved from the Nixon to the Trump administrations. Although experts might differ on what has been included or left out of these volumes, the author would remind the reader of what Robert Wilson Lynd has stated — "the art of writing history is the art of emphasizing the significant facts at the expense of the insignificant. And it is the same in every field of knowledge. Knowledge is power only if a man knows what facts not to bother about."[9]

Definitions, Analytical Frameworks, Statistical Sources

The study of political terrorism is complicated by the absence of a general agreement in academia and the U.S. and other governments on the definitions of terrorism and state-sponsored terrorism, typologies of terrorist groups, and the most appropriate statistics on terrorism. In this multi-volume chronicle, the author used the following terms, frameworks, and statistics in writing this chronicle of anti-American terrorism at home and abroad.

Definitions

Anti-Americanism — This term refers to "any hostile action or expression that becomes part and parcel of an undifferentiated attack on the foreign policy, society, culture and values of the United States."[10]

Anti-American Sentiment — This "is dislike, fear, or hostility toward the United States or the American people and their culture, business practices and technology, or the policies of their government, especially the foreign policy practices of the United States. Common contemporary negative stereotypes of Americans include the assertions that Americans are aggressive, arrogant, ignorant, overweight, poorly dressed, obsessed with making money, too moralistic, too materialistic, liberated and obnoxious. Other criticisms originate from a perception that the United States military acts as 'the world's policeman'".[11]

---

[9] https://www.azquotes.com/author/9163-Robert_Wilson_Lynd.

[10] Alvin Rubinstein and Donald Smith, "Anti-Americanism in the Third World," Annals (AAPSS), vol. 497, May 1988, p. 35.

[11] https://en.wikipedia.org/wiki/Anti-Americanism. Accessed January 13, 2017.

Terrorism — The U.S. Department of State definition of terrorism is based on Section 2656f(d) of Title 22, United States Code: "premeditated, politically motivated violence perpetrated against non-combatant targets by subnational groups or clandestine agents." The FBI defines terrorism as "the unlawful use of force or violence against persons or property to intimidate or coerce a government, the civilian population, or any segment thereof, in furtherance of political or social objectives." The Department of Defense definition of terrorism is "the calculated use of unlawful violence or threat of unlawful violence to inculcate fear; intended to coerce or to intimidate governments or societies in the pursuit of goals that are generally political, religious, or ideological."[12] The reader can find that countless articles, book chapters, and books have been written that address the problems of defining terrorism.[13] Since there is no right or generally accepted definition of terrorism, this multi-volume work will use the U.S. Department of State definition of terrorism as it is an acceptable "working" definition of terrorism.

Anti-American Terrorism — This term refers to the political terrorist activity carried out by states, sub-national groups, or individuals against U.S. interests (military, diplomatic, business, aviation, tourist, private citizens) at home or abroad.

Internal Terrorism — This term refers to all terrorist activity on U.S. soil, including the combination of domestic terrorism, foreign spillover terrorism, and foreign incursion terrorist activities.

Domestic Terrorism — This term refers to the political terrorist activity carried out in the U.S. by individuals and/or groups inspired by or associated with primarily U.S.-based grievances and movements that espouse extremist ideologies of a political, religious, social, racial, or environmental nature.[14]

Foreign Spillover Terrorism — This term refers to the political terrorist activity carried out in the U.S. by foreign terrorists or sympathetic American

---

[12] https://www.state.gov/j/ct/rls/crt/2017/282851.htm; http://www.fbi.gov/about-us/investigate/terrorism/terrorism-definition; and http://usacac.army.mil/cac2/call/thesaurus/toc.asp?id=29533. Accessed February 6, 2017.

[13] See, for example, Bruce Hoffman. *Inside Terrorism* (New York: Columbia University Press, 2006), pp. 1–41. This is the best discussion of the problems in defining terrorism and contains one of the best academic-proposed definitions of terrorism.

[14] https://www.fbi.gov/investigate/terrorism. Accessed February 6, 2017.

citizens against foreign interests because of foreign grievances/issues/events/ events/developments. For example, Palestinian terrorists coming into the U.S. to attack Israeli targets or Armenian Americans carrying out an attack on a Turkish target in the U.S. on behalf of Armenian terrorist organizations. U.S. targets inside the U.S. are not directly attacked by foreign spillover terrorism.

Foreign Incursion Terrorism — This term refers to the political terrorist activity carried out in the U.S. against U.S. targets by foreign terrorists or American citizens inspired or directed by foreign terrorist organizations or movements, for example, Al-Qaeda's attacks on September 11, 2001, the 2013 Boston Marathon bombings or the 2009 Ft. Hood shootings.

Anti-American Terrorism Overseas — This term refers to the political terrorist activity carried out by domestic or foreign terrorists in other countries against U.S. interests overseas, for example, German terrorists attacking U.S. military bases and personnel in Germany; Palestinian, Iranian, Lebanese terrorists attacking U.S. targets in Germany.

International Terrorism — This term refers to the political terrorist activity involving the citizens or territory of more than one country.

Threat Analysis — This involves a continual process of compiling and examining all available information concerning potential terrorist activities by terrorist groups which could target a facility or person. A threat analysis will review the factors of a terrorist group's existence, capability, intentions, history, and targeting, as well as the security environment within which friendly forces operate. Threat analysis is an essential step in identifying the probability of a terrorist attack and results in a threat assessment. Threat drives response. The more accurate the threat assessment, the more effective the response will be. Overestimating the terrorist threat will result in the application of excessive protective security measures. Under-estimating the terrorist threat will increase the exposure of U.S. targets to a terrorist attack.

Anti-terrorism — This term describes the efforts to prevent, dissuade or deter terrorist attacks and to diminish their adverse effects when they do occur. Anti-terrorism is defensive in nature and relies heavily on the intelligence function. Typical anti-terrorism activities are focused on instilling vigilance, identifying threats, hardening potential targets, forecasting probable attacks and neutralizing harmful effects.[15]

Counter-terrorism — This term is used to describe the efforts used to counteract terrorists and actively thwart terrorist attacks. Accordingly, counter-terrorism is offensive in nature and relies heavily on the operations function. Typical counter-terrorism efforts are focused on identifying and capturing terrorists and/or actively defending a target from attack.[16] For the purposes of this four-volume work, the term "counter-terrorism" will include both anti-terrorism and counter-terrorism measures.

Analytical Frameworks

Political terrorism in the post-World War II era has appeared in five manifestations:

- The urban terrorist group.
- The rural insurgent organization's terrorist arm.
- State-sponsored terrorism by a state's intelligence service or through surrogates.
- Lone wolf terrorists.
- Autonomous terrorist cell.

The differences between a rural insurgent organization and an urban terrorist group are as follows:

- A rural-based insurgent group focuses its operations in rural areas where it can develop hidden bases, training camps, and safe havens. They generally have over 1,000 operatives and either control or have significant influence over territory. They have a military structure and wear some type of military uniform. Terrorism is only a tactic for the insurgent group and is used more often in urban areas. Insurgent groups will directly confront military forces. Insurgent organizations usually establish a special unit tasked to engage in urban terrorism in the capital and other major cities.

---

[15] http://fieldcommandllc.com/anti-terrorism-vs-counter-terrorism-tactical-edge-summer-2011-pp-68-70/. Accessed February 21, 2017.
[16] Ibid.

- An urban terrorist group carries out most of its attacks in cities, most often capitals and major secondary cities. They do not have a central base. The organization is spread out in safehouses in apartments and houses. They generally have less than 250 people who are contained in various functional cells deployed in several cities. They do not control or have significant influence over territory. They wear no uniforms. For these groups, terrorism is a strategy. Attacks are relatively infrequent, and they avoid direct clashes with military forces.

The above five manifestations can be further divided into two major categories of terrorist activity:

Organizational or Command Terrorism — This term refers to the political terrorist activity carried out by an individual or sub-unit that is directed or coordinated by a recognized command structure of a larger, parent terrorist organization or state intelligence service. The urban terrorist group, the rural insurgent organization's terrorist arm, and state-sponsored terrorism compose this category.

Leaderless Terrorism — This term refers to the political terrorist activity carried out by an individual or small cell of like-minded individuals who are not under the direct command and control of a larger, parent terrorist organization. It is primarily a manifestation of a violent arm of a social/political movement. It consists of lone wolf terrorists and autonomous terrorist cells or ATCs. A lone wolf terrorist is defined as an individual who does not belong to any organized terrorist group and carries out a terrorist attack for political, religious, or social objectives. They have been primarily males and are often driven by personal conscience or political grievance. The individual can carry out a single attack or a series (campaign) of terrorist attacks. All terrorism-related functions and actions are carried out by the individual without outside aid. An autonomous terrorist cell (ATC) is defined as two or more individuals with a similar grievance and mindset who decide to engage in political terrorist activity but do not belong to or are not under the direct command and control of a larger parent terrorist organization. All tasks, functions, and acquisitions are carried out primarily by this self-recruited, self-organized, and self-directed cell. They take their targeting, tactical, and timing cues from hints, guidance, messages, and exhortations that appear on the grievance-related common propaganda organ(s) of the militant arms of social/political movements. ATCs deduce their mission, they do not receive orders. ATCs are usually associated with a broader social/political/religious movement that has a stated grievance, an identified enemy, and a proposed solution.

A political, social, or religious movement is defined as a collection of disparate individuals and groups who have accepted the movement's common grievance, agreed on the sources or protagonists of the grievance, and engage in a lightly coordinated effort to redress this grievance — either through peaceful or violent means. Most movements have an informal "common propaganda organ(s)" — a web site, a magazine, radio station, newsletter, or journal that propagates the grievance of a movement. It acts as a central forum for debate, discussion, and lessons learned and is the repository of the movement's activities. It is run and maintained by an activist cadre within the relevant movement. It transmits the messages, instructions, and analyses of the movement's guides, strategists, and interpreters. A movement emerges, it is not created. The appearance of any movement is an informal and gradual process. A movement cannot be monolithic as there is no central leadership to impose uniformity or discipline heresy. Anyone can become an adherent of the movement simply by accepting the movement's mind-set and program. A movement has no detailed plan, which would require some type of central leadership to develop it. A movement operates on generalities and broad goals. It is essentially the ad hoc spreading of a grievance to a scattered collective of receptive individuals. Individuals in the movement can rise to various degrees of influence and notoriety by riding on the movement's common propaganda organs, thereby acquiring more and more readers and supporters. This attraction of followers translates into authority within the movement. Since a movement has no leaders per se, structure, headquarters, membership list, operational code, or oaths of loyalty, a movement cannot be measured for the level of influence, number of adherents, and what measure of success it has had. Movements are not defeated, they are eroded, mostly by internal as opposed to external developments. This four-volume work will be examining the anti-abortion movement, anti-nuclear movement, animal rights movement, environmental movement, anarchist movement, the Islamic revival movement, the Global jihadist movement, and the anti-Vietnam War movement.

Key Typology

This work will examine the anti-American terrorist threat at home and abroad by analyzing the activity of four distinct, major anti-American terrorist strains over 12 U.S. presidential administrations:

(1) The left-wing terrorist strain (composed of Marxist, Maoist, and anarchist militants).

(2) The state-sponsored terrorist strain.

(3) The secular Palestinian terrorist strain.

(4) The Islamic revolutionary terrorist strain.

Two additional terrorism strains — ethnonational and right-wing — will also be surveyed, although these strains rarely focus on targeting U.S. interests overseas. Due to the operational area and tactics of ethnonational terrorist organizations and their terrorist activities, especially in the capitals and other major cities, these groups pose an indirect threat to U.S. citizens transiting, visiting, living, or working in these cities. In the 1970s and 1980s, ethnic terrorist and insurgent groups were responsible for the deaths of 17 Americans, mostly in Africa and Asia. Many of these deaths were incidental, due to Americans being in the wrong place at the wrong time. Right-wing terrorism has caused periodic problems for U.S. interests overseas, mostly in Latin America, particularly in El Salvador and Guatemala, in the 1980s. Of the 13 Americans killed in right-wing attacks in the 1980s, 12 were killed in these two countries. Right-wing groups in Latin America directly targeted Americans as a response to the U.S. policy that was critical of right-wing dictatorships in Latin America and interference in internal politics. One American was accidentally killed in the 1980s when the right-wing, loyalist, paramilitary terrorist group Ulster Volunteer Force (UVF) attacked a pub in County Tyre in Northern Ireland on November 30, 1989. The ethnonational and right-wing terrorist strains were more security irritants than major security threats to U.S. overseas interests in the 1970s and 1980s.

All six of the above terrorist strains were composed of either terrorist groups, insurgent organizations, or state sponsors of terrorism. This anti-American terrorist threat overseas in the post-World War II period primarily took the form of command or organizational terrorism. In the U.S., organizational terrorism was the primary manifestation of the terrorist threat in the 1970s and 1980s. Beginning in the mid-1990s, it would shift to leaderless terrorism by lone wolf terrorists.

(1) *Left-Wing Terrorist Strain*

The left-wing terrorist strain is composed of Marxist, Maoist, and anarchist terrorists, terrorist groups, and insurgent organizations whose objective is the overthrow of democratic and democratic-oriented governments. It also includes anarchist elements that shun formal organizations and instead operate under the concept of leaderless terrorism. Marxist/Maoist terrorist groups have emerged predominantly in Western Europe and Latin America. In Europe, these groups were byproducts of the social, new left, anti-Vietnam War, and student protest movements of the 1960s, especially in Germany, France, Italy, Great Britain, Belgium, and the Netherlands. Militant leftists assessed that civil protests and demonstrations were ineffective and that armed struggle was necessary. This growing militancy took place in parallel to the increased U.S. involvement in Vietnam during the 1960s. In Latin America, Marxist/Maoist terrorist groups and insurgent organizations surfaced during the 1960s as Cuba exported its revolutionary principles, agents, and programs into the region which contained many right-wing dictatorships that failed to address the growing gap between the rich and poor. This created a fertile environment for Marxist and Maoist revolutionaries. The primary driver for most of these Latin American groups was a desire to reorganize society along socialist lines, remove foreign business interests and redistribute land and wealth. The Marxist/Maoist terrorist groups that emerged in Western Europe were small, urban terrorist organizations. In Latin America, larger, rural-based Marxist/Maoist insurgencies also surfaced. This left-wing terrorist strain began to weaken in the late 1980s as communist regimes in the Soviet Union and Eastern Europe imploded or fragmented. This development eventually forced Cuba to reduce its logistical support to Latin American left-wing terrorist groups and insurgent organizations as it was no longer receiving military, financial, and economic subsidies from the Soviet Union to replenish or supplement Cuba's revolutionary aid to the region.

The left-wing terrorist strain has carried out more terrorist attacks against U.S. interests overseas than any of the other three anti-American terrorist strains. However, due to its tendency to engage in primarily discriminate tactics, it has caused fewer U.S. fatalities. This strain targeted U.S. interests due to the ideological makeup of these groups. The core elements of the ideological platform of these groups, organizations, and individuals that make up this strain are anti-capitalism, anti-fascism, and anti-imperialism. The United States is seen as the primary representative of these elements. The left-wing strain is also anti-Israel, therefore, U.S. support for Israel was another grievance for this strain. Other issues that aggravated this strain were as follows: (1) U.S. involvement in Vietnam, (2) the stationing of U.S. military personnel in Western European countries, Japan, and the Philippines, (3) the deployment of Pershing II and Cruise missiles in Western Europe, (4) U.S. support for various dictatorships in Latin America, and (5) U.S. conflict with the Soviet Union, North Vietnam, and Communist China.

The anarchist component of this strain has also engaged in anti-American terrorist activity overseas, but not to the level and extent of the Marxist and Maoist terrorist groups and insurgent organizations. Anarchist terrorist activity is found primarily in Western Europe and Latin America. The anarchist terrorist activity aimed at U.S. interests overseas has consisted primarily of property damage attacks on U.S. banks, multinationals, and diplomatic facilities and has been carried out by lone wolf anarchists or small autonomous anarchist terrorist cells. Anarchist terrorist organizations are rare. Given that anarchist elements did not generally claim responsibility for their attacks, or claimed them weeks or months after the attack, it is sometimes problematic trying to determine if a bombing or arson attack in Europe or Latin America came from the Marxist, Maoist or anarchist scene. The advent of the Internet has re-energized world-wide anarchism as anarchists, previously isolated and disconnected with each other, now, via websites, have a common global agitation/propaganda channel to exchange ideas, publicize activities and problems, call for international actions and solidarity, and share messages from imprisoned anarchists worldwide.

(2) *State-Sponsored Terrorist Strain*

The state-sponsored terrorist strain consists of states that engaged in or supported terrorist activity in other countries directed at other states and/or dissident exiles and carried out by their intelligence services or contracted non-state terrorist groups. This strain emerged as an international terrorist threat around 1979 and began to dissipate in 1992. This strain has killed more Americans overseas than any other strain. State-sponsored attacks were generally indiscriminate, mass-casualty attacks that involved mid-air bombings or hijacking of commercial air-crafts, and vehicular suicide attacks. This strain targeted U.S. interests overseas as a result of U.S. political, economic, military, security, and diplomatic support for Israel; the U.S.'s general involvement in Middle Eastern affairs to include the stabilization of Lebanon; and U.S. policies and goals that clashed with or obstructed the regional strategic objectives of these terrorist states. The primary state sponsors of anti-American terrorism have been Libya, Iran, Iraq (during the Saddam Hussein period), Syria, and Cuba. State-sponsored terrorism can be defined as direct or indirect involvement of a government in the planning, sup-port, or implementation of a political terrorist act, using official or non-official groups, directed at its own citizens overseas or foreign interests, for purposes of coercion and widespread intimidation to bring about the desired political or stra-tegic objective.

A state will use its intelligence service to engineer and manage terrorist operations. The intelligence service could use its own agents to carry out such operations, but this entails a significant risk since if the agent is captured or leaves an evidence trail (as Libyan intelligence agents did for the December 1988 Pan Am 103 operation), the state could be implicated. It is generally safer for the intelligence service to hire a non-state terrorist group that shares some of the terrorist state's regional objectives and/or its perceived enemies. In this case, the target is consistent with the group's targeting pattern and the state's, thereby making it difficult to attach paternity to the operation if no formal claim is issued. Given that a state would not claim public responsibility for a terrorist attack, it is generally difficult to implicate a state in a terrorist operation due to the state's ability to camouflage its involvement. State-sponsored terrorism is, in theory, the most dangerous terrorist strain in the world. If a state makes the decision to engage in or support terrorist attacks on its perceived enemies, then that state can deploy all the resources of the state in this endeavor. Unlimited money, technology, false documents, weapons, intelligence support, and military training can be applied to its terrorist operations. The involvement of a state in a terrorist operation also has the potential to ignite an inter-state conflict, especially if the operation is aimed at another state.

Israel, France, Pakistan, and the U.S. are the only countries that have responded to state-sponsored terrorism with retaliatory military strikes that could, according to international law, have led to inter-state conflicts. The United States has carried out retaliatory military strikes against Libya (1986), Iraq (1993), Sudan (1999), and Afghanistan (1999 and 2001). In all cases, the U.S. claimed that these states ordered terrorist attacks on U.S. targets or permitted known anti-American terrorist groups to use their countries as a base for anti-American terrorist attacks. After the Iranian/Syrian backed bombing in October 1983 of the French Paratrooper barracks in Beirut that killed 58 soldiers, French warplanes retaliated by striking Iranian Revolutionary Guard facilities in the Beqaa Valley in Lebanon in November 1983. Israel initiated military incursions into Lebanon in 1982 (First Lebanon War) and 2006 (Second Lebanon War) to neutralize anti-Israeli Palestine Liberation Organization (PLO) terrorist actors based in southern Lebanon. Thus, the international community and the U.S. has made stopping or controlling state-sponsored terrorism a major counter-terrorism objective, using military force as well as economic and political pressures.

(3) *The Secular Palestinian Terrorist Strain*

The Secular Palestinian terrorist strain was composed of a dozen secular Palestinian terrorist groups and insurgent organizations that engaged in terrorist attacks inside and outside Israel and advocated either a democratic, Marxist, or Islamic political agenda with the goal of establishing an independent Palestinian state in place of the state of Israel. This strain was primarily active during 1968–1988. The Palestinian terrorist strain targeted U.S. interests overseas due to U.S. political, economic, military, security, and diplomatic support for the state of Israel. For some of the Marxist Palestinian terrorist groups, targeting of the U.S. was also driven by their anti-imperialist and anti-capitalist ideological platform. The Marxist organizations saw the Palestinian struggle as part of a wider uprising against Western imperialism. They also aimed to unite the Arab world by over-throwing "reactionary" regimes. The secular Palestinian terrorist strain emerged as an international terrorist problem in the late 1960s when several of these orga-nizations decided to engage in extensive terrorist activity outside the state of Israel and consequently endanger the international security environment, including international aviation. This strain underwent a transformation in the late 1980s, when its overseas operations waned, and the secular nature of the Palestinian ter-rorist threat was initially supplemented by and later replaced by a rising Islamic terrorist component of the Palestinian nationalist movement, specifically the Al-Qassam Brigades of Hamas and the Al-Quds Brigades of the Palestine Islamic Jihad.

The secular Palestinian terrorist strain was never ideologically or operation-ally united. It was ostensibly composed of 12 Palestinian terrorist organizations that disagreed over the ultimate ideological makeup of the Palestinian state, tac-tics, negotiation with Israel, and whether to initiate and/or continue terrorist attacks outside Israel. In addition, there were personality clashes between leaders of these Palestinian groups and conflict caused by different groups aligning with different Arab states. All these conflicts created a terrorist strain that spent an inordinate amount of operational energy on intra-Palestinian and inter-Arab attacks, that is, various secular Palestinian terrorist groups attacked one another, and some were used by various Arab states to attack other Arab states. In fact, about 30% of all secular Palestinian terrorist attacks in the 1980s were directed at other Palestinians and Arab states.

Throughout the decades of the 1960s and 1970s, this terrorist strain became synonymous with international terrorism. In fact, this strain introduced the prob-lem of international terrorism to the world. It then dominated the international terrorist threat environment until the early 1980s when it shared the terrorist threat production with the state-sponsored and Islamic revolutionary terrorist strains. The operational output of the secular Palestinian terrorist strain from 1968 to 1987 was as follows: responsible for 602 terrorist attacks directed against 28 different nationalities in 62 countries on five continents.[17] This was an operational output and geographic scope that remains unmatched in the modern history of political terrorism. Despite this output, within the larger context of international terrorist attacks, this strain only accounted for about 5% of such attacks from 1968 to1984.[18] It was not the total number of Palestinian terrorist attacks that defined its terrorist threat image during this period, but the innovative and media magnetic nature of its operations against Western and Israeli targets.

The 12 major organizational components of this terrorist strain were as follows:

- Fatah — The Revolutionary Council (also known as the Abu Nidal Organization or ANO).
- Arab Nationalist Youth Organization (ANYO).
- Black September Organization — Fatah (BSO).
- Democratic Front for the Liberation of Palestine (DFLP).
- Lebanese Armed Revolutionary Faction (LARF).
- Popular Front for the Liberation of Palestine (PFLP).
- Popular Front for the Liberation of Palestine — General Command (PFLP-GC).
- Popular Front for the Liberation of Palestine — Special Command (PFLP-SC).
- Arab May 15th Organization.
- Saiqa.
- Popular Struggle Front (PSF).
- The Carlos Group.

Of these 12 organizations, the mainline PFLP, Abu Nidal's Fatah Revolutionary Council, and Yasir Arafat's Fatah Black September Organization were the major international terrorist pollutants in the 1970s and 1980s due to their operational output, wide operational area, and indiscriminate tactics. These three organizations accounted for about 50% of all external Palestinian terrorist attacks during this period.

The primary targets of this Palestinian terrorist threat were (1) Israeli/Jewish, (2) Western, and (3) Arab. The Israeli/Jewish targets involved official Israeli

---

[17] See section on "Palestinian statistics" for sources used to compile these statistics on Palestinian terrorist attacks.

[18] Ariel Merari and Shlomi Elad. *The International Dimension of Palestinian Terrorism* (Boulder: Westview Press, 1986), p. 7. This was a Jaffee Center for Strategic Studies (Tel Aviv University) study.

targets outside Israel including El Al airlines, and prominent Jewish personalities, synagogues, and businesses. Western targets consisted primarily of European and U.S. targets. The Arab targets were other Palestinians, and official personnel and facilities, commercial airlines and airline offices of Syria, Jordan, Saudi Arabia, Egypt, Iraq, and Kuwait. The tactics employed were primarily explosive attacks, letter bombs, assassinations, rocket attacks, aircraft hijacking, and barricade and hostage incidents. The Palestinian terrorists were innovative in their tactics. Although they were not the first terrorists to hijack an airplane, they were the first to hijack an aircraft for the purposes of political blackmail. From 1968 to 1982, only 24% of terrorist-related aircraft hijackings were carried out by Palestinian groups.[19] However, the tactic came to be associated primarily with Palestinian terrorists. They were the first terrorist group to carry out attacks against aircraft and passengers on the ground. This took place on December 26, 1968, when Palestinian terrorists attacked an El Al aircraft on the tarmac in Athens. They were the first to blow up aircraft in mid-air. The first time this occurred was on February 21, 1970 when Palestinian terrorists blew up a Swissair aircraft going from Zurich to Tel Aviv. They were the first to seize hostages in non-aircraft situations. This took place when the PFLP stormed and seized hostages in the Philadelphia and Intercontinental hotels in Amman, Jordan on July 9, 1970.

Palestinian terrorists were also the first to attempt to use shoulder-fired rockets and surface to air missiles against commercial aircraft. The former took place on January 13 and 17, 1975 when Carlos and members of the PFLP-Special Operations Group fired an RPG-7 at Yugoslav aircraft on the tarmac in Paris. The latter occurred on September 5, 1973 when five members of the Black September Organization were arrested near Fiumicino airport in Rome for plotting to shoot down an El Al aircraft with a surface-to-air missile. The Palestinians were not the first to seize diplomatic hostages; Croatian terrorists accomplished this on February 10, 1971 when they occupied the Yugoslav embassy in Goteborg, Sweden. Like terrorist aircraft hijackings, the diplomatic barricade and hostage tactic became associated primarily with Palestinian terrorists. However, of the 48 barricade and hostage incidents directed at diplomatic facilities worldwide, only 13, or 27%, were carried out by Palestinian terrorists.[20] Palestinian terrorists were also the first to hijack multiple aircraft in a single operation — the September

---

[19] Ibid. The CIA study "Terrorist Skyjackings: A Statistical Overview of terrorist skyjackings from January 1968 through June 1982," published July 1982, p. 2 noted that Palestinian terrorists were only responsible for 20% of all "skyjackings" from 1968 to June 1982, at https://www.scribd.com/doc/53824134/Terrorist-Skyjackings-A-CIA-Report. Accessed June 10, 2017.

[20] Merari and Elad, *International Dimension of Palestinian Terrorism*, p. 9.

1970 hijacking and attempted hijacking of five aircraft: one hijacking failed, one plane was blown up on the ground in Cairo, and three were eventually diverted to Dawson's Field in Jordan. The next seizure of multiple aircraft would take place 41 years later by al-Qaeda in the United States.

What made the Palestinian terrorist strain so dangerous was its international dimension and its skillful exploitation of the media. Palestinian terrorists attracted and recruited non-Palestinians to join their organizations. For example, the Venezuelan Marxist revolutionary Illich Ramirez Sanchez, popularly known as "Carlos," members of the Japanese Red Army, and various European nationalities worked with Palestinian terrorist groups to different degrees. Given that many European left-wing terrorist groups considered the U.S. and Israel as enemies, Palestinian terrorists used their training camps in South Yemen, Jordan, and later Lebanon to train members of these sympathetic groups. In addition, in order to support their international operations, Palestinian terrorist groups established extensive logistical, financial, and support networks in other regions, usually involving Palestinian and Arab students, tourists, businessmen, and other members of the Palestinian diaspora. The primary operational area of the Palestinian terrorist threat was Western Europe, followed by the Middle East and South Asia. It was the terrorist activities of Palestinian terrorists outside Israel that prompted the use of the term "spillover terrorism," which means terrorist activity that spills from one region to another. However, the primary contribution of this threat to the modern history of terrorism is that it demonstrated the utility and advantages of the international arena as a desired operational area for discontented and militant ethnic and religious elements. In the assessment of the secular Palestinian terrorist leaders, the decision to operate internationally provided the following[21]:

Propaganda Benefits — It attracted the attention of the international community to the plight of the Palestinians.

Security Benefits — It was impossible to protect all Israeli and Jewish (and American) targets worldwide. The international area provided the Palestinian terrorists with more targets that had little or no protective security measures.

The Element of Surprise — The geographical scope of the Palestinian threat was enlarged, so predicting or prioritizing possible Israeli and Jewish targets was extremely difficult for the security services.

---

[21]Condensed and modified from Merari/Elad, pp. 10–12.

Cadre Benefits — The operatives' chances for escape after attacks were higher outside Israel than inside. Western Europe was very attractive in this regard due to its open borders, compact geographical area, excellent transport systems, large Palestinian diaspora, sympathetic left-wing militants and terrorist groups, and, in certain cases, sympathetic governments willing to give in to terrorists' demands. This last factor also fostered another benefit — lighter sentences for captured Palestinian terrorists, compared to what they would receive in Israel. During the 1960s and early 1970s, there was a tendency for some European governments to release imprisoned Palestinian terrorists when subjected to extortion demands during Palestinian terrorist aircraft hijackings or barricade and hostage incidents.

Morale Booster — Palestinian terrorists encountered difficulties in carrying out consistent terrorist operations inside Israel. This led to the capture or killing of Palestinian terrorists. Given the higher rate of success in carrying out attacks outside Israel, the international operations boosted the morale of organizational members and the Palestinian community in general.

Threat Projection — Any terrorist organization that could carry out attacks outside its primary targeted country (in this case, Israel) demonstrated an enhanced operational capability and posed a wider geographic threat than the one that only operated in a domestic environment.

These six benefits of external operations were weighed against the following negatives:

Damage to the Cause — Operating in the international arena, especially if a group attacked civilian targets or engaged in indiscriminate attacks, could antagonize international public opinion and tarnish the groups' cause.

Logistical Strain — It took more resources to fund and support external operations. There were travel costs, safe houses, communication costs, funding support networks, and procuring false documents.

Constituency Stress — External operations might cause supporters and sympathizers to question the use of resources that might be better deployed for internal operations on the soil of the primary targeted enemy. Which would produce more satisfaction and pride among Palestinian terrorist supporters and sympathizers — internal or external anti-Israeli operations?

Counter-Terrorism Blowback — Engaging in internal operations usually only triggered a counter-terrorism response from the targeted country. External operations, depending on the geographic scope and frequency of attacks, would trigger other countries to engage in counter-terrorism operations against the terrorist organization and possibly lead to increased counter-terrorism support to the primary targeted country.

As the pros and cons above indicate, Palestinian external operations were clearly a double-edged sword. Most if not all the Palestinian organizations believed that attacks inside Israel were necessary. For some groups, external operations were simply a supplement to the internal operations. However, Israeli internal and border security measures made it difficult and costly for the Palestinian terrorist organizations to engage in a sustained terrorist campaign inside Israel. External operations offered a temporary opportunity to strike at Israel and Jewish targets overseas and thus foster the viability and visibility of the Palestinian armed struggle. Some groups saw the benefits of external operations but questioned the specific tactic of aircraft hijackings which provoked a higher level of international condemnation due to the number of innocent civilians involved.

This clash between internal and external operations and the pros and cons of aircraft hijackings plagued several of the Palestinian terrorist groups, triggering dissent, debate, and splits. There was disagreement over the utility of external operations between the two major Marxist groups — the DFLP, which opposed them, and the PFLP which was in favor.[22] The DFLP opposed external operations, especially aircraft hijackings, because it felt such operations "furthered individualism and created personal myths, in the process leaving the masses in the position of mere onlookers."[23] In other words, hijackings fostered personal notoriety for some hijackers, such as Carlos and Leila Khaled.[24] The DFLP believed that revolution without mass mobilization was impossible.

From the beginning, Arafat, Fatah, and the nationalist umbrella entity he constructed, the Palestine Liberation Organization (PLO), opposed external

---

[22] Merari/Elad, p.29.

[23] Ibid.

[24] Leila Khalid was the first woman to hijack an airplane. She participated in two hijackings of a U.S. plane in 1969 and an Israeli plane in 1970. She was 25 when she hijacked the TWA plane in 1969, attractive, and became the subject of an iconic photo of her wearing a *keffiyeh*, an Arabic headdress, holding an AK-47. See Timur Moon, "Leila Khaled — hijacked by destiny," *Al-Jazeera*, October 17, 2002, at http://www.aljazeerah.info/Opinion editorials/2002 Opinion editorials/Oct 2002 op eds/Oct 17, 2002 op eds.htm. Accessed June 5, 2016.

operations as a detriment to the Palestinian cause and a stain on Arafat's perceived image of himself as a statesman and leader of the Palestinian cause. However, three developments eventually convinced Arafat of the necessity of acquiescing to the temporary use of international terrorism. Firstly, after the PFLP initiated external operations against Israel targets in 1968, Arafat noticed how these operations boosted the morale of the Palestinians and attracted more recruits to the PFLP. Secondly, after the Jordanian onslaught of the Palestinian bases in Jordan in 1970, there were young Fatah members who wanted to take revenge on Jordan. Thirdly, having lost a base in Jordan to mount operations inside Israel and having failed to initiate a successful campaign of terrorist attacks from inside Israel, Arafat and Fatah were searching for relevance and prestige. The solution was to create a clandestine and deniable channel for Fatah militants to vent their frustration against Jordan and to allow Fatah to compete with the PFLP for the hearts and minds of young Palestinians. This channel was Black September or BSO. The BSO, formed in 1970, was not a formal, centralized organization but an informal floating collection of Palestinian militants, groups, and militant European supporters that were loosely directed by Fatah's intelligence service — "Jihaz el Razd" (Reconnaissance). The BSO had no formal membership or leadership. Independent operations could be conducted.[25] Arafat and Fatah always denied any links between Fatah and the BSO. However, the U.S. government believed that the BSO was controlled by Fatah.[26] In the CIA "President's Daily Report" for September 8, 1972, it is noted that "the Black September Organization is not a distinct fedayeen, but rather a cover name that Fatah — the largest and most heavily funded group — uses for terrorist operations."[27]

The BSO initially engaged in revenge attacks against Jordanian targets, then expanded its targets to Israeli and Western targets. Yasir Arafat and Fatah closed Black September down, in September 1973, on the third anniversary of its founding, by the "political calculation that no more good would come of terrorism abroad."[28] As a result of a meeting in July 1974 in Cairo of the Palestine National Council, Arafat ordered the PLO to withdraw from acts of violence outside the

---

[25] Christopher Dobson. *Black September: Its Short, Violent History* (New York: MacMillan Press, 1974), p. 42.

[26] Oswald Johnston, "U.S. Intelligence Analysis: Olympic Terrorists Linked to al-Fatah," *Washington Star*, September 12, 1977, CIA FOIA document # RDP80-01601R000-300300003-6.

[27] CIA, "President's Daily Report," September 8, 1972, p. A1, CIA FOIA document # RDP79T00936A011100080001-5.

[28] Benny Morris. *Righteous Victims: A History of the Zionist-Arab Conflict, 1881–2001* (New York, Vintage Books, 2001), p. 383.

West Bank, the Gaza Strip and the rest of the land of Israel.[29] Fatah did however continue to initiate selective, periodic attacks outside Israel using special external units from its intelligence apparatus. However, sustained external "campaigns" were over. The public renunciation of external operations by Arafat and the PLO in 1988 and his decision to take part in negotiations with Israel for less than the whole territory of Palestine triggered dissent within Fatah and the Palestinian nationalist movement in general. It led to the establishment in 1974 of a "rejectionist front" composed of the PFLP, PFLP-GC, Popular Struggle Front, and the Arab Liberation Front. The rejectionists opposed any negotiations with Israel. While moderate Arab states supported Arafat and the PLO, radical Arab states like Syria, Iraq, and Libya supported the rejectionists. This split between the pro-Arafat factions and the Palestinian rejectionist groups eventually caused an extensive intra-Palestinian and inter-Arab terrorist campaign during the 1980s which was fought primarily in the Middle East and Western Europe.

The secular-oriented Palestinian terrorist strain began to dissipate in the late 1980s primarily as a result of four developments: (1) the disintegration of the Soviet Union in 1988, (2) the ongoing momentum for negotiations between Israel and the PLO that eventually led to the 1991 Madrid Conference and the 1993 Oslo Accords, (3) the 1990/1991 Gulf War and the U.S. response (especially constructing a multinational coalition) which intimidated Syria and Libya, traditional state sponsors of Palestinian terrorism, and (4) the 1987 implosion of the most active and dangerous secular Palestinian terrorist actor in the 1980s — the Abu Nidal Organization. While some secular Palestinian terrorist organizations carried out periodic attacks in the 1990s, Palestinian external operations had essentially ceased. It lasted for 20 years, from 1968 to 1988, and polluted the security environments in Western Europe, South Asia, and the Middle East. During the decade of the 1960s and 1970s, this was the most dangerous and dominant terrorist strain in the world for Israel, the U.S., and the West.

(4) The Islamic Revolutionary Terrorist Strain[30]

The Islamic revolutionary terrorist strain consists of Islamist revolutionary terrorist groups, insurgent organizations, and individual Muslims and converts

---

[29] Merari/Elad, p. 34.

[30] Islam is an Arabic word that means "submission" or "surrender" to the will of God. Muslims believe that Islam is God's final and perfect religion. Mohammad is God's prophet and he lived around 570–632 AD. It is the second largest religion in the world behind Christianity. The primary authoritative sources in Islam are the Koran, scriptures considered to be the verbatim word of God, and the

who believe that it is necessary to engage in militant, defensive jihad (armed struggle) to return Islam to a position of domination in the world by (1) replacing secular Muslim governments ("apostate regimes") with Islamic states,[31] (2) expelling Western cultural, economic, and political influences from Muslim societies, (3) guiding Muslims back to the true path of Islam, (4) recapturing lost Muslim lands, and (5) creating the conditions for the re-establishment of an Islamic caliphate. There have been two forms of Islamic revolutionary terrorism: domestic and global jihadists. There has been no single, monolithic Islamic revolutionary movement or flagship Islamic revolutionary terrorist or insurgent group. In fact, in the late 2010s, two flagship groups, al-Qaeda and the Islamic State in Iraq and Syria (ISIS) became competitors. Unity was problematic and continues to be so.

Those who believe that it is more important to direct this violence at apostate Muslim regimes or the "near enemy" ("lesser enemy") are referred to as "domestic jihadists." Those who contend that the primary enemy of Islam and the "puppeteer" of these apostate regimes are the United States — "far enemy ("greater enemy") — and its allies are termed "global jihadists."[32] Both frame this violence

---

Sunnah, the traditions of Islam based on the Hadith — words and deeds of Mohammad, as recorded by his contemporaries. The most important point about Islam is that it is more than a religion. It is a way of life. It dictates all aspects of a Muslim's life — social, political, economic, physical, and spiritual. In Islam, politics and religion are inseparable. Islam is divided into two main branches: the Sunni and Shia. The former makes up over 80% of Muslims in the world. The Shia is the minority branch. The division took place after the Prophet Muhammad's death over the proper way his successor should be chosen. Shia believed that the successors should come from those who are direct descendants of the prophet while the Sunni opined that was not necessary. This and other issues have led to tensions and conflict between the two branches.

There are also different schools of thought and sects in Islam. The one that is most relevant to this work is the Wahhabi doctrine within the Sunni branch. Founded in the 18th century by Muhammad ibn Abd al-Wahhab, the Wahhabis are the most conservative Muslim group and are found mainly in Saudi Arabia. Adherents dislike being called by that name, preferring instead to be called Salafis. They rigorously oppose all practices not sanctioned by the Koran and are considered to be ultra-conservative, fundamentalist, and puritanical. The global jihadist movement that emerged in the 1990s and continues to this day is primarily Salafi-oriented.

[31] "Apostate" regimes are ones that the jihadists believe are not ruling their countries according to the strict tenets of Islam and Islamic law. In addition, apostate regimes allow Western cultural, political, and economic influences to undermine Islamic cultural and religious mores.

[32] Typing Islamic revolutionary terrorists into domestic and global jihadists is not the only way to categorize jihadist terrorist activity in the world since 1979. Some academics use different terminology and a broader typology. For example, Fawaz Gerges in his book *The Far Enemy: Why Jihad Went Global* (New York: Cambridge University Press, 2005) uses terms like "internal jihadists" or "religious nationalists" instead of domestic jihadists. In place of "global jihadists," Fawaz uses the term

under the concept of a militant, defensive form of jihad. A jihadist is a Muslim or convert to Islam who believes that militant jihad is an obligation for Muslims given the current conditions of Islam and Muslims in today's world. This Islamic revolutionary terrorist strain has evolved through three separate periods:

- 1979–1989: when Iranian-directed, Shia jihadist elements were ascendant;
- 1990–1997: a period of transition from domestic to global jihadist;
- 1998–present: when Sunni/Salafi global jihadist elements are dominant.

To date, this strain has not carried out as many anti-American terrorist attacks overseas as the left-wing terrorist strain nor killed as many Americans overseas as the state-sponsored strain. The Shia Islamic revolutionary terrorist organizations in the 1980s played a role of varying degrees in the 1983 and 1984 suicide attacks on the U.S. Embassies and U.S. Marine barracks in Beirut. However, the author has included the American death toll from these attacks in the state-sponsored terrorist threat column as the objectives of these attacks sprung more from Iranian and Syrian foreign policy considerations than local jihadist motivations. Within the Islamic revolutionary terrorist strain, it is also necessary to place Palestinian Islamic terrorist groups that surfaced in the 1990s and 2000s — al-Qassam brigades of Hamas and the al-Quds brigades of Palestine Islamic Jihad. These two groups represented the face of Palestinian terrorism that, at the time, limited itself to attacks primarily in Israel, the Gaza strip, and the West Bank.

The operational, as opposed to ideological, formation of this Islamic revolutionary terrorist strain began around 1979 when Ayatollah Khomeini led Shia Islamic revolutionaries in an overthrow of the secular Iranian regime and replaced it with an Islamic state or the Islamic Republic of Iran. Not content with this internal success, Khomeini wanted to export his revolutionary model to neighboring states with significant Shia minorities. The most important experiment was in Lebanon where Iran fostered the formation in 1982 of a Shia terrorist organization called Hezbollah (Party of God) which emerged from a discontented Shia population in Lebanon. It was this union between the Islamic state of Iran and the Lebanese Hezbollah that provided the operational spark for the emergence of the

---

"transnational jihadists." He adds a third category in his typology of jihadists called "irredentist jihadists" which he defines as groups struggling to recapture lost Muslim lands that are now under the rule of non-Muslims — like in Palestine, Chechnya, Mindanao, Andalusia, and Kashmir. See pages 2–3 and 11. In general, however, there is agreement that the two main types of jihadists in the world today are domestic jihadists and global jihadists and that there are disagreements and tensions between the two types.

Islamic revolutionary terrorist strain that would dominate the anti-American overseas terrorist environment over the next four decades and the U.S. internal threat environment in the 2000s and 2010s. Khomeini was the most significant global jihadist evangelist in the modern era. He believed that it was Islam's manifest destiny to rule the world and that the U.S. was the primary enemy of Islam. Khomeini died on June 3, 1989. In his last will and testament that was read to the Iranian people on June 4, he wrote: "The U.S. is the foremost enemy of Islam. It is a terrorist state by nature that has set fire to everything everywhere and its ally, the international Zionism, does not stop short of any crime to achieve its base and greedy desires, crimes that the tongue and pen are ashamed to utter or write."[33] The identification of the U.S. as the "Great Satan" and the primary enemy of Islam was a cornerstone of the global jihadist political and ideological platforms.

It was also in 1979 that the Soviet Union invaded Afghanistan and triggered a subsequent anti-Soviet mujahideen war, lasting from 1979 to 1989. While Shia Islamic revolutionaries were focused on Lebanon and the Gulf state's arena, Sunni Islamic revolutionaries were congregating in Afghanistan to fight the Soviets and eventually plant the seeds of the Sunni terrorist flagship — al-Qaeda. Khomeini's death in 1989 signaled the decline of the Shia as the primary generator of jihadist anti-American terrorism and the defeat of the Soviets in Afghanistan the same year marked the start of a transition period. In this period, the victorious Sunni Islamic revolutionary elements in Afghanistan and elsewhere discussed and debated what to do next — return to their respective countries and confront the near enemy or prepare for a global jihad against the far enemy? Al-Qaeda was the first major operational manifestation of this nascent global jihadist movement.

Since 1983, this Islamic revolutionary terrorist strain posed the greatest threat to U.S. interests at home and abroad. The main ideological and theological drivers of this threat (Shia/Salafi; near vs. far enemy) have changed over time, but the U.S. has been consistently painted as the primary enemy of Islam and the primary obstacle preventing the Islamic revolutionaries from attaining victory. In the first period of the evolution of this jihadist threat, the Islamic revolutionary terrorist organizations worked with states, Iran and Syria. This did not take place in the second period and has not to date occurred in the third period. If a new metamorphosis takes place in this jihadist threat, the most dangerous outcome would be that global jihadist terrorists receive the direct and full support of one

---

[33] Khomeini's last will and testament in English at http://server32.irna.com/occasion/ertehal/english/will/lmnew1.htm. Accessed on January 2, 2016.

or more Muslim states. This combination of state support for a global jihadist terrorist organization would represent a dangerous manifestation of anti-American terrorism.

(5) Ethnonational Terrorist Threat

The Ethnonational terrorist strain is composed of terrorist groups and insurgent organizations that seek a separate ethnic state, reunification of a splintered ethnic homeland, recovery of a lost ethnic homeland, or more autonomy for their ethnic community.[34] Ethnonational militant organizations arise from discontented ethnic communities with historical and/or contemporary grievances with the state that has, as a result of conquest or treaty, absorbed the ethnic community/region. The most prevalent are as follows: (1) freedom to speak and teach their own language, (2) to have input into the educational curriculum, (3) equal opportunities for its ethnic community, (4) more say over the administration of its ethnic region, and (5) the fair sharing of revenue from the exploitation of prized resources in its ethnic region. In some cases, militant ethnonational groups seek independence — essentially a belief that only the complete separation of their ethnic region from the state will provide long-term security for their ethnic community. In other cases, militants are engaging in armed struggle against the state in order to acquire more autonomy for their ethnic region, that is, a greater participation in administering the affairs of their region. These ethnonationalist terrorist and insurgent groups implement a strategy of attrition against the central government of the state, which they usually refer to as the "center." Their intent is to create social, economic, and political instability in their homeland by engaging in bombings, kidnappings, assassinations, and other forms of physical and psychological intimidation. They believe that the successful application of this strategy will over time cause the center to perceive the discontented ethnic region as ungovernable and/or too costly, that is, not worth the financial drain, casualty toll, or loss of international prestige to keep it within the state. At the minimum, the state could then be compelled to agree to some degree of autonomy for the discontented

---

[34] For background information on ethnonational terrorism, see Daniel Byman, "The Logic of Ethnic Terrorism," *Studies in Conflict and Terrorism*, Vol. 21, #2, April–June 1998, pp. 149–169; Dennis Pluchinsky, "Ethno-National Terrorism: Themes and Variations," *FOA Report on Terrorism*, edited by Gunnar Jervas, Defense Research Establishment (FOA), Stockholm, Sweden, Report #FOA-R-00788-170-SE, June 1998, pp. 41–52; and Dennis Pluchinsky, "Ethnic Terrorism and Insurgencies," in Albrecht Schnabel and Rohan Gunaratna, editors, *Understanding and Managing Insurgent Movement* (Singapore: Marshall Cavendish, 2006), pp. 25–47.

ethnic region or accede to independence. In contrast to left-wing and jihadist terrorist and insurgent organizations, ethnonational groups do not seek the overthrow of the central government. Instead, they seek to pressure the government to relinquish administrative control or territorial paternity over their ethnic region through of strategy of attrition.

The implementation of this strategy of attrition involves ethnonational attacks at three different operational levels: (1) attacks in their respective ethnic homelands, (2) attacks outside their homeland but within the targeted or containing state, and (3) attacks outside the targeted country, that is, in the international arena. Most of the attacks by an ethnonationalist terrorist or insurgent group take place at the first level. However, these groups also believe that to apply adequate pressure on the targeted state, they need to periodically carry out attacks at the second level, in most cases, in the capitals, to pressure the governments to meet their demands. Such attacks have multiple objectives: (1) to demonstrate the threat projection of the group, (2) to embarrass the government and security forces, (3) to attract more national publicity, (4) to bring the conflict and its consequences directly to the general populace of the targeted state, and (5) to diminish tourism revenues by scaring foreigners. Most ethnonational militant groups operate only at these two levels. However, some carry out operations at the third level, attacking outside the targeted state. Third-level operations have the following benefits: (1) they amplify the group's threat projection, (2) they attract international publicity, (3) they frame the conflict as an international problem, and (4) they take place in an environment where targets are generally softer, that is, security awareness is lower and protective security measures are less stringent. As noted previously, it was this last benefit that also convinced the Palestinian terrorist leaders to hit Israeli targets outside of Israel. The ethnonational terrorist group that carried out the most attacks at this third level was the Irish Republican Army (IRA). It has carried out over two dozen terrorist attacks against British targets on the European continent. Other groups like the Basque Homeland and Liberty (ETA), the Liberation Tigers of Tamil Eelam (LTTE), Sikh extremists, and Kashmiri extremists also operated at the third level but in a much more episodic and limited way.

The IRA spoke for many ethnonationalist terrorist and insurgent groups that operate or would like to operate at the third level when it made the following statement concerning its attacks on British overseas targets:

> *"Overseas attacks also have a prestige value and internationalize the war in Ireland. The British government has been successful in suppressing news about the struggle in the North. With its huge propaganda*

machine administered by ambassadors and officials, one example being Peter Jay when he was in America, it can spread a rosy picture which does much to undermine the people's sacrifices and completely ignores the people's suffering. But we have kept Ireland in the world headlines, our struggle is kept in the news, and sooner or later an expression of discontentment probably from the English people rather than from the army, will snowball and the British government's ability and will to stay, which we are sapping, will completely snap."[35]

Ethnonational terrorist and insurgent groups do not usually target U.S. interests overseas. However, when these groups operate at level two, most of the attacks take place in the capitals. The strategic nature of such attacks is that they are usually planned as indiscriminate, mass-casualty attacks. As a result, such indiscriminate operations undermine the security environment for Americans (and other foreigners), transiting, living, visiting, and working in these capital cities. This increases the possibility of an American being accidentally caught up in one of these attacks. In fact, from 1960 to 2017, 28 Americans were accidentally killed overseas in ethnonationalist terrorist attacks in capital cities. If an ethnonationalist terrorist group is involved in sustained operations in the capital or other major cities in the targeted state, the U.S. government may issue a travel warning or advisory for that city. In general, ethnonationalist terrorist and insurgent groups avoid direct attacks on foreign targets as it could damage international sympathy for the group and its cause.

While nationalism is the main ideological driver for these groups, many ethnonational terrorist and insurgent groups incorporate Marxist-Leninism into their ideological platform. For example, renowned groups such as the Kurdistan Workers Party (PKK) in Turkey, the Irish Republican Army (IRA) in Great Britain, the Basque Homeland and Liberty group (ETA) in Spain, the Liberation Tigers of Tamil Eelam (LTTE) in Sri Lanka, and the Quebec Liberation Front (FLQ) in Canada emerged from leftist milieus and consider themselves to be socialist organizations. There is another complex dimension to ethnonational terrorism. It is a sub-category within this terrorist threat category called "global" ethnonational terrorism, represented by militant Palestinian, Croatian, and Armenian terrorist groups. For various reasons, these groups made the decision to operate primarily outside their ethnic homelands in the international arena. It has already been discussed as to why Palestinian terrorist groups decided to

---

[35] Republican News (Belfast), February 23, 1980 — from an interview with an IRA spokesman (in author's possession).

strike at Israeli targets outside of Israel. This leads to the question as to whether the Palestinian terrorist strain should be subsumed into the ethnonational strain. The position of the author is that the secular Palestinian terrorist threat, while it had an objective (establishment of a Palestinian state in the place of Israel) contained within the ethnonational terrorist strain, was so unique in its targets, tactics, state support, and operational area that it required a separate terrorist threat category — secular Palestinian terrorist strain:

- Secular Palestinian groups directly targeted U.S. interests, whereas ethnic groups generally do not.
- Secular Palestinian terrorist groups attacked targets of over a dozen countries while ethnic terrorist groups generally avoid attacks on foreign targets.
- Secular Palestinian groups carried out aircraft hijackings; ethnic groups generally do not.
- Secular Palestinian groups received state support and periodically carried out terrorist attacks on behalf of Arab states, while ethnic terrorist groups rarely have state sponsors.
- Secular Palestinian groups trained non-Palestinian terrorists in their training camps; ethnic groups do not usually incorporate foreigners into their groups.
- Secular Palestinian groups initially had the objective of recovering their lost homeland which meant the destruction of the state of Israel. Ethnic terrorist groups are not trying to destroy or overthrow the state but are simply trying to pressure it into giving in to their demands for more autonomy or independence.
- The fragmentation and intra-Palestinian fighting far exceeded that found in most ethnic terrorist groups.

Another better example of global ethnonational terrorism would be Croatian terrorists and organizations. Croatian terrorists operated primarily in the international arena in the 1970s and early 1980s. Their targets were official Communist Yugoslav personnel and facilities and their objective was a free and independent Croatian state. All these Croatian groups were émigré groups with tenuous and limited links to militant elements in Croatia. Given the autocratic nature of the communist regimes in Belgrade and Zagreb, it was difficult for militant Croatian terrorist groups to emerge and operate inside Croatia. Like the situation with the militant Palestinian nationalists, it was easier for Croatian militants, especially those living outside Yugoslavia, to strike at Yugoslav targets outside of Yugoslavia. The most notorious Croatian terrorist attacks were as follows: the 1971 seizure of the Yugoslav consulate in Goteborg, Sweden; the 1972 mid-air bombing of a

Yugoslav airliner that killed 27 people; the 1972 hijacking of a Swedish airliner to force Sweden to release several imprisoned Croatian militants; the 1976 hijacking of a TWA plane in New York; and the 1980 seizure of the Yugoslav consulate in Chicago, Illinois. From 1962 to 1982, militant Croatian terrorists carried out 128 anti-Yugoslav terrorist attacks worldwide. This campaign also triggered a response of state-sponsored terrorism by Communist Yugoslavia. It has been estimated that the Yugoslav intelligence services carried out some 46 attacks against Croatian émigrés worldwide during this same period.[36] It should also be noted that several of these Croatian terrorist attacks were examples of "leaderless terrorism," that is, carried out by autonomous terrorist cells that had no connections with Croatian terrorist organizations.

Militant Armenian terrorist groups are another example of a global ethnic terrorist group. These groups were active in the international arena from 1975 to 1986. Their objectives were somewhat of a deviation from ethnonationalist groups in general in that the Armenian groups initiated a campaign of international terrorism against Turkish targets worldwide in revenge for the reported genocide by Turkey in 1915 of an estimated 1.5 million Armenians who were reportedly expelled from Turkey and forced to trudge into Syria. They also demanded that the Turkish government officially acknowledge this genocide. The desire for an independent Armenian homeland was mentioned by these Armenian groups, but it was not the focus of their terrorist campaign in the 1970s and 1980s. Demographic realities in southeastern Turkey, overlapping territorial claims with Kurdish ethnonational groups, and the existence of an Armenian republic in the Soviet Union undermined their efforts for an independent Armenian entity in Turkey. Militant Armenian groups carried out 30 assassinations, 16 attempted assassinations, 129 bombings, 19 attempted bombings, one airport attack, and three embassy seizures during the 1975–1986 period. Most of these attacks were directed at Turkish targets. However, 38 non-Turkish persons were killed and 357 injured as a result of these attacks.[37] These militant Armenian groups carried out these attacks in 22 countries including Turkey. The two most active groups were the Armenian Secret Army for the Liberation of Armenia (ASALA) and the Justice Commandos Against the Armenian

---

[36] Information and statistics on militant Croatian terrorist activities and those of the Yugoslav secret police or UDBA are derived from Dennis Pluchinsky, "Political Terrorism in Western Europe," in Yonah Alexander and Kenneth Myers, editors, *Terrorism in Europe*, (New York: St. Martin's Press, 1982), pp. 59–60, 63.

[37] Information and statistics on militant Armenian groups are derived from two unclassified studies by Andrew Corsun, *Armenian Terrorism: 1975–1980*, U.S. Department of State, Office of Security, Threat Analysis Group, (August 1981), and an updated version *Armenian Terrorism: 1984–1987* (September 1988).

Genocide (JCAG). Both groups also used various commando names for different operations and for various thematic terrorist campaigns. Armenian militant groups were second only to the secular Palestinians in the level and scope of their international terrorist activity in the late 1970s and early 1980s.

The international operations of secular Palestinian, Croatian, and Armenian terrorists created another problem for countries that contained significant diasporas of these ethnic groups. Members of these diasporas would engage in legal and illegal activities to promote the cause of the ethnic terrorist group operating in their homeland. Legal activities consisted of demonstrations and lobbying host country elected officials to try and attract sympathy and political support for the militants' cause. Illegal activities included procuring weapons, bomb-making equipment, communication devices, fundraising schemes, recruitment, and supporting attacks in the host country. There have been numerous examples of Palestinian-Americans, Croatian-Americans, and Armenian-Americans joining the militant groups and carrying out attacks. In the U.S., such actors are examples of "foreign spillover" terrorism. For example, the September 1976 hijacking of TWA flight 355 in New York was carried out by five terrorists, including two Croatian-Americans. A total of 16 Armenian-Americans have been convicted of terrorist- or terrorism-related crimes in the United States.[38] Some Tamil-Americans have supported the ethnonational insurgent group, the Liberation Tigers of Tamil Eelam (LTTE), which operated on Sri Lanka with the objective of establishing an independent Tamil state in the north. The LTTE established a support branch in the United States. The head of the U.S. branch was arrested in April 2007. He raised millions of dollars for the LTTE, which were laundered to the terrorist group through charitable front organizations such as the Tamil Rehabilitation Organization (TRO). In June 2009, four supporters of the LTTE pleaded guilty in a New York federal court to terrorism charges, including funneling money and weapons to the LTTE and trying to bribe U.S. officials to remove the group from the terrorism list. In January 2009, four men pleaded guilty in New York to terrorism violations in connection with their efforts to acquire surface-to-air missiles, missile launchers and hundreds of assault rifles for the LTTE.[39] Although the ethnonational terrorist threat does not directly target U.S. interests overseas, as the above discussion suggests, this threat does create

---

[38] http://armenians-1915.blogspot.com/2006/04/605-armenian-terrorism-ethnic-terror.html. Accessed January 22, 2016.

[39] http://www.adl.org/terrorism/symbols/liberation_tigers_te1.asp, and http://www.justice.gov/usao/nye/pr/2007/2007Apr25.html. Accessed February 2, 2017.

security and diplomatic problems for the United States — at home and abroad. Similar problems arose in other countries also.

All four of the above anti-American terrorist strains and the ethnonational terrorist threat form a multi-dimensional terrorist threat package that have polluted the security environment for U.S. facilities and personnel overseas for the past six decades. Each threat strain was driven by a different goal, ideology, strategy, and sets of tactics and targets. The geographic scope of each strain's operational area varied. Some strains triggered terrorist activity — logistical or offensive — on U.S. soil. Each one presented a different level of terrorist threat to U.S. interests and each strain's lifespan was different. The common thread however that ran through all these different threat strains was the belief that the United States was directly or indirectly responsible for one or more of their grievances and that sympathizers in the U.S. could be a good source of funding and other support. All the terrorists, terrorist groups, and insurgent organizations within each threat believed that violence was the only effective means to address these grievances.

Why the U.S.?

Of all the countries in the world, why were U.S. interests overseas targeted the most by groups and states that carried out international terrorist attacks? The U.S. faced a multi-dimensional overseas terrorist threat composed of left-wing, secular Palestinian, Islamic revolutionary, and state-sponsored terrorism. Its interests were attacked worldwide, but mostly in Western Europe, Latin America, and the Middle East. Confronting this overseas terrorist threat was costly, complicated, and controversial — internally and internationally. In general, the four anti-American terrorist strains noted above targeted U.S. interests overseas for one or more of the following reasons[40]:

- Opposition to U.S. foreign policy in general.
- Opposition to the "capitalist exploitation" of their country by U.S. multinationals.

---

[40] Ivan Eland, "U.S. Arrogance, Intervention Fuel Anti-American Terrorist Attacks," The Independent Institute, September 19, 1999, at http://www.independent.org/newsroom/article.asp?id=1070. Accessed January 5, 2016; Barry Rubin and Judith Colp Rubin, Anti-American Terrorism and the Middle East (New York: Oxford University Press, 2002), pp. 4–5; CIA, Research Study: "International and Transnational Terrorism — Diagnosis and Prognosis," April 1976, pp. 12–13.

- Perception of the United States as a symbol of world capitalism and thus a logical target for any Marxist or Maoist terrorist or insurgent group.
- Perceived arrogance of the U.S. for its tendency to intervene in overseas conflicts: U.S. targets had a high symbolic value for "anti-imperialists" of both nationalistic and ideological persuasion.
- Opposition to specific American policies, such as military, economic, security, and diplomatic assistance to a government these groups or states opposed.
- Realization that attacking U.S. interests would attract more publicity for the terrorists' political cause.
- Perception that the U.S. was the primary obstacle to accomplishing the terrorists' worldwide goal.
- Punishment of the U.S. for supporting unpopular secular and religious regimes in their countries.
- Perception that U.S. cultural and economic influence was undermining their religious and cultural values and mores.
- Realization that it would be difficult for them to attack U.S. interests in the U.S.
- Its support for Israel.
- Its extensive involvement in Middle Eastern affairs for decades.
- U.S. targets had a high "embarrassment quotient" for the governments where the anti-American attacks took place.
- Jealousy: The U.S. was rich, powerful, influential, had large economic, cultural, political, and military footprints overseas; it was a superpower.[41]
- As the 1999 U.S. Commission on National Security in the 21st Century noted: "Much of the world will resent and oppose us, if not for the simple fact of our preeminence, then for the fact that others often perceive the United States as exercising its power with arrogance and self-absorption."[42]

---

[41] Terrorist attacks on the other superpower — the Soviet Union — were less frequent than those against the U.S. From 1975 to October 1985, there were 174 international terrorist attacks aimed at Soviet targets overseas — six kidnappings, 89 bombings, 51 armed attacks, 20 arsons, one each of assaults, hostage barricades, and skyjacking, and five other types of attack. These attacks took place in 39 different countries. Most anti-Soviet attacks took place in the U.S. — 33 since 1975. Source: U.S. Department of State, "Briefing Paper — Terrorism," October 16, 1985, at Department of State FOIA Reading Room, at https://foia.state.gov/Search/results.aspx?searchText=Terrorism+overview&beginDate=&endDate=&publishedBeginDate=&publishedEndDate=&caseNumber=. Accessed March 5, 2017.

[42] The United States Commission on National Security/21st Century, "New World Coming: American Security in the 21st Century: Major Themes and Implications," September 15, 1999, p. 8, at http://www.au.af.mil/au/awc/awcgate/nssg/nwc.pdf. Accessed March 4, 2016.

In sum, the U.S. was targeted for its political, economic, and cultural composition, its superpower status, its frequent military deployments overseas, and its foreign policies.

U.S. Footprint Overseas

A terrorist, terrorist group, insurgent organization, or state sponsor of terrorism that wants to deliver an anti-American message has two major options: carry out an attack in the U.S. or hit U.S. interests overseas. While the former may be more desirable, the latter is easier. The U.S. has a perceived reputation of possessing stringent internal security controls at its borders, airports, and ports. In addition, the Federal Bureau of Investigation has had an international reputation for diligence and effectiveness. The security environment in the U.S. has been perceived by most terrorist groups, insurgent organizations, and state sponsors of terrorism as being high risk. Whether the U.S. deserved this reputation is arguable, but this was the overseas perception of many terrorist actors. Another factor may have been that the U.S. had such large and extended diplomatic, economic, military, and aviation footprints overseas that it made more sense to attack U.S. targets overseas as it was easier, cheaper, and less risky.

No other military in world history has been so widely deployed as that of the United States.[43] From 1970 to 1990, roughly 20% of all U.S. military forces were stationed overseas — the figures were 32% in 1950 and 31% in 1969. In 1968, there were 1.2 million U.S. military personnel overseas. From 1972 to 1984, the average was over half a million U.S. military personnel overseas.[44] This overseas deployment of U.S. military forces was concentrated in Europe and Asia. In total, the U.S. had a military presence in 54 countries — or about 40% of the world.[45]

The U.S. had the largest diplomatic footprint overseas. In 1970, the U.S. had 117 diplomatic posts. In 1984, it had 233 diplomatic posts in over 170 countries.[46] Thus, the two official footprints of the U.S. overseas — military and

---

[43] Tim Kane, "Global U.S. Troop Deployment, 1950–2003," Heritage Foundation, Report #04-11 on National Security and Defense, October 27, 2004, at http://www.heritage.org/research/reports/2004/10/global-us-troop-deployment-1950-2003. Accessed April 7, 2017.

[44] Report of the Secretary of Defense Casper W. Weinberger to the Congress, February 4, 1985, p. 303, CIA FOIA document #RDP90B01390R000100050003-1.

[45] Kane, "Global U.S. Troop Deployment ...".

[46] U.S. Department of State, Office of the Historian, History of the Bureau of Diplomatic Security of the United States Department of State, p. 199; GAO Report: "Overseas Staffing: U.S. Government

diplomatic — were widespread. The U.S. also had a large economic footprint overseas with the distribution of U.S. businesses and subsidiaries in most of the countries in the world. As the terrorist threat against U.S. interests overseas evolved, U.S. military and diplomatic targets became hardened in terms of their protective security measures. This left U.S. businesses as a more attractive target for terrorists "because of their number and high visibility."[47] In 1985, the high watermark of the anti-American terrorist threat overseas, "U.S. business-related targets accounted for about 30% of all terrorist attacks against U.S. interests, more than against diplomatic and military targets combined."[48] These terrorist attacks on U.S. businesses caused casualties, property damage, increased protective security measures, high premiums for kidnap ransom insurance, and an adverse effect on efficiency and productivity as companies became hesitant to send advanced equipment or key people to high-risk areas. U.S. multinationals such as IBM, Pan Am, TWA, Citibank, Coca-Cola, McDonalds, Exxon, ITT, Xerox, Mobil, American Express, Bank of America, Chase Manhattan, and Chemical Bank of New York were all companies associated in the mind of the overseas public with the "American way of life."[49] In terms of hijackings, U.S. airlines were just behind Israel's El Al airline in terms of attractiveness and value for international terrorists.

Overseas anti-American terrorism actors in the 1970s and 1980s had both motivations and opportunities to carry out attacks on U.S. interests. Any country that has its overseas interests consistently and lethally targeted by terrorists is presented with multi-dimensional political, diplomatic, public relations, and protective security problems. The U.S. terrorism problem was compounded by the fact that it was also confronted with a domestic and foreign spillover terrorist threat. While not as acute as the overseas threat, it was still a concern and a consumer of valuable psychological and physical resources. The U.S. was faced with the worst-case threat scenario for a country — a persistent internal and overseas terrorist threat. It is within this context that the evolution of U.S. counter-terrorism policy and programs from Nixon through Trump should be seen.

Diplomatic Presence Abroad," Document # GAO/T-NSIAD-95-136, April 6, 1995, p. 2, at http://archive.gao.gov/t2pbat1/153940.pdf. Accessed June 6, 2017.

[47] U.S. Department of State, "Terrorist Attacks on US Businesses Abroad," March 1986, p. 1.

[48] Ibid.

[49] U.S. Department of State, "Terrorist Attacks Against U.S. Business: A Statistical overview of international terrorist attacks against U.S. business personnel and facilities from January 1968- December 1981," June 1982, p. 4.

Terrorism Statistics

The statistics used in these volumes are straightforward. They come mostly from U.S. government terrorism databases. These databases were later accused of being inaccurate, too narrow, or politicized. However, these accusations do not undermine these databases' functions and values to analysts and policy makers at the time. Threat assessments, terrorism research papers, protective security resource allocation, counter-terrorism policy and programs were based on these prevailing statistics. The later claims that they may have been inaccurate has no bearing on how they were used at the time. To understand the existing terrorist threat and the government's response to that threat, it is necessary to know what statistics were being used at the time. Retrospectives have little value to understanding history as it was taking place. For Volumes I and II, the author used the statistics that were collected and published at the time. The subsequent criticism and modifications of those databases will be addressed in latter sections.

Statistics on terrorism provide only limited illumination of the nature and extent of the international or internal terrorist threats. Statistics are simply one analytical tool. They are not infallible. They require interpretation which means the injection of subjectivity. Moreover, there is no one generally accepted terrorism database in the world.

This four-volume study will use three key terrorism statistics to help illustrate the anti-American terrorist threat overseas:

- The number of international terrorist attacks.
- The number of anti-American terrorist attacks.
- The number of American deaths overseas in terrorist-related incidents.

For the internal terrorist threat, the following two statistics will be utilized:

- The number of terrorist incidents in the U.S.
- The number of people killed in the U.S. in terrorist-related incidents.

As a terrorism threat analyst for the U.S. Department of State for 28 years, the author believes that macro-statistics that measure all terrorism in the world (internal and international) have nominal value in assessing the terrorist threat to U.S. interests overseas or in the U.S. The reasons for the author's position will be explained in Volumes I and II.

Statistics from Vinyard Software, the U.S. Department of State, the Federal Bureau of Investigation, and the U.S. Federal Aviation Administration will be used. Some will disagree with using government statistics on terrorism. However flawed the government's statistics were, it is important to note that it was these statistics that were used by intelligence analysts and policy makers at the time to make assessments and decisions. In later years, these statistics may have been modified or found to contain some errors, but this has no relevance to the past assessments made by intelligence analysts with the prevailing statistics. In addition to the government statistics noted above, the author has compiled a chronology of lethal, anti-American terrorist incidents overseas, and one on the lethal terrorist attacks inside the U.S. These chronologies can be found in the appendices in each volume.

U.S. Government's Annual Report on International Terrorism

The U.S. government first initiated an earnest and organized effort to collect, collate, analyze, and disseminate data on international terrorism in the summer of 1975. At that time, the CIA's Office of Political Research (OPR) began to use and expand a database called "International Terrorism: Attributes of Terrorist Events" or ITERATE. This database was created by Edward Mickolus who had just joined the CIA. This database was first publicly identified by the government in April 1976 when CIA/OPR published the first unclassified U.S. government assessment on international terrorism. It was titled "Research Study: International and Transnational Terrorism — Diagnosis and Prognosis."[50] A follow-up study was released in July 1977 — "International Terrorism in 1976."[51] These two studies created the foundation for the release of the U.S. government's most significant unclassified series on international terrorism — an annual report that began in 1976 and continues to the present.[52]

---

[50]This study was written by OPR analysts David L. Milbank and Edward Mickolus (document #PR 76 10030) and can be found at https://www.cia.gov/library/readingroom/docs/DOC_0000658249.pdf. Accessed July 1, 2017.

[51]This study was also complied by Milbank and Mickolus (document #RP-77-10034U). It examined international terrorist activity in 1976 but was released in July 1977 because end-of-year data had to be collated, checked, and analyzed. It then had to be written and cleared. As might be expected, unclassified studies underwent a lengthy clearance process at the agency in the late 1970s. This study can be found at https://www.cia.gov/library/readingroom/document/cia-rdp80m01048a0011000 20126-1. Accessed July 1, 2017.

[52]Additional information on these two CIA studies is contained in Chapters 7 and 12 in Volume I.

Both of these seminal studies on international terrorism specifically noted that the definitions and judgments were those of the "authors," and not the CIA's. The stated goals of the studies were "to cast the problem of internationalized terror into clear perspective and to provide the reader with a framework for a more systematic grasp of the subject." The 1976 study also noted in the foreword that the "statistics presented also break new ground." This was because they were drawn from ITERATE. The study's statistical charts showed international and transnational terrorist activity from 1968 to 1975.[53] With accurate prescience, the studies warned that the definitions used in them, the figures, and the statistical inferences were "bound to draw some critical comment." The subsequent controversies that developed over the government's data on international terrorism concerned definitions, criteria, whether internal terrorist incidents should be included, and whether the data would be politicized by an administration.

The groundbreaking April 1976 study presented international terrorism and transnational terrorism as two different designations. International terrorism was when an action was "carried out by individuals or groups controlled by a sovereign state," whereas transnational terrorism was carried out by "basically autonomous non-state actors, whether or not they enjoy some degree of support from sympathetic states." In the follow-up July 1977 study, the term "transnational terrorism" was dropped and never appeared again. The focus of the database and subsequent studies by the CIA would be on "international terrorism." There was no intent to try and collect data on worldwide internal terrorism. This rejection of collecting worldwide internal terrorist attacks was a reasonable decision. The term "international" terrorist incident was later refined to mean "incidents that involve the citizens or the territory of more than one country." This would include foreign spillover terrorism and foreign incursion terrorism. An international terrorist attack was easier to identify and track and provided more value to

---

[53] The year 1968 is generally accepted as the beginning of the modern era of the international terrorist threat. Most databases use 1968 as the front end of their data collection. For example, see Bruce Hoffman, *Inside Terrorism* (London: Victor Gollancz, 1998), p. 67; Jeffrey D. Simon, *The Terrorist Trap: America's Experience with Terrorism* (Indiana: Indiana University Press, 1994), p. 97. The U.S. government has also used 1968 as the front end of its statistical database on international terrorist attacks. See Central Intelligence Agency, Directorate of Intelligence, International Terrorism in 1976, Document #RP77-10034U, July 1977, pp., 11, 13, and 15 and Central Intelligence Agency, National Foreign Assessment Center, Patterns of International Terrorism: 1980, Document #PA81-10163U, June 1981, pp. 4–9, and 21. The Jaffee Center for Strategic Studies at Tel Aviv University in Israel also used 1968 as the starting point for its extensive study on Palestinian terrorism, see, Ariel Merari and Shlomi Elad, *The International Dimension of Palestinian Terrorism* (Colorado: Westview Press, 1986), pp. 7, 130.

anti-American terrorism threat assessment than worldwide internal terrorist incidents. In an April 1984 speech, the Director of Central Intelligence, William Casey, noted that "by definition, international terrorism is the kind that most directly impacts on U.S. interests... there is no way we can keep track of all the terrorism in the world; there are just too many incidents in too many places."[54]

Because international terrorist incidents, by definition, involve the citizens or the territory of more than one country, it is difficult for a country where the attack took place to deliberately conceal the incident. Internal terrorist incidents carried out by domestic terrorists could be ignored, denied, hushed up, or not counted in government internal terrorism reports in a way that international incidents could not. In addition, most international terrorist incidents generally take place in the capitals and other major cities where there is more media and therefore a higher probability of press reporting. Many internal/domestic terrorist incidents take place in rural areas where the government can deny, refuse to report or confirm the attack; or the major city media might overlook the attack or be unable to obtain reliable information. Furthermore, it is often difficult to confirm attacks that take place in remote areas of the larger countries. Theoretically, given that internal terrorist incidents worldwide significantly outnumber international terrorist incidents, there is a greater possibility of a database recording entity missing some internal terrorist incident. From 1977 to 1989, there was an average of over 2,800 worldwide terrorist incidents annually.[55] However, the highest number of international terrorist incidents recorded in one year during the 1970s and 1980s was 666 incidents in 1987. More importantly, anti-American terrorist attacks are found within the number of international terrorist incidents. Any attack by an internal terrorist group against an American target would be classified as an international terrorist attack. The total number of international terrorist attacks reflected the prevailing trend or pattern of the terrorist threat to foreign interests worldwide, developments that the U.S. government needed to monitor.

Except for macro-statistical reasons, there is a little direct value in assessing the terrorist threat to U.S. interests overseas knowing that there were 700 domestic terrorist attacks in country X if none of them involved U.S. or foreign interests. Monitoring domestic terrorist incidents can be helpful in assessing the indirect terrorist threat to Americans overseas. Should these attacks take place in major cities and involve indiscriminate, mass-casualty attacks, then the U.S. Department of State would use that data to issue U.S. Department of State — travel warnings

---

[54]CIA, "Draft of DCI Speech on Terrorism," dated December 5, 1984, CIA FOIA document # CIA-RDP86M00886R00100010003-9.

[55]https://ourworldindata.org/terrorism. Accessed on June 15, 2018.

and alerts to American travelers going or living overseas. While Americans are not being directly targeted, given the type (indiscriminate, mass casualty) and location (capital and other major cities) of the attacks, American tourists, diplomats, businesspersons, and military personnel could become accidental victims of terrorism by being in the wrong place at the wrong time. However, one would not need to record every internal terrorist incident to assess this risk, but only those that took place in a major city and were indiscriminate, mass-casualty attacks. The U.S. government's limiting of the collection of terrorist incidents overseas to international and anti-American terrorist incidents was simply a calculation of what are the most valuable, detectable, manageable, and relevant terrorism statistics when assessing the threat to U.S. interests overseas.

Over the next 39 years, the U.S. government's annual report on international terrorism would undergo many changes, which were intended to enhance the value and accuracy of the report. Some changes were cosmetic, some were wordsmithing, some were additions, and some were statistical modifications. There were adjustments to definitions, modifications of data fields, criteria refinements to what type of incident should be included, and changing paternity of the report's publication. This annual publication would be titled "International Terrorism," "Patterns in International Terrorism," "Patterns in Global Terrorism," and is currently referred to as "Country Reports on Terrorism." This annual report was initially published by Central Intelligence Agency's Office of Political Research and National Foreign Assessment Center (from 1977 to 1980). Since 1981, it has been published by the State Department's Office of the Coordinator for Combatting Terrorism. The CIA's terrorism database "ITERATE" provided the data for all these publications until 2005 when the database was renamed "Worldwide Incidents Tracking System" or WITS. The WITS served as the annual report's database until 2011 when the government turned over statistical support for the annual report to the University of Maryland's National Consortium for the Study of Terrorism and Responses to Terrorism (START) and its "Global Terrorism Database."[56] This was a major mistake by the U.S. government to surrender its responsibility for keeping international terrorism statistics to a private entity, albeit an academic institution.

A database that tracks global developments is a manpower-intensive operation that requires worldwide assets. Anyone can enter a terrorist attack into a database. The accuracy comes from the ability to acquire credible information on

---

[56] For a study of the evolution of the U.S. government's annual report on international terrorism, see Dennis Pluchinsky, "The Evolution of the U.S. Government's Annual Report on Terrorism: A Personal Commentary," *Studies in Conflict & Terrorism*, March 2006, pp. 91–98.

the details of the attack and the accurate assignment of responsibility to a specific group. In some cases, the responsibility is not known until foreign law enforcement and intelligence investigations are complete. Academic and public entities rely more on open source reporting from the media. Although the USG database was unclassified and used open source reporting, it also had access to worldwide reporting assets and other unclassified and classified sources to confirm the specifics of an attack. In addition, during the year, government terrorism analysts were convened monthly to discuss what should or should not be counted as a terrorist attack as initial open source reporting is not always immediately accurate. These government analysts were experts with access to comparative classified information, and special open source reporting (some embassy reporting on incidents were unclassified) whose opinions were anchored in experience and expertise, as opposed to a revolving cadre of interns, students, or contractors hired to enter data into public sector terrorism databases. At present (2019), the U.S. government (Department of Homeland Security) pays a public entity attached to a university to maintain its terrorism database. The government is misusing its money for a contracted task that was and could be carried out by government personnel more accurately and effectively for less money (government analysts do receive salaries, but there are no overhead costs). Despite some definitional, tagging, and methodological flaws in the past, the U.S. government developed, operated, and maintained the most accurate, extensive and quoted database on international terrorism and anti-American terrorist attacks and casualties in the world.

In 1988, Congress, based on Public Law 100-204, required the State Department to publish this annual report. In 1991, based on Title 22 of the U.S. Code 2656f(a), Congress mandated that the State Department provide Congress a full and complete annual report on terrorism for those countries and groups meeting the criteria noted in the responsible act. It noted that the Secretary of State "shall transmit to the Speaker of the House of Representatives and the Committee on Foreign Relations of the Senate, by April 30 of each year, a full and complete report." Title 22 also required that this report should contain "to the extent practicable, complete statistical information on the number of individuals, including United States citizens and dual nationals,[57] killed, injured, or kidnapped by each

---

[57] The issue of dual nationality in terrorism-related casualty statistics surfaced more with dual American–Israeli citizens than any other nationality. According to the U.S. Department of State, "The concept of dual nationality means that a person is a national of two countries at the same time. Each country has its own nationality laws based on its own policy. Persons may have dual nationality by automatic operation of different laws rather than by choice. U.S. law does not mention dual nationality or require a person to choose one nationality or another. A U.S. citizen may naturalize in a foreign state without any risk to his or her U.S. citizenship. Dual nationals owe allegiance to both the United

terrorist group during the preceding calendar year." The report also defined terrorism as "premeditated, politically motivated violence perpetrated against non-combatant targets by subnational groups or clandestine agents." The key to this definition is "non-combatants." It was not until the 1991 edition of Patterns of Global Terrorism that a "non-combatant" was defined for the first time. The term

> *is interpreted to include, in addition to civilians, military personnel who at the time of the incident are unarmed and/or not on duty. Examples given were: (1) the assassination of Col. James Rowe in April 1989 in Manila, Philippines, (2) the car-bomb killing of Capt. William Nordeen, U.S. Defense Attaché, in Athens in June 1988, (3) the deaths of two U.S. servicemen in the bombing of the La Belle disco in West Berlin in April 1986, and (4) the killing of four off-duty U.S. Embassy Marine guards in a café in El Salvador in June 1985. We also consider as acts of terrorism attacks on military installations or armed military personnel when a state of military hostilities does not exist at the site, such as bombings against U.S. bases in Europe, the Philippines, or elsewhere.*

The term "non-combatant" was not defined by Congress in Title 22 of the U.S. Code 2656.

As anticipated by Milbank and Mickolus in 1976, the government's annual report on terrorism would be controversial in some respects. In addition to whether domestic terrorist incidents worldwide should be tracked, the most serious concern was if an administration would distort the statistics for political purposes? The fear was that various administrations would use the report to justify how they perceive and measure the terrorist threat and to support certain counter-terrorism policies, programs, and approaches. Four years after the annual report's formation, this controversy emerged for the first time. On April 24, 1981, the *New York Times* published an article titled "Data on Terrorism Under U.S. Revision," which reported that the USG's statistics on international terrorist incidents were "being revised to include 'threats' as well as actual acts of politically motivated violence." The article noted that Tony Quainton, the

---

States and the foreign country. They are required to obey the laws of both countries, and either country has the right to enforce its laws," at https://travel.state.gov/content/travel/en/legal/travel-legal-considerations/Advice-about-Possible-Loss-of-US-Nationality-Dual-Nationality/Dual-Nationality.html. Accessed May 6, 2017. No one knows for sure how many Americans are also citizens of other lands because neither the U.S. nor other governments keep track. This sometimes leads to confusion in terms of whether an "American" was killed in a terrorist attack or not.

Director of the State Department's Office for Combatting Terrorism, "indicated that the change would approximately double the number of terrorist incidents counted by the United States in the last 12 years." The article then stated that some Democratic members and staff officials of Congress said they feared the statistical revisions were motivated by a Reagan administration desire to justify a more rigid foreign policy abroad and might also be cited by conservatives to justify increased surreptitious surveillance of political dissidents at home. Representative Don Edwards, a Democrat of California and Chairman of the House subcommittee that oversees the FBI, was quoted as stating that "terrorism is actually decreasing and disagreeing with the new statistical criteria." The *Times* article also reported that the publication of the 1981 annual report was delayed "because of disputes among Government agencies as to the nature, extent, and gravity of terrorism." One Senate staff official was quoted as saying that "C.I.A. analysts were also being 'pushed' or encouraged to expand the definition of terrorist incidents to include 'all acts of violence intended to impact on a wider audience than the victims of the violence.'" By that definition, said the official, "the shooting of President Reagan by John Hinckley would be a terrorist act." This claim of politicizing the annual report's statistics also surfaced some 23 years later. In a letter sent to the Secretary of State on May 17, 2004, Democratic Congressman Henry Waxman charged that the decline in terrorism in 2003, as reported in the annual Patterns of Global Terrorism for 2003 was inaccurate due to flawed statistics.[58]

Other changes would take place in this annual report immediately after the 9/11 attacks. These annual reports presented statistics on international terrorist and anti-American terrorist incidents that were valuable and timely in assessing the terrorist threat to U.S. interests overseas. In later years, academics would snipe

---

[58] This controversy will be covered in more detail in Volume III which will examine the Clinton and George W. Bush administrations. Further information on this controversy can be found at Stephen Alter "The 2003 Annual Report on Global Terrorism: An Information System Failure?," *Communications of the Association for Information Systems*, August 2004, Vol. 14 , Article 4, at http://aisel.aisnet.org/cais/vol14/iss1/4. Accessed June 5, 2017; Susan Glasser, "Global Terrorism Statistics Debated," *Washington Post*, May 1, 2005; Dennis Pluchinsky, "The Evolution of the U.S. Government's Annual Report on Terrorism: A Personal Commentary," *Studies in Conflict & Terrorism*, 29:91–98, 2006: Raphael Perl. "The Department of State's Patterns of Global Terrorism Report: Trends, State Sponsors, and Related Issues," Congressional Research Service, June 1, 2004, at http://fpc.state.gov/documents/organization/33630.pdf. Accessed August 6, 2017; and May 17, 2004 Letter from Congressman Henry Waxman to Secretary of State Colin Powell, re: Patterns of Global Terrorism 2003 at https://fas.org/irp/congress/2004_cr/waxman051704.pdf. Accessed September 4, 2017.

at the U.S. government's exclusion of internal terrorist incidents in its database in the 1970s, 1980s, and 1990s.[59] The criticism would center on the following:

- It was a mistake to exclude domestic terrorist attacks from terrorism databases.
- Only 3% of the attacks by government designated anti-U.S. groups were directed at U.S. targets.
- 99% of attacks targeting the United States did not occur on U.S. soil but were aimed at U.S. targets in other countries.
- The U.S. State Department's claim that one-third of all terrorist attacks worldwide were directed at the United States.
- International terrorist attacks account for less than 3% of terrorist attacks in the world.

The problem is that none of the above conclusions are surprising. Government analysts knew in the 1980s that (1) most of the terrorist attacks against U.S. targets took place overseas, (2) no anti-American terrorist group focused solely on the U.S., and (3) international terrorism was less than 1% of all terrorist attacks worldwide.[60] Moreover, it is unlikely that the State Department would make the statement that one-third of *all* worldwide terrorist attacks were aimed at the U.S. The State Department policy was to note that one-third or so of "international terrorist" incidents were directed at the U.S. It has also been pointed out that "between 1969 and 2009, there were 38,345 terrorist incidents around the world. Of these attacks, 7.8 percent (2,981) were directed against the United States."[61] However, no one in the U.S. government in the 1970s or 1980s ever stated publicly that a large percentage of worldwide terrorist incidents were directed at U.S. targets. The U.S. government was correct to concentrate its collection and analysis of data on international terrorist incidents and not worldwide domestic

---

[59] See, for example, Gary LaFree, Sue-Ming Yang, Martha Crenshaw. "Trajectories of terrorism: Attack patterns of foreign groups that have targeted the United States, 1970–2004," *Criminology & Public Policy*, 2009, Volume 8, Issue 3, pp. 445–473; at https://cisac.fsi.stanford.edu/publications/ trajectories_of_terrorism_attack_patterns_of_foreign_groups_that_have_targeted_the_united_ states_19702004/. Accessed June 7, 2017.

[60] In a previously noted December 1984 speech by DCI Casey, he stated that "perhaps only 1 or 2 percent of all terrorist incidents are international incidents." CIA, "Draft of DCI Speech on Terrorism," dated December 5, 1984, CIA FOIA document # CIA-RDP86M00886R00100010003-9.

[61] Todd Sandler, "The analytical study of terrorism: Taking stock," *Journal of Peace Research*, August 13, 2013 at http://journals.sagepub.com/doi/full/10.1177/0022343313491277.

terrorist attacks. Those who criticize this focus do not understand the finer points of terrorist threat analysis. More data are not always more valuable.

Of all the statistical measurements, it is the number of American deaths and the number of anti-American attacks that shape, along with the news coverage of them, the public's perception of the terrorist threat. Therefore, these are the two statistical measurements that are used to gauge the operational impact of each of the four anti-American terrorism strains tracked in this four-volume study. The number of injuries should not be overlooked as some injuries can cause a lifetime of suffering. However, it is fatalities that appear to register more with the American public, as injuries can heal, and property damage can be replaced, but death is irreversible. A single death creates expanding ramifications within the victim's family and friends, and potentially a loss to humanity, as the victim could have later invented a device, written, painted, or composed a masterpiece, or become a prominent military or political leader. A terrorist attack on a government, diplomatic, military, or business target is a cut on the nation, with some larger or more serious than others, but rarely debilitating or fatal for the nation. The death of an individual is a human tragedy that gets lost in the macro-political and security ripples of the attack.

This four-volume work will present in each volume a chronology of terrorist attacks overseas that have killed Americans (civilians, military, government, businesspersons, missionaries, contractors, and diplomats) during the discussed administration.

Recording the number of Americans killed overseas from 1950 to 2018 for these four-volumes was tedious as each incident in the chronology had to be confirmed with at least two other sources. Several chronologies consulted did not follow up on injured Americans who later died of their injuries. There was also confusion over the deaths of dual Israeli–U.S. citizens. During the conflicts in Iraq and Afghanistan, there were confusion and inaccuracies over the death of DOD contractors in those conflicts. The U.S. government's annual publication on terrorism also changed how it counted American deaths in terrorist-related incidents. Finally, in certain incidents in Africa and Latin America when no terrorist group claimed credit for an attack that killed an American, the possibility of drug and criminal gangs had to be considered as the perpetrator of the attacks. When ISIS emerged in Iraq in 2014 and then established a "caliphate," some Americans went on to join ISIS and fight. Moreover, some Americans went to join Kurdish groups that were fighting against ISIS. If they were killed in a confrontation with ISIS, were they killed by terrorists and should they be counted as a terrorist-related death? The criteria for establishing if an American was killed in a terrorist-related attack has shifted over time as unique conditions emerged.

It should also be noted that the U.S. government has changed its criteria for recording terrorist incidents over the past 34 years. For example, before 1989, the U.S. counted violence by Palestinians against other Palestinians in the Occupied Territories as international terrorism as the Palestinians were considered stateless persons. Beginning in 1989, those Palestinian incidents were no longer counted.[62] Another example is that from 1977 to 2004, the U.S. government terrorism database recorded primarily international terrorist incidents. Beginning in 2005, the statistics used in the government's annual report on terrorism included both overseas internal and international terrorist incidents. From 1977 to 2004, the U.S. government counted all Americans killed overseas in terrorist-related incidents. Beginning in 2005, the government only published the fatality total of "U.S. private citizens," leaving out the deaths of U.S. diplomats, and other government personnel who were killed in terrorist-related attacks. The author has taken these adjustments into account when compiling the statistics on anti-American terrorism.

In compiling the number of international terrorist incidents and anti-American terrorist incidents, and the number of Americans killed in terrorist-related incidents overseas, the author relied on the following sources for Volumes I and II[63]:

1. The U.S. government's unclassified annual reports on international terrorism from 1977 to 1992, titled successively as "International Terrorism" and "Patterns of Global Terrorism."
2. The State Department's annual unclassified publication "Political Violence Against Americans" from 1987 to 1992. This publication recorded terrorist acts and violent anti-American demonstrations and thus presented a broader picture of the threat to U.S. interests overseas from political violence.
3. Special unclassified statistical charts on international terrorism and anti-American terrorist attacks overseas in the 1970s and 1980s, released in 1994 and 1998 by the State Department's Office for Combatting Terrorism.
4. Jaffee Center for Security Studies (Tel Aviv, Israel), JCSS Project on Terrorism, Annual Reviews of International Terrorism (focus on secular Palestinian terrorist activity).
5. The RAND-St. Andrews Chronology of International Terrorism.
6. Central Intelligence Agency, *Research Study: International and Transnational Terrorism: Diagnosis and Prognosis*, Unclassified. PR-76-10030, April 1976. Author — David Milbank, 45 pages with foldout chart.
7. U.S. Department of State, Office for Combatting Terrorism, *Terrorist Attacks Against Diplomats: January 1968 — June 1981*, December 1981, 16 pages.

---

[62] U.S. Department of State, *Patterns of Global Terrorism 1989*, p. 1.

[63] As subsequent volumes are published, additional sources may be used.

8. U.S. Department of State, Office for Combatting Terrorism, *Terrorist Attacks Against U.S. Businesses: January 1968 — December 1981*, June 1982, 20 pages.

9. U.S. Department of State, Office for Combatting Terrorism, *Terrorist Skyjackings: January 1968 — June 1982*, July 1982, 24 pages.

10. U.S. Department of State, Office for Combatting Terrorism, *International Terrorism: Hostage Seizures: January 1968 — December 1982*, March 1983, 26 pages.

11. U.S. Department of State, Office for Combatting Terrorism, *Terrorist Incidents Involving Diplomats: January 1968 — April 1983*, August 1983.

12. U.S. Department of State, Office for Combatting Terrorism, *Terrorist Bombings: January 1977 — May 1983*, September 1983, 19 pages.

13. Central Intelligence Agency, Significant International Terrorist Incidents: 1968–1981 — an unclassified chronology of international terrorist incidents, 200 double-sided pages.

14. RAND Corporation, *International Terrorism: A Chronology — 1968 to 1974* (Document # R-1597-DOS/ARPA), March 1975.

15. ITERATE database at Vinyard Software.

16. The excellent published chronologies on terrorism by Ed Mickolus, Todd Sandler, and Susan Simmons. Multiple volumes cover from 1968 to 2015.

It should also be noted that contrary to what has been written,[64] the U.S. Department of State never maintained a database on international terrorism. The international terrorism statistics used in its annual, unclassified report on international terrorism from 1982 to around 2004 were based on the CIA's ITERATE database.

All aircraft hijacking statistics from 1961 to 1985 come from Office of Civil Aviation Security, Federal Aviation Administration, "Aircraft Hijackings and Other Criminal Acts against Civil Aviation Statistical and Narrative Reports — Updated to January 1, 1986," Publication date: May 1986, pp. 2 and 228 (in author's possession).

All statistics on the secular Palestinian terrorist strain were collated from the following sources:

1. Ariel Merari and Shlomi Elad, *The International Dimensions of Palestinian Terrorism* (Colorado: Westview Press, 1986). This book was published by the Jaffee Center for Strategic Studies (JCSS), Tel Aviv University.

---

[64] Gary LeFree, Sue Ming Yang, and Martha Crenshaw, "Trajections of Terrorism: Attack Patterns of Foreign Groups that have Targeted the United States, 1970–2004," *Criminology and Public Policy*, Volume 8, Issue 3, 2009, p. 448.

2. JCSS annual assessments of International Terrorism or the "Inter" series for 1986, 1987, 1988, and 1989.
3. Dennis Pluchinsky, "Middle Eastern Terrorist Activity in Western Europe in the 1980s: A Decade of Violence," in Yonah Alexander and Dennis Pluchinsky, editors. *European Terrorism: Today and Tomorrow* (Washington, D.C.: Brassey's, Inc, 1992), pp. 1–41.
4. CIA, "Chronology of Significant Fedayeen Terrorist Incidents — July 1968 — October 15, 1973," published October 1973, at https://www.cia.gov/library/readingroom/docs/DOC_0005764836.pdf. Accessed January 6, 2017.
5. CIA, Directorate of Intelligence, Intelligence Memorandum: Palestine Arab Terrorist Organizations, December 2, 1966, at https://www.cia.gov/library/readingroom/docs/CIA-RDP79T00826A001400010080-2.pdf. Accessed March 6, 2017.
6. Israeli Ministry of Foreign Affairs, at http://mfa.gov.il/MFA/Foreign Policy/Terrorism/Palestinian/Pages/Victims%20of%20Palestinian%20Violence%20and%20Terrorism%20sinc.aspx. Accessed January 10, 2017.
7. The author's personal chronology of Middle Eastern terrorist attacks in Western Europe from 1980 to 1989. Used for the author's several published journal articles and book chapters on Middle Eastern spillover terrorist activity in Western Europe in the 1980s.

The Internal Terrorist Threat in the U.S.

The internal terrorist threat is composed of domestic and foreign spillover terrorist activity. The following two statistics were utilized to analyze the internal terrorist threat in the U.S. — the number of terrorist incidents in the U.S. and the number of people killed in the U.S. in terrorist-related incidents. To assess the terrorist threat inside the U.S., Volumes I and II relied on the FBI's annual reports of internal and international terrorist incidents in the U.S. from 1980 to 1992 which contained a chronology of attacks and statistical charts. This annual report was the premier unclassified government assessment of the domestic and foreign spillover terrorist threats in the U.S. Like the government's annual report on international terrorism, the evolution of the definition of terrorism colored what was included or excluded as a terrorist incident. The FBI did not record its first eco-terrorist attack until November 1987 when it reported an attack in Arizona by the Evan Meacham Eco-Terrorist International Conspiracy. Although it recorded attacks by Eric Rudolph as terrorism, the FBI did not classify attacks on abortion clinics as acts of domestic terrorism. Consequently, some 367 anti-abortion murders, attempted murders, kidnappings, and bombing and arson attacks and attempts are not counted in the FBI's internal terrorist statistics.[65] As a result, the author used other sources when counting eco-terrorist and anti-abortion attacks.

Since the FBI issued no public annual reports on internal terrorism in the 1970s, other government and media sources were used to determine the number of attacks. Therefore, internal terrorism statistics in the 1970s are less accurate than those in the 1980s. As of August 2017, the U.S. government "does not keep a publicly available list of domestic terrorist incidents (foiled plots or attacks) ... this makes it especially challenging for anyone trying to develop a sense of this particularly diverse threat."[66] Moreover, unlike the U.S. Department of State which publishes a list of "foreign terrorist organizations," the federal government does not generate an official and public list of domestic terrorist organizations and individuals.[67]

In addition to its annual report on terrorism in the U.S., FBI officials would occasionally provide the number of terrorist attacks in the U.S. in speeches or in interviews with the press.

Other sources used for the number of terrorist attacks in the U.S. were as follows:

- Bryan Burrough's 2015 book *Days of Rage: America's Radical Underground, the FBI, and the Forgotten Age of Revolutionary Violence.*
- The U.S. Senate, Committee on the Judiciary, Subcommittee to Investigate the Administration of the Internal Security Act and other Internal Security Laws, Report: Terroristic Activity: Interlocks Between Communism and Terrorism, Part 9, May 7, 1976. Beginning on p. 721 this report contains a chronology of "Guerrilla Acts of Sabotage and Terrorism in the United States: 1965–1970."
- Law Enforcement Assistance Administration's (LEAA), National Advisory Committee on Criminal Justice Standards and Goals, "Report of the Task Force on Disorders and Terrorism," March 2, 1977, Appendix 6 — Chronology of Incidents of Terroristic, Quasi-Terroristic in the United States from January 1965 — March 1976, pp. 507–595, at https://babel.hathitrust.org/cgi/pt?id=umn.31951p008901837;view=1up;seq=542. Accessed October 6, 2017. In the 1970s, terrorist attacks killed many U.S. law

---

[65] National Abortion Federation data on violence against clinics and providers, at https://5aa1b2xfmfh2e2mk03kk8rsx-wpengine.netdna-ssl.com/wp-content/uploads/2016-NAF-Violence-and-Disruption-Statistics.pdf. Accessed March 9, 2017.

[66] Jerome P. Bjelopera, "Domestic Terrorism: An Overview," Congressional Research Service Report #R44921, August 21, 2017, p. 40.

[67] Ibid., p. 9.

enforcement officials, see the Officer Down website at http://www.odmp.org/search/this_day_in_history. Accessed March 10, 2016.

- https://ourworldindata.org/terrorism. Accessed January 29, 2019.

All statistics and attacks of Puerto Rican terrorism in the U.S. are based on chronologies of Puerto Rican terrorist attacks found from the following sources:

1. http://www.latinamericanstudies.org/puertorico/FALN-incidents.pdf. Accessed June 7, 2017.
2. Movement of National Liberation Towards People's War for Independence and Socialism in Puerto Rico: In Defense of Armed Struggle — Documents and Communiques from the Revolutionary Public Independence Movement and the Armed Clandestine Movement. January 1979, pp. 40–49, at http://www.scribd.com/doc/99105307/Towards-People-s-War-for-Independence-and-Socialism-in-Puerto-Rico#scribd. Accessed May 6, 2017.
3. William Sater. Puerto Rican Terrorists: Possibly Threat to U.S. Energy Installations? RAND Corporation, #N-1764-SL, October 1981, pp. 21–30, at https://www.rand.org/content/dam/rand/pubs/notes/2005/N1764.pdf. Accessed March 6, 2017.
4. Federal Bureau of Investigation, Counterterrorism Division, Counterterrorism Threat Assessment and Warning Group:
   - "Terrorism in the United States 1999," FBI Publication #0308. Chronology of Terrorist Activity in the United States: 1980–1999, pp. 54–61.
   - "Terrorism 2000/2001," FBI Publication #0308. Chronology of Terrorist Activity in the United States: 1990–2001, pp. 535–37.
   - U.S. District Court, Eastern District of New York. "Sentence Memorandum of the United States in the Case of the U.S. Government vs. Julio Rosado, Andres Rosado, Ricardo Romero, Steven Guerra, and Maria Cueto," Document #CR 83-0025, dated May 20, 1983, p. 6, found at http://www.latinamericanstudies.org/puertorico/FALN-memo.pdf. Accessed July 4, 2017.

All statistics on Armenian terrorism come from the following sources:

1. Andrew Corsun, "Armenian Terrorism: A Profile," Department of State Bulletin: The Official Monthly Record of United States Foreign Policy,

Special Issue Terrorism, Volume 82, Number 2065, August 1982, pp. 31–35. This is published for the public by the Department of State.

2.   Anat Kurz and Ariel Merari, "ASALA — Irrational Terror or Political Tool," Jaffee Center for Strategic Studies #2," Tel Aviv University (Colorado: Westview Press, 1985).

3.   Declassified CIA study on Armenian terrorism, dated January 1984, accessed at http://www.foia.cia.gov/sites/default/files/document_conversions/89801/ DOC_0005462031.pdf. Accessed November 6, 2016.

Statistics on Croatian terrorist attacks in the U.S. came from the following sources:

1.   An unpublished, unclassified statistical study on "Yugoslav-Related Terrorist Attacks, 1962–July 1982," U.S. Department of State, Office of Security, Threat Analysis Group. Six pages of statistical charts.

2.   CIA, National Foreign Assessment Center, Memorandum — Yugoslav Émigré Extremists, May 29, 1980, pp. A1–A8, at https://www.cia.gov/ library/readingroom/docs/CIA-RDP85T00287R000101220002-6.pdf. Accessed October 5, 2017.

Statistics on Jewish Defense League (JDL) attacks inside the United States are based on the author's chronology compiled from the following sources: (1) Southern Poverty Law Center at www.splcenter.org and (2) Anti-Defamation League at www.adl.org.

Each volume in this four-volume work will contain appendices that will include a statistical snapshot for each administration listing the following: (1) number of international terrorist attacks, (2) the number of anti-American terrorist attacks overseas, (3) the percentage of anti-American terrorist attacks in the international terrorist incidents total, (4) the number of Americans killed in overseas terrorist attacks, (5) the number of terrorist attacks in the U.S., and (6) the number of people killed in the U.S. in terrorism attacks. These appendices will also include chronologies of lethal terrorist attacks against Americans overseas and a chronology of lethal attacks in the U.S. that took place during the covered administrations.

As noted previously, there is no generally accepted terrorism database in the world today. The author has identified the above statistical sources used to compile the statistics used in the text. The author has been analyzing terrorism for over 42 years and has applied the experience and expertise he acquired over those years in the selection of statistical sources. Some may disagree with the selections.

Terrorist Communiques

The author has made extensive use of excerpts of terrorist communiques in this four-volume work. Terrorists communicate with their actions and words. A terrorist attack is a form of communication as it signals to the target audience the intentions and capabilities of the terrorists. It is however a form of esoteric communication as the intended message of the attack can sometimes be obscure. Most terrorists will follow-up an attack with a written communique explaining more concisely and in more detail the reasons behind the attack. It is the combination of the attack and the communiqué that transmits the terrorist organization's message to the various targeted audiences. Terrorist communiqués are one of the several methods of terrorist communications. Terrorist leaders may give interviews, speeches, or write articles. Terrorist organizations and/or their overt political fronts may publish recurring newsletters, magazines, or journals. Terrorist organizations may give clandestine press conferences.

Terrorist organizations have a need to explain their actions to their members, supporters, sympathizers, constituency, the targeted population, and the international community. This explanation is usually in the form of written communiqués. There are three types of terrorist communiqués:

- *Terrorist attack communiqués* — An attack communiqué claims responsibility for a specific operation and explains why that target was attacked.
- *Terrorist strategic communiqués* — Strategic communiqués comment on broad domestic and/or international political developments or explain strategic shifts by the terrorist group.
- *Terrorist special events communiqués* — Special communiqués comment on the death of a leader, arrests of members, anniversary dates, hunger strikes, cease fires, etc.

An analyst who reads every written communiqué from a terrorist group will develop an analytical feel for the grammar, sentence structure, terminology, and ideological view of the author. Any changes in authors should be detected. While communiqués do not provide the timing, location, and target of the next terrorist attack, they sometimes provide hints of a targeting shift, internal dissent, new grievance, or a growing weariness for armed struggle.

In the 1960s, 1970s, and 1980s, many terrorist communiqués were delivered to various news agencies, sent to sympathetic newsletters or magazines, or simply left at the attack site. For law enforcement, the physical aspects of the communiqués and the envelope, if used, could provide forensic evidence such as saliva from the stamp or envelope, fingerprints, and type of paper and typewriter used. With the advent of the Internet and the tendency for terrorist groups to issue e-communiques and videos, these evidentiary benefits disappeared.

The importance of terrorist communications, especially terrorist communiqués, should not be underestimated. These communiques provide a small peek through an admittedly opaque window into a terrorist organization. In 1974, when Italian General Carlo Alberto Dalla Chiesa created an anti-terrorism unit in Turin, Italy, he selected ten top-notch police officers to target the Red Brigades (Brigate Rosse) terrorist group, at the time, the most dangerous group in Italy. This special anti-terrorism unit "succeeded, among other things, in capturing Renato Curcio and Alberto Franceschini, two of the top BR leaders."[68] In October 1979, the author was the European analyst for the State Department's Threat Analysis Group. During an official visit to Italy to discuss the terrorist threat to U.S. interests in Italy with Italian intelligence and law enforcement, the author was told that Della Chiesa had candidates for his special anti-terrorism unit read all the communiques by the Red Brigades and, based on their analysis of the communiques, predict, as closely as possible, the next attack of the Red Brigades. Those who were the most accurate were picked for the unit. Italy's top anti-terrorism official recognized the importance of reading and analyzing terrorist communiques. Della Chiesa was and remains the most famous and successful Italian anti-terrorism official in Italian history. As a result of his success in neutralizing the Red Brigades terrorist group, on May 1, 1982, he was appointed as prefect for Palermo to address the violence of the Second Mafia War. Four months later, he and his wife were murdered in Palermo by the Mafia.

---

[68] Deirdre Pirro, "Carlo Alberto Dalla Chiesa: A man alone," The Florentine, May 21, 2009, at www. theflorentine.net/lifestyle/2009/05/carlo-alberto-dalla-chiesa/.

Introduction to Volume I

The early stages of anti-American terrorism overseas began developing during the Eisenhower–Carter administrations. This first volume describes the overseas developments and responses by the Eisenhower, Kennedy, and Johnson administrations that created grievances against the U.S., thus fueling anti-American terrorism in the coming decades. Although the decade of the 1950s did not witness significant anti-American terrorist activities overseas, it did provide seeds for the three future anti-American terrorist strains that formed in the subsequent decades: secular Palestinian, Islamic revolutionary and left-wing.

Consider the following:

- The state of Israel emerged in 1948 out of the 1947–1948 war between Palestinian Arabs and their Arab allies, and Jews which was a response to the United Nations' partition plan. The U.S. under President Truman was the first country to recognize the new state of Israel. The U.S. crystallized its support for Israel during the Eisenhower, Kennedy, and Johnson administrations in the 1950s and 1960s. This contributed at the time to festering Arab and Islamic resentment of the U.S. and led to the targeting of U.S. interests by secular Palestinian and Islamic revolutionary terrorists in the subsequent decades.
- The U.S.- and U.K.-engineered 1953 coup in Iran contributed to the conditions for the 1979 Islamic revolution in Iran that in turn launched the Islamic revolutionary terrorism strain.
- The U.S.-backed 1954 coup in Guatemala contributed to the image of the United States as an imperialist power with designs in Latin America, thereby

providing the ideological rationale for an emerging left-wing terrorist strain in Latin America.

- The U.S.'s growing presence in Vietnam in the late 1950s put the U.S. on a road to an extended, costly, and controversial 15-year war that fueled anti-American sentiment and terrorist attacks in Latin America, Western Europe, and the U.S. throughout the 1960s and 1970s.
- The 1958 Cuban revolution, led by Fidel Castro, that overthrew the U.S.-supported Batista government led to the establishment of an eventual Soviet-supported communist regime in Cuba. This created a communist beachhead in the hemisphere that was used to export, support, and foster similar revolutions in Latin America — in America's "backyard." Cuba became the first state sponsor of anti-American terrorist activity in the post-war period and harbors wanted U.S. terrorists to this day. Part of Cuba's support also went to the Puerto Rican terrorist groups, such as the FALN and Macheteros, which carried out attacks on U.S. soil.

The above "seeds" of anti-American terrorism germinated in the 1960s. Two anti-American terrorist strains developed and grew: left-wing and secular Palestinian. In the late 1960s, the terrorist threat to U.S. interests overseas developed an international dimension. This occurred when secular Palestinian terrorists made the strategic decision to operate outside the Middle East and struck at Israeli, U.S., and other Western targets. Furthermore, left-wing terrorist and insurgent organizations in Latin America increased their targeting of U.S. interests there in response to the U.S. support for right-wing regimes and Cuban agitation. In Western Europe, left-wing terrorist groups emerged from student protest movements against the Vietnam War, university-related issues, the continued stationing of U.S. military troops in Europe, and nuclear power and nuclear weapon concerns.

While foreign policy decisions by the Eisenhower, Kennedy, and Johnson administrations inadvertently planted the seeds of anti-American terrorism that grew in the subsequent decades, it was the Nixon, Ford, and Carter administrations that confronted the first of the four distinct phases of the international terrorist threats that plagued the U.S. over the next five decades. In this first phase, the U.S. government concluded that international terrorism was not a transient but a long-lasting national security concern that required, for the first time, a policy and organizational response. Volume I outlines that response and details the terrorist groups, insurgent organizations, and states that targeted U.S. military, business, diplomatic, and government interests overseas, the events and developments that triggered those attacks, and the tactics, targets, locations, and motivations of these attacks. It examines the evolution of the anti-American terrorist threat overseas and the internal terrorist threat from the Nixon to the Carter administrations (1969–1980), especially during the 1970s.

During the Nixon and Ford administrations, the left-wing and secular Palestinian strains escalated their activities. As in the 1960s, the left-wing threat was concentrated in Western Europe and Latin America, while the secular Palestinian threat was active in the Middle East, Africa, Western Europe, and Asia. Their attacks involved kidnapping, aircraft hijacking, barricade and hostage incidents, assassinations, letter bombs, and the use of anti-armor rockets. It is important to note that given the relative rarity of international terrorism in the 1970s, the Nixon administration, the first to confront the international terrorist threat, had no counter-terrorism template or precedents from previous administrations for guidance. This also applied to the internal terrorist threat that the Nixon administration faced. This internal threat was composed of domestic and foreign spillover terrorism threats. The domestic terrorist threat, that is, indigenous terrorist groups that attacked U.S. targets in the U.S., was caused primarily by two developments: (1) opposition to the Vietnam War and (2) the rising militancy of black nationalists in response to the perceived racial injustices, oppression, and discontentment and disillusionment in the black urban areas. This domestic threat from left-wing and militant black organizations produced property damage bombings and periodic assassinations of mostly police officers. From the perspective of the Nixon administration, its supporters, a significant section of the American population, and U.S. law enforcement and intelligence agencies, America was under attack by young black and white subversives who might have been receiving aid and advice from foreign interests.

Compounding the internal terrorist threat were activities of foreign spillover terrorist groups operating in the U.S. These were groups that were composed of foreigners and/or sympathetic American citizens who engaged in terrorist activities on U.S. soil against foreign targets because of their overseas grievances. For example, Cuban-Americans carrying out attacks against Cuban targets and other countries' interests which maintained diplomatic and/or economic relations with the Castro regime; Armenian-Americans who attacked Turkish targets in U.S.; and Serbian and Croatian-Americans who struck at Yugoslav targets on U.S. soil. Foreign spillover terrorism polluted the security environment in the U.S. by using America as a battleground to advance or address overseas grievances.

The Nixon administration faced an embryonic but growing international terrorist threat overseas with no counter-terrorism playbook for reference and a complex and rising internal terrorist threat against which U.S. law enforcement and intelligence agencies had no effective law enforcement tools to utilize. It was the internal terrorist threat that eventually created legal, moral, and political problems for the Nixon administration and U.S. law enforcement and intelligence agencies. Under political pressure from the Nixon administration, there was the tendency to push and breach the legal envelope in counter-terrorism investigations in the late 1960s and the early 1970s. After President Nixon's resignation in August 1974, a media, congressional, and public backlash during the Ford administration led to internal and external restraints imposed on the FBI, CIA, DOD, and NSA. The results were greater domestic surveillance restrictions and increased Congressional and Department of Justice oversight of U.S. law enforcement and intelligence agencies. For subsequent administrations, these imposed restrictions and oversight initiated a debate over and search for an acceptable and effective balance between security and civil rights. To date, that balance has not been found and it shifts from time to time.

The international terrorist threat overseas was a security concern but not a front-burner issue for the Nixon administration. At the time, the administration was involved in a series of high-risk and crucial foreign policy issues such as: (1) opening relations with China, (2) engaging in negotiations on the Strategic Arms Limitation Talks (SALT) with the Soviet Union, (3) ending the Vietnam War, and (4) dealing with the Middle East Yom Kippur War and the 1973 oil crisis. From July 1973 onward, overlaying these foreign policy issues was the evolving Watergate investigation and scandal. Still, the Nixon administration addressed the growing international terrorist threat overseas by constructing a basic counter-terrorism package consisting of rudimentary policies and a satisfactory organizational structure. Considering the era, and given the administration's foreign policy priorities, the Nixon administration's counter-terrorism effort was an acceptable, if flawed, attempt to deal with the overseas terrorist threat. Internally, the Nixon administration faced the high-water mark of the historical internal terrorist threat in the U.S. No presidential administration before or since has confronted such a quantity and mix of internal terrorism actors. It was the response to this internal terrorist threat that tainted the Nixon administration.

The two-year Ford administration essentially kept most of the Nixon administration's counter-terrorism organization and adhered to most of its policies on hostage-taking, emphasis on the criminality of terrorism, building international counter-terrorism cooperation, developing protective security measures at home and abroad, and not allowing terrorists to influence U.S. foreign policy. Like the Nixon administration, overseas and domestic terrorism was not a major priority for Ford, even though the Ford administration confronted an internal terrorist threat that consisted of militant black, left-wing, and Puerto Rican separatist terrorist groups and Cuban exile, Croatian, and Armenian foreign spillover terrorists.

Under the Nixon and Ford administrations, the field of terrorism analysis was in its infancy both inside and outside the government. In the following decade, it became an academic and think-tank industry and a resource magnet for government intelligence and law enforcement agencies. In the 1970s, it was too early to declare or imply a "war on terrorism." For Nixon and Ford, it was essentially a skirmish, not an existential threat. The same was true for President Carter.

The terrorist threat to U.S. interests overseas did not significantly increase during the Carter administration. There were 1,882 international terrorist attacks of which 648, or 34%, were aimed at U.S. targets, resulting in the deaths of 39 Americans. During the Nixon and Ford administrations, there were 2,789 international terrorist attacks of which 1,204, or 43%, were aimed at U.S. targets, resulting in the deaths of 95 Americans. Considering the fact that Nixon and Ford had eight years in office and Carter only four, the numbers are similar. However, the Nixon administration faced more high-impact terrorist attacks than Carter: the 1970 Dawson's Field hijackings in Jordan — the only time multiple planes have been hijacked; the 1972 attack on the Munich Olympics — the only time Olympic athletes were attacked; the 1972 attacks on the Lod Airport in Israel that resulted in the deaths of 17 American citizens; and the 1973 brutal murders of the U.S. Ambassador and his deputy in Khartoum, Sudan on orders from PLO chairman Yasir Arafat.

It was during the Carter administration that two new anti-American terrorist strains started to emerge — state-sponsored and Islamic revolutionary.

The state-sponsored strain surfaced as a major concern as a result of the increased agitational and terrorist activities of Muammar Qaddafi's Libya. While the U.S. had a hostile relationship with Libya under Nixon and Ford, Libya became more radical, aggressive, and willing to directly confront the U.S. during the Carter administration. For example, it plotted an assassination attempt in late 1977 against the U.S. Ambassador in Cairo; it allowed a mob attack on the U.S. Embassy in Tripoli in 1979; it was suspected of involvement in a 1980 attempted assassination of a Libyan student in Ft. Collins, Colorado; and it twice authorized Libyan fighter aircraft to buzz U.S. reconnaissance planes over the Gulf of Sidra in 1980. As for Islamic revolutionary terrorism, the following were the indicators of a rising Islamic militancy during the Carter administration: the 1979 overthrow of the Shah of Iran and later seizure of the U.S. Embassy in Tehran in which U.S. diplomats were held hostage for 444 days; the 1979 seizure of the Grand Mosque in Mecca, Saudi Arabia by Islamic revolutionaries; the 1979 mob attack by Muslims on the U.S. Embassy in Islamabad, Pakistan in which two Americans were killed; and the flocking of young Muslims to "foreign fighter" detachments to confront the 1979 Soviet military incursion into Afghanistan. Few in government or academia at the time could have predicted the level and scope of the international and anti-American terrorist activities that emerged later in the 1980s from these developments.

Internally, the Carter administration faced a terrorist threat composed of periodic bombings by left-wing domestic groups and bombings and assassinations by foreign spillover groups. The latter caused the administration diplomatic problems and created issues between various federal and local authorities over protective security responsibilities and reimbursement of expenses. Objectively, the internal terrorist threat was lower during the Carter administration than the Nixon and Ford administrations. The Carter administration did take initiatives to strengthen U.S. counter-terrorism efforts. It established the first dedicated U.S. counter-terrorism rescue force and demonstrated the will to use it when, in April 1980, the President deployed it in a failed attempt to rescue the American hostages in Iran. The Carter administration also recognized the danger of state-sponsored terrorism. The Carter administration supported the use of tabletop training exercises to manage terrorist incidents, especially weapons of mass destruction attacks. The administration also increased security around U.S. nuclear facilities and added more support for the Nuclear Emergency Support Team (NEST). Like the Nixon administration, the Carter administration worked to develop measures, programs, and policies to deal with the terrorist threat. As was the case during the Nixon and Ford administrations, the issue of terrorism during the Carter administration was not politicized by the two major political parties. In general, the counter-terrorism efforts received bipartisan support.

The first phase of the international terrorist threat against U.S. interests overseas formed and developed during the Nixon, Ford, and Carter administrations. It was a new government concern that was addressed gradually, reactively, and partially. Given the level and scope of the overseas and internal terrorist threats in the 1970s, an objective analysis of this response indicates that it was sufficient but not very forward-looking. The next phase of the international terrorist threat took place in the 1980s during the Reagan and George H.W. Bush administrations. In this phase, the U.S. government confronted overseas, for the only time in its history, all four strains of anti-American terrorism. The 1980s, which coincided with President Ronald Reagan's two terms, became the apex of the anti-American terrorist threat in the post-war era — quantitatively and qualitatively — and in its geographic scope.

Chapter 1

The Prologue: Eisenhower, Kennedy, and Johnson Administrations

We wanted to put the Palestinian question in front of international opinion. All the time we were being dealt with as refugees who only needed human aid. That was unjust. Nobody had heard our screams and suffering. All we got from the world was more tents and old clothes. After 1967, we were obliged to explain to the world that the Palestinians had a cause.

—Leila Khalid, Palestinian Hijacker in 1968, 1969[1]

The 1950s: The Eisenhower Administration — Iran, Guatemala, Cuba, and Vietnam — Planting the Seeds of Anti-American Terrorist Activity

In the immediate post-World War II period, the United States was engaged in a "cold war" with the Soviet Union that involved countering and containing Soviet moves around the world to expand communism. This situation compelled the Eisenhower administration to continue the U.S. doctrine of containment against the Soviet Union as outlined by the National Security Council Report 68 (NSC-68) issued on April 14, 1950, during the presidency of Harry S. Truman and to initiate a covert action policy to undermine Soviet expansionism as outlined in the National Security Council document NSC 162/2 of October 30, 1953. As a result

---

[1] BBC, "Transcripts: The guerrilla's story," January 1, 2001, at http://news.bbc.co.uk/2/hi/in_depth/uk/2000/uk_confidential/1090986.stm. Accessed June 6, 2017.

of this doctrine and policy, the United States became involved, directly or indirectly, in several controversial international situations that unintentionally led to long-term terrorism problems for the United States and other countries. In August 1953, the United States and Great Britain orchestrated a *coup d'état* against the democratically elected government of Iranian Prime Minister Mohammad Mosaddegh. The coup's trigger was the Iranian government's 1951 nationalization of the British-owned Anglo-Iranian Oil Company (AIOC).

At the time, Iran's oil was Britain's single largest overseas investment. The Iranian government claimed that the AIOC was taking 85% of Iranian oil profits.[2] The coup resulted in 26 years of dictatorship under Mohammad-Reza Shah Pahlavi, who relied heavily on U.S. support to maintain power until the Shah was overthrown in February 1979 by Islamic revolutionaries. Their leader, Ayatollah Ruhollah Khomeini, then established an Islamic republic in Iran. The 1979 Iranian revolution turned out to be a traumatic event for the United States as it created a virulent anti-American, Middle Eastern state and triggered the emergence of the anti-American terrorism strain — Islamic revolutionary terrorism. It could be argued that the U.S. constructed the 1953 coup in Iran and planted some of the seeds for the formation of this strain.

In Latin America, the 1954 Guatemalan *coup d'état* was a covert operation organized by the United States to overthrow Jacobo Árbenz Guzmán, the democratically elected president of Guatemala. The coup trigger was the Guzman government's initiating of policies that the U.S. felt were communist-oriented and could lead to the emergence of a Soviet client state in the western hemisphere. It did not help that Guzman also threatened to nationalize hundreds of thousands of uncultivated acres owned by United Fruit, a U.S. corporation with extensive plantation holdings in eight Latin American countries. Guzman was replaced by Col. Carlos Castillo Armas, a ruthless right-wing dictator who abolished the Guzman land reforms, the secret ballot, taxes on foreign investments, and civil rights. Over the next four decades, the succession of military rulers waged counter-insurgency warfare, destabilizing the Guatemalan society. There were numerous U.S. military interventions to support the dictators, and these actions further radicalized the left in Guatemala and elsewhere in Latin America.[3] Thus, the image of the

---

[2] See, for example, Donald N. Wilber, "Overthrow of Iranian Premier Mossadeq of Iran November 1952–August 1953," CIA Historical Paper #208, Clandestine Service History, written March 1954 and published in October 1968, at http://www.webcitation.org/5hOKk6ByB. Accessed May 9, 2017.
[3] Gerald K. Haines, CIA History Staff Analysis, "CIA and Guatemala Assassination Proposals, 1952–1954," June 1995, at https://nsarchive2.gwu.edu/NSAEBB/NSAEBB4/docs/doc01.pdf. Accessed September 9, 2017; and Nicholas Cullather, CIA History Staff, "Operation PBSUCCESS

U.S. as an imperialist puppeteer in Latin America emerged and continues to this day. The subsequent five decades of violence caused the deaths and disappearances of more than 140,000 Guatemalans, while some human rights activists put the death toll as high as 250,000.[4]

In Cuba, throughout the 1950s, American business interests were pervasive and extremely profitable in President Fulgencio Batista's dictatorial government. At the beginning of 1959, U.S. companies owned about 40% of the Cuban sugar lands, almost all the cattle ranches, 90% of the mines and mineral concessions, 80% of the utilities, and practically all the oil industry — and supplied two-thirds of Cuba's imports.[5] The United States government, however, said then Senator John F. Kennedy, "lacked the imagination and compassion to understand the need of the Cuban People — which lacked the leadership and vigor to move forward to meet those needs — and which lacked the foresight and vision to see the inevitable results of its own failures."[6] The result was a peasant revolt led by Fidel Castro and welcomed by most Cubans who seized power on January 1, 1959 and initiated land reforms. In time, a Soviet client state emerged that fostered and supported leftist insurgent and terrorist organizations in Latin America that targeted U.S. interests throughout the region for over five decades.

In Vietnam, the communist Ho Chi Minh led a revolt in 1954 against France which was attempting to re-establish its pre-war colonial rule. The U.S. provided France with massive military aid, but France was nevertheless decisively defeated by the Viet Minh at the battle of Dien Bien Phu from March to May 1954 and withdrew from the country. This led to the partitioning of Vietnam into a communist North and non-communist South Vietnam. In South Vietnam, the U.S. assumed growing influence in and over the government which confronted an increasingly serious communist insurgency. The U.S. government viewed involvement in the war as prevention of a communist takeover of South Vietnam as part of its wider strategy of containing communism. This was the "Domino

— The United States and Guatemala, 1952–1954," 1994, at https://nsarchive2.gwu.edu/NSAEBB/NSAEBB4/docs/doc05.pdf. Accessed May 9, 2017; and Kate Doyle and Peter Kornbluh, editors, "CIA and Assassinations: The Guatemala 1954 Documents," National Security Archive Electronic Briefing Book No. 4, at https://nsarchive2.gwu.edu/NSAEBB/NSAEBB4/. Accessed July 7, 2017.

[4] Kate Doyle, "Guatemala — 1954: Behind the CIA's Coup," Consortium News, 1997, at http://www.consortiumnews.com/archive/story38.html. Accessed July 9, 2017.

[5] Senator John F. Kennedy, "Remarks at Democratic Dinner, Cincinnati, Ohio, October 6, 1960," John F. Kennedy Presidential Library, at http://www.jfklibrary.org/Research/Ready-Reference/JFK-Speeches/Remarks-of-Senator-John-F-Kennedy-at-Democratic-Dinner-Cincinnati-Ohio-October-6-1960.aspx. Accessed March 7, 2016.

[6] Ibid.

Theory," which was developed in the Eisenhower administration and argued that if one country fell to communist forces, then all the surrounding countries would follow. U.S. military advisors first arrived in Vietnam in 1950. U.S. involvement escalated in the early 1960s, with U.S. troop levels tripling in 1961 and tripling again in 1962. U.S. combat units were deployed beginning in 1965.[7] U.S. interference in South Vietnam's elections and its support for the corrupt, repressive ex-Japanese collaborator Ngo Dinh Diem as president in South Vietnam further antagonized the left in Latin America, North America, and Western Europe. The Vietnam issue evolved into a major fuel pellet for Marxist, Maoist, and anarchist terrorist activities against U.S. targets during the 1960s and 1970s.

The above seminal events in U.S. foreign policy in the 1950s created some of the conditions that nurtured the development of the left-wing and Islamic revolutionary terrorist strains in subsequent decades. However, in the decade of the 1950s, there were very few terrorist attacks directed at U.S. interests overseas. Although there are no U.S. government official statistics on terrorism for the 1950s, it is possible to construct an adequate, representative chronology of anti-American terrorist attacks from open sources. This open-source survey indicates that from 1950 to 1959, there were 19 reported anti-American terrorist attacks in Greece, Turkey, Vietnam, Cuba, Argentina, Cyprus, Indonesia, Tunisia, Ecuador, Chile, Egypt, Jordan, and Lebanon.[8] The attacks were spread out among all these countries, so there was not a sustained terrorist campaign against U.S. interests. They were episodic and mostly property-damage attacks aimed at U.S. diplomatic facilities and U.S. Information Service (USIS) facilities. Only five Americans were killed in terrorist-related incidents overseas. On April 27, 1950, Indonesian militants kidnapped and killed two Americans — Yale Sociology Professor Raymond Kennedy and Robert James Doyle, *Time-Life* Far Eastern correspondent in Tomo, on Java Island in Indonesia.[9] On June 16, 1956, U.S. Vice Consul William P. Boteler was killed during the bombing of a restaurant in Nicosia, Cyprus by the militant Greek Cypriot group the National Organization of Cypriot Fighters or EOKA. Three other U.S. diplomats were also injured.

The bomb was intended for a British target in the restaurant. Colonel George Grivas, head of EOKA, immediately issued a statement denying a deliberate

---

[7] See, "Vietnam War Statistics and Facts," 25th Aviation Battalion website, at http://25thaviation.org/facts/id430.htm. Accessed January 12, 2011. The figures come from the Church Committee report on the 1963 Diem Coup.

[8] See chart C in the appendix — Anti American Terrorist Incidents Overseas from 1950 to 1969.

[9] http://www.time.com/time/magazine/article/0,9171,812438,00.html#ixzz1C4TQx043. Accessed June 6, 2016.

attempt to target American citizens. He further warned American officials, for their own safety, to avoid the establishments patronized by "our British enemy."[10] On July 8, 1959, Viet Cong guerrillas armed with small arms and homemade bombs attacked the U.S. 7th Infantry Advisory Detachment at Bien Hoa. American advisors Major Dale Buis and Master Sergeant Chester Ovnard, who were watching a movie in the mess hall, were killed along with a Vietnamese mess attendant and an Army of the Republic of Vietnam (ARVN) soldier. Buis and Ovnard were the first Americans killed in a terrorist attack in Vietnam. At the time, there were about 2,000 U.S. military and civilian officials in country. The Military Assistance Advisory Group (MAAG) arrived in South Vietnam on November 1, 1955.

Americans were also kidnapped in Cuba. In 1958, 12 Americans working for two U.S. companies in Cuba were kidnapped by Cuban rebels in two separate incidents. The rebels demanded that the U.S. government stop its support to the Batista government. These demands were not met, but all 12 Americans were eventually released unharmed. The incident that caused the most concern for the Eisenhower administration was the June 28, 1958 kidnapping of 29 U.S. sailors on a bus near Guantanamo Bay by Cuban rebels led by Raul Castro, Fidel's brother.[11] This incident is significant and revealing in several ways. It triggered a clash between Raul and Fidel over the merits of the kidnapping of Americans. Raul Castro felt that the kidnapping would attract publicity for the rebels' cause, put pressure on the U.S. to stop supplying weapons to the Batista government, and create "human shields" to deter the government from bombing rebel positions. However, Fidel Castro criticized the kidnapping because it "threatened to turn international public opinion against the rebels," and the Batista government could exploit this incident by attacking or killing Americans in Cuba and blame it on the rebels. These are pros and cons of hostage-taking that all insurgent and terrorist groups must weigh in planning such an operation.

This incident, more than the other hostage-taking incidents in Cuba involving Americans, provoked a clash between Congress and President Eisenhower on how to deal with this situation. Pressure was put on Eisenhower by the media,

---

[10]The Boteler incident is taken from Ted Gup. *Book of Honor: Covert Lives and Classified Deaths at the CIA* (New York, Doubleday, 2000), p. 90.

[11]Gitmo kidnapping incident condensed from Simon, *The Terrorist Trap*, pp. 54–59; See also, "24 U.S. Navy Men Missing In Cuba; Kidnapping Seen," *New York Times*, June 29, 1958, p. 1; "U.S. Opens Parley With Cuba Rebels," *New York Times*, July 2, 1958, p. 12; Herbert L. Matthews, "Castro's Kidnappings Show War Is Still On: But Methods He Uses Have Cost Him Support of Friends in U.S.," *New York Times*, July 6, 1958, p. E-4; "Grandstand Kidnaping," *Time Magazine*, July 7, 1958, p. 33; "Dealing with Kidnapers," *Time Magazine*, July 14, 1958, p. 17; "All Free," *Time Magazine*, July 28, 1958, p. 34.

Congress, his own cabinet, and the hostages' family members to take more direct, aggressive steps to deal with this crisis.[12] It should be noted that at this time the administration was also dealing with other hostage incidents involving the seizure of American military personnel by communist countries. On June 8, 1958, nine U.S. soldiers were captured by Soviet military personnel when their helicopter made a forced landing near Zwickau, East Germany. They were eventually released on July 19, 1958. On June 27, 1958 a U.S. Air Force C-118, reportedly the personal aircraft of Allen Dulles, then director of the Central Intelligence Agency, was shot down over Soviet Armenia. Nine crew members were captured. They were released by the Soviet on July 7, 1958.[13] When these two incidents are combined with the Gitmo incident, 47 American servicemen were held as hostages in June 1958. President Eisenhower did not succumb to the hardline pressure to deal with the incidents and used a more measured, low-key, diplomatic approach that eventually succeeded in releasing the 29 American servicemen from Gitmo, and the 18 U.S. military personnel held in East Germany and Soviet Armenia.

The June 1959 Guantanamo Bay hostage incident was the fourth time in U.S. history that the U.S. government had to deal with an overseas hostage situation involving Americans.[14] Up until the Eisenhower administration, there was no formal U.S. policy on hostage-taking and kidnapping. During the 1958 Guantanamo Bay hostage incident, Secretary of State John Foster Dulles and President Eisenhower both stated publicly that the U.S. would not give in to blackmail and to do so would only encourage others to use Americans as hostages.[15] It could be argued that U.S. hostage policy in the modern era was first formulated at this time. During the 1950s, however, there were no virulent

---

[12] "Eisenhower Vows Aid for Captives," *New York Times*, July 3, 1958, p. 4. President Eisenhower is quoted as saying at the time that "We are not disposed to do anything reckless that would create consequences for them that would be final."

[13] "Aircraft Downed During the Cold War and Thereafter," at http://sw.propwashgang.org/shootdown_list.html. Accessed June 7, 2017.

[14] The first took place on October 11, 1784 when Moroccan pirates seized the U.S. brigantine "Betsey" with its 10 American merchant seamen. The second incident took place on September 3, 1901 when Miss Ellen Stone, a Protestant missionary from Haverhill, Massachusetts, was kidnapped in Bulgaria by a Macedonian terrorist organization known as the "International Macedonian Revolutionary Organization" that demanded $110,000 in gold — $1,000,000 today — for her release. The third hostage situation occurred on May 18, 1904, when an alleged American industrialist named Ion Perdicaris was kidnapped along with his stepson in Tangier, Morocco by a brigand named Raisuli, known as "Last of the Barbary Pirates." These incidents will be discussed in more detail in Chapter 2 — The Nixon administration — in the section on hostage-taking policy.

[15] Jeffrey Simon, *The Terrorist Trap* (Indiana: Indiana University Press, 2001), pp. 56–57.

anti-American terrorist organizations operating overseas and the terrorist threat to U.S. personnel and facilities overseas was low, except for Cuba and Vietnam.

The 1960s: The Kennedy and Johnson Administrations — The Advent of the Left-Wing and Secular Palestinian Terrorism Strains

The U.S. counterinsurgency era, in terms of the military and the intelligence establishments, began with the Kennedy administration. "The Eisenhower emphasis on offensive, unconventional, covert war against undesirable governments was matched by Kennedy's overt and covert war against the internal enemies of friendly governments. This latter task, the counterinsurgency dimension of political warfare, became a principal public plank of Kennedy's foreign policy."[16] However, political terrorism, while seen as part of the tactical options of large insurgent organizations, was not singled out as a unique problem that required special counter-terrorism policy, organizations, and programs. This assessment took place later during the Nixon administration.

The low terrorist threat for U.S. interests overseas in the 1950s continued into the early 1960s. From 1960 to 1964, there were 23 anti-American terrorist attacks overseas, all but one in Latin America. All but one of these incidents were carried out by left-wing terrorists.[17] The two most serious incidents both involved kidnapping of U.S. military personnel in Venezuela in 1963 and 1964 by a left-wing terrorist organization. On November 27, 1963, four members of the pro-Cuban Armed Forces of National Liberation (FALN) kidnapped U.S. Army Attaché and Deputy Chief of the U.S. Military Mission in Venezuela, Colonel James K. Chenault, in Caracas. Immediately after the kidnapping, a woman called the American embassy to announce: "We just want him for propaganda purposes. We will not harm him." The terrorists mistakenly believed he was a close relative of General Claire Lee Chennault who was an American military aviator best known for his leadership of the "Flying Tigers" and the Republic of China Air Force in World War II. As the Venezuelan police initiated a dragnet

---

[16]"The Kennedy Crusade — A Dynamic National Strategy to Defeat the Communists," found at www.statecraft.org, chapter 6. Accessed May 17, 2017.

[17]It should be noted that the U.S. government has not published unclassified statistics on anti-American terrorist activity in the 1950s and from 1960 to 1964. The first year that the government recorded anti-American terrorist activity was for 1965 and that total was first published publicly in Central Intelligence Agency, *Research Study: International and Transnational Terrorism: Diagnosis and Prognosis*, Unclassified. PR-76-10030, April 1976. Author — David Milbank, 45 pages with foldout chart.

against leftists in order to find the kidnappers, the FALN phone calls became more threatening. The group offered to exchange Chenault for 70 leftists recently jailed by the government. "Unless our comrades are turned loose, we will not be responsible for the safety of the North American." The Venezuelan government gave in to the demands and Col. Chenault was released 8 days later.[18]

On October 3, 1964, Lt. Col. Michael Smolen, Deputy U.S. Air Force Attaché in Caracas, was kidnapped by two FALN terrorists in front of his home.[19] The group claimed the attack was in protest of U.S. interference in Venezuelan affairs. A police dragnet found Smolen on October 12 and freed him. His kidnappers tried unsuccessfully to swap him for the life of a young Viet Cong terrorist, Nguyen Van Troi, who was executed in Saigon, South Vietnam on October 18. Troi was arrested for a May 1963 attempt to assassinate U.S. Defense Secretary Robert McNamara and U.S. Ambassador Henry Cabot Lodge by planting a bomb under a bridge their motorcade would cross over. Troi's pending execution became a *cause célèbre* for leftists and communist elements throughout the world and attracted extensive media attention. On September 26, 1965, the Viet Cong executed two American prisoners — Captain Humberto "Rocky" Versace and SFC Kenneth M. Roraback — in retaliation. The FALN's other sensational exploits included the theft of five world-famous French paintings in January 1963; the hijacking of the merchant ship Anzoategui, in February 1963, and the kidnaping of an internationally known Spanish soccer star, Alfredo di Stefano, in August, 1963.

At the start of the decade, the U.S. signaled its opposition to the Castro regime in Cuba and recognized the fertile environment in Latin America for the spread of communism — poverty and popular discontent with dictatorial regimes in the region, for example in Argentina, the Dominican Republic, Ecuador, Guatemala, Honduras, and Peru. President Kennedy established the Alliance for Progress in 1961 which aimed to establish economic cooperation between North and South America and to aid Latin America. Unfortunately, the effort failed to achieve intended improvements for the poor and middle classes largely due to the corruption of the anti-communist ruling classes that the U.S. was reluctant to challenge.[20] In 1961, Kennedy authorized an unsuccessful CIA

---

[18] The Chenault incident is taken from "Venezuela: Time to Finish the Communist Bridgehead," *Time Magazine,* December 6, 1973, at http://www.time.com/time/magazine/article/0,9171,898097,00. html#ixzz1C4z8oPsE. Accessed November 7, 2017.

[19] "Venezuelan Terrorists Kidnap U.S. Colonel and Threaten Him," *New York Times,* October 10, 1964, at https://www.nytimes.com/1964/10/10/archives/venezuelan-terrorists-kidnap-us-colonel-and-threaten-him.html. Accessed September 8, 2017.

[20] "Alliance for Progress," John F. Kennedy Presidential Library and Museum, at https://www.jfklibrary.org/JFK/JFK-in-History/Alliance-for-Progress.aspx. Accessed October 5, 2018.

effort to invade Cuba at the Bay of Pigs, following an Eisenhower administration plan.[21] Castro responded to growing U.S. belligerence to his regime by aligning Cuba with the Soviet Union for protection. This led to the implantation of Soviet missiles on Cuba which triggered the 1962 Cuban Missile Crisis. Given the affinity and admiration Latin Americans felt for the Castro revolution in Cuba, these actions by the United States only reinforced the imperialist/interventionist image of the United States. It was the U.S. policy in Latin America and the successful revolution in Cuba that largely fostered the conditions for the onset of a multi-decadal left-wing terrorist threat against U.S. interests in Latin America.

In the first half of the 1960s, Venezuela was the hot spot for anti-American terrorist activities. Castro's first candidate in Latin America to export his model of a communist revolution was Venezuela. The leftist elements there were responsive to his direction and support, and the country had abundant oil resources. Although several leftist organizations emerged there in opposition to the government, the FALN was the primary terrorist threat confronting U.S. interests overseas from 1961 to 1964.[22] It was responsible for seven of the 23 anti-American terrorist attacks during the period including the two kidnappings of U.S. military personnel noted above. The FALN was a pro-Cuban Marxist–Leninist guerrilla organization that began operations in Venezuela in 1962. Its membership included elements opposed to the government of President Rómulo Betancourt: dissident military officers, radical members of the Venezuelan Communist Party, and leaders of the Movement of the Revolutionary Left, a breakaway splinter faction of Betancourt's ruling Democratic Action Party. The Betancourt government supported Cuba's expulsion from the Organization of American States and broke diplomatic relations with the Castro government in December 1961. The FALN emerged in mid-1962 and initiated rural and urban guerrilla activities throughout the remainder of the 1960s. This activity reached its height in 1962 and 1963, when the FALN sabotaged U.S. subsidized oil pipelines and bombed a Sears Roebuck warehouse and the U.S. Embassy in Caracas. Ultimately, the FALN's efforts to disrupt the December 1963 elections proved futile. The group

---

[21] In a sense, Kennedy's failed Bay of Pigs invasion also contributed to Cuban exile terrorism in the U.S. in the late 1960s and in the 1970s as some of these Cuban American terrorists were trained by the CIA for this incursion. The skills they received were later used to carry out terrorist attacks against Cuban targets, Cuban exiles in the U.S., and foreign interests in the U.S. that had diplomatic and economic relations with Castro's Cuba.

[22] CIA, Office of Current Intelligence, "Memorandum: Terrorism in Venezuela," September 16, 1963, Document # 2366/66, at CIA FOIA, document # RDP79T00429A001200030018-5.

suffered from internal conflicts, and the government later implemented a "pacification" program aimed at armed opposition elements. The FALN's operational capability diminished afterward. In 1963, the FALN had about 500 full-time operatives. In 1966, that number was reduced to 250.[23] The FALN was no longer a major anti-American terrorism actor. It is interesting to note that the FALN was the first terrorist organization in the post-war period to hijack a ship. In February 1963, nine FALN terrorists hijacked the 3,127-ton government-owned freighter *Anzoátegui* only a few hours after it left the port of La Guaira bound for Houston and New Orleans. The main purpose of the operation was to embarrass Venezuela's President Betancourt and force him to cancel his scheduled state visit to the U.S. in late February. Betancourt did not do this. However, the terrorists did attract a lot of international publicity as they evaded naval search operations by the U.S. and Venezuela.[24] The terrorists surrendered in Rio de Janeiro on March 23, 1963.

Beginning in early August 1964, President Johnson was confronted by a growing problem in the Congo. It would lead to the emergence of a major international hostage crisis involving Americans in the Congo, which at the time was involved in a civil war. This hostage crisis was just one episode during the "Congo Crisis" — a time of internal conflict in the Republic of the Congo between 1960 and 1965. The crisis started after the Congo became independent from Belgium in 1960 and concluded with the entire country under the rule of Joseph-Désiré Mobutu in 1965. Over the next four years, as the Republic of the Congo installed a series of prime ministers, the United States repeatedly attempted to create a stable, pro-Western regime through vote buying and financial support for pro-Western candidates.[25] This desire for a stable, pro-Western government was policy under Presidents Kennedy and Johnson. However, the "Congo Crisis" developed into another proxy conflict

---

[23] "Venezuela: War on Subversion," *Time Magazine*, December 23, 1966, at http://www.time.com/time/magazine/article/0,9171,840765,00.html#ixzz1CGJn5DgG. Accessed July 9, 2017.

[24] "Venezuela: The Saga of the *Anzoategui*," *Time Magazine*, February 22, 1963. http://www.time.com/time/magazine/article/0,9171,828017,00.html#ixzz1CGEFPmDy. Accessed August 4, 2017.

[25] https://history.state.gov/milestones/1961-1968/congo-decolonization, accessed June 5, 2019. See also, See Major Thomas P. Odom. Dragon Operations: Hostage Rescues in the Congo, 1964–1965, Leavenworth Papers, #14, at https://babel.hathitrust.org/cgi/pt?id=uc1.31210015350026&view=1up&seq=1, accessed June 5, 2019; Nina Strochlic, "Argo in the Congo: The Ghosts of the Stanleyville Hostage Crisis." The Daily Beast, July 12, 2017, at https://www.thedailybeast.com/argo-in-the-congo-the-ghosts-of-the-stanleyville-hostage-crisis, accessed June 5, 2019.

in the Cold War, in which the United States and the Soviet Union supported opposing factions. In 1963–1964, various tribal rebellions against the central government took place in the Congo. The largest of these were the Simba ("lion") rebels. In August 1964, the Simba captured the key city of Stanleyville and declared a new rebel state called the People's Republic of the Congo. Its capital was Stanleyville and it had a president. This new state was supported by the Soviet Union, China, and Cuba which supplied it with arms and military advisors. After seizing Stanleyville, the rebels announced that all Americans, and later all Europeans, would be held as prisoners.

By late 1964, the central Léopoldville government, supported by Western powers, carried out several successful military operations against the communist-backed Simba rebellion. The Simba rebels, fearing certain defeat, resorted to taking hostages of the local white population in areas under their control. On October 28, the Simba rebels arrested all foreigners, including Belgians and 40 Americans. Five U.S. diplomats from the U.S. Consulate in Stanleyville were also captured. Several negotiations by the central government and Western powers with the rebels failed. This led to the construction of a U.S. – Belgian rescue operation codenamed "Red Dragon." In November, it was sent into the Congo. During the operation 31 hostages, including two Americans, died. "Red Dragon" was the most complicated, international hostage-rescue raid in the post-war period. It was also the first time that the CIA constructed "an instant air force" of mercenary Cuban pilots to try and contain the Simba rebellion.[26] Shortly after the Stanleyville raid, Cuban revolutionary Che Guevara addressed the U.N. General Assembly on December 11, 1964, publicly denouncing the operation as an "unacceptable intervention. A case without parallel in the modern world," that illustrated "how the rights of peoples can be flouted with absolute impunity and the most insolent cynicism."[27] In April 1965, Guevara, along with a small unit of Cuban fighters, arrived in Dar es Salaam, Tanzania and made their way to the Congo where they led rebellions against the central government for six months, until their retreat on November 20, 1965.

The second half of the 1960s (1965–1969) saw the initial development of the secular Palestinian terrorist strain and the expansion of the left-wing terrorist

---

[26] Odom, Dragon Operations…, p. 6.
[27] Address by Ernesto Che Guevara to the U.N. General Assembly, New York on December 11, 1964. Social justice website at http://www.sojust.net/speeches/che_un.html. Accessed August 6, 2017.

strain throughout Latin America and Western Europe. Anti-American terrorist activity increased noticeably:

	1960–1964	1965–1969
Anti-American attacks	23	143
Locations	4 countries	31 countries
Targets	Diplomatic, business	Government, business, diplomatic
American deaths	0	7
Kidnappings	2	2

In the second half of the decade, all but eight of the 143 anti-American attacks were carried out by left-wing terrorists. Of the eight, secular Palestinians carried out seven attacks and an ethno-national terrorist group carried out one. Latin America continued to be the primary location for anti-American terrorism, accounting for 60% of the 143 attacks. Western Europe was second with 13%. Compared to the first half of the decade, the number of countries in Latin America where anti-American attacks occurred increased from three (Bolivia, Venezuela, Uruguay) to 11 (Bolivia, Venezuela, Uruguay, Chile, Guatemala, Brazil, Peru, Argentina, Colombia, Ecuador, and the Dominican Republic). The three high-threat countries were Argentina (44 anti-American attacks), Brazil (17 attacks, including one death), and Guatemala (four attacks: one attempted assassination and three deaths). The first American killed in a terrorist attack in Latin America in the post-war period was Robert R. Smetek. He was killed on August 4, 1966 when a powerful bomb exploded in the ground floor lady's room of the Binational Center in Bogota, Colombia. Two other Americans (Thomas and Carolyn Withers) were also injured in the attack which was linked to the presidential inauguration. The pro-Chinese Communist Party of Colombia, Marxist–Leninist, claimed responsibility for the act.

The first U.S. military officers killed in Latin America in the post-war period were Col. John D. Webber, the Commander of MAAG in Guatemala, and Lt. Cdr. Ernest A. Munro, the Head of the Naval Section in the MAAG. They were assassinated on January 16, 1968 in Guatemala City by the left-wing terrorist group, the Rebel Armed Forces (FAR). The group cited the U.S. creation of Guatemalan Army assassination squads and revenge for the January 12 killing of Rogelia Cruz Martinez, Miss Guatemala of 1950, by the right-wing group "La Mano Blanco." The first U.S. diplomat killed overseas in the post-war period was also killed in Guatemala. On August 28, 1968, U.S. Ambassador John Gordon Main, was killed when a kidnapping attempt by the FAR failed. Main's car was blocked by two terrorist vehicles in downtown Guatemala City and the ambassador was shot as he tried to escape by running away. FAR claimed that it wanted to kidnap the ambassador and demand the release of a FAR leader. Most of the left-wing terrorist attacks on U.S. targets in Latin America, however, remained low-level bombings designed to cause property damage against U.S. government, diplomatic, and business targets in the region. Most attacks in the region were carried out against U.S. government facilities such as binational centers, Peace Corps buildings, and USIS libraries.

Since the end of World War II, the U.S. has deployed an array of programs in various host countries overseas to provide cultural, educational, and information activities on the United States. The U.S. government's relationship with these programs has varied from supervision, to funding, to support, to general cooperation. The brick and mortar fronts of these programs were binational centers, U.S. information service libraries, Amerika Haus (in Germany), and U.S. cultural centers. These are places where host country citizens can go to learn about the United States and various exchange programs. These places were generally established in the capitals and other major cities. During the 1950s, 1960s, and 1970s, they had few security measures. If an anti-American terrorist group wanted to send a violent message to the United States government at little risk to their operatives, bombing or throwing a Molotov cocktail at one of these buildings was the easiest option. These facilities were particularly attractive for left-wing terrorists in Latin America and Western Europe. Of the 166 anti-American terrorist attacks that happened overseas from 1960 to 1969, 67 (40%) were directed at these cultural facilities.[28]

It is in the second half of the 1960s that the secular Palestinian terrorist threat emerged. Following the 1947 United Nations Partition Plan and the 1948 British withdrawal, and 1947–1948 Civil War between the Palestinian Arabs and Jews, the state of Israel was established on May 14, 1948. The U.S. was the first country to recognize Israel.[29] Afterward, some Palestinian nationalists conducted a terrorist campaign against Israeli targets inside the Jewish state throughout the 1950s and 1960s.[30] The Israeli defeat of the combined Arab armies in the 1948 war and then the June 1967 "Six Day War" was a traumatic event for Palestinian nationalists who concluded that they had to take the initiative themselves and not depend

---

[28] See chart C in appendix — Anti-American Terrorist Incidents Overseas from 1950 to 1969.

[29] https://www.state.gov/r/pa/ei/bgn/3581.htm. Accessed July 4, 2017.

[30] See Ministry of Foreign Affairs, Israel, "Which Came First- Terrorism or Occupation — Major Arab Terrorist Attacks against Israelis Prior to the 1967 Six-Day War," at http://www.mfa.gov.il/MFA/Terrorism. Accessed August 4, 2017.

on the Arab nations to defeat Israel. The U.S. supported Israel in these conflicts, and this contributed substantially to festering Arab and Islamic resentment of the U.S. During the 1950s and 1960s, the U.S. emerged as the primary supporter of Israel in the region and was subsequently embroiled in decadal conflicts in the Middle East and numerous quests for their resolutions. During these decades, militant Palestinian groups formed and soon concluded that they needed to attract international attention and sympathy for their cause by operating in the international arena. It is in the late 1960s that the secular Palestinian terrorism strain became a major terrorism problem for the U.S. and the West. Its first operational manifestation took place on July 22, 1968 when three members of the Popular Front for the Liberation of Palestine (PFLP) hijacked El Al Flight 426 scheduled to go from Rome to Tel Aviv. The plane was diverted to Algiers by the hijackers. Negotiations with the hijackers lasted for 40 days. Both the hijackers and the passengers, including 21 Israeli hostages, were eventually freed. This was the first hijacking carried out by Palestinian terrorists and the first attack by a Palestinian terrorist group outside the Middle East.

The first U.S. target hit by Palestinian terrorists occurred on August 29, 1969 when TWA Flight 840 out of Rome was hijacked by PFLP terrorists. The PFLP believed that Yitzak Rabin, then the Israeli Ambassador to the United States, was scheduled to be aboard the flight. The hijackers said they were the "Che Guevara Commando Unit of the PFLP." They read a statement: "We have kidnapped this American plane because Israel is a colony of America and the Americans are giving the Israelis Phantom jets." Passengers were eventually taken off the plane in Syria and the plane was then damaged with explosives, though not destroyed. Most of the passengers and crew members were Americans. They were all eventually released unharmed, except for two Israeli hostages who were released in December of that year in return for 71 Syrian and Egyptian soldiers held by Israel. In addition to this hijacking, there were other incidents in 1969 linked to secular Palestinian terrorists. On August 9, a bomb planted by suspected Palestinians exploded at an Olympic Airlines office in Athens, injuring two American tourists. On November 27, Palestinian terrorists threw hand grenades into the Athens office of El Al, killing a Greek child and injuring three Americans. On December 21, PFLP terrorists were arrested in Athens while trying to board a TWA plane flying from Tel Aviv to Athens to New York. They were planning to hijack the aircraft. On December 27, Leon Holtz, 48, a tourist from Brooklyn, New York, was killed when PLO terrorists fired shots at a tourist bus near Hebron in the West Bank. The key question for the U.S. government in late 1969 was whether these attacks were a temporary burst of Palestinian terrorist activity or were they a harbinger of things to come. The answer came in the next decade with such spectaculars as the September 1970 PFLP hijacking of four airliners on the same day.

The 1960s ended with an event that had a serious long-term effect on the terrorist threat to U.S. interests overseas and contributed to the state-sponsored terrorist strain. On September 1, 1969, a small group of junior military officers led by Colonel Muammar el-Qaddafi staged a bloodless *coup d'état* in Libya against King Idris while he was in Turkey for medical treatment. The Libyan Arab Republic was created, and an active anti-American proponent of state-sponsored terrorism emerged.

In summation, terrorist activity in the 1960s directed at U.S. targets overseas was not as sustained, widespread, or lethal as in the subsequent decades. The birth of international terrorism occurred in the late 1960s when some Palestinian nationalist leaders made the political and strategic decision to engage in political terrorist activity against Israeli and other targets in the international area. This decision internationalized terrorism, which to this point had been primarily a domestic security problem. Most of the terrorist activity in the first half of the 1960s was carried out by domestic terrorist organizations against domestic targets in their country of origin. Few attacks spilled over into the international arena. The secular Palestinian nationalist leaders changed all that when they decided to engage in aircraft hijackings, embassy seizures, assassinations, bombings, and mid-air bombings against Israeli, Jewish, and other foreign targets outside Israel. Still, the most dominant anti-American terrorist strain in the 1960s was the left-wing strain. It started in Latin America in the first half of the decade, amplified in the second half and spread to Western Europe in the next decade.

Foreign Spillover Terrorism in the United States

Beginning in 1964, for the first time an overseas conflict triggered terrorist activity on U.S. soil. This activity was carried out by militant elements in the large exiled Cuban American population residing in the United States, especially in and around Miami, Florida. These militants opposed the communist regime in Cuba. They engaged in operations on U.S. soil and in Cuba. In the United States, this terrorist activity was aimed at official Cuban targets and those of other countries with diplomatic or economic relations with Cuba. Although this activity was considered to be a domestic terrorist activity, it was essentially triggered by reaction to an overseas development — Castro's communist regime in Cuba. The first major attack took place on December 11, 1964 when a 3.5-inch bazooka rocket was fired at the United Nations headquarters building from across the East River. The rocket was fired by a timing device, but fell short and hit the water. It could have caused many casualties if had it hit the glass façade of the UN building which was 900 yards away and within the range of the rocket. The attack took place during a protest by Cuban exiles at the front entrance against Che Guevara, the Cuban Minister of Industry, who was giving a speech at the time in the General Assembly.[31]

Anti-Cuban terrorist activity picked up in 1967–1968. During this period, about 34 attacks were carried out in Miami, New York, Los Angeles, Chicago, and New Jersey. They were primarily bombings. Targets of the attack were the Cuban Mission to the U.N.; Canadian, Finnish, Yugoslav, British and Mexican diplomatic facilities; Japanese, Canadian, and Mexican national tourism offices; French, Japanese, and Mexican airline offices; a Shell oil building, and a Japanese bank. No U.S. targets were attacked.[32] There were about a dozen anti-Castro militant groups with a presence in the United States. The most notorious were Cuban Action, Cuban National Liberation Front, Alpha 66, and Omega 7. The apex of this terrorist activity took place in the 1970s when Cuban exile groups carried out attacks in the United States and 17 other countries.[33]

U.S. Counter-Terrorism Responses

There were no specific U.S. counter-terrorism policies, programs, or organizations developed during the 1950s and 1960s as terrorism was not perceived as a special problem but simply a sub-component of insurgencies. If the terrorism issue was addressed, it was from the perspective of counterinsurgency strategy which was the prevailing irregular warfare concern under the Eisenhower, Kennedy, and Johnson administrations. Both Eisenhower and Johnson faced major hostage-taking incidents — Eisenhower in 1958 with the Cuban rebel seizure of 29 American servicemen and Johnson in 1964 during the Congo crisis. Johnson's crisis was more complex as it involved an incident with multiple nationalities and thereby several other countries were involved in the process. In this case, the coordination was effective. Eisenhower used quiet diplomacy and approached the issue by not painting the rebels into a corner with hardline rhetoric and saber-rattling.[34] It was a low-key approach that worked. The Eisenhower

---

[31] Homar Bigart, "Bazooka Fired at U.N. as Cuban Speaks: Launched in Queens, Missile Explodes in East River," *New York Times*, December 12, 1964, p. 1.

[32] "Opposition to Fidel Castro" at http://en.academic.ru/dic.nsf/enwiki/565980. Accessed May 7, 2017.

[33] Jim Mullen, "The Burden of a Violent History," *Miami New Times*, April 20, 2000.

[34] Jack Raymond, "Eisenhower Vows Aid for Captives," *New York Times*, July 3, 1958, p. 4.

administration did publicly articulate U.S. policy on hostage-taking and kidnappings in a way that was later endorsed by subsequent administrations. On July 1, 1958, Secretary of State John Foster Dulles commented at a press conference on the fate of four Americans held in Communist China, nine in East Germany, nine in the Soviet Union and 45 in Cuba:

> *I can't think of anything that would be worse than, in effect, to pay blackmail to get people out. We are willing to use any proper methods to get them out short of paying blackmail. If we started doing that, then that would only encourage further efforts to use Americans as hostages.*[35]

During the Eisenhower administration, the problem of a sustained terrorist threat — internal or international — did not exist. Consequently, the United States did not devote much attention or resources to the issue.

While the left-wing terrorist threat formed and advanced during the Kennedy and Johnson administrations, there was no identification of this threat as a major national security issue. For example, there were 99 National Security Action Memoranda (NSAM) issued by the Johnson administration between November 26, 1963 and October 18, 1968.[36] None dealt directly or indirectly with the issue of terrorism. Terrorism was never listed as a specific topic of discussion at the NSC meetings in the Kennedy and Johnson administrations.

Summation

Although the decade of the 1950s did not produce significant anti-American terrorist activity overseas, it did provide seeds for future anti-American terrorist strains that formed in subsequent decades. The U.S.-engineered 1953 coup in Iran contributed to the conditions for the 1979 Islamic revolution in Iran that in turn launched the Islamic revolutionary terrorism strain. The U.S-engineered 1954 coup in Guatemala contributed to the portrait of the United States as an imperialist power with designs in Latin America, thereby providing ideological rationale for an emerging left-wing terrorist strain in Latin America. The U.S.'s

---

[35] Jack Raymond, "Dulles Rules Out Blackmail to Get Americans Freed," *New York Times*, July 2, 1958, p. 1.

[36] NSAMs are issued by the president or his national security advisors either to relay policy statements or to request action programs. Lyndon Baines Johnson Presidential Library and Museum, "National Security Action Memoranda (NSAM)," at www.lbjlib.utexas.edu/johnson/archives.hom/NSAMs. Accessed July 3, 2017.

growing presence in Vietnam in the late 1950s put the U.S. on a road to an extended, costly, and controversial 15-year war that fueled anti-American sentiment and terrorist attacks in Latin America, Western Europe, and the U.S. throughout the decades of the 1960s and 1970s. The fourth significant event that took place in the 1950s that contributed to anti-American terrorist activity in later decades was the overthrow of the U.S.-supported Batista government in Cuba by Cuban revolutionaries led by Fidel Castro. This created a communist beachhead in the hemisphere that was used to export, support, and foster similar revolutions in Latin America — in America's "backyard." Cuba became the first state sponsor of anti-American terrorist activity in the post-war period.

In the 1960s, one anti-American terrorist strain formed and began its development (left-wing) and two (state-sponsored and secular Palestinian) were in the early stages of their development. However, it was not until the late 1960s that the terrorist threat to U.S. interests overseas assumed an international dimension when secular Palestinian terrorists left the Middle East to strike at Israeli, U.S., and other Western targets. The primary terrorist threat that confronted U.S. interests overseas in the 1960s was domestic left-wing terrorists operating in Latin America. The tactics used by these groups were generally property damage bombings and arsons with periodic lethal attacks and kidnappings. However, the tactics were discriminate. There were no mass-casualties or indiscriminate attacks like those that surfaced in the 1980s and 1990s. Unfortunately, the secular Palestinian hijackings of commercial airliners in the late 1960s were a harbinger of things to come — terrorist attacks designed to harm or endanger innocent civilians and carried out in a global arena. The number of anti-American terrorist actors also increased significantly. The decade of the 1970s builds on the anti-American terrorist activity in the 1960s and lays the foundation for the 1980s — the high-water mark of anti-American terrorist activity in the post-war era.

Mohammed Mossadegh (right), Iranian prime Minister with President Truman in October 1951.

Source: Wikimedia Commons.

CIA HISTORICAL REVIEW PROGRAM
RELEASE AS SANITIZED
2003

12 May 1975

MEMORANDUM

SUBJECT: CIA's Role in the Overthrow of Arbenz

In August 1953, the Operations Coordinating Board directed CIA to assume responsibility for operations against the Arbenz regime. Appropriate authorization was issued to permit close and prompt cooperation with the Departments of Defense, State and other Government agencies in order to support the Agency in this task. The plan of operations called for cutting off military aid to Guatemala, increasing aid to its neighbors, exerting diplomatic and economic pressure against Arbenz and attempts to subvert and or defect Army and political leaders, broad scale psychological warfare and paramilitary actions. During the period August through December 1953 a CIA staff was assembled and operational plans were prepared.

Following are the specific operational mechanisms utilized by the Agency in the overall missions against the Arbenz government:

a. Paramilitary Operations. Approximately 85 members of the CASTILLO Armas group received training in Nicaragua. Thirty were trained in sabotage, six as shock troop leaders and 20 others as support-type personnel. Eighty-nine tons of equipment were prepared. The support of this operation was staged inside the borders of Honduras and Nicaragua

.........There were an estimated 260 men in Honduras and El Salvador for use as shock troops and specialists, outside of the training personnel that had been sent to Nicaragua.

b. Air Operations. The planning for providing air operational support was broken down into three phases; i.e. the initial stockpiling of equipment; the delivering of equipment to advance bases by black flight; and the aerial resupply of troops in the field. Thirty days prior to D-day, a fourth phase, fighter support, was initiated. There were approximately 80 missions flown during the 14-29 June 1954 period, by various type aircraft such as C-47's, F-47's and Cessnas which were used to discharge cargo, distribute propaganda and for strafing and bombing missions.

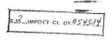

SECRET

Internal CIA memo describing the CIA's role in the overthrow of Guatemalan President Arbenz.
Source: CIA FOIA reading room.

President Eisenhower and Secretary of State John Foster Dulles (on left) greet South Vietnamese President Diem on arrival in Washington, D.C. on May 8, 1957.

Source: U.S. Department of Defense.

Cuban rebel leader Fidel Castro.

Source: Wikimedia Commons.

U.S. Ambassador to Guatemala John Gordon Meins, killed by Rebel Armed Forces (FAR) terrorists on August 28, 1968.

Source: U.S. Department of State.

Cuban Dictator Col. Fulgencio Batista is met on his arrival in Washington, D.C. on November 10, 1958 by Sumner Wells, The Undersecretary of State, and Gen. Malin Craig, the Chief of Staff of the U.S. Army.

Source: Wikimedia Commons.

Bomb damage to the U.S. Binational Center in Rancagua, Chile on March 16, 1968. U.S. binational centers were frequent targets of left-wing terrorists in Latin America.

Source: U.S. Department of State.

MEMORANDUM

THE WHITE HOUSE

WASHINGTON

~~CONFIDENTIAL~~   Wednesday, July 12, 1967 -- 4:30 PM

MEMORANDUM FOR THE PRESIDENT

SUBJECT: Congo Situation Report

1. Mobutu has reported to McBride that the mercenaries in Kisangani
   (formerly Stanleyville) fled the city by truck convoy at noon today our
   time. Destination unknown.

2. McBride has refused Mobutu's suggestion that we supply a C-130 for
   reconnaissance to find out where the mercenaries are going. Congolese
   planes can and should do this job.

3. The Red Cross mission to Kisangani is now fully set up and will leave
   at 10:00 tonight our time. We have no word on what happened to the
   hostages when the mercenaries fled. If they were unharmed, the job
   of the Red Cross plane will be to forestall any Congolese excesses as
   the Congolese army occupies the city.

4. McBride has made a strong demarche to Mobutu that a great deal depends
   on his ability to keep his soldiers from harming the white population in
   Kisangani and other cities. Mobutu has responded with a radio announcement that restrictions on travel by foreigners, curfews, and other measures
   directed against the white community will be lifted tonight.

5. McBride has worked up several more proposed mercy missions for the
   C-130's in addition to the food flight now on the way to Bukavu. The first
   would be another food delivery to the Kisangani area tomorrow.

6. All C-130 missions not required for emergency protection of Americans
   must now be approved in Washington by the Joint Chiefs.

Walt W. Rostow

July 1967 Congo situation report for President Johnson.

Source: Lyndon B. Johnson Presidential Library.

November 1964 — U.S. aircrews and Belgian Paracommandos at Kamina airfield in southern Congo prior to Stanleyville flight — Operation Red Dragon.

Source: Wikimedia Commons.

July 24, 1967 — President Johnson (seated) confers with (background L-R): Marvin Watson, FBI Director J. Edgar Hoover, Sec. Robert McNamara, Gen. Harold Keith Johnson, Joe Califano, Sec. of the Army Stanley Rogers Resor, on responding to the urban riots in Detroit and other cities.

Source: LBJ Presidential library.

Chapter 2

The Nixon and Ford Administrations (1969–1976) — The Overseas Threat

Overview

The 1960s ended with the acceleration of Palestinian terrorism into the international arena, the birth of a left-wing Marxist/Maoist terrorist and insurgent threat in Latin America, and the takeover of the Libyan government by Colonel Muammar el-Qaddafi, who proceeded to establish an anti-American regime that caused major terrorism problems for the U.S. over the next three decades. International terrorism emerged as a nascent security concern to the international community toward the end of the Johnson administration. This concern grew during the succeeding Nixon administration, and that administration responded to this new threat by developing an initial, elementary set of U.S. counter-terrorism components. Over the next 45 years, as the international terrorist threat escalated, became more complex, and experienced several evolutions, so did U.S. counter-terrorism policy, programs, organizational components, and actions. The Nixon administration, however, laid the foundation for this counter-terrorism edifice. In addition to a rising overseas terrorist threat against American interests emanating from secular Palestinian and leftist terrorist groups, the Nixon administration also confronted an escalating and more serious internal terrorist threat stemming from domestic left-wing, right-wing, Jewish, and Puerto Rican separatist groups, and from foreign spillover terrorism carried out by militant Croatians, Armenians, and Cuban exiles living in the U.S. In retrospect, the Nixon administration faced the most multifaceted internal terrorist threat in the U.S. history. Overseas, the United States was witnessing and experiencing the advance of the internationalization of political terrorism. After Nixon, the Ford administration essentially faced the same terrorist actors at home and abroad and maintained most of Nixon's counter-terrorism policies, programs, and structures.

During the Nixon and Ford administrations, 95 Americans were killed in 1,204 anti-American overseas terrorist attacks and 76 were killed in internal terrorist attacks. The most significant overseas terrorist attacks during these administrations were the 1970 Dawson's Field hijackings, which ushered in the modern era of spectacular televised terrorist attacks, the 1972 Munich Olympics attack, and the 1973 Khartoum attack in which two U.S. diplomats were murdered by Palestinian terrorists. The most noteworthy domestic terrorist attacks were the 1971 bombing by the Weather Underground of the U.S. Capitol, the 1972 bombing by the Weather Underground of a wing of the Pentagon, and a series of terrorist attacks by black militants that killed 17 police officers — the most killed by domestic terrorists in U.S. history. Puerto Rican separatism also emerged under both the Nixon and Ford administrations to carry out over 300 terrorist attacks on Puerto Rico and the U.S. mainland, including the January 1975 bombing of the historic Fraunces Tavern in New York City which killed four people and injured 60 others. Internally, there were also two assassination attempts on President Ford — in 1974 in Sacramento by Lynette Squeaky Fromme and in 1975 in San Francisco by Sara Jane Moore. The Ford administration experienced the first hijacking of an American aircraft on U.S. soil by a terrorist cell for political objectives in September 1976 when TWA Flight 355 was hijacked out of New York City by Croatian terrorists. The U.S. was confronted with the most lethal terrorist bombing in 55 years when unknown terrorists detonated a large bomb in a baggage area in New York's LaGuardia Airport's main terminal in 1975, killing 11 people.

The most active terrorist regions for anti-American terrorism during the Nixon and Ford administrations were Western Europe and Latin America. The primary anti-American terrorism actors were left-wing Marxist and Maoist insurgent and terrorist organizations in Western Europe and Latin America, and militant Palestinian organizations out of the Middle East. Nixon and Ford were also the first to confront the problem of foreign spillover terrorism on U.S. soil, for example, militant Cuban exiles, militant Croatian and Armenian émigré groups, and the Jewish Defense League. They added to an internal security environment already infected with Puerto Rican separatism and left-wing terrorist organizations, such as the United Freedom Front, the Weather Underground Organization, the May 19 Communist Organization, and the Black Liberation Army.

It is extremely difficult to ascertain how many political terrorist groups were active worldwide during the Nixon/Ford administrations. The CIA's National Foreign Assessment Center in a research paper titled "International Terrorism in 1979" published in April 1980 contained an appendix of "names and acronyms used by groups claiming responsibility for international terrorist attacks from 1968 to 1979."[1] There are 374 terrorist group names listed in this appendix. It is noted that some of these names are cover names and were only used one time. Of these 374 terrorist group names, only about 50 engaged in persistent anti-American terrorist activity in the 1970s.

In response to this evolving terrorist threat at home and abroad, Nixon and Ford advocated new domestic laws, lobbied for international treaties, developed counter-terrorism organizational structures, and established some counter-terrorism policies. They constructed a fundamental and nascent U.S. counter-terrorism toolbox. Subsequent administrations were compelled to add, subtract, or modify these tools.

The Record

The Overseas Terrorist Threat

Left-wing Terrorist Threat

Left-wing Marxist/Maoist terrorism emerged as an anti-American threat during the Johnson administration and continued to advance through the Nixon and Ford administrations. This threat was geographically concentrated in Latin America and Western Europe where left-wing terrorist groups and insurgent organizations attacked U.S. diplomatic, military, and business targets and private U.S. citizens. The tactics employed were primarily bombings, assassinations, and kidnappings. The attacks were generally discriminate in nature. In the 1960s, nine major left-wing terrorist organizations were operating — all but one in Latin America.[2] In the 1970s, 25 more major left-wing terrorist groups emerged. This means that in the 1970s there were 34 of these groups active — 17 in Latin America, 15 in Western Europe, one in Asia, and one in the Middle East.

---

[1] Central Intelligence Agency, National Foreign Assessment Center, "International Terrorism in 1979 — A Research Paper," April 1980, Unclassified document number PA-80-10072U, 25 pages. Appendix on pages 19–25. https://www.cia.gov/library/readingroom/document/cia-rdp86b00985r000 200260002-1. Accessed July 6, 2016.

[2] The groups were: Revolutionary Movement 13th November (MR-13) in Guatemala, the Rebel Armed Forces (FAR) in Guatemala (MR-13 merged into FAR in 1963), the Armed Forces of National Liberation in Venezuela, the Tupamaros in Uruguay, the Revolutionary Left Movement (MIR) in Chile, the People's Revolutionary Vanguard (VPR) in Brazil, the Movement of the Eighth (MR-8) in Brazil, and the Montoneros in Argentina. In Iran, there was the People's Mujahedin of Iran (MEK).

All the 10 Americans killed overseas in terrorist incidents during the Johnson administration were killed by left-wing terrorists in the Republic of the Congo, South Vietnam, Colombia, Dominican Republic, Guatemala, and Brazil. Of the 95 Americans killed overseas in terrorist incidents during the Nixon and Ford administrations, 20 were killed by left-wing terrorists in Germany, Greece, the Philippines, Uruguay, Argentina, Iran, and Lebanon. These 20 deaths consisted of 12 U.S. military personnel, two U.S. diplomats, one private U.S. citizen, one U.S. government official, and four U.S. businesspersons. In terms of the targets of anti-American terrorist attacks overseas during the Nixon and Ford administrations, most were bombings aimed at U.S. business interests — around 32%. The primary triggers for these attacks were: (1) U.S. involvement in South Vietnam, (2) U.S. support for military or dictatorial regimes in Latin America, the Philippines, and Iran, (3) the terrorist's ideological, political, and economic perception of the United States as a "capitalist" and "imperialist" superpower in conflict with the communist bloc and the third world, and (4) the stationing of U.S. military troops in Western Europe, Latin America, and Asia.

Western Europe

In Western Europe during the Nixon and Ford administrations, five Americans were killed by left-wing terrorist organizations. They were all killed in Greece (one) and West Germany (four). It was in these countries that the left-wing, anti-American terrorist threat was being molded by terrorist organizations that adopted lethal operations and demonstrated an operational acumen and resilience. Other left-wing terrorist organizations were developing in Spain, Turkey, and France. However, they had not yet advanced to the level of the Red Army Faction in West Germany and Revolutionary Organization 17 November in Greece. In the 1960s, the left-wing terrorist threat was anchored in Latin America. In the 1970s, it expanded into Western Europe. It remained in these two regions for the next four decades.

In the 1970s, Western Europe had the most active terrorist environment in the world. From 1970 to 1979 there were 3,988 international terrorist incidents worldwide of which 1,706, or, 43% occurred in Western Europe. Of the 1,591 anti-American terrorist attacks worldwide in this decade, 617, or 39%, attacks took place in Western Europe. The European security landscape at this time was polluted by the activities of Marxist/Maoist, ethno-national, and Palestinian terrorists. There were 15 major left-wing terrorist groups active in Western Europe in the 1970s:

- Red Army Faction (RAF) in West Germany.
- Movement 2 June (M2J) in West Germany.

- Red Brigades (RB) in Italy.
- Angry Brigade in Great Britain.
- The Liberation Army of the Workers and Peasants of Turkey, the armed wing of Communist Party of Turkey/Marxist-Leninist in Turkey.
- Turkish People's Liberation Army (TPLA).
- Revolutionary Cells (RZ) in Germany.
- Revolutionary Popular Struggle (ELA) in Greece.
- Revolutionary Organization 17 November (17N) in Greece.
- First of October/Anti-Fascist Resistance Group (GRAPO) in Spain.
- Prima Linea in Italy.
- Revolutionary Left (Dev Sol) in Turkey, later renamed Revolutionary People's Liberation Party-Front or DHKP/C.
- International Revolutionary Action Group in France, Spain, and Belgium.
- Direct Action in France.
- Marxist–Leninist Armed Propaganda Unit (MLAPU) in Turkey.

Many of these groups referred to themselves as "fighting communist organizations" (FCO) to distinguish themselves from the traditional communist parties in Western Europe that participated in ruling coalitions and power-sharing arrangements with non-communist parties in order to acquire political power.[3] For the FCOs these parties failed in their mission to mobilize the proletariat into a revolutionary mass organization that would seize power from the capitalist, imperialist state. The FCOs believed that the governments of these states had forced these communist parties to play by the "bourgeois" political rules. As a result, these communist parties had been effectively channeled by the bourgeois political parties into a parliamentary process where they had no hope of defeating the ruling political parties. In time, these communist parties assumed a cloak of respectability and legality. Their revolutionary zeal dissipated, and they abandoned the proletariat. They became part of the system they had intended to overthrow. Consequently, it fell to the FCOs to fill this revolutionary void left by these traditional communist parties. Italy in the 1970s presents a good example of this clash. The Italian Communist Party (CPI), led by Enrico Berlinguer in the 1970s, had around 1.5–1.8 million members and attracted about 30% of the vote in Italy during elections. The CPI opposed the armed struggle by the Italian RB terrorist group who was also targeted for killing many CPI members or trade unionists close to the CPI. The party asked the Soviet Union to put pressure on the Communist Czechoslovakia security service, to withdraw its support to the RB.

---

[3] For background on these FCOs, see Yonah Alexander and Dennis Pluchinsky, *Europe's Red Terrorists: The Fighting Communist Organizations* (London: Frank Cass Publishers, 1992).

The Soviet Union refused to do so.[4] The RB in the 1970s had around 600 full-time operatives living a clandestine lifestyle.[5]

The 15 terrorist groups above combined to form the Marxist/Maoist terrorist threat in Europe during the 1970s. Eleven of these groups targeted, in a limited or expanded terrorist campaign, U.S. interests in their respective countries. Most of the Marxist/Maoist terrorist attacks in Western Europe against U.S. interests were bombings designed to cause property damage. Assassination was the next preferred tactic, followed by kidnapping. Of the 20 Americans killed by left-wing terrorist groups worldwide during the Nixon and Ford administrations, five were killed in Western Europe.

Turkey

In Turkey, there was an active terrorist environment made up of both left- and right-wing terrorist groups. The left-wing terrorist threat began to emerge in the late 1960s and continued into the early 1970s. In the late 1960s, economic problems in Turkey triggered a wave of social unrest marked by street demonstrations, labor strikes, and political assassinations. Left-wing workers' and students' movements were formed that generated terrorist organizations that carried out bombing attacks, robberies, and kidnappings. This rise in left-wing violence produced a violent reaction from right-wing nationalist organizations. From the end of 1968, and increasingly during 1969 and 1970, left-wing violence was matched and surpassed by far-right violence, notably from the Grey Wolves, the militant arm of the extreme-right-wing Nationalist Movement Party, whose objective was to unify all Turkish people in one state. Turkey's government was not capable of dealing with this escalating violence as splits took place in the major political parties. This in turn produced a political stalemate on the legislative front, further hampering the government's ability to contain the violence.

By January 1971, Turkey appeared to be in a state of chaos. Universities had ceased to function and became battlegrounds between left and right. Factory workers were on strike. Militant organizations started to coalesce and engage in bank robberies, bombings, and assassinations. U.S. targets began to be attacked. The left-wing terrorist campaign against U.S. interests in Turkey began in January 1970 when a bomb exploded at the entrance of the U.S. Consulate in Istanbul

---

[4]Background on CPI from https://en.wikipedia.org/wiki/Italian_Communist_Party. Accessed July 9, 2017, Membership numbers of the PCI found at https://web.archive.org/web/20131110124209/http://www. cattaneo.org/archivi/adele/iscritti.xls. Accessed July 11, 2017.

[5]Alexander and Pluchinsky, *Europe's Red Terrorists*, p. 194.

causing minor damage. In November, three bombs exploded in the U.S. officer's open mess (club) in a military installation in Ankara. Three other bombs detonated at the U.S. military annex in Ankara, causing minor to moderate damage. In February 1971, three TPLA terrorists kidnapped James Finley, a U.S. airman stationed in Turkey. After 17 hours, he was released unharmed. On March 4, five TPLA terrorists kidnapped four U.S. Air Force airmen, and demanded a ransom of $400,000, which the U.S. and Turkish governments did not pay. The police dragnet against the kidnappers forced them to search for a way out of this predicament. The four airmen "escaped" four days later when the terrorists conveniently left the airmen unguarded in an apartment near the U.S. Embassy in Ankara.[6]

Campus and street violence in Turkey continued to spiral out of control. Consequently, the Turkish military issued an ultimatum to the civilian government in March 1971. It demanded "the formation, within the context of democratic principles, of a strong and credible government, which will neutralize the current anarchical situation and which, inspired by Atatürk's views, will implement the reformist laws envisaged by the constitution," putting an end to the "anarchy, fratricidal strife, and social and economic unrest." If the demands were not met, the army would "exercise its constitutional duty" and assume direct control over the state. In April, the military declared martial law in 11 of 67 Turkish provinces, including the major urban areas and Kurdish regions. The military quickly banned youth organizations, prohibited union meetings, proscribed leftist (but not right-wing) publications, and declared strikes to be illegal.[7] After the military took over in April 1971, it imposed stringent security measures, engaged in a massive crackdown on leftist organizations, used torture, imposed death sentences, and forced left-wing terrorists to hide in order to survive.[8] Some hid in Turkey while others went to Western Europe, in particular Germany which had a large Turkish immigrant population. Key leaders were also arrested or killed during shoot-outs. As a result of the military crackdown, anti-American terrorist attacks in Turkey subsided, until the late 1970s when the left-wing terrorist groups were able to regroup and initiate a new terrorist campaign.

---

[6] Albert Parry. *Terrorism: From Robespierre to Arafat* (New York: Vanguard, 1976), p. 443.

[7] Section on 1971 military coup in Turkey condensed from the Associated Press, "Turkish Regime is Ousted by the Military Leaders; No Move Made to Take Over Actual Rule — Step Follows Unrest Military Chiefs in Turkey Oust Regime," March 13, 1971, at http://www.allaboutturkey.com/darbe. htm. Accessed June 21, 2017, and http://en.wikipedia.org/wiki/Military_coup_in_Turkey,_1971. Accessed September 1, 2017.

[8] According to the *Anatolian News Agency* on March 12, 1972, during 1971, 3,759 people were tried by military tribunals for political or terrorist offenses.

By 1973, the military had stabilized the security situation and therefore returned most of its control of the state back to the civilian leadership. However, the fragmented political system did not correct the situation, and consequently, the problems that provoked the 1971 coup continued. The economy did not recover sufficiently. Left- and right-wing terrorist organizations re-emerged from hiding and exile, and by the late 1970s, instability returned. From 1977 to 1979, over 5,000 people died in Turkey as a result of political violence. In 1977, the death toll was 231. In 1978, it rose to 1,170 and then approached 2,000 in 1979.[9]

At the beginning of the decade, Turkish left-wing groups avoided lethal attacks on U.S. targets, carrying out instead property damage bombings and kidnappings in which the victims were eventually released unharmed. At the end of the decade, some Turkish left-wing terrorist groups authorized lethal attacks on Americans. Mapping left-wing terrorist groups in Turkey is difficult because these groups had the tendency to fragment and change group names. For example, DHKP/C was originally formed in 1978 as Dev Sol (Revolutionary Left), a splinter faction of Dev Yol (Revolutionary Way), which in turn broke away from the People's Liberation Party-Front of Turkey (THKP-C), a splinter of Dev Genç (Revolutionary Youth Federation). MLAPU was also a splinter group from the DHKP/C. The TPLA also split from Dev Genç in January 1971. The internal issues that caused this fractionalization were disagreements over strategy, tactics, targets, and leadership personality clashes.

At the beginning of the 1970s, the most active left-wing group was the TPLA, composed of some 200–500 operatives at various times. The group's most spectacular attack took place on March 26, 1972 when 11 terrorists attacked a NATO base in Unye on the Black Sea coast and kidnapped two British radar operators and one Canadian radar operator. The TPLA demanded the release of three imprisoned comrades who were under a death sentence for kidnapping U.S. servicemen the previous spring. As it had done consistently in the past, the Turkish government refused to accede to the demands. Four days later, government forces surrounded the mountain village hideout of the kidnappers. The terrorists refused to surrender and engaged the security forces in a lengthy shootout. The three hostages were killed by the terrorists and 10 of the TPLA operatives were killed. A note found near the dead kidnappers stated: "To Traitors, Pro-American Dogs, these English agents are part of the NATO forces which occupy our country, and as the revolutionaries of an occupied country we consider it our

---

[9] *Washington Post*, August 13, 1980; *Milliyet* (Istanbul), September 2, 1980; and *Cumhuriyet* (Istanbul), June 7, 1980.

basic right and a debt of honor to execute them."[10] This incident soured whatever support the TPLA received from the Turkish people. Killing unarmed hostages does not present a terrorist organization in a positive light, especially to the general population, and the group's constituency and supporters.

On May 3, 1972, four TPLA operatives hijacked a Turkish airliner at Istanbul airport with 68 people aboard. The plane was forced to fly to Sofia, Bulgaria. The hijackers demanded the release of six imprisoned colleagues. Again, the Turkish government refused the demands. The hostages were released the next day and the terrorists received political asylum in Bulgaria. The TPLA tried this tactic again on October 22 — hijacking an aircraft to Bulgaria. Again, no concessions were provided by the government and the terrorists received asylum. By 1973, the TPLA was severely damaged operationally by police arrests and an increase in public tips to the police.[11] As the decade ended, two groups emerged to replace the TPLA: MLAPU and Dev Sol. Both groups posed terrorist threats to U.S. interests in Turkey in the 1980s and 1990s.

West Germany

Left-wing terrorism crystallized in West Germany after the police killing of a student on June 2, 1967 in West Berlin during an anti-Shah of Iran protest. The Shah was on a state visit and attended the city's Opera House that evening. A protest took place outside. The protestors were violently attacked, not only by the city police but also by Iranian SAVAK secret police agents who accompanied the Shah. A 26-year-old student, Benno Ohnesorg, was shot and killed by a policeman. This incident marked a turning point for the German left. It convinced some that it was necessary to escalate from protests to armed actions. For them, the killing of Ohnesorg and the violent crackdown on the protestors demonstrated what they considered to be the true fascist nature of the German state. It has been reported that one blonde-haired woman was crying uncontrollably that night in a West Berlin leftist center. In anger, she exclaimed: "This fascist state means to kill us all. We must organize resistance. Violence is the only way to answer violence. This is the Auschwitz generation, and there's no arguing with them!"[12] That woman was Gudrun Ensslin who became a co-founder of the RAF terrorist group

---

[10] The details of the Unye kidnappings are from Parry, *Terrorism: From Robespierre to Arafat*, pp. 444–445.

[11] Edgar O'Balance. *The Language of Violence: The Blood Politics of Terrorism*, (San Rafael, California: Presidio Press, 1979), p. 143.

[12] Stefan Aust, *The Baader-Meinhof Group* (London: The Bodley Head, 1987), p. 44.

and a key operational leader along with Andreas Baader. Ensslin participated in that anti-Shah protest.

In West Germany, there were three major left-wing terrorist entities that emerged in the 1970s: RAF, or M2J,[13] and RZ. The first two engaged in lethal terrorist attacks while the RZ limited itself generally to property damage attacks. The RAF and M2J were terrorist organizations. The RZ conducted its first attack in 1973 and emerged from the student protest movements of the late 1960s. The RZ was a "leaderless" terrorist entity in that it was not a structured group and had no central leadership. It was more of a "mindset." Individuals, if they agreed with the RZ's grievances and operational concept, established their own autonomous cells and took independent actions against relevant local targets. RZ cells had no connections with other cells. You could not join a preexisting RZ cell, you had to form your own. Consequently, when police arrested one cell, it rarely led to other RZ cells. RZ "adherents" (as opposed to members) were sometimes referred to as "legal" or "part-time" terrorists since many held normal jobs and carried out their attacks in the evenings or weekends. The RZ sought to exploit local issues. Under this strategy, termed the "connection strategy" by the German authorities, RZ targets changed with public concerns.[14] In the 1970s, RZ attacks on nuclear-related targets paralleled the growing domestic concern over nuclear issues. The RZ had cells in West Berlin, Frankfurt, Dusseldorf, Heidelberg, Wiesbaden, Mainz, and Bochum. Membership was estimated to be around 30–60.

RZ cells and adherents collectively debated and discussed various issues, grievances, and operations in a mimeographed, clandestinely distributed, periodic magazine called "Revolutionarer Zorn" (Revolutionary Rage). One unique development concerning the RZ was a spinoff known as Red Zora.[15] It was originally created as a women's subset of the RZ. However, it became more independent and focused on women-related issues and targets (porn shops, cinemas, bars, firms deemed to exploit women, and government agencies because of the government's rigid abortion laws). It is to date the only all-female terrorist entity ever constructed in the history of terrorism. Red Zora began its communiqués with "On [date of attack], the women of the Revolutionary Cells carried out an attack

---

[13] The group took its name from June 2, 1967 when German police shot and killed the student Benno Ohnesorg during an anti-Shah of Iran protest in West Berlin.

[14] CIA, Directorate of Intelligence, Terrorism Review, "Group Profile: West Germany's Revolutionary Cells," May 12, 1983, pp. 3–6. CIA FOIA document #RDP84-00893R000100160001-3.

[15] The movement took its name from a book written in 1941, "Red Zora and Her Gang," which tells the story of a red-haired Croatian girl called Red Zora who commands a gang of orphans committed to righting injustice.

against the [name of target]." Red Zora did not carry out any attacks against U.S. targets in Germany in the 1970s.

The RZ did target U.S. interests in West Germany in the 1970s, carrying out about 6–7 attacks. From 1973 to 1982, the RZ was responsible for 25 attacks. Of those, 14 were aimed at U.S. targets, mostly U.S. military facilities.[16] In November 1973, an RZ cell bombed the International Telephone and Telegraph (ITT) offices in West Berlin and Nuremberg and caused over $200,000 in damages.[17] In a communiqué claiming responsibility for the attacks, the RZ cell stated that "we attacked the ITT branches, because ITT is responsible for the torture and murder of women, workers, and peasants."[18] The communiqué also accused the ITT of aiding the September 1973 "CIA-backed coup" of the socialist Salvatore Allende government in Chile. Three years later, an RZ cell bombed the U.S. Army V Corps headquarters in Frankfurt and the U.S. Air Force Officer's Club at Rhein Main Air Base. In December 1979, an RZ cell bombed the Frankfurt office of the Morgan Trust Company of New York. The RZ also carried out occasional "solidarity" attacks with revolutionaries in other countries. Some RZ members felt that it was necessary to get more involved with the international revolutionary movement and consequently joined Palestinian terrorist groups in carrying out joint operations. RZ members gravitated in particular toward Waddi Haddad's faction of the Popular Front for the Liberation of Palestine (PFLP) and a small group associated with the PFLP led by Ilich Ramerez Sanchez (aka: Carlos and the Jackal), a Venezuelan Marxist revolutionary. These RZ members are sometimes referred to as the RZ "international wing." They were the exception and not the rule for RZ cells and individual members.[19]

The following were the two most notorious international operations involving RZ terrorists:

- The December 1975 Carlos-led attack on the Organization of the Petroleum Exporting Countries (OPEC) Ministerial meeting in Vienna that involved Palestinian terrorists and former RZ terrorist Hans-Joachim Klein and former M2J member Gabriele Kröecher-Tiedemann.

---

[16] CIA, Terrorism Review, "Group Profile: West Germany's Revolutionary Cells," p. 6. CIA FOIA document # RDP84-00893R000100160001-3.

[17] "West German ITT Offices Bombed," The Associated Press, November 19, 1973.

[18] J. Smith and Andre Moncourt, *The Red Army Faction: A Documentary History — Volume I: Projectiles for the People* (Quebec: Kersplebedeb Publishing, 2009), p. 437.

[19] See also, CIA, Terrorism Review, "Group Study: The International Revolutionary Cells," December 9, 1982, pp. 9–10, CIA FOIA document # RDP84-00893R000100050001-5.

- The June 1976 hijacking of an Air France plane by Palestinians and RZ terrorists Wilfried Bose and Brigitte Kuhlmann. The latter ended with the famous Israeli long-distance counter-terrorism operation at Entebbe airport in Uganda that freed the passengers/hostages.

Given that the RZ was not a centrally structured organization but more of a mindset or operational approach, individuals who considered themselves to be part of the RZ could engage in whatever sideline operations they wanted. The only downside for these individuals was they might be criticized by other RZ adherents in the magazine "Revolutionary Rage." Compared to its lethal competitors, the RAF and M2J, the RZ suffered fewer arrests and fewer casualties to its adherents but carried out more terrorist attacks than the RAF and M2J combined. The latter two groups, however, carried out more high-profile and high-impact operations than the RZ. At the heart of the RZ operational concept was "wholesale" or "mass-militancy," that is, RZ operations were designed to be inexpensive, tactically simple, low risk, casualty free, and involve low manpower. The idea was to inspire others to engage in similar actions by demonstrating that the average person could carry out an attack without specialized training, hard-to-find bomb ingredients, and a lot of money.

> *Carry out actions primarily from the point of view of bringing about the perpetration on a wholesale basis — that is, implementing them at places and carrying them out with means that make it possible for the people to carry them out and identify with them.*[20]

The leaderless terrorism propagated by the RZ created investigative problems for the German police agencies. This operational concept surfaced again, in a systematic and more lethal way, in the 2000s when the global jihad movement adopted it and called it "jihad of the individual and small cell." Beginning in 2014, the Islamic State in Iraq and Syria perfected this operational concept by using the Internet for agitation, propagation, and avocation of jihadist leaderless terrorism.

The M2J was ideologically anti-American, but it did not carry out any attacks against U.S. interests in the 1970s. It was the RAF that evolved into the primary terrorist threat against the U.S. interests in West Germany over the next three

---

[20]Revolutionaere Zorn (Revolutionary Rage) # 4, January 1978, p 17; see also CIA, Terrorism Review, May 12, 1983, "Group Profile: West Germany's Revolutionary Cells," pp. 3–6 at CIA FOIA document # RDP84-00893R00010016001-3.

decades.[21] The RAF was a small (less than 30 hardcore members) Marxist–Leninist, urban terrorist group that emerged in West Germany in 1970. The roots of this group, often referred to inaccurately as the Baader–Meinhof Group,[22] go back to the violent student protests in West Germany during the late 1960s that were triggered by the Vietnam War. The goal of the RAF was to destroy the current West German state and replace it with a vaguely defined "proletarian dictatorship." The group considered itself to be part of the international revolutionary movement and counted as its "enemies," imperialism, capitalism, and fascism, in all their various forms and practitioners. All RAF terrorist attacks were directed against symbolic targets that represented one or more of these enemies. In June 1970, during its formative year, about 20 RAF members received training at a PFLP training camp in Jordan. The RAF members encountered severe problems in adjusting to the desert training camp and culture of the Palestinians. They criticized the training program (essentially the program was geared toward rural, insurgent scenarios while the RAF wanted training relevant to their urban, terrorist mission), they complained about the food (one RAF member demanded that a Coca-Cola machine be installed), and lack of sufficient ammo for target practice, and they antagonized their hosts by demanding segregated accommodations (no woman had been trained in that camp before) and to be allowed to sunbathe in the nude.[23] As a result, the RAF members were eventually expelled from the camp in the fall of 1970. They returned to West Germany where they established safe houses, procured weapons and false documents, and carried out a series of bank robberies to prepare for the launch of their urban terrorism campaign. This campaign began in May 1972 when the RAF carried out six bombing attacks that month, two against U.S. targets and four against German targets. It was clear

---

[21] For the most accurate English language accounts of the evolution of the RAF, see Stefan Aust, *Baader-Meinhof: The Inside Story of The RAF* (London: Oxford University Press, 2008), and Jillian Becker, *Hitler's Children: Story of the Baader-Meinhof Terrorist Gang* (London: DIANE Publishing Company, 1998). For a good collection of translated RAF communiqués, see the J. Smith and Andre Moncourt book noted previously. For a detailed and accurate chronicle of RAF anti-U.S. operations, see Dennis Pluchinsky, "An Organizational and Operational Analysis of Germany's Red Army Faction Terrorist Group (1972–1991), in Yonah Alexander and Dennis Pluchinsky, editors, *European Terrorism: Today and Tomorrow* (Washington, D.C.: Brassey's, 1992), and Dennis Pluchinsky, "The Red Army Faction: An Obituary," *Studies in Conflict and Terrorism*, Volume 16, July 1993.

[22] The RAF was in reality a product of Andreas Baader and Gudrun Ensslin. Ulrike Meinhof was a famous leftist writer at the time of the group's formation so the German press attached her name to Baader's. However, Ensslin was Baader's girlfriend and played a key formative and operational role in the RAF.

[23] Aust, *The Baader-Meinhof Group*, pp. 65–75.

from these attacks that the RAF intended to discriminately kill people and not just cause property damage.

The RAF's first high-profile attack took place on May 11, 1972 when it bombed the U.S. Army V Corps headquarters building in Frankfurt, killing 1st Lt. Paul A. Bloomquist, and injuring 13 other American servicemen. In the communiqué claiming responsibility for this attack, the RAF noted that this attack took place "on the day on which the U.S. imperialists began a mine blockade against North Vietnam" and warned that "West Germany and West Berlin are no longer a safe hinterland for the extermination strategy in Vietnam." The communiqué continued: "They must know that their crimes against the Vietnamese people have created for them, new bitter enemies, and that there will no longer be any place in the world where they can be safe from attacks by the revolutionary guerrilla units." The RAF demanded "immediate suspension of the mine blockade against North Vietnam," the "immediate suspension of bomb attacks on North Vietnam," and "the withdrawal of all U.S. troops from Indochina."[24] On May 15, the RAF planted a bomb under the car of a West German Federal High Court judge. The bomb detonated, but the judge's wife was in the car. She was severely crippled from the attack. On May 24, the RAF detonated two cars packed with 50 and 60 pounds of explosives, respectively, outside the mess hall and computer center of the European headquarters of the U.S. Army in Heidelberg, killing three American soldiers — Captain Clyde R. Bonner, Specialist Ronald A. Woodward, and Specialist Charles Peck. In a communiqué, the RAF stated that "In the last seven weeks, the American air force has dropped more bombs on Vietnam than were dropped on Germany and Japan during World War II." It claimed that the German people "want nothing to do with the crimes of American imperialism and the support it receives from the ruling class here, because they have not forgotten Auschwitz, Dresden, and Hamburg."[25]

The Heidelberg attack was the last attack carried out by the first generation of RAF members. In June 1972, the founders and five top leaders of the RAF (Andreas Baader, Gudrun Ensslin, Ulrike Meinhof, Jan-Carl Raspe, and Holger Meins) were all arrested at different locations. These arrests crippled the RAF organizationally and operationally. However, these imprisoned RAF leaders were able to supervise from prison the emergence of a second generation of RAF operatives whose primary objective was to force the release of their imprisoned

---

[24] Communiqué excerpts from Dennis Pluchinsky, "An Organizational and Operational Analysis of Germany's Red Army Faction Terrorist Group (1972–1991), p. 57.

[25] Smith and Moncourt, *The Red Army Faction: A Documentary History*, (Quebec: Kersplebedeb Publishing, 2009), p. 178.

comrades. The public and high-profile trials of these RAF leaders were held in a specially constructed courtroom in Stammheim prison in Stuttgart from 1975 to 1977. During this trial period, a second generation of RAF terrorists engaged in a series of "prisoner liberation operations." The first operation was the April 1975 seizure of the West German Embassy in Stockholm, Sweden by six RAF members. They stated that the purpose of the operation was "to free 26 political prisoners in the Federal Republic of Germany" and then proceeded to name them, including the top five RAF leaders noted above. During the embassy seizure, the RAF killed the German military and economic attaches. The German government refused to give in to the demands of the terrorists, forcing the terrorists to try and escape from the embassy at which time the terrorists' explosives were accidentally detonated, killing one terrorist and seriously injuring another who later died. The other four RAF terrorists were arrested. The operation failed, and it took two more years for the RAF to mount another prisoner liberation operation.

Greece

Greece also had an active left-wing terrorist environment in the 1970s, especially in the second half of the decade. Left-wing opposition to the rule of the military junta in Greece from 1967 to 1974 laid the foundation for the emergence of anti-American terrorism in Greece in the 1970s. The junta justification for the military takeover was an alleged communist conspiracy that had infiltrated key sectors of the government, press, and academia, and thus, the military had to intervene to prevent a communist coup. The junta proceeded to repress political freedoms and civil liberties, political parties were dissolved, freedom of the press was suspended, military courts were established, and torture employed. Many Greeks believed that the U.S. supported the Greek junta. While there is "no evidence the U.S. assisted the coup, the colonels later won the open backing of President Richard Nixon and his then-national security adviser, Henry Kissinger."[26] President Nixon's vice president, Spiro Agnew, a Greek American, went to Athens and "publicly threw his arms around dictator Georgios Papadopoulos, an act many Greeks have not forgotten."[27]

A significant event took place on November 17, 1973 during Greek student strikes and protests against the junta at the National Technical University of Athens. In response, the junta sent in a tank to crush the protests. Twenty-eight Greek students were killed. The future Greek Marxist terrorist group, 17N took

---

[26]Ray Moseley, "Thousands decry U.S. in streets of Athens," *The Chicago Tribune*, November 17, 1999.

[27]Ibid.

its name from this event. Given the dictatorial nature of the junta and its use of torture and other repressive measures, it was difficult for opposition elements to engage in armed struggle to challenge the junta. The junta however was over-thrown in July 1974. The first major Greek left-wing terrorist group to form in the post-junta era was ELA. It carried out several anti-American attacks from 1975 to 1979. The attacks were primarily bombings at U.S. military and business inter-ests. In 1975, the ELA firebombed the U.S. Air Force commissary in Athens. In the 1970s, the ELA was the most active left-wing terrorist group in Greece, but it posed only a low terrorist threat at the time, given its tendency to engage in pri-marily property damage attacks.

There were other smaller left-wing groups and anarchist terrorist cells active in Greece in the late 1970s, but none had the organizational ability and opera-tional record of the ELA.[28] The Greek press reported that from 1974 to March 1980, there were six political assassinations, 300 bombings, 80 Molotov cocktail attacks, and 180 vehicle fire bombings in Greece.[29] The U.S. Embassy reported that in 1975 there were 200 bombings of U.S. employee vehicles in Greece. In 1976, there were 120 vehicle bombings and 84 in 1977.[30] Only one American was killed in Greece by left-wing terrorist groups during the 1970s. On December 23, 1975, Richard Welch, the CIA's station chief in Athens, was shot and killed out-side his home in Athens by three masked members of a previously unknown group called the "Revolutionary Organization 17 November." Political assassina-tions were unusual in Greece at this time and the well-planned operation initially confused the Greek police. At the time, left- and right-wing terrorist groups made false claims so the police initially dismissed the 17N claim.[31] In its communiqué claiming credit for the Welch assassination, the group said that "the CIA was responsible for and supporting the military junta," and that this "is the first time in Greece that it paid for its contribution to the events in Cyprus."[32]

---

[28]The attacks were mostly bombings of vehicles and buildings. Greek leftists used names like "L.A.O.S.-11," "Popular Resistance Sabotage Group," "Independence, Liberation, and Resistance," "Greek Anti-Dictatorship Youth," "People's Resistance Organized Army," and "National Youth Resistance Organization" — to name a few.

[29]*Athens Post*, March 2, 1980.

[30]George Kassimeris. *Europe's Last Red Terrorists: The Revolutionary Organization 17 November* (London: Hurst and Company, 2001), p. 74.

[31]Ibid., p. 73.

[32]Ibid., p. 110. The Greek junta sponsored a military coup by EOKA-B on Cyprus on July 15, 1974 which overthrew Archbishop Makarios III, the Cypriot president. EOKA-B was a Greek Cypriot paramilitary organization formed in 1971. It followed a right-wing nationalistic ideology and had the ultimate goal of achieving the enosis (union) of Cyprus with Greece. At this time, Cyprus was a hot

Wherever you turn your eyes, there is the finger of the CIA that you find behind each event: behind the execution of heroic [communist activist] Beloyiannis, behind the Zurich and London treaties, behind the 1961 election of rigging and violence, behind the apostasy and the overthrow of George Papandreou in 1965, behind the 1967 military coup and the seven-year tyranny and, most recently, behind the betrayal of Cyprus and the resultant rivers of tears, blood, pain, and 200,000 refugees and with Kissinger expressing his 'humanitarian concerns.'[33]

In the Welch communiqué, 17N expressed some of the sentiments and grievances that other European left-wing Marxist/Maoist terrorist groups held toward the United States:

Enough is enough. The American imperialists and their domestic agents must understand that the Greek people are not a flock of sheep. They must also understand that this time the people won't swallow their lies, provocations and poisonous propaganda; they have realized that the Americans have tied the government's hands behind its back so it has no independence of action and thus can do absolutely nothing. The main slogan of the 1973 Polytechnic uprising "out with the Americans" remains today unfulfilled. The Americans are not out and what is worse, the monopolies have moved here from Lebanon and the CIA moved its Middle East headquarters from Beirut to Athens. For the Americans, Greece continues to be a xefrago ambeli [author's note: it means "open field," that is, to foreign intervention] *like it was throughout the dictatorship. A Latin American Banana Republic in the Southern Mediterranean.*[34]

The Welch assassination could have been interpreted at the time as possibly an aberration and not the beginning of a sustained and prolonged anti-American terrorist threat in Greece. When a new terrorist group forms, its intentions, capabilities, strategy, tactics, and operational area are initially unknown. It is difficult to deduce these components from a single attack. 17N could have been a fictitious

---

spot between Greece and Turkey because 18% of the population was made up of Turkish Cypriots and 80% of Greek Cypriots. There were frequent inter-communal ethnic tensions and violence on the island between 1963 and 1974. The EOKA-B overthrow of Makarios caused Turkey to invade Cyprus on July 20, 1974 and occupy the northern part of the island. From the perspective of the Greek left, the U.S. supported the junta which lost part of Cyprus to Turkey.

[33] Ibid.

[34] Ibid., p. 111.

name used by criminals or Greeks who had a personal vendetta against the U.S. It could have been a few leftists who formed a cell, carried out the attack, issued a communiqué, and were never heard from again. On December 14, 1976, however, 17N appeared again and assassinated Evangelos Mallios, an alleged police torturer under the military junta. To further its credentials and attract more publicity, 17N, ten days after the Mallios killing, issued a communiqué which was published on December 24 in the French newspaper *Liberation* that claimed the Mallios attack and provided extensive details on how it carried out the Welch killing.[35] What tipped the scale on whether or not 17N was a potentially transient or long-term

---

[35] Ibid., p.74. The following is an example of the operational details on the Welch assassination provided by 17N in the Liberation communiqué:

The former station chief of the CIA, Stacy Hals, left Athens on May 30, 1975 and Welch arrived in Athens on June 15. Before moving into Hals' residence on July 9, Welch stayed at the home of his deputy. At this time, Welch also got a new driver. We found out about Welch's name and his profession by simple means which we will not disclose at this time. [Author's note: The English-language newspaper Athens News published a list of CIA employees in Athens. In addition, Welch's name appears on a list of names of the 100 chiefs of the CIA network around the world published in an American magazine entitled Counterintelligence. At that time, he was the station chief in Lima, Peru.]

Welch used to leave with his driver at around 8:30 am and return home between 6:30 pm and 7:30 pm. In contrast to his deputy, Welch did not go out much and he would never stay out after 11 pm. On weekends beginning in September, Welch would use a second car, a white Mustang with CD plate number 3181 which he always kept in the garage.

On Tuesday evening, November 11, at 6:30 pm, Welch went to the movies (the Astron cinema in Ambelokipi) with his wife and another woman. That night he drove the white Mustang and left the movies at 10 pm. When they returned home at 10:30 pm, the black Ford [Welch's official car] was parked in front of the main entrance to the villa. The situation was ideal for our operation. While Welch was putting the Mustang into the garage, the two women entered the house. Welch then went out into the street to move the Ford into the garden. We walked right past him, and it was very easy for us to kill him. There was absolutely no one else around. We give you these few facts to prove that we had decided to kill Welch and began to study Welch's movements as soon as he arrived in Athens.

The communiqué then refers to the actual assassination on December 23. The operatives were waiting outside Welch's house for him to return.

At 10:23 pm we saw the black Ford pass us. We began to follow it at a slow pace. They eventually stopped in front of the garden gate, at right angles to the sidewalk, in order to enter. The chauffeur got out of the car and opened the rear door to let Mrs. Welch out. He then turned to open the garden gate. At that time we pulled up right behind the Ford. Three of us with hoods over our faces got out of the car. Seeing us, they turned toward us and our comrade ordered 'hands up high' and he moved towards the right rear door from which Welch stepped out. All this time the second comrade was threatening the chauffeur and Mrs. Welch. Our third comrade went to the right side of the car to prevent Welch from escaping into the house. The comrade who was to shoot Welch again ordered

terrorist threat was its publication in April 1977 of a 28-page communiqué that contained a politically astute, from the perspective of the leftist milieu, assessment of the current political situation in Greece and arguments of the need for violence. This was a group that was being directed by some shrewd political strategists who correctly assessed a rising anti-American sentiment in Greece and calculated that it was time to engage in assassinations, not bombings of unoccupied vehicles, as previous left-wing terrorists and anarchists had done. It was the first Greek left-wing terrorist group that instituted assassinations as a preferred tactic. To this point, left-wing political assassinations were rare and except for the ELA, few groups demonstrated any staying power in their terrorist activities. 17N was to shape the left-wing terrorist threat to American interests in Greece for the next two decades and develop into one of the most enigmatic terrorist groups in the history of modern terrorism. 17N posed a serious terrorist threat to U.S. interests in Greece in the 1980s and 1990s.[36]

Latin America

In the 1970s, Latin American had the second most active terrorist environment in the world, behind only Western Europe. From 1970 to 1979 there were 3,988 international terrorist incidents worldwide of which 1,056, or 26%, occurred in Latin America. Of the 1,591 anti-American terrorist attacks worldwide in this decade, 582, or 37%, took place in Latin America. The Latin American security landscape at this time was polluted primarily by left-wing terrorist and insurgent organizations. Unlike Western Europe, Latin America was not affected by ethnonational and Palestinian terrorism. There were 17 major left-wing terrorist and insurgent groups active in Latin America in the 1970s:

- Revolutionary Movement 13th November (MR-13) in Guatemala.
- Rebel Armed Forces (FAR) in Guatemala (MR-13 merged into FAR in 1963).

'hands up high.' Welch, who spoke Greek very well, answered in English 'what!' At that instant, our comrade fired three rounds with his Colt .45 ...

The communiqué then notes:

Neither Mrs. Welch nor the chauffeur bear direct responsibility for the crimes committed by the CIA against our people. Our decision was that Welch and only he should be executed. That was the reason we made certain to exclude the possibility of injuring others, even by chance.

[36]For an excellent history of terrorism in Greece, see John Brady Kiesling, *Greek Urban Warriors: Resistance and Terrorism 1967–2012* (Athens: Lycabettus Press, 2014).

- Armed Forces of National Liberation in Venezuela.
- Tupamaros in Uruguay.
- Revolutionary Left Movement (MIR) in Chile.
- People's Revolutionary Vanguard (VPR) in Brazil.
- Montoneros in Argentina.
- 19th of April Movement (M-19) in Colombia.
- Revolutionary Armed Forces of Colombia (FARC).
- Red Flag or Bandero Roja in Venezuela.
- 23rd of September Armed Communist League (LC-23) in Mexico.
- People's Revolutionary Party (ERP) in Argentina.
- Farabundo Martí National Liberation Force (FMLN) in El Salvador.
- Popular Liberation Front (FPL) in El Salvador.
- Popular Revolutionary Bloc (BPR) in El Salvador.
- Revolutionary Vanguard in Peru.
- Revolutionary Movement 8th of October (MR-8) in Brazil.

Of the 20 Americans killed overseas by left-wing terrorists during the Nixon and Ford administrations, three were killed in Latin America — one diplomat, one government employee, and one businessman. Anti-American terrorist attacks took place in Mexico, Venezuela, Brazil, the Dominican Republic, Uruguay, Colombia, El Salvador, Guatemala, and Argentina in the 1970s. However, the most active countries for anti-American terrorism were Argentina, Uruguay, and El Salvador (starting in 1979). Of the 582 anti-American terrorist attacks in the region during this decade, the majority were low-level bombings aimed at property damage to U.S. business and diplomatic interests. In fact, U.S. businesses were targeted the most. In this decade, there were more kidnappings than assassinations of Americans, especially in Argentina. Given the number of left-wing terrorist groups operating in the region in this decade and the large number of anti-American terrorist incidents that took place, it was fortunate that only three Americans were killed. However, considering the large number of kidnappings and attempted kidnappings of Americans during this time, it is clear that many of the left-wing groups in Latin America considered Americans more valuable alive than dead. The terrorist threat to U.S. interests in the region was the highest in Argentina during this decade.

Argentina

In the 1970s, there were five left-wing terrorist organizations operating in Argentina: Liberation Armed Forces (FAL), Revolutionary Armed Forces (FAR),

Peronist Armed Forces (FAP), the Montoneros, and the People's Revolutionary Army (ERP). The FAL, active from 1962 to 1972, merged with the ERP. The FAR, active from 1966 to 1973, merged with the Montoneros. The FAP, active from 1968 to 1973, split and some members gravitated toward the ERP and others to the Montoneros. By 1973, the two most active left-wing groups were the Montoneros and the ERP. Both posed a serious terrorist threat to U.S. interests in Argentina. The Montoneros formed in 1970 out of a confluence of Roman Catholic groups, university students in social sciences, and fascist supporters of Juan Domingo Perón. It was the militant wing of the Peronist movement which sought to destabilize the incumbent military government that it saw as a pro-American regime.[37] The Montoneros had some 2,500 combatants and 11,000 sympathizers. It attacked Argentinian government, political, business, military, and foreign targets in Argentina, especially foreign firms, in an effort to halt foreign investment and involvement in the Argentine economy. After Peron assumed the presidency in late 1973, he attempted to negotiate a halt to the terrorism, but the Montoneros refused. By 1974, the spilt was complete and the Peronist regime became the group's target. The Peronist government outlawed the group in mid-1975, and security forces moved against them. After overthrowing Peron in 1976, the Argentine military had free rein against the Montoneros. Over a three-year period, using torture, illegal detentions, and widespread dragnets, the police and military succeeded in forcing most of the group's members into exile. By early 1977, the group's strength was down to 300 members. By late 1979, there were 200 members.[38]

The Montoneros killed two Americans in Argentina during this decade. On February 26, 1975, John P. Egan, the U.S. Consular agent was kidnapped by the Montoneros in Cordoba. Egan was killed 48 hours later when the Argentine government refused the terrorists' demand for the release of four of its imprisoned comrades. The group is also suspected of killing a U.S. businessman and his two bodyguards in Buenos Aires on December 2, 1977. It also carried out numerous

---

[37] Peronism, named after Argentinian military and political leader Juan Peron, can be defined as an authoritarian populism rooted in the masses. It calls for a strong centralized government with authoritarian tendencies; freedom from foreign influences, a third way approach to economics which purported to be neither socialist nor capitalist, but to incorporate elements of both; and the combination of nationalism and social democracy. Source: http://en.wikipedia.org/wiki/Peronist June 17, 2018. Conflict emerged between Juan Peron and the Montoneros when he returned to Argentina in 1973. There was a split between the left (Montoneros) and right wing of the Peronists. In 1974, Peron withdrew his backing of the Montoneros.

[38] CIA, *Terrorism Review*, November 12, 1982, pp. 17–19 at https://www.cia.gov/library/readingroom/docs/CIA-RDP84-00893R000100030001-4.pdf. Accessed July 7, 2017.

kidnappings and attempted kidnappings of American and Argentine executives working for American companies in Argentina. In many cases, ransom was paid by the companies. The Montoneros carried out what is probably a record for ransom paid during a kidnapping. On September 19, 1974, it killed the chauffeur and a manager and then kidnapped Juan and Jorge Born, directors of Bunge and Born, one of the largest international trading companies in Latin America. The ransom demand was for $60 million. If not paid, the brothers would be tried in a people's court. The group later added the requirement that the company had to publish the Montoneros' communiqué in major newspapers.[39] Eventually, the company agreed to pay the ransom and the brothers were released nine months later. The Argentine government opposed the ransom payment which it said equaled one-third of the country's defense budget. $1.2 million of the ransom was paid in food and clothing and distributed to the slum areas.[40] At the time, it was the largest ransom payment made to a political terrorist group.

On September 16, 1974 about 40 Montoneros bombs exploded throughout Argentina, targeting foreign companies. The targets included three Ford showrooms, Peugeot and IKA-Renault showrooms, Goodyear and Firestone tire distributors, the pharmaceutical manufacturers Riker and Eli Lilly, the Union Carbide Battery Company, the Bank of Boston, Chase Manhattan Bank, the Xerox Corporation, and the soft drink companies, Coca-Cola and Pepsi-Cola. The group also discouraged foreign investment in Argentina by blowing up executives' homes. The Montoneros peak operating years were from 1973 to 1974.

The People's Revolutionary Army (ERP) was the military branch of the Workers' Revolutionary Party in Argentina. The ERP had a Maoist orientation but received aid from Cuba. The ERP launched its terrorist campaign against the Argentine military dictatorship in 1969. The avowed aim of the ERP was a communist revolution against the Argentine government in pursuit of "proletarian rule." It used bombings, assassinations, kidnappings, and armed assaults against domestic and foreign targets in Argentina from 1969 to about 1977. At its height, it had several hundred members and several thousand supporters and sympathizers. The ERP worked with the Montoneros on certain operations.

In addition to carrying out bombings of U.S. firms in Argentina, the group also carried out kidnappings, some of which resulted in the deaths of the victims.

---

[39] This communiqué was published in the *Washington Post*, June 19, 1975, p. A28. The company noted that it was being forced to publish the communiqué and made 11 points of "clarification" that preceded the communiqué. The *Washington Post* noted that it was a paid advertisement.

[40] Brian Michael Jenkins, J. J. Johnson, *International Terrorism: A Chronology (1974 Supplement)*, RAND Corporation, 1976, Document Number: R-1909-1-ARPA, p. 14.

On May 21, 1973, the ERP shot two Ford Motor company executives as they left the factory in Buenos Aires. One of the Ford executives, Luis Giovanelli, died on June 25 from his wounds. The ERP issued a communiqué stating the two men were shot while resisting a kidnapping attempt. On November 22, 1973, John Swint, a U.S. citizen and general manager of Transax (a transmission and axle plant owned by the Ford Motor Company) and two of his bodyguards were shot and killed in Cordoba in an ERP ambush. The ERP carried out numerous kidnappings and attempted kidnappings of American and Argentinian executives working for American companies in Argentina. In many cases, ransom was paid by the companies. For example, on June 18, 1973, the ERP kidnapped U.S. citizen John R. Thompson, president of the Firestone and Tire and Rubber Company in Buenos Aires. He was released on July 6 after a reported record payment at the time of $3 million by the Firestone Rubber Company. The ERP's peak operating years were from 1973 to 1974.

Both the Montoneros and ERP were severely damaged operationally during the "Dirty War" in Argentina beginning in 1976. In March 1976, Isabel Perón was ousted and a military junta installed, led by General Jorge Rafael Videla. The junta redoubled its anti-guerilla campaign, leading to the so-called "Dirty War". The "Dirty War" was a period of state-sponsored violence in Argentina from 1976 until 1983. Victims of the violence included several thousand left-wing activists, including trade unionists, students, journalists, Marxists, and Peronist guerrillas and sympathizers. Some 10,000 of the "disappeared" were Montoneros, and "guerrillas" of the People's Revolutionary Army (ERP). Estimates of the number of people who were killed or "disappeared" ranged from 10,000 to 30,000.[41] It was also during this period that right-wing death squads like the Argentine Anticommunist Alliance emerged. The junta relied on mass illegal arrests, torture, and executions without trial to stifle any political opposition. The U.S. was also a key provider of economic and military assistance to the Videla regime. U.S. Department of State documents obtained by the National Security Archive under the Freedom of Information Act show that in October 1976, Secretary of State Henry Kissinger and high-ranking U.S. officials gave their full support to the Argentine military junta and urged them to hurry up and finish the "Dirty War" before the U.S. Congress cut military aid.[42] Remnants of the Montoneros lingered into 1978–1979, but by 1977, the group was effectively finished.

---

[41] https://www.britannica.com/event/Dirty-War. Accessed August 6, 2017.
[42] Daniel A. Grech, "Transcript: U.S. OK'd 'Dirty War'," the *Miami Herald*, December 4, 2002, p. 1. See also http://www.gwu.edu/~nsarchiv/NSAEBB/NSAEBB104/index.htm. Accessed July 6, 2018. It was the State Department's defense of the Argentine government at the time that led to the elevation

Mexico

During the 1970s, there were about nine left-wing terrorist groups operating in Mexico.[43] None had more than several hundred members. The most powerful terrorist organization was LC-23, which was based in Guadalajara. The group took its name from an aborted attack by a left-wing group on September 23, 1965 on the Mexican Army barracks at Madera, in the state of Chihuahua. The league emerged around 1973 and carried out a series of robberies, bombings, kidnappings, and assassinations. The first significant anti-American terrorist attack in Mexico by left-wing terrorists took place on May 4, 1973 when Terrence J. Leonhardy, the U.S. Consul General in Guadalajara, was kidnapped by members of the Federation of Revolutionary Students (FER).[44] They demanded the release of 30 "political prisoners" (26 men and four women) from Mexican jails and $80,000 in ransom for the release of Leonhardy. The government agreed to their demands and the released terrorists were flown to Cuba. FER also kidnapped the British Consul General in Guadalajara on October 10, 1973, who was eventually released unharmed. Mexican left-wing terrorist groups carried out bombing attacks throughout the 1970s against U.S. businesses (Pepsi Cola, Union Carbide, Coca Cola, Sears, etc.) and U.S. diplomatic interests in Mexico. An American Express executive was kidnapped on July 19, 1975 in Mexico City for $80,000 in ransom. On August 9, 1977, William A. Weinkamer, an American businessman was kidnapped in Mexico City and then released after $100,000 in ransom was paid. Mexican employees of U.S. companies were occasionally shot when they tried to stop leftist agitators from distributing propaganda leaflets at the factories. On January 20, 1977, an American businessman (Mitchel Andreski, president of

---

of the State Department's "Coordinator" for Human Rights to a "Bureau" of Human Rights headed by an assistant secretary of state. Some members of Congress felt that the State Department's testimony during a Senate Foreign Relations Committee meeting on human rights abuses was an overly apologetic defense of the Argentine government. (*Source*: Michel Kraft, who was Senator Clifford Case's (R-NJ) foreign policy and defense legislative assistant at the time. Case was the ranking Republican member on the Foreign Relations Committee.) See also, Karen DeYoung, "Newly Declassified Papers Reveal U.S. Tensions on Argentina's 'Dirty War'," *Washington Post*, August 9, 2016, p. A8.

[43] FBI Legal attaché (LEGAT) Mexico City, Memorandum: Characterization of Mexican Revolutionary Terrorist and Guerrilla Groups, Dated March 11, 1974, at http://www.gwu.edu/~nsarchiv/NSAEBB/NSAEBB307/doc02.PDF. Accessed June 7, 2018.

[44] FER was created in December 1969 as a Marxist-oriented student-dominated, worker–peasant–student alliance. FER leaders came from university professors and students in Guadalajara and Mexico City. FER operated under the direction of the 23rd of September Communist League.

the Duraflex Corporation) and a Mexican associate were shot and killed in Mexico City by members of the LC-23 when they tried to prevent the group from handing out propaganda leaflets. The left-wing terrorist activity reached a point where *Time* magazine published an article on September 16, 1974 entitled "MEXICO: State of Semi-Siege."[45] The U.S. Embassy in Mexico City issued an Airgram on January 4, 1974 entitled "The Current Security Situation in Mexico: An Appraisal," in which it concluded that "politically motivated crime in Mexico represents a serious annoyance to the GOM [Government of Mexico] … however, existing guerrilla groupings at present constitute no threat to the stability of the GOM, nor have their existence and activities."[46] During the 1970s, Mexico was also the scene of a half dozen bombings of Cuban and Soviet targets by militant anti-Castro exiles.

Left-wing terrorist groups were also active in Guatemala, Brazil, Uruguay, the Dominican Republic, Colombia, Venezuela, and El Salvador during the 1970s. However, compared to the terrorist groups in Argentina, these groups presented only a low threat to U.S. interests in those countries. Like all left-wing terrorist groups, these groups periodically bombed U.S. business and diplomatic facilities. Assassinations and kidnappings were relatively rare. The following are some of the more notable attacks in these countries:

- On March 6, 1970, five members of FAR kidnapped Sean M. Holly, the U.S. Labor Attaché, in Guatemala City, Guatemala and threatened to kill him if the government did not release four imprisoned terrorists. The government agreed, and Holly was released on March 8.
- On March 24, 1970, Lt. Col. Donald J. Crowley, U.S. Air Attaché, was kidnapped by six members of the Maoist group "Dominican Popular Movement" (MPD) in Santo Domingo, the Dominican Republic using the commando name of the "United Anti-Reelection Command." The MPD opposed Dominican President Balaguer's re-election and demanded the release of 24 imprisoned political prisoners. Within 60 hours, the government released 20 political prisoners, the most prominent of whom was the MPD Secretary-General Maximiliano Gomez, who were then flown into exile. Crowley was released on March 26.

---

[45] http://www.time.com/time/magazine/article/0,9171,908684,00.html#ixzz1KwWHDA7r.
[46] Page 13 of Airgram, at http://www.gwu.edu/~nsarchiv/NSAEBB/NSAEBB307/doc01.PDF. Accessed June 9, 2018.

- On July 31, 1970, Daniel A. Mitrione, a public safety advisor with the U.S. Agency for International Development, was kidnapped in Montevideo by the Tupamaros terrorist group. He was killed on August 10, 1970 when a demand to release 115 imprisoned Tupamaros was not met.[47]
- On June 18, 1973, FAR kidnapped Robert Galvez, the General Manager of Corn Products, a U.S. company, in Guatemala and received $50,000 in ransom.
- On September 27, 1974, Barbara Hutchison, the director of the U.S. Information Service in Santo Domingo was kidnapped by the 12th of January Liberation Movement and later released in exchange for safe passage for the terrorists out of Guatemala.
- On August 5, 1975, Donald Cooper, a Sears Roebuck executive, was kidnapped from his home in Bogota, Colombia and later released on November 2.
- On February 27, 1976, William Niehous, the Owens-Illinois director in Venezuela, was kidnapped by terrorists who identified themselves as part of a small left-wing group named the Argimiro Gabaldon Revolutionary Command. Rather than ask for a ransom payment, the group demanded that Owens-Illinois (1) pay each of its 1,600 Venezuelan employees $116 as compensation for its "exploitation"; (2) distribute 18,000 packages of food to needy families; and (3) buy space in Venezuelan and foreign newspapers for a lengthy manifesto, written by the extremists, denouncing the company and the Caracas government. Otherwise, they implied, Niehous would be killed. The manifesto criticized Owens-Illinois as "one of the many multinationals that plunder the country" and called for Venezuelans to "strengthen their fight for socialism."[48] It was published in the *New York Times*, *Times of London*, and *Le Monde*. Owens-Illinois also paid $116 in bonuses to its 1,600 employees

---

[47] According to the National Security Archive, the Nixon administration recommended a "threat to kill detained insurgent Raul Sendic and other key MLN-Tupamaros prisoners (who were captured on August 7) if Mitrione is killed." The secret cable on August 9, 1970 from U.S. Secretary of State William Rogers, made public by the National Security Archive on August 11, 2010 for the first time, instructed U.S. Ambassador Charles Adair: "If this has not been considered, you should raise it with the Government of Uruguay at once." The cable was sent on the same day that the Tupamaros were going to kill Mitrione and was an attempt to delay the killing. During the 10 days Mitrione was kidnapped, the U.S. went to great lengths to secure his release. Nixon administration officials pressured the Uruguayan government to negotiate, offer ransom, and, in the words of President Richard Nixon himself, "spare no effort to secure the safe return of Mr. Mitrione," at https://nsarchive2.gwu.edu/NSAEBB/NSAEBB324/. Accessed June 6, 2017.

[48] Niehous incident details from "Venezuela: Terror and Takeover," *Time Magazine*, April 19, 1976.

in Venezuela. The terrorists later added a $2.3 million ransom for his release. Negotiations broke down and Niehous was eventually rescued by Venezuelan forces in June 1979.[49]

Other Regions

Of the 20 Americans killed during the Nixon and Ford administrations by left-wing terrorist groups, five were killed in Western Europe and three in Latin America. The other 12 were killed in Iran (6), Lebanon (1), and the Philippines (5).

Philippines

The primary anti-American terrorist group in the Philippines in the 1970s was the New People's Army (NPA). The NPA was formed in 1969 as the military wing of the Maoist-oriented Communist Party of the Philippines. The objective of the NPA was to overthrow the current government and replace it with a communist regime. The NPA started out with several hundred members but increased its strength throughout the 1970s, especially when Philippine President Ferdinand Marcos declared martial law on September 21, 1972. At the end of the decade, it consisted of about 20,000 members. President Marcos lifted the martial law on January 17, 1981. The NPA identified the U.S. as a primary enemy in a December 1971 communique:

> *U.S. investments in Asia are most concentrated in the Philippines and continue to expand in the Philippines. According to conservative 1972 estimates, which do not fully take into account the current market value of all U.S. assets in the country, U.S. direct investments alone amount to three billion dollars. These comprising eighty per cent of foreign investments in the country are strategically located and enjoy a high rate of profit. To protect these against the people, U.S. imperialism does not only keep firm control over Philippine politics and the local reactionary armed forces but also under unequal military treaties, maintains as its*

---

[49] Office for Combatting Terrorism, U.S. Department of State, "Terrorist Attacks on U.S. Businesses: January 1968 — December 1981," Released June 1982, 20 pages. For additional information on terrorism in Venezuela at this time see CIA, Directorate of Intelligence, Intelligence Memorandum: Status of Insurgency in Venezuela, No. 2048/68, October 31, 1968, at https://www.cia.gov/library/readingroom/docs/DOC_0000126963.pdf. Accessed September 6, 2017.

ultimate weapon its own military personnel and military installations on Philippine soil.

Since the resumption of our people's war, U.S. military and police advisers on 'counterinsurgency' have been increasing and participating in training and military operations against the people. The sale and free grant of military materiel to the local reactionary armed forces have been stepped up. U.S. aircraft flown by U.S. pilots have been involved in reconnaissance and bombing operations against us. U.S. 'green beret' reconnaissance teams have deployed under the cover of 'civic action' in various parts of the countryside. A.I.D., Peace Corps and other ostensibly U.S. civilian personnel have been used for intelligence purposes by the U.S. 'country team' composed of the U.S. ambassador, the C.I.A. station chief, JUSMAG chief, A.I.D. director and U.S.I.A. head.[50]

The NPA was responsible for all five American deaths in the country during the Nixon and Ford administrations. On April 2, 1970, two American servicemen at Clark Air Force base were kidnapped by elements of NPA outside the air base. On April 14, their bodies were found in a shallow grave. On April 13, 1974, three U.S. Navy officers were shot and killed by the NPA near Subic Bay.

Iran

In Iran, six Americans were killed in terrorist attacks during the Nixon and Ford administrations. All were killed by People's Mujahedin of Iran (MEK). The MEK is a militant Islamic-Marxist organization founded in 1965 by a group of Iranian college students as a political movement. The MEK was originally devoted to armed struggle against the Shah of Iran, capitalism, and "Western imperialism," but with the establishment of the Islamic Republic of Iran in 1979, it advocated the overthrow of the Islamic regime in Iran. In the 1970s, the MEK was the most active and violent terrorist organization that confronted the Shah's regime. The MEK also opposed U.S. support to the Shah and, as a result, the group targeted U.S. interests in Iran. On November 30, 1971, the MEK carried out an attempted kidnapping of the U.S. Ambassador to Iran, Douglas MacArthur II, in Tehran. In May 1972, the group attempted to assassinate USAF Brig. Gen. Harold Price,

---

[50] New People's Army, "Specific Characteristics of our People's War," December 1, 1971, at http://www.philippinerevolution.net/cgi-bin/cpp/pdocs.pl?id=scpwe;page=08. Accessed June 9, 2017.

who was wounded in the attempt. On June 2, 1973, two MEK gunmen shot and killed a U.S. military advisor, Lt. Col. Lewis Hawkins, who was working for the U.S. Army Military Aid and Assistance Group in Tehran. On May 21, 1975, the MEK shot and killed two U.S. Air Force officers, Col. Paul Shaffer and Lt. Col. Jack Turner, in Tehran as they were being driven to their offices. On August 28, 1976, three American officials of Rockwell International (William C. Cottrell, Robert R. Krongard, and Donald G. Smith) were assassinated in Tehran by the MEK as they were being driven to work at an Iranian Air Force installation.

The Palestinian Terrorist Threat

Having emerged in the late 1960s, the Palestinian terrorist threat escalated in the 1970s. In retrospect, the 1970s was the most active decade for Palestinian terrorist activity outside Israel. From 1970 to 1979, Palestinian terrorists carried out 293 terrorist attacks outside Israel, compared to 19 during 1968–1969.[51] The decision by militant Palestinian nationalist groups to engage in terrorist operations outside Israel was based on two assessments. The non-Marxist groups determined that it was a strategic necessity given their loss of Jordan in 1970 as a base of operations and their difficulties in carrying out guerrilla operations inside Israel. The Marxist groups appreciated this necessity but also felt more ideologically comfortable operating in the international arena because they were part of an international revolutionary movement against world imperialism and capitalism, led by the United States. While it was generally agreed within the Palestinian nationalist movement that external operations were necessary, disagreement over tactics and targets was prevalent in the beginning of the decade and these conflicts eventually led to splits within some groups.

Of the 293 Palestinian terrorist attacks outside Israel, 41 were aimed at U.S. military and diplomatic interests, U.S. aircraft, and U.S. private citizens. Of the 119 Americans killed overseas by terrorism from 1970 to 1979, 71 were killed by Palestinian terrorists and affiliated groups like the Japanese Red Army. However, only 41 of these 71 Americans were killed in attacks that directly targeted U.S. interests. The remaining 30 Americans were killed during attacks on non-U.S. targets and were simply in the wrong place at the wrong time. The U.S. was targeted because of its support for Israel and, from the perspective of the left-wing

---

[51] Merari and Elad, *The International Dimension of Palestinian Terrorism*, p. 107.

Palestinian terrorist organizations, as a leader of "world imperialism."[52] The Palestinian terrorist threat was not concentrated in the Middle East but spilled out of the Middle East into other regions, especially Western Europe. In essence, the Palestinian terrorist threat was geographically wider, and its tactics were more indiscriminate.

Americans were killed in Palestinian terrorist attacks in Switzerland, Lebanon, Jordan, West Germany, Austria, Israel, Italy, Sudan, Greece, and the West Bank and Gaza strip. Fifty-eight Americans were killed in mid-air bombings of aircraft and assaults on airport terminals and aircraft on the ground. The groups that either claimed credit for or were prime suspects in these attacks on Americans were the PFLP, Popular Front for the Liberation of Palestine — General Command (PFLP-GC), the Black September Organization (BSO), Fatah dissidents, the Japanese Red Army or JRA (on behalf of the PFLP), the Arab Nationalist Youth Organization for the Liberation of Palestine, and the Democratic Front for the Liberation of Palestine. In addition, there were 11 Palestinian terrorist incidents in the United States during the 1970s that will be addressed in detail in the "foreign spillover terrorism" section in this chapter.

The first significant terrorist attack by Palestinians in the 1970s that killed Americans overseas took place on February 21, 1970 when a bomb exploded on Swissair Flight 330 out of Zurich to Tel Aviv. A barometric-triggered, parcel bomb detonated in the aft cargo compartment of the aircraft about nine minutes

---

[52]"The enemy includes not only Israel, but also the Zionist movement, world imperialism led by the USA and reactionary powers bound to imperialism." George Habash, PFLP leader, as quoted in Merari and Elad, p. 20. Palestinians and Arabs perceived that the U.S. was blindly pro-Israel during the 1970s and took Israel's side in almost all disputes with the Palestinians and other Arab countries. In October 1973, Egypt and Syria, with additional Arab support, staged a surprise attack on Israeli forces occupying their territory — the Sinai and Golan Heights — since the 1967 war, thus starting the Yom Kippur War. To help Israel, the U.S. initiated "Operation Nickel Grass," a strategic airlift operation to deliver tanks, artillery, ammunition, and supplies to Israel in October and November. These resupply missions were critical to the Israeli military during the conflict and led to the oil-exporting Arab states within OPEC to carry out their previously declared threats to use oil as a "weapon." The result was a complete oil embargo on the United States, and restrictions on other countries. This in turn helped trigger the 1973 oil crisis. After the Yom Kippur War, the United States quadrupled its foreign aid to Israel and replaced France as Israel's largest arms supplier. In the United Nations, the U.S. cast its very first veto on September 10, 1972 on a Syria/Lebanon resolution "Complaint Over Israeli Aggression Against Lebanon." From 1972 to 1976, the U.S. vetoed six resolutions critical of Israel. (Jewish Virtual Library, "UN Security Council: U.S. Vetoes of Resolutions Critical of Israel — 1972 to 2011," at http://www.jewishvirtuallibrary.org/jsource/UN/usvetoes.html. Accessed September 6, 2017). In the 1970s, the United Nations was perceived by the Palestinians as being generally hostile to Israel and the U.S. was often its sole defender in that organization.

after take-off causing the plane to crash, killing everyone on board. The passenger list included six Americans and 14 Israelis. Sabotage was immediately suspected due to the anger in Arab countries triggered by the sentencing the previous December of three Palestinians to 12 years imprisonment by a Swiss court. In Beirut, a spokesman for Ahmed Jibril's PFLP-GC claimed responsibility. However, worldwide condemnation of the attack forced the group to withdraw its claim of responsibility.[53] The PFLP-GC considered a foreign airliner that flew to Israel to be a legitimate target. The increased effective protective security measures being implemented on El Al planes made them difficult to target, and thus, foreign aircraft became more attractive and were vulnerable. Jibril was an engineer by training whose hobby was "tinkering ... he loved devices and gadgets and considered himself something of an inventor."[54] He also had an "obsession for airplanes" and has been called the world's first "techno terrorist."[55] He hired Marwan Kreeshat as the PFLP-GC's chief bomb maker.

From a PFLP-GC safe house in Sofia, Bulgaria, Kreeshat worked on developing a bomb that was reliable, would explode in mid-air, and would take down an aircraft. The idea was to plant such a device on an El Al or foreign aircraft flying from Europe across the Mediterranean Sea to Israel. The bomb had to be timed to explode over the sea so that no forensic evidence could be discovered. Kreeshat came up with a barometric device that, when it reached a certain altitude, would initiate a timer that would detonate the explosives over the sea. The barometric device was concealed in an East German produced transistor radio that was provided by the East German foreign espionage agency or HVA.[56] The PFLP-GC had four members test the barometric device in the 2,887-foot-high Feldberg Mountain near Frankfurt.[57] The device was then wrapped as an airmail parcel. Two devices were prepared. One caused the above Swissair Flight 330 explosion. However, the time set on the timing device was off and the plane crashed on land. On the same day, a second device was put aboard an Austrian Airlines flight with 121 people aboard en route from Frankfurt to Vienna to Tel Aviv. This device exploded but failed to bring down the plane and the pilot was

---

[53] *New York Times*, February 22, 1970.

[54] Information on the Swissair Flight 330 was compiled from Samuel M. Katz. *Israel vs. Jibril: The Thirty-Year War Against A Master Terrorist* (New York: Paragon House, 1993), p. 23–31.

[55] Ibid., p. 23.

[56] Ibid., p. 28.

[57] Edgar O'Ballance. *The Language of Violence: The Blood Politics of Terrorism* (California: Presidio Press, 1979), p. 79.

able to land it safely. Police uncovered parts of the device and figured out the bomb's construction.

The barometric-triggered bomb was designed to ensure that there would be mass-casualties and that bomb evidence would be destroyed. Previously used timed-bombs were set for a specific time. If a plane was delayed on the ground, the bomb could explode in a de-pressurized cabin, and given the small amount of explosives contained in these mid-air bombs, the casualties would have been low. In addition, there was the possibility of bomb fragments being found and providing the authorities evidence of its construction and paternity. The barometric-timed bomb ensured that the bomb would explode in a pressurized cabin, thereby creating mass-casualties and likely spreading debris for miles, reducing the possibility of bomb fragments being found. It was also the PFLP-GC that developed the false-bottom suitcase bomb. It was first utilized on July 28, 1971 in combination of using an unwitting female carrier or "mule" to carry a "gift" to Israel for her Palestinian boyfriend.[58] All these creative ideas were a by-product of a targeting decision by Palestinian terrorist groups to focus on commercial aircraft. As airlines developed general security measures and specific ones to counter a particular tactic, the terrorists had to find a new method to bypass security. This was in essence a dialectical process between terrorist creativity and counter-terrorism measures,

---

[58] Information on PFLP-GC incidents and Marwa Khreesat from https://wikispooks.com/wiki/Marwan_Khreesat, and Samuel M. Katz. *Israel vs. Jibril: The Thirty-Year War Against A Master Terrorist* (New York: Paragon Press, 1993), pp. 22–59. Jibril later used these devices again but had them transported into Israel via unwitting women who were enticed by Palestinian boyfriends to go to Tel Aviv. In 1971, he used a Dutch girl and a Peruvian woman to carry the devices. In 1972, he used two English girls to bring the device aboard an El Al aircraft on August 16 flying from Rome to Tel Aviv. Source: Claire Sterling. *The Terror Network* (New York: Berkley Books, 1981), p. 257. Palestinian terrorist groups were not the first to develop the "letter" or "parcel" bomb sent to individuals. However, they were the first groups to carry out a letter bomb campaign, such as the one that took place in September 1972 when 64 mail bombs were mailed by Palestinian terrorists from Amsterdam to various Israeli targets in Europe, the Americas, Australia, and Africa. Another terrorist weapon that emerged in the first phase of the international terrorist threat was surface-to-air missiles, specifically the Soviet SA-7. This weapon had the potential to cause havoc with tourism and the travelling public. On September 5, 1973, five BSO terrorists were arrested in Rome with surface-to-air missiles (Soviet SA-7). On January 21, 1976, five terrorists were arrested in Nairobi, Kenya with SA-7s, intending to take down an El Al flight. See, John Kamau, "How Mossad threw Kenya into the line of terrorist fire, *The Daily Nation* (Nairobi, Kenya), January 17, 2014, at https://www.nation.co.ke/lifestyle/saturday/How-Mossad-threw-Kenya-into-the-line-of-terrorist-fire/1216-2150206-d8y286/index.html. Accessed January 20, 2019.

one that continues to the present day, as terrorists attempt to come up with new ways of smuggling explosives aboard commercial and cargo aircraft.

From May to September 1970, there were several assassinations and kidnappings of U.S. personnel in Jordan:[59]

- On May 10, the U.S. Military attaché (Major Bob Perry) was assassinated in his home in Amman in front of his wife and kids. On June 10, the PFLP claimed responsibility for the attack.
- On June 7, the chief of the Political Section at the U.S. Embassy, Morris Draper, was forcibly taken from his car in Amman as he was going to a party. The PFLP demanded the release of 40 imprisoned terrorists in Jordan. Draper was released 22 hours later. On the same day, U.S. Army Captain Robert Potts, from the defense attaché's office, and his wife were injured when PFLP terrorists fired on them at a roadblock in Amman.
- On June 9, PFLP terrorists seized the Philadelphia and Intercontinental hotels in Amman holding over 60 foreigners as hostages, including seven Americans, and one U.S. Foreign Service officer. The hostages were released unharmed on June 12. The seizure was designed to pressure the Jordanian government not to continue its assault on PFLP camps in Jordan.
- On September 9, 1970, U.S. Staff Sergeant Ervin Graham, assigned to the defense attaché's office, was kidnapped by the Palestine Liberation Army in Amman. He was held for eight days and released.
- On September 10, U.S. Cultural Affairs officer John Stewart was kidnapped by the Palestine Liberation Army in Amman. He was held, interrogated, and released 28 hours later. All these operations in Amman were directed at U.S.

---

[59] In July, 1970, the U.S. introduced the "Rogers Plan" that called for a cease-fire in the War of Attrition (1967–1970) between Egypt and Israel and for Israel's negotiated withdrawal from territories occupied in 1967, according to the United Nations Security Council Resolution 242, but the plan also mentioned that the West Bank was to be under King Hussein of Jordan's authority and that was unacceptable for the more radical Palestinian organizations. Moreover, during the summer, in accordance with the Rogers Plan, Jordan tightened security along the long Israeli-Jordanian border, denying the Palestinian guerrillas access to Israeli targets. For anti-Hashemite (the Hashemites are the ruling royal family of Jordan) Palestinians, this betrayal was the last straw. On the first of September, the truce between Palestinian guerrillas and the Jordanian regime was shattered by an assassination attempt against King Hussein. Hussein survived the attempt, but his country was plunged into civil conflict as the full extent of Palestinian unrest was unleashed. On September 16, King Hussein responded by declaring martial law and, the following morning, unleashing his military on the Palestinian insurgency. In America, President Nixon denounced the Palestinian guerrillas. Source: "Black September in Jordan" at https://en.wikipedia.org/wiki/Black_September_in_Jordan. Accessed June 6, 2017.

interests to harass and punish the U.S. for pressuring Jordan to close its borders with Israel and for its overall support for Jordan during the failed Palestinian uprising.

The September 1970 crisis in Jordan also triggered one of the most notorious hijacking operations in the modern history of terrorism.[60] On September 6, 1970, the PFLP launched a multi-plane hijacking operation. Four aircraft were hijacked and one attempt failed. TWA Flight 741 en route from Frankfurt to New York with 145 passengers was hijacked and diverted to Dawson's Field, a remote desert airstrip near Zarka, Jordan. Swissair Flight 100 from Zürich was hijacked and diverted to Dawson's Field. Pan Am Flight 93 was hijacked and diverted first to Beirut and then to Cairo rather than the small Dawson's Field airstrip. There was an attempt to hijack El Al Flight 219 from Amsterdam, but this failed when one hijacker, Patrick Arguello, was shot and killed. His partner, the female Palestinian terrorist Leila Khaled, was captured and turned over to British authorities in London. On September 9, the fourth and last plane hijacked was BOAC Flight 775, going from Bombay to London, via Bahrain, where the hijacking occurred. This hijacking was a direct response to the British detention of Leila Khaled in Great Britain. The BOAC plane was forced to Dawson's Field. A total of 114 Americans were aboard the four planes. None were killed, but several were injured during the hijackings. The terrorists demanded the release of imprisoned comrades in various European countries and Israel.

On September 7, the hijackers held a press conference for 60 members of the media who had made their way to what was being called "Revolution Airport." About 125 hostages were transferred to Amman, while the American, Israeli, Swiss, and West German citizens were held on the planes. These hijackings further aggravated the fall crisis in Jordan as it directly and publicly challenged the authority of the Jordanian government. On September 17, King Hussein declared

---

[60] *Background*: during the 1967 Six Day War, in which Jordan entered at the urging of Egyptian President Nasser, Israel drove back Jordanian forces and captured the Jordanian-occupied West Bank. Thousands of Arab Palestinian West Bankers fled to Jordan, where they became increasingly problematic to King Hussein's Jordanian government. Palestinian nationalists essentially created a virtual state within Jordan. Between 1968 and 1971, there were hundreds of violent clashes between Palestinian "Fedayeen" and Jordanian security forces. Cross-border attacks by the Palestine Liberation Organization (PLO) into Israel were followed by Israeli reprisals that caused high Jordanian civilian and military casualties. There were also several Palestinian assassination attempts on King Hussein and Jordanian government officials and diplomats inside and outside Jordan. This Palestinian threat to Jordan's stability was also disconcerting to the Nixon administration, which along with Great Britain, supported the Hashemite Kingdom.

martial law in Jordan. This act accelerated the hijacking negotiations between the PFLP and Western governments. By September 30, a deal was concluded for the release of all the airplane hostages in return for the release of Leila Khaled in Great Britain and three PFLP members in a Swiss jail. The September 1970 uprising by Palestinian militant organizations in the Palestinian enclaves and refugee camps in Jordan is known in Palestinian history as the "Black September," when King Hussein established military rule and moved to quash the militancy of Palestinian organizations and restore his rule over the country. The subsequent violence resulted in the deaths of thousands of people, the vast majority Palestinian. The conflict lasted until July 1971 with the expulsion of the PLO and thousands of Palestinian fighters to Lebanon, thereby planting the seeds for Palestinian agitation and conflict there for the next two decades. Several Palestinian terrorist organizations subsequently used the commemorative name "Black September" when claiming responsibility for terrorist attacks in and outside the Middle East.[61]

While Palestinian terrorist organizations had already made the decision to engage in external operations, the events of September 1970 contributed to an intensification of this activity as Palestinian groups retaliated against Jordanian targets and, increasingly, went after U.S. targets. Before 1970, militant Palestinian nationalists saw the U.S. as an adversary because of U.S. support for Israel. Attacks on U.S. targets were sporadic and mostly carried out by the Marxist PFLP. After 1970, U.S. support for Jordan during the Palestinian–Jordanian conflict created another grievance against the U.S. for militant Palestinians. Subsequently, terrorist attacks on U.S. targets became more frequent and were carried out by both the PFLP and Fatah, through its Black September terrorist arm. The two largest militant Palestinian terrorist organizations were now increasingly targeting Western and U.S. interests. The September events contributed to the expulsion of militant Palestinians from Jordan to Lebanon, thereby adding to the political and sectarian instability and civil warfare in Lebanon including the emergence of Islamic revolutionary terrorism in that country. The ramifications of September 1970 for the evolution of Middle East terrorism cannot be understated. It acted as an accelerator, launching Palestinian terrorist

---

[61] Fatah used the name for a special terrorist group that focused on attacking Jordanian targets as well as other countries from 1971 to 1973. Abu Nidal's Fatah Revolutionary Council also used the name as a cover to attack Jordanian targets in the mid-1980s. For background information on the BSO, see Christopher Dobson. *Black September: Its Short, Violent History* (New York: Macmillan Publishers, 1974).

activity through the 1970s and eventually producing 293 Palestinian terrorist attacks outside Israel during the decade.

The following were some of the more notable attacks by Palestinian terrorist groups and their allies involving Americans:

- On May 8, 1972, five terrorists from the BSO hijacked a Sabena flight on a Vienna–Athens–Tel Aviv route and forced the plane to land at Lod Airport in Israel. The terrorists demanded the release of 317 Fedayeen prisoners, or they would blow up the plane and all aboard. Israeli security forces stormed the plane killing three of the terrorists. Five passengers were injured, one of them an American, later died.

- On May 30, 1972, three members of the Japanese Red Army (Kozō Okamoto, Tsuyoshi Okudaira, and Yasuyuki Yasuda) fired machine guns and threw grenades at passengers arriving from an Air France flight at Lod Airport in Israel. Among the 28 killed were two terrorists (Okudaira and Yasuda), eight Israelis, one Canadian, and 17 Americans (Puerto Rican Catholic pilgrims). In the letter claiming official responsibility for the attack carried out by the Japanese Red Army, the PFLP referred to it as Operation Deir Yassin. This was to portray the attack as revenge for the 1948 Deir Yassin massacre of Arabs by Jewish Irgun terrorists during the fighting following the U.N. vote to establish the state of Israel. The letter also stated that the operation was carried out by the Squad of the Martyr Patrick Arguello. Patrick Arguello had been killed two years earlier, on September 6, 1970 on an Israeli El Al jet he had attempted to hijack together with PFLP member Leila Khaled. Kozo Okamoto was the only terrorist who survived and was captured.[62] The attack attracted worldwide publicity and attention not only because of the number of fatalities and the target and location of the attack but also because Japanese terrorists were involved. This is the first time that non-Palestinians carried out a major international terrorist attack in support of the Palestinian cause.

---

[62]On July 23, 1973, PFLP and JRA operatives hijacked Japan Air Lines Flight 404, demanding Okamoto's release in exchange for the hostages on board; Israel refused to comply. Okamoto was released in 1985 after 13 years in prison, as part of the "Jibril Agreement," an exchange of prisoners between Ahmed Jibril's PFLP-General Command and Israel for captive Israeli soldiers. After his release, Okamoto ended up in Lebanon, where, as of 2019, he remains. On August 12, 2018, Fatah's official Facebook page posted a photo of Okamoto and information about him, including the note "a Japanese fighter who carried out an attack against the Zionists in Palestine." Okamoto is referred to as an "international revolutionary." There was also a posting on Fatah's Facebook page on Okamoto on May 18, 2016, at https://www.memri.org/reports/official-fatah-facebook-page-honors-japanese-terrorist-kozo-okamoto. Accessed October 7, 2017.

"It was not merely the carnage that attracted worldwide attention. People asked how is it that Japanese come to Israel to kill Puerto Ricans on behalf of Palestinians?"[63] The answer was that the Japanese were from the left-wing Japanese Red Army terrorist group that was sympathetic to the Palestinian cause and saw the JRA as part of a broader anti-imperialist movement. The death of 17 Americans in this attack was the largest death toll at the time of Americans killed in a single terrorist incident.[64] In 1988, this was exceeded when 189 Americans were killed in the mid-air bombing of Pan Am 103.

- On September 5, 1972, eight BSO terrorists assaulted the Olympic village in Munich, Germany, the site of the summer games of the XX Olympiad, and seized 11 Israeli athletes, including weightlifter David Berger, an American Israeli from Cleveland, Ohio. The terrorists initially demanded the release and safe passage to Egypt of 234 Palestinians and non-Arabs jailed in Israel, along with two German terrorists held in German prisons, Andreas Baader and Ulrike Meinhof. Negotiations eventually concluded with the German government deceiving the terrorists and allowing them to go to a nearby military airfield with the hostages where a plane was supposed to be waiting to

---

[63] Brian Michael Jenkins, Special to CNN, "Why terrorists attack airports," *CNN Online*, January 25, 2011.

[64] On December 3, 2009, American victims of the 1972 Lod Airport terrorist attack went to a federal court in Puerto Rico to try holding the North Korean regime responsible for its role in supporting the JRA and PFLP. In this case, lawyers for the plaintiff argued that in the months up to the massacre, JRA and PFLP met with North Korean officials who provided "Military and other training; training bases; facilities for, inter alia, training, storage of weapons and explosives and the maintenance and operation of a leadership command and operational infrastructure; safe haven; lodging; means of communication and communications equipment; financial services, including banking and wire transfer services; and means of transportation." Source: Calderon-Cardona v. Democratic People's Republic of Korea criminal complaint, at http://www.investigativeproject.org/documents/misc/347. pdf. Accessed June 6, 2017. On July 24, 2010, a U.S. federal court in Puerto Rico awarded the plaintiff $378 million against North Korea over the Lod airport attack. As the Court wrote in its decision: "As a matter of its official policy, North Korea provided training, resources, weapons and safe haven to the JRA and the PFLP during the period relevant to this case. Defendants ran roughly 30 terrorist training camps from 1968 to 1988 within North Korea's borders; those camps specialized in terrorist and guerilla warfare training. These camps serviced in excess of 10,000 terrorists, including members of the JRA and PFLP, and provided courses lasting from three to eighteen months." The Court also found that members of North Korea's military and intelligence agencies served as instructors in the training camps. This was the first time that North Korea was held accountable in a U.S. court for its support of terrorism over many decades. The U.S. State Department put North Korea on its official list of states that sponsor terror in 1988, a fact that made it possible, along with the 1996 Anti-Terrorism and Effective Death Penalty Act, for American victims to sue the North Korean government and collect against their assets in the United States.

let them leave Germany. At the airfield, a failed German counter-terrorism rescue resulted in the deaths of all the 11 hostages (who were blown up by the terrorists) and eight terrorists, and one German policeman. In response to the Munich Olympics attack, the Israeli government quickly constructed a special hit team (Operation Wrath of God) that was tasked to track down and kill all those Palestinians involved in this attack. From 1973 to 1976, 12 Palestinian terrorists were killed in the Middle East and Western Europe by suspected Mossad agents.[65] The attack on the Munich Olympics was a seminal international terrorist event. The attack, although aimed at Israel, affected the international community because the attack took place during the most important international sporting event in the world, thereby assuring maximum publicity for the terrorists. The selection of Germany, with its past treatment of Jews, only amplified that publicity. This attack also underlined the need for governments to construct a professional counter-terrorist rescue unit. In a sense, it was also an attack that "keeps on giving," that is, during every subsequent Olympics the host country has allocated millions of dollars in protective security measures so as to prevent "another Munich." However, the security record of the post-Munich Olympic Games indicates that, to date, few terrorist organizations ever seriously considered mounting an attack on an Olympic game. The Munich attack was also the catalyst for the initial development of U.S. counter-terrorism policy, constructing a counter-terrorism organizational entity, and for putting terrorism on the radar screen of the U.S. Intelligence Community.

- On March 1, 1973, eight BSO terrorists seized the Saudi Arabian Embassy in Khartoum as guests were leaving from a diplomatic reception. They demanded the release of 60 Palestinians held in Jordan, all Arab women detained in Israel, Sirhan Sirhan (assassinated Senator Robert F. Kennedy in Los Angeles on June 5, 1968), and imprisoned members of the Baader–Meinhof terrorist group in Germany. When negotiations failed, the terrorists on March 2 killed the U.S. Ambassador Cleo Noel, the U.S. Deputy Chief of Mission George C. Moore, and the Belgian Charge who were among the hostages. The terrorists surrendered the next day. They were sentenced by the

---

[65] For information on the BSO attack on the Munich Olympics and the Israeli response, see David B. Tinnin, *The Hit Team: The Unprecedented Inside Story of a Top Secret Israeli Anti-terrorist Squad* (Boston: Little, Brown, and Co., 1976), and Simon Reeve, *One Day in September* (New York: Arcade Publishing, 2006). "Since World War II, Israel has conducted more state-sanctioned assassinations than any other country in the world" — CIA, Center for the Study of Intelligence, *Studies in Intelligence*, Vol. 62., No. 3 (Unclassified Articles from September 2018), p. 60.

Khartoum government to life sentences, but the Sudanese President Numaryi later reduced the sentence to seven years and had the terrorists deported to Egypt. President Sadat reportedly released them to the PLO. It has been reported that the NSA had intercepted a call prior to the attack and alerted the State Department, but the warning failed to reach the American diplomats in Khartoum in time.[66] It was later discovered that the terrorists were targeting DCM George C. Moore as they believed he was a CIA agent responsible for the massacre of Palestinians in Amman, Jordan in September 1970.[67]

- On August 5, 1973, two terrorists claiming to be from the "Seventh Suicide Squad," but belonging to the Ahman Abd-Al Ghaffur's group of Fatah dissidents, opened fire with machine guns and hand grenades on passengers in Athens waiting to board a TWA flight to New York. It was later learned that they were ordered to attack the TWA flight to Tel Aviv, but the passengers were already on board the plane. Among the five people killed were three Americans. Fifty-five other people were wounded, and 35 people were seized as hostages. The two terrorists eventually surrendered to Greek police and were expelled to Libya on May 5, 1974.

- On December 17, 1973, after police discovered weapons in the luggage of an Arab traveler at Rome's Fiumicino airport, four other Arabs opened fire in the crowded transit lounge. The gunmen said that they belonged to the Arab Nationalist Youth Organization for the Liberation of Palestine. The terrorists then took several Italian hostages and Lufthansa ground crew members and then encountered a Pan American 707 (Flight 110) that was loading passengers for a flight to Beirut. The terrorists threw hand grenades into the plane killing 29 passengers, including 14 American employees of the Arab American Oil Company ARAMCO. The terrorists, with their several hostages, then hijacked a Lufthansa aircraft to Athens and eventually flew to Kuwait where they surrendered to Kuwaiti authorities. They released their hostages after receiving a safe conduct guarantee. On March 2, 1974, the terrorists were flown from Kuwait to Cairo, where they were to be tried by the PLO, but Egyptian authorities did not release them. The five Pan Am terrorists were later flown to Tunis in response to the demands of four

---

[66]Adam Goldman, Randy Herschaft, "Mystery terrorist deported: Convicted bomb plotter never yielded secrets in U.S. prison," *Associated Press*, March 5, 2009. For additional information on the killing of the two U.S. diplomats in Khartoum, see "The Terrorist Attack on the Saudi Embassy — Khartoum 1973," Association for Diplomatic Studies and Training, at http://adst.org/2013/02/the-terrorist-attack-on-the-saudi-embassy-khartoum-1973/. Accessed July 21, 2017.
[67]David A. Korn. *Assassination in Khartoum* (Indiana: Indiana University Press, 1993), p. 214. George C. Moore was not a CIA agent.

Palestinian terrorists who hijacked a British Airways VC-10 jetliner on November 22, 1974. They went to Libya in December with the BA hijackers and two additional Palestinian terrorists were released by the Netherlands. Libya reportedly imprisoned all 11, but they later appeared to have been freed.[68]

- On September 8, 1974, the pilot of a TWA flight 841 from Tel Aviv to New York radioed that he was having trouble with one engine. The plane went into a deep-nose dive and crashed into the Ionian Sea. All 88 passengers, including 17 Americans were killed. On January 11, 1975 investigators from the U.S. and Britain announced that tests of some debris from the aircraft conclusively showed that a high explosive had gone off in the rear cargo compartment of the plane. The Organization of Arab Nationalist Youth for the Liberation of Palestine issued a press statement in Beirut stating that a member of their organization exploded a bomb he was carrying around his waist. The anonymous caller said that a member of the group — a Chilean of Palestinian descent — blew himself up with the passengers on board the plane, which he said was carrying Israeli secret service squads. If the statement is true, this would be one of the world's first terrorist suicide attacks.[69]

- On June 16, 1976, the U.S. Ambassador to Lebanon Francis E. Meloy, Jr., the U.S. Embassy Economic Counselor Robert O. Waring, and their Lebanese driver were kidnapped at a roadblock in Beirut by PFLP gunmen. Their bullet-ridden bodies were found later.[70]

---

[68]"Guerrilla Committee to Question Five Arab Hijackers in Kuwait," *New York Times*, December 28, 1973, at https://www.nytimes.com/1973/12/28/archives/guerrilla-committee-to-question-five-a-rab-hijackers-in-kuwait.html. Accessed July 6, 2017; "P.L.O. Reports Detaining 26 for a Trial in Hijacking," *New York Times*, November 28, 1974, at https://www.nytimes.com/1974/11/28/archives/plo-reports-detaining-26-for-a-trial-in-hijacking-plo-reports.html. Accessed August 23, 2017; Juan de Onis, "Challenge to Arafat: Hijacking Seen as Challenge to Arafat," *New York Times*, November 23, 1974, at https://www.nytimes.com/1974/11/23/archives/challenge-to-arafat-hijacking-seen-as-challenge-to-arafat.html. Accessed May 4, 2017.

[69]"U.S. Bound Plane With 88 Crashes in Sea Off Greece," *New York Times*, September 9, 1974, at https://www.nytimes.com/1974/09/09/archives/usboundplane-with-88-crashes-in-sea-off-greece-all-on-t-w-a-flight.html. Accessed June 6, 2017; Richard Within, "Evidence Indicates Explosion Caused TWA Crash Off Greece That Killed 88," *New York Times*, October 27, 1974, at https://www.nytimes.com/1974/10/27/archives/evidence-indicates-explosion-caused-twa-crash-off-greece-that.html. Accessed September 6, 2017. The full National Transportation Safety Board investigative report on this incident can be read at www.fss.aero/accident-reports/dvdfiles/US/1974-09-08-US.pdf. Accessed October 6, 2017.

[70]For information on the Meloy assassination, see Association for Diplomatic Studies and Training, "Moments in U.S. Diplomatic History, A Completely Lawless Place — Beirut and the Assassination

The above attacks were generally aimed at U.S. targets, either diplomats or American aircraft. These attacks on U.S. targets killed 41 of the 71 Americans killed in Palestinian-related terrorist attacks during the decade. The remaining 30 Americans killed in the 1970s during Palestinian terrorist attacks were simply in the wrong place at the wrong time. For example:

- On February 23, 1970, suspected Palestinian militants fired on a tourist bus in Halhul, in the West Bank, killing one American woman, Barbara Ertle, wife of Reverend Theodore Ertle, of Michigan and wounding two other Americans.
- On January 16, 1972, an American nurse was killed and a number of people were injured when terrorists opened fire on their car in the Gaza strip.
- On October 18, 1973, five members of the Lebanese Socialist Revolutionary Organization stormed the Bank of America in Beirut and took 39 hostages. The group made a number of demands to include that the bank pay them $10 million dollars to help "finance the Arab war effort against Israel" and the Lebanese government release all fedayeen guerrillas. When the government refused their demands, the terrorists killed one of the hostages, a Lebanese American citizen. Two of the terrorists were killed when police stormed the bank. The other two were arrested.
- On November 21, 1975, Michael Nadler, an American–Israeli from Miami Beach, Florida, was killed when axe-wielding terrorists from the Democrat Front for the Liberation of Palestine, a PLO faction, attacked students in the Golan Heights.
- On August 11, 1976, two terrorists from the PFLP attacked passengers preparing to board an El Al aircraft at Yesilkoy airport in Istanbul. Four persons, including one American, Harold Rosenthal of Philadelphia, Pennsylvania, an aide to U.S. Senator Jacob Javits, were killed in the attack.

---

of Ambassador Meloy and Robert Waring," at http://adst.org/2013/06/a-completely-lawless-place-the-assassination-of-ambassador-meloy-and-robert-waring-beirut-june-16-1976. Accessed June 7, 2017; CIA, "Talking Points: June 26, 1986, Lebanon: Update on the Assassination of Ambassador Francis E. Meloy," at https://www.cia.gov/library/readingroom/docs/DOC_0006116800.pdf. Accessed August 7, 2017; and Joseph Fitchett, "Killing of U.S. Ambassador in Beirut Laid to Leftist Plotters," *New York Times*, June 19, 1977, p. 24; James M. Markham, "U.S. Ambassador and Aide Kidnapped and Murdered in Beirut Combat Sector, *"New York Times*, June 17, 1976, at https://www.nytimes.com/1976/06/17/archives/us-ambassador-and-aide-kidnapped-and-murdered-in-beirut-combat.html. Accessed November 23, 2017; and U.S. House of Representatives, Committee on International Relations, Special Subcommittee on Investigations, Hearing — The Assassination of American Diplomats in Beirut, Lebanon, July 27, 1976, at https://babel.hathitrust.org/cgi/pt?id=purl.32754074 689757;view=1up;seq=8. Accessed November 6, 2018.

Given the threat environment at the time, all these Americans were traveling to relatively high-threat areas — Israel, the Occupied Territories, Turkey, and Lebanon. The odds of becoming an accidental victim of terrorism in such countries is obviously higher than if one were traveling to low- or medium-threat areas. This pattern of some Americans ignoring travel warnings from the U.S. Department of State became more pronounced in the next decade, especially in Lebanon.

"Foreign Fighters" in the Palestinian Cause

In addition to the active targeting of Western interests in and outside the Middle East, Palestinian terrorist organizations created additional security problems by attracting and training "foreign fighters" or non-Palestinian terrorists to work for the Palestinian cause. Some European and Latin American leftists went to the Middle East to join Palestinian terrorist groups while others stayed in their countries and helped these groups logistically or with propaganda. Palestinian terrorist groups also provided logistical, financial, and training support to various left-wing groups like the German RAF and the Turkish People's Liberation Army.[71] There were also those who joined the Palestinian terrorist organizations and participated in terrorist operations. The two most important non-Palestinian terrorism actors that emerged in the 1970s were a group of Japanese leftists who were collectively referred to as the "Japanese Red Army" (JRA) and those German and Latin American leftists who orbited around the infamous Carlos group. Both the JRA and the Carlos group were anti-American in their ideological makeup and periodically attacked U.S. targets.

Ilyich Ramirez Sanchez (aka Carlos or the Jackal), a Venezuelan leftist, emerged in the 1970s and developed into an infamous international terrorist, compliments of the European press.[72] In 1970–1971, Carlos became a member of the PFLP, was trained and mentored by Wadi Haddad,[73] and assigned to a

---

[71] See, for example, O'Balance, *Language of Violence*, p. 141; and Parry, *From Robespierre to Arafat*, p. 442.

[72] In the author's opinion, the most accurate books written on Carlos are the following: Colin Smith, *Carlos: Portrait of a Terrorist* (New York: Hold, Reinhart, 1976); John Follain, *Jackal: The Secret Wars of Carlos the Jackal* (London: Weidenfeld and Nicolson, 1998); David Yallop, *To the Ends of the Earth: The Hunt for the Jackal* (London: Jonathan Cape, 1993); Wilhelm Dietl, *Carlos: Das Ende eines Mythos* (Koln: Bastei Lubbe, 1995); and Fritz Schmaldienst and Klaus-Dieter Matschke, *Carlos-Komplize Weinrich: Die Internationale Karriere eines Deutschen Top-Terroristen* (Frankfurt: Eichborn, 1995).

[73] Haddad was the head of the military wing of the PFLP. He pioneered the use of aircraft hijacking for political purposes. He planned the first Palestinian terrorist hijacking that took place in July 1968

Western European cell, first in London then Paris. In December 1973, he carried out his first terrorist act for the PFLP, a failed assassination attempt in London on Joseph Sieff, a Jewish businessman and vice president of the British Zionist Federation. The attack was in revenge for the June 28, 1973 Mossad car bombing assassination of Mohamed Boudia, a PFLP leader, in Paris. In January 1974, Carlos planted bombs at the Israeli Hapoalim Bank in London. In August 1974, he detonated car bombs outside three pro-Israeli French newspaper offices in Paris. On September 15, 1974, Carlos threw a hand grenade into the "Drugstore Saint Germain" in Paris killing two and injuring 34. It is believed that this attack was in support of the September 13 seizure of the French Embassy in The Hague by the JRA. In this seizure, the French ambassador and 10 other people were taken hostage. On January 13 and 17, 1975, Carlos, and a new accomplice, RZ terrorist Johannes Weinrich, carried out two failed shoulder-fired, rocket-propelled grenade attacks on El Al airliners at Orly Airport in Paris.[74] In June 1975, Carlos shot and killed two French policemen who tried to arrest him. This incident drove the French government to pursue Carlos over the next 19 years and finally abduct him in the Sudan in 1994.

In December 1975, Carlos led a six-person commando (including two Germans — Hans-Joachim Klein, a former RZ terrorist, and Gabriele Kröcher-Tiedemann, a former 2JM member) that assaulted an OPEC Ministerial meeting in Vienna, seizing over 60 hostages and exchanging several of the ministers for ransom. Carlos' failure to kill the finance minister of Iran and the oil minister of Saudi Arabia, and suspicions that he may have kept some of the ransom money, forced the PFLP to expel him. Reportedly, Waddi Haddad of the PFLP told Carlos:

Stars are very bad at following instructions. You have not followed my instructions. There is no room for stars in my operational teams. You can go.[75]

---

when an El Al plane was seized on its way from Rome to Tel Aviv. His avocation of terrorist attacks outside Israel eventually clashed with new PFLP policy and he was expelled in 1973. He then established the PFLP-External Operations group. Haddad also was responsible for attracting and using "foreign fighters" for the Palestinian cause. His most famous recruits were Carlos and the Japanese Red Army, in addition to some German, Dutch, and Italian left-wing extremists. He died or was assassinated in East Germany in 1978. Haddad was the most dangerous and notorious Palestinian terrorist of his generation.

[74] This is one of the few instances where a terrorist group attacked the same target twice in succession. Weinrich became Carlos's chief lieutenant over the next 23 years.

[75] Follain, *Secret Wars of the Jackal*, p. 99.

In the late 1970s, Carlos was briefly arrested in Yugoslavia and then went to Iraq and Yemen where he began to form his own group "The Organization of Arab Armed Struggle," composed of Syrian, Lebanese, and German terrorists. In the 1970s, Carlos was not involved in any anti-American terrorist attacks or plots. However, like the JRA and independent German terrorists, he underlined the growing threat of non-Palestinian terrorism actors gravitating toward the Palestinian cause and carrying out attacks with or on behalf of them. In the 1970s, Carlos acquired an international reputation as a brave, audacious, dashing, and intelligent terrorist. In retrospect, it was more myth than reality. His reputation was more a product of the Western press attempting to sensationalize terrorism during this decade. Yet, Carlos was involved in the attacks noted above and he courted and used the publicity given him. In fact, he reveled in it. More so than even his mentor Wadi Haddad, Carlos, especially in the late 1970s, became the public face for the international terrorist threat that had intensified during the decade.

The Japanese Red Army was a name used to describe a dozen or so militant Japanese leftists who left Japan to join the Palestinian nationalist movement.[76] They coalesced as a group around 1971 with a woman named Fusako Shigenobu as one of their leaders. The JRA's stated goals were to overthrow the Japanese government and monarchy and to start a world revolution. However, the political conditions in Japan and police pressure forced members to leave and to go to the Middle East where they linked up with the PFLP and Wadi Haddad. In the 1970s, the JRA worked for Haddad by carrying out the following operations:

- The May 1972 Lod Airport massacre in Israel that killed 17 Americans.
- The July 1973 hijacking of a Japan Airlines (JAL) plane over the Netherlands.
- The January 1974 attack on a Shell facility in Singapore.
- The September 1974 seizure of the French Embassy in The Hague, Netherlands.
- The August 1975 seizure at the AIA building housing several embassies in Kuala Lumpur, Malaysia. The hostages included the U.S. Consul, six to seven other Americans, and the Swedish *chargé d'affaires*. The Japanese government released three JRA terrorists in exchange for the hostages, and the terrorists were flown to Libya.[77]

---

[76] For additional information on the JRA, see William R. Farrell, *Blood and Rage: The Story of the Japanese Red Army* (Toronto: Lexington Books, 1990).

[77] For background on this incident, see Association for Diplomatic Studies and Training (ADST), "More Moments in U.S. Diplomatic History: Terror on the 9th Floor — The Kuala Lumpur Hostage

- The September 1977 hijacking of JAL Flight 472 over India forced to land in Dacca, Bangladesh. The Japanese Government freed six imprisoned JRA members and paid a $6 million ransom.

The JRA was one of the more notorious international terrorist groups operating in the international arena in the 1970s. The group acted as an extension of the PFLP but did have its own agenda, primarily the release of imprisoned comrades in Japan. After the successful September 1977 hijacking of the JAL plane, the group disappeared in Lebanon and became operationally silent. It did not emerge again until 1986 when some of its members offered their services to Libya in an anti-American terrorism campaign that lasted from 1986 to 1988.

Ethno-National Terrorist Threat

In the 1970s, ethno-national terrorist groups were responsible for the deaths of six Americans. Given that such groups do not directly target U.S. interests, the low toll is not a surprise. One of the few areas where ethno-national terrorist groups directly targeted U.S. interests in the 1970s was in Ethiopia. From 1885 to 1941, Eritrea was governed by Italy. In 1942, British military forces expelled Italy from Eritrea and Great Britain ruled it under a U.N. mandate until 1952 when the United Nations combined Eritrea into neighboring Ethiopia as per U.N. resolution 390(A) under the prompting of the United States. While Eritrea gained some measures of autonomy, the resolution stopped short of creating an independent republic in Eritrea. As a result, various Eritrean liberation groups emerged over the next 20 years whose objective was to secede from Ethiopia and create an independent Eritrea. Eritrean nationalist violence in the region increased throughout the 1960s and 1970s. The Eritrean Liberation Front (ELF) was the main independence movement in Eritrea at this time, but there were several splinter groups that formed also, like the Eritrean People's Liberation Front. In the 1970s, the ELF either claimed responsibility for or was suspected of having carried out the following attacks against Americans:

- On January 11, 1970, an American soldier serving in Ethiopia was shot and killed by the ELF in a tavern in Asmara.

Crisis," May 1990 Interview with Robert Dillon, a Foreign Service officer in Kuala Lumpur at the time, at http://adst.org/2013/07/terror-on-the-9th-floor-the-kuala-lumpur-hostage-crisis/. Accessed August 6, 2017.

- In March 1970, five members of a National Geographic film team, including the American producer, were kidnapped by the ELF. No ransom demands were made, and the hostages were released 17 days later.
- On April 21, 1970, a U.S. Peace Corps Volunteer (Jack Fry) and his wife were kidnapped from a train by the ELF. No ransom demands were made, and they were released five days later.
- On March 26, 1974, four Tenneco Oil Company employees, including three Americans, were kidnapped by the ELF — General Command (ELF/GC) after the company helicopter made an emergency landing in Massawa due to bad weather. After long negotiations with the company, the employees were released.
- On April 8, 1974, a rocket was fired at the U.S. Navy's Kagnew tracking station in Asmara by the ELF.
- On May 27, 1974, four ELF members assaulted the American Evangelical Mission Hospital in Ghinda, near Asmara and kidnapped two nurses, one Dutch and one American. The Dutch nurse was found shot to death. The American nurse was released on June 22.
- On January 8, 1975, three bombs were thrown through the main entrance of the USIS library in Asmara, causing no casualties and minor damage.
- On July 14, 1975, two U.S. employees of Collins International Service Company were kidnapped from the U.S. Navy's Kagnew station transmitter near Asmara by the Popular Liberation Forces. The employees were released on May 3, 1976.
- On September 12, 1975, the ELF attacked the U.S. Navy's Kagnew communications facility near Asmara and kidnapped two U.S. military personnel. They were released by the ELF in the Sudan on January 8, 1976.
- On December 21, 1975, Ronald B. Michalke, a U.S. citizen employed by the Collins International Service Company at the U.S. Navy's Kagnew communications base near Asmara, was kidnapped by the ELF. He was released on June 2, 1976.
- On March 27, 1977, Don McClure, an American missionary, was shot and killed outside his home in Gode by suspected ELF members.

The U.S. was not the only Western country targeted by Eritrean separatists. British and Italian targets were periodically attacked. However, U.S. interests were targeted the most. The direct targeting of Americans in Ethiopia may have been a result of lingering resentment for U.S. support for the 1952 federation of Ethiopia and Eritrea. It could have been prompted by the realization that kidnapping foreigners, especially Americans, would embarrass the Ethiopian government and attract media attention. It could also be attributed to growing left-wing elements within the ELF who saw attacks on U.S. targets as being part of an international anti-imperialist struggle. Whatever the reasons, this anti-American terrorist activity was concentrated in the first half of the decade.

The only other incidents in the 1970s where U.S. interests were directly targeted by ethno-national terrorist groups were in Northern Ireland and Quebec. On March 17, 1974, the IRA assaulted the U.S. Naval Communications station in Londonderry, Northern Ireland in an attempt to steal weapons and ammunition. One guard and three U.S. sailors were seized but as the IRA commando entered a facility, an alarm went off. The IRA members fled the scene with one U.S. sailor who was later released. On June 21, 1970, Canadian authorities uncovered a plot by the Quebec Liberation Front (FLQ) to kidnap the U.S. Consul General, Harrison W. Burgess. In the 1960s, the FLQ carried out several attacks on U.S. targets in Quebec including two bombings in 1965 and 1968 on the U.S. Consulate in Montreal and a 1968 bombing of a Seven-Up factory in Mont-Royal. However, like the IRA, the FLQ was not an inherently anti-American terrorist group. It should also be noted that on May 16, 1975, suspected Catalan militants bombed a Pan Am office in Barcelona, causing minor damage. However, this may have been carried out by leftist elements in Barcelona, as the stated reason for the attack was to protest against the use of U.S. military force in the Mayaguez incident.[78]

In Indonesia, an American engineer working for Mobil Oil was killed in Sumatra on November 29, 1977 by terrorists from the Free Aceh Movement. The terrorists left pamphlets warning Americans and other foreigners to leave the region. Aceh is a region in Indonesia on the northern part of the island of Sumatra. Aceh nationalists were discontented over various issues, including the distribution of Aceh's natural resource wealth, to include oil. There was an Aceh Insurgency on the island from 1976 to 2005, during which over 15,000 lives were believed to have been lost. The initial goal of this insurgency was independence.

There were other Americans killed in ethno-national terrorist incidents. In April 1977, an American missionary was killed in Zaire by terrorists from the National Liberation of the Congo (FLNC). Two Americans were killed in Rhodesia (now Zimbabwe) in 1978 and 1979 by the Zimbabwe African National Liberation Army. Both appeared to have been targets of opportunity.

---

[78] On May 12, 1975, the American container ship SS Mayaguez was attacked and seized by Khmer Rouge forces off the coast of Cambodia. On May 14, U.S. military forces assaulted the captured ship and in the ensuing conflict, 18 U.S. military personnel and 20–25 Khmer Rouge were killed.

Despite the above incidents, the primary terrorist threat that ethno-national groups presented to U.S. interests overseas was their periodic bombing campaigns in the capitals — places where Americans visit, work, study, transit, and meet. One such example took place on July 17, 1974 in London when the IRA bombed the lower level of the Tower of London, killing one person and injuring 41 tourists, including four Americans. As the European ethno-national terrorist groups intensified their terrorist activity in the 1980s, more Americans were killed or injured in these capital-area attacks, although they were not the intended targets.

Greek left-wing terrorist group "Revolutionary Organization 17 November" assassination of U.S. diplomat.

Source: U.S. Department of State.

Attack site of December 1975 November 17 Assassination of U.S. diplomat Richard Welch.

Source: U.S. Department of State.

December 2, 1972–Beirut, Lebanon: Secular Palestinian terrorist attack on U.S. Embassy using M-28 rockets concealed in and fired from car trunk.

Source: U.S. Department of State.

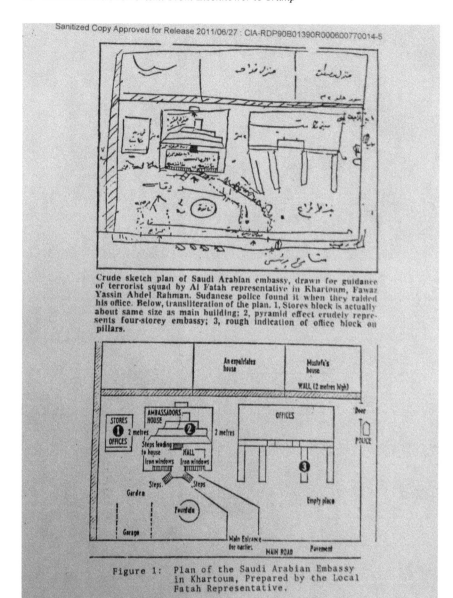

Crude sketch plan of Saudi Arabian embassy, drawn for guidance of terrorist squad by Al Fatah representative in Khartoum, Fawaz Yassin Abdel Rahman. Sudanese police found it when they raided his office. Below, transliteration of the plan. 1, Stores block is actually about same size as main building; 2, pyramid effect crudely represents four-storey embassy; 3, rough indication of office block on pillars.

Figure 1:   Plan of the Saudi Arabian Embassy in Khartoum, Prepared by the Local Fatah Representative.

Black September terrorists' surveillance sketches of Saudi Embassy in Khartoum. Attack took place in March 1973.

Source: CIA FOIA reading room.

On August 19th, 1974, recently appointed Ambassador to Cyprus, Rodger Davies, was shot dead during a Greek Cypriot protest outside the U.S. Embassy.

Source: U.S. Department of State.

WANTED RECHERCHÉ

ILICH RAMIREZ- SANCHEZ - FPS 827669A

ALIASES: "CARLOS", CLARKE, CENON MARIA (26-8-45 - N.Y., USA); GEBHARD, GLEN (1-3-50 - N.Y., USA);
MARTINEZ-TORRES, CARLOS ANDRES (4-5-47 - BOLTERO, PERU); EUSEPI, MASSIMO (24-1-48,
BELLEGRA, ITALY); MULLER-BERNAL, ADOLFO JOSE (CHILEAN NATIONALITY).

BORN: 12 OCT., 1949	NE: 12 OCTOBRE 1949
P.O.B.: VENEZUELA	LIEU DE NAISSANCE: VENEZUELA
HEIGHT: 5'9"	TAILLE: 5'9"
HAIR: CURLY, THICK, BROWN, SHORT	CHEVEUX: BOUCLES, ABONDANTS BRUNS ET COURTS
BUILD: FAIRLY HEAVY	CORPULENCE: ASSEZ FORTE
SPEAKS SPANISH, ARABIC, RUSSIAN	PARLE: L'ESPAGNOL L'ARABE ET LE RUSSE
HOLDS VENEZUELAN PASSPORT NO. 498056	DETIENT UN PASSEPORT VENEZUELIEN NO 498056

WARRANT FOR THE ARREST OF THE ABOVE-NAMED IS HELD BY THE REGIONAL COURT, VIENNA, AUSTRIA, FOR STRONG SUSPICION OF PARTIALLY COMMITTED PARTIALLY ATTEMPTED MURDER EXTORSIONATE KIDNAPPING AND TRESPASSING.

ALSO WANTED BY FRENCH AUTHORITIES FOR LOCATION.

EXTREMELY DANGEROUS AND WILL NOT HESITATE TO OPEN FIRE.

IF LOCATED ARREST AND ADVISE THE COMMISSIONER RCMP, OTTAWA, ONT.

UN MANDAT POUR L'ARRESTATION DU SUSNOMME EST DETENU PAR LA COUR REGIONALE DE VIENNE, AUTRICHE, OU IL EST FORTEMENT SOUPCONNE DE TENTATIVE ET DE COMMISSION PARTI-ELLES DE MEURTRE, D'ENLEVEMENT AVEC EXTORSION ET D'INTRUSION.

AUSSI RECHERCHE PAR LES AUTORITES FRANCAISES EN VUE DE DECOUVRIR SON LIEU DE REFUGE.

EXTREMEMENT DANGEREUX ET N'HESITERAIT PAS A FAIRE USAGE DE SES ARMES.

SI DÉPISTÉ, ARRÊTER ET EN INFORMER LE COMMISSAIRE, GRC, OTTAWA, ONT.

DANGEROUS   DANGEREUX

SPECIAL WANTED CIRCULAR
NO. 247 - APRIL 29, 1976
RCMP IDENTIFICATION SERVICES

CIRCULAIRE SPÉCIALE DE PERSONNES
RECHERCHÉES NO 247, LE 29 AVRIL 1976
SERVICES DE L'IDENTITE DE LA G.R.C.

1976 Wanted poster of the infamous terrorist "Carlos".

Source: Author's personal collection.

April 30, 1970 — President Richard Nixon points to a map of Cambodia during a Vietnam War press conference.

Source: Nixon Presidential Library.

Chapter 3

The Nixon and Ford Administrations (1969–1976) — The Internal Threat

The Internal Terrorist Threat

The internal terrorist threat in the U.S. consisted of two components: domestic and foreign spillover terrorism. During the Nixon and Ford administrations, there were an estimated 1,000 terrorist attacks in the U.S. that killed 76 people, including 31 law enforcement officers (28 during the Nixon administration). The largest number of terrorist-related law enforcement deaths in the U.S. history took place during the Nixon administration. This was a direct by-product of the terrorist activities of black militant groups.

Domestic Terrorist Threat

The emergence of domestic terrorist organizations in the United States in the late 1960s and early 1970s was directly linked to the racial riots and campus unrest that developed during this period.

Racial/Campus Violence

The 1960s was marked by growing student protests on university campuses and racial riots and other urban civil disturbances in major U.S. cities. All these developments provided fuel to left-wing and black militants who believed that more violent actions were required to redress the grievances that triggered these campus and urban disorders. A U.S. government commission reported that from 1965 to 1968, there were 329 "important" racial disturbances that took place in 257 cities, resulting in nearly 300 deaths, 8,000 injuries, 60,000 arrests, and property losses in the hundreds of millions of dollars.[1] The largest and most damaging race riots took place in 1965 (Los Angeles Watts riots) and in 1968 (Detroit riots). The growing urban disturbances compelled President Johnson to establish in 1967 the National Advisory Commission on Civil Disorders, also known as the Kerner Commission after its chair, Illinois Governor Otto Kerner, Jr. This commission was charged with investigating the causes of race riots in the United States and providing recommendations for the future.

The Kerner Report suggested that the causes of these urban riots were black Americans' frustration and feelings of powerlessness regarding the extremely high rates of unemployment and underemployment, poverty, police brutality, and inadequate public services. It also opined that the racism of white Americans was essentially responsible for the explosive mixture leading to the uprisings. In terms of what should be done to alleviate these issues, the commission suggested that the Federal government intervene to improve housing, education, employment opportunities, and social services for African Americans and to dismantle discriminatory practices in education, employment, the police force, and criminal court systems.[2] Its most famous quote was the conclusion that the United States is moving toward two societies — one black, one white; separate and unequal. The conclusions of the report were not universally accepted. In fact, while President Johnson accepted the report, he did not support the conclusions, and minimal efforts were made to address the problems identified by the Commission.[3] In April 1968, one month after the release of the Kerner report, rioting broke out in more than 100 cities following the assassination of civil rights leader Martin Luther King, Jr.

The inner neighborhoods of many major cities, such as Detroit, Los Angeles, Newark and New York, were burned out. National Guard and Army troops were called out. At one-point machine gun units were stationed on the steps of the Capitol building in Washington to prevent

---

[1] http://www.heritage.org/research/lecture/the-kerner-commission-report, Accessed January 7, 2017. See also, U.S. Senate. Committee on Government Operations, Permanent Subcommittee on Investigations, "Riots, Civil and Criminal Disorders," Part 15, March 4, 1969, p. 2950. The chart/table of all these disorders can be found in Part 13 of these committee reports, pp. 2762–2777.

[2] http://www.eisenhowerfoundation.org/docs/kerner/Kerner_Contents.pdf and http://www.blackpast.org/aah/national-advisory-commission-civil-disorders-kerner-commission#sthash.kUzzBHfF.dpuf. Accessed June 6, 2018.

[3] http://freedomcenter.org/voice/kerner-commission-established-day-1967. Accessed June 17, 2017.

rioters from burning it down. Every summer from 1964 through 1970 was a "long hot summer."[4]

Developing in parallel to the racial riots of the late 1960s was growing campus unrest over the nature and purpose of the university, specific university rules that limited political activity on campus, opposition to the Vietnam War, empathy for the conditions of black Americans in the urban areas, and a general disillusionment with the country's direction and policies. It could be argued that the student protests at the University of California's Berkeley campus from 1964 to 1966 opened this era of campus unrest. Later, campus protests at Columbia (1968), Kent State (1970), and Jackson State (1970) contributed to its evolution. While there are no reliable statistics on the number of campus protests or actions from 1964 to 1970, it is clear that 1970 was the high-water mark for this campus unrest. The key trigger event was President Nixon's April 30 announcement that U.S. forces would invade Cambodia. The objective of the Cambodian incursion was to defeat some 40,000 People's Army of Vietnam and Viet Cong troops who were using the eastern border regions of Cambodia as a safe zone for cross-border operations into South Vietnam. In a televised speech to the nation, President Nixon stated he had warned the North Vietnamese that if increased enemy activity in Laos or Cambodia was detected, he would take action. Increased enemy activity was detected in Cambodia and in order to "guarantee the continued success of our withdrawal and Vietnamization programs, I have concluded that the time has come for action." Nixon emphasized that "this is not an invasion of Cambodia ... once enemy forces are driven out of these sanctuaries and once their military supplies are destroyed, we will withdraw."

Nixon also referenced the growing campus violence and opposition to the Vietnam War:

My fellow Americans, we live in an age of anarchy, both abroad and at home. We see mindless attacks on all the great institutions which have been created by free civilizations in the last 500 years. Even here in the United States, great universities are being systematically destroyed. Small nations all over the world find themselves under attack from within and from without. If, when the chips are down, the world's most powerful nation, the United States of America, acts like a pitiful, helpless giant, the forces of totalitarianism and anarchy will threaten free nations and free institutions throughout the world.

---

[4]https://en.wikipedia.org/wiki/Law_and_order_(politics). Accessed March 4, 2018.

I realize that in this war there are honest and deep differences in this country about whether we should have become involved, that there are differences as to how the war should have been conducted. But the decision I announce tonight transcends those differences.[5]

After the speech, Secretary of State William Rogers commented that night: "The kids are going to retch."[6]

The campuses exploded as students interpreted the Cambodian action as an escalation of the Vietnam War. On May 2, the Reserve Officers' Training Corps building was burned down on Kent State University in Kent, Ohio. On May 3, the Governor of Ohio, Jim Rhodes, angrily stated:

We've seen here at the city of Kent especially, probably the most vicious form of campus-oriented violence yet perpetrated by dissident groups. They make definite plans of burning, destroying, and throwing rocks at police and at the National Guard and the Highway Patrol.... We are going to eradicate the problem. We're not going to treat the symptoms. And these people just move from one campus to the other and terrorize the community. They're worse than the brown shirts and the communist element and also the night riders and the vigilantes. They're the worst type of people that we harbor in America. Now I want to say this. They are not going to take over [the] campus. I think that we're up against the strongest, well-trained, militant, revolutionary group that has ever assembled in America.[7]

On May 4, the Ohio National Guard was sent in to qualm demonstrations on the Kent State campus protesting the U.S. military incursion into Cambodian. In circumstances that remain unknown, national guardsmen fired on the students, killing four and injuring nine others. The killing of the four students in turn ignited more campus protests all over the country. Many were already taking place due to the U.S. military incursion into Cambodia. On May 15, mostly black students at Jackson State University in Jackson, Mississippi were protesting

---

[5]Full text of this speech found at http://www.presidency.ucsb.edu/ws/?pid=2490. Accessed June 7, 2016.

[6]Tim Weiner, *One Man Against the World: The Tragedy of Richard Nixon* (New York: Henry Holt and Co., 2015), p. 87.

[7]*President's Commission on Campus Unrest*, pp. 253–254, at https://files.eric.ed.gov/fulltext/ED083899.pdf. Accessed July 5, 2017.

against historical racial intimidation, harassment by white motorists traveling through the campus, and the Kent State killings. The situation escalated due to unsubstantiated rumors of a white person being killed, rocks being thrown at motorists, and fires being started on campus. The students were confronted by a large contingent of well-armed city and state police. Ultimately, police shot and killed two students and injured 12 others.[8] By May 10, "448 campuses were still affected by some sort of student protest or were completely closed.... By the end of May 1970, one half of approximately 2,500 colleges and universities experienced some sort of protest activity."[9] This wave of campus unrest caused the president on June 13, 1970, to establish the "President's Commission on Campus Unrest," which became known as the Scranton Commission after its chairman, former Pennsylvania Governor William Scranton. Scranton was asked to study the dissent, disorder, and violence breaking out on college and university campuses, particularly the national student strike that was going on at the time. The student strike was both a general protest against the Vietnam War and a specific response to the American invasion of Cambodia and the Kent State killings. The focus of the commission was the student protests in the 1960s, the black student movement, university response to campus disorder, the law enforcement response, university reform, and the Kent State and Jackson State shootings. The commission concluded that the Kent State killings were unjustified and that campus unrest increased as the perception grew that the war was lasting longer and escalating. The recommendations of the commission were at best general and philosophical and lacked any practical utility to mitigate student unrest.[10]

This growing campus violence also generated an unprecedented "Open Letter to College Students" by FBI Director J. Edgar Hoover, dated September 21, 1970, in which he praised this generation of youth and their independent ideas but then warned them of eight ploys or traps that "extremists," "communists," and "Trotskyites" have used or will use to "lure you into their activities." He notes that they will:

1. encourage you to lose respect for your parents and the older generation;
2. convince you that your college is irrelevant and a tool of the establishment;

---

[8] Whitney Blair Wyckoff, "Jackson State: A Tragedy Widely Forgotten," National Public Radio, May 3, 2010, at http://www.npr.org/templates/story/story.php?storyId=126426361. Accessed September 7, 2016.

[9] The Report of the President's Commission on Campus Violence, September 1970, p. 18, at http://files.eric.ed.gov/fulltext/ED083899.pdf. Accessed March 11, 2017.

[10] Ibid., see section on "recommendations," pp. 7–13.

3. wrap complex issues in slogans and clichés;
4. envelop you in a mood of negativism, pessimism, and alienation toward yourself, your school, and your nation;
5. encourage you to disrespect the law and hate the law enforcement officer;
6. tell you that any action is honorable and right if it's sincere and idealistic in motivation;
7. encourage you to believe that you, as a student and citizen, are powerless by democratic means to effect change in our society; and
8. encourage you to hurl bricks and stones instead of logical argument at those who disagree with your views.[11]

Student unrest was due to a plethora of developing issues like women's liberation, student rights, alternative life styles, free speech, environmentalism, drug experimentation, communal living, sexual liberation, racial inequality, urban poverty, the military draft, youth voting rights (persons could be drafted at 18 but were not able to vote until 21), and students questioning the moral and spiritual health of America. Many of these issues intertwined with the Vietnam War which began under Kennedy but escalated under Johnson and Nixon. Although the anti-Vietnam War movement was multi-generational and involved a multitude of diverse local and national groups, it was the college students who were the engine of this movement. The Vietnam War had a direct impact on the lives of male college students who were subject to the draft. Overlaying all these issues were generational traumatic events like the 1962 assassination of President Kennedy, the 1968 assassination of Robert Kennedy, the 1968 assassination of Martin Luther King, Jr., Nixon's 1970 decision to authorize military incursions into Cambodia, and the 1970 shootings of four Kent State students by the Ohio National Guard and two Jackson State students by local law enforcement. From the perspective of the students, the country appeared to have lost its moral compass.

This increasing social and political violence on campuses and in volatile urban areas compelled both the Johnson and Nixon administrations to deploy the U.S. military to assist domestic law enforcement (local police, state police, and National Guard units) more frequently and with more troops than any period since the Civil War.[12] The scope and level of this deployment of the U.S. military

---

[11] http://www.nixonlibrary.gov/virtuallibrary/releases/jul10/58.pdf. Accessed October 7, 2016.

[12] The 1878 Posse Comitatus Act was promulgated to prevent U.S. military personnel from acting as law enforcement agents on U.S. soil, except "in cases and under circumstances expressly authorized by the Constitution or Act of Congress." Various presidential administrations, especially those after the 9/11 attacks, have modified, updated, and expanded parts of the act. However, as of 2019, the

in non-war time remains unmatched to this day. Inserting the U.S. military in domestic law enforcement situations is a key indicator as to the seriousness of a destabilizing domestic development. The multiple deployments of the U.S. military by the Johnson administration to quell incidents of domestic violence underlined the volatility of the domestic environment that the Nixon administration was facing in 1969. This was also reflected in Nixon's 1968 campaign theme of restoring "law and order." This theme resonated with the "silent majority" of Americans who felt that the demonstrations, riots, and political violence in the universities and urban areas were getting out of control and needed to be checked. The law and order issue was a key factor in Nixon winning the presidency in 1968.[13]

Domestic Terrorist Organizations

Since the mid-1960s a confluence of three anti-establishment protest strains had developed in the U.S.: (1) the "hippie" counterculture movement, (2) "New Left" activism and militancy, and (3) "Black Power" militancy. These three strains were anchored primarily in the universities and urban areas and attracted mostly disillusioned white and disgruntled black youths — some searching for purpose in their lives, some using political violence to camouflage their internal criminal and psychotic dispositions, some seeking new experiences, while others sought to

---

philosophical heart of the act remains. On July 24, 1967, at the request of Governor George Romney, President Johnson deployed federal troops to help quell riots in Detroit. When the riots were finally controlled, the resultant damage was 43 dead, 2,000 injured, 4,000 fires, 5,000 homeless, and a large part of Detroit, the fifth largest city in the U.S., "lay in ruins." The assassination on April 4, 1968 of Rev. Martin Luther King Jr. in Memphis, Tennessee triggered riots in over 100 cities and 29 states. Federal troops were deployed in Chicago, Washington, D.C., and Baltimore to assist the police and National Guard forces which were eventually federalized. "The U.S. government also realized the effectiveness of a new tactic, the prepositioning of troops. From 1968 to 1973, the government repositioned troops six different times, covering such events as an antiwar demonstration at Yale University in 1970, both the Republican and Democratic presidential nominating conventions in Miami, Florida in 1972, and Richard Nixon's second inauguration in January 1973. Troops were not needed but it showed a federal propensity to intervene quickly which had never been seen in the past." *Source*: http://www. globalsecurity.org/military/library/report/1995/SLP.htm. Accessed March 11, 2017.

   The U.S. military also engaged in collecting data on U.S. citizens during the 1960s. Military intelligence units acquired data from local police reports and the FBI which was then used to compile dossiers on Americans. This operation was exposed publicly in 1970 and ended the same year. "U.S. Army Intelligence Command and the Home Front," at http://www.globalsecurity.org/intell/ops/steephill.htm. Accessed June 7, 2017.

[13] https://en.wikipedia.org/wiki/Law_and_order_(politics). Accessed August 6, 2018.

redress real and perceived social, educational, economic, and political grievances. Adding more fuel to these strains were the Vietnam War and the 1968 assassination of civil rights leader Rev. Martin Luther King, Jr. The Vietnam War was perceived by many, mostly white radicals as an indictment of America's capitalist and imperialist policies, while the King assassination underlined to mostly dissatisfied urban black moderates and militants the failure of America's social and racial policies. These developments led to campus unrest, urban riots, and growing political violence — organized and disorganized.

One of the by-products of this disillusionment of student and black activists was the emergence of domestic terrorist organizations that engaged in arson attacks, bombings, and periodic assassinations. Prior to the Nixon administration, the domestic terrorist activity that took place in the U.S. was carried out by individuals and small independent cells of anarchists, militant members of the labor movement, and local militant members of white supremacist organizations. This terrorist activity was not centrally controlled or directed but was instead local, ad hoc, and leaderless. It was during the Nixon administration that organizations devoted to political terrorism first surfaced and engaged in terrorist activity across the country.

As one writer put it:

> *Imagine if this happened today. Hundreds of young Americans — white, black, and Hispanic — disappear from their everyday lives and secretly form urban guerrilla groups. Dedicated to confronting the government and righting society's wrongs, they smuggle bombs into skyscrapers and federal buildings and detonate them coast to coast. They strike inside the Pentagon, inside the U.S. Capitol, at a courthouse in Boston, at dozens of multinational corporations, at a Wall Street restaurant packed with lunchtime diners. People die. They rob banks, dozens of them, launch raids on National Guard arsenals, and assassinate policemen, in New York, in San Francisco, in Atlanta. There are deadly shoot-outs and daring jailbreaks, illegal government break-ins, and a scandal in Washington. This was a slice of America during the tumultuous 1970s, a decade when self-styled radical 'revolutionaries' formed something unique in postcolonial U.S. history; an underground resistance movement.*[14]

---

[14]Bryan Burrough, *Days of Rage: America's Radical Underground, the FBI, and the Forgotten Age of Revolutionary Violence* (New York: Penguin Press, 2015), p. 3.

In retrospect, the Nixon administration confronted a domestic terrorist threat in the United States that reached its historical high-water mark in the early 1970s. The following statistical snapshots of just bombings partially underscore the severity of this domestic terrorist threat environment in the early 1970s:

- According to the 1970 U.S. Senate Sub-Committee on Investigations, from January 1969 to April 7, 1970, there were 4,330 bombings in the U.S. — 3,355 incendiary, 975 explosives — and 1,175 attempted bombings that resulted in the deaths of 43 people and caused $21.8 million in property damage.[15]
- According to the New York City Police Commissioner, from January 1969 to May 1970, there were 368 bombings in New York City — more than twice as many as in the eight preceding years.[16]
- During an 18-month period in 1971 and 1972, the FBI reported more than 2,500 bombings on U.S. soil, nearly five a day.[17]
- According to the U.S. Senate Committee on the Judiciary, Subcommittee to Investigate the Administration of the Internal Security Act, and other Internal Security Laws, the May 1975 issue of the FBI Reports notes 2,041 bombing incidents in the United States and Puerto Rico in 1974. A total of 24 people were killed and 206 injured in connection with these incidents.[18]

In addition to terrorist bombings, there were frequent assassinations of mostly law enforcement personnel. During the Nixon administration, 47 people were killed in the U.S. by domestic terrorist organizations. Of those 47, 28 were law enforcement officers who were shot. This remains the largest number of police

---

[15]Wade Greene, "The Militants Who Play with Dynamite," *New York Times*, October 25, 1970.

[16]"Bombings Here Reaching Gigantic Proportions, Leary Tells Senators," *New York Times*, July 17, 1970, p. 1.

[17]Burrough, *Days of Rage*, p. 5.

[18]U.S. Senate, Committee on the Judiciary, Subcommittee to Investigate the Administration of the Internal Security Act and other Internal Security Laws, Report: Terroristic Activity: Interlocks Between Communism and Terrorism, Part 9, May 7, 1976, p. 707. This report also contains on p. 721 a chronology of "Guerrilla Acts of Sabotage and Terrorism in the United States: 1965–1970." The problem with the bombing statistics for the 1970s was that there were not many reliable sources that breakdown the bombing statistics into criminal, political, and personal grudge bombings. This statistical flaw does not undermine the core assumption that there were more political bombings in the 1970s than in any other decade in American history. Moreover, the majority of those political bombings were carried out from 1970 to 1974.

fatalities from domestic terrorist attacks under any administration in U.S. history.

During the Nixon administration, there were five significant domestic terrorist organizations operating in the United States: The Black Panther Party (BPP), the Weather Underground Organization (WUO), the New World Liberation Front (NWLF), the Symbionese Liberation Army (SLA), and the Black Liberation Army (BLA). The WUO and NWLF generally engaged in property damage bombings and tried to avoid causing injuries to innocent bystanders. The BPP, SLA, and BLA however carried out mostly assassinations. All carried out bank robberies to fund their operations. All these organizations were left-wing with the WUO and NWLF expressing solidarity with similar left-wing terrorist organizations in Latin American and Western Europe and considering themselves to be part of the international revolutionary movement. The Ku Klux Klan and other white supremacist terrorist groups were relatively inactive in the 1970s. The Klan was severely debilitated by internal dissention, federal court cases, FBI infiltration, and fractionalization. In 1974, David Duke founded the Knights of the Ku Klux Klan and moved the Klan into mainstream politics and promoted non-violence and legality.[19] From 1970 to 1975, the domestic terrorism landscape in the U.S. was shaped and dominated by left-wing organizations. The two places that acted as flashpoints for this threat were the New York City and San Francisco Bay areas.

The goals of these left-wing terrorist groups were eclectic, murky, and implausible in attainment. At no point did any of these groups have significant support from the general population or their own constituencies. They were all caught up in the revolutionary aura of the 1960s that was growing in Latin America, Africa, and Western Europe. The plight of blacks in urban America, the rigidity of the university curriculums, the independence movements in colonial Africa, the Vietnam War, the publication of Regis Debray's book *Revolution in the Revolution?* in 1967, Franz Fanon's *The Wretched of the Earth* in 1961, Carlos Marighella's *Mini-manual of the Urban Guerrilla* in 1969, and the romantic images of Che Guevara and the Tupamaros in Latin America, all contributed to this emerging revolutionary narrative and mythology.

Black Panther Party for Self-Defense

The Black Panthers was a black extremist organization that was founded in 1966 by black nationalists Huey P. Newton and Bobby Seale in Oakland, California. It

---

[19] https://www.splcenter.org/fighting-hate/extremist-files/ideology/ku-klux-klan. Accessed May 6, 2016.

operated primarily during the Johnson and Nixon administrations. It advocated the use of violence and guerilla tactics to overthrow the U.S. government. It emerged from the Student Nonviolent Coordinating Committee (SNCC), one of the most important organizations in the civil rights movement in the U.S. in the 1960s. More hardline black nationalists expressed dismay over the slow pace of the civil rights movement and demanded more militant revolutionary social and political change and "black power." The Panthers advocated militant self-defense of minority communities against the U.S. government and fought to establish revolutionary socialism through mass organizing and community-based programs. The organization launched more than 35 Survival Programs and provided community help, such as education, tuberculosis testing, legal aid, transportation assistance, ambulance service, the manufacture and distribution of free shoes to poor people, and the Free Breakfast for Children Program that spread to every major American city with a BPP chapter.[20] The Panthers also published its founding manifesto titled "What We Want, What We Believe," a 10-point program for "Land, Bread, Housing, Education, Clothing, Justice and Peace." The Party also demanded exemptions for African Americans from military service in Vietnam. However, it also adopted and applied a violent, racist rhetorical style and paramilitary organization and tactics. It was the Panthers who first used the term "pigs" to describe the police and used the slogan "off the pigs" which meant kill the policeman.[21]

The Panthers were a militant political organization in the late 1960s and members were involved in a series of violent shootouts with the police, other black organizations, and even in some internal feuds. The party had a decentralized, underground "violent" arm that was called different names but ultimately was known as the Black Liberation Army or simply the "army." In January 1969, the BLA was officially mentioned by the party in its "Rules of the Black Panther Party" which stated in rule #6 that "no member can join any other army force

---

[20] http://www.britannica.com/topic/Black-Panther-Party. Accessed May 10, 2017.

[21] The Oxford English Dictionary cites an 1811 reference to a "pig" as a Bow Street Runner — the early police force in London, named after the location of their headquarters. Before that, the term "pig" was used to describe someone who is intensely disliked. In the U.S., the modern, well-known usage of the term started in the 1960s when it was frequently and consistently used by anti-Vietnam War protestors. The Blank Panther usage had a more ominous application. Other explanations of the term involve the gas masks worn by the riot police in that era, or the pigs in charge of George Orwell's *Animal Farm* who were oppressing the other animals. With the wave of controversial police shootings in 2015 in the U.S., the term was once again being thrown at policemen. http://forums.officer.com/t73948/. Accessed September 6, 2017.

other than the BLACK LIBERATION ARMY."[22] There were no accurate numbers in terms of how many policemen were killed by the Panthers and how many Panthers were killed by the police. The latter number was a controversial issue as the Panthers and its supporters were propagating the idea that some 28 members were killed by police. Moreover, the FBI and police were engaged in a "centrally directed drive ... to decimate and perhaps even annihilate the Black Panther Party through outright, unprovoked killings."[23] The Panthers pointed to the 1969 shooting of Fred Hampton, the party's leader in Chicago, by police during an FBI/Chicago Police Department raid, and the shooting by prison guards of the party's ideologist George Jackson, during a 1971 prison escape, as testaments to this accusation.[24]

In terms of the number of BPP members killed by police, it appears that the total is around 10 and not 28.[25] As for the number of policemen killed by the BPP, the estimate varies between 5 and 12.[26] The Black Panthers were also involved in

---

[22] As quoted in William Rosenau's excellent article "'Our Backs Are Against the Wall': The Black Liberation Army and Domestic Terrorism in 1970s America," *Studies in Conflict and Terrorism*, Volume 36, 2013, p. 178.

[23] Albert Parry. *Terrorism: From Robespierre to Arafat* (New York: Vanguard Press, 1976), p. 306.

[24] On Hampton's death, see Christianna Silva, "Who Was Fred Hampton, the Black Panther Shot and Killed in His Bed by Chicago Police 48 Years Ago?," *Newsweek*, December 4, 2017, at https://www.newsweek.com/fred-hampton-black-panther-shot-killed-chicago-730503, Accessed May 6, 2017; and Ted Gregory, "The Black Panther Raid and the death of Fred Hampton," *Chicago Tribune*, December 19, 2007, at https://www.chicagotribune.com/news/nationworld/politics/chi-chicagodays-panther-raid-story-story.html. Accessed May 4, 2017; and https://www.democracynow.org/2009/12/4/the_assassination_of_fred_hampton_how. Accessed June 6, 2017; On Jackson's death, see Craig Marine, "Exit the Dragon / It's been 30 years since George Jackson died in a pool of blood at San Quentin. His death still reverberates in America," *SFgate*, August 9, 2001, at https://www.sfgate.com/bayarea/article/EXIT-THE-DRAGON-It-s-been-30-years-since-George-2888071.php. Accessed July 5, 2016; Wallace Turner, "Two Desperate Hours: How George Jackson Died," *New York Times*, September 3, 1971, at https://www.nytimes.com/1971/09/03/archives/two-desperate-hours-how-george-jackson-died-two-desperate-hours-how.html. Accessed September 4, 2017; and https://blackagendareport.com/content/george-jackson-forty-years-ago-they-shot-him-down. Accessed February 4, 2017.

[25] The most accurate and extensive analysis of the killings of Black Panther members by police is found in Edward J. Epstein's article "The Black Panthers and the Police: A Pattern of Genocide?," The *New Yorker Magazine*, February 13, 1971, at http://www.edwardjayepstein.com/archived/panthers.htm. Accessed June 5, 2017.

[26] The author's chronology indicates that militant black nationalists (includes BPP killings) had killed 30 people from 1967 to 1975, including 19–25 law enforcement officers. The Officer Down Memorial Page states that "Members and former members of the group were responsible for the murders of at least 15 law enforcement officers and the wounding of dozens more across the nation," at http://www.odmp.org/officer/5125-police-officer-john-f-frey. Accessed July 5, 2016. The *Police Magazine* states that "Between the fall of 1967 to the end of 1970, as a result of confrontations between police and

shoot-outs and assassinations with other rival black extremist groups like the U.S. Organization or "United Slaves," "The Black Guerrilla Family," and the "Simbas." There were also several intra-BPP assassinations. On May 21, 1969, Alex Rackley, a Panther member was murdered by other members because they suspected him of being a police informant. In the spring of 1971, the Huey Newton and Eldridge Cleaver factions of the Black Panthers engaged in retaliatory assassinations of each other's members, resulting in the death of four people. On June 15, 1969, J. Edgar Hoover declared, "the Black Panther Party, without question, represents the greatest threat to internal security of the country." However, according to Hoover, it was not so much the shootings that were the threat but the Panthers' Free Children's Breakfast Program because it was an infiltration of the black communities designed to attract support and members.[27]

At its height, the BPP grew from an Oakland-based organization into an international one with chapters in 48 states in North America and support groups in Japan, China, France, England, Germany, Sweden, Mozambique, South Africa, Zimbabwe, Uruguay, and elsewhere.[28] From the mid-1970s through the 1980s, the activities of the BPP all but ceased. FBI pressure and informants contributed to its demise as many of the Panther leadership had become entangled in criminal trials, were serving long prison sentences, or were killed in police shootouts. The Panthers were also riven with internal disputes and personality clashes. The big split came in 1971 when Panther leaders Huey Newton and David Hilliard favored a focus on community service while Eldridge Cleaver, the minister of information, embraced a more militant strategy. As a black nationalist website summed it up:

> *The internal strife, division, intrigue, and paranoia had become so ingrained that eventually most members drifted or were driven away. Some continued the struggle on other fronts and some basically cooled out altogether. The BPP limped on for several more years, then died what seemed a natural death.[29]*

Although the BPP was diminishing, there were other successor militant black nationalist organizations that rose to take its place.

Black Panthers, nine police officers were killed and 56 were wounded," at http://www.policemag.com/blog/gangs/story/2012/09/the-black-panther-party-1-of-2.aspx. Accessed September 6, 2017.
[27] https://www.pbs.org/hueypnewton/people/people_hoover.html. Accessed May 6, 2016.
[28] Ibid.
[29] http://www.thetalkingdrum.com/bla2.html. Accessed July 5, 2017.

Weather Underground Organization

The WUO was a militant splinter group from the radical campus organization Students for the Democratic Society or SDS which in turn was part of the anti-Vietnam War movement. The SDS operated primarily during the Johnson and Nixon administrations. According to the government, the SDS was directly involved in 247 arson cases and 462 personal injury incidents, and 300 other miscellaneous episodes of destruction to other facilities or property from October 1969 to October 1970.[30] The WUO was primarily active in the U.S. from 1969 to 1974 and was considered the number one domestic terrorist threat in the United States at that time. It was composed mostly of white college students and graduates who generally came from a middle class or privileged background. Over its lifespan, the WUO had between 40 and 70 members in various cities. Its goal was to create a clandestine revolutionary party for the violent overthrow of the U.S. Government. In 1970, the organization issued a "Declaration of a State of War" against the United States government. The WUO members were very sympathetic to the goals and activities of the militant black organizations like the BPP, the BLA, and the George Jackson Brigade (GJB). The SDS and WUO praised these black organizations in their publications and even wanted to join these organizations "whenever the blacks would let them, which was not always, since by degrees many Panthers were growing more and more anti-honky and segregationist."[31] The militant black organizations looked down on the SDS and WUO organizations. Black Panther chairman Bobby Seale castigated the SDS as a "bunch of those jive bourgeois national socialists and national chauvinists."[32] Very few whites became members of militant black organizations in the early 1970s.

From 1969 to 1974, the WUO was responsible for about 44 terrorist incidents, mostly bombings.[33] Its targets were generally government targets, banks, and U.S. multinational companies. The organization attempted to minimize casualties to innocent people by calling in evacuation warnings before the bombs exploded. The group issued written communiqués that explained the reasons behind each of the

---

[30] Bruce E. Johnson, "Nixon Asks An FBI Role In Campus Bomb Probes," *The Harvard Crimson*, September 23, 1970, at http://www.thecrimson.com/article/1970/9/23/nixon-asks-an-fbi-role-in. Accessed June 6, 2016.

[31] Albert Parry. *Terrorism: From Robespierre to Arafat*, p. 308.

[32] Ibid.

[33] http://en.wikipedia.org/wiki/List_of_Weatherman_actions. Accessed July 7, 2016. In a March 1975 WUO magazine titled "Osawatomie," the organization claimed credit for 25 terrorist bombings over the past five years. Parry, *Terrorism from Robespierre to Arafat*, p. 340.

bombings. For example, the organization bombed the U.S. Capitol in 1971 ("in protest of the US invasion of Laos"), the Pentagon in 1972 ("in retaliation for the US bombing raid in Hanoi"), and the U.S. Department of State in 1975 ("in response to escalation in Vietnam"). The WUO was the largest domestic terrorist organization with the broadest geographical operational area of any terrorist organization in U.S. history. It carried out attacks in San Francisco, Chicago, New York City, Boston, Washington, D.C., Sacramento, and Oakland. The organization started to decline in 1973 after the United States reached a peace accord in Vietnam. Combined with Nixon's resignation in August 1974, the anti-war movement lost its key issue and its major protagonist, and as a result, a volatile era of revolutionary violence came to an end.

New World Liberation Front

The NWLF was a left-wing terrorist organization that was active from 1974 to 1980. It operated primarily during the Ford and Carter administrations. It was the most enigmatic domestic terrorist group in U.S. history. It carried out more terrorist attacks than any other left-wing group in U.S. history. Its origin and expiration are obscure. No book or major journal article has been written on this group. Bryan Burrough's 2015 book *Days of Rage* contains the most extensive and prescient analysis of the group. It is known that the name first appeared on August 5, 1974 when it was used to claim responsibility for an unsuccessful bombing of an insurance agency in the Burlingame area of San Francisco. There are no reliable estimates of membership or the number of attacks carried out by the organization which at times appeared to be an umbrella organization whose name was used by various militant cells and groups. Based on the FBI wanted lists and arrests at the time, a rough estimate would be between 10 and 15 members. The NWLF had several "combat units" that functioned with some degree of autonomy under the overall control of the "Central Command." This is an organizational concept that left-wing terrorist groups in Western Europe and Latin America also used — they would name a specific attack team after a famous Marxist revolutionary leader or after one of their dead comrades. In the NWLF, individual cells/units such as the Lucio Cabanas Combat Unit, the Emiliano Zapata Combat Unit, the Nat Turner/John Brown Combat Unit, the May 19 Combat Unit, the Sam Melville/Jonathan Jackson Combat Unit, as well as the People's Force #1, People's Force #2, People's Force #3, and People's Force #4 of the NWLF Central Command, all claimed credit for numerous actions. There were nine different unit names used. The use of the different names is what makes ascertaining the number of attacks the organization carried out difficult to assess.

It is possible that the same people were involved in several of these combat units and were simply trying to project a larger operational reach for the NWLF. The more combat units that claimed credit for attacks, the greater the perception of the public and left-wing milieu that the NWLF was a sizable organization.

A rough estimate would be that terrorists using the name of the NWLF carried out between 65 and 100 bombings in the San Francisco area.[34] The NWLF's attacks were focused mainly on local, concrete political issues rather than abstract symbolic protest. The bombings were directed at power stations, banks, office buildings, and motor vehicles, without causing a single injury to anyone. The bombing targets of the NWLF have included several West Coast business facilities: Dean Witter and Company, General Motors (four times), Adolph Coors Company (five times), ITT (five times), and Pacific Gas and Electric (over 30 times). The organization's most notorious bombings were the February 1976 bombing of the Hearst Castle in San Simeon built by publishing magnate William Randolph Hearst that caused around $1 million in damage and the December 1976 attempted bombing of the home in San Francisco of Supervisor Diane Feinstein — a future Senator from California who became the first female Speaker of the House. Some of the NWLF "combat units" were more vitriolic in their rhetoric than others. The following is a communiqué from the "Jonathan Jackson/Sam Melville Unit" of the NWLF claiming responsibility for the August 1975 bombing of a police station:

> *The explosion at the Emeryville Station of Fascist Pig Repression is a warning to the rabid dogs who murder our children in cold blood. Remember pigs: every time you strap on your gun, the next bullet may be speeding towards your head, the next bomb may be under the seat of your car...*[35]

---

[34] A RAND corporation research paper in May 1980 stated that the NWLF carried out 70 bombings between 1974 and 1978 in the San Francisco bay area and "the group was credited with 26 bombings in other cities of northern California and may be associated with a number of bombings in other Western states." Brian Jenkins, "Terrorism in the United States," May 1980, Research Paper #6674, p. 9. Bryan Burrough in his book *Days of Rage* (p.353) quotes a *San Francisco Chronicle* "box score" of Bay area bombings as follows: the NWLF carried out 64 bombings, the Chicano Liberation Front with nine, the Zapata unit with eight, and the Americans for Justice with six (p. 353). Burrough also quotes an FBI agent referring to San Francisco at this time as the "Belfast of North America" (p. 345).

[35] Communiqué published in the underground magazine *Dragon*, issue #2, September 1975, p. 20 is in the author's possession. This Jonathan Jackson/Sam Melville Unit of the NWLF should not to be confused with the Sam Melville/Jonathan Jackson Unit name that was also used by the United Freedom Front. See also, *Dragon*, Issue #9, June 1976, at http://www.freedomarchives.org/ Documents/Finder/DOC514_scans/SLA%20Dragon/514.SLA.Dragon9.Jun1976.Periodical.pdf. Accessed June 6, 2017.

domestic terrorist organization in U.S. history.[46] Over 70% of the BLA incidents took place in the New York area, followed by California, and Georgia.

It should also be noted that the only two domestic terrorism hijackings in the 1970s were carried out by black militants:

- On July 31, 1972, Delta Airlines Flight 841 was hijacked by three men and two women, some of whom were affiliated with the BLA. Upon landing in Miami, they demanded a $1 million ransom in exchange for the passengers — the largest ransom of its kind at that time. After releasing the passengers, the hijackers forced the plane to fly to Boston for refueling then continued to Algeria where they sought asylum and to join Black Panther Eldridge Cleaver's "Afro-American Liberation Army." The U.S. government requested the Algerian government to seize the plane and money. The terrorists were briefly taken into custody by Algeria but were eventually released after a few days and disappeared.[47]

- On November 27, 1971, Charles Hill, Ralph Lawrence, and Albert Finney were driving a carload of weapons to Louisiana for the Republic of New Afrika (RNA) militant group. They murdered New Mexico State Police officer Robert Rosenbloom during a traffic stop and escaped to Albuquerque where at gunpoint they hijacked a TWA 727 to Cuba. The RNA was a social movement that proposed the creation of an independent African American majority country situated in the southeastern United States, the payment of several billion dollars in reparations for the damages inflicted on Africans and their descendants by chattel enslavement, and a referendum of all African Americans in order to decide what should be done with regard to their citizenship. The RNA was involved in a small number of shootouts with police and FBI agents. The group's militancy led FBI officials to raid RNA bases. A 1971 raid in Jackson, Mississippi led to the death of one policeman and the arrest

---

[46] https://en.wikipedia.org/wiki/Black_Liberation_Army. Accessed June 7, 2018. Once again, the statistics on terrorist-caused police deaths are confusing. In a newspaper article titled "A Brave Man Remembers another Era of Attacks on Police" by Bill McKelway in the *Richmond Times-Dispatch* on September 2, 2015, the author notes that "by June 1973, according to the New York Daily News, some three years of Black Liberation Army mayhem had taken the lives of 23 New York officers and left an additional 880 wounded," at http://www.richmond.com/article_4b76bfd2-e2a8-5b16-990e-4391806ec010.html. Accessed September 4, 2018.

[47] FBI Newark Press Release, "International Fugitive Captured After More Than 40 Years," September 27, 2011, at https://www.fbi.gov/newark/press-releases/2011/international-fugitive-captured-after-more-than-40-years. Accessed June 6, 2018.

The NWLF, like most left-wing terrorist organizations, also had its own common propaganda organ — a magazine booklet titled "The Urban Guerilla" or TUG. The TUG acted as a repository of NWLF attack communiqués, reprints of articles from other left-wing magazines, commentaries on political developments in the world, operational training articles, letters to the central command and its responses, and as a forum for debate.[36] Prior to the publishing of the TUG, the NWLF communicated primarily through the newsletter *Dragon* which was published by the Bay Area Research Collective in Berkeley, California. The NWLF was one of the first domestic terrorist groups to develop above-ground spokespersons who would explain and rationalize the group's actions. This was adopted by the other groups and terrorist entities like the Animal Liberation Front and Earth Liberation Front in the 1990s.

Symbionese Liberation Army

The SLA was a self-styled left-wing terrorist group active between 1973 and 1975. It operated primarily during the Nixon and Ford administrations. The SLA adopted its program and propaganda from Latin American revolutionaries. The slogan of the group was — "death to the fascist insect that preys on the life of the people." The SLA embraced Marxist French journalist Régis Debray's concept of "urban propaganda." The concept involved the use of selected violence — assassinations, kidnappings, bank robbery, etc. — aimed at capturing media attention and through it popular support.[37] The SLA comprised around 12–15 mostly white members and carried out about 24 terrorist attacks including bombings, bank robberies, assassinations, and the only successful political kidnapping in U.S. history.[38] It was led

---

[36] *The Urban Guerrilla* #4, published in late 1976, has 56 pages and numerous black and white maps and photos. Such revolutionary magazine booklets were usually distributed at universities and in left-wing book stores. The people who published TUG had their own press and darkroom facilities and were open to other left-wing organizations. TUG printers also did commercial printing to pay the rent and buy printing supplies. This issue of the TUG had three articles in the "manual of warfare" section dealing with "heavily armed," "detonations," and "fertilizer explosive." The man behind TUG was Jacques Regiers (Burrough, *Days of Rage*, p. 349). Regiers acted as the unofficial public relations spokesperson for the NWLF. He claimed that he received NWLF communiqués and passed them on to the press (Burrough, p. 347). This approach was later used by Craig Rosebraugh and David Barbarash who acted as public spokespersons for the Earth Liberation Front and Animal Liberation Front, respectively. The ELF and ALF were terrorist entities that were active in the late 1980s and 1990s.

[37] http://www.slate.com/articles/news_and_politics/explainer/2002/01/what_is_the_symbionese_liberation_army.html. Accessed June 5, 2017.

[38] Ann W. O'Neill, "Prosecutors Seek to Cite SLA Violence," *Los Angeles Times*, September 19, 2000.

of an RNA member for the police officer's death. Six other prominent RNA members were also arrested.[48]

The record indicates that militant black nationalists from various groups, which used assorted operational names, killed at a minimum 30 people from 1967 to 1975, including 19–25 law enforcement officers. No U.S. domestic terrorist group or aggregate has to date equaled this bloody toll. The emergence of militant black nationalism was due to a confluence of events and developments in the U.S. in the 1960s and early 1970s, such as the ones listed here:

- The assassination of Malcolm X in 1965.
- The assassination of Martin Luther King, Jr. in 1968.
- The 1965 Watts riots in Los Angeles, the 1967 riots in Detroit and Newark, and the 1968 riots in Washington, D.C.
- The Vietnam War and the resultant anti-war movement in the U.S.
- A perceived need for alternatives to non-violent National Association for the Advancement for Colored People (NAACP) — a civil rights organization in the United States. (U.S.), Southern Christian Leadership Congress (SCLC) — a civil rights organization that originated during the Civil Rights Movement of the 1960s. (U.S.), Congress of Racial Equality (CORE) — an African-American civil rights organization in the United States, Student Nonviolent Coordinating Committee (SNCC) — a US civil-rights student organization active in the 1960s.
- The perception that civil rights reforms are insufficient.
- Linkage of the struggle of Black people with anti-colonial struggles abroad.
- Rise of a black separatist agenda — need for the cultural, political, and economic separation of African Americans from white society.
- Rise of black pride as seen in the political slogan "Black Power" and in the "black is beautiful" catchphrase.

Puerto Rican Separatism

Both the Nixon and Ford administrations were also confronted by terrorist activities by Puerto Rican separatists. Puerto Rico was a colony of Spain for over 400 years. In 1897, it was given limited sovereignty by Spain. From April to August 1898, the U.S. was involved in the Spanish–American War over the issue of Cuban independence. The result of the U.S. winning this war was the 1898 Treaty of Paris which

---

[48] https://www.frontpagemag.com/point/205629/leader-black-communist-terrorist-group-elected-daniel-greenfield. Accessed May 5, 2017.

was an agreement that dictated that Spain relinquish nearly all of the remaining Spanish Empire, especially Cuba, and cede Puerto Rico, Guam, and the Philippines to the United States. While an independence movement quickly surfaced in Puerto Rico in the early 1900s, it was not until the Truman administration in the 1950s that militant separatists emerged on the U.S. mainland. In 1952, Puerto Rico's first elected governor, Luis Muñoz Marin, signed the island's commonwealth pact with the United States in which Puerto Rico was now a commonwealth of the U.S. Puerto Rican nationalists were furious as the 1952 referendum limited the options to only two choices: continuing the colonial status or the proposed new commonwealth status. There were no options for statehood or independence.[49]

The two most notorious Puerto Rican terrorist attacks during the 1950s were the following:

- On November 1, 1950, two Puerto Rican terrorists, Griselio Torresola and Oscar Collazo, attempted to assassinate President Harry S. Truman while he was staying at the Blair House, across the street from the White House. One uniformed U.S. Secret Service agent, Leslie Coffelt, and Torresola were killed.[50] Collazo was wounded and captured. He was convicted of murder and sentenced to death, but President Truman commuted his sentence to life. After Collazo served 29 years in a federal prison, President Jimmy Carter commuted his sentence to time served and he was released in 1979. Both Torresola and Collazo were members of the Puerto Rican Nationalist Party.

- On March 1, 1954, four Puerto Rican terrorists, Lolita Lebrón, Rafael Cancel Miranda, Andres Figueroa Cordero, and Irving Flores Rodríguez, sprayed 30 rounds from semi-automatic pistols from the visitor's section down to the

---

[49] It should be noted that in various plebiscites since the 1950s, few Puerto Ricans have voted for independence:
- 1967: 1% voted for independence;
- 1993: 4.4% voted for independence;
- 1998: 2.54% voted for independence;
- 2012: 6% voted for independence.
http://ushistoryscene.com/article/puerto-rico. Accessed May 6, 2017.

[50] For more detailed information on these attacks, see Stephen Hunter and John Bainbridge. *American Gunfight: The Plot to Kill Harry Truman — And the Shoot-Out That Stopped It* (New York: Simon & Schuster, 2005). The most detailed history of Puerto Rican terrorism is Professor Michael Gonzalez-Cruz's article "Clandestine Armed Struggle — 1960–1999" (in Spanish), at http://www.cedema.org/index.php?ver=verlista&grupo=145&nombrepais=Puerto%20Rico&nombregrupo=Otros%20Documentos. Accessed June 6, 2017; and Ronald Fernandez, *Los Macheteros: The Wells Fargo Robbery and the Violent Struggle for Puerto Rican Independence* (New York: Simon & Schuster, 1987).

chamber of the U.S. House of Representatives, wounding five congressmen. All four terrorists were captured. All four were members of the Puerto Rican Nationalist Party. The terrorists were tried and convicted in federal court and were essentially given life imprisonment. It is interesting to note that this was the first time that a woman led a terrorist cell attack in the U.S. and one of the few times in the world that a woman led a terrorist attack. In 1978 and 1979, all four terrorists were pardoned by President Jimmy Carter; all four returned to Puerto Rico. It was speculated that Carter released the four "as part of an elaborately crafted prisoner swap to secure the release of American CIA agents jailed in Cuba by Fidel Castro's government."[51] All four terrorists received a hero's welcome when they returned to the Island.[52]

While the above Puerto Rican terrorist attacks were episodic, it was the Nixon, Ford, and Carter administrations that faced to varying degrees a sustained Puerto Rican terrorist campaign on Puerto Rico and on the U.S. mainland. Eight Puerto Rican separatist terrorist groups operated on the U.S. mainland and on Puerto Rico: Armed People's Movement (MAP), People's Revolutionary Commandos (CRP), Armed Liberation Commandos (CAL), Armed Forces of Popular Resistance (FARP), Organization of Volunteers for the Puerto Rican Revolution (OVRP), Armed Revolutionary Independence Movement (MIRA), Armed Forces of National Liberation (FALN), and the Macheteros. The three terrorist groups that were the most dangerous and active were the MIRA, FALN, and Macheteros.[53]

---

[51] Manuel Roig-Franzia, "When Terror Wore Lipstick," Cover Story. *Washington Post Magazine*, February 22, 2004, at https://www.washingtonpost.com/archive/lifestyle/magazine/2004/02/22/a-terrorist-in-the-house/293c52cd-8794-47bd-9960-9c7a871e009c/. Accessed May 4, 2017. This article is a lengthy interview with Lolita Lebrón. Additional information on the terrorists involved in the attack on the House of Representatives can be found at Douglas Martin, "Lolita Lebrón, Puerto Rican Nationalist, Dies at 90," *New York Times*, August 3, 2010, p. A17 at http://www.nytimes.com/2010/08/03/us/03lebron.html?_r=0 accessed May 4, 2017, and Mireya Navarro, "40 Years After Attacks, Time Has Softened Zeal," *New York Times*, October 21, 1990, at http://www.nytimes.com/1990/10/21/us/40-years-after-attacks-time-has-softened-zeal.html. Accessed May 6, 2017. It is also interesting to note that Albizu Campos, the imprisoned leader of the Puerto Rican Nationalist Party, corresponded with Lolita Lebrón whom he never met. Was she radicalized by him through this correspondence? This issue of remote radicalization surfaces more prominently in the post-9/11 era as global jihadists used the Internet to radicalize young Muslims and converts worldwide, at https://en.wikipedia.org/wiki/Pedro_Albizu_Campos. Accessed April 3, 2017.

[52] http://content.time.com/time/magazine/article/0,9171,947395,00.html. Accessed May 4, 2018. Another example of the adage "one man's terrorist is another man's freedom fighter."

[53] These eight terrorist groups were active for roughly the following periods: MAP (1960–1965), MIRA (1968–1972), CAL (1967–1972), CRP (1977–1982), FALN (1974–1984), Macheteros

All these groups came from the same lineage and cooperated with each other to varying degrees, to include occasional joint operations or coordinated attacks conducted on Puerto Rico and on the mainland. In some cases, one group evolved into another. The number of members in each group and the number of attacks carried out by each group are difficult to accurately assess — approximations are the norm. The differences between these groups, aside from minor ideological variations, were in tactics, targets, and operational area. All these groups had as their stated goal to free Puerto Rico from "Yanki colonial domination" and considered themselves to be "part of the international workers revolution and all people fighting for national liberation." These groups were engaged in armed struggle on "two fronts, one in Puerto Rico and the other on the U.S. mainland."[54] These groups saw the first front as being the most important and also understood that it was necessary to carry out attacks on the U.S. mainland. The FALN and MIRA focused their attacks on the U.S. mainland while the others operated mostly on Puerto Rico where from 1967 to 1978 there were over 200–300 terrorist incidents.[55] At times, they also sought the release of incarcerated Puerto Rican

---

(1978–1985), FARP (1978–1982), and OVRP (1978–1986). Some of the groups continued politically after they gave up armed struggle. The author warns that terrorist groups do not have specific birth dates and death dates. Many groups expire slowly without any official notice of their demise. All statistics and attacks of Puerto Rican terrorism are based on a chronology of Puerto Rican terrorist attacks, at http://www.latinamericanstudies.org/puertorico/FALN-incidents.pdf. Accessed May 6, 2017; Movement of National Liberation. *Towards People's War for Independence and Socialism in Puerto Rico: In Defense of Armed Struggle — Documents and Communiques from the Revolutionary Public Independence Movement and the Armed Clandestine Movement.* January 1979, pp. 40–49, at http://www.scribd.com/doc/99105307/Towards-People-s-War-for-Independence-and-Socialism-in-Puerto-Rico#scribd. Accessed July 4, 2018, hereafter referred to as "Movement of National Liberation Documents"; William Sater, "Puerto Rican Terrorists: Possibly Threat to U.S. Energy Installations?," RAND Corporation, #N-1764-SL, October 1981, pp. 21–30, at https://www.rand.org/content/dam/rand/pubs/notes/2005/N1764.pdf. Accessed May 4, 2017. Federal Bureau of Investigation, Counterterrorism Division, Counterterrorism Threat Assessment and Warning Group, "Terrorism in the United States 1999," FBI Publication #0308. Chronology of Terrorist Activity in the United States: 1980–1999, pp. 54–61; and Federal Bureau of Investigation, Counterterrorism Division, "Terrorism 2000/2001," FBI Publication #0308. Chronology of Terrorist Activity in the United States: 1990–2001, pp. 535–537.

[54] Quotes are from FALN Communiqué #1, dated October 26, 1974. All subsequent Puerto Rican separatist terrorist groups' communiqués noted in this chapter can be found at http://www.latinamericanstudies.org/separatists.htm. Accessed June 6, 2017; and the Documentation Center for Armed Movements (CEDEMA) at http://www.cedema.org/index.php?ver=mostrar&pais=16&nombrepais=Puerto%20Rico. Accessed May 7, 2017.

[55] Movement of National Liberation Documents, "Chronology of Armed Struggle in Puerto Rico and the U.S.: 1967–1978," pp. 40–49.

terrorists, who they considered "political prisoners," from U.S. jails and prisons and the removal of all U.S. military installations from Puerto Rico. There were also accusations at the time of Cuban involvement in these groups as a counter-weight to the U.S. support for anti-Castro groups in the U.S. and in Cuba.[56]

Armed Revolutionary Independence Movement

In 1967, the MIRA was founded and led by Filiberto Ojeda Ríos. Rios became the man most responsible, directly or indirectly, for over 30 years of Puerto Rican terrorism on Puerto Rico and the U.S. mainland. The MIRA operated primarily during the Johnson and Nixon administrations. The goal of MIRA was to free Puerto Rico from American "colonial" rule. It is considered to be the first major Puerto Rican terrorist group to initiate a sustained terrorist campaign in the U.S., primarily in New York City.[57] The MIRA first surfaced in Puerto Rico on February 15, 1969 when it bombed a police station, bank, and Howard Johnson's hotel in San Juan. It first appeared on the U.S. mainland on December 21, 1969 when it bombed a bank, a Puerto Rican office, and Woolworth's Department store in New York City. The number of group members is unknown but is most likely

---

[56] Brian Jenkins. *Terrorism in the United States.* RAND Corporation, Report # P-6474, May 1980, p. 14. See also U.S. District Court, Eastern District of New York. "Sentence Memorandum of the United States," Document #CR 83-0025, dated May 20, 1983, p. 106, endnote 1, found at http://www. latinamericanstudies.org/puertorico/FALN-memo.pdf. Accessed July 6, 2018; U.S. Senate, Committee on the Judiciary, "The Cuban Connection in Puerto Rico: Castro's Hand in Puerto Rico and U.S. Terrorism," Part 6, July 30, 1975; Edmund Mahony, "A Rocket Attack, An FBI Revelation," The Hartford Courant, November 12, 1999; and The Heritage Foundation. Latin American Backgrounder #655 on Latin America — Cuba's Terrorist Connection, June 4, 1988, at http://www.heritage.org/research/reports/1988/06/cubas-terrorist-connection. Accessed April 3, 2917. The evidence is clear that the Cuban intelligence service interacted with Puerto Rican separatists. Moreover, this relation-ship was not surprising.

[57] The first Puerto Rican terrorist group to emerge in the post-World War II era was the MAP around 1961–1965. The MAP was more rural based and was short-lived. The first Puerto Rican urban terrorist group was the CAL. It carried out its first attack in September 1967 when it burned down five U.S.-owned stores in the Santa Rosa, Bayamon shopping center in Puerto Rico. In its initial communiqué on February 22, 1968, the group stated that it wanted to engage in "national liberation through armed action, end the monopoly control industry and commerce in Puerto Rico from US firms, and expel all American companies on the Island." CAL is reported to have carried out more than 45 terrorist attacks from 1968 to 1972 that caused over $15 million in damage. All of its attacks were carried out in Puerto Rico (Source: Armando Andre, "20 Years of Terrorism in Puerto Rico," *The San Juan Graphic Chronicle*, 1987, at http://www.latinamericanstudies.org/puertorico/macheteros1.htm. Accessed May 4, 2017). A 1968 interview with CAL leader Alfonso Beal can be found at "Movement of National Liberation Documents," pp. 53–57.

less than 50 in Puerto Rico and the U.S. mainland. It only attacked unprotected targets. From 1968 to 1973, the U.S. government attributed around 200 incendiary bombings in New York City and a series of bombings in San Juan, Puerto Rico to MIRA.[58] MIRA's most serious attack on the U.S. mainland took place on May 1, 1970 when it carried out two bombings of cinemas in the Bronx which injured 10 people. The MIRA New York cell may have been composed of just a single operative or three at the most.[59]

MIRA may also have been involved in the assassination of one or more U.S. sailors near San Juan, Puerto Rico on March 5, 1970.[60] Although no group claimed responsibility for this attack, the MIRA and CAL were the primary suspects since they were the only two Puerto Rican terrorist groups active on the island at this time. An unsigned communiqué was issued for this attack and stated that it was carried out "to avenge the death of the young student Antonia Martinez." Martinez was killed on March 4 by a policeman during a riot at the University of Puerto Rico. The communiqué noted that "for every student who falls die several representatives of the Armed Forces, as Yankee aggression against the unarmed and defenseless student body ... will not go unpunished."[61] The operational zenith of MIRA in New York City and in Puerto Rico was from late 1969 to 1971. By 1972, the group was neutralized by arrests to include Rios, who escaped to New York City after he was arrested in Puerto Rico in 1970 and failed to show up for his trial.

---

[58] U.S. District Court, Eastern District of New York. "Sentence Memorandum of the United States in the Case of the U.S. Government vs. Julio Rosado, Andres Rosado, Ricardo Romero, Steven Guerra, and Maria Cueto," Document #CR 83-0025, dated May 20, 1983, p. 6, found at http://www.latinamericanstudies.org/puertorico/FALN-memo.pdf. Accessed September 4, 2017. Hereafter referred to as "1983 Sentencing Memorandum."

[59] Burrough, *Days of Rage*, pp. 326–327.

[60] This March 5 attack on one or more U.S. sailors may or may not have taken place. In a RAND Corporation report titled "Puerto Rican Terrorists: A Possible Threat to U.S. Energy Installations" by William Sater (Report # N-1764-SL, October 1981, p. 25), two U.S. sailors are reported to have been killed by MIRA on March 5, 1970 in Puerto Rico. However, the Department of the Navy, Naval Historical Center, in its official list "Casualties: U. S. Navy and Marine Corps Personnel Killed and Wounded in Wars, Conflicts, Terrorist Acts, and Other Hostile Incidents," does not list any Navy or Marine personnel killed in Puerto Rico in 1970 (http://www.ibiblio.org/hyperwar/AMH/AMH-USNchron.htm. Accessed June 6, 2017). Andre, "20 Years of Terrorism in Puerto Rico," notes that an attack on a U.S. Marine named Ruben Humphrey, 21, was carried out on March 7, 1970. He notes further that the attack was carried out by Rios using a .38 caliber pistol to shoot Humphrey in the head and chest.

[61] Andre, "20 Years of Terrorism in Puerto Rico."

Armed Forces of National Liberation

After the dissolution of the MIRA, Filiberto Ojeda Rios fled to New York City where around 1974 he began the construction of a successor terrorist group to MIRA called the Armed Forces of National Liberation or FALN. The birth of the FALN in New York City and Chicago had multiple fathers to include Rios, Oscar Torres, Oscar Lopez-Rivera, Willie Morales, and even the Weather Underground and Cuban Intelligence Services. All contributed to its emergence to varying degrees. Another important contributor was Maria Cueto, then director of the National Commission on Hispanic Affairs, who provided significant logistics to the group.[62] The FALN operated during the Ford, Carter, and Reagan administrations. The MIRA and the FALN both embraced the standard Puerto Rican separatist goal of independence of Puerto Rico from the United States. However, in its published political program, the FALN outlined some additional objectives and positions:

> *An armed struggle whose minimum goal is national independence and the release of all Puerto Rican political prisoners.... Priority on armed struggle in Puerto Rico over the armed struggle in the United States (first front over the second front).... Development of a 'rearguard' armed struggle throughout the breadth of the United States on internationalist principles of organization, which include the active participation of the American people in the armed struggle.*[63]

Although the FALN placed a priority on armed struggle in the first front or Puerto Rico, most of the group's attacks took place in the second front or the United States. As a result, the group established working relationships with several black and white left-wing terrorist organizations in the United States and these groups adopted the cause of Puerto Rican independence. Like all ethnic-based terrorist groups, the FALN took advantage of large Puerto Rican populations in New York City, Chicago, and Philadelphia to recruit and hide. However, the FALN never received significant support from these Puerto Rican communities in the U.S., from Puerto Ricans in Puerto Rico, or from the Puerto Rican Independence Party — the most active and well known independence party in

---

[62] Background on the FALN comes primarily from Burrough, *Days of Rage*, pp. 317–332, and 380–406; the "1983 Sentencing Memorandum," p. 6; and the "Puerto Rican Separatist" section at http://latinamericanstudies.org/separatists.htm. Accessed June 4, 2017.

[63] http://www.latinamericanstudies.org/puertorico/FALN-political-position.pdf. Accessed April 3, 2017.

Puerto Rico.[64] There are no reliable estimates as to the number of operatives in the FALN in the 1970s. This is not surprising given that attempting to assess the number of members in a clandestine organization is by definition difficult. The fact that FALN members were trained to not acknowledge membership to anyone, including family members and other FALN members, makes such an assessment even more problematic.[65] Based on the number of FALN members arrested in the United States from 1975 to 1983, a reasonable estimate would be that the FALN had between 50 and 75 operatives. This does not include sympathizers or supporters within the various Puerto Rican communities.

The number of FALN terrorist attacks is somewhat easier to discern, although there are wide variations. Most of the FALN attacks were claimed either through a typed communiqué or a phone call. However, the group did not claim credit for every attack. A reasonable estimate of the number of FALN terrorist attacks on the U.S. mainland between 1974 and 1983 would be between 120 and 130 incidents. This includes attempted bombings. Property damage is estimated at around $5 million. Six deaths and more than 100 injuries have also been attributed to the FALN.[66] The FALN's primary tactics were bombings and incendiary devices. The FALN generally attacked soft targets like U.S. businesses, banks, department stores, government buildings, police stations, and airports. While it carried out a few operations in Puerto Rico, the bulk of the FALN attacks were carried out in the "second front," primarily in the New York City area, Chicago, and Washington, D.C.

The FALN's first publicly claimed attack on the U.S. mainland took place on October 26, 1974. On that day, the day before the "Day of Solidarity with the Independence of Puerto Rico" held by the Puerto Rican Socialist Party in Madison Square Garden in New York City, the FALN bombed five targets in New York City — Rockefeller Center, the Banco de Ponce, the Chemical Bank, Exxon Mobil, and Union Carbide. All these companies had economic interests in Puerto Rico and benefited from the "colonial regime." The bombings caused property damage

---

[64]Ward Morehouse III, "Puerto Rican terrorists, with low grass-roots support, change tactics," *The Christian Science Monitor*, January 7, 1983, at http://www.csmonitor.com/1983/0107/010749.html. Accessed May 6, 2017.

[65]According to Freddie Mendez, a FALN member who provided evidence to the FBI and was put into the witness protection program, FALN members led double lives as normal people, and as terrorists, did not socialize with each other, practiced compartmentalization, and even wore "pillowcases with eye slits" at planning sessions. Burrough, *Days of Rage*, p. 480. See also Section II of the "1983 Sentencing Memorandum."

[66]A chronology of FALN incidents from 1974 to 1983 can be found at the end of the "1983 Sentencing Memorandum," and Sater, "Puerto Rican Terrorists," pp. 21–29.

of over $1 million. The FALN claimed responsibility for these attacks in a typed "Communique #1," dated October 26. In this communiqué, the group noted that these attacks were carried out in "commemoration of the October 30, 1950 uprising in Puerto Rico against Yanki colonial domination" and to reinforce "our demands for the release of the five Puerto Rican political prisoners, the longest held political prisoners in the hemisphere."[67] On December 11, 1974, the FALN set up an ambush for New York City policemen, calling in a false distress call to entice the police to a booby-trap bomb hidden in a building. One policeman was seriously injured. On January 24, 1975, the FALN bombed the historic Fraunces Tavern in New York City during the lunch hour. The bomb killed 4 people, injured 60 others, and caused extensive property damage. At the time, it was the most lethal terrorist attack in New York City since the 1920 wagon bombing in Wall Street by anarchists that killed 38 people. In a phone call, the FALN directed the police to a phone booth in the Financial District where they found Communique #3, dated January 24, 1975 that opened "We, FALN, the Armed Forces of the Puerto Rican Nation take full responsibility for the especially detonated bomb that exploded today at Fraunces Tavern with reactionary corporate executives inside."[68]

The communiqué explained that the Fraunces Tavern bomb was in retaliation for "the CIA ordered bomb" on January 11, 1975 that killed three and injured 11, one a child, in a restaurant in Mayaguez, Puerto Rico. The communiqué noted that two of those killed — Angel Luis Chavonnier and Eddie Ramos — were "two innocent young workers who supported Puerto Rican independence." It noted that the "Yanki government is trying to terrorize and kill our people to intimidate us from seeking our rightful independence from colonialism ... they do this in the same way as they did in Viet Nam, Guatemala, Chile, Argentina, Mexico, the Congo, Algeria and in many other places including the United States itself ... but this CIA/Colby method will fail." At the end of the communiqué, the

---

[67] The five prisoners were Oscar Collazo, Lolita Lebrón, Rafael Cancel Miranda, Andres Figueroa Cordero, and Irving Flores. Collazo was involved in the 1950 attack on President Truman while he was in the Blair House and the other four were involved in the 1952 shootings in the U.S. House of Representatives. Quotes from FALN Communique #1, dated October 26, 1974, at http://www.latina-mericanstudies.org/puertorico. Accessed June 5, 2017.

[68] Communique #3, at http://www.latinamericanstudies.org/puertorico/FALN-3.pdf. Accessed August 5, 2017. An excellent description of the Fraunces Tavern bombing can be found at Mara Bovsun, "Justice Story: FALN bomb kills 4 at Fraunces Tavern, where George Washington said farewell to troops," *New York Daily News*, January 21, 2012, at http://www.nydailynews.com/new-york/justice-story-faln-bomb-kills-4-fraunces-tavern-george-washington-farewell-troops-article-1.1008711. Accessed December 4, 2017.

FALN again demanded the release of five Puerto Rican prisoners being held in the U.S. The FALN's most disturbing operation occurred on October 27, 1975, the anniversary of its first bombing in New York City a year earlier. During a one-hour period, 10 pipe bombs exploded in New York City, Chicago, and Washington, D.C. The U.S. Department of State, Bureau of Indian Affairs, five banks, the United Nations building, the Sears Tower, and IBM Plaza were all hit. Damage was estimated at a quarter of a million dollars.[69]

The FALN issued Communique #6, dated October 27, 1975, claiming responsibility for these attacks. The communiqué demanded "the immediate independence of Puerto Rico and the unconditional release of the five Puerto Rican nationalist prisoners ... as well as other Puerto Rican Political Prisoners in Yanki colonial and neo-colonial prisons." Further evidence of a relationship between the FALN and Cuba can be found in this communiqué. The FALN "especially acknowledge the moral support given to our organization by the Cuban people and government in a speech made by Prime Minister Fidel Castro in August in which he said that the Cuban government would do all it could to support the FALN." The communiqué also expresses "our solidarity with all the organizations waging armed struggle within the U.S. against Yanki imperialism abroad and capitalist exploitation of the North American working class."[70] Puerto Rican separatist terrorism was a major terrorism problem for both the Nixon and Ford administrations. It was responsible for periodic terrorist activity well into the late 1990s.

During the Ford administration, two new left-wing terrorist organizations also surfaced: The George Jackson Brigade and the Red Star Brigade and Sam Melville/Jonathan Jackson Unit.

George Jackson Brigade

The GJB was a small, left-wing terrorist group based in Seattle, Washington, which was named after George Jackson, a dissident prisoner and Black Panther member shot and killed during an alleged escape attempt at San Quentin Prison in 1971. The GJB operated primarily during the Ford and Carter administrations. The group saw itself as acting as a catalyst for a revolution of the masses to overthrow the present government and establish a communist state. Its attacks and communiqués were carried out to demonstrate that the masses were being

---

[69]Burrough, *Days of Rage*, p. 332.

[70]Communique #6, at http://www.latinamericanstudies.org/puertorico/FALN-6.pdf. Accessed December 4, 2018.

oppressed by the state and U.S. multinational corporations and to inspire the masses to revolt. They were attempting to substitute violence for the absence of a mass struggle. The group also felt it could "boost" ongoing struggles with the bombing of selected, symbolic targets. For example, the struggle of prisoners for better conditions, City Light utility workers who were on strike, and grievances of the United Farm Workers. The group was composed of only six to seven members. However, only four to five were operating at one time as some were arrested or killed at various times. One member, Bruce Seidel, was killed and two, Ed Mean and John Sherman, were arrested during a bank robbery attempt of a Pacific National Bank in January 1976. In March 1976, Sherman escaped from his detention and one county deputy was shot. In July 1976, Mark Cook was captured.

From May 1975 to December 1977, the group robbed eight banks and a state liquor store and carried out two failed bank robberies. It detonated about 18 pipe bombs — mainly targeting government buildings, electric power facilities, Safeway stores, and companies accused of racism.[71] It generally claimed responsibility for its attacks in written communiqués issued to the public. In various communiqués, the group tried to justify their various acts of violence by linking the attacks to specific strikes, protests, or conflicts. For example, on September 5, 1975, the group bombed the FBI office in Takoma, Washington. The next day, it bombed the Bureau of Indian Affairs in Everett, Washington. Why? To bring attention and demonstrate solidarity with the American Indian Movement. On June 26, 1975, the Pine Ridge reservation, an Oglala Lakota Native American reservation located in the U.S. state of South Dakota, was the location of a shoot-out between AIM activists and the FBI and their allies, which became known as the 'Pine Ridge Shootout'. Two FBI agents, Jack Coler and Ronald Williams, and an AIM activist, Joe Stuntz, were killed.[72]

---

[71] Chronology of GJB attacks from Seattle Police Department Intelligence Division and FBI documents at FBI Records: The Vault, at https://vault.fbi.gov/George%20Jackson%20Brigade%20. Accessed June 6, 2017. These documents also contain several GJB communiqués and other investigative reports.

[72] The American Indian Movement (AIM) was founded in July 1968 in Minneapolis, Minnesota. It was initially formed to address American Indian sovereignty, treaty issues, spirituality, and leadership, while simultaneously addressing incidents of police harassment and racism against Native Americans forced to move away from reservations and tribal culture. Its most notorious incident took place on February 27, 1973 when about 200 AIM and Oglala Lakota activists occupied the hamlet of Wounded Knee. The occupation followed the murder of an Oglala Lakota man and the failed impeachment of the tribal president Dick Wilson who AIM members accused of corruption. They also demanded a restoration of treaty negotiations with the U.S. government and correction of U.S. failures to enforce

The GJB first appeared on May 31, 1975 when it bombed an office of the Department of Social and Health Services in Olympia, Washington. The group claimed the action was in support of state prison inmates' demands. On May 31, a communiqué was released by the group and posted in a telephone booth in Seattle, Washington, in which it claimed responsibility for the bombing. The communiqué criticized the criminal sentencing process and notes the hypocrisy "that allows Nixon and gang to escape justice while the poor and confused are made examples of by the court." It noted that "the Amerikan people support the most notorious criminals in existence: U.S. imperialism. Our high standard of living come from the plunder of the "free" world, especially the Third World countries ... if people want a better society, they can start by becoming active feminists, anti-racists, and anti-imperialists. The ruling class is white, male, and imperialist."[73]

The group carried out several attacks against Safeway Food stores in the northwest. In one communiqué, the group explained why it targeted the stores:

Safeway is one of the largest corporations in the world. It is the world's largest food chain and a powerful agribusiness and imperialist. Safeway has effectively monopolized all facets of the food processing, distribution, and retailing industry on the west coast.... As a large grower, Safeway has consistently and violently oppressed the farmworkers and fought their struggle for a union. Safeway makes its super profits by charging poor and working people outrageous inflated prices for nutritionally deficient and chemically poisoned food... it is not surprising that Safeway has been the target of bombings and armed actions up and down the west coast throughout 1975.[74]

---

treaty rights. This occupation led to a 71-day armed stand-off at the Pine Ridge reservation. AIM activist Leonard Peltier was convicted on two counts of first-degree murder for the deaths of the FBI agents and sentenced to two consecutive terms of life in prison, after a trial which is still contentious. He remains a cause for Indian rights activists who believe he is innocent. As of 2019, he remains imprisoned. For more information, see https://www.britannica.com/topic/American-Indian-Movement. Accessed July 4, 2017. See also, https://aimovement.org/; and http://indians.org/articles/american-indian-movement.html. Accessed December 6, 2017.

[73] Daniel Burton-Rose. *Creating a movement with Teeth: A Documentary History of the George Jackson Brigade* (Publisher: Oakland, Calif.: PM Press, 2010), pp. 77–78, at http://www.worldcat.org/title/creating-a-movement-with-teeth-a-documentary-history-of-the-george-jackson-brigade/oclc/555670667/viewport. Accessed June 4, 2017. See also, Daniel Burton-Rose, *Guerrilla USA: The George Jackson Brigade and the Anticapitalist Underground of the 1970s* (Berkeley: University of California Press, 2010).

[74] Ibid., pp. 84–85.

The GJB robbed or tried to rob ten banks. These operations were referred to as "expropriations." In Western Europe, left-wing terrorist groups called them "proletarian expropriations." The group explained its actions in a subsequent communiqué:

> *Yesterday, the George Jackson Brigade expropriated about $4,200 from the Factoria Branch of the Ranier National Bank.... Armed expropriation is a vital part of our work. Apart from the everyday cost of living (which is as a terrible burden for us as it is for everyone else); weapons, ammunition, explosives, medical supplies, vehicles, etc., cost an enormous amount of money. We will continue to take this money from the ruling class and its state. Most people understand that the banks and the state are the real robbers of all society; and that the profit motive is the biggest robbery in history. But we will under no circumstances steal so much as a penny from small businesses or from the working people. When we robbed the liquor store, for example, it was necessary to take the manager's entire purse because the liquor store's money was in it. The day after the robbery we returned the manager's purse with all her own personal money (about $45). We are not prepared at this time to provide a detailed analysis of the politics of armed robberies, but we feel it is necessary to claim these robberies to counter the attempt by the police to hide these actions from the people.*[75]

By the end of the Ford administration, the group had been reduced to three-four members.

The Red Star Brigade and Sam Melville/Jonathan Jackson Unit

During the Ford administration, a new small, left-wing terrorist group formed in the northeast. It never had more than eight members and was active from October 1975 to September 1984. Several of the members had families and lived somewhat normal lives in the suburbs with jobs and children. This helped them blend into the community and not attract any attention. It took the FBI seven years to find them. The group was initially known as the Red Star Brigade, then the Sam Melville/Jonathan Jackson Unit (during the Ford and Carter administrations) and

---

[75] Ibid., p. 105.

later the United Freedom Front (UFF) during the Reagan administration.[76] During their trials in the mid-1980, they were also known as the "Ohio 7." The founding leaders of this group were Raymond "Luc" Levasseur and Thomas Manning — both Vietnam veterans and former prison inmates. Initially, the two men and several others formed a small group which called itself the "Red Star Brigade" and conducted several bank robberies under that name from October to December 1975 in Augusta and Portland, Maine that netted the group around $16,000. In April 1976, there was a split in the small group. The original members of the Red Star North Brigade, including Levasseur, Patricia Gros, and Thomas and Carol Manning, stayed together and became known as the Sam Melville–Jonathan Jackson Unit. The other faction gave up armed struggle. By 1977, both Levasseur and Manning were on the FBI's Most Wanted List.

Between 1975 and 1984, the Red Star Brigade/Melville–Jackson Unit/UFF carried out at least 19 dynamite bombings, two shootings against policemen that killed one, and ten bank robberies that netted $900,000.[77] All the attacks took place in the northeastern United States and the group claimed responsibility with written, numbered communiqués. The group targeted corporate buildings, courthouses, and military facilities. The UFF always phoned in warnings to evacuate before the bombs went off. A 1976 bombing at a Boston courthouse however did injure 22 people. In a communiqué, the group blamed courthouse security for failing to heed a warning to evacuate the building.[78] The group's stated targets

---

[76] Both leaders of the UFF Raymond Levasseur and Tom Manning, served prison terms and were advocates of prison reform and prison issues. The initial name of the group is instructive. Sam Melville was a white prisoner killed in the 1971 Attica Prison Uprising in New York where he was serving time for involvement/connection to the bombings in 1969 of facilities belonging to the United Fruit Company, Marine Midland, Department of Commerce, Army Induction Center, Standard Oil, Chase Manhattan Bank, General Motors, and the New York City Criminal Courts. Jonathan Jackson, the 17-year-old black militant and brother of George Jackson, was killed in August 1970 during a failed attempt to free three militant blacks during a courtroom session in a courthouse in San Rafael, California.

[77] Statistics compiled from 1984 Indictment from U.S. District Court, District of Massachusetts, U.S. vs. Raymond Levasseur, Patricia Gros, Thomas Manning, Carol Manning, Jaan Laaman, Barbara Curzi, Richard Williams, and Christopher King; and U.S. District Court, E.D. New York, No. 85 Crim 143, 619 F.Supp. 775 (1985), UNITED STATES of America, Plaintiff, vs. Raymond Luc LEVASSEUR, Jaan Karl Laaman, Thomas William Manning, Richard Charles Williams, Carol Ann Manning, Patricia Gros and Barbara Curzi, Defendants, October 7, 1985, at http://www.leagle.com/decision/19851394619FSupp775_11330/UNITED%20STATES%20v.%20LEVASSEUR. Accessed June 6, 2017.

[78] Sam Melville-Jonathan Jackson Unit Communique #1, dated April 22, 1976 (in author's possession).

were American corporations that continued to do business with South Africa, the American government's support for Latin American rightist dictatorships, and anyone it perceived as associated with racism and economic injustice in America. To disguise their activities, members conducted relatively normal lives living in the suburbs, holding jobs, and raising children.

During the Ford administration, the group carried out three bombings and two bank robberies. It bombed two courthouses in Boston and Lowell, Massachusetts and a First National Bank office in Boston. A communiqué claiming responsibility for the July 4, 1976 bombing of the First National Bank was devoted solely to the issue of Puerto Rican independence. The communiqué noted that the attack was in support of "independence for Puerto Rico and the immediate release of the national prisoners," a reference to the five Puerto Rican terrorists who the FALN and Macheteros also wanted released. The communiqué ended as follows:

> *Today, our unit attacks an institution that lives off the sweat and blood of the poor and working masses of people and that is a pillar of U.S. imperialism. With these actions we grow stronger and extend our support to the struggle for a free and independent Puerto Rico — a struggle to the death!*[79]

Assassination Attempts on President Ford

It should also be noted that President Ford was confronted with two assassination attempts during his term. On September 5, 1975, Lynette "Squeaky" Fromme, a Charles Manson Family cult member, attempted to kill Ford by firing a .45 caliber automatic pistol at him from several feet away while he was outside the California State Capitol building in Sacramento. Luckily, her gun failed to fire. There was no bullet in the firing chamber but there was in the magazine. Fromme wanted to make a statement to people who refused to halt environmental pollution and its effects on Air, Trees, Water, and Animals. For her crime, Fromme spent 34 years in prison and was released on August 14, 2009 — two years and eight months after Ford's death in 2006.[80] President Ford gave video testimony in Fromme's

---

[79] Sam Melville–Jonathan Jackson Unit, Communique #3, dated July 4, 1976 (in author's possession).

[80] https://en.wikipedia.org/wiki/Gerald_Ford_assassination_attempt_in_Sacramento. Accessed May 4, 2017. See also *Time* Magazine, September 15, 1975 when Lynette Fromme appeared on the cover. For more detailed information on Fromme, see Jess Bravin, *Squeaky: The Life and Times of Lynette*

trial and it was the first time in U.S. history that oral testimony was given by a sitting president in a criminal trial.[81]

On September 22, 1975 in San Francisco, as President Ford was heading for the car to go to the airport, Sara Jane Moore pulled out a 0.44 caliber pistol from her purse. She pointed the gun at Ford who was about 40 feet away. She fired one shot that passed within a few feet of Ford. A person standing next to her grabbed her before she could fire a second shot. She was sentenced to life in prison, and escaped in 1979, but was captured four hours later. Moore was 77 years old when she was released in 2007. There has been speculation that she was not working alone when she carried out this attack. She had connections with an underground radical organization called Tribal Thumb. This group was founded in 1973 by Earl Lamar Satcher, a convict and former BPP member. Property that Satcher owned in northern California was used as a safe house/ retreat for group members and fugitives. Moore was believed to have used the place for target practice.[82] Moore was the first woman to fire a shot at a sitting president and the first person who attempted to assassinate a president to be released from prison.

Foreign Spillover Terrorism in the United States

Foreign spillover terrorism is a security concern for many countries. Such terrorist activity pollutes the internal security environment of a country, especially those that are already confronted with domestic terrorism. Terrorist organizations that have an international operational footprint are the primary sources of foreign spillover terrorism. In the 1970s, Armenian, Croatian, and Cuban terrorist organizations carried out attacks in several regions of the world, especially Western Europe and Latin America. The United States, in addition to having its interests

---

Alice Fromme (New York: St. Martin's Press, 1997); Ronald Kessler, *In the President's Secret Service: Behind the Scenes with Agents in the Line of Fire and the Presidents They Protect* (New York: Crown Forum, 2010), pp. 49–51.

[81] http://www.nbcnews.com/news/other/video-gerald-ford-recalls-seeing-would-be-assassins-hand-weapon-f8C11011972. Accessed June 3, 2016.

[82] http://www.classroomhelp.com/lessons/Presidents/ford_assassination_attempt.html. Accessed December 4, 2017; "2 in Radical Group Jailed in Shooting," *New York Times*, March 15, 1983, at http://www.nytimes.com/1983/03/15/us/2-in-radical-group-jailed-in-shooting.html. Accessed December 21, 2016. For more detailed information on Moore, see Geri Spiele, *Taking Aim at the President: The Remarkable Story of the Woman Who Shot at Gerald Ford* (New York: Palgrave Macmillan, 2008).

targeted overseas by foreign terrorist actors, was also confronted with this problem. Foreign spillover terrorism first emerged inside the United States in the mid-1960s when anti-Castro, Cuban exiles conducted terrorist attacks here. In the 1970s, the problem of foreign spillover terrorism in the United States significantly increased. The four major protagonists were the following: (1) Anti-Castro, Cuban exiles, (2) Anti-Turkish, Armenian terrorists, (3) Anti-Yugoslav, Croatian and Serbian terrorists, and (4) Anti-Soviet, Jewish Defense League (JDL)[83]. All four were products of grievances that originated overseas but were operationally redressed on U.S. soil. The terrorist activities of these four foreign spillover terrorism actors polluted a U.S. internal security environment already aggravated by terrorist activity from domestic left-wing, right-wing, Puerto Rican separatists, and animal rights militants. In many cases, these overseas grievances inspired American citizens from the four above mentioned ethnic groups to engage in or support terrorist attacks in the United States, either autonomously or under the guidance of a foreign-based leadership. These terrorist organizations did not directly target U.S. interests overseas. Their activities in the U.S. simply aggravated the internal security environment by causing casualties and property damage, increasing the investigative workload of federal, state, and local law enforcement agencies, and forcing the government's implementation of diplomatic protective security measures since many of the attacks were aimed at foreign diplomatic facilities and personnel.

---

[83] The author believes that the JDL was more of a foreign spillover group than a domestic group. The JDL emerged in the late 1960s to protect Jews, Jewish cemeteries, and synagogues from violence in the New York City area. The group's declared purpose was to combat anti-Semitism in the public and private sectors of life in the United States. By 1970, the JDL developed into an ultra-nationalist militant youth movement. It was the Soviet Jewry issue that moved the JDL into the limelight. This issue concerned the right of Jews in the Soviet Union to emigrate. The JDL adopted this issue and as a result carried out 39% of its violent actions against Soviet targets in the U.S. (source: Bruce Hoffman, "Terrorism in the United States and the Potential Threat to Nuclear Facilities," RAND Corporation, document # R-3351-DOE, January 1985, p. 15, at https://www.ncjrs.gov/pdffiles1/Digitization/101049NCJRS.pdf. Accessed January 15, 2017). Around 80% of all JDL violent actions were aimed at foreign targets in the U.S. When it did target U.S. targets, those targets were connected with overseas issues. For example, in 1972, the JDL bombed the office of a promotor in New York City who brought Soviet cultural and musical groups to the U.S. for tours. In 1985, it killed the regional director of the American–Arab Discrimination Committee. Therefore, the author believes that JDL terrorism was driven more by overseas events and developments and less by grievances against the U.S. The JDL never attacked a U.S. government, military, or law enforcement target in the U.S. There will be disagreement on the classification of the JDL as a foreign spillover terrorist group.

Anti-Castro, Cuban Exile Terrorism

Background: When Fidel Castro overthrew the Cuban government in 1959, President Eisenhower officially recognized the Castro government. However, the U.S. became concerned over Cuba's reforms in agriculture and its nationalization of U.S-owned industries. In response, in October 1960, the U.S. prohibited all exports to Cuba. This contributed to Castro moving closer to the Soviet Union as he began to consolidate trade relations with the Soviet Union and sought to find a counter-weight to U.S. hostility. Cuba thus became a "privileged client-state" of the Soviet Union. This closer relationship with the Soviet Union prompted the U.S. to break off all diplomatic relations with Cuba in January 1961. During the Kennedy administration, the U.S. perceived that the Castro regime, with support from the Soviet Union, was serving as a beachhead to induce and support other communist movements elsewhere in Latin America. The U.S. detected growing Cuban financial and military support for left-wing terrorist and insurgent organizations in the region. Consequently, the U.S. began to construct new clandestine operations designed to destabilize the Cuban government. The U.S. started to encourage and support Cuban exile groups in the U.S. that opposed Castro.[84] The apex of this support was the failed April 1961 Bay of Pigs invasion. The Bay of Pigs invasion involved a U.S.-trained force of about 1,500 Cuban exiles who planned to invade southern Cuba with support from the U.S. in order to topple the Castro regime. It was during this early 1960s period that tensions between Cuba and the United States started building and climaxed in 1962, after U.S. spy planes

---

[84] It has been reported that the CIA's Cuba-targeted counterintelligence office "had its headquarters at an old Navy blimp center on the south campus of the University of Miami, cover-named Zenith Technical Enterprises and code-named JM Wave. It was a headquarters that soon became the 'company's' largest, with an annual budget of over $50 million, branch offices in 54 dummy corporations, and a permanent staff of 300 Americans who employed and controlled approximately 6,000 Cuban exile agents. There were literally dozens of exile groups under the CIA's umbrella. After the Bay of Pigs disaster, their number only increased. They were a vast army, with the best and the brightest receiving special paramilitary training at Forts Jackson, Knox and Benning ... Years later, sitting in the plush dining room of Washington's Army-Navy Club, the CIA's then-chief of counterintelligence James Angleton mused: "The concept of Miami was correct. In a Latino area, it made sense to have a base in Miami for Latin American problems, as an extension of the desk. If it had been self-contained, then it would have had the quality of being a foreign base of sorts. It was a novel idea. But it got out of hand, it became a power unto itself. And when the target diminishes, it's very difficult for a bureaucracy to adjust. What do you do with your personnel? We owed a deep obligation to the men in Miami. It was a question of, how many could remain on? We didn't have the slots. And when people found there weren't jobs to be had, we had some problems." The above excerpt from Joe Crankshaw and Gloria Marina, "Miami a Hotbed for Terrorism," *Miami Herald*, November 29, 1976.

photographed Soviet construction of intermediate-range missile sites on Cuba, resulting in the Cuban Missile Crisis. The failure of the Bay of Pigs operations caused President Kennedy to authorize a CIA clandestine operation known as the Cuba Project (also known as "Operation Mongoose") which was aimed at removing Castro by fueling anti-Castro sentiments in Cuba and attempting to kill Castro. The Cuba Project was at "its core a coordinated program of political, psychological, and military sabotage, involving intelligence operations as well as assassination attempts on key Cuban political leaders."[85] Peter Kornbluh, director of the Cuba Documentation Project at the National Security Archive and a specialist on U.S. policy toward Cuba claims that "throughout most of the 1960s, rolling back the Cuban revolution through violent exile surrogates remained a top U.S. priority."[86] Many anti-Castro Cubans went to work for U.S. intelligence and compiled long résumés of covert activities.[87]

There was an interesting proposed corollary to the Cuba Project known as "Operation Northwoods." In a Joint Chiefs of Staff Memorandum for the Secretary of Defense, titled "Justification for U.S. Military Intervention in Cuba (TS)," and dated March 13, 1962, the objective of the plan was stated as follows[88]:

This plan, incorporating projects selected from the attached suggestions, or from other sources, should be developed to focus all efforts on a specific ultimate objective which would provide justification for US military intervention. Such a plan would enable a logical build-up of incidents to be combined with seemingly unrelated incidents to camouflage the ultimate objective and create the necessary impression of Cuban rashness

---

[85] There are no accurate statistics as to how many terrorist attacks were carried out by Cuban American exiles in Cuba. Both the exiles and Cuban government had reasons to inflate the number of attacks. The U.S. government has not published any official statistics. According to one account that appears to use Cuban government statistics, since 1960, there have been over 800 terrorist attacks in Cuba that have killed 3,478 people and injured 2,099 others. Keith Bolender, *Voices from The Other Side: An Oral History of Terrorism Against Cuba* (Pluto Press, 2010), p. 2.

[86] Tristram Korten and Kirk Nielsen, "Anti-Castro Cuban exiles who have been linked to bombings and assassinations are living free in Miami — Does the U.S. government have a double standard when it comes to terror?" Salon.com, January 14, 2008, at http://www.salon.com/news/feature/2008/01/14/cuba/print.html. Accessed June 4, 2017.

[87] Ibid., see also, Julia E. Sweig and Peter Kornbluh, "Cuban Exile on Trial," *Los Angeles Times*, January 12, 2011.

[88] Joint Chiefs of Staff Memorandum for the Secretary of Defense, "Justification for U.S. Military Intervention in Cuba," March 13, 1962, at http://www.gwu.edu/~nsarchiv/news/20010430/northwoods.pdf. Accessed June 3, 2017.

and irresponsibility on a large scale, directed at other countries as well as the United States.[89]

This memorandum was very specific on how this objective could be accomplished:

> We could develop a Communist Cuba terror campaign in the Miami area, in other Florida cities and even Washington. The terror campaign could be pointed at Cuban refugees seeking haven in the United States. We could sink a boatload of Cubans en-route to Florida (real or simulated). We could foster attempts on lives of Cuban refugees in the United States even to the extent of wounding in instances to be widely publicized. Exploding a few plastic bombs in carefully chosen spots, the arrest of Cuban agents and the release of prepared documents substantiating Cuban involvement also would be helpful in projecting the idea of an irresponsible government.[90]

"Operation Northwoods" was never officially accepted and the proposals included in the plan were never executed. However, the U.S. government's objective of overthrowing Castro coincided with the goals of some hundreds of thousands of Cubans who fled to the U.S. to escape the communist regime in Cuba.[91] There was a confluence of vested interests, and this resulted in the U.S. government employing Cuban exiles to engage in political violence against the Castro regime. It is not far-fetched to contend that there probably were more assassination attempts against Castro than any other world leader, past and present.[92] Castro's 1958 revolution in Cuba triggered a wave of Cuban immigration to the

---

[89] Ibid., p. 5; "Cuban exiles, in pay of CIA, spied in U.S. for 10 years," *The Miami News*, January 4, 1975, p. 1.

[90] Ibid., pp. 8–9.

[91] "From January 1, 1959 to October 22, 1962, 248,070 Cubans emigrated to the United States." Maria Cristina Garcia. *Havana USA: Cuban Exiles and Cuban Americans in South Florida, 1959–1994* (University of California Press, 1997), p. 13.

[92] The U.S. Senate's Church Committee of 1975 stated that it had confirmed at least eight separate CIA-run plots to assassinate Castro. See also, Duncan Campbell, "638 ways to kill Castro," *The Guardian*, August 3, 2006; Central Intelligence Agency, "Inspector General's Report on Plots to Assassinate Fidel Castro," May 23, 1967, approved for release in 1993 under the CIA Historical Review Program. The report describes the various capers the CIA engaged in during their attempts to "eliminate" Fidel Castro, at http://www.parascope.com/mx/articles/castroreport.htm. Accessed June 6, 2017.

U.S. and eventual U.S. hostility toward the regime. These developments combined to facilitate the emergence of two terrorism problems for the United States. The first was an aircraft hijacking problem that emerged in the U.S. in the 1960s. The second problem was the development in the 1960s and 1970s of anti-Castro terrorist activity in the U.S. carried out by militant Cuban exile groups.

The exodus from Communist Cuba contributed to the emergence of internal aircraft hijackings in the 1960s as some Cuban exiles sought to return to Cuba by seizing U.S. aircraft and forcing them to fly to Cuba. At first, the hijackings involved anti-Castro Cubans hijacking planes from Cuba and escaping to the U.S., but that changed in 1961, after the U.S. broke diplomatic relations with Cuba. During the late 1960s, it was common for U.S. commercial planes to be hijacked and diverted to Cuba. From 1961 to 1968, 21 aircraft were hijacked to Cuba and all but one were taken to Cuba.[93] Most of these hijackings were carried out as a political statement or conducted by homesick Cubans as a way around the U.S. travel ban to Cuba. There was a surge in hijackings of U.S. planes from 1968 to 1972, peaking in 1969.[94] These hijackings to Cuba became so common that U.S. pilots who flew in the southern United States carried maps of Havana's airport, and the Swiss Embassy in Washington, D.C., which handled U.S. affairs in Cuba, had forms prepared in advance for U.S. requests for Cuba to return the aircraft.[95] The wave of Cuban hijackings declined around 1972 as a result of new anti-hijacking laws and better protective security measures at airports. Moreover, Cuba made hijacking a crime in October 1970, and in December 1970, 50 countries approved the Convention for the Suppression of Unlawful Seizure of Aircraft, commonly known as the Hague Convention. This convention outlined the responsibilities of the signatories in terms of capturing and bringing the hijackers to trial. In 1973, the United States and Cuba reached an agreement that allowed either country to request the extradition of a hijacker. This agreement was mutually beneficial to both countries as many Cubans had hijacked planes from Cuba and forced them to fly to the United States and vice versa.

U.S. government tolerance for anti-Castro militancy, albeit overseas, also had domestic consequences. The second terrorism problem caused by Castro's revolution in Cuba was the emergence of terrorist activity in the U.S. by Cuban exile groups that were aimed primarily at Cuban and Cuban-related targets. Most

---

[93] Timothy Naftali, *Blind Spot: The Secret History of American Counterterrorism* (New York: Basic Books, 2005), pp. 19–20.

[94] For a chronology of aircraft hijackings between the U.S. and Cuba, at http://en.wikipedia.org/wiki/List_of_Cuba-US_aircraft_hijackings. Accessed June 7, 2017.

[95] Naftali, *Blind Spot*, p. 20.

Cuban exiles in the United States were content to form political organizations to initially lobby the U.S. government to oppose and overthrow Castro's regime. When an overthrow appeared unlikely, the exiles advocated for trade and travel negotiations so that exiles could visit families in Cuba. However, there was always a minority element within the Cuban American community that advocated, engaged in, and supported the use of violence against Cuban interests in and outside the U.S. This attitude produced the formation of about a dozen militant organizations[96] like Alpha 66, Commandos L, Abdala, the Insurrectional Jose Marti Movement, 17th of April Movement, the Cuban Revolutionary Directorate, Joven Cuba, Revolutionary Alliance, the National Christian Movement, the Cuban Revolutionary Council, the Cuban Nationalist Movement (CNM), the Cuban National Liberation Front (FLNC), Cuban Power (el Poder Cubano), and the 2506 Brigade.[97] The last four groups gathered on June 11, 1976 in Santo Domingo and formed a group called the "Coordination of United Revolutionary Organizations" or CORU, which the FBI classified as a terrorist umbrella organization. Orlando Bosch was selected as its leader.[98]

CORU initiated a terrorist campaign in Miami, Trinidad, Guyana, and Mexico. By one account, Cuban militant exile groups carried out attacks in 16 countries.[99] CORU claimed responsibility for the October 6, 1976 mid-air bombing of Cubana Flight 455 from Barbados to Jamaica, killing 73 people, in what was at the time the deadliest terrorist airline attack in the Western hemisphere. Four anti-Castro Cuban exiles were later arrested and tried for this attack. The

---

[96] In the words of Lieutenant Tom Lyons, head of a special tactical investigation bureau to combat terrorism set up by the Miami Metro Public Safety Department: "Even trying to identify a group and its membership is almost impossible. A few years ago, there were about 105 different groups. Now the names have changed. Some people hold multi-memberships. We're getting death lists with 15 to 30 people on each, all of them different. All from different organizations, or maybe they're the same organization with different names. Some exiles often switch from one group to another for personal or ideological reasons. What can I tell you?" As quoted in Dick Russell, "Little Havana's Reign of Terror," *New Times*, October 29, 1976. An unclassified CIA report titled "International Terrorism in 1979," op cit., noted 37 "names" used by anti-Castro terrorist organizations (p.20).

[97] In claiming responsibility for some terrorist attacks, the above organizations used operational pseudonyms like Omega 7, M-17, Latin American Anti-Communist Forces or ELAC, GIN, Youth of the Star, the Zero organization, and El Condor.

[98] Miami Field Office, FBI, Memo # 2-471, dated August 15, 1978, titled "Coordination of United Revolutionary Organizations," at http://www.gwu.edu/~nsarchiv/NSAEBB/NSAEBB153/19780816. pdf. Accessed June 4, 2017.

[99] Jim Mullen, "The Burden of a Violent History," *Miami New Times*, April 20, 2000.

Venezuelan intelligence service was also implicated in this attack.[100] In fact, CORU sent statements to news organizations two months before the Cubana de Aviación explosion warning that "very soon we will be attacking jetliners in flight."[101] Although some CORU planning and financial activity took place in the United States, CORU refrained from carrying out terrorist attacks on U.S. soil until the late 1970s. CORU was also involved in the September 21, 1976 remote-detonated car-bombing assassination of Orlando Letelier, a former Chilean diplomat, and Ronni Moffitt, his 25-year-old American associate, in Washington, D.C. Four Cuban exiles were involved in the assassination on behalf of the Chilean National Intelligence Directorate, or secret police, known as DINA.[102] In fact, President Pinochet of Chile "personally ordered his intelligence chief to carry out the murders ... and decided to 'stonewall' the U.S. investigation in order to hide his 'involvement' ..."[103] The Letelier assassination was the first act of political violence against a Chilean exile in this country. The Letelier assassination was, until September 11, 2001, the most flagrant and infamous international terrorist attack in the U.S. capital.[104] Despite the emergence of CORU, there was little coordination and centralization of Cuban exile terrorist activity in the 1960s and 1970s.

---

[100] "Luis Posada Carriles — The Declassified Record: CIA and FBI Documents Detail Career in International Terrorism; Connection to U.S.," National Security Archive Electronic Briefing Book No. 153, at http://www.gwu.edu/~nsarchiv/NSAEBB/NSAEBB153. Accessed June 6, 2017.

[101] Kirk Nielsen, "Terrorists, but Our Terrorists: Where can terrorists find safe harbor? If you're of the Cuban exile variety, right here," *Miami New Times*, December 20, 2001.

[102] Kenneth Bredemeier, "Cuban Exiles Guilty in Letelier Death," *Washington Post*, February 15, 1979, p. A1. On February 14, 1979, three anti-Castro Cuban exiles were convicted on all counts in connection with the 1976 assassination of Letelier and the Directorate of National Intelligence was implicated as the masterminds of the attack. See also, declassified U.S. government report titled "The Letelier Case: Background and Factual Summary," at https://foia.state.gov/Search/results.aspx?searc hText=The+Letelier+Case%3A+Background+and+Factual+Summary&beginDate=&endDate=&pub lishedBeginDate=&publishedEndDate=&caseNumber. Accessed June 3, 2017.

[103] U.S. Department of State, Memorandum from George P. Shultz to the President, "Pinochet and the Letelier-Moffitt Murders: Implications for U.S. Policy," dated October 6, 1987, at https://nsarchive2.gwu.edu/NSAEBB/NSAEBB532-The-Letelier-Moffitt-Assassination-Papers/letelierdocument.pdf. Accessed June 5, 2017.

[104] David Binder, "Opponents of Chilean Junta Slain in Washington by Bomb in his Auto," *New York Times*, September 22, 1976; Saul Landau and Ralph Stavins, "This is how it was done: An account of the murder of Orlando Letelier and Ronni Moffitt," *The Nation*, March 26, 1977; "Did Chilean Agents Seek Exiles as Assassins?" *Miami Herald*, November 9, 1976.

The nexus of anti-Castro, Cuban exile terrorism in the United States was Miami, Florida.[105] In the late 1960s, there were about 1.5 million Cubans living in the United States. The majority lived in the Miami area, about 400–500,000 Cubans. The Cuban American community, especially in the Miami area, was never unified. There was infighting among the various political and social organizations over goals and methods and competition for the hearts and money of the Cuban American community. Some wanted the U.S. to adopt a more hardline, isolationist attitude toward the Castro regime while others believed it was better to coexist with the regime and engage in cultural and economic exchanges and allow travel to Cuba in order to undermine the communists. Militant groups were in competition with each other for the hearts and minds, and wallets of Cuban exiles living in Latin America. Some exile militant groups were also involved in criminal activities and some of their attacks were driven by criminal rather than political motives. There were also personal vendettas, or feuding inside the local "Cuban Mafia." To further complicate the Cuban exile terrorism landscape, some Latin American countries used the Cuban exiles for their own anti-Castro purposes.[106] Cuban intelligence agents also operated in the U.S. during this time. Historically, the government of Cuba has considered its principal target in the United States to be the anti-Castro groups. The Cuban intelligence services actively directed assets in the United States to report on the plans, objectives, goals, and personnel of the various anti-Castro groups. The Intelligence services were known to use their assets in the United States to attempt to confuse and fragment the exile community. There were reports that the Cuban intelligence service had a special unit called the "Exile Immigration Division" that was charged with targeting members of the Cuban American community.[107] All of these elements combined to create a confusing and shifting terrorism landscape

---

[105] See, U.S. Senate, Committee on the Judiciary, Subcommittee to Investigate the Administration of the Internal Security Act and Other Internal Security Laws, *Hearings — "Terroristic Activity — Terrorism in the Miami Area,"* May 6, 1976, at http://www.latinamericanstudies.org/belligerence/judiciary-committee-5-6-1976.pdf. Accessed May 4, 2016; and International Association Chiefs of Police, "Needs Assessment Study: Terrorism in Dade County," July 1979, at http://www.latinameri-canstudies.org/belligerence/Terrorism_Dade_County.pdf. Accessed June 7, 2017.

[106] Juan DeOnis, "Anti-Castro Extremists Tolerated, If Not Encouraged, by Some Latin American Nations," *New York Times*, November 15, 1976.

[107] In March 2011, Roberto Hernandez Del Llano, a Cuban agent and a major in the state security division of the Cuban Interior Ministry, testified that a separate wing of the intelligence agency, the Exile Immigration Division, targeted members of the Cuban American exile community, saying its "fundamental duty is looking for, locating and liquidating Luis Posada Carriles." Luis Posada Carriles was a prominent militant Cuban American exile leader. Will Weissert, "Cuba out to kill militant on trial in US," *Associated Press*, March 30, 2011.

in the Miami area. This landscape triggered the creation of one of the first joint counter-terrorism task forces in the United States:

> *In October 1975, an anti-terrorist coordinating committee composed of representatives from the Dade County Public Safety Department, the city of Miami Police Department, the FBI, the U.S. Customs, Immigration, and Naturalization, and the Bureau of Alcohol, Tobacco, and Firearms met to coordinate at a supervisory level a cooperative effort between federal and state law enforcement agencies on terrorism in the Dade County area.*[108]

As in the 1960s, Cuban exile terrorism in the 1970s targeted perceived external and internal enemies. The primary external enemy was the Castro government and its diplomatic, commercial, and cultural facilities in and outside the United States. Secondary external enemies were those countries who maintained diplomatic, commercial, and cultural ties with Cuba, primarily other communist countries and certain Western countries like Japan, Great Britain, France, Canada, and Latin American countries like Costa Rica, Venezuela, Panama, and Mexico. In addition, if a Latin American country arrested a key Cuban exile militant, it was pressured to release the militant with a series of terrorist attacks. In 1976, when

---

[108] U.S. Senate Hearings, Committee of the Judiciary, Sub-Committee to Investigate the Administration of the Internal Security Act and other Internal Security Laws. *Terroristic Activity: Terrorists in the Miami Area*, Part Eight., May 8, 1976, p. 609. Despite this effort of coordination, there was still tension between the FBI, CIA, and Dade County law enforcement authorities. For example, in early 1976, "when the reign of terror began to escalate in Miami, the Metro Police placed an unusual request to CIA headquarters. They wanted a list of all exiles trained in bomb-making and, if possible, an accounting of all C-4 and C-3 plastic explosives left behind when the CIA closed its school. So far, the list has not been received" — Dick Russell, "Little Havana's Reign of Terror," *New Times*, October 29, 1976. Moreover, "The Miami Police Department's relationship with the FBI on terrorism cases has been compromised by an unexplained leak and the association of some Cuban detectives who socialized with suspected terrorists or sympathized with the goals of anti-Castro militants. Three police officers between 1977 and 1980 were disciplined or asked to be transferred because of their associations with suspected terrorists or anti-Castro militants, *The Herald* learned. In 1979, some of the department's secret intelligence reports, including intercepted plans for a bombing attack at Miami International Airport, fell into the hands of suspected terrorists. Terrorism investigations have been hurt by the FBI's distrust of local police and the agency's traditional reluctance to share information or work closely with local detectives" (*Source*: Jim McGee, "FBI agents, police stub toes in terrorism investigations," *Miami Herald*, December 15, 1983). To underline the active terrorist environment in the Miami area at this time, it was reported that from April 1975 to October 1976, there were more than 100 bombings and an average assassination of one a week (*Source*: Dick Russell, "Little Havana's Reign of Terror," op. cit.).

Orlando Bosch was arrested by Venezuelan authorities for the bombing of Cubana Flight 455, his supporters within a 9-month period placed five bombs in Venezuelan establishments. The targets were two VIASA (Venezuelan Airlines) ticket offices (in San Juan and Miami), a Venezuelan Air Force DC-9 at the Miami International Airport, the Venezuelan Mission to the U.N. in New York City, and the Venezuelan Consulate in San Juan. The internal enemies were Cuban Americans who the militants felt were too sympathetic to the Castro regime, opposed the militants, or did not provide adequate financial support to the militants. Cuban exile terrorism was carried out primarily in Latin America and the United States with a few attacks in Western Europe, mostly in Spain.

From 1970 to 1979, Cuban exile groups in the United States carried out at least 119 bombings aimed at British, Mexican, Spanish, Canadian, Japanese, Yugoslav, Cuban, Panamanian, Russian, Costa Rican, Dominican, and French diplomatic missions and tourist offices in New York City, Miami, Chicago, and Los Angeles. These countries were targeted because they had friendly relations with Cuba. In addition, some of these bombings were aimed at Cuban exile interests that were owned by persons suspected of not supporting the militant exile groups. U.S. targets, such as courthouses and federal law enforcement agencies, were occasionally targeted when Cuban exile terrorists were arrested. For example, from December 3 to 4, 1975, Cuban exile terrorists placed eight bombs in the Miami, Florida area. Most of these bombs were placed in government buildings such as post offices, social security offices, the State Attorney's office in Miami, and even in the Miami FBI office. During the 1970s, 13 Cuban exiles were assassinated in the United States by suspected rival militant groups. Most of these assassinations took place in the Miami area. Outside Cuba and the United States, Cuban exile groups have been linked to the deaths of 79 people, including 73 killed on October 6, 1976 when a bomb exploded on a Cuban airliner en route from Cuba to Barbados. Of the 73 dead, 57 were Cubans, 11 Guyanese — most of them students on scholarships in Cuba — and five were North Korean cultural officials. An additional terrorism by-product of the Cuban exile terrorist activity was that Castro, to get even with the United States, provided financial and logistical support to the Armed Forces of the National Liberation Front (FALN), a Puerto Rican separatist group that was responsible for about 100 bombings in New York City, Chicago, and Washington, D.C. in the 1970s.[109]

---

[109] Joe Crankshaw and Gloria Marina, "Miami a Hotbed for Terrorism," *Miami Herald*, November 29, 1976. "Federal investigators have identified one of the bombers working with FALN as Filiberto Ojeda Rios, 42, a member of the Cuban Directorate of Intelligence (DGI) or secret police. Ojeda Rios, code-named 'Ruben', was identified in at least nine FALN bombings last year."

Omega 7

While there were over a dozen Cuban exile terrorist groups active in the U.S. in the 1960s and the first half of the 1970s, one group emerged during the Ford administration that became the most notorious — Omega 7. This Miami, Florida-based anti-Castro Cuban terrorist group was formed on September 11, 1974, by Eduardo Arocena. The name Omega 7 comes from the fact that there were seven original members from different anti-Castro Cuban factions.[110] The number of individuals actively participating in this group was believed to be less than 20 members. However, Omega 7 was condoned and supported by the Cuban Nationalist Movement (CNM), whose membership and resources were considerably larger. The CNM, a violent anti-Castro Cuban exile group, was founded in 1960. However, pressure on the CNM as a result of the September 21, 1976 car-bomb assassination of the former Chilean Ambassador Orlando Letelier, and the arrest of Armando Santana, its leader in the late 1970s, essentially destroyed the CNM.

The main areas of operation for the Omega 7 were the New York, New Jersey, and Miami, Florida areas. Its primary targets were representatives of the Cuban government, or any individual, organization, facility, or business that dealt with, or supported in any way, the communist government of Fidel Castro, including Cuban Americans in the U.S. The group carried out 36 (33 in the Miami, Florida area) attacks during the Ford administration.[111] The majority of the Omega 7 attacks were bombings, followed by shootings and assassinations. Its terrorist attacks were usually well-planned and flawlessly executed. Many of the Omega 7 members were veterans of the U.S.-supported failed 1961 Bay of Pigs invasion of Cuba who were trained in demolition, intelligence, and commando techniques. Their expertise, combined with the financial resources available to them through the exiled Cuban community in the U.S., gave the Omega 7 an almost unlimited potential for terrorist activity. After Omega 7 was formed, it remained independent of both the CNM and several other militant Cuban exile

---

[110]The origin of the group's name is murky. A statement issued by the organization in late 1979 seemed to offer a partial explanation. "'We shall continue to struggle in foreign lands until we reach the 'Omega' stage to complete plans of bringing the struggle to Cuban soil,' the statement said. "Omega" is the last letter of the Greek alphabet. Joseph B. Treaster, "Suspected Head of Omega-7 Terrorist Group Seized," *New York Times*, July 23, 1983, at http://www.nytimes.com/1983/07/23/nyregion/suspected-head-of-omega-7-terrorist-group-seized.html. Accessed May 3, 2016.

[111]http://www.latinamericanstudies.org/belligerence/Cuban-Militant-Organizations-AB-225.pdf. Accessed August 4, 2016; and http://www.eurekaencyclopedia.com/index.php/Category: Anti-Cuba_Terrorist_Campaign. Accessed May 3, 2016.

groups, although individuals from the various groups continued to associate with each other.

Omega 7 committed its first act of terrorism on February 1, 1975, when it detonated a bomb at the Venezuelan consulate in New York City to protest that government's recent resumption of diplomatic relations with Cuba. In June 1976, it set off a bomb at the Cuban Mission to the United Nations. Then, on September 16, 1976, the group bombed a Soviet cargo ship docked in Port Elizabeth, New Jersey, where Arocena worked as a longshoreman. Arocena himself swam out to plant the bomb on the ship's hull with magnets. While Omega 7 was active, a significant portion of the Cuban exile community in the U.S., especially in the Miami and New York/New Jersey area, saw the terrorist attacks against Cuban officials and Castro supporters in the U.S. as part of the Cuban people's struggle against Communist Cuba. Like most anti-communist terrorist groups, Omega 7 members believed they were liberators of the Cuban people and wanted to see Cuba free of Castro and communism. The Cuban diaspora in the U.S. provided money to these militant groups and rarely provided information on them to law enforcement agencies. It should be noted that intimidation by these groups played a role in these services. Omega 7 continued its terrorist activity at a higher rate during the Carter administration.

Anti-Turkish, Armenian Terrorism

Background: Armenians contend that in 1915 the Ottoman Empire implemented the deliberate and systematic destruction of Armenians during and after World War I. It was carried out through massacres and deportations, with the deportations consisting of forced marches designed to lead to the death of the Armenians. The total number of Armenian fatalities is generally believed to have been around 1.5 million. Armenians consider this event to be the first modern genocide. The starting date of the genocide is traditionally noted to be April 24, 1915. On that date, Ottoman authorities arrested around 250 Armenian intellectuals and community leaders in Constantinople. To this day, the Republic of Turkey, the successor state of the Ottoman Empire, denies that the word genocide is an accurate description of the events. However, as of 2019, 32 countries have officially recognized the events of the period as genocide, and most genocide scholars and historians accept this view.[112] After the genocide, Armenian militants engaged in

---

[112] "Armenian Genocide Recognition" at https://en.wikipedia.org/wiki/Armenian_Genocide_recognition. Accessed June 3, 2017. On October 29, 2019, the U.S. House of Representatives passed a bill by 405-11 vote recognizing this genocide. On December 12, 2019, the U.S. Senate unanimously passed a similar resolution recognizing the genocide. As of January 2020, there has been no action of the President.

a sporadic terrorist campaign against Ottoman leaders who they thought were responsible for the genocide. As a result, a secret organization called "Nemesis," which was a reference to the Greek goddess of revenge, was established in the 1920s to track down and execute those Ottoman leaders. From 1920 to 1922, eight Ottoman leaders were assassinated in Berlin, Rome, Constantinople, Tbilisi, and Tajikistan. The most prominent victim was Talat Pasha or target "Number One," one of the primary architects of the Armenian genocide who was hiding out in Berlin. He was killed there by a 24-year-old Armenian student on March 15, 1921. The assassin told the German police after his arrest: "It is not I who am the murderer; it is Talat. I have lived only to revenge."[113] The Nemesis group also executed several Armenian spies and traitors, who, by denouncing their ethnicity to Turkish authorities, were responsible for their deaths. Nemesis was either disbanded or adopted another operational name following the incidents of the early 1920s. About 50 years later, a new sustained terrorist campaign by militant Armenians was directed at Turkey.

In the 1970s, a younger generation of Armenians, especially in the Armenian diaspora, who believed that the non-violent approaches by their parents consistently failed to compel the Turkish government to admit to the genocide and to pay reparations, decided to engage in a terrorism campaign against the Turkish state. The event that triggered the emergence of Armenian terrorist organizations took place on January 27, 1973, when Gourgen Yanikian, a 78-year-old Armenian emigrant who survived the Armenian genocide, shot and killed two Turkish diplomats in Los Angeles. He reportedly stated afterward: "I'm not Gourgen M. Yanikian but unacknowledged history coming back for the 1,500,000 Armenians whose bones desecrate my invisible existence."[114] Yanikian's revenge attack inspired some Armenian youth to use violence to compel the Turkish government to admit to the genocide and pay reparations. They also sought revenge.

---

[113] As quoted in an obituary of the assassin, Solomon Teilirian, in *Time* magazine of June 6, 1960. Teilirian died in San Francisco in 1960. The assassination of Talat Pasha was the subject of an Armenian movie in 1982 called "Assignment Berlin." For more information on the Armenian organization "Nemesis," at http://www.operationnemesis.com/. Accessed June 4, 2016, and Jacques Derogy, *Resistance and Revenge: The Armenian Assassination of Turkish Leaders Responsible for the 1915 Massacres and Deportations*, Trans. A. M. Barret, (Transaction Publishers, 1990); and "Operation Nemesis" at https://en.wikipedia.org/wiki/Operation_Nemesis. Accessed May 4, 2017.

[114] Richard G. Hovannisian, "The Armenian Genocide: Wartime Radicalization or Premeditated Continuum?" in *The Armenian Genocide: Cultural and Ethical Legacies*. Edited by Richard G. Hovannisian (New Brunswick, NJ: Transaction Publishers, 2007), p. 72. Yanikian claimed that 26 of his relatives were killed during the Armenian genocide and after. He received a life sentence for the killings, was paroled in 1984, and died that year at 88 years.

The first Armenian terrorist organization to emerge was the Armenian Secret Army for the Liberation of Armenia or ASALA. This group surfaced in 1975 in Beirut, Lebanon, initially, under the name of "The Prisoner Kurken Yanikian Group." The group's first attack took place on January 20, 1975 when it bombed the Beirut offices of the World Council of Churches. The group's first acknowledged killing was the assassination of the Turkish diplomat in Vienna on October 22, 1975. The two most notorious ASALA attacks were the following: (1) the August 7, 1982 Esenboga airport attack in Ankara, Turkey when ASALA targeted non-diplomat civilians for the first time — nine people were killed and 82 injured in the attack, and (2) the July 15, 1983 Orly airport attack in Paris when a suitcase bomb exploded at the Turkish Airlines check-in desk, killing eight people.

A second Armenian terrorist organization called the Justice Commandos of Armenian Genocide (JCAG) also emerged in 1975 and was an ideological competitor of ASALA. It could be argued that JCAG formed as a response to ASALA in order to compete for the support of the discontented Armenian youth in the diaspora. JCAG was a more right-wing, nationalist organization while ASALA was a Marxist-Leninist organization influenced by the Palestinian nationalist movement. Left-wing Armenian youths observed how Palestinian terrorism overseas attracted attention to the Palestinian cause. Both the Armenians and Palestinians believe they lost their homelands, and both had large diaspora communities. ASALA and JCAG understood that terrorism would attract international attention for their cause, that is, acknowledgement of the Armenian holocaust of 1915. While both ASALA and JCAG formally called for the establishment of an independent Armenia consisting of northeastern Turkey, northern Iran, and Soviet Armenia, it is clear that their more attainable objectives were the following: (1) to take revenge on the Turkish state, (2) to attract attention to the Armenian cause, (3) to force the Turkish government to admit to the 1915 genocide, and (4) to compel the Turkish government to pay reparations to the Armenian people.

As competitors for the hearts, minds, and money of the Armenian diaspora, both organizations periodically claimed responsibility for each other's actions. In addition, both groups had the tendency to use different commando names when carrying out attacks. ASALA used commando names such as "The Orly Group," "The 3rd of October Organization," "Yanikian Commandos," "The June 9 Organization," "Youth Action Group," "May 28 Armenian Organization," "Armenian Group of 28," "The Zaven Apetian Commando," "Yeghia Keshishian Suicide Commando Van Operation," "Khirimian Harik Suicide Commando," and "New Armenian Resistance." JCAG changed its operational name in 1983 to the "Armenian Revolutionary Army" and also used the name "Greek-Bulgarian-Armenian Front."

Armenian terrorists were operational from 1973 to 1983 and carried out 214 terrorist attacks in 23 countries, mostly in Western Europe and the United States.[115] They killed 31 Turkish diplomats and their family members, and 38 innocent bystanders, including three Americans. They injured 353 persons. Tactically, Armenian terrorists carried out bombings, rocket attacks, car bombings, assassinations, arson attacks, embassy seizures, and grenade attacks. As for targets, they attacked airline offices, tourist offices, embassies, diplomats, airports, and train stations. While JCAG only attacked Turkish targets, ASALA hit Turkish, French, Swiss, and some U.S. targets. France, Switzerland, and the United States were targeted because they arrested and imprisoned Armenian terrorists. The last known Armenian terrorist attack was by ASALA on December 19, 1991, when it attempted to assassinate the Turkish Ambassador to Budapest.

Armenian terrorism emerged in the decade of the 1970s but did not reach its operational peak until the 1980s. Both ASALA and JCAG were formed in 1975, 60 years after the Armenian massacre. Why did two Armenian terrorist groups emerge at that time to take revenge on Turkey? First, as previously noted, the 1973 assassination of two Turkish diplomats by a 78-year-old survivor of the 1915 Armenian genocide who lost 26 members of his family in the genocide acted as an inspirational spark for some Armenian youth in the Armenian diaspora, especially in Lebanon, the birthplace of ASALA. Second, these same youths had observed how successful militant Palestinian nationalists had been in using international terrorist activity to attract international attention to their cause. From its inception in January 1975, ASALA received support from the Palestine Liberation Organization (PLO), in particular the Marxist Popular Front for the Liberation of Palestine (PFLP).[116] Third, in the late 1960s and early 1970s, terrorism emerged

---

[115] All statistics on Armenian terrorism come from the following sources: (1) Andrew Corsun, "Armenian Terrorism: A Profile," *Department of State Bulletin: The Official Monthly Record of United States Foreign Policy*, Special Issue - Terrorism, Volume 82, Number 2065, August 1982, pp. 31–35, and (2) Anat Kurz and Ariel Merari, *ASALA — Irrational Terror or Political Tool*, Jaffee Center for Strategic Studies #2, Tel Aviv University (Colorado: Westview Press, 1985). See also, Declassified CIA study on Armenian terrorism, dated January 1984, at http://www.foia.cia.gov/sites/default/files/document_conversions/89801/DOC_0005462031.pdf, May 4, 2017. For extended academic studies on Armenian Terrorism, see Michael Gunter, *Pursuing the Just Cause of their People — A Study of Contemporary Armenian Terrorism*, (Westport: Greenwood Press, 1986), and Francis P. Hyland, *Armenian Terrorism: The Past, the Present, the Prospects* (Boulder: Westview Press, 1991).

[116] Kurz and Merari, *ASALA — Irrational Terror*, p. 16.

for some militants as a preferred and attractive method to address political and social grievances. Ethnic and left-wing militant organizations were forming to redress historical and current complaints — real or imagined — of their respective constituencies. These three developments produced a conducive environment for the emergence of a militant Armenian organization. In addition, a 1974 report by a United Nations committee on the rights of man failed to mention the 1915 Armenian genocide.[117] It appeared that the international community, subjected to Turkish diplomatic pressure, was ignoring the Armenian genocide.

Terrorist organizations are generally formed not by committees, conferences, or conventions but by one or more "militant activists" — individuals who believe that armed struggle is the only effective option to redress the grievances of their discontented constituency. In ASALA's case, that man was Hagop Hagopian. Hagopian received his terrorist training from Wadi Haddad, the head of the PFLP's "foreign operations branch" in the late 1960s. He reportedly participated in several PFLP attacks, including the February 6, 1974 takeover of the Japanese embassy in Kuwait.[118] Hagopian's acquaintances at the time were key PFLP and JRA operatives, and the notorious international terrorist Carlos.[119] Around 1973, Abu Iyad, the deputy chief and head of intelligence for the PLO, and the second most senior official in Yasir Arafat's Fatah political party, asked Hagopian why no one had yet created an Armenian group similar to his own Palestinian Black September Organization.[120] Hagopian, along with another Armenian, Kevork Ajemian, accepted this challenge and established ASALA in Beirut in late 1974. In the late 1970s, ASALA never had more than a dozen operatives. However, ASALA's initial attacks in 1975 worried the right-wing Armenian Revolutionary Federation or "Dashnaks" which saw the ASALA "actions" as enticing to young Armenians, including its own youth group. To mitigate the flow of young Armenians to ASALA, the Dashnaks set up JCAG, an alternative Armenian terrorist organization, in October 1975. From this point on, ASALA and JCAG,

---

[117] Ibid.

[118] Markar Melkonian, *My Brother's Road: An American's Fateful Journey to Armenia* (New York: I.B. Tauris, 2005), p. 76. This is an excellent book that provides background and insights into the development of ASALA and the internal feuds within the group. These feuds eventually led to the assassination of Hagop Hagopian on April 28, 1988 in Athens. Initially, the Turkish government was the primary suspect. However, the author believes that given the number of enemies Hagopian made within ASALA, this was most likely a settlement of accounts within ASALA.

[119] Ibid. Illich Ramirez Sanchez, aka: Carlos, was a Venezuela Marxist revolutionary who attained international notoriety by carrying bold terrorist attacks in the 1970s and 1980s, initially, on behalf of the Palestinian movement, later on behalf of states like Libya, Iraq, and Syria.

[120] Ibid., pp. 76–77.

occasionally using different operational aliases, competed in attacking Turkish targets worldwide. From 1975 to 1979, Armenian terrorists carried out 42 attacks in 14 countries that primarily consisted of bombings and also involved 11 assassinations and two attempted assassinations.

Aside from Yanikian's assassination of two Turkish diplomats in Santa Barbara, California in January 1973, there were only two additional Armenian attacks in the U.S. in the 1970s. On October 26, 1973, there was an attempted bombing of the Turkish Information Office in New York City. A previously unknown group calling itself the "Yanikian Commandos" claimed responsibility and demanded the release of Yanikian. Since neither ASALA nor JCAG were formed at the time, it is likely that the New York incident was carried out by disgruntled Armenian youths who were inspired by Yanikian's assassinations. Similarly, on April 4, 1973, Armenian youths in Paris threw tear gas grenades at the offices of the Turkish Consul General and Turkish airlines. Any acts of suspected Armenian terrorism carried out before January 1975 cannot be attributed to any militant Armenian organization, but to individuals. The only other Armenian terrorist attack carried out in the U.S. in the 1970s occurred on October 3, 1977 when a bomb detonated at the house of Professor Stanford Shaw, who taught Ottoman history at the University of California in Los Angeles. Shaw wrote a book that stated that the Turks never carried out genocide against the Armenians. Responsibility for the attack was claimed by an "Armenian Group of 28." The "28" most likely refers to May 28 — the commemoration of the declaration of the Armenian republic in 1915. It is unlikely the 1977 attack was carried out by either ASALA or JCAG. It was probably carried out by one or two Armenians in the Los Angeles area, operating independently, who were inspired by the ASALA and JCAG attacks taking place overseas. Similar examples of American citizens being externally inspired to carry out terrorist attacks would emerge after the 9/11 attacks. By the time of the bombing of Professor Shaw's house, ASALA and JCAG were notorious in the Armenian American community in the Los Angeles area. However, neither group had an operational presence in the U.S. Supporters and sympathizers yes, but no offensive cells. The above three attacks were most likely examples of Armenian leaderless terrorism.

In 1978, a young Armenian American from California named Monte Melkonian left the U.S. to go to Iran and eventually ended up in Beirut where he ultimately contacted ASALA. Melkonian became one of the key leaders and operatives of ASALA in the 1980s. He also became the highest-ranking Armenian American in ASALA. Armenians began to arrive in the United States in the late nineteenth century, most notably after the Hamidian Massacres of 1894–1896 that were carried out by the Ottoman Empire against Armenians. The 1915 massacre of Armenians also contributed to an increase in Armenian immigration to the U.S. This wave of Armenian immigration lasted until the mid-1920s. Subsequent Armenian immigrant flows took place in the 1960s and 1970s as a result of instability in Middle Eastern countries where Armenians lived. These immigrations resulted in the presence of about 475,000 Armenians in the United States. Most Armenians lived in Los Angeles, Boston, New York, Detroit, Chicago, and San Francisco. More importantly, the Armenian American community consisted largely of descendants of the survivors of the Armenian massacres in the 1890s and the subsequent 1915 Armenian genocide.[121] It could be argued that there was a high sensitivity among Armenian Americans to the genocide issue and an inherent tendency to sympathize or support ASALA and JCAG in their attacks on Turkish targets. This sympathetic environment contributed to the burst of ASALA and JCAG terrorist activity in the U.S. in the 1980s.

Anti-Yugoslav, Croatian Terrorism

Background: Another example of foreign spillover terrorism in the United States was the activities of militant Croatian and, to a lesser extent, Serbian émigré elements directed at Yugoslav targets in the United States. The Socialist Federal Republic of Yugoslavia was founded in 1946 as a multi-ethnic communist federation consisting of the socialist republics of Croatia, Slovenia, Macedonia, Serbia, Bosnia and Herzegovina, and Montenegro. The two most important and largest republics were Croatia and Serbia. Although composed of different ethnic groups, ethnic tensions in Communist Yugoslavia were effectively managed by the government using oppressive measures. In the 1970s, however, a nationalist movement emerged in Croatia that demanded more rights for Croatia, greater civil rights, democratic reform, the decentralization of the Yugoslav economy, and the use of the Croatian language in schools and media. This has been referred to as the "Croatian Spring." Croatian nationalists believed that Yugoslav state authorities were imposing the Serbian language as the official language. The Yugoslav leadership interpreted the Croatian Spring as an attempt at restoration of Croatian nationalism, dismissed the movement as chauvinistic, and arrested most of its important leaders. In a controlled communist state like Yugoslavia, militant Croatian nationalists found it difficult to consistently operate inside Yugoslavia.

---

[121] Information on Armenian immigrant flows into the U.S. from Kirakosian, Arman Dzh. (ed.), *The Armenian Massacres, 1894–1896: U.S. Media Testimony* (Detroit: Wayne State University Press, 2004), p. 11.

As a result, the most active Croatian militants were living outside Yugoslavia, primarily in Western Europe and the United States. They formed Croatian resistance organizations like the Croatian National Resistance (CNR, aka: OTPOR), the Croatian Revolutionary Brotherhood, and the Croatian Revolutionary Movement or Ustashi. Their objective was to establish an independent Croatian state. Their support came from the Croatian émigré communities worldwide. It is from within these communities that Croatian émigré terrorism emerged. Some of this terrorist activity was orchestrated by the Croatian resistance organizations mentioned earlier while other attacks were carried out by individuals or autonomous cells — examples of leaderless terrorism. Some attacks were carried out inside Yugoslavia, but most took place outside.

Like Palestinian and Armenian terrorist organizations, Croatian terrorists sought publicity for their cause. Publicity appears to have been the primary motive for these attacks since it was extremely doubtful that such attacks would force the Yugoslav government to give Croatia its independence. As was the case with Cuban exile terrorism, some of the Croatian émigré attacks were aimed at other Croatian émigrés. Unlike Palestinian (Israel) and Armenian (Turkey) terrorists, Croatian émigré terrorists carried out most of their attacks against their primary enemy (Yugoslavia) but also attacked other countries that arrested their operatives. Like Palestinian and Armenian terrorists, it was younger Croatians who fueled the use of political terrorism to redress their grievances. An unfortunate but logical by-product of this émigré terrorism was the brutal response by the Yugoslav intelligence service, the Department of State Security or UDBA. The UDBA was as ruthless, maybe even more so, as the Soviet KGB in liquidating opponents overseas. It has been reported that the UDBA assassinated 72 émigrés from 1960 to 1990, mostly Croatians and Serbians, including four émigrés in the United States.[122] These assassinations served three objectives. Two of

---

[122] http://en.wikipedia.org/wiki/UDBA. Accessed May 4, 2017. Given that these attacks were carried out by an intelligence agency, it is impossible to accurately assess how many assassinations, kidnappings, or bombings were carried out by the UDBA overseas. The author's estimate is that between 65 and 100 Croatian and Serbian émigrés were killed by the UDBA from 1960 to 1989. Partial investigations were undertaken in the Republic of Croatia after it gained independence in 1991; they revealed that the Yugoslav government, through its intelligence-security services, had liquidated 73 Croatian emigrants, of which five are still missing. In a book by Božo Vukušić, secretary of the "The Commission to Certify Postwar Victims of the Communist System Abroad," and the "Committee to Certify War and Postwar Victims," it is written that agents of the Yugoslav secret service killed 69 Croatian emigrants throughout the world between 1946 and 1990, while eight are listed as missing (their disappearance is assumed to be connected to actions of the Yugoslav services). Also, 24 unsuccessful assassinations are recorded, the victims having survived after suffering various degrees of

the objectives were ones that any state engaged in an assassination campaign against dissidents overseas had: (1) eliminate political agitators opposed to the regime, and (2) scare other dissidents and émigrés both at home and abroad. Another objective was to plant in the minds of the host country's government that these killings of émigrés were simply in-fighting among themselves.

Most of these UDBA assassinations took place in Germany, a key battlefield between Croatian émigrés there and the UDBA. In Munich, a whole section of a cemetery was set-aside for Croats assassinated by the UDBA.[123] In fact, after the Fourth Plenary Session of the Yugoslav Communist Party in 1966, the UDBA was reorganized as the State Security Service and one of its listed functions was "to act against anti-Yugoslav political émigrés."[124] During the 1960s, it has been estimated that the UDBA carried out 20 assassinations, four attempted assassinations, and three kidnappings of Croatian and Serbian dissident exiles outside Yugoslavia.[125] Additionally, the UDBA carried out terrorist attacks in an attempt to implicate Croatian and Serbian dissident exile groups. It also infiltrated many of these dissident exile groups. Yugoslav émigrés and some neutral observers claimed that the West ignored the UDBA assassinations because they wanted President Tito to remain in power as a counter-weight to the Soviet Union.[126]

---

injury. Three emigrants were kidnapped, and four kidnap attempts failed, as the victims succeeding in saving themselves" (Source: Ivo Lucic, "Bosnia and Herzegovina and Terrorism, *"National Security and The Future*, 3–4 (2) 2001, p.116). See also, Tomislav Sunic and Nikola Stedul, "Marshal Tito's Killing Fields: Croatian Victims of the Yugoslav Secret Police ... 1945–1990," at http://tomsunic.com/?p=457. Accessed May 9, 2018; and http://studiacroatica.blogspot.com/2010/02/dr-john-r-schindler-agents-provocateurs.html. Accessed May 9, 2018.

[123] Sasha Uzunov, "ASIO'S Poor Record," March 2, 2010, ASIO is the Australian Security Intelligence Organisation, at http://www.scoop.co.nz/stories/HL1003/S00021.htm. Accessed June 23, 2018.

[124] Carl Savich, "Yugoslav Dissidents during the Cold War," July 3, 2007 at http://www.serbianna.com/columns/savich/090.shtml, June 6, 2017.

[125] Tomislav Sunic and Nikola Stedul, "Croatian Victims of the Yugoslav Secret Police Outside former Communist Yugoslavia, 1945–1990," posted on February 17, 2002, at http://www.andrija-hebrang.com/eng/marshal_tito.htm.

[126] "Tito was useful to the West, so UDBA crimes were mostly ignored, even when Yugoslav agents killed abroad, frequently. During the Cold War, UDBA assassinated many more people in the West than the Soviet bloc did, but it has received very little attention — then or since." From a published interview with Dr. John R. Schindler on February 11, 2010. https://ante-rokov-jadrijevic.blogspot.com/2010/02/interview-dr-john-r-schindler_08.html, Accessed June 9, 2018. The *New York Times* reported on August 9–10, 1979 — "The Senate Foreign Relations Committee maintained that the Yugoslavian government conducted extensive intelligence gathering in the United States to spy on and harass their citizens in this country. This was supposedly part of the tacit approval granted by the FBI, CIA, and the State Department. President Carter denied the allegations as not substantiated. In the

From 1962 to 1969, there were 30 terrorist attacks directed against Yugoslav targets outside Yugoslavia.[127] Most, if not all, of these attacks can be attributed to Croatian and Serbian émigré terrorists. Most of these attacks were carried out in West Germany. During this period, three Yugoslav diplomats were assassinated in Stuttgart (Sava Milovanovic), West Berlin (Anton Kolendic), and Bad Godesburg (Momcilo Popovic), Germany, and one was wounded in Munich (Andrija Klaric). In the 1960s, six anti-Yugoslav attacks took place in the United States as well as five attacks on Croatian and Serbian émigrés.

It was in the 1970s that the émigré-UDBA terrorism war escalated[128] From 1970 to 1979, it is estimated that the UDBA killed 28 Croatian émigrés, attempted to kill 13 others, kidnapped one and attempted to kidnap four other émigrés.[129] The first major anti-Yugoslav terrorist attack in the 1970s occurred on February 10, 1971, when two Croatian separatists seized the Yugoslav Consulate in Gothenburg, Sweden for about 24 hours. They demanded that a Croatian nationalist be released from Yugoslav imprisonment. On February 11, they surrendered

---

case of the Yugoslavia government, this goes back to 1969, when at that time a confidential source advised the U.S. government that UDBA agents based here sought to destroy anti-Communist émigré groups. The report further alleged that the Yugoslav consul general in San Francisco engaged in attempts to monitor and intimidate Yugoslav citizens living in the United States and waged war of threats and blackmail. The State Department took no action and the Senate report does not indicate whether the agents are still active." Even Libyan leader Colonel Qaddafi complained about the West's indifference to UDBA attacks. In an interview with the German *Der Spiegel* magazine, he said. "Tito sends his agents to the Federal Republic of Germany in order to liquidate Croatian opponents. But Tito's prestige doesn't suffer at all in Germany. Why should Tito be allowed those things and why am I not allowed to do the same? Moreover, I have never given a personal order to have somebody killed in foreign countries." Op. Cit., Sunic and Stedul, "Croatian Victims of the Yugoslav Secret Police," at http://studiacroatica.blogspot.com/2010/02/dr-john-r-schindler-agents-provocateurs.html. Accessed June 3, 2017.

[127] Unless otherwise noted, all statistics on Anti-Yugoslav terrorist attacks come from unclassified statistical study on "Yugoslav-Related Terrorist Attacks, 1962–July 1982," U.S. Department of State, Office of Security, Threat Analysis Group. Six pages of statistical charts. See also chronology at CIA, National Foreign Assessment Center, Memorandum — Yugoslav Émigré Extremists, May 29, 1980, pp. A1—A8. CIA FOIA document # RDP85T00287R000101220002-6; see also, CIA, Directorate of Intelligence, Intelligence Memorandum: Croatian Émigré Activity, Document #2069/72, September 15, 1972, CIA FOIA document # RDP85T00875R001100130099-4; CIA, Eastern European Intelligencer, #125, July 5, 1972, Document #OCI-0926-72, CIA FOIA document #RDP-79B00864A001200020111-4; FBI, "Overview of Terrorism in the U.S.," April 1983 Lecture to CIA Training Class, pp. 23–24, CIA FOIA document # RDP87S00869R000200280002-3.

[128] See, for example, Malcolm Browne, "Croatian Exiles and Tito's Police Fight Clandestine War Worldwide," *New York Times*, September 12, 1976, p. A1.

[129] Op. Cit., Sunic and Stedul. "Croatian Victims of the Yugoslav Secret Police ..."

and were brought before the Swedish criminal justice system. The two-man group said they belonged to "Jadran" or the Black Legion. The Yugoslav ambassador to Sweden said they were part of the "Ustashi."[130] Western Europe, in particular Sweden and Germany, became the primary operational area for anti-Yugoslav attacks in the 1960s and 1970s. Over 67% of all anti-Yugoslav attacks during these decades took place in these two countries.[131] A confidential memo from the Foreign Ministry in Belgrade to the Yugoslav military mission in West Berlin, dated August 28, 1970 stated the following:

> *With reference to Instruction No. 3827 of 7 May 1970, the following instructions are given at the request of the state secretary and in connection with the recommendation of the cabinet of the president of the republic and the Federal Executive Council:*
>
> *Embassies and other auxiliary offices of the Socialist People's Republic of Yugoslavia are advised to take supplementary measures designed to enhance control over Yugoslav citizens and hostile emigrant organizations ... it is therefore the duty of Yugoslav representative offices to investigate tendencies for political reorientation ... the state security service will initiate certain technical measures and will publicize the requisite disinformation ... to conduct a 'cleanup of the terrain' in West Berlin.*[132]

Attacks were also carried out in France, Austria, Norway, the United States, Paraguay, and Belgium.[133] The most notorious anti-Yugoslav attacks outside the

---

[130] Dan Hansén, doctoral dissertation, "Crisis and Perspectives on Policy Change: Swedish Counter-terrorism Policymaking." Chapter 3 — Croatian Terrorism Challenges Security Policy Structures, at http://www.crismart.org/upload/PDF%20volumes/Volume%2034.pdf. Accessed June 6, 2017. The Ustaša or Croatian Revolutionary Movement was a Croatian fascist, ultranationalist and terrorist organization that was active between 1929 and 1945. Its members murdered hundreds of thousands of Serbs, Jews, Roma (Gypsies) and anti-fascist or dissident Croats in Yugoslavia during World War II, at https://en.wikipedia.org/wiki/Usta%C5%A1e. Accessed July 9, 2018.

[131] According to the West German Federal Criminal Police or BKA, from 1967 to mid-1982, 40 Yugoslav émigrés were killed in West Germany in "obviously politically motivated killings." Claus Bienfait, "Belgrade's Long Reach — Murder of Yugoslavs in the FGR," *Die Welt* (Hamburg), May 7, 1982, pp. 33—35.

[132] Ibid.

[133] Dennis Pluchinsky, "Political Terrorism in Western Europe: Some Themes and Variations," in Yonah Alexander and Kenneth Myers, editors. *Terrorism in Europe* (NY: St. Martin's Press, 1984), pp. 59–60.

United States in the 1970s were the following: (1) the 1971 assassination of the Yugoslav ambassador in Stockholm, (2) the 1972 bombing of a train from Dortmund, Germany to Athens that killed one person, (3) the 1972 hijacking of an SAS plane, and (4) the 1976 assassination of the Yugoslav Consul General in Frankfurt. The January 27, 1972 mid-air bombing of Yugoslav aircraft (JAT Flight 367) on a domestic route that killed 26 people has been attributed to Croatian terrorists, but there is controversy over this attribution.[134] In addition to the above major attacks, there were a half dozen attempted assassinations of Yugoslav diplomats and bombings of Yugoslav diplomatic facilities, airline offices, tourist offices, and businesses in Western Europe. Croatian terrorists were also attempting to establish a base in Paraguay but that failed when they accidentally killed Uruguay's Ambassador to Paraguay, Carlos Abdala, who they thought was a visiting Yugoslav official. One Croatian was subsequently jailed.[135]

In the 1970s, especially from 1978 on, the United States also became a key operational area for anti-Yugoslav terrorists. Both Serb and Croatian militants were active in the United States, but the Croatians were the most active. The United States has a relatively large Croatian population. In 1980, there were about 252,972 Croatian Americans. Most lived in Pennsylvania, Illinois, Ohio, California, New York, Wisconsin, and Indiana.[136] Several of the Croatian resistance organizations previously noted were present in the U.S., especially the CNR or OTPOR. As with Cuban Americans and Armenian Americans, the majority of Croatian Americans supported the non-violent Croatian nationalist organizations. A minority of Croatian Americans had engaged however in terrorist activity against Yugoslav targets and other Croatian Americans in and outside the United States. From 1970 to 1979, there were 24 anti-Yugoslav attacks in the United States, 14 of which took place from 1978 to 1979. Moreover, Croatian émigrés carried out five terrorist attacks against non-Yugoslav targets in the United States. These five attacks were aimed at four U.S. and one West German targets — a bookstore, New York's Grand Central Station, a TWA plane, an American Airlines plane, and a West German Consulate. In addition to these 24 Croatian terrorist attacks, there were three-six assassinations of Serbian and Croatian émigrés in the United States during the decade.[137] The majority of this terrorist activ-

---

[134] Ben Leach, "Serbian Flight attendant's fall from 10,000 meters was 'hoax'," *The Daily Telegraph*, January 14, 2009.

[135] Alan Riding, "Paraguay Accepts Terrorist and Stir Is Minor," *New York Times*, December 27, 1987.

[136] https://en.wikipedia.org/wiki/Croatian_American. Accessed June 6, 2017.

[137] A range of three-six is used because responsibility for the attacks was not claimed and some attacks on Croatian émigrés in the U.S. were carried out by other Croatians.

ity took place in New York City, Chicago, and San Francisco, while fewer attacks took place in Los Angeles, Cleveland, and Pittsburg. The attacks consisted primarily of bombings but there were also assassinations, an aircraft hijacking, and a barricade and hostage incident.

The most notable Yugoslav émigré terrorist attack on U.S. soil during the Ford administration was a hijacking. On September 10, 1976, five Croatian terrorists hijacked TWA Flight 355 out of New York with 85 passengers and crew. The five terrorists were Frane Pesut, Mark Vlasic, Petar Matavic, Zvonko Bušić (cell leader), and Julienne Bušić, his wife. The terrorists had also planted a bomb in a locker at the Grand Central Station in New York City. NYPD explosive ordinance disposal (EOD) officer Brian Murray was killed when the bomb exploded after the bomb squad removed the explosive device from the locker and transported it to the department's range at Rodman's Neck in the Bronx. Three other officers were also injured in the explosion. The terrorists planted the bomb in the locker as proof that they had explosives on the plane (in fact, the "bomb" on the plane was a Crock-Pot filled with Silly-Putty, wires, and electrical tape) and were serious in their intent. They left instructions in the locker on how to defuse the bomb. They later claimed that they did not intend to kill or injure anyone during this hijacking operation. During the hijacking, they demanded that five major U.S. newspapers (the *New York Times*, the *Washington Post*, the *Chicago Tribune*, the *Los Angeles Times*, and the *International Herald Tribune*) publish their 1,600-word "appeal to the American People" and a 2,500-word declaration of independence for the 4.4 million Croatians, who were a fifth of Yugoslavia's population at the time. The eight-page "Appeal to the American People" manifesto stated in part that:

> *We decided to undertake this particular action for many reasons ... our goal was to present an accurate picture of the brutal oppression taking place in Yugoslavia ... we expect peace-loving forces in the world to describe us as terrorists, criminals, and murderers.... Those fighting for national liberation have always been described in such terms.... The point to be made here, obviously, is not to conclusively define terrorism, an impossible and unnecessary task, but, rather, to explain the ultimate necessity for our extreme decision and to ask others to judge this decision objectively and unemotionally.... We must remember that todays' 'terrorists' are often tomorrow's policymakers, having participated in the formation of a new, independent state. Such was the position of the*

supporters of the Declaration of Independence, after the American colonies were freed from British subjugation.[138]

According to the terrorists, if the manifestos were published, the hostages would be released. If they were not, another hidden bomb would be detonated in a "highly busy location" in the U.S. After the publication of their manifestos, the hijackers surrendered on September 12 at the Charles de Gaulle airport in France and freed the passengers and crew members who had been held captive for 30 hours. None of the passengers or crew members were injured. The terrorists were given the option of returning to the United States to stand trial or be tried in France. They opted to go back to the U.S. In May 1977, all five Croatian terrorists were convicted. Bušić's wife and the others were paroled in the late 1980s after serving about a dozen years. The Republic of Croatia declared its independence from Yugoslavia in 1991, and sympathizers there called for Zvonko Bušić's release. On July 23, 2008, Zvonko Bušić, who served 32 years in prison for the TWA hijacking, was released and returned to Croatia to a hero's welcome.[139] In 2013, at the age of 67, Bušić killed himself.

The five-person cell that carried out this hijacking was not connected to any Croatian organization. It was an "autonomous terrorist cell," or a leaderless terrorist cell. In an interview in October 2004, Julienne Bušić provided some insights into the hijacking operation.[140] When asked who came up with the hijacking idea, she responded:

My husband had the idea, and it came from sheer desperation. The Yugoslav Secret police had been assassinating Croatian dissidents around the world, many of them our friends and even relatives. We were shot at twice, once in Berlin, and another time in Frankfurt. We moved

---

[138] As quoted in Ovid DeMaris, *Brothers in Blood*, pp. 386–387.

[139] The description of the TWA 355 hijacking was compiled from the *New York Times*, September 12, 1976, p. 1, and "Skyjackings: Bombs for Croatia," *Time Magazine*, September 20, 1976, at http://www.time.com/time/magazine/article/0,9171,946611. Accessed May 4, 2016; see also, Luke John Gensler, "Pots, Putty, and Wires: Croatian Separatist Terrorism and the Hijacking of TWA 355," a thesis submitted to the faculty of the University of North Carolina at Chapel Hill in partial fulfillment of the requirements for the degree of Masters of Arts in the Department of Russian and Eastern European Studies, Chapel Hill, 2014, at https://cdr.lib.unc.edu/indexablecontent/uuid:79f86eb6-6181-46df-b98e-21748a5a24a6. Accessed June 6, 2017.

[140] Julienne Bušić quotes from Philip Baum, "Zvonko & Julienne Busic: an ASI exclusive interview," *Aviation Security International Magazine*, October 2004, at http://www.avsec.com/interviews/busic.htm. Accessed June 3, 2017.

to the United States and still the threats continued. All our legal attempts to bring the situation to the attention of the press and authorities failed. At the time, the U.S. and Yugoslavia were close allies and America was not interested in criticizing Tito. Even the FBI told us they couldn't do anything until something actually happened which would, of course, have been too late. So we had the choice of waiting to be killed and living in constant fear or sacrificing our freedom to alert the world to Tito's state-terrorism, which was how many journalists and policymakers referred to his government, including the former US ambassador to the former Yugoslavia, Laurence Silberman. The one and only goal of the hijacking was to force the world media to print the truth about the human rights abuses in former Yugoslavia, the imprisonment of dissidents, the murders and assassinations. To force them to do their job, in other words.

She was asked why they selected the TWA flight from New York to Chicago. She replied:

It was sheer chance, because TWA was one of the international lines and we thought, incorrectly, that it could fly non-stop to Europe. As for the route, that also was arbitrarily chosen.

In terms of picking the other terrorists, she noted:

Only my husband and myself until the end, when he chose three other Croatian men he felt were trustworthy, plus a Croatian dissident relative in Europe, Bruno Bušić, who wrote the leaflets that were ultimately dropped during our flight over several major cities in the U.S., Canada, and Europe. Bruno was murdered soon thereafter in Paris, in 1978, shot five times in the back and head by the Yugoslav Secret Police, probably partly due to their belief that he'd been involved in our case.

As for the reason of planting a bomb in the Grand Central Station locker that killed an NYPD EOD officer, Bušić stated:

Real explosives were left in an isolated locker at Grand Central Station, and their only purpose was to convince the authorities there were real weapons on the plane so that the leaflets would be printed. Detailed deactivation instructions were also left along with the explosives in the actual locker.

The hijacking of TWA Flight 355 was up to that time the most prominent example of a "foreign spillover terrorist" operation on U.S. soil — five Croatian Americans engaged in a terrorist act against a U.S. target as a result of overseas political situation that did not directly involve the United States.[141]

It should also be noted that Croatian terrorists were among the suspects in the December 29, 1975 bombing at a TWA baggage area in LaGuardia airport that killed 11 people and injured 75 others. The bomb, which had the force of 20 sticks of dynamite, exploded in a coin-operated locker. There was the potential for a higher casualty toll as 15 minutes before the explosion hundreds of passengers from two flights were at the baggage carousel.[142] It was the highest death toll from a bomb explosion in New York City since the September 16, 1920 Wall Street wagon bomb that killed 38 and injured 143. Zvonko Bušić, who was involved in the September 1976 hijacking of TWA Flight 355, was a later suspect in this bombing.[143] However, no evidence has been uncovered to date to implicate any individual or organization in this bombing. Like the 1920 Wall Street bombing, the 1975 LaGuardia bombing remains unsolved.[144] There has been recent speculation that the UDBA may have carried out the LaGuardia bombing and that the bomber may have been an FBI informant. The attack was not meant to cause mass casualties, but a faulty timer caused the bomb to explode prematurely. Reportedly, whenever an UDBA agent showed up in the U.S. with the secret mission of assassinating a Croatian or Serbian exiled dissident, he would usually offer his services to the FBI, which wanted confidential informants inside the brash and violent Balkan émigré community. With a degree of FBI protection, the assassin was reportedly then free to do his hit and get away with it.[145]

---

[141] Zvonko and Julienne Bušić have their own website at http://www.zvonkobusic.com/. Accessed June 3, 2018.

[142] Wendy Wenner, "Bomb Rips LaGuardia Airport, 11 Killed, 75 injured," *Burlington (Vermont) Banner*, December 30, 1975, p. 1.

[143] Al Baker, "Terrorist's Release Reopens Wound of Unsolved Bombing," *New York Times*, August 9, 2008.

[144] "LaGuardia Christmas bombing remains unsolved 27 years later," John Springer, Court TV, CNN, at http://articles.cnn.com/2002-12-24/justice/ctv.laguardia_1_limo-airport-shuttle-smoke?_s=PM:LAW. Accessed June 6, 2017.

[145] John R. Schindler, "Why Hasn't Washington Explained the 1975 LaGuardia Airport Bombing?" *The Observer*, January 4, 2016, at http://observer.com/2016/01/why-hasnt-washington-explained-the-1975-laguardia-airport-bombing/. Accessed May 4, 2017. There is no additional confirmation at this time of the claims that the FBI allowed UDBA assassins to operate in the U.S.

Outside the U.S., Croatian terrorists carried out 41 attacks from 1970 to 1977, but only three attacks from 1978 to 1979. There was a clear shift away from Western Europe to the United States in the late 1970s that continued into the early 1980s. The reason for this operational shift was unclear, but it may have been dictated by increased police pressure on Croatian terrorist activity in Western Europe, especially in Sweden and West Germany, where 67% of all Croatian terrorist attacks in Western Europe took place from 1962 to 1977. In 1976, the West German government outlawed several Croatian extremist groups. Confronted by Croatian terrorist activity and a rising left-wing terrorist threat, the German government instituted stricter anti-terrorism legislation. In Sweden, Croatian terrorist activity peaked in 1971–1972. As a result, Sweden promulgated the core of its anti-terrorist legislation during 1973–1974. The fact is that the last Croatian terrorist attack in Sweden took place in 1972. Under police pressure in Western Europe and given the large Croatian diaspora in the United States, the U.S. became the preferred operational area for Croatian terrorists from 1978 onward.

Anti-Soviet, Jewish Terrorism

Background: The JDL was founded by Rabbi Meir Kahane in New York City in 1968. "Never again" is the official slogan of the JDL. This slogan refers to the JDL's adherence to the principle that unless a constant vigilance is maintained to battle against anti-Semitism, the Holocaust will reoccur. While headquartered in New York City, the JDL had chapters located in several of the larger metropolitan areas of the United States. In its early years, the JDL was a militant Jewish organization whose stated goals were to (1) serve as the premier Galut (exile)-based activism force in defense of Jews, Judaism, and righteous non-Jews, (2) to advocate, educate, and inspire the Jewish people in such notable areas as authentic Torah Judaism, self-defense (including firearms ownership), and security, and (3) to vigorously oppose all manifestations of Jew hatred.[146] The Southern Poverty Law Center (SPLC) defines the JDL as "a radical organization that preaches a violent form of anti-Arab, Jewish nationalism."[147] The JDL initiated a series of harassments, demonstrations, and physical attacks against Soviet offices and personnel in New York at the end of 1969 and continued over the next two years. JDL actions included forcefully occupying some offices, spray-painting Hebrew slogans that proclaimed "the Jewish nation lives," and disrupting public

---

[146] http://www.jdl.org/index.php/about-jdl/mission-history/. Accessed June 5, 2017.

[147] http://www.splcenter.org/get-informed/intelligence-files/groups/jewish-defense-league. Accessed May 3, 2018.

meetings. In 1970, the JDL initiated a terrorist campaign to attack Soviet establishments in the U.S. in order to pressure the USSR to change its anti-Semitic policies, to include the repression of the 2.1 million Jews living in the Soviet Union, who were often jailed and refused exit visas to emigrate to Israel. The JDL decided that violence was necessary to draw attention to their plight, assuming that Moscow would respond to the strain on Soviet–United States relations by permitting more emigration to Israel. The Soviet Union was the JDL's primary target. However, it also targeted anyone it considered was a threat to the survival of radical Jewish nationalism. This included foreign diplomats, domestic radical-right organizations, Arab and Muslim activists, journalists and scholars, and Jewish community members who were simply not "Jewish enough." The JDL attacked Arab, Iranian, Iraqi, Egyptian, Palestinian, Lebanese, French, and German targets in the United States.

The FBI closely monitored the JDL and Rabbi Meir Kahane out of concern that the group's protests and violent action could hurt diplomatic relations with the Soviet Union. On August 29, 1970, the Soviet government newspaper *Izvestia* "protested repeated attacks by members of the Jewish Defense League against Soviet diplomats in New York and demanded better U.S. protection."[148] Declassified FBI documents suggested that FBI Director J. Edgar Hoover, starting at least as early as 1970, ordered aggressive infiltration and surveillance of the group, while reporting even seemingly benign details to the White House.[149] JDL attacks on Soviet targets were increasing in the early 1970s to the point that by the fall of 1971, President Nixon feared that Kahane would wreck the Strategic Arms Limitation Talks (SALT).[150] Another ingredient in the growing JDL problem for the United States was the accusation that some of the Israeli political leaders were behind the JDL. This also put a strain on U.S.–Soviet relations.[151] From 1970 to 1987, the JDL was one of the most active foreign spillover terrorist organizations in the United States.

---

[148] *New York Times*, August 30, 1970. As quoted in Donald Neff, "Jewish Defense League Unleashes Campaign of Violence in America," *Washington Report on Middle East Affairs*, July/August 1999, pp. 81–82, at http://www.washington-report.org/backissues/0799/9907081.html. Accessed June 5, 2017.

[149] Marc Perelman, "Secret FBI Files Reveal Hoover's Obsession with Militant Rabbi," The *Jewish Daily Forward*, February 24, 2006, at http://www.forward.com/articles/1100/#ixzz1FO8IRYs0. Accessed June 6, 2017.

[150] Robert I. Friedman, "Rabbi Kahane," 1987 article for the Alicia Patterson Organization, at http://aliciapatterson.org/APF1004/Friedman/Friedman.html. Accessed September 3, 2017.

[151] Robert I. Friedman, *The False Prophet: Rabbi Meir Kahane* (Brooklyn, NY: Lawrence Hill Books, 1990), pp. 105–107, as quoted in Donald Neff, "Jewish Defense League Unleashes Campaign of

Like militant Armenian, Cuban, and Croatian organizations in the United States, the JDL had an antagonistic relationship with its more moderate counterparts in the United States — conventional Jewish political and social organizations, such as B'nai B'rith's Anti-Defamation League — which regarded the JDL as a marginal group and an embarrassment to the American Jewish community.

The JDL emerged as a terrorist organization on September 27, 1970 when two JDL members, Avraham and Nancy Hershkovitz, were arrested at the Kennedy airport in New York City in an alleged plot to hijack an Arab airliner. The two were carrying firearms and explosives. They were later indicted on six counts by a grand jury but pleaded guilty only to a charge of passport falsification. From 1970 to 1979, 30 terrorist incidents in the United States can be attributed to the JDL.[152] All but five took place in the New York area. Of these five incidents one occurred in Washington, D.C., one in New Jersey, and three in Los Angeles. Of the 30 terrorist incidents, 26 were bombings. The other four incidents involved an attempted aircraft hijacking (noted previously) and three shooting incidents. In the 1970s, only one person was killed in a JDL attack. This took place on January 26, 1972 when a bomb exploded in impresario Sol Hurok's Manhattan office, killing his receptionist, Iris Kones, 27, while Hurok and 12 others were injured. The JDL was suspected because Hurok, as an impresario, organized the appearance of Soviet performers to the United States. Of these 30 terrorist incidents in the 1970s, eight were directed at Soviet diplomatic and government facilities in the United States. The other targets involved an Arab airliner, Iraqi, Polish, and Egyptian targets, a Nazi war criminal, a Russian bookstore,

---

Violence in America." The two Israeli politicians were Yitzhak Shamir, Prime Minister of Israel from 1983 to 1984 and from 1986 to 1992, and Geula Cohen, leader of the Jewish extremist party Tehiya and a member of the Knesset at the time. Friedman contends that "Shamir and Cohen were at the center of a group that masterminded the league's often violent campaign against Soviet targets during its heyday in the late 1960s and early 1970s, seriously threatening détente." See also, Robert I. Friedman, "How Shamir Used JDL Terrorism," *The Nation*, October 31, 1988.

[152] Statistics on JDL attacks inside the United States are based on the author's chronology compiled from the following sources: (1) Southern Poverty Law Center at www.splcenter.org and (2) Anti-Defamation League at www.adl.org. Other sources have stated the following on the number of JDL terrorist attacks, "According to the FBI, the JDL was responsible for at least 37 terrorist acts in the United States in the period from 1968–1983, while the International Terrorism: Attributes of Terrorist Events (ITERATE) database developed on behalf of the United States Central Intelligence Agency by Edward F. Mickolus recorded 50 such incidents from 1968–1987, making the JDL second only to the Puerto Rican FALN (q.v.) as the major internal terrorist group." Sean Anderson and Stephen Sloan, *Historical Dictionary of Terrorism* (New Jersey: Scarecrow Press, 1995), at http://www.securitymanagement.com/library/000248.html. Accessed May 3, 2017.

three vehicles, a Democratic Party office, a communist party headquarters office, a service station, Arab apartment tenants, as well as the impresario Sol Hurok.

In addition to these attacks, there were half a dozen plots that never materialized. For example, in February 1973, members of the JDL had planned to use a "drone airplane" in 1971 to bomb the Soviet Mission to the U.N. Another plot was discovered on May 24, 1972, when, in an apparent effort to disrupt U.S.–Soviet relations, four people, two of whom were reported to be members of the JDL, were arrested in New York City and charged with bomb possession and burglary in a conspiracy to blow up the Long Island residence of the Soviet Mission to the U.N. President Nixon was on an official visit to Moscow at the time. On August 4, 1972, the two JDL members pleaded guilty and were sentenced to three years in prison. In many of these incidents, the action would be clandestinely claimed in the name of the JDL or fictitious subgroups like the "Jewish Defenders," "United Jewish Underground," "Jewish Direct Action," and "New Jewish Defense League." However, afterward, an official JDL spokesman would publicly disavow the group's responsibility.

Up until 1975, most JDL attacks were aimed at official Soviet facilities in the United States. However, from 1976, there was a slight shift toward more non-Soviet targets. On November 10, 1975, the U.N. General Assembly adopted, by a vote of 72 to 35 (with 32 abstentions), its Resolution 3379, which stated as its conclusion: Zionism is a form of racism and racial discrimination. The following year, JDL members began targeting diplomats of all nations who had voted for this U.N. resolution. The first such incident occurred on January 6, 1976, when three JDL members in Philadelphia were charged by the police with invading and vandalizing the Mexican Consulate, to protest Mexico's vote for the U.N. resolution. The JDL continued to engage in terrorist attacks even after its founder, Rabbi Kahane, emigrated to Israel in 1971 to establish a right-wing political party called Kach. This party was eventually designated a "foreign terrorist organization" by the U.S. Department of State in 1994.

Palestinian Terrorism — Foreign Incursion Terrorism

Secular Palestinian terrorist activity outside Israel increased throughout the 1970s. There was also a corresponding increase in the United States. Compared to Croatian and Armenian émigrés and Cuban exiles in the United States, the number of Palestinians here was small — about 100,000 by 1985.[153] Palestinian terrorist groups did not consider the United States an ideal operational area. It

---

[153] http://www.everyculture.com/multi/Pa-Sp/Palestinian-Americans.html. Accessed June 6, 2017.

may have been strategically attractive in that the U.S. was the primary supporter for the state of Israel. However, no Palestinian terrorist group made the effort in the 1970s to construct a logistical infrastructure here to support sustained offensive operations. What occurred were periodic foreign incursion attacks.

According to one account, only 11 Palestinian terrorist incidents were carried out inside the United States in the 1970s.[154] Five incidents took place in 1972, four in 1973, and one in both 1977 and 1978. The five incidents in 1972 were letter bombs sent to the U.S. leaders including President Nixon, Secretary of State William Rogers, and Secretary of Defense Melvin Laird. This was part of the Palestinian terrorist letter bomb campaign that was aimed at Israeli and other targets worldwide and lasted from roughly September to December 1972 and involved around 200 letter bombs.[155] Four of the other incidents were low-level bombings like the July 25, 1977 bombing at the home of the leader of the Israeli lobby in Washington, D.C. The last two incidents were the most significant Palestinian terrorist attacks inside the U.S. — an attempted car bombing in New York City in March 1973 and the assassination of an Israeli defense attaché in Washington, D.C in July 1973.

On January 12, 1973, a Black September terrorist named Khalid Duhham al-Jawari, an Iraqi, flew to Boston via Montreal and then to New York City.[156] Working with several other people, he began scouting targets for a terrorist attack, rented three cars, and then constructed bombs for the vehicles. On March 4, 1973, he drove the three automobiles filled with bombs made of gasoline, propane tanks and Semtex, and parked them in front of several Israeli targets in the area including the First Israel Bank and Trust Company, the Israel Discount Bank, and at El-Al's cargo terminal at the JFK airport. Alarm clocks and an electronic timer were used as the timing devices. Black September propaganda, concealed in Hebrew language newspapers, was also placed in the cars. The car bombs were supposed to detonate at noon that day with the arrival of Israeli Prime Minister

---

[154] Merari and Elad, *The International Dimension of Palestinian Terrorism*, p. 116.

[155] Ibid., p.133.

[156] This incident was reconstructed from the following sources: *Associated Press*, "Freedom looms for convicted terrorist: Man behind 1973 N.Y. bomb plot to be released Feb. 19," January 24, 2009; and *Associated Press*, "U.S. Agency helped uncover 1973 NYC plot to kill Golda Meir," February 3, 2009; see FBI Report at https://www.cia.gov/library/readingroom/docs/CIA-RDP75B00380R0005000600 08-7.pdf. Accessed June 3, 2018; and George Lardner Jr., "U.S. Fights Efforts of Terrorists," *Washington Post*, March 18, 1973, at https://www.cia.gov/library/readingroom/docs/CIA-RDP75B00380R000500060004-1.pdf. Accessed May 4, 2018.

were under suspicion of being "Arab terrorists or extremists" underlined the large Palestinian "suspects" footprint in the U.S. at the time.

While the Alon assassination was a discriminate attack aimed at an Israeli diplomat, the car bombings plot in New York was an indiscriminate attack, even though the targets were all Israeli. Had the car bombs detonated, it is certain that some American citizens would have been killed or injured. Given the deliberate murders of two U.S. diplomats in Khartoum by the BSO two days before the New York car bombs were to detonate, it is clear that Yasir Arafat's Fatah and its BSO terrorist arm, were sending a message to the United States. Unlike the Croatian, Armenian, and Cuban terrorist organizations that operated on U.S. soil, Palestinian terrorists were actively targeting U.S. interests overseas. To supplement these overseas attacks with attacks on U.S. soil would have created major security problems for the United States. The July 1973 car bombings plot in New York City, however, turned out to be an aberration and not the beginning of an operational trend. In general, after this incident, secular Palestinian terrorist groups did not qualitatively or quantitatively increase their offensive operational activity on U.S. soil. In the 1970s, secular Palestinian terrorism was the primary example of foreign incursion terrorism in the U.S.

Protests against the Vietnam War in Washington, D.C.

Source: Lyndon B. Johnson Presidential Library.

August 24, 1970 bombing of the Army Mathematics Research Center (AMRC) at the University of Wisconsin-Madison campus as a protest against the university's research connections with the U.S. military during the Vietnam War. One person killed.

Source: University of Wisconsin Digital Collections — with permission.

FBI wanted posters published shortly after the 1970 bombing of Sterling Hall at the University of Wisconsin.

Source: Wikimedia Commons.

Patty Hurst joins Symbionese Liberation Army (SLA). Photo shows Hurst, on right, with SLA leader DeFreeze in robbing a San Francisco bank on April 15, 1974. It was her first crime as a professed SLA member.

Source: U.S. Federal Bureau of Investigation.

WANTED BY THE FBI

BANK ROBBERY
INTERSTATE FLIGHT - POSSESSION OF HOMEMADE BOMB, ROBBERY, RECEIVING STOLEN PROPERTY, ASSAULT WITH FORCE
DONALD DAVID DE FREEZE

Photograph taken 1973   Date photographs taken unknown   FBI No. 606,723 D

Aliases: Don Cinque DeFreeze, Donald John DeFreeze, Donald DeFrez, John DeFriele, David DeFrieze, Donald DeFrieze, Donald DeFrize, David Kenneth Robinson, Steven Robinson, Donald David Thomas, "Cin," "Cinque," "Cynque"

DESCRIPTION

Age: 30, born November 16, 1943, Cleveland, Ohio

Height:	5'9" to 5'11"	**Eyes:**	Brown
Weight:	150 to 160 pounds	**Complexion:**	Medium brown
Build:	Medium	**Race:**	Negro
Hair:	Black	**Nationality:**	American

Occupations: Autobody shop worker, carpenter, chef, painter, restaurant manager, service station attendant, stationary engineer, typist, key punch operator

Scars and Marks: Scar on bridge of nose, scars on forehead, face, left arm and wrist, right elbow and palm of right hand, appendectomy scar

Remarks: Reportedly drinks plum wine, may be wearing tinted glasses

Social Security Number Used: 042-34-4002

Fingerprint Classification: 9 S 1 R 10I 12
S 1 U 00I

CRIMINAL RECORD

DeFreeze has been convicted of robbery, possession of homemade bomb, possession of stolen property, assault with force, and forgery.

CAUTION

DE FREEZE, AN ESCAPEE FROM A PENAL INSTITUTION, REPORTEDLY HAS HAD NUMEROUS FIREARMS IN HIS POSSESSION AND ALLEGEDLY HAS FIRED ON LAW ENFORCEMENT OFFICERS TO AVOID ARREST. DE FREEZE, WITH ACCOMPLICES, ALLEGEDLY ROBBED A BANK USING AUTOMATIC WEAPONS. TWO INDIVIDUALS WERE KNOWN TO HAVE BEEN SERIOUSLY WOUNDED DURING SHOOTING AT THE BANK. DE FREEZE SHOULD BE CONSIDERED ARMED AND EXTREMELY DANGEROUS.

A Federal warrant was issued on February 8, 1974, at Salinas, California, charging DeFreeze with unlawful interstate flight to avoid confinement after conviction for robbery, possession of homemade bomb, receiving stolen property, and assault with force (Title 18, U. S. Code, Section 1073). Also on April 16, 1974, a Federal warrant was issued at San Francisco, California, charging DeFreeze with bank robbery (Title 18, U. S. Code, Sections 2113(a), (d)).

IF YOU HAVE ANY INFORMATION CONCERNING THIS PERSON, PLEASE NOTIFY ME OR CONTACT YOUR LOCAL FBI OFFICE. TELEPHONE NUMBERS AND ADDRESSES OF ALL FBI OFFICES LISTED ON BACK.

C. M. Kelley

DIRECTOR
FEDERAL BUREAU OF INVESTIGATION
UNITED STATES DEPARTMENT OF JUSTICE
WASHINGTON, D. C. 20535
TELEPHONE, NATIONAL 8-7117

Entered NCIC
Wanted Flyer 473
April 17, 1974

FBI wanted poster on Donald De Freeze, leader of the Symbionese Liberation Army and organizer of the 1974 kidnapping of Patricia Hearst, the granddaughter of American publishing magnate William Randolph Hearst.

Source: U.S. Federal Bureau of Investigation.

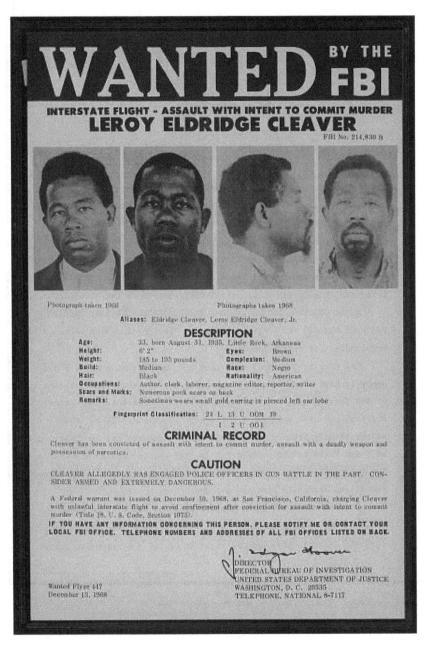

FBI Wanted Poster on Eldridge Cleaver, an early leader of the Black Panther Party. Newton eventually broke from the party led by Huey Newton. This split seriously weakened the party.

Source: U.S. Federal Bureau of Investigation.

de LIBERACIÓN NACIONAL PUERTORRIQUEÑA
ARMED FORCES OF PUERTO RICAN NATIONAL LIBERATION

COMMUNIQUE NO.1   OCTOBER 26, 1974

Today, commando units of FALN attacked mayor Yanki corporations
in New York City. These actions have been taken in commemoration
of the October 30, 1950 uprising in Puerto Rico against Yanki
colonial domination. These bombings are also to accent the seriousness
of our demands for the release of the five Puerto Rican political
prisoners, the longest held political prisoners in the hemisphere:

OSCAR COLLAZO, LOLITA LEBRON, RAFAEL CANCEL MIRANDA, ANDRES
FIGUEROA CORDERO and IRVING FLORES, and the immediate and unconditional
independence of Puerto Rico.

The corporations that we bombed are an integral part of Yanki
monopoly capitalism and are responsible for the murderous policies
of the Yanki government in Puerto Rico, Latin America, and against
workers, peasants and Indios throughout the world. It is these
corporations which are responsible for the robbery and exploitation
of Third World countries in order to make greater profit and increase
their capital. They are the ones which often decide who shall govern
countries, who shall live and who shall die.

For these reasons these corporations and the criminals who run
them are the enemies of all freedom loving people, who are struggling
for self determination and the right to decide their own destinies.

FALN Communique #1 on October 1974 bombings in New York City.

Source: Author's personal collection.

Turkish diplomats and family members killed by the Armenian Secret Army for the Liberation of Armenia, and the Justice Commandos of the Armenian Genocide in the 1970s and 1980s.

Source: Assembly of Turkish American Associations.

FBI Director J. Edgar Hoover.

Source: Federal Bureau of Investigation.

Joan Chesimard, aka: Assata Shakur, a member of the Black Liberation Army, convicted of the murder of NJ State Trooper Werner Foerster in 1973. Escaped from prison in 1979, fled to Cuba where as of 2019 she remains.

Source: U.S. Government.

Chapter 4

The Nixon and Ford Administrations (1969–1976): The Response — The Overseas Threat

The Response

The Nixon and Ford administrations began at the dawn of a new era in American history that was marked by a growing internal terrorism threat and an embryonic but rising and dangerous international terrorism threat overseas. They were the first administrations to face such a double-edged terrorist threat. The Nixon administration was the first to confront a major terrorist threat to civilian aviation, diplomats, and diplomatic facilities. It was the first to deal with the possibility of terrorists using surface-to-air missiles against civilian aircraft and possibly stealing nuclear materials. While hijackings, kidnappings, hostage-taking, and assassinations of American citizens occurred before 1969, the U.S. government had neither formulated an overall policy in response to these incidents nor designed a plan for unilateral, bilateral, or multilateral action to prevent them.[1] While there were countries that faced an internal terrorist threat, few had their overseas interests targeted as much as the U.S. Israel was in a similar situation beginning in the late 1960s. Like the U.S., Israel at the time was also in the process of searching for an effective response against the same set of terrorism problems.[2]

---

[1] U.S. Department of State. Office of the Historian. Press Release, September 19, 2005. Foreign Relations of the United States, 1969–1976, Volume E-1, Documents on Global Issues, 1969–1972, at https://history.state.gov/historicaldocuments/frus1969-76ve01/pressrelease. Accessed June 4, 2017.

[2] For an excellent analysis of Israeli counter-terrorism policy and actions, see Daniel Byman, *A High Price: The Triumphs and Failures of Israeli Counterterrorism* (New York: Oxford University Press, 2011).

Candidate Richard Nixon did not devote a great deal of attention to the issue of international terrorism during his election campaign nor did he mention it in his first 1969 inaugural address. It was also not on the list of priority foreign policy issues to be addressed during the first year of his administration. The initial set of pressing foreign policy and security issues consisted of Vietnam, China, the Soviet Union, Latin America, and the Middle East. Some of the developments in these regions did, however, spark anti-American terrorism. Vietnam became a trigger for both domestic and overseas terrorism against the U.S. while U.S. policies in the Middle East and Latin America generated anti-American attacks in those regions. Any presidential administration faced with both an internal and overseas terrorist threat would for obvious political reasons attempt to address the internal threat first. Given that the Nixon campaign also made domestic law and order a key campaign issue, it was not surprising that the administration directed its initial counter-terrorism attention and efforts at stemming the growing domestic political violence emanating from the universities and black urban areas. Domestic terrorism became a domestic political issue and international terrorism overseas was more of a foreign policy issue. Of the two, the former evolved into a national security issue. For the Nixon administration, international terrorism overseas was simply a security "concern" that periodically affected U.S. foreign policy objectives and bilateral relationships. Of the Nixon administration's 206 National Security Study Memoranda (NSSM) from 1969 to 1974, none fully addressed the terrorism issue.[3] Of the 264 National Security Decision Memoranda from 1969 to 1974, none fully addressed the terrorism issue.[4]

---

[3] The NSSMs were the main tools for studying and deciding upon issues of national security and foreign policy. The NSSMs commissioned studies for NSC consideration. The process began with the identification of an issue requiring a presidential decision. This could be done by the President, a National Security Council member, or by the NSC staff. The following NSSMs made a cursory reference to the issue of terrorism: #102 — *The President's Annual Review of American Foreign Policy*, dated September 21, 1970, addressed 20 topics, Topic #20 was "New Tasks for Diplomacy" (hijacking, narcotics, pollution, space); #137 — *The President's Annual Review of American Foreign Policy*, dated September 22, 1971, addressed 21 topics, Topic #21 was "New Tasks for Diplomacy" (hijacking, narcotics, pollution, space); #185 — *Policy Towards Libya*, dated June 5, 1973, one-line reference to Libyan support for international terrorism; #188 — *The President's Annual Review of American Foreign Policy* dated October 24, 1973, addressed 19 topics, Topic #19 was "Multilateral Cooperation" (hijacking, narcotics, pollution, space, and international terror), at https://nixonlibrary.gov/virtuallibrary/documents/nationalsecuritystudymemoranda.php. Accessed June 3, 2017.

[4] https://nixonlibrary.gov/virtuallibrary/documents/nationalsecuritydecisionmemoranda.php. Accessed May 7, 2016. NSDM #254, dated April 27, 1974, briefly addresses the issue of domestic safeguard of nuclear power plants and makes a short reference to the possibility of terrorists attacking such facilities.

Overseas Terrorist Threat

In the last year of the Johnson administration, Palestinian terrorists initiated an international terrorist campaign against overseas Israeli interests by hijacking an El Al plane out of Rome in July 1968 and attacking an El Al plane at Athens airport in December 1968. However, the Johnson administration did not assess these acts as the start of a new dangerous security phenomenon or potential national security problem. Johnson was preoccupied at the time with the Vietnam War. The Nixon administration was the first to realize that the growing overseas international terrorist threat against U.S. interests that initially emerged under the Johnson administration was not an aberration but a probable trend.[5] It was not a short-term threat, as the issues that fostered this anti-American terrorism were core issues, not peripheral or transient, and thus could not be easily remedied. Addressing this threat would require a unique set of policies, strategies, actions, organizations, and counter-terrorism tools. The administration also recognized that since this was a global problem requiring international remedies, the U.S. had to assume an international leadership role in pursuit of multilateral remedies. Given that international terrorism was a new developing security problem, the administration had no templates or historical precedents to consult. Moreover, no other country had been compelled to address this issue, so the U.S. could not copy any existing effective counter-terrorism elements.[6] These factors help explain some of the inconsistencies of the Nixon administration as it searched for ways to address and counter this new threat. There were mistakes made and opportunities lost. Some of the policies were ad hoc.[7] In retrospect, however, the Nixon

---

[5] Jeffrey D. Simon, *The Terrorist Trap: America's Experience with Terrorism* (Indiana: Indiana University Press, 2001), Second Edition, p. 97; Timothy Naftali, *Blind Spot: The Secret History of American Counterterrorism* (New York: Basic Books, 2006), p. 33; and Yonah Alexander and Michael B. Kraft, *Evolution of U.S. Counterterrorism Policy, Volume One* (Westport: Praeger Security International, 2008), p. xxxvi.

[6] In fact, the Department of State sent out Airgram A-7676, dated October 8, 1974, to all U.S. diplomatic posts worldwide asking posts to collect data on host country law and policy concerning international terrorism. The Airgram stated the following: "It is important for our handling of particular incidents and for longer range planning that we have adequate information concerning approaches to terrorism taken by nations throughout the world." The Airgram then asked posts to collect information on 11 specific questions. Source: Foreign Relations of the United States, 1969–1974, Volume E-3, Documents on Global Issues, 1973–1976, Document 217, at www.history.state.gov. Accessed June 23, 2017.

[7] Secretary of State William Rogers stated in a meeting on April 13, 1970 that "for the present we should follow an ad hoc policy on kidnappings." Action Memorandum from Deputy Under Secretary of State for Administration (Macomber) to Under Secretary of State for Political Affairs (Johnson),

administration performed credibly given the circumstances and constructed a satisfactory counter-terrorism foundation for future administrations to build on. The Ford administration built on this foundation with only minor additions and modifications.

The terrorist threat to U.S. interests overseas emanated from left-wing terrorist and insurgent groups in Western Europe and Latin America and Palestinian terrorists operating primarily in Western Europe, the Middle East, and Africa. Whereas the left-wing groups were mostly discriminate in their tactics, it was clear that Palestinian terrorists were not hesitant to engage in indiscriminate, mass casualty attacks, and thus aircraft and airports became more prominent targets. Moreover, communist and some Arab states were becoming involved in supporting or supervising certain left-wing and Palestinian terrorist organizations. These terrorist and insurgent groups were carrying out bombings, assassinations, hijackings, and kidnappings of U.S. businesses and diplomatic and military facilities and personnel. The emerging anti-American terrorist threat was international, dangerous, and complex. The priority counter-terrorism tasks for the U.S. were to help find and arrest members of the anti-American terrorist and insurgent groups, ensure that there were effective internal legislation and international conventions to counter the threat, develop counter-terrorism relationships with allies and other countries, deploy the necessary protective security resources overseas, and develop an organizational structure in the government that would manage and coordinate the U.S. response to the international terrorist threat.

During the first four years of the Nixon administration, a series of major international terrorist attacks took place overseas that convinced the administration that a specialized organizational structure had to be established in the government to manage this problem. In 1969, TWA 840 was hijacked by Palestinian terrorists — the first time Palestinians terrorists hijacked a U.S. aircraft. In 1969, the U.S. Ambassador in Brazil was kidnapped by left-wing terrorists — the first kidnapping of a U.S. Ambassador in U.S. history. In 1970, four commercial planes, including TWA 741, were hijacked and diverted to an abandoned airfield in Jordan while a Pan Am Flight 93 was hijacked to Cairo. There were a total of 153 Americans on these planes. In 1972, Japanese terrorists attacked passengers at the Lod Airport in Israel, killing 17 Puerto Rican Catholic pilgrims, and Palestinian terrorists seized 11 Israeli athletes during the Olympic Games in Munich. An examination of the memos from Secretary of State William Rogers

---

Washington, April 3, 1970. Foreign Relations of the United States, 1969–1976, Volume E-1, Documents on Global Issues, 1969–1972, Document 39, at https://history.state.gov/historicaldocuments/frus1969-76ve01/d39. Accessed May 4, 2018.

and National Security Advisor Henry Kissinger to President Nixon and an analysis of the administration's counter-terrorism actions before and after the September 5–6, 1972 Munich Olympics hostage-taking incident clearly indicate that the Munich attack was the pivotal event that prompted the administration's formation of a more permanent counter-terrorism infrastructure and strategy.[8]

Given the international nature of the terrorist threat, it was reasonable for the State Department to assume the lead role in dealing with the issue. On September 18, the State Department established "an ad hoc interagency committee to coordinate intelligence data regarding terrorist organizations and their activities and to improve exchanges of such information with other countries."[9] It consisted of representatives from the FBI, CIA, INS, NSA, Customs, ATF, Secret Service, and Treasury. The Secretary of State noted on September 21 that "all these organizations are giving the highest priority to the problem before us."[10] Since terrorists were attacking U.S. interests in multiple countries, it was sensible and prudent to set up counter-terrorism intelligence relationships with other countries in order to share information and analysis. It was also crucial to coordinate the sharing of information among the U.S. federal intelligence and law enforcement agencies as well as with the local police. Terrorism was a new field in intelligence and law enforcement and a new problem for policymakers. What type of information should be collected on terrorist organizations and who should collect it? How should a terrorist threat be assessed? Should a database on terrorism be established and what fields should be used? What were the country's vulnerabilities at home and abroad? What counter-terrorism tools would the country need to mitigate the threat? On September 15, 1972, the CIA underlined the growing attention to this issue by publishing a "Weekly Situation Report on International Terrorism" (WSRIT) that was distributed to policymakers and other government

---

[8]These memos can be found in Foreign Relations of the United States, 1969–1976, Volume E-1, Documents on Global Issues, 1969–1972, Chapter 1, U.S. Policy Towards Terrorism, Hijacking of Aircraft, and Attacks on Civil Aviation, at http://history.state.gov/historicaldocuments. Accessed May 6, 2017.

[9]Memorandum from Secretary of State Rogers to President Nixon, Washington, September 18, 1972. Foreign Relations of the United States, 1969–1976, Volume E-1, Documents on Global Issues, 1969–1972, Document 102, at https://history.state.gov/historicaldocuments/frus1969-76ve01/d102. Accessed July 4, 2017. See also, Tad Szulc, "U.S. Sets up Intelligence Group to Combat Terrorism," *New York Times*, September 9, 1972, p. 4.

[10]Memorandum from Secretary of State Rogers to President Nixon, Washington, September 21, 1972. Foreign Relations of the United States, 1969–1976, Volume E-1, Documents on Global Issues, 1969–1972, Document 103, at https://history.state.gov/historicaldocuments/frus1969-76ve01/d103. Accessed August 4, 2016.

agencies.[11] The WSRIT listed terrorist events that intelligence sources said would or might occur, reviewed past terrorist events for lessons learned, and analyzed past terrorist activities as a means of predicting future happenings.

The State Department continued to emphasize the terrorism issue by setting up two additional special committees within the department in mid-September. One was established to "stimulate and coordinate international actions against terrorism" chaired by Assistant Secretary of State for Near Eastern and South Asian Affairs Joseph Sisco and the other "to protect foreign persons and property in the United States" chaired by Deputy Under Secretary of State for Management William Macomber. These two committees were later subsumed into a new executive branch committee on terrorism. It was Kissinger who came up with the idea of forming a special U.S. government group to manage and coordinate U.S. policy on terrorism. He saw it, however, as only a token action in response to the Munich attack that might "encourage the American Jewish community to lessen its attacks on détente" — basically an interest group buyout. Nixon wanted this counter-terrorism group to be more than a gesture. Alexander Haig, Nixon's Deputy Assistant for National Security Affairs, perceived this proposed group to be a "charade."[12] Nevertheless, on September 25, 1972, 19 days after the end of the Munich hostage seizure, Nixon established the Cabinet Committee to Combat Terrorism (CCCT). It was the first U.S. executive-level entity that was tasked with addressing and monitoring the terrorism issue — at home and abroad. The Cabinet Committee was established to consider the most effective means by which to prevent terrorism in the United States and abroad; to take the lead in establishing procedures to ensure that the federal government could take appropriate action swiftly, and to effectively respond to acts of terrorism; to coordinate the collection of intelligence worldwide; to consider the most effective means by which to protect installations abroad, foreign diplomats and diplomatic installation in the United States; to evaluate such programs and activities and make recommendations for their implementation; to devise procedures for reacting swiftly and effectively to acts of terrorism that occurred; and to make recommendations to the Director, Office of Management and Budget, concerning funding for these activities.[13]

---

[11] Naftali, *Blind Spot*, p. 55.

[12] Kissinger, Nixon, and Haig characterizations of this group from Naftali, *Blind Spot*, p. 58.

[13] https://nixonlibrary.gov/forresearchers/find/textual/central/subject/FG355.php. Accessed June 5, 2017. See also, Memorandum from the President for the Secretary of State titled "Action to Combat Terrorism," dated September 25, 1972. Foreign Relations of the United States, 1969–1976, Volume E-3, Documents on Global Issues, 1973–1976, Terrorism (Documents 203–228), at http://history.state.gov/historicaldocuments/frus1969-76ve01/ch1. Accessed May 23, 2017.

The CCCT was composed of the Secretary of State, who served as the chairperson, Secretary of the Treasury, Secretary of Defense, Secretary of Transportation, the Attorney General, the Ambassador to the United Nations, Director of the Central Intelligence Agency, Assistant to the President for National Security Affairs, and the Director of the Federal Bureau of Investigation.

Seemingly confirming the perceived cynical nature of the committee, it reportedly only met once, on October 2, 1972.[14] In the view of the CCCT members "there has been no compelling reason to convene more frequently since its ten statutory Cabinet-level members are kept fully informed by its dynamic Working Group, which is in close contact as issues arise and incidents occur."[15] The committee's responsibilities were delegated to a "Working Group on Terrorism" (WGT) chaired initially by Joseph F. Donelan, Jr., Deputy Under Secretary of State for Administration. He was later succeeded by the State Department representative, Armin Meyer, who was given the title "Special Assistant to the Secretary of State for Combatting Terrorism." Meyer was a Middle Eastern specialist. The WGT met more than 100 times between 1972 and 1977.[16] The Carter administration disbanded the CCCT in 1977.[17] Although flawed by inexperience and misperceptions, the CCCT and its WGT was a seminal organizational step in developing and coordinating U.S. counter-terrorism policy and strategy. Every subsequent presidential administration established a similar executive-level body to address the terrorism issue.

---

[14] Jeffrey D. Simon. *The Terrorist Trap: America's Experience with Terrorism* (Bloomington, Indiana: Indiana University Press, 1994), p. 108.

[15] This contention that the CCCT met only once during its existence is noted by Naftali, p. 59; Tucker, p. 13; Simon, p. 108; and a Memorandum from the Acting Secretary of State (Ingersoll) to President Ford, Washington, February 18, 1975. Foreign Relations of the United States, 1969–1976, Volume E-3, Documents on Global Issues, 1973–1976, Document 221 at https://history.state.gov/historical-documents/frus1969-76ve03/d221. Accessed December 23, 2017. However, Memorandum from Secretary of State Rogers to President Nixon, Washington, March 8, 1973, subject: Post-Khartoum Actions. Foreign Relations of the United States, 1969–1976, Volume E-3, Documents on Global Issues, 1973–1976, Document 208 states that Secretary Rogers "called a March 13 meeting of the principals of the Cabinet Committee to Combat Terrorism to consider specific recommendations from the Working Group ...." It is possible that the March 13 meeting never took place, at https://history.state.gov/historicaldocuments/frus1969-76ve03/d208. Accessed May 4, 2017.

[16] Simon, *The Terrorist Trap*, p. 108.

[17] Tucker, *Skirmishes at the Edge of Empire*, p. 13.

Hostage-Taking

Of the 77 international hostage-taking incidents that took place between 1968 and 1975, American diplomats and representatives overseas were the targets in more than one-third of these incidents.[18] Of all the terrorist tactics, hostage-taking is the one that causes the most difficulties for governments. Hostage-taking incidents include kidnappings, hijackings of transportation targets — aircraft, trains, buses, etc. — and barricade and hostage incidents. In hijacking and barricade incidents, the government at least knows the location of the terrorists and hostages, whereas in kidnappings, the hostage and terrorist's location are unknown. Terrorist hostage-takers usually demand the release of imprisoned comrades, ransom, a change of government policy, or some other concession. The country where the incident takes place has the primary responsibility to address the situation. Other countries may have an interest if their citizens are involved. The more countries involved in the incident, the more complex a resolution becomes due to different policies and approaches to the incident. The country where the incident takes place may want to make concessions to secure the safe release of the hostages while the hostages' countries may have a no concessions policy. While it is generally recognized that giving in to terrorists could encourage more hostage-taking, in the 1970s there was no universally accepted policy. A country's hostage-taking policy was a product of its values, mores, previous experience with terrorism, and mindset of its leaders.

The following were some of the questions that the U.S. had to address in constructing this policy:

- Should it be flexible or inflexible?
- Does the government pay ransom for the release of Americans kidnapped, hijacked, or seized in a barricade incident?
- Does the government give in to the political demands of hostage-takers (release imprisoned members, cease an ongoing military action, or change foreign policy)?
- Does the government put pressure on the host government to pay ransom or give in to the demands of the hostage-takers?
- When should the U.S. government consider a hostage-rescue attempt?[19]

---

[18]Brian Jenkins, "RAND Research on Terrorism," August 1977, Document P-5969, p. 5, at http://www.rand.org/content/dam/rand/pubs/papers/2008/P5969.pdf. Accessed January 2, 2016.

[19]The implication here is that the U.S. had a trained hostage rescue force. It appears that the first attempt to develop such a force was in 1973 by then Army Chief of Staff General Creighton Abrams. He established two Ranger battalions — one at Ft. Stewart, Georgia and one at Ft. Lewis, Washington.

- Does the government engage in a post-incident dragnet to find the hostage-takers to arrest/kill?
- Should the government publicly state its policy on hostages?
- How publicly involved should the President be?

Aircraft Hijacking

One of the first alarming terrorism tactics that the U.S. and international community confronted was aircraft hijacking, also referred to as skyjacking or air piracy. The first aircraft hijacking by political terrorists in modern history took place on February 21, 1931 when several Arequipa rebels hijacked a mail plane in Peru and used it to drop propaganda leaflets. Most of the hijackings carried out after the 1930s took place in Eastern Europe and involved people seeking escape from communist rule. For example, from 1947 to 1958, there were 23 hijackings of which 20 were carried out by people escaping communist countries.[20] The first aircraft hijacking by political terrorists for the purposes of political blackmail occurred on July 22, 1968 when Palestinian terrorists hijacked an El Al Plane to Algiers to force Israel to release imprisoned Palestinian terrorists. Although only 24% of all terrorist-related hijackings from 1968 to 1982 were carried out by Palestinians, aircraft hijacking became synonymous with Palestinian terrorism.[21] The first U.S. aircraft hijacked by political terrorists was carried out on August 28, 1969 when TWA Flight 840 en route to Tel Aviv from Rome was hijacked by Palestinian terrorists who took the plane to Damascus, Syria. In addition to hijacking aircraft, terrorists also started to plant bombs on aircraft to explode in mid-air and to attack aircraft and passengers while the plane was on the airport tarmac or at the boarding gate. Consequently, the safety and security of aircraft and airports became a priority for the U.S. and the international community in general. Terrorist attacks on aircraft and airports attract considerable publicity for the groups, create leverage/hostage problems for governments, potentially create mass casualties, and require multinational cooperation and coordination to resolve. This last point was a legal and management dilemma for the international

---

See Bernard Weinraub, "U.S. is Training Units to Fight Terrorists," *New York Times*, October 20, 1977, p. 17.

[20] O'Ballance, *Language of Violence*, p. 67.

[21] Ariel Merari and Shlomi Elad. *The International Dimension of Palestinian Terrorism*. Jaffee Center for Strategic Studies in Tel Aviv (Colorado: Westview Press, 1986), p. 7. In the author's opinion, this is the best analysis of Palestinian terrorism in its early stages.

community and one that the Nixon administration wanted to address immediately.

The September 6, 1970 hijackings of four aircraft (TWA, Swiss Air, BOAC, and Pan Am) and an attempted hijacking of one other (El Al) by members of the Popular Front for the Liberation of Palestine (PFLP) was a seminal event in the history of aircraft hijackings. These hijackings forced the U.S. to reassess the international terrorist threat. This was the first and only time in history that five commercial aircraft were targeted for hijacking in a single terrorist campaign.[22] The campaign was operationally unique as was the subsequent terrorist propaganda and media performance. On September 7, the PFLP hijackers held a press conference for 60 members of the media at Dawson's Field, now renamed "Revolution Airport." This hijacking spectacle was the first time that terrorists engaged the media in public to propagate their cause. At the conclusion of the Dawson's Field operation, the PFLP wanted to stage a final and lasting media event. After the hostages were taken off all the planes and removed from the area, the terrorists blew up all three planes — after alerting the media in advance — so that the explosions "were recorded and seen on television screens all over the world." [23] The objectives of a terrorist hijacking were now leverage and publicity. George Habash, the founder of the PFLP, articulated the latter in a 1970 interview when he stated: "When we hijack a plane it has more effect than if we killed a hundred Israelis in battle."[24] Aircraft hijackings also caused some of the international audience to ask themselves what would cause these hijackers to do some-

---

[22]The original aim of the campaign was to hijack three aircraft to Dawson's Field in Jordan. Two hijackings were successful (TWA, Swiss Air) but one attempt failed (El Al). As a result, a fourth aircraft was targeted and successfully hijacked (Pan Am). A fifth plane, a British BOAC plane, was also hijacked three days later. However, the hijacking of the British plane was carried out to force the release of a terrorist, Leila Khalid, who was in British custody after failing to hijack the El Al plane. Khalid was eventually released by the British government. The TWA, Swiss Air, and BOAC aircraft were flown to Dawson's Field while the Pan Am plane was flown to Cairo. The PFLP demonstrated operational flexibility in these hijackings. It was only on September 11, 2001 that terrorists were able to seize four aircraft at once. However, 9/11 was not a hijacking operation. The 9/11 terrorists would have preferred that the plane be empty as they only wanted the planes to use as flying bombs. In a hijacking, the terrorists seize passengers to be able to negotiate with the government for certain demands. The 9/11 hijackers had no intention to engage in negotiations with the U.S. government. For an excellent interview by Phillip Baum, editor of *Aviation Security International* magazine, with Leila Khalid in 2000 on the El Al hijacking attempt, see "Leila Khalid: In Her Own Words," at https://web. archive.org/web/20060324074350/http://www.asi-mag.com/editorials/leila_khaled.htm. Accessed June 1, 2018.

[23]O'Ballance, *Language of Violence*, p. 90.

[24]As quoted in Hoffman, *Inside Terrorism*, p. 66.

thing like this, thereby triggering an exploration of the terrorists' cause. Coinciding with the increase in terrorist hijackings in the late 1960s and early 1970s was the confluence of three factors: (1) expansion of commercial airline routes so that terrorists now had more opportunities in more places to hijack planes from targeted countries, (2) the development and expansion of the visual media, that is, TV, and (3) the absence of protective security measures at airports and on aircraft. It was a perfect storm for terrorists hijacking aircraft.

The Dawson's Field hijackings also caused consternation for the Nixon administration as two U.S. planes were involved and there were a total of 153 Americans on all the five aircraft targeted. According to Nixon's chief of staff, H.R. "Bob" Haldeman, as recorded in his diary on September 7, 1970, these hijackings "opened Nixon's eyes" and Nixon was "very anxious to develop some dramatic administration action about hijackings, need tough shocking steps, especially guards on planes."[25] In his October 23, 1970 address to the U.N. General Assembly, Nixon noted eight problems which the U.N. had to address. Number Seven was "to put an end to sky piracy and the kidnapping and murder of diplomats."[26] In May 1973, the administration warned:

> *Crimes against civil aviation continue to be a major threat. The number of aircraft hijackings has grown throughout the world since the first such incident, the diversion of an American plane to Cuba in May 1961. Aircraft of nations representing the full range of the political spectrum have been affected, including Soviet, Israeli, German, Belgian, British, Mexican, and American planes.*[27]

The aircraft hijackings carried out by Palestinian terrorist groups (extortion hijackings) were different than the ones in the 1960s carried out by homesick Cubans, criminals, or leftist activists (transport hijackings) who hijacked U.S.

---

[25] Stephen Collinson, "Nixon's own 9/11: When terrorism came of age," *CNN*, July 29, 2015, at http://www.cnn.com/2015/07/27/politics/terrorism-1970s-richard-nixon. Accessed January 2, 2019.

[26] December 21, 1970 Memorandum from Secretary of State Rogers to President Nixon. Foreign Relations of the United States, 1969–1976, Volume V, United Nations, 1969–1972, Document 20, at https://history.state.gov/historicaldocuments. Accessed December 4, 2017.

[27] Fourth Annual Report to the Congress on United States Foreign Policy, May 3, 1973 issued by the White House in the form of a 234-page booklet entitled *U.S. Foreign Policy for the 1970's: Shaping a Durable Peace; A Report to the Congress by Richard Nixon, President of the United States, May 3, 1973*, at https://history.state.gov/historicaldocuments/frus1969-76v38p1/d9. Accessed December 17, 2016.

aircraft to Cuba.[28] In the latter case, there was little violence, the passengers were not at risk, and there were few political demands. The hijackers simply wanted transportation to Cuba. The Palestinian extortion hijackings were designed to instill fear in the passengers and targeted governments so that the government would give in to the hijacker's demands. The risk to the passengers and crew was high. The hijacking would be successful for the hijackers when their demands were met and the hijackers safely escaped, by going either to a friendly or sympathetic country or to a country that did not have an extradition treaty with the government of the hijacked planes. In some cases, hijackers who were arrested were subsequently freed when their colleagues carried out another hijacking to force their release. These extortion hijackings presented three problems for governments: (1) How to prevent hijackers from getting on planes with weapons and explosives? (2) Whether to give in or not to the hijackers' demands? (3) How to bring the hijackers to justice? The solutions to these three problems consisted of the following: (1) the application of increased security measures at airports and on planes, (2) a stated policy of not negotiating with terrorists, (3) to develop a counter-terrorism rescue capability, and (4) to advocate and advance international conventions that required states to arrest, try, convict, and sentence hijackers or to extradite them to the targeted country of the hijacking.

From 1968 to 1973, 58, or 89%, of the 65 private U.S. citizens killed as a result of terrorism overseas were killed in six incidents involving mid-air bombing of aircraft, assaults on airports, or assaults on aircraft on the tarmac. Attacks on aviation-related targets were increasing, and more Americans were being caught up in these incidents. As a result, the Nixon administration actively engaged in diplomatic efforts to construct international conventions to tackle this problem. These efforts resulted in two international conventions: the 1970 Hague Convention and the 1971 Montreal Convention. The 1970 Hague Convention for the Suppression of Unlawful Seizure of Aircraft (effective in the U.S. in 1971) compelled states to

---

[28]The Kennedy administration responded to these hijackings by employing, for the first time, armed guards on civilian planes in August 1961. In September 1961, Kennedy signed Public Law 87–197, an amendment to the Federal Aviation Act of 1958, which made it a crime to hijack an aircraft, interfere with an active flight crew, or carry a dangerous weapon aboard an air carrier aircraft. In March 1962, Attorney General Robert Kennedy swore in FAA's first "peace officers" as special U.S. deputy marshals who worked as safety inspectors for the FAA. They were only used as armed marshals on flights when specifically requested to do so by airline management or the FBI. In October 1966, President Johnson signed the Department of Transportation Act (Public Law 89–670), bringing 31 previously scattered federal elements, including FAA, under the wing of one Cabinet-level department, the new Department of Transportation (DOT), at http://www.faa.gov/about/history/historical_perspective/media/historical_perspective_ch3.pdf. Accessed December 5, 2017.

prohibit and punish hijacking of only civilian aircraft that take off or land in a place different from its country of registration. The Hague Convention also required that a party to the treaty must prosecute an aircraft hijacker if no other state requests his or her extradition for prosecution of the same crime. The 1971 Montreal Convention for the Suppression of Unlawful Acts against the Safety of Civil Aviation (effective in the U.S. in 1973) addressed attacks on or sabotage of civil aircraft either in flight or on the ground, or destruction of or damage to air navigation facilities when this was likely to endanger the safety of aircraft in flight.[29] The potential for aircraft hijackings at home and those taking place abroad persuaded Nixon on September 11, 1970 to order the immediate deployment of armed federal agents on United States commercial aircraft to counter the increasing threat of air piracy by unbalanced individuals and terrorist organizations.

The air marshal program was originally created by President Kennedy in 1962 as a response to increased hijackings of U.S. aircraft to Cuba. He ordered that federal law enforcement officers be deployed to act as security officers on certain high-risk flights in the southeastern U.S.[30] In addition, new security measures were implemented by the Federal Aviation Administration (FAA), the airlines, and various government law enforcement agencies. Nixon's federal air marshal order was short-lived and only in operation until 1974. At its height, the program had almost 2,000 air security officers from the U.S. Customs Service to

---

[29] The first international convention to address the aircraft hijacking problem was the 1963 Convention on Offences and Certain Other Acts Committed on Board Aircraft (implemented in 1969) which addressed any acts impinging on the safety of persons or property on board civilian aircraft while in-flight and engaged in international air navigation. The groundwork for this 1963 convention was laid by the 1958 Montreal Draft convention, the 1959 Munich Draft convention, and the 1962 Rome Draft convention, which addressed the question of hijacking for the first time.

[30] The FAA, Air Transport Association, and Air Line Pilots Association all had reservations about placing armed sky marshals in an aircraft. The obvious concern was that gunfire in the pressured cabin of an aircraft could easily result in passengers being killed or vital parts of the aircraft being hit. This concern was somewhat mitigated when each "sky marshal" was issued special ammunition for his .38 caliber handgun to prevent damage to the aircraft skin and critical control components if a shoot-out were to take place in the aircraft. The bullets in these handguns were special, light-weight, hollow-point ones that expand at impact with a rapid loss of velocity. This resulted in good knockdown of the target but poor penetration, thereby minimizing the possibility of penetration of the airplane skin. Still, at the time, airline officials "remained traditionally opposed to the use of force on board airplanes." This attitude was reinforced by the fact that most of the hijackings at this time involved trips to Cuba and that the hijackings were relatively "passive." *Criminal Justice Monograph*, Vol. III, No. 5, 1972, Robert T. Turi, Charles M. Friel, Robert B. Sheldon, John P. Matthews, "Descriptive Study of Aircraft Hijacking," Institute of Contemporary Corrections and the Behavioral Sciences, Sam Houston State University, pp. 121–122, at http://files.eric.ed.gov/fulltext/ED073315pdf. Accessed June 6, 2018.

fly on commercial airlines and conduct pre-departure inspection. However, following the mandatory passenger screening enacted by the FAA at U.S. airports beginning in 1973, the customs security officer force was disbanded and by 1974, armed sky marshals were a rarity on U.S. aircraft.[31] In a March 9, 1972 statement "About Air Transportation Safety," the administration touted as follows:

> *The sky marshal and passenger screening programs conducted jointly by the Government and the airlines since that time have progressively reduced the hijacker's chances of success. From a onetime high of 83 percent, the success average of hijacking attempts diminished to 44 percent last year and now to only 25 percent thus far in 1972. Our efforts will continue until we reduce that rate to zero.[32]*

In 1973, metal detection and X-ray devices became mandatory at all airports. The FAA required all airlines to screen passengers and carry-on baggage for hidden weapons. The policy became a model for all airports worldwide, spawning the X-ray screening industry.[33] Although the new security measures led to longer check-in times and some passenger inconvenience, they also led to a dramatic reduction in the number of U.S. hijackings.[34] In March 1973, the United States and Cuba were able to reach an agreement that allowed either country to request the extradition of a hijacker. The agreement came about through an exchange of diplomatic notes. It was in Cuba's interest to make the agreement because many Cubans had hijacked planes from Cuba and forced them to fly to the United States. The agreement allowed either country to consider extenuating circumstances when the hijackers acted "for strictly political reasons and were in real and imminent danger of death without a viable alternative, provided there was no financial extortion or physical injury" to crew, passengers, or other persons. In March 1974, the International Civil Aviation Organization (ICAO), a specialized

---

[31] "Riding the Planes: Sky Marshals redefined airline security in the 1970s," U.S. Customs and Border Protection document, at http://www.cbp.gov/sites/default/files/documents/ridingtheplanes.pdf. Accessed December 17, 2017. Accessed March 9, 2015. Across the life of the program, agents "... made 3,828 arrests, some in-flight; seized or detained 69,317 potentially lethal weapons; and made 248 hard narcotic seizures and 1,667 marijuana and dangerous drug seizures."

[32] Statement about Air Transportation Safety, March 9, 1972. The American Presidency Project, University of California, Santa Barbara, at http://www.presidency.ucsb.edu/ws. Accessed June 6, 2017. Search of President Nixon's Public Papers from 1969 to 1974 using the search term "terrorism."

[33] http://www.tc.faa.gov/logistics/grants/success/invision.pdf. Accessed July 17, 2016.

[34] Scott McCartney, "The Golden Age of Flight," *Wall Street Journal*, July 22, 2010.

agency of the United Nations charged with coordinating and regulating international air travel, met in Chicago and adopted Annex 17, which established Standards and Recommended Practices for international aviation security. Annex 17 created standard procedures and guidance for the Civil Aviation Industry on how to safeguard the industry against acts of unlawful interference. Of relevance are Chapter 4 "Preventive Security Measures" and Chapter 5 "Management of Response to Acts of Unlawful Interference."[35]

In August 1974, the U.S. passed the Anti-Hijacking Act to implement The Hague and Montreal international conventions. This act was designed to prevent nations from adopting a permissive posture toward illegal activities such as the commandeering of aircraft, by providing penalties for hijackers and for nations that shield or fail to take adequate precautions against hijackers. The act gives the President the power to terminate air service between an offending nation and the United States if the President determines that the offending nation has acted inconsistently with its obligations under the anti-hijacking conventions. In addition, the Secretary of Transportation, with the approval of the Secretary of State, can withhold, revoke, or impose conditions on the U.S. operating authorities of the airlines of any nation that does not effectively maintain and administer security measures equal to, or above, ICAO minimum standards. With the signing of these international conventions in the 1970s, airplane hijacking fell sharply, especially in the United States.

According to an unclassified U.S. government study on "Terrorist Skyjackings," the number of attempted skyjackings reached a high in 1969–1970, declined slightly in 1971–1972, and decreased by half in 1973. The decline was attributed primarily to increased security measures.[36]

Kidnappings and Assassinations: Protection of U.S. Officials Overseas

Another terrorism concern for the U.S. was the terrorist targeting of U.S. officials (government, diplomats, and military) overseas. U.S. officials and facilities were being assassinated, bombed, kidnapped, and involved in barricade and hostage situations during the Nixon administration.[37] In 1968, 82% of all

---

[35] http://aviationknowledge.wikidot.com/aviation:icao-annex-17:security:safeguarding-international-c; and http://www.icao.int/Security/SFP/Pages/Annex17.aspx. Accessed December 2, 2016.

[36] U.S. Department of State. "Terrorist Skyjackings: A Statistical overview of terrorist Skyjackings from January 1968 through June 1982," published July 1982, p. 1.

[37] See for example, U.S. House of Representatives, Committee on Internal Security, "Staff Study: Political Kidnappings: 1968–1973," August 1, 1978.

Table 4.1

Year	Hijackings in the U.S.	Hijackings Overseas[a]
1970	25	49
1971	25	30
1972	26	30
1973	2	20
1974	3	17
1975	6	13
1976	2	14

[a] U.S. Department of Transportation, Bureau of Transportation Statistics, "Pocket Guide to Transportation — 2004," Figure 3 Worldwide Civil Aviation Hijackings, at http://www.rita.dot.gov/bts/sites/rita.dot.gov.bts/files/publications/pocket_guide_to_transportation/2004/html/figure_03.html. Accessed December 17, 2017.

anti-American terrorist attacks overseas were aimed at U.S. diplomatic, government, and military targets. In 1969, it was 55% and in 1970, 78%.[38] Of the 87 Americans killed overseas by political terrorists from 1968 to 1974, 22, or 25%, were U.S. diplomatic, government, and military personnel. However, the terrorists' seizure of Americans, through kidnappings, hijackings, or barricade and hostage incidents, was the most serious terrorist problem that could confront the U.S. government. Such incidents were designed to extract political or financial concessions from the U.S. or the country where the incident took place. The following hostage situations involving Americans took place during the 1968–1974 period:

- August 1969 — Hijacking of TWA plane to Damascus, Syria.
- June 1970 — Terrorists seized the Philadelphia and Intercontinental hotels in Amman, Jordan.
- July 1970 — Hijacking of Olympic Airline flight in Lebanon.
- September 1970 — Dawson's Field hijackings — 144 Americans on four aircraft.
- May 1972 — Hijacking of Sabena Airline flight to Israel.
- September 1972 — Munich Olympics seizure (Dual Israeli–American held).

---

[38] Statistics from Central Intelligence Agency, National Foreign Assessment Center, "International Terrorism in 1977: A Research Paper," RP 78-10255U, August 1978, pp. 9–12.

- March 1973 — Seizure of Saudi Embassy in Khartoum (two U.S. diplomats held).

All these hostage situations involved Palestinian terrorists.

Another emerging terrorism problem for the Nixon administration was the growing number of political kidnappings worldwide. In 1968 and 1969, there was one recorded political kidnapping worldwide each year. In 1970, there were 32. In 1968, there was one political kidnapping of an American and two in 1969. In 1970, there were 17.[39] Most of these kidnappings were aimed at U.S. officials, including military personnel. From 1968 to 1973, there were 23 attempted or successful terrorist kidnappings of U.S. officials overseas, of which sixteen involved U.S. diplomats, six U.S. military personnel, and one U.S. Peace Corps volunteer. Four of those U.S. citizens were eventually killed. Sixteen of these attacks took place in 1970:

- August 1968 — A failed kidnapping of the U.S. Ambassador John Gordon Main in Guatemala led to his death.
- September 1969 — The U.S. Ambassador in Brazil was kidnapped.
- September 1969 — The U.S. Consul General in Ethiopia was kidnapped.
- March 1970 — The U.S. Labor Attaché was kidnapped in Guatemala.
- March 1970 — The U.S. Air Attaché was kidnapped in the Dominican Republic.
- April 1970 — Two U.S. military personnel were kidnapped in the Philippines and later found dead.
- April 1970 — There was an attempted kidnapping of a U.S. Consul General in Brazil.
- April 1970 — A U.S. Peace Corps volunteer was kidnapped in Ethiopia.
- May 1970 — The Assistant U.S. Naval Attaché was kidnapped in South Africa.
- June 1970 — The Chief of the Political Section at the U.S. Embassy in Jordan was kidnapped.
- June 1970 — A plot by the Quebec Liberation Front (FLQ) to kidnap U.S. Consul General Harrison W. Burgess was discovered by the police. Weapons, explosives, and communiqués for the kidnapping were found in a safe house. The FLQ was planning to ask for the release of 13 political prisoners.
- July 1970 — There was an attempted kidnapping of a U.S. Embassy officer in Bolivia.

---

[39] Ibid.

- July 1970 — There was an attempted kidnapping of two U.S. Embassy personnel in Uruguay.
- July 1970 — A U.S. Agency for International Development official was kidnapped in Uruguay and later killed.
- August 1970 — A U.S. diplomat was kidnapped in Uruguay.
- August 1970 — A U.S. Agency for International Development Public Safety officer was kidnapped in Uruguay.
- September 1970 — An enlisted man assigned to the Defense Attaché Office was kidnapped in Jordan.
- September 1970 — A U.S. Cultural Affairs officer was kidnapped in Jordan.
- November 1970 — There was an attempted kidnapping of the U.S. Ambassador and his wife in Iran.
- February 1971 — A U.S. Airman was kidnapped in Turkey.
- March 1971 — Four U.S. Airmen were kidnapped in Turkey.
- January 1973 — The U.S. Ambassador in Haiti was kidnapped.
- May 1973 — The U.S. Consul General in Mexico was kidnapped.

Most of these political kidnappings were carried out by left-wing terrorist groups or insurgent organizations with a few carried out by Palestinian terrorists.

The protection of diplomats overseas is the primary responsibility of the host country. This is stated in Article 22 of the 1961 Vienna Convention Diplomatic Relations and Optional Protocols. The increase in attacks on diplomatic targets worldwide created two dilemmas for the U.S. government: (1) concern over attacks on its diplomatic interests overseas, and (2) protection of foreign diplomatic interests in the U.S. When Nixon formed the CCCT in 1972, he charged it with "the physical protection of U.S. personnel and installations abroad." The U.S. government's strategy to deal with this threat was to: (1) lobby for regional and international conventions that would protect diplomats and punish those who threaten or carry out attacks against "internationally protected persons and facilities," (2) develop political and technical measures to protect U.S. diplomatic interests overseas, and (3) develop protective security programs, increase resources, and work out a division of responsibility among U.S. federal and local law enforcement agencies for the protection of internationally protected persons and facilities in the U.S.

In 1970, the U.S. advocated that terrorism was a criminal offense and not a political offense.[40] It recognized however that terrorism can arise from real and

---

[40] U.S. Department of State, Office of the Historian, Foreign Relations of the United States, Nixon-Ford Administrations, Volume E-1, Documents on Global Issues. Document 43. Position Paper on

perceived political grievances. The U.S. position was that these political grievances should be addressed through non-violent political channels and measures. Given that Latin America was becoming a high-terrorist threat region for U.S. diplomats,[41] the U.S. actively lobbied the Organization of American States (OAS) to adopt a convention concerning terrorist attacks on foreign officials. Secretary of State Rogers declared that "the kidnapping of foreign officials by private groups for ransom purposes is a phenomenon new to the history of international relations."[42] On February 2, 1971, the OAS passed a "Convention to Prevent and Punish the Acts of Terrorism Taking the Form of Crimes Against Persons and Related Extortion That Are of International Significance." Article 2 of this convention states that "kidnapping, murder, and other assaults against the life or personal integrity of those persons to whom the state has the duty to give special protection according to international law, as well as extortion in connection with those crimes, shall be considered common crimes of international significance, regardless of motive."[43] On February 3, the State Department noted that the convention was the "first time that any international agreement has specified that the murder or kidnapping of representatives of states are not to be considered as political offenses whose perpetrators are sheltered by asylum."[44]

On September 25, 1972, the U.S. submitted a draft convention on the "Prevention and Punishment of certain acts of International Terrorism" to the U.N. General Assembly. This convention was "ahead of its time in serving as a counterpart to neutrality laws for low-intensity conflict settings ... that is, it sought to establish that carrying on civil struggle on the territory of a third state was impermissible."[45] In a September 22 memorandum to the Secretary of State

---

Inter-American Convention on Terrorism and Kidnapping. Prepared in the U.S. Department of State, Washington, D.C., December 31, 1970, at https://history.state.gov/historicaldocuments/frus1969-76ve01/d43. Accessed July 5, 2016.

[41] Latin America accounted for 37% of all international terrorist incidents worldwide in 1968, 43% in 1969, and 40% in 1970. It accounted for 70% of all anti-American terrorist incidents in 1968, 54% in 1969, and 46% in 1970. Statistics from Central Intelligence Agency, National Foreign Assessment Center, "International Terrorism in 1977: A Research Paper," RP 78-10255U, August 1978, pp. 9–12.

[42] As quoted in Tucker, *Skirmishes at the Edge of Empire*, p. 3.

[43] http://www.oas.org/juridico/english/treaties/a-49.html. Accessed November 4, 2017.

[44] As quoted in Tucker, *Skirmishes at the End of Empire*, p. 3.

[45] John Norton Moore, "Legal Mechanisms to Combat Terrorism," Testimony before the U.S. Senate Judiciary Subcommittee on Security and Terrorism, Liability of Civil and Criminal Actions against Yasir Arafat's Palestine Liberation Organization, April 23, 1986, p. 194, at https://www.ncjrs.gov/pdffiles1/Photocopy/105320NCJRS.pdf. Accessed May 3, 2017. At the time of his testimony, Moore was the Director of the Center for Law and National Security at the University of Virginia and Chairman of the Standing Committee on Law and National Security of the American Bar Association,

from the State Department's legal advisor, the views of the government on this issue are spelled out[46]:

- Its objective "is to single out acts of political violence which occur both outside the State of the nationality of the perpetrator and outside the State against which the act is directed." In other words, it focused on spillover terrorism that impacted on parties not involved in the trigger conflict.
- To be covered, "an act is required to be directed against civilians rather than members of the Armed Forces of a State in the course of military hostilities."
- The convention would "exclude civil violence in which a national is acting against his own government within the territory of his State." This means it would not cover domestic terrorism committed in countries where, for example, "wars of liberation" were taking place. The reason for this exclusion was to "single out the recent internationalization of violent acts abroad, and to increase the chances for agreement."
- Within the scope of the covered acts listed in the draft convention, "anyone who unlawfully kills, causes serious bodily harm or kidnaps another person commits an offense of international significance." States party to this convention would be "required to extend their jurisdiction over such offenses, make such offenses punishable by severe penalties, and to extradite or prosecute alleged offenders found in their territory."

At the end of this memorandum, the author provides examples of terrorist acts that would and would not be covered by this draft convention:

Terrorist Acts Covered

(1) The Munich Tragedy and any other case of a Palestinian attack on Israeli citizens abroad.
(2) The assassination of the Foreign Minister of Jordan in Egypt.

---

and he formerly served as Counselor on International Law to the Department of State and in that capacity drafted the 1972 United States Convention on Terrorism.

[46]U.S. Department of State. Office of the Historian. *Foreign Relations of the United States, 1969– 1976*, Volume E-1, Documents on Global Issues, 1969–1972, Document 105. Information Memorandum on the Draft Convention for the Prevention and Punishment of Certain Acts of International Terrorism, from the Legal Adviser of the Department of State (Stevenson) to Secretary of State Rogers, Washington, September 22, 1972, at https://history.state.gov/historicaldocuments/frus1969-76ve01/d105. Accessed December 3, 2016.

(3) The recent mailings of explosive devices to Israeli diplomats.
(4) The Croatian hijacking in Switzerland (though the hijacking Conventions would take precedence).

Terrorist Acts Not Covered

(1) The Lod Airport attack.
(2) Palestinian attacks on Israel if committed within Israel.
(3) Attacks by liberation groups in Southern Africa within the territory of the State attacked.
(4) Acts by or against members of the Armed Forces of a State in the course of military hostilities.[47]

On December 12, 1972, the U.S. draft convention was defeated in the U.N. General Assembly by a vote of 74 to 36 in favor of one to study terrorism's "underlying causes."[48] As on all terrorism-related proposals, the Arabs and Africans were the principal stumbling blocks.[49] They opposed the criminalization of terrorism as they felt that some political grievances, especially national liberation movements, could justify using political violence.

In December 1973, the U.N. General Assembly adopted a "Convention on the Protection and Punishment of Crimes Against Internationally Protected Persons, including Diplomatic Agents." The U.S. mission at the U.N. and the State Department's Legal Adviser's office engaged in "careful, imaginative, and effective diplomacy" to get this convention passed.[50] This convention criminalized the commission of murders or kidnappings of internationally protected persons as well

---

[47] For a detailed and interesting perspective on this point, see Jordan J. Paust, "Terrorism and the International Law of War," *Military Law Review*, Vol. 64, Spring 1974, pp. 1–36.

[48] U.S. Department of State, Office of the Historian, *Foreign Relations of the United States*, Nixon-Ford Administrations, Volume E-3, Documents on Global Issues, Document 204. Memorandum from the President's Assistant for National Security Affairs (Kissinger) and the Assistant to the President for Domestic Affairs (Ehrlichman) to President Nixon, Washington, January 17, 1973, at https://history.state.gov/historicaldocuments/frus1969-76ve03/d204. Accessed June 4, 2017.

[49] U.S. Department of State, Office of the Historian, *Foreign Relations of the United States*, Nixon-Ford Administrations, Volume E-1, Documents on Global Issues. Document 120. Telegram 5582 from the Mission to the United Nations to the Department of State, New York, December 15, 1972, 0221, at https://history.state.gov/historicaldocuments/frus1969-76ve01/d120. Accessed November 16, 2016.

[50] U.S. Department of State, Briefing Memorandum titled "Major Problems in Combatting Terrorism," from Lewis Hoffacker, Special Assistant on Terrorism to the Secretary of State, Dated October 4, 1973. Document #211, Foreign Relations of the United States, 1969–1976, Volume E-3, Documents on Global Issues, 1973–1976, Terrorism (Documents 203–228), at http://history.state.gov/historical-documents/frus1969-76ve01/ch1. Accessed May 23, 2018.

as violent attacks against the official premises, private accommodation, or means of transport of such persons. Signatories of the convention also agreed to criminalize the attempted commission or threatened commission of such acts. "Internationally protected persons" was a term created by the convention and referred explicitly to heads of state, heads of government, foreign ministers, ambassadors, other official diplomats, and members of their families. A central provision of the convention was that a signatory to the treaty must either (1) prosecute a person who commits an offense against an internationally protected person or (2) send the person to another state that requests his or her extradition for prosecution of the same crime.[51] By the end of 1974, the convention had been signed by 25 states, and it came into force on February 22, 1977 after it had been ratified by 22 states. The U.S. was the first country to sign the convention on December 28, 1973 and the 17th country to ratify it.[52] These actions in international and regional organizations highlight the determined and extensive diplomatic effort the U.S. undertook to corral international support to address the terrorism dilemma.

As the international terrorist threat continued to rise, terrorist attacks on diplomatic targets in general were increasing worldwide as follows[53]:

Year	No. of Incidents
1968	80
1969	79
1970	204
1971	145
1972	200
1973	174
1974	136
1975	131
1976	174
1977	155
1978	255

[51] Convention on the Prevention and Punishment of Crimes against Internationally Protected Persons, including Diplomatic Agents 1973, at http://legal.un.org/ilc/texts/instruments/english/conventions/9_4_1973.pdf.

[52] http://www.unodc.org/pdf/crime/terrorism/Commonwealth_Chapter_6.pdf. Accessed December 21, 2017.

[53] U.S. Department of State, "Terrorist Incidents Involving Diplomats: A Statistical Overview of International Terrorist Incidents involving Diplomatic Personnel and Facilities from January 1968 through April 1983," Published August 1983.

Terrorist attacks against U.S. diplomatic facilities and personnel overseas significantly increased in the early 1970s. In 1969, there were 26 incidents. In 1970, there were 96 and in 1971, there were 97. In 1972, there were 93.[54] The geographic footprint of the Department of State was also expanding. In 1940, the Department of State had 58 diplomatic posts, but by 1970, that number had ballooned to 117.[55] The U.S. now had more people and facilities to protect. In fact, at the time, the U.S. had the largest diplomatic footprint of any country in the world. Moreover, since the end of World War II, the U.S. had deployed an array of programs in various host countries overseas to provide cultural, educational, and information activities on the United States. The U.S. government's relationship with these programs has varied from supervision, to funding, to support, to general cooperation. The brick and mortar representations of these programs were binational centers, U.S. information service libraries, Amerika Haus (in Germany), and U.S. cultural centers. These were places where host country citizens could go to learn about the United States and various exchange programs. These places were generally established in the capitals and other major cities. During the 1950s, 1960s, and 1970s, they had few security measures. These made for soft targets for any terrorist group who wanted to make an anti-American statement with an attack. Of the 166 anti-American terrorist attacks that took place overseas from 1960 to 1969, 67, or 40%, were directed at these cultural facilities.[56] This soft underbelly of the semi-official U.S. presence overseas was also expanding. By the 1960s, there were 113 binational centers in 19 Latin American countries.[57]

---

[54] Statistics from Central Intelligence Agency, National Foreign Assessment Center, "Patterns of International Terrorism: 1980," PA 81-10163U, June 1981, p. 4.

[55] U.S. Department of State, Office of the Historian. *History of the Bureau of Diplomatic Security of the United States Department of State*, p. 199, at http://www.state.gov/m/ds/rls/rpt/c47602.htm. Accessed May 8, 2017. All references and information on the Office of Security or SY (the predecessor to the Bureau of Diplomatic Security) comes from this 441-page history. Hereafter, referred to as "DS History."

[56] Statistic based on author-compiled chronology of anti-American terrorist attacks from 1950 to 2019.

[57] Wilson P. Dizard, Jr., *Inventing Public Diplomacy: The Story of the U.S. Information Agency* (Boulder: Lynne Rienner Publishing, 2004), p. 181. The United States Information Agency (USIA), an agency of the executive branch of government, was known overseas as the United States Information Service (USIS). Binational Centers are autonomous, foreign institutions dedicated to the promotion of mutual understanding between the host country and the United States. English teaching is usually a major component of their cultural, educational, and information activities. Binational Centers often work in close cooperation with USIS posts overseas but are independent in their financial and administrative management. Binational Centers are found mostly in Latin America. Unfortunately, they have been perceived by terrorist groups as representing a U.S. footprint in their

The most prominent and prevalent official U.S. footprint in any country was the U.S. Embassy. The highest representative was the U.S. Ambassador. U.S. military interests were also attractive targets, but most U.S. military personnel lived on secure bases while U.S. diplomats lived outside the embassy and were more vulnerable to terrorist attack. The most direct way to attack the United States in a foreign country was to attack the U.S. Embassy, consulate, ambassador's residence, and U.S. diplomats. Such attacks attracted the most publicity and caused the most embarrassment to the host country. Another problem for the State Department was that before World War II, U.S. embassies were staffed almost exclusively by the State Department. By 1960, State Department employees were frequently in the minority as many other U.S. government agencies wanted overseas representation.[58] This contributed to the increase in U.S. government employees in U.S. diplomatic facilities from other U.S. government agencies. This in turn created security problems for State Department employees as terrorists perceived the diplomatic facilities, especially embassies, to be a base for spying and therefore anyone working there was spy. In other words, embassy officials who were engaged in purely diplomatic endeavors were being painted with the same brush as CIA operatives.

The protection of U.S. diplomatic facilities and personnel overseas rested with the State Department, specifically its undersized Office of Security. In the 1960s, SY's responsibilities in the State Department were centered on background investigations of employees, protection of classified information, and counter-intelligence. Prior to 1965, the protective security focus of SY was on the protection of the Secretary of State and visiting foreign dignitaries, whose visits to the U.S. were increasing.[59] President Kennedy hosted 74 official visits from

---

countries. By 1970, the USIA had established posts in over 150 countries. In many cases, they were small outposts in regions where they were the only USG presence (Dizard, p. 157).

[58] Ibid., p. 156.

[59] Ibid., p. 201. In early 1965, SY organized an ad hoc interagency committee to study terrorism, and particularly the isolated attacks against U.S. posts and installations in Latin America. The result was a "comprehensive guidance document" titled "The Protection of U.S. Personnel and Installations Against Acts of Terrorism in Latin America," that SY sent to all Chiefs of Mission in Latin America. Although implementation of the documents' recommendations was subject to the decision of the Chief of Mission, the guidance document requested that all missions set up Security Watch Committees. SY tasked the Watch Committees to evaluate the state of security in their country and to devise and implement measures to improve post security. U.S. Department of State, Office of the Historian. History of the Bureau of Diplomatic Security of the United States Department of State, p. 201. The 100th year anniversary of the Bureau of Diplomatic Security took place in 2016.

1961 to 1962 compared to the 32 during Eisenhower's first two years.[60] Such visits strained the SY work load. In the mid-1960s, SY had just over 300 special agents and security officers, with 245 in domestic assignments and 55 overseas.[61] The murder of U.S. Ambassador John Gordon Mein in Guatemala in 1968 during a failed kidnapping, and the kidnapping of the U.S. Ambassador in Brazil in 1969 "sent shock waves through the department" in part, because Ambassador Mein was the first U.S. Ambassador killed in the performance of duty.[62] Since the mid-1960s, SY was becoming more involved and devoted more resources to the protection of U.S. diplomatic facilities and personnel overseas. Given that U.S. diplomatic facilities represented the official face of the United States overseas, they were often the target of protests, violent and non-violent. For example, during the June 1967 Six-Day war between Israel, the United Arab Republic (Egypt), Jordan, and Syria, mobs attacked 22 U.S. embassies and consulates in Arab countries with damage ranging from broken windows to gutted buildings. Anti-Vietnam protests also took place in front of U.S. diplomatic facilities in Western Europe.[63] Such anti-American protests at U.S. diplomatic facilities in the 1960s were a harbinger of things to come as U.S. diplomatic facilities were seized, ransacked, and burned down in the 1980s and 1990s. In addition to these protests, there was a wave of kidnappings and assassinations of diplomats in general, but U.S. diplomats in particular, that caused the State Department and SY to construct new protective security measures, programs, and guidelines overseas. Although there was no significant increase in SY manpower at this time, SY evolved over the next four decades into the largest protective security organization in the world.[64]

In an April 2, 1970 internal State Department memorandum, the heads of the Latin American Bureau and SY assessed some of the weaknesses in the overseas

---

[60] U.S. Department of State, Bureau of Diplomatic Security, *The Diplomatic Security Service — Then and Now: The First Century of the Diplomatic Security Service*, historical study released in April 2016, p. 40, at https://www.state.gov/documents/organization/255554.pdf. Accessed June 23, 2018.

[61] Ibid., p. 48.

[62] *DS History*, p. 202.

[63] *DS History*, p. 52.

[64] By 1975, SY's staff had shrunk to just under 200, with 139 special agents in domestic assignments and 57 overseas. In 1976, as a result of a growing terrorist threat overseas, 168 special agents were added to SY for a total of 364 personnel. By 1984, the SY staff included 426 special agents and security officers, 312 of them in domestic positions and 151 overseas, many as regional security officers assigned to protect U.S. diplomatic facilities overseas. *DS History*, p. 48. The evolution of SY's responsibilities, especially overseas, and the increase in its manpower and budget were directly linked to the growing overseas terrorist threat.

protective security program. There were no guidelines in place to link the terrorist threat to a required level of protective security measures; the Ambassador was not explicitly required to determine the threat level at post and invoke commensurate protections; and the State Department "does not know at any given time in any given country what the degree of danger of kidnapping is or what measures the Ambassador has invoked."[65] It was also suggested that a mobile reserve of equipment (partially and fully armored cars, communications equipment, etc.) be created that could be utilized when the kidnapping risk in a particular country was deemed to be high. To fix these weaknesses, a four-phase plan that outlined "graduated responses" to threats against U.S. missions and staff was established. The four phases were "Early Warning," "Clear Existence of Threat," "Clear Existence of Intense Threat," and "Unacceptable Level of Threat." Each level required the missions to implement certain protective security measures. A mobile reserve of equipment and people was established in Washington, D.C. for dispatch to troubled areas when the need arose and the U.S. Intelligence Board required intelligence agencies to place "a high priority" on the acquisition of intelligence relating to "plans, targets, etc. of potential kidnappers in an area from which we receive danger signals."[66]

The State Department also sent out security guidelines to all missions on personnel and facility protective security measures.[67] These measures consisted of avoiding patterns on travel routes, arrival and departure times; increased security awareness when leaving the mission compound; using locally manufactured vehicles when possible; removal of diplomatic license plates in certain situations; defensive driver training; use of fully or partially armored vehicles; and installing

---

[65]U.S. Department of State, Office of the Historian, Foreign Relations of the United States, Nixon-Ford Administrations, Volume E-1, Documents on Global Issues, Document 37. Memorandum titled "Kidnapping of U.S. Officials Abroad," from Deputy Assistant Secretary of State for Inter-American Affairs (Hurwitch) and Deputy Assistant Secretary of State for Security (Gentile) to Deputy Under Secretary of State for Administration (Macomber), Washington, April 2, 1970, at https://history.state. gov/historicaldocuments/frus1969-76ve01/d37. Accessed July 6, 2017.

[66]Ibid.

[67]U.S. Department of State, Office of the Historian, Foreign Relations of the United States, Nixon-Ford Administrations, Volume E-1, Documents on Global Issues. Document 114. Memorandum titled "Status of USG Actions Against Terrorism," from Richard Kennedy of the National Security Council Staff to the President's Assistant for National Security Affairs (Kissinger), November 1, 1972, at https://history.state.gov/historicaldocuments/frus1969-76ve01/d114. Accessed November 6, 2017; U.S. Department of State, Office of the Historian, Foreign Relations of the United States, Nixon-Ford Administrations, Volume E-3, Documents on Global Issues, Document 210. Memorandum titled "Combatting Terrorism," from the Secretary of State to the President, June 27, 1973, at https://history. state.gov/historicaldocuments/frus1969-76ve03/d210. Accessed May 5, 2017.

mobile radios in embassy vehicles. SY also augmented Marine Security Guard forces for several embassies, such as those in Brazil and Argentina; replaced older vehicles of embassy motor pools; expanded the use of "follow" cars for Ambassadors; and provided more money for mission security expenses. Embassies built or upgraded fences and walls at chanceries and Ambassadors' residences, installed emergency generators, upgraded lighting, and added vault doors and window grills.[68] SY also outlined a four-stage sequence that U.S. posts should follow in case they required additional protection. The first stage was to approach the host government, which bore the primary responsibility for providing security for foreign missions. The thinking was that if the host country provided extra guards and an incident occurred (e.g., a shoot-out), it would be a local issue under the responsibility of the host government, not a diplomatic incident between the United States and the host nation. The second stage was for U.S. posts to examine the possibility of hiring local, reputable, professional guards. If that was not possible, then, the third stage was that U.S. security officers might be made available. The fourth stage was to hire additional Marine Security Guards. This was to be a last resort, partly due to questions of immunity and jurisdiction. Moreover, since many Marines had served a tour of duty in Vietnam, the Commandant of the Marine Corps made clear that it was "somewhat unfair to ask that a 20-year-old veteran of Vietnam, whose reflexes have been sharpened by combat, [to] exercise the restraint and cool judgment" required on protective security assignments.[69] This surge of increased and updated packages of protective security procedures, measures, and manpower in the late 1960s/early 1970s was not duplicated again until after the April 18, 1983 vehicular suicide attack on the U.S. Embassy in Beirut, Lebanon that killed 63 people, including 17 Americans.

Policy on Hostages in Hijackings, Kidnappings, and Barricade and Hostage Incidents

Historical Background

The U.S. government policy on hostage-taking had slowly evolved from the founding of the country. From around 1784 to 1815, the United States had been at war with the pirates of North Africa and their sponsoring potentates of Morocco, Tunis, Libya, and Algiers. Four American presidents, namely, Washington, Adams, Jefferson, and Madison, had paid tribute to various Arab

---

[68] *DS History*, p. 203.
[69] Ibid, pp. 204–205.

leaders, negotiated contracts and treaties, endured the hostage-taking or enslavement of some 700 Americans and the capture of 35 American ships, and paid millions of dollars in tribute and ransom to secure the freeing of American hostages.[70] When the U.S. was a colony of Great Britain, it was protected by the British Navy and British treaties with the Barbary States. However, even then when a few American ships were captured, it was private American citizens who collected the ransom payments to free the American sailors. Immediately after the American Colonies declared and won their independence, British authorities made it a point to notify the Barbary States that her former possessions in America were no longer protected under British treaties with the Barbary States. At the time, the American continental navy was disbanded, the American colonies' economy was weak, and the Mediterranean remained a key commerce route for the U.S. Prior to the American Revolution, "an average of 100 American ships transported 20,000 tons of goods annually to Mediterranean ports ... whose markets consumed one-sixth of America's wheat exports and one-fourth of its exported fish."[71] In the immediate post-revolutionary years, the U.S. was ruled by a Confederation government established in 1781 that was broke, weak, and had no power to tax. In 1788, with the approval of the Confederation Congress, the Articles of Confederation were replaced by the United States Constitution in 1789 that established a stronger central government. It is certain that the problem of the Barbary States and its pirates had considerable influence on the debate that ratified the new constitution.[72]

---

[70] http://middleeast.about.com/od/usmideastpolicy/qt/barbary-pirates-victory-message.htm. Accessed May 6, 2017.

[71] Joseph Wheelan. *Jefferson's War: America's First War on Terror 1801–1805* (New York: Carrol and Graf Publishers, 2003), p. 36. See also, Brian Kilmeade. *Thomas Jefferson and the Tripoli Pirates: The Forgotten War That Changed American History* (New York: Penguin Random House, 2015); Martha Elena Rojas, "'Insults Unpunished': Barbary Captives, American Slaves, and the Negotiation of Liberty," *Early American Studies: An Interdisciplinary Journal*, Vol. 1, no. 2 (Fall 2003), 159–186; Gardner W. Allen, *Our Navy and the Barbary Corsairs*, (Boston: Houghton, Mifflin and Company, 1905); Joshua E. London. *Victory in Tripoli: How America's War with the Barbary Pirates Established the U.S. Navy and Shaped a Nation* (New Jersey: John Wiley & Sons, 2005).

[72] Christopher Hitchens, "Jefferson Versus the Muslim Pirates: America's first confrontation with the Islamic world helped forge a new nation's character," *The City Journal*, Spring 2007. Hitchens notes that "Many a delegate, urging his home state to endorse the new document, argued that only a strong federal union could repel the Algerian threat. In *The Federalist* No. 24, Alexander Hamilton argued that without a "federal navy ... of respectable weight ... the genius of American Merchants and Navigators would be stifled and lost." In No. 41, James Madison insisted that only a union could guard America's maritime capacity from "the rapacious demands of pirates and barbarians." John Jay, in his letters, took a "bring-it-on" approach; he believed that "Algerian Corsairs and the Pirates of Tunis and

The new United States government began operations in 1789 with George Washington elected as the first President on April 30.[73] However, the Confederation Congress was the first American entity that had to address the issue of the seizure of American ships and citizens by the Barbary Coast pirates. The first significant attack on a United States ship took place in October 1784 when "The Betsey," a 300-ton ship from Boston, was attacked 100 miles from Africa's western coast, in the Atlantic. The ship's 10 American merchant seamen were captured, but released in mid-1785 with Spain's assistance. This was the first act of piracy against the United States and inaugurated the era of the Barbary Coast pirates.[74] The next year, the U.S. ships "Maria" and "Dauphin" were seized by the pirates with 21 seamen and passengers. In early 1786, the U.S. Minister to France, Thomas Jefferson, and Minister to England, John Adams, met in London with the ambassador from Tripoli and asked him why Tripoli was attacking U.S. ships when they were not at war?

> *The Ambassador answered us that it was founded on the Laws of the Prophet, that it was written in their Koran that all nations who should not have acknowledged their authority were sinners, that it was their right and duty to make war upon them wherever they could be found, and to make slaves of all they could take as prisoners and that every Musselman (Muslim) who should be slain in battle was sure to go to Paradise.*[75]

Afterwards, Jefferson estimated that the U.S. would have to pay more than $1.3 million to make peace with all the Barbary States and ransom U.S. hostages.[76] Adams concluded that the U.S. did not have the ships, money, and public support

---

Tripoli" would compel the feeble American states to unite, since "the more we are ill-treated abroad the more we shall unite and consolidate at home," at http://www.city-journal.org/html/17_2_urbanities-thomas_jefferson.html. Accessed May 7, 2017.

[73] http://www.lewis-clark.org/article/3165. Accessed May 5, 2018, and https://en.wikipedia.org/wiki/Articles_of_Confederation. Accessed June 6, 2017.

[74] For a more extensive study of this era, see Wheelan, *Jefferson's War*. The seizure of U.S. ships and hostages during this period produced: (1) the first example of state-sponsored terrorism against the U.S., (2) the first "arms for hostages" situation, (3) the first deployment of the U.S. military in a counter-terrorism operation, and (4) part of the opening line to the U.S. Marine Corp hymn — "from the halls of Montezuma to the shores of *Tripoli*." In addition, the Tripoli Monument at the U.S. Naval Academy is the oldest U.S. military monument in the United States. See also, https://en.wikipedia.org/wiki/First_Barbary_War. Accessed June 6, 2016.

[75] Wheelan, *Jefferson's War*, p. 41.

[76] Ibid., p. 41.

for a war with the Barbary States and argued that paying ransom and tribute was the better course. Jefferson opposed paying any type of ransom or tribute. The U.S. government essentially had two choices: (1) declare war and build up a large, expensive U.S. Navy to convoy U.S. merchant ships in the Mediterranean; the declaration of war would also drive up shipping insurance rates, or (2) pay off the pirates. The latter would, however, most likely encourage other Barbary States to demand equal or even higher payoffs. Given the state of the finances of the new U.S. government and ignoring moral and ethical issues, the U.S. Congress decided to pay the tribute and ransoms. Although the two were separate issues, they were linked in this situation. American officials at the time were more prone to pay for the release of American hostages than pay tribute to the Barbary States. The two issues were linked because by paying tribute or a bribe to the Barbary States, the U.S. would in theory stop the seizure of Americans ships and citizens. It became more of a question of whether it was cheaper to pay ransom for each ship and American citizen versus an annual tribute. Some Barbary States initially required both.

In 1790, Jefferson was appointed as the Secretary of State under George Washington's administration. In a December 30, 1790 message to the U.S. Congress, Jefferson assessed the problem with the Barbary States and outlined some options. He presented three: ransom, prisoner exchange, or military. Congress ignored his entreaties. The idea of war was simply too expensive as it would involve rebuilding an American Navy. Jefferson tried to find a way to respond militarily to the Barbary States without adding more financial debt to the U.S. In his "Proposal to Use Force against the Barbary States," he proposed that three frigates be sent to confront Algerian ships in the Mediterranean. They would also capture Turkish and Greek vessels. The captives from these ships would be sold in slave markets on Malta, just as Christian captives were sold in slave markets in Algiers. This was a hardline eye for an eye approach by Jefferson. The U.S. Congress ignored his proposal.[77]

The Maria hostages were eventually released in late 1794. By then, a third of the original hostages had died and the U.S. was compelled to pay a ransom of $642,500 cash (about $10 million in today's dollars) for the captives' release and $21,600 worth of powder, shot, oak planking, and masts in annual tribute. This could be considered the first "arms for hostages" deal in U.S. history.[78] In 1795, Algeria came to an agreement that resulted in the release of 115 American sailors they held, at a cost of over $1 million. This amount totaled about one-sixth

---

[77] Ibid., pp. 57–59.

[78] Simon. *The Terrorist Trap*, p. 32.

of the entire U.S. budget.[79] President John Adams went along with the Europeans who were paying tributes to the Barbary States for peace in the Mediterranean. Congress, in 1795, authorized payment of cash, munitions, a 36-gun frigate, and an annual tribute of $21,600 worth of naval supplies. Ransom rates were officially set for those Americans already in Barbary prisons; $4,000 for each passenger, $1,400 for each cabin boy.[80]

Jefferson was elected the third U.S. President in March 1801. He changed Washington's and Adam's policies toward the Barbary States. After arguing for a military response to the Barbary States for 17 years to no avail, he now sent the U.S. Navy and Marines to Tripoli to deal militarily, if necessary, with the Barbary States. These actions set the stage for military incidents that would establish the lore and legacy of both the U.S. Navy and Marines:

- Lt. Stephen Decatur, who led a daring commando mission to board and recapture the Philadelphia — a U.S. ship that had run aground in Tripoli harbor. He set her on fire under the enemy's nose on February 16, 1804. British admiral, Horatio Nelson reportedly called this "the most bold and daring act of the age."[81]
- William Eaton, who led an invasion force of U.S. Marines, dissident Tripolitans, Arabs, and European mercenaries 520 miles through the desert to the outskirts of Derna, Tripoli in a daring ground campaign. This action forced the surrender of Tripoli and freed those Americans who had been kidnapped and were made slaves.
- Marine Lt. Presley O'Bannon, Eaton's most trusted officer, planted the Stars and Stripes atop the battlement at Derna, the first American flag-raising on hostile foreign soil.
- The U.S. Marine Corps Hymn "From the Halls of Montezuma to the shores of Tripoli." The Tripoli phrase refers to actions during the First Barbary War and the Battle of Derna. It became the official hymn of the corps in 1929 and is the oldest official song in the U.S. armed forces.
- Due to the hazards of boarding hostile ships, Marines' uniforms had a high leather collar to protect against cutlass slashes. This led to the nickname "Leatherneck" for U.S. Marines.

---

[79] https://en.wikipedia.org/wiki/First_Barbary_War. Accessed June 4, 2017.

[80] Thomas Jewett, "The U.S. Wages War Against The Barbary States To End International Blackmail and Terrorism," at https://www.varsitytutors.com/earlyamerica/early-america-review/volume-6/terrorism-early-america. Accessed June 7, 2017.

[81] Spencer Tucker. *Stephen Decatur: A Life Most Bold and Daring* (Naval Institute Press, 2005), p. xi.

- Today, behind Preble Hall at the U.S. Naval Academy in Annapolis, one can find the "Tripoli Monument," the oldest U.S. Military Monument, dedicated to the six naval officers killed during the Barbary War.

In June 1805, a treaty was signed between the U.S. and Tripoli ending hostilities. The U.S. had demonstrated that it could flex its overseas military strength when necessary and other powers in the region certainly took notice. It was a debutante event for the U.S. as a potential global power. However, the problem of Barbary piracy was not fully settled. In 1807, Algiers had reverted to taking American ships and seamen hostage. The U.S. was understandably distracted by the preludes to the War of 1812 and was unable to respond to the Algiers provocation until 1815, with the Second Barbary War.[82] In 1815, after a brief interval of recovery from the War of 1812 with Britain, President James Madison asked Congress for permission to dispatch Stephen Decatur once again to North Africa, seeking a permanent settling of accounts with Algiers. Algiers was defeated and had to pay compensation, release all hostages, and promise not to offend again. In December 1815, President Madison declared that the Barbary wars were over. The Barbary States, although they did not capture any more U.S. ships, began to resume raids in the Mediterranean and despite punitive British bombardments did not end their practices until the French conquest of Algeria in 1830.[83]

At the end of the second war with the Barbary States, what then, was the U.S. policy on hostage-taking situations involving Americans overseas? The reading of letters and official documents of Washington, Adams, Jefferson, and Madison indicates that they all preferred a stronger response to the seizure of American ships and citizens by the Barbary States and pirates. The debate was more about money and capability than principle. The U.S. economy was weak, the government had no money and was in debt to some European countries, and the country had a weak navy. The prevalent political and financial calculations at the time suggested it was better to pay ransom and tribute than to respond with military actions. Only Jefferson consistently argued as Ambassador to France and then as Secretary of State that a forceful response was necessary. In the end, Jefferson, as President, applied force and it did eventually lead to a cessation of attacks on American vessels. However, what was the official U.S. government policy on hostage-taking after the two Barbary wars? U.S. policy on paying tribute to other nations to buy peace was clear. President James Madison and his Secretary of State James Monroe in an official letter to the leader of Algiers that was signed

---

[82] https://en.wikipedia.org/wiki/First_Barbary_War. Accessed May 5, 2017.
[83] https://history.state.gov/milestones/1801-1829/barbary-wars. Accessed October 3, 2017.

by both of them stated that "the United States, while they wish for war with no nation, will buy peace with none, it being a principle incorporated into the settled policy of America, that as peace is better than war, war is better than tribute."[84] While Jefferson and the other founding fathers recognized that paying ransom for captured Americans only enticed others to do the same, they were willing to pay ransom for the captured American citizens. Jefferson also recognized that the more attention or concern the government showed toward the hostages, the more this increased their value to their captors.[85] Ultimately, Washington, Adams, Jefferson, and Madison established no consistent official policy in dealing with American hostages held overseas. It would be 117 years before another American was held captive by "terrorists."

On September 3, 1901, 17 members of the Internal Macedonian-Adrianople Revolutionary Organization (IMRO), a Macedonian terrorist organization that demanded autonomy for a large portion of the geographical region of Macedonia from its Ottoman Turkish rulers, kidnapped Ellen Stone, an American Protestant missionary working in Macedonia, and 12 of her traveling companions. After a few hours, 11 of her companions were released. Stone and her Bulgarian companion Katerina Tsilka however remained as captives. The goal of the kidnapping was to obtain a large ransom to aid the financially struggling IMRO which had been fighting the Ottomans with guerrilla tactics since 1896.[86] The kidnappers initially asked for $110,000 (about $1 million in today's dollars) ransom from the United States. Stone's kidnapping quickly became a *cause célèbre* in the U.S., and U.S. newspapers and the world press sensationalized the incident.[87] The fact that Tsilka was in her fifth month of pregnancy only amplified the interest that further increased when on January 3, 1902 she gave birth to a baby girl while still in captivity.[88] The American Board of Commissioners for Foreign Missions, a

---

[84] Robert Greenhow. *The History of the Present Condition of Tripoli with Some Accounts of the Other Barbary States* (Richmond: T. H White, 1835), p. 46 at https://books.google.com/books?id=YMwRA AAAYAAJ&pg=PA46%7C#v=onepage&q&f=false. Accessed June 3, 2017.

[85] Wheelan, *Jefferson's War*, p. 50; Simon, *The Terrorist Trap*, p. 31.

[86] For an excellent history of the IMRO, see Duncan Perry, *Politics of Terror: The Internal Macedonian Revolutionary Organization* (North Carolina: Duke University Press, 1988).

[87] See Library of Congress, Topics in Chronicling America — The Kidnapping of Ellen Stone, at https://www.loc.gov/rr/news/topics/missStone.html, accessed June 6, 2017, for examples of the front-page newspaper headlines on the Stone kidnapping in the U.S.

[88] Laura Beth Sherman. *Fires on the Mountain: the Macedonian Revolutionary Movement and the Kidnapping of Ellen Stone* (New York: Columbia University Press, 1980); and Teresa Carpenter, *The Miss Stone Affair: America's First Modern Hostage Crisis* (New York: Simon and Shuster, 2003) are the best books on this incident. Many of the details of the Stone kidnapping come from these two sources.

religious organization, announced on September 28 that it could not pay the ransom. The U.S. government also stated that it would not pay the ransom. President Theodore Roosevelt stated that "using public money to pay ransom was illegal unless it was authorized by an act of Congress."[89] In October, the relatives of Miss Stone appealed to the American public to help raise the ransom money. "Sunday School children from coast to coast were emptying their piggy banks into collection plates."[90] They eventually raised about ½ of the ransom or $66,000. Over the next five months, various private and diplomatic actors engaged in efforts to contact the hijackers to negotiate for a reduction in the initial ransom price. The U.S. also put diplomatic pressure on both the Bulgarian and Ottoman governments which in turn sent out troops and police to find the kidnappers.

While there was still no publicly announced U.S. policy on paying ransom, President Theodore Roosevelt stated the following in a confidential memorandum to a top State Department official:

> *Equally of course the government has no power whatever to guarantee the payment of the money for the ransom. As far as I can see, all that can be done is to say we shall urge upon Congress as strongly as possible to appropriate money to repay the missionaries in the event of its proving impossible to get from the Turkish or other government the repayment ... that the American government has no power to pay the ransom of anyone who happens to be captured by brigands or savages.*[91]

In addition, the President and the U.S. government did nothing to stop the collection and payment of the ransom by private organizations. As noted above, the President did state that he would try to get Congress to reimburse for the ransom. The President was involved in the ongoing Stone kidnapping, held meetings with various private organizations on the issue, and was engaged with the State Department on diplomatic developments. The U.S. did agree to become the "custodian" of the ransom funds that were raised by private donations.[92] It was also reported that the State Department would use a "secret fund" to supplement the private donations if the full ransom amount was not reached.[93] The government also thought that it might get the reimbursement from either the Bulgarian or

---

[89]Carpenter, *The Miss Stone Affair*, p. 33.

[90]Ibid., p. 56.

[91]Ibid., p. 30.

[92]*New York World* Newspaper, October 7, 1901, p. 1.

[93]*San Francisco Call* Newspaper, October 9, 1901, p. 8.

Ottoman governments. The U.S. had no legal grounds to demand the ransom money from the Bulgarian government; at the same time, demanding it from the Ottoman government would only encourage the rebels to commit more kidnappings of American missionaries. After almost 6 months in captivity, Ms. Stone and her companion were released on February 23, 1902 after a ransom payment of 14,000 Turkish gold liras or about $66,000 that was paid from a U.S. State Department account in the Ottoman Bank branch in Thessaloniki.[94] The issue of reimbursement of the Miss Stone ransom was a controversial one for Congress. Between 1908 and 1912, the Senate approved four times a draft bill to that end, but it was defeated four times in the House of Representatives. The law was finally passed on March 21, 1912, 10 years after the end of the Miss Stone kidnapping affair.[95]

After her release, Ms. Stone wrote her memoirs, and from 1903 to 1904 gave over 50 lectures around the United States on the kidnapping incident. In her comments, she clearly sympathized with the Macedonian rebels who kidnapped her. She apparently suffered from the psychological phenomenon in which hostages express empathy and display positive feelings toward their captors, to the point of defending and identifying with them. In 1973, this condition was called the "Stockholm Syndrome" after a bank robbery in Sweden in which bank employees became emotionally attached to their captors, rejected assistance from government officials at one point, and even defended their captors after they were freed from their six-day ordeal.[96] Ellen Stone's companion Katerina Tsilka also wrote her memoirs and engaged in her own tour of the U.S. in 1903. Unfortunately, just before Miss Stone's memoirs were to be printed, the manuscript was burned in a fire in her hometown. She died there in 1927 at 81.

IMRO's career in the international spotlight reached its apex in 1934 when Vlado Chernozemski, an IMRO operative working with the Croatian Ustashe movement assassinated King Alexander of Yugoslavia.[97] The assassination, the first captured on film (newsreel) and watched around the world, prompted

---

[94] www.novinite.com/articles/122679/Bulgaria+and+USA+in+the+Miss+Stone+Affair%3A+Terrorism+As+It+Once+Was#sthash.L8XRlIVG.dpuf. Accessed June 6, 2017.

[95] Ibid., and Carpenter, *The Miss Stone Affair*, p. 205.

[96] https://en.wikipedia.org/wiki/Stockholm_syndrome. Accessed June 6, 2017.

[97] In 1927, Chernozemski proposed to the IMRO Central Committee that he would enter the main conference building of the League of Nations in Paris and detonate grenades attached to his person, in order to attract the attention of the world and generate publicity over the question of the Bulgarians in Macedonia, but his proposal was rejected. This would have been the first terrorist attack on an international organization and one of the first terrorist suicide attacks in modern history, at https://en.wikipedia.org/wiki/Vlado_Chernozemski. Accessed October 4, 2018.

the League of Nations to convene a working group to combat international terrorism. As a result of the assassination of King Alexander, the League of Nations adopted on November 16, 1937 a "Convention on the Prevention and Punishment on Terrorism" — the first international debate and convention on terrorism.[98] The assassination can be considered one of the first modern international terrorist attacks in the 20th century carried out by a terrorist organization. It involved a Bulgarian terrorist seeking independence for Macedonian territory working with a Croatian terrorist organization that killed a Yugoslav king on French territory using a German automatic pistol.

The next hostage-taking dilemma for President Theodore Roosevelt and the U.S. occurred on May 18, 1904 when a reported Greek American citizen, Ian Perdicaris, and his stepson, a British citizen, were kidnapped by a Moroccan brigand named Raisuli, in Tangier, Morocco.[99] Raisuli had previously kidnapped other foreigners in Morocco. Although Raisuli was a claimant to the throne of Morocco and well-educated, he was widely regarded as a bandit and as such earned the reputation as the "Last of the Barbary Pirates."[100] Upon being notified of the kidnapping on May 19, the U.S. Consul General in Tangier immediately telegraphed the U.S. State Department and stated "situation serious … request man-of-war to enforce demands." Roosevelt had encountered a similar situation two years earlier with the kidnapping of the American missionary Ellen Stone.

---

[98]The convention was signed by 24 members, but not the U.S. For analysis on this convention, see Ben Saul, "The Legal Response of the League of Nations to Terrorism," *Journal of International Criminal Justice*, Vol. 4, No. 1, 2006, pp. 78–102. To see the original text of this convention, see https://www.wdl.org/en/item/11579/view/1/26/. Accessed June 6, 2017. To watch the video of King Alexander's assassination, at http://www.britishpathe.com/video/assassination-of-king-alexander/query/king+alexander+assassination. Accessed May 5, 2018.

[99]For more information on this incident, see John Hughes, *House of Tears: Westerners' Adventures in Islamic Lands*, (New York: Lyons Press, 2005). For those who want to see Hollywood's version of this incident, watch the 1975 John Milius film *The Wind and the Lion*. Raisuli demanded $70,000 in ransom and the U.S. eventually put pressure on France and Great Britain to pressure the Sultan to pay the money, which he eventually did. Perdicaris also suffered from the "Stockholm Syndrome," a hostage condition that was identified in 1973 by Nils Bejerot, a Swedish criminologist and psychiatrist, after he analyzed the victims' reactions to the 1973 bank robbery and their status as hostages. This condition is defined as one which causes hostages to develop a psychological alliance with their captors as a survival strategy during captivity.

[100]The details of the Perdicaris incidents have been condensed from Barbara W. Tuchman, "Perdicaris Alive or Raisuli Dead," *American Heritage* magazine, Volume 10, Issue 5, August 1959, at http://www.americanheritage.com/content/%E2%80%9Cperdicaris-alive-or-raisuli-dead%E2%80%9D. Accessed May 6, 2017. In the author's opinion, this is the most accurate and detailed analysis of this incident.

Similar to that incident, the Perdicaris kidnapping provided Roosevelt with another opportunity to apply his "big stick diplomacy" in a crisis situation where once again he had the opportunity to make the Navy the vehicle to flex American overseas power.[101] Roosevelt immediately dispatched four warships — the entire South Atlantic Squadron — to proceed to Tangier along with several companies of U.S. Marines. He later reinforced this fleet to Tangier with three more warships for a total of seven. All this took some time. Therefore, the British and U.S. Consuls in Tangier both agreed that they had to pressure the Moroccan government to give in to Raisuli's demands.

The abduction of an American and British citizen had put the foreign colony in Tangier in an uproar that would soon become panic if the kidnap victims were not rescued. European residents, increasingly agitated, were flocking in from outlying estates, voicing indignant protests, petitioning for a police force, guards, and gunboats. On May 22, the Moroccan government received Raisuli's demands:

- prompt withdrawal of government troops from the Rif (region in the north);
- dismissal of the Bashaw (Pasha) of Tangier;
- arrest and imprisonment of certain officials who had harmed Raisuli in the past;
- release of Raisuli's partisans from prison;
- payment of an indemnity of $70,000 to be imposed personally upon the Bashaw;
- appointment of Raisuli as governor of two districts around Tangier (the two richest);
- relief of these two districts of taxes and cession of them to him absolutely;
- safe conduct for all Raisuli's tribesmen to come and go freely in the towns and markets;
- a British and American guarantee of fulfillment of the terms by the Moroccan government.

Secretary of State John Hay and Roosevelt both agreed that the demands were preposterous and responded by sending more warships to Tangier and trying to get the French to add pressure on the Moroccan government. In his diary, Hay, who served as a private secretary and assistant to President Lincoln, wrote "I hope they may not murder Mr. Perdicaris ... but a nation cannot degrade itself to

---

[101] "Perdicaris Incident: T. Roosevelt Uses Kidnapping for Big-Stick Diplomacy, Election Insurance," May 18, 2012, at http://burnpit.legion.org/2012/05/perdicaris-incident-t-roosevelt-uses-kidnapping-big-stick-diplomacy-election-insurance. Accessed October 3, 2017.

prevent ill-treatment of a citizen."[102] Like the Ellen Stone incident, the American public and press were paying close attention to the Perdicaris incident. As Barbara Tuchman wrote:

> *Back in America, the Perdicaris case provided a welcome sensation to compete in the headlines with the faraway fortunes of the Russo-Japanese War. A rich old gentleman held for ransom by a cruel but romantic brigand, the American Navy steaming to the rescue — here was personal drama more immediate than the complicated rattle of unpronounceable generals battling over unintelligible terrain. The President's instant and energetic action on behalf of a single citizen fallen among thieves in a foreign land made Perdicaris a symbol of America's new role on the world stage.*[103]

On May 29, Raisuli threatened to kill his hostages if all his demands were not met in two days. As this was weighing on the U.S. government, an unusual letter was received by the State Department on June 1. Its writer questioned whether Perdicaris was an American citizen. He claimed that Perdicaris gave up his American citizenship and was a Greek citizen and that this could be checked by contacting Greek officials. On June 4, the State Department tasked the U.S. Ambassador in Athens to investigate. On June 7, the Ambassador telegraphed that Perdicaris had indeed been naturalized as a Greek on March 19, 1862. Upon hearing the information, Roosevelt reasoned that, since Raisuli thought Perdicaris was an American citizen, it made little difference. On June 8, the Moroccan government, succumbing to various international pressures, gave in to all Raisuli's demands. However, the U.S. did not convey to the Moroccan government or to the American public the fact that Perdicaris was not an American citizen. Despite agreeing to Raisuli's demands, the Moroccan government dragged its feet in resolving the kidnapping to the chagrin of the U.S. government. The U.S. was trapped. It was impossible to reveal Perdicaris' status now and equally impossible to withdraw the fleet and leave him, whom the world still supposed to be an American, at the brigand's mercy. On June 21, the U.S. Consul delivered an ultimatum to the Moroccan government to keep its word and resolve the kidnapping. On that same day, the Republican National Convention met in Chicago. At this point, domestic politics started to take advantage of the Perdicaris incident.

---

[102] Tuchman, "Perdicaris Alive or Raisuli Dead."
[103] Ibid.

There was little chance that Roosevelt would not be given the nomination. However, there was an unenthusiastic air to the convention as Roosevelt had strong-armed the delegations and convention. Roosevelt knew he had the nomination sewed-up, but he was worried lest the dislike and distrust of him so openly exhibited at the Chicago Convention should gather volume and explode at the ballot box. Something was needed to uplift and energize the delegates at the Chicago convention and to attract the media. Roosevelt had the reputation at the time of being able to create news and to dramatize himself to the public. He was considered at the time to be the "master press agent of all time."[104] On June 22, Secretary of State Hay sent a telegram to Tangier stating that "this Government wants Perdicaris alive or Raisuli dead." The telegram was also given to the press at home. However, Hay did not release to the press a conditional or restrictive additional sentence in his telegram that told the U.S. Consul to "not land marines or seize customs without Department's specific instructions." At the Chicago Convention, a key Republican speaker read out only the catchy phrase that the government wanted "Perdicaris alive or Raisuli dead." According to contemporary accounts, the convention was electrified. Delegates sprang up onto their chairs and hurrahed. Flags and handkerchiefs waved. The attitude of the delegates toward Roosevelt had shifted and the convention re-energized, along with the media. After nominating Roosevelt by acclamation, the convention departed in an exhilarated mood. Roosevelt was later elected in November by the largest popular majority ever before given to a presidential candidate.[105]

In Morocco, a settlement had been reached before receipt of the telegram. Raisuli was ready at last to return his captives. Only afterward, when it was all over, did the State Department inform the Consul that Perdicaris was not an American citizen. The U.S. Consul was highly indignant, and he compelled Perdicaris to write a full confession of his 40-year-old secret. The letter contained no remorse. On September 3, Secretary of State Hay wrote to his Assistant Secretary Adee that the Perdicaris incident was "a bad business ... we must keep it excessively confidential for the present." They succeeded. Administration officials in the know held their breath during the presidential election campaign, but no hint leaked out either then or during the remaining year of Hay's lifetime or during Roosevelt's lifetime. As a result of the Perdicaris incident, Roosevelt's administration proposed a new citizenship law which was introduced in Congress in 1905 and enacted in 1907, but the name

---

[104] Ibid.
[105] Ibid.

of the man who inspired it was never mentioned during the debates. The truth about Ion Perdicaris remained unknown to the public until historian Tyler Dennett gave it away — in one paragraph in his biography of John Hay titled *John Hay: From Poetry to Politics* published in 1933:

> *More than two weeks before the telegram was sent the Department of State had reason to suspect that Perdicaris was not, in fact, an American citizen and, therefore, not entitled to the protection of the United States.... The information in the Department was not complete when the famous telegram was drafted, but Gaillard Hunt, then in charge of the Citizenship Bureau, felt justified in showing the correspondence to the Secretary. Hay requested him to take it across the street and show it to the President. To the latter it was quite unwelcome, and Hunt returned with the instruction to send the telegram at once.*[106]

Like the Ellen Stone situation, Perdicaris came to admire and befriend Raisuli who pledged to protect his prisoner from any harm.[107] Perdicaris later said: "I go so far as to say that I do not regret having been his prisoner for some time.... He is not a bandit, not a murderer, but a patriot forced into acts of brigandage to save his native soil and his people from the yoke of tyranny." Like Ellen Stone, Perdicaris wrote about his captivity first in *Leslie's Magazine* and later in the *National Geographic Magazine*.[108]

---

[106] Tyler Dennett, *John Hay: From Poetry to Politics* (New York: Dodd, Mead, and Co., 1933), p. 402. Dennett notes the sources of this paragraph as follows: Personal conversation with the late Gaillard Hunt; Archives of the Department of State: A. H. Slocumb, Fayetteville, N. C., to the Department, May 30, 1904; Secretary of State to Jackson and Gummere, June 4; Jackson to Department, June 7; June 10; Gummere to the Department, July 14, enclosing a personal letter of apology and explanation from Perdicaris to Gummere; Hay Papers: Adee to Hay, September 1, 1904. The correspondence was held very confidentially in the Department until November 8, 1905. The Republican campaign managers in the summer of 1904 were much concerned least it be made public. See also, John Blackwell, "1904: Perdicaris Alive or Raisuli Dead," *The Trentonian*, at http://www.capitalcentury.com/1904. html. Accessed May 5, 2017.

[107] For an excellent background on Raisuli, see Charles Somerville, "Raisuli The Bandit: The Kidnapper of Perdicaris," *New York Tribune*, July 10, 1904, pp. 5–6, 18, at http://chroniclingamerica. loc.gov/lccn/sn83030214/1904-07-10/ed-1/seq-32/. Accessed August 4, 2017. In 1975, Hollywood made the film *The Wind and the Lion* loosely based on the Perdicaris incident. The closing narration of this film was taken from the actual letter that Raisuli wrote to President Roosevelt after the incident.

[108] Paul Baepler, Research Article: Rewriting the Barbary Captivity Narrative: The Perdicaris Affair and the Last Barbary Pirate, *Prospects*, Vol. 24, October 1999, pp. 177–211.

President Eisenhower was the next U.S. president to confront a hostage situation involving Americans overseas. On June 28, 1958, Cuban rebels seized 29 U.S. sailors traveling on a bus from Guantanamo Bay where the U.S. had a military base. Several other Americans were also seized a few days earlier. The rebels were led by Raul Castro, Fidel's brother. The rebels had two objectives in seizing the American military personnel: (1) to attract publicity for their cause and (2) to use them as human shields to pressure the Batista government to stop bombing rebel positions.[109] However, Fidel Castro was concerned that the hostage seizure would have a negative effect on international public opinion. The U.S. Congress and the media wanted Eisenhower to take a more hardline approach to this incident, but he wanted to apply a more patient and diplomatic approach which included contacting the Cuban rebels. Even his Secretary of State, John Foster Dulles, was putting pressure on Eisenhower. In a July 1 press conference, Dulles said that the U.S. would never "pay blackmail to get people" and doing so "would only encourage further efforts to use Americans as hostages."[110] The next day, Eisenhower held a press conference. Dulles sent the President talking points that suggested a strong approach to dealing with the rebels. Eisenhower, however, took an opposite approach at the press conference stating that "we are trying to get live Americans back and we are not disposed to do anything reckless that would create consequences for them that would be final."[111] Giving the rebels time to think about their situation without the worry of a U.S. military action apparently helped the rebels realize that they had miscalculated the benefits of this incident. The U.S. military personnel were gradually released by the Cuban rebels. As Jeffrey Simon points out:

> *The pragmatic Eisenhower succeeded in preventing the hostage episode from turning into a full-blown crisis that could affect the cautious approach the United States was pursuing towards the Cuban Revolution at that time. He also did not fall into the terrorist trap of escalating rhetoric or hasty action that would increase the risk to the hostages' safety. By using such terms as 'trying to convince' the rebels of their 'errors,' and not issuing any ultimatums, he avoided putting their backs against the wall and leaving them no room to save face.*[112]

---

[109] Simon, *The Terrorist Trap*, p. 54. Condensed details of this hostage incident are taken from Simon's excellent book, pp. 53–58.

[110] Ibid., p. 56.

[111] Ibid., p. 57.

[112] Ibid.

Six years later, in August 1964, a major international hostage crisis involving Americans took place in the Congo. The Congo received its independence from Belgium in June 1960. This created an internal power vacuum that led to tribal and political conflict over a four-year period. In June 1964, the U.N. pulled out. On August 6, 1964, rebel elements seized Stanleyville, the capital of the Katanga province. Initially, the whites were treated well by the Simba rebels. However, after U.S.-supported Congolese forces began to make consistent military gains against the communist-backed Simba rebels, the rebels' attitude changed, and they began to round up whites in the city. Over the next two months, about 1,600 foreigners were rounded up and held as hostages by the Simbas, including 600 Belgians and about 40 Americans, including five U.S. diplomats assigned to the U.S. Consulate who were seized on September 5 after hiding inside the communication vault of the consulate. The five U.S. diplomats seized were Michael Hoyt (Consul), David Grinwis (Vice-Consul), Ernest Houle, and two communications officers, James Stauffer and Donald Parkes.[113] This was the first time that American diplomats had been held hostage by militants. Several of the diplomats were subjected to false executions — a hostage-takers' tactic that would surface again in Tehran in 1979 when 52 U.S. diplomats were seized by militant Iranian students. The Simba rebels made threats to kill the white hostages if the central government bombed Stanleyville. They demanded that the U.S. cease its support to the Congolese government. There were rumors and media reports of hostages being mistreated and paraded around the city. There were even rumors of cannibalism. Dr. Paul Carlson, an American missionary, became the public face of the American hostages. The rebels charged that he was an "American spy and an American major." The rebels announced that Carlson had been "tried" as a spy and sentenced to death. However, his execution kept being postponed.[114]

The U.S. did not know initially how to react to this hostage situation. President Johnson was advised that any unilateral U.S. military action would seriously aggravate the Congo situation and lead to increased anti-U.S. sentiment in Africa. Therefore, it made more sense to try and construct a multinational

---

[113] Consul Hoyt became the first American diplomat to be held hostage by terrorists/rebels and to write his memoirs of the incident. See, Michael Hoyt, *Captive in the Congo: Return to the Heart of Darkness* (Annapolis: Naval Institute Press, 2000). See also interview with Mike Hoyt in "Lessons Learned from a Former Hostage," Association for Diplomatic Studies and Training, at http://adst.org/2012/10/lessons-learned-from-a-former-hostage. Accessed May 5, 2017 and interview with William E. Schaufele, Jr. the Congo Desk Officer at State from 1964 to 1965 in "Operation Dragon Rouge," Association for Diplomatic Studies and Training, at http://adst.org/2012/09/operation-dragon-rouge/. Accessed July 3, 2017.

[114] "Congo: The Hostages," *Time Magazine*, November 27, 1964, at http://www.time.com/time/magazine/article/0,9171,871387,00.html#ixzz1CGtC1U20. Accessed September 23, 2017.

response. The U.S. began to discuss with Belgium, which had 600 of its citizens as hostages, the possibility of a rescue attempt involving Belgian paratroopers being transported on U.S. military transport planes. Secretary of Defense Robert McNamara advised President Johnson that "it'll be dangerous if the paradrop is carried out, but it'll be dangerous if it isn't, and under the circumstances, the danger of carrying it out is less than the danger of not carrying it out." It seemed that a paratrooper rescue mission was the only viable option. Johnson feared both that the Congo would fall into leftist hands and that the United States would find itself dragged into a ground war in a country of no strategic importance. On November 23, from his ranch in Texas, Johnson spoke on the phone with acting Secretary of State George Ball — "Is this in any way going to involve us in getting us in there and getting us tied down there?" the president asked.[115]

In a phone conversation between Secretary of State Dean Rusk and Belgium Foreign Minister Paul Spaak in October, Spaak wanted to know what the U.S. position was on a rescue mission. Rusk said that since the paratroopers would be Belgian, whatever Belgium wanted to do was fine with the U.S. and that the U.S. could provide transport planes; however, the decision was Belgium's. Spaak replied, "Do you mean that the great United States of America is leaving this decision to Belgium?" Rusk said yes, and Spaak replied: "That's incredible, no decision affecting Belgium has ever been made in Belgium before!"[116] After negotiations with the Simba rebels by the United Nations, Belgium, and the United States failed, Belgium and the U.S. constructed a hostage rescue operation code-named "Red Dragon." It was launched on November 24, 1964 following a strike by CIA-piloted B-26s against Stanleyville Airport, and consisted of five U.S. Air Force C-130s bearing 340 troops of the 1st Battalion, Belgian Paracommando Regiment. The operation involved the coordination of air and land operations and multiple paratroop drops. At the end of the rescue operation, 31 hostages were dead, including two Americans. The Americans killed were Dr. Paul Carson and missionary Phyllis Rhine.[117] This was the first U.S. and first international hostage-rescue operation in the modern era. In retrospect, it was the most complex multinational hostage-rescue operation of the Cold War. The Congo was clearly just a pawn in the Cold War global chessboard.

---

[115] Quotes are from Nina Strochlic, "Argo in the Congo: The Ghosts of the Stanleyville Hostage Crisis," *The Daily Beast*, November 23, 2014, at http://www.thedailybeast.com/articles/2014/11/23/argo-in-the-congo-the-ghosts-of-the-stanleyville-hostage-crisis.html. Accessed September 23, 2018.

[116] As quoted in Simon, *The Terrorist Trap*, p. 90.

[117] Major Thomas P. Odom, "Dragon Operations: Hostage Rescues in the Congo, 1964–1965," U.S. General Command and Staff College, The Leavenworth Papers #14, at http://www.cgsc.edu/carl/resources/csi/odom/odom.asp. Accessed September 3, 2017.

Shortly after the Stanleyville raid, the Soviet leaders decried the rescue mission as an act of imperialist aggression. In response, American embassies across the world were stoned, and in Cairo, the new John F. Kennedy Library was burned to the ground. Communist China announced support for the rebels and Fidel Castro sent Che Guevara to the United Nations,[118] where on December 11, 1964, he denounced American actions as an "unacceptable intervention … a case without parallel in the modern world," that illustrated "how the rights of peoples can be flouted with absolute impunity and the most insolent cynicism."[119] The rescue operation also triggered a burst of protests in Africa with many accusing the U.N. Security Council of supporting a neocolonialist government and Western economic and political interests. Twenty-two African and Asian member states requested the Security Council to meet on December 9 to consider the rescue operation which they called "the Belgian and American aggression against the Congo." What followed was one of the most acrimonious debates in the Security Council's history, taking 17 sessions to complete.[120] Belgian and U.S. representatives were shocked and perplexed by the ugly tone of the debate. Spaak, the Belgian foreign minister, called it "violent" and "insulting." U.S. Ambassador Adlai Stevenson referred to it as "irrational, irresponsible, insulting and repugnant language."[121] Spaak argued that "the Stanleyville operation was not a military operation … it was not a matter of helping the Congolese National Army … it was a question of saving between 1,500 and 2,000 persons whose lives were in danger… it was to save people who were regarded as hostages by the rebel authorities." Stevenson argued that the intervention "was exactly what we said it was when we notified this Council at the very beginning — nothing more and nothing less than a mission to save the lives of innocent people of diverse nationalities." The Security Council eventually passed Resolution 199 (1964) unanimously. It appealed for a cease-fire and requested all states to refrain from intervening in the domestic politics of the Congo. As a result, the U.S. and

---

[118] Nina Strochlic, "Argo in the Congo."

[119] Address by Ernesto Che Guevara to the U.N. General Assembly, New York on December 11, 1964. Social justice website at http://www.sojust.net/speeches/che_un.html. Accessed October 4, 2016. In April 1965, Guevara, along with a small unit of Cuban fighters, arrived in Dar es Salaam and made their way to the Congo where they led rebellions against the central government for six months, until their retreat on November 20, 1965.

[120] The International Commission on Intervention and State Sovereignty. *The Responsibility to Protect: Research, Bibliography, Background* (Ottawa: International Development Research Centre, 2001), pp. 51–52, http://web.idrc.ca/openebooks/963-1/. Accessed May 6, 2016.

[121] All quotes from Ibid.

Belgium were able to argue that this request implicitly referred, not simply to their military action but also to alleged Soviet support for the rebel forces.[122]

From the first to the 36th President of the United States, a span of 174 years, the United States was confronted with five major episodes of Americans being held hostage overseas by terrorists.[123] Six Presidents were involved in resolving these incidents — Washington, Adams, Jefferson, Theodore Roosevelt, Eisenhower, and Johnson. Although no publicly announced U.S. policy on overseas hostage-taking was declared, it is clear from public and private statements by these Presidents, their Secretaries of State, and other government officials that the U.S. preference was not to give in to the political demands of terrorists. The argument was consistent — that to do so only encourages more hostage-taking incidents against Americans and it projects a sign of weakness. In all these five episodes, there were debates and disagreements within the government over how to manage them. In all these five incidents, the press and public opinion also played an agitational role as they were generally in favor of taking action. In these episodes, Americans appeared to want a strong president who would engage in saber-rattling to protect Americans abroad. The temperament and character of the president ultimately shaped how the government would respond as he was the primary target of the pressure from the Congress, media, and public to do something.

There was also the question as to how publicly involved the President should become in such incidents. Less public involvement could be misinterpreted by the media and public, while more involvement would enhance the importance and therefore the value of the hostages. Some of these episodes were relatively simple while others were more complex. The hostage-taking episodes involving the Barbary Coast States and pirates and the Congo situation were the most difficult as they involved multiple actors that had to be persuaded and managed. In two of the episodes, hostage-rescue operations were carried out — in the Congo and a delayed response against the Barbary States. U.S. military force was displayed in the Stone and Perdicaris incidents, but it was more for show than offensive action. While the U.S. government's preference was not to give in to the demands of the terrorists, it did condone paying ransom to release the hostages. The U.S. did pay

---

[122] Ibid.

[123] In addition, as Jeffrey Simon points out in his book *The Terrorist Trap* (pp. 53–54, 95–96), there were four incidents in which U.S. military personnel were held hostage by four Communist States — East Germany, the Soviet Union, Communist China, and North Korea. Dealing with a state as opposed to a terrorist organization while difficult is qualitatively different. A miscalculation by a state could lead to interstate war.

ransom to the Barbary Coast States to release imprisoned Americans and it allowed and facilitated the paying of ransom in the Ellen Stone case.

The Nixon Administration

Terrorist hostage-taking creates the most counter-terrorism policy problems for governments. These situations can become complicated as more countries are involved. The relevant players could be: (1) the country where the incident is taking place, (2) the country that is targeted for political demands, (3) those other countries whose nationalities are also involved in the incident, and (4) the nationality of the hijackers. The cooperation of all these players is necessary for a successful resolution to the incident. A resolution is enhanced if all the players are reading from the same policy sheet. They agree on generally accepted counter-terrorism principles, a policy on hostage-taking, and have signed or ratified international conventions on terrorism. In the early 1970s, the international community was subjected to a wave of aircraft hijacking extortions, kidnappings, and barricade and hostage incidents such as the 1972 Palestinian seizure of 11 Israeli athletes at the Munich Olympics and the 1973 seizure of the Saudi Embassy in Khartoum, Sudan, where two U.S. diplomats were killed. There were international conventions on hijackings in place so the responsibilities of the various parties in such an incident were understood. It was also recognized that states have certain responsibilities in terms of protecting foreign diplomats in their countries. However, there was no international convention of how states must respond to terrorist extortion or ransom incidents. This was left to each state to address in each incident. Some countries acquiesced to the demands of terrorists, while others did not. While it was generally recognized that giving in to the demands of terrorists would only encourage similar incidents against the country giving in, few countries were willing to refuse such demands and have their citizens or foreigners under their protection killed. A country may be able to implement this policy in the case of a single hostage, but when dozens are held the resolve weakens. The United States did not have a consistent publicly stated policy on hostage situations since its founding, or at least one that was tested.

There is no publicly available information to suggest that officials in the Nixon administration had studied the historical hostage-taking episodes noted previously to extract any lessons learned. The administration almost faced its first test of this policy on August 29, 1969 when two terrorists, including the infamous female terrorist Leila Khaled, from the "Che Guevara Brigade of the Palestinian Liberation Movement" (aka PFLP) hijacked TWA Flight 840 in Rome that was en route to Tel Aviv and diverted it to Damascus, Syria.[124] There were Americans and American crew members on this plane. This was only the second Palestinian hijacking at the time. The first was against an El Al plane in July 1968. The fact that it was aimed at the U.S. was not unexpected as the U.S. was perceived by Palestinian militants as the primary supporter — politically and militarily — of Israel. In fact, the hijackers read the following statement on the plane: "We have kidnapped this American plane because Israel is a colony of America and the Americans are giving the Israelis Phantom jets."[125] Prior to this hijacking, Palestinian terrorists detonated a bomb near the U.S. Embassy in Beirut on May 27, 1967, attempted to bomb a U.S. Cultural Center in Tel Aviv on September 29, 1967, and detonated a small bomb on August 21, 1968 in the garden of the U.S. Consulate in East Jerusalem. It was only a matter of time before Palestinian terrorists went after U.S. targets in earnest. The hijacking of TWA 840 was the opening salvo in that campaign. The U.S. of course condemned the hijacking and called on Syria to resolve the issue quickly. The Department of State, rather than the National Security Council, was designated the lead agency to handle this incident in order to distance the President from the incident.[126] Since this was the first time that political terrorists had hijacked a U.S. airliner, the media turned it into a major news story which in turn triggered a debate over how the incident was being handled.[127] The hijacking was following the script of previous U.S. hostage-taking episodes.

After TWA 840 landed in Damascus, the passengers and crew were taken off the plane and a timed explosive device, which apparently had been placed in the forward part of the aircraft by the hijackers, detonated and caused considerable damage to the cockpit and forward cabin areas. On August 30, Syria released all the passengers and crew but kept six Israelis. Therefore, the U.S. no longer had a direct interest in this incident, except in making sure the TWA aircraft was returned. The U.S. thereafter focused its diplomatic energy on securing the release of the Israeli passengers, and making sure Israel did nothing rash. Eventually, the four female Israelis were released but two Israeli men were kept as hostages. Israel now pressured the U.S., stating that if U.S. diplomatic efforts did not work, Israel would take unilateral action. Additional pressure was being

---

[124] For an eyewitness account of this hijacking by U.S. Foreign Service Officer Thomas D. Boyatt, see "The Hijacking of TWA 840," *Foreign Service Journal*, December 1969, pp. 4–6.

[125] Edward E. Mickolus. *Transnational Terrorism: A Chronology of Events, 1968–1979* (Westport: Greenwood Press, 1980), p. 132. Hereafter referred to as "Mickolus, 1968–1979."

[126] Naftali, *Blind Spot*, p. 36.

[127] Ibid.

put on TWA by the Israeli Consulate General in New York. Clyde Williams, a TWA executive, noted "he has been continually harassed by the Israeli Consulate General in New York ... the harassment has been so bad that his New York office has not opened today ... he has been receiving telephone calls at home ... there has been an organized effort to dictate to TWA what it should do in connection with the hijacking incident and they have received threats that were not veiled."[128] The two Israelis could not be released because Israel consistently refused to release the two Syrian pilots who Syria claimed landed in Israel by mistake. In talks with the U.S., Israel consistently threatened to take military action against Syria. Israel also wondered why all the other passengers who were released did not stay in Damascus until all passengers, including the Israelis, were freed. The U.S. considered this proposition as "unfeasible."[129]

The U.S. put a full court diplomatic press on Syria to return the two Israelis. The U.S. believed that the hijacking caught the Syrians by surprise and now posed a dilemma for them.[130] It believed that Syria was looking for a way to save face. Syria had to receive something in return if it released the Israelis. The U.S. took the following actions:

- The U.S. reached out to the Soviet Union to put pressure on Syria.
- It encouraged many governments with influence in Damascus to make their views known to Syrian authorities.
- It convened an emergency session of the special committee of ICAO which the U.S. believed would result in a further communication by that organization to the Syrians.
- It reached out to the Director General of the International Air Transport Association (IATA) to mobilize the resources of that organization.

---

[128] U.S. Department of State, Office of the Historian, Foreign Relations of the United States, Nixon-Ford Administrations, Volume E-1, Documents on Global Issues. Document 10. U.S. Department of State, Memorandum of Conversation, Washington, August 31, 1969, at https://history.state.gov/historicaldocuments/frus1969-76ve01/d10. Accessed June 4, 2017.

[129] U.S. Department of State, Office of the Historian, Foreign Relations of the United States, Nixon-Ford Administrations, Volume E-1, Documents on Global Issues. Document 11. Telegram 147525 from the Department of State to the embassy in Israel and the consulate in Jerusalem, August 31, 1969, 1331, at https://history.state.gov/historicaldocuments/frus1969-76ve01/d11. Accessed September 6, 2017.

[130] Ibid. Document 13. Telegram 7222 from the embassy in Lebanon to the Department of State, September 1, 1969, 1233, at https://history.state.gov/historicaldocuments/frus1969-76ve01/d13. Accessed May 9, 2018.

- It convened a meeting of the NATO Council in order to encourage U.S. European allies to keep up the momentum on this matter.
- It contacted the International Committee for the Red Cross to determine what if anything that organization, which at the time had two representatives in Damascus, could do.
- It sought the intervention of the World Health Organization (WHO) since one of the Israeli passengers being held was returning from a WHO meeting and was working on a WHO project, bearing in mind that WHO had been active in Syria.
- It continued to urge the Israelis to exercise restraint and to allow time for U.S. efforts to be played out.
- It explored the possibility of organizing a broad boycott by the principal carriers using the new Damascus airport as a means of bringing further pressure.
- It explored the possibility of attempting to block Syria's candidacy for a seat on the Security Council.[131]

It became clear also that the PFLP had placed the Syrian government in a very volatile situation. The Syrian government had to play along with the PFLP as it was a supporter of the Palestinian cause. The PFLP had even asked the Syrians to get some of its members released from Israel, but the Syrians had said no.[132] In late October, the Syrian government released the two hijackers who then went to Jordan. There was no trial for the hijackers. The U.S. concluded that the only way to resolve this incident was for both sides to agree to an exchange. The U.S. increased its pressure on Israel to reconsider its opposition to an exchange of the two Syrian pilots for the two Israelis, one of whom turned out to have served in the Israeli intelligence services. This last fact, however, was not known to the Syrians. The U.S. tried to find an exchange scenario acceptable to the Israelis. It suggested that Israel could release the two pilots quietly in Italy.[133] Israel held

---

[131] Ibid. Document 15. Memorandum from Secretary of State Rogers to President Nixon, Washington, September 2, 1969, at https://history.state.gov/historicaldocuments/frus1969-76ve01/d15. Accessed October 4, 2017.

[132] Ibid., Document 16. Department of State Memorandum of Conversation, Washington, September 3, 1969, at https://history.state.gov/historicaldocuments/frus1969-76ve01/d16. Accessed December 4, 2017.

[133] Ibid., Document 18. Department of State Information Memorandum from the Assistant Secretary of State for Near Eastern and South Asian Affairs (Sisco) to Secretary of State Rogers, Washington, September 5, 1969, at https://history.state.gov/historicaldocuments/frus1969-76ve01/d18. Accessed June 4, 2016.

firm, arguing that it could not agree to any kind of exchange, contending that this would only encourage further hijackings.[134] Israeli Foreign Minister Eban reiterated that the idea of linking the release of the two Israelis with Israel's release of the two Syrian pilots in its custody was intolerable. He argued that each time Israel captured a Syrian prisoner of war, Syria would simply hijack an Israeli plane.[135] Finally, as a result of U.S. pressure on Israel, and the good offices of the International Red Cross and the Italians, a deal was worked out. The release of passengers and the TWA aircraft was pursuant to a three-cornered agreement developed through the International Red Cross under which: (1) Israeli passengers would be released from Damascus; (2) simultaneously, 13 Syrians, including two Syrian MIG pilots, would be turned over to Syrian authorities in the Golan Heights; and (3) approximately 24 hours later, about 50 Egyptian nationals would be handed over to Egypt in exchange for two Israeli Air Force pilots downed in action over Egypt.[136] On December 5, 1969, the Syrian Government permitted the departure from Damascus of the hijacked TWA aircraft as well as two Israeli passengers who had been detained since the hijacking took place on August 29. The PFLP gained nothing. No Palestinian-hijacked aircraft was ever diverted to Damascus again.

Given that the Americans on the TWA 840 plane were immediately released by Syria, the U.S. did not face a hostage predicament. However, the U.S. did demonstrate that it did not have a problem with another country giving in to terrorists' demands to resolve the incident. The U.S. put pressure on Israel to release

---

[134] Ibid., However, Israel did give in to terrorists in an earlier incident. On July 23, 1968, El Al Flight 426 was hijacked in Rome by three PFLP terrorists. The plane was en route from London to Lod Airport in Tel Aviv but diverted to Algiers. There were 38 passengers and 10 crew members aboard the aircraft. Algerian authorities immediately released 26 non-Israeli passengers while 22 Israeli passengers (including crew) were held as hostages. Another 10 passengers (including 3 stewardesses) were released after 5 days. Seven crew members and five Israeli passengers were held for 39 days in Algeria. On September 1, the remaining hostages were released in exchange for 16 convicted Arab prisoners held in Israel. It remains the longest hijacking on record. It was also the first and only successful hijacking of an El Al plane. Afterwards, El Al and the government of Israel instituted strict security measures.

[135] U.S. Department of State, Office of the Historian, Foreign Relations of the United States, Nixon-Ford Administrations, Volume E-1, Documents on Global Issues. Document 26. Memorandum of Conversation Between Secretary of State Rogers and Israeli Foreign Minister Eban, New York, September 23, 1969, at https://history.state.gov/historicaldocuments/frus1969-76ve01/d26. Accessed December 23, 2017.

[136] Ibid., Document 36. Telegram 203374 from the Department of State to Secretary of State Rogers in Bonn, December 5, 1969, 2331Z, at https://history.state.gov/historicaldocuments/frus1969-76ve01/d36. Accessed August 4, 2017.

two Syrian pilots in exchange for Israeli hostages. One could argue that this was a U.S. diplomatic solution to prevent the possibility of a military incident between Israel and Syria that could have increased tensions in the already volatile Middle East. Israel faced its first hijacking hostage incident a year earlier when the PFLP hijacked an El Al plane. Israel gave in to the demands of the hijackers then and released some imprisoned Palestinian terrorists. After that, Israel was determined not to give in to hostage-takers again.[137]

The first hostage policy test for the Nixon administration occurred on September 4, 1969, the week after the TWA 840 hijacking, when U.S. Ambassador Charles Burke Elbrick was kidnapped at a road block in Rio de Janeiro, Brazil by left-wing terrorists from the Revolutionary Movement 8th October (MR-8). The terrorists demanded the release of 15 left-wing political prisoners and the publication of a three-page MR-8 manifesto. If the demands were not met within 48 hours, MR-8 threatened to carry out "revolutionary justice," by executing Elbrick. In the Elbrick incident, the U.S. followed the prevailing policy at the time for countries whose diplomats were kidnapped and that was to "encourage the host government to meet the kidnappers' demands."[138] The Nixon administration pressured a "reluctant Brazilian government hard" to meet the kidnapper's demands to free Elbrick unharmed. This decision by the Brazilian government almost provoked a revolt in the ranks of the military.[139] In fact, Brazilian paratroopers in Rio de Janeiro went to the airport to try and prevent the released political prisoners from taking off. However, they were ordered to refrain from stopping the plane and to return to their barracks. The government published the requested MR-8 communiqué and released 15 political prisoners who were then flown to Mexico where they received asylum. Many of them ended up in Cuba. Elbrick was released on September 7, having been held hostage for 78 hours and having suffered minor head trauma from being pistol-whipped during the kidnapping.[140] The U.S. was grateful to the Brazilian government. It increased its military aid team in Brazil and trained Brazilian law enforcement and military personnel in counter-insurgency techniques at Ft. Gulick in Panama.[141] As for the kidnapping ledger in Brazil, from 1969 to 1979, the Brazilian government released 129

---

[137] Byman, *A High Price*, p. 42.

[138] Tucker, *Skirmishes at the Edge of Empire*, p. 9.

[139] David Korn. *Assassination in Khartoum*, pp. 111–112.

[140] This incident was portrayed somewhat accurately in the American film "Four Days in September," released in 1997 and starring Alan Arkin as Ambassador Elbrick.

[141] Brian Train, "Urban Guerrilas in Brazil," MIT Western Hemisphere Project, at http://web.mit.edu/ hemisphere/events/mnm03-1m/brazil-train.shtml. Accessed November 4, 2016.

political prisoners to acquire the freedom of kidnapped foreign diplomats.[142] Given that Brazil was ruled by an authoritarian military dictatorship at the time, one can only conclude that these releases were due to the pressure of the governments of the foreign diplomats and not desired government policy.[143] Elbrick was the first and only U.S. Ambassador who was ever kidnapped and ransomed. In a June 18, 1971 speech in Philadelphia, Ambassador Elbrick stated that it was unwise for a government to negotiate and to give in to the demands of terrorists even if as a result of following such a policy he would have "disappeared" during the Brazil kidnapping. This attitude was reportedly consistent with those of the other U.S. Foreign Service officers.[144] He admitted however that several U.S. diplomats would have to "disappear" before a terrorist group received the message that a government would not give in.[145]

Elbrick's kidnapping in Brazil led State Department's SY to create two new programs. First, SY officials turned the pilot project for armored vehicles into the formal Protective Security Vehicle Program. This enabled SY not only to purchase fully protective security vehicles but also to install mobile radios in embassy vehicles, obtain kits to armor existing cars, and buy automobiles equipped with "high-performance features." The vehicles went to "high-risk" posts such as Saigon, Beirut, and Montevideo. By 1972, SY could claim some success for the armored vehicle program. In Phnom Penh, Cambodia, a bomb exploded near the embassy's armored vehicle, and the *chargé d'affaires*, the

---

[142] Korn, *Assassination in Khartoum*, p. 112.

[143] In December 2014, Brazil's National Truth Commission delivered a damning 2,000-page report on the killings, disappearances, and torture committed by government agents during the country's 1964–1985 military dictatorship. The work exhaustively details the military's "systematic practice" of arbitrary detentions and torture, as well as executions, forced disappearances, and hiding bodies. It documents 191 killings and 210 disappearances committed by military authorities, as well as 33 cases of people who "disappeared" and whose remains were discovered later. The commission noted that these numbers certainly do not correspond to the total number of deaths and disappearances but only to those cases where it was possible to prove. *The Guardian*, December 10, 2014 at http://www.theguardian.com/world/2014/dec/10/rousseff-tears-brazilian-report-details-torture-killings-military-regime. Accessed December 13, 2017.

[144] "Secretary Rogers had told me a few months ago that a survey made of the Foreign Service, in which he had asked what would be the attitude of a member of the Foreign Service, in the event if he were captured and held hostage — what would be the attitude as to what our Government should do. It was unanimous that the United States Government should not submit to demands for blackmail or ransom." Remarks by President Nixon at a Ceremony Honoring Slain Foreign Service Officers (killed in Khartoum, Sudan), March 6, 1973, at http://www.presidency.ucsb.edu/ws/index.php?pid=4132&st=Terrorism&st1=. Accessed June 4, 2017.

[145] Carol Edler Baumann. *The Diplomatic Kidnappings: A Revolutionary Tactic of Urban Terrorism* (The Hague: Martinus Nijhoff Publishers, 1973), p. 77.

chargé's guard, and the chauffeur walked away unharmed.[146] The second program SY created was the Mobile Reserve and Emergency Action Teams. The Mobile Reserve consisted of a reserve of personnel and equipment that could be temporarily sent to a post where kidnapping and terrorism threats were high. SY officials organized personnel into Emergency Action Teams, the forerunner of Mobile Tactical Security Teams. The teams were three squads of 4–5 people each and were assigned as emergencies dictated. Once at post, an Emergency Action Team immediately conducted a "detailed physical survey" and determined the host government's capability of protecting U.S. diplomatic personnel. The squad also made recommendations for enhancing post security and provided temporary security services. If needed, the team could request additional Marine Guards for the Ambassador's residence or other post buildings.[147]

U.S. policy at this point appeared to be to encourage governments to give in to kidnappers' demands to save American lives. This policy was followed on March 6, 1970 when four Rebel Armed Forces terrorists kidnapped Sean M. Holly, the U.S. Labor Attaché in Guatemala City, Guatemala and threatened to kill him in 48 hours if the government did not release four political prisoners. The government agreed and released two of the prisoners. Holly was released on March 8. It has been suggested that the U.S. government encouraged the Guatemalan government to give in to the demands of the terrorists.[148] In an April 2, 1970 State Department "action" memorandum from William B. Macomber, Jr., the Deputy Under Secretary of State for Administration, to the Under Secretary of State for Political Affairs, a U.S. policy on hostages was discussed. The memo noted that the first thing the government should do was to make "general statements at appropriate levels of the U.S. Government deploring kidnapping of public officials or private citizens as a crime and decrying the use of such methods as a political weapon." The memo then outlined the pros and cons of three options for the U.S. in hostage-type situations:

Option #1 — Apply pressure to the extent necessary to persuade the host government to comply fully with the kidnapper's terms.

<u>Pros</u>: Maximizing the chances of recovering a U.S. official or his or her dependent whose life was in immediate danger.

---

[146] *DS History*, p. 205.

[147] Ibid., p. 206.

[148] Tucker, *Skirmishes at the Edge of Empire*, p. 9.

<u>Cons</u>: The kidnappers would have gained their ends; they or others would become encouraged to repeat the performance; it would make compliance with the kidnappers' terms a major issue in our relations with the host country; the U.S. could encounter considerable public and Congressional concern or criticism.

Option #2 — Express our expectation that the host government would do everything reasonable to obtain the freedom of the kidnapped official, recognizing, however, that the determination of what is reasonable would be made by the host government.

<u>Pros</u>: We would have acknowledged the importance of the life at stake and avoided the possibility of the problem becoming a major issue in our relations; since each case might be decided differently by the host government, the resultant uncertainty as to the outcome of their demands could deter some potential kidnappers; since it was possible that the U.S. might be faced with the reverse situation, this course of action would create a reciprocal basis for the U.S. President to decide in a given case that might occur in the U.S.

<u>Cons:</u> This could quite probably result in the eventual torture and/or death of a U.S. official or dependent; another disadvantage would be Congressional and public criticism from some quarters; hazardous pay might have to be paid to U.S. personnel serving in areas where substantial danger of kidnapping existed.

Option #3 — Urge the host government to refuse publicly the kidnappers' demands.

<u>Pros:</u> If we were to adopt this course, we should probably announce it immediately and publicly for its deterrent potential — its main advantage.

<u>Cons</u>: The near certainty that one or more U.S. officials or their dependents would suffer torture and/or death as the kidnappers tested our will.

Macomber recommended that "the second option above be followed as U.S. policy in the event a kidnapping should take place before the ultimate policy decision is reached by the President."[149]

---

[149] U.S. department of State, Office of the Historian, Foreign Relations of the United States, Nixon-Ford Administrations, Volume E-1, Documents on Global Issues. Document 38. Action Memorandum from Deputy Under Secretary of State for Administration (Macomber) to Under Secretary of State for

It appears that the U.S. followed Option #2 during the July 31, 1970 kidnapping of Daniel A. Mitrione, a U.S. public safety advisor, by the National Liberation Movement (known as the "Tupamaros") terrorists, in Montevideo, Uruguay.[150] A Brazilian diplomat and another U.S. diplomat were also seized around the same time as part of a Tupamaros kidnapping campaign aimed at foreign diplomats. The kidnappers demanded the release of approximately 150 Tupamaros being held in jail in return for the three hostages they had taken. The Uruguayan government refused to concede to the kidnappers' demands as a matter of policy but also on a legal point. The country was a democracy and as such was governed by the separation of powers. The executive branch had no power over the judicial branch which was holding the prisoners.[151] The Brazilian government wanted the Uruguayan government to concede to the demands of the terrorists. During the Eldrick kidnapping 10 months earlier, the Brazilian government acquiesced to the kidnappers' demands and saved his life. The Brazilian government was now asking the U.S. to support them for a similar resolution by the Uruguayan government. The U.S. was walking a diplomatic tightrope as it did not want to put pressure on the Uruguayans to give in to the kidnappers but also wanted to support the Brazilians. The U.S. focused its efforts on trying to convince the Uruguayans to maintain open communication channels with the terrorists and to employ a public relations strategy of seeking a humanitarian outcome and criticizing the Tupamaros' tactics.[152] The U.S. also proposed a "funding operation" to free Mitrione. This was like the Ellen Stone incident, where the State Department was willing to secretly give funds to help with the private ransom payment to free Stone. In the Mitrione case, the U.S. government was willing to provide some money to the Uruguayan government to provide a "reward," not ransom, to individuals who provided information that would produce a hostage release.[153] Ultimately, the Uruguayan government stood fast and the Tupamaros killed Mitrione. His body was found on August 10.

After Mitrione's death, the Uruguayan ambassador to the U.S. told the U.S. Secretary of State that his government had previously made a policy decision not

---

Political Affairs (Johnson), Washington, April 2, 1970, at https://history.state.gov/historicaldocuments/frus1969-76ve01/d38. Accessed June 5, 2017.

[150] This kidnapping and Mitrione's subsequent killing became the basis for the Costa-Gavras film *State of Siege*.

[151] The most extensive and accurate description of this kidnapping is Donald Ronfeldt, "The Mitrione Kidnapping in Uruguay," The RAND Corporation, Document N-1571, August 1987, http://www.rand.org/pubs/notes/N1571.html. Accessed October 5, 2017.

[152] Ibid., p. vi.

[153] Ibid., p. 47.

to give in to kidnappers who seize foreign diplomatic personnel in Uruguay — with one exception. If a U.S. diplomat was kidnapped, the government would make an "ad hoc" decision on whether to give in or not.[154] It is clear that even with this favoritism toward the U.S., the Uruguayan government had determined that to give in to the Mitrione kidnappers was not "legally possible or honorable."[155] In 1987, in an interview, one of the leaders of the Tupamaros stated that the group had not planned to kill Mr. Mitrione. If the government did not give in, they wanted to hold him indefinitely instead of killing him. Critically, the kidnappers encountered a breakdown in communications after the Uruguayan security forces captured the leaders of the operation, who were unable to send instructions to those holding him. On August 7, a week after the kidnapping, government forces arrested the group's leadership, and several days later, it arrested the group's replacement leadership. Consequently, the terrorist cell holding Mitrione lost all contact with the leadership and was on its own. When the stated deadline to kill Mitrione came, the cell decided to carry out the threat.[156]

After Mitrione's death, the State Department publicly denied that it pressured the Uruguayan government to give in to the kidnappers' demands stating that it only asked the government to do everything "practicable." On August 10, 1970, Carl Bartch, the spokesman for the State Department, issued a major policy announcement concerning kidnapping in Latin America. He noted that the U.S. believed that if it "presses governments to accede to such extreme demands that would serve, in our view, only to encourage other terrorist groups to kidnap Americans with the expectation that if they have an American prisoner, the U.S. government would support the kidnappers' demands against host governments. Such a policy carried with it greater risk for Americans overseas."[157] This can be considered the first U.S. government public statement on its policy toward hostage-taking. While it was mentioned regarding kidnappings in Latin America, the key philosophical point was that giving in to the demands of hostage-takers only encourages terrorists and increases the terrorist threat to Americans overseas. It could be deduced that this was a "no concessions" policy. The statement implies that consenting to the demands of terrorists would be counter productive.

---

[154] Ibid., p. 50.

[155] Ibid.

[156] Shirley Christian, "Uruguayan Clears Up 'State of Siege' Killing," *New York Times*, June 21, 1987, at   http://www.nytimes.com/1987/06/21/world/uruguayan-clears-up-state-of-siege-killing.html. Accessed November 3, 2017.

[157] Ronfeldt, "The Mitrione Kidnapping," pp. 52–53.

On January 23, 1973, U.S. Ambassador Clinton E. Knox was kidnapped by three terrorists in Port-au-Prince, Haiti. He was then forced to call the U.S. Consul General Ward L. Christensen, who then joined Knox at his residence where he was also taken as a hostage. The terrorists demanded the release of 30 prisoners and $1 million. Negotiations brought the number of prisoners down to 12 and a ransom of $70,000. Deputy Under Secretary of State Macomber, accompanied by Marvin Gentile, the Director of State's SY, flew to Haiti, and told the Haitian President, Dictator Jean-Claude "Baby Doc" Duvalier, that the United States would neither pay ransom payments nor grant concessions to the gunmen.[158] Duvalier disagreed, and successfully negotiated the release of Knox after 18 hours in captivity. The three terrorists and the 12 released prisoners were flown to Mexico which offered them asylum but also took the ransom money. The kidnapping was claimed by the Coalition of National Liberation Brigades, a Haitian anti-Duvalier exile group. As a result of this kidnapping, the U.S. decided to make it standard procedure to notify a host government as early as possible in a hostage situation that it was not U.S. policy to make concessions to hostage-takers.[159] After Knox's kidnapping, Armin Meyer, head of the Office for Combatting Terrorism, drafted a Department of State instruction for all diplomatic and consular posts that outlined the Administration's new hostage policy. However, no senior Department of State official, including Secretary of State Rogers and Deputy Under Secretary Macomber, would sign the memorandum as the policy appeared to be "too callous," and the instruction was not sent.[160] It is clear that NSC Director Kissinger had apparently adopted a policy of no negotiations, no deals, and no concessions sometime after the Knox incident. The policy change was not written down, reviewed for its implications, formalized, or even announced.[161]

The incident that contributed the most impetus to the evolution of U.S. policy on hostage-taking incidents took place on March 1, 1973 when eight Black September Organization (BSO) terrorists seized the Saudi Arabian Embassy in Khartoum, Sudan and held U.S. Ambassador Cleo Noel and Deputy Chief of Mission (DCM) George Curtis Moore, along with the Saudi ambassador, his wife and four children, and the Belgian and Jordanian *chargés d'affaires* as hostages.

---

[158] *DS History*, p. 216.

[159] Tucker, *Skirmishes at the Edge of Empire*, p. 9. Details on incident are from Mickolus, *Transnational Terrorism: A Chronology of Events, 1968–1979*, p. 371.

[160] Korn, *Assassination in Khartoum*, pp. 116–121; Tucker, *Skirmishes at the Edge of Empire*, p. 9. Tucker had access to Armin Meyer's unpublished memoirs and notes. At the time, Meyer was chairman of the Working Group on Terrorism.

[161] Ibid, p. 110.

They were all attending a farewell dinner in honor of Mr. Moore.[162] The terrorists demanded the release of 60 Palestinians held in Jordan, including BSO leader Abu Daoud, all Arab women detained in Israel, Sirhan Sirhan (assassin of Senator Robert F. Kennedy in Los Angeles on June 5, 1968), and imprisoned members of the Baader-Meinhof terrorist group in Germany. The terrorists later reduced their demand to release imprisoned Palestinians from 60 to 17. On March 2, the State Department sent a cable to the U.S. Embassy in Khartoum instructing the embassy to notify the Sudanese government that U.S. policy is not to negotiate with hostage-takers. The U.S. did not, however, pressure the Sudanese to adopt this policy. This was the first time the policy of no negotiations, no deals, no concessions had been stated in an officially approved document.[163] The Sudanese government still engaged in negotiations with the terrorists. The U.S. also talked to the hostage-takers through a third party suggesting that the U.S. had no problem with free passage for the terrorists if they released all the hostages unharmed. This was the so-called "Bangkok Solution."[164] However, it was clear that the U.S. would not meet any of the demands of the hostage-takers.[165] Neither would Germany or Jordan. On March 2, there was a controversial news conference in Washington, D.C. where a reporter asked President Nixon about the terrorists' demand to release Sirhan Sirhan. In an apparent off the cuff response, Nixon replied that "as far as the United States as a government giving in to blackmail demands, we cannot do so and will not do so ... the position of the ambassador, once so greatly sought after, now, in many places ... is quite dangerous ... but it is a problem and it is a risk that an ambassador has to take."[166] The U.S. did send several State Department officials, including William B. Macomber, Jr., the Deputy Under Secretary of State for Administration, to Khartoum to work the incident. According to one account, Macomber "had no instructions on what he

---

[162] It was learned later that DCM Moore "had possibly been at least vaguely aware of being under surveillance but had discounted it." Moreover, Ambassador Noel had also been advised to be cautious, but, with his deep experience in Khartoum, had said on the very day of the Saudi Embassy seizure, "Nothing will happen to me in the Sudan." Association of Diplomatic Studies and Training. Moments in U.S. Diplomatic History. "The Terrorist Attack on the Saudi Embassy — Khartoum, 1973." ADST 1999 Interview with Robert E. Fritts, DCM Moore's replacement. http://adst.org/2013/02/the-terrorist-attack-on-the-saudi-embassy-khartoum-1973/ November 7, 2017.

[163] Korn, *Assassination in Khartoum*, p. 128.

[164] The term "Bangkok Solution" resulted from a December 1972 incident, during which four terrorists of the BSO entered the Israeli Embassy in Bangkok and took hostages. Thai officials allowed the four men safe passage out of Thailand in exchange for releasing their hostages.

[165] Tucker, *Skirmishes at the Edge of Empire*, p. 9.

[166] Ibid.

was exactly to do once he arrived" there.[167] This became irrelevant as Macomber and his party had to stop in Cairo due to sandstorms in and around Khartoum.

The consensus has been that the terrorists, upon hearing Nixon's hardline policy, decided to kill the two U.S. and Belgian hostages. Late in the evening on March 2, the terrorists took the hostages down to the basement of the Saudi Arabian Embassy. The BSO terrorists allowed Noel and Moore to write "last words" to their wives, who were together throughout at the ambassador's residence in Khartoum. The terrorists then put the two Americans up against the wall and shot them with over 40 rounds.[168] The diplomats were previously beaten, and their bodies mutilated. The terrorists surrendered the next day and the remaining hostages were released unharmed. In June 1974, they were sentenced by the Khartoum government to life sentences, but Sudanese President Numaryi later reduced the sentence to seven years and had the terrorists deported to Egypt where President Sadat released them to the PLO. These actions antagonized the U.S., especially the State Department's Foreign Service officers.

After the Khartoum incident, the BSO issued a communiqué in Beirut. It warned that it would continue to attack "Zionist and American imperialism and their agents in the Arab world." The BSO claimed that the Khartoum operation was not aimed "at bloodshed but had sought the release of our imprisoned heroes ... as a result of the arrogance and obstinacy of the American imperialism, represented by Nixon's statement and by the attitude of the hireling tools in Jordan, our revolutionaries carried out the death sentences on three hostages ..." The BSO accused DCM Moore of being "the plotting brain of the American Central Intelligence Agency and one of those directly responsible for the September massacres." The communiqué continued: "Those who ostensibly weep today over the execution of three enemies of the Arab nation, for which the United States has been directly responsible, realize that thousands of the sons of this people have been atrociously slaughtered and that thousands of others are suffering all kinds of torture in Jordanian and Israeli jails ...."[169] This communiqué clearly implies that Nixon's hardline statement was a trigger for the executions. U.S. foreign service officers in the Department of State came to believe this also.[170] However, an argument could be made that the terrorists had planned to kill the Americans regardless of Nixon's statement. Ideally, the terrorists wanted to accomplish some of their demands to save some face. However, none of the relevant countries were

---

[167] Simon, *The Terrorist Trap*, p. 109.

[168] Mickolus, *Transnational Terrorism: 1968–1979*, p. 377.

[169] Ibid.

[170] *DS History*, pp. 216–218.

giving in to the terrorists' demands. Therefore, the terrorists now faced the decision of whether to seek free passage out of Sudan in exchange for the hostages (the Bangkok Solution), surrender, or kill the hostages.

One of the objectives of the Khartoum operation was most likely to restore face after the recent BSO hostage-taking failure in Bangkok, Thailand. On December 28, 1972, four BSO terrorists attacked the Israeli Embassy building in Bangkok and held the Israeli Embassy staff as hostages. After 19 hours of negotiations, the hijackers agreed to abandon the embassy in exchange for safe conduct and were flown to Egypt. The BSO leadership was reported to be very upset with the behavior of its operatives in settling the incident. BSO militants felt that the Bangkok terrorists had shown weakness in not killing any of the hostages and that the BSO had lost face and credibility among Palestinians and the Arab world.[171] Why then would the BSO leadership accept another "Bangkok Solution" in Khartoum?[172] Consider also that information later surfaced that neither the U.S. nor the Sudanese government knew at the time that the terrorists had planned to take the two American diplomats to the United States (most likely on a plane supplied by the Sudanese government) in order to kill them on American soil.[173] In addition, according to the Sudanese government, when the "executions" were not carried out promptly on deadline, a prodding message was transmitted from the PLO in Beirut: "What are you waiting for?"[174] The leadership in Beirut did not want another Bangkok result. Either they get their demands or they kill some hostages. Immediately after the executions of the two U.S. diplomats and a Belgian diplomat on March 2, a Beirut newspaper published a statement from a BSO spokesman who stated that "this operation will teach the world to respect what we say ... we will not allow ourselves to be deceived again or subject our demands to bargaining."[175] In other words, Nixon's statement was not the reason for the

---

[171] Dobson, *Black September*, p. 109.

[172] Dobson believes that the Khartoum operation was a result of several factors: (1) to restore BSO prestige after the Bangkok failure, (2) the realization that seizing Israeli hostages would not succeed as Israel would never give in and therefore seizing high-profile foreign hostages would be more advantageous, (3) the Saudi King had threatened to stop collecting taxes for the PLO from Palestinians working in Saudi Arabia, (4) there was growing anger among Arabs of increasing American support for Israel, and (5) Libya's Qaddafi was angry with the Sudan President for not allowing Libyan airborne forces to pass over Sudan to help the Ugandan President Idi Amin in an internal conflict. *Black September*, pp. 112–113. The BSO terrorists had hoped to capture the British and West German ambassadors and Emperor Haile Selassie of Ethiopia. Had this taken place, the terrorists would have been in a better bargaining position.

[173] Ibid., p. 115, and Mickolus, *Transnational Terrorism: 1968–1979*, p. 378.

[174] "Arresting Arafat," *The New Republic*, December 30, 1985, p. 12.

[175] Korn, *Assassination in Khartoum*, p. 174.

executions but simply an excuse. The BSO had every intention of killing one or more hostages in this attack to make a point and correct the impression of BSO weakness left by the Bangkok incident. The initial demands of the terrorists and even their revised demands of prisoner releases had no possibility of being met by the U.S., Israel, and West Germany. It was as if the BSO leadership knew in advance that hostages would be eventually killed. The two U.S. diplomats were at the top of the list.

It has also been argued that "one of the primary goals of the operation was to strike at the United States because of its efforts to achieve a Middle East peace settlement which many Arabs believe would be inimical to Palestinian interests."[176] Allowing the two U.S. hostages to live would not send as strong and pointed a message to the U.S. as killing them.

> *The Khartoum operation was an intoxicating success for Arafat. It drew the Nixon administration to launch secret negotiations with him, through an intermediary, Richard Helms, ambassador to Iran and CIA head through 1973. The contacts were conducted with Ali Hassan Salameh, 'Arafat's right-hand man,' as Helms put it, and Black September's operations officer. Nixon and Kissinger wanted to moderate Arafat's policies and prevent further terror attacks (against Americans; the others didn't count). For his part, the Palestinian leader leveraged the attacks to conduct diplomatic negotiations, unbeknownst to Israel and Jordan.[177]*

Arafat wanted to attract the attention of the U.S. and to signal how Fatah and the BSO could become a terrorism problem for the U.S. Until the attack in Khartoum, no American was deliberately killed by Palestinian terrorists controlled by Arafat. The PFLP and PFLP-GC had killed Americans, including the April 1970 assassination of the U.S. military attaché in Jordan. However, neither group was under Arafat's control. It is also true that the BSO killed David Berger, a dual Israeli American citizen during the Munich barricade and hostage incident in 1972. It is not known if the BSO terrorists knew that Berger was an American citizen. Given

---

[176]U.S. Department of State, Office of the Historian, Foreign Relations of the United States, 1969–1976, Volume E-6, Documents on Africa, 1973–1976, Sudan, Document 217. Intelligence Memorandum, Washington, dated June 1973, titled "The Seizure of the Saudi Arabian Embassy in Khartoum," athttps://history.state.gov/historicaldocuments/frus1969-76ve06/d217. Accessed June 6, 2017.

[177]Amir Oren, "For Yasir Arafat, Crime Certainly Paid," *Haaretz*, August 26, 2011, at http://www.haaretz.com/israel-news/for-yasser-arafat-crime-certainly-paid-1.380812. Accessed May 5, 2017.

that Arafat controlled Fatah, the largest Palestinian component within the PLO, its active involvement in anti-American terrorism operations would significantly increase the terrorist threat for U.S. interests overseas. One of the esoteric messages of the Khartoum incident was "talk with us or there will be more Khartoums." In 1973, after the BSO killed the two U.S. diplomats in Khartoum, then Secretary of State Henry Kissinger dispatched General Vernon Walters, CIA deputy director, to a November 3 meeting with Ali Hassan Salameh, the "Red Prince," to tell the PLO that such actions would not be tolerated. The message: "Stop killing Americans or there would be serious consequences."[178] There was one report that indicated that the CIA was prepared to begin a campaign of attacks against PLO facilities.[179]

In July 1973, CIA Officer Robert Ames wrote a memorandum for then U.S. Ambassador to Iran and former CIA Director Richard Helms titled "Contacts with Fatah Leadership." He noted:

> *During my stay in Beirut on 9–10 July I contacted a close associate of Fatah leader Yasir Arafat on the basis of a letter he sent to me requesting a meeting. As you know, I had a useful meeting with this fellow in the past and his position in Fatah is fully established.... My contact said that significant changes had taken place in the Palestinian Movement since I had last seen him in early March 1973. He reiterated what he said at that time, which was shortly after the Khartoum murders. The fedeyeen have no plans to go after individual Americans or American interests; Khartoum had made its point of causing the USG to take fedeyeen terrorist activity seriously.... Arafat wanted the USG to know that he had "put the lid on" American operations by the fedeyeen and that the lid would stay on as long as both sides could maintain a dialogue.... My contact stated that fedeyeen activity would be confined to two areas: Jordan and Israel, in that priority.[180]*

---

[178] Edwin Black, "Justice Department is Considering Indicting PLO Chief Yasir Arafat," *The Palm Beach Jewish World*, November 27, 1985; Simon Reeve. *One Day in September* (New York: Arcade Publishing, 2000), p. 203.

[179] Black, "Justice Department Is Considering ..."

[180] As quoted in Aland Berlind, "Partners in Capital Crime," *American Diplomacy*, October 2012, at http://www.unc.edu/depts/diplomat/item/2012/0712/comm/berlind_partners.html#note6. Accessed August 4, 2017. Berlind's primary source for this memo is Memorandum for the Ambassador re: Contacts with the Fatah Leadership, July 18, 1973, at https://www.cia.gov/library/readingroom/docs/73_1499655.pdf. Accessed October 23, 2017. Berlind was DCM in Khartoum (following the

The Khartoum attack was both an Arafat provocation and a probe of the U.S. government's desire to talk with the PLO. After Khartoum, the U.S. did not want to be included in the BSO targeting box and Arafat did not want the U.S. coming after Fatah and the BSO. What came out of Khartoum was a mutual self-defense pact. In that sense, Khartoum was a success for Arafat. The U.S. was also now in direct contact with the PLO through established channels.

However, the Khartoum incident also triggered three controversies for the United States that continue to this day:

- First, did the State Department receive prior information of a BSO attack in Khartoum?
- Second, was the U.S. government aware that the order to kill the two American hostages came directly from Yasir Arafat?
- Third, whatever happened to the intercepted tapes and transcripts from the Khartoum incident?

On February 28, 1973, the National Security Agency listening post in Cyprus picked up radio traffic including Arafat, Salah Kalaf (a cofounder of Arafat's PLO faction, Fatah), and others strongly suggesting that a BSO operation was about to be conducted in Khartoum. These messages were originating from then Fatah HQs in Shatilla refugee camp where the Fatah radio headquarters were located.[181] Jim Welsh, a Navy analyst at NSA in the U.S. with a Palestinian portfolio, read the intercept and helped draft a message warning the U.S. Embassy in Khartoum that a BSO operation was imminent. Welsh has stated that he recognized the voice of Arafat telling his aides, Abu Jihad and Abu Iyad, to carry out the attack. Welsh and his NSA colleagues marked the message for transmission with a "Zulu" (second highest to "Critic") precedence. For reasons still unknown, the message was assigned a lower priority by a watch officer at State; if it was ever sent, it arrived much too late. Given that the intercept information did not contain any references to U.S. targets or contain specific targeting, tactical, timing, and location information, it is likely that the information was too general to act on. Welsh claimed that when he demanded that the State Department's failure be investigated, his NSA superiors told him such a campaign would cost him his security clearance and result in his transfer from Washington to a Navy fueling ship. Welsh backed

---

Sudanese release of the killers in 1974) and Athens, political advisor at the U.S. mission to NATO as well as serving earlier tours in Greece, Ghana, and Belgium.

[181] March 2003 Interview of James Welsh, at http://www.freerepublic.com/focus/news/857344/posts. Accessed September 23, 2016.

down.[182] It is a mystery as to whether the State Department Operations Center did send a cable to the American Embassy in Khartoum with the NSA intercept information. If it did, that cable has not surfaced. It may have been destroyed.[183]

At the time of the attack in Khartoum, the U.S. and Israel were monitoring Fatah communications in Beirut and Khartoum.[184] On March 2, 1973, the NSA and Israeli intelligence intercepted an ultra-high frequency radio phone message from a PLO radio command center in Beirut to the terrorists in Khartoum. This intercept was relayed immediately by both to Washington. Using coded instructions, Arafat's closest Fatah associate in Beirut, Salah Khalaf, directed the murder of Noel, Moore, and the Belgian charge. The code word for the executions was "Nahr al-Bard" or Cold River.[185] Arafat was present in the command center when the message was sent, and he personally congratulated the terrorists after the execution of the three diplomats.[186] The uncertainty centers on whether Arafat verbally gave or confirmed the kill orders. If he did, what and where is the evidence?

On April 13, 1973, Charles W. Bray III, the State Department spokesman, publicly stated for the first time that the BSO and PLO were interconnected.[187] On May 12, 1973, the following exchange in Washington took place between Kissinger and Israeli Foreign Minister Abba Eban:

---

[182] Information on the NSA intercepts and NSA analyst Jim Welsh compiled from Amir Oren, "For Yasir Arafat, Crime Certainly Paid," Haaretz, August 26, 2011, at http://www.haaretz.com/israel-news/for-yasser-arafat-crime-certainly-paid-1.380812. Accessed July 4, 2017; and author email and phone conversations with Welsh in April 2016.

[183] U.S. Senate, Committee on the Judiciary, Subcommittee on Security and Terrorism, 99th Congress, Liability of Civil and Criminal Actions against Yasir Arafat's Palestine Liberation Organization, "Legal Methods to Combat Terrorism," April 23, 1986, p. 306, at https://www.ncjrs.gov/pdffiles1/Photocopy/105320NCJRS.pdf. Accessed June 4, 2018.

[184] Neil C. Livingstone and David Halevy. *Inside the PLO* (N.Y: Quill/William Morrow, 1990), pp. 282–184.

[185] On February 20, 1973, Israel's Shayetet 13, Unit 707, and Sayeret Tzanhanim commandos jointly raided the PLO's Nahr al-Bard training camp concealed in a refugee camp outside Tripoli, Lebanon. They killed around 40 terrorists. It was called "Operation Bardas 54–55." Livingstone and Halevy, *Inside the PLO*, p. 281, also point out that during one conversation between Arafat and the Khartoum terrorists, Arafat stated "glory and immortality to the martyrs of the Nahr al-Bard and Libyan aircraft." The latter reference was to the February 21, 1973 Israeli downing of a Libyan passenger jet. Thus, the Khartoum operation was to avenge the Israeli raids on the training camp and a Libyan aircraft — payback for Qaddafi.

[186] David B. Ottaway, "Arafat Implicated in Envoy's Deaths, the *Washington Post*, April 5, 1973; Livingstone and Halervy, *Inside the PLO*, pp. 279–181.

[187] Oswald Johnson, "Palestinian Linked to Black September," *Washington Star*, April 13, 1973.

Kissinger — *During the Khartoum incident, someone suggested we ask you for help. You would have blown up Beirut.*

Eban — *You know that it was from Beirut that the phone call went to finish them off.*

Kissinger — *We know that.*[188]

A June 1973 "Intelligence Memorandum" on Khartoum, released by the State Department's Office of the Historian in 2006, concluded that "...The Khartoum operation was planned and carried out with the full knowledge and personal approval of Yasir Arafat, Chairman of the Palestine Liberation Organization (PLO), and the head of Fatah..." and that after executing the three diplomats, "thirty-four hours later, upon receipt of orders from Yasir Arafat in Beirut to surrender, the terrorists released their other hostages unharmed and surrendered to Sudanese authorities."[189] It is one thing to approve an operation and another to personally give the order to execute the three hostages. The U.S. simply acknowledged that there was a connection between the BSO and Fatah and that Arafat knew of or approved the Khartoum incident. This is as far as the U.S. would go on the Khartoum incident. Despite the evidence, there was no official implication that Arafat gave the execution order. Nor did Israel come forward with a similar statement. Given that the BSO was a terrorist arm of Fatah, that Arafat was in the command center for the Khartoum operations, and that he gave the order for the attack and the subsequent order to the terrorists to surrender, it seems improbable that he did not give or confirm the most important order of the entire operation — to kill two U.S. diplomats. It appears that there was a "smoking gun" — tapes and transcripts of these communications between Beirut and Khartoum.

---

[188] Berlind, "Partners in Capital Crime." Berlind's primary source was: "Memorandum of Conversation, Washington, May 12, 1973, as found in National Archives, Nixon Presidential Materials, NSC Files, Kissinger Office Files. Other participants: Israeli Ambassador Simcha Dinitz, Israeli Minister Amir Idan, NSC Staffers Harold Saunders and Peter W. Rodman."

[189] U.S. Department of State, Office of the Historian, Foreign Relations of the United States, 1969–1976, Volume E-6, Documents on Africa, 1973–1976, Sudan, Document 217. Intelligence Memorandum, Washington, dated June 1973, titled "The Seizure of the Saudi Arabian Embassy in Khartoum," at https://history.state.gov/historicaldocuments/frus1969-76ve06/d217. Accessed September 4, 2017. See also, U.S. Department of State, Office of the Historian, Foreign Relations of the United States, 1969–1976, Volume XXV, Arab-Israeli Crisis and War, 1973. Document 41. Back channel message from the Egyptian Presidential Adviser for National Security Affairs (Ismail) to the President's Assistant for National Security Affairs (Kissinger), dated March 20, 1973, footnote #3, at https://history.state.gov/historicaldocuments/frus1969-76v25/d41. Accessed October 4, 2017. Its statement also acknowledged Arafat's direct involvement in the Khartoum attack.

The evidence clearly indicates that such communication intercepts existed. Arafat's voice was reportedly monitored and recorded in the many message exchanges with the Khartoum terrorists.[190] In fact, Khartoum telegram #471, dated March 3, 1973, which was sent to the State Department states that the "embassy has obtained notes and documents of BSO instructions, floor plan of action, allocation of duties for each terrorist by name, and recitation of communications (based on tapes) between al-Fatah in Beirut to terrorists in Saudi Embassy in Khartoum ... documents reportedly obtained from desk drawer of al-Fatah Khartoum office."[191] Over a decade later, then U.S. United Nations Ambassador Vernon Walters confirmed in an interview with journalist Edwin Black that in 1973, when Walters was deputy director of the CIA, he was told of the existence of such a tape. Walters said he did not actually hear the tape but that the existence of the tape "was common knowledge at the time among all sorts of people in the government."[192]

An Israeli journalist at the time of the Khartoum incident later wrote that he immediately learned in 1973 "that Israeli intelligence had succeeded in intercepting radio-telephone transmissions between Yasir Arafat and his Beirut aides and the Palestinian murderers in Khartoum" and that then Israeli Prime Minister Golda Meir "ordered that the incriminating intelligence material be passed on to the CIA and Nixon's White House through the proper channels." However, the U.S.'s "own wiretapping services based in Cyprus received the exact same criminal transmissions between Arafat in Beirut and his hit men in Khartoum."[193] In 2002, this same journalist asked the then Israeli Prime Minister Ariel Sharon to

---

[190] U.S. Senate, Committee on the Judiciary, Subcommittee on Security and Terrorism, 99th Congress, Liability of Civil and Criminal Actions against Yasir Arafat's Palestine Liberation Organization, "Legal Methods to Combat Terrorism," April 23, 1986, p. 4 and 7, at https://www.ncjrs.gov/pdffiles1/Photocopy/105320NCJRS.pdf. Accessed May 5, 2018.

[191] Copy of telegram appears in U.S. Senate, Committee on the Judiciary, Subcommittee on Security and Terrorism, 99th Congress, Liability of Civil and Criminal Actions against Yasir Arafat's Palestine Liberation Organization, "Legal Methods to Combat Terrorism," April 23, 1986, p. 139, at https://www.ncjrs.gov/pdffiles1/Photocopy/105320NCJRS.pdf. Accessed September 23, 2017.

[192] "Arresting Arafat," *New Republic* Magazine, December 30, 1985, p. 12. It was also reported that Deputy U.S. U.N. Ambassador Charles M. Lichenstein noted that "Vernon Walters has said that many people spoke to Mr. Walters at the time of the assassination and told him that the U.S. government possessed a recording of Arafat ordering the executions. Source: Bill Kritzberg, "Meese may consider indictment of Arafat," *Washington Times*, December 18, 1985.

[193] Covering Up for Arafat, *Jerusalem Post*, June 14, 2006. http://www.jpost.com/Israel/Covering-up-for-Arafat December 5, 2016.

ask Mossad chief Ephraim Halevy to bring him the files on these Israeli intercepts. Sharon later told the journalist that he had "repeatedly asked Halevy to bring him the material but that Halevy had come back empty handed."[194] It was not until October 1985 that the Israeli government for the first time stated in an Israeli Ministry of Foreign Affairs white paper titled "The Threat of PLO Terrorism" on page 24 that "the order to kill the diplomats had been phoned to the terrorists personally by Yasir Arafat."[195] NSA analyst James Welsh, who listened to the intercepted messages and read the transcripts, has consistently stated since 1973 that the tapes and transcripts existed. Welsh was the Palestinian communications analyst for NSA from 1969 to 1974 and worked with the SIGINT materials that were being intercepted between the Fatah command center and the BSO hostage-takers in Khartoum. In a March 2003 interview, Welsh stated:

> *The tapes were made. Some were made in Cyprus and others at the embassies in Beirut and Khartoum. NSA (and CIA) possessed them and there never was any doubt when I was there that it was Arafat's voice directing the operation from the initial intercept on February 28 (the day before!) to its end on March 2.*[196]

In an email statement sent to U.S. Senator John Kyl on October 25, 2000, Welsh, referring to the Khartoum incident, noted that:

> *Over the next week, we awaited the arrival of the field intercept tapes and transcriptions. At least we would be able to gain valuable insight into this terrible affair and maybe even someday help punish those responsible. We waited. Finally, I remember asking when would the tapes arrive? I was puzzled by the answer. Oh, they've been looked at and there isn't much there. !!!!!????? Wait a minute. Then, how could the field guys have given us all this detailed information that we based the warning message on and which in fact occurred two days later? Something was not right. In addition, our folders with all our materials*

---

[194] Ibid.

[195] U.S. Senate, Committee on the Judiciary, Subcommittee on Security and Terrorism, 99th Congress, Liability of Civil and Criminal Actions against Yasir Arafat's Palestine Liberation Organization, "Legal Methods to Combat Terrorism," April 23, 1986, p. 7, at https://www.ncjrs.gov/pdffiles1/Photocopy/105320NCJRS.pdf. Accessed August 5, 2016.

[196] March 2003 Interview of James Welsh, at http://www.freerepublic.com/focus/news/857344/posts. Accessed July 23, 2016.

of the hostage crisis were never returned to us from the higher levels to which they had gone during the crisis.[197]

In 1986, Congress requested the then Attorney General Ed Meese to investigate Arafat's involvement in the executions of Noel and Moore in Khartoum. On February 12, 1986, 47 U.S. senators petitioned Meese "to assign the highest priority to completing this review, and to issue an indictment of Yasir Arafat if the evidence so warrants."[198] On April 21, 1986, the Justice Department notified Congress that it did not plan to seek prosecution of PLO Chairman Yasir Arafat for the murders of the two U.S. diplomats because the U.S. lacked legal jurisdiction and enough evidence. The DOJ letter noted that a law passed in 1976 giving U.S. courts clear authority to prosecute terrorists for the murder of U.S. diplomats abroad could not be applied retroactively to the 1973 killings as it would violate the *ex post facto* clause in Article 1, Section 9 of the Constitution.[199] In 1973, there was no Federal criminal liability for the murder of U.S. diplomats abroad. In addition, the DOJ could not find the key evidence — the intercept tapes or transcriptions:

Notwithstanding our legal analysis, we reviewed the evidence available to determine if admissible evidence existed that might support such an indictment. Although much has been alleged about evidence implicating Arafat in planning the takeover of the Saudi Arabian Embassy and directing the terrorists to murder Ambassador Noel and Charge d'Affaires Moore, the evidence currently available from key departments and agencies within our government and from other sources is insufficient for prosecutive purposes.[200]

---

[197] Email from James Welsh to Senator John Kyl, dated October 25, 2000, at http://www.debbieschlussel. com/2811/too-late-state-dept-admits-arafat-ordered-murder-of-american-diplomats-exclusive-nsa-palestinian-analyst-contacts-schlussel/. Accessed December 23, 2016.

[198] U.S. Senate, Committee on the Judiciary, Subcommittee on Security and Terrorism, 99th Congress, Liability of Civil and Criminal Actions against Yasir Arafat's Palestine Liberation Organization, "Legal Methods to Combat Terrorism," April 23, 1986, pp. 40–41, at https://www.ncjrs.gov/pdffiles1/ Photocopy/105320NCJRS.pdf. Accessed June 23, 2017.

[199] U.S. Senate, Committee on the Judiciary, Subcommittee on Security and Terrorism, 99th Congress, Liability of Civil and Criminal Actions against Yasir Arafat's Palestine Liberation Organization, "Legal Methods to Combat Terrorism," April 23, 1986, pp. 47–48, at https://www.ncjrs.gov/pdffiles1/ Photocopy/105320NCJRS.pdf. Accessed June 6, 2017.

[200] Ibid., p. 47.

In April 1986, Senator Jeremiah Denton convened a subcommittee of the Senate Judiciary Committee for a one-day hearing on the possibility of bringing Arafat to justice for crimes including the murders of Noel and Moore. Mark Richard, Deputy Assistant Attorney General, Criminal Division, reiterated that there was no legal ground for a federal prosecution of Arafat based on his role in the murders. He noted again that:

> *The Department conducted an extensive search both within our govern-*
> *ment and from other sources to determine if admissible evidence is*
> *available to support criminal prosecution in this country. We enlisted the*
> *assistance of the State Department and various components of the intel-*
> *ligence community to obtain and verify information alleging Arafat's*
> *complicity in the planning of the Embassy takeover and the murder of*
> *our diplomats. We have analyzed all of the materials available and have*
> *determined that the evidence currently available is plainly insufficient*
> *for prosecutive purposes, even if there were a legal basis for instituting*
> *charges against Arafat.*[201]

The DOJ did not find the "evidence" because it was most likely destroyed. The *Chicago Sun-Times* journalist Thomas B. Ross in a June 13, 1974 article "Cover-Up in '73 Sudan Slaying of Diplomats" wrote that "reliable sources" stated that the State Department's SY "discovered the destruction of cables dealing with the murders of the three diplomats":

> *This destruction was discovered when security officers came across a*
> *cable ordering the U.S. Embassy in Khartoum to destroy the copies of*
> *the cables. That led to a master index in which the destroyed cables were*
> *listed by serial numbers and the discovery that there were no copies in*
> *the file.*[202]

Ross suggested that some of the cables dealt with Sudanese interrogations where the terrorists stated that they killed the diplomats after hearing Nixon's press comments that the U.S. would not give in to the demands of hostage-takers and cables that "dealt with the bungled U.S. effort to negotiate the release of the diplomats." The presumed destruction of the cables was clearly designed to protect President Nixon and his administration. If government officials were willing to

---

[201] Ibid., p. 67.
[202] Ibid., p. 306.

destroy cables to protect the administration, would they hesitate to destroy intercept tapes and transcriptions to further the administration's foreign policy goals
in the Middle East?

In February 2002, an Israeli journalist spent several days at the U.S. National
Archives in College Park, Maryland researching the Khartoum attack. He
searched BSO, NSC, and Khartoum files. He also searched "the Nixon Project,"
an archive within the National Archives created when Congress confiscated
Nixon's papers. He found many files missing and concluded that "it looked like
monkey business in the National Archives." He also found "no reference in the
National Archives to an NSA telephone intercept, never officially acknowledged
to exist, and although Israel has repeatedly confirmed publicly it intercepted
Arafat's orders, there is no reference to that information either." His research at
the State Department's archives also produced no information on the tapes.[203]

As previously noted, NSA analyst James Welsh, with access to the information, Khartoum telegram #471, and NSC advisor Kissinger all verified the existence of U.S. intercepts of communications between the Fatah in Beirut and BSO
terrorists in Khartoum. A 1973 CIA Intelligence memorandum implied their
existence. The then CIA Deputy Director Vernon Walters stated that the existence
of these tapes was well-known in the U.S. government. Despite all this evidence,
a DOJ investigation in 1986 on behalf of Congress could not find these tapes or
transcriptions.[204] Moreover, several U.S. and Israeli journalists who sought the
tapes or transcripts at the National Archives and State Department's Historian
Office have not been able to find them. What happened to these U.S. intercept
tapes and the transcriptions? Khartoum telegram #471 clearly states that the
"embassy has obtained" documents and transcripts of messages from a BSO safe
house in Khartoum. The normal course of action would have been to send these
back to the State Department in Washington. It is also very likely that copies were
sent back to CIA headquarters. Where are these documents? If they cannot be
found, they were either destroyed or intentionally misfiled. If they were destroyed,
then a criminal action was carried out by someone in the government. If they were
misfiled, someone should have found them by now. What is clear is that there was
a cover-up to prevent these tapes and transcripts from ever becoming public.

---

[203] Russ Braley, "Sidebar: Nixon tapes and the Arafat's murders in Khartoum," *Behind the News in
Israel*, March 4, 2004, at http://israelbehindthenews.com/sidebar-nixon-tapes-and-the-arafats-mur-
ders-in-khartoum/4169/. Accessed December 23, 2016.

[204] Howard Kurtz, "Prosecution of Arafat Rejected," *Washington Post*, April 22, 1986, at https://www.
washingtonpost.com/archive/politics/1986/04/22/prosecution-of-arafat-rejected/48dfd125-27f9-4f0a-
90e5-1cdc82e585a5/?utm_term=.aad219240e5a. Accessed September 27, 2016.

Given the record of the Nixon administration, which erased tapes and engaged in illegal cover-ups and dirty tricks, the wanton destruction of the Arafat tapes and transcripts is not inconsistent with the administration's mindset of occasionally operating outside the law. But why destroy these tapes and transcripts which could have been used as political blackmail against Arafat?

It is perplexing as to why Israel has not released these tapes. They clearly intercepted the communications between Fatah in Beirut and the BSO terrorists in Khartoum. If there is a recording of Arafat personally ordering the executions of the two U.S. diplomats, why did the Israelis not release the tapes at the time to tarnish Arafat's image even more and undermine any movement toward consultations between the U.S. and the PLO? Israel may have had internal and external political considerations at the time preventing it from releasing the tapes. However, the tapes could have been released after Nixon's death in 1994 and Arafat's in 2004. The disposition of the Arafat intercept tapes in Israel and the United States remains a mystery.

The Khartoum incident was a seminal event in terms of the evolution of U.S. policy on hostage-taking. For the first time, the U.S. made a public statement on its policy — the U.S. will not give in to the demands of hostage-takers. The U.S. had hinted that it had or was developing a policy like this. On August 10, 1972, a State Department spokesman publicly stated that the government would not press another government to accede to the demands of kidnappers holding Americans because it would encourage other terrorists to kidnap Americans. Sometime in February 1973, after Ambassador Knox's kidnapping, Kissinger had adopted an unpublished, privately held policy of no concessions, no negotiations, and no deals — without any debate or discussion on this policy.[205] President Nixon's statement on March 2, 1973 of no deals simply put the policy on public record, albeit unintentionally. The U.S. government could have backtracked on the President's statement or provided some context or framework to the policy. It did not. It appears that both Kissinger and Nixon believed that this was the most effective policy. In remarks made at the State Department during a ceremony honoring the slain Foreign Service Officers Noel and Moore on March 6, 1973, the President reinforced that policy when he stated:

They were willing to risk their own lives in order that others might live. They were willing also to have their Government take a position of no compromise with terrorism, because they knew that once that compromise was entered into that it could lead to consequences that would be

---

[205] Korn, *Assassination in Khartoum*, p. 110.

far worse in the years ahead. I was noting a well-intentioned comment by one individual who raised a question as to whether the United States, in this instance, might have been better advised to bring pressure on another government to release 60 who were held in prison in order to save the lives of two.

I disagree with that. All of us would have liked to have saved the lives of these two very brave men, but they knew and we knew that in the event we had paid international blackmail in this way, it would have saved their lives, but it would have endangered the lives of hundreds of others all over the world, because once the individual, the terrorist, or the others, has a demand that is made, that is satisfied, he then is encouraged to try it again. And that is why the position of your Government has to be one in the interest of preserving life, of not submitting to international blackmail or extortion anyplace in the world. That is our policy and that is the policy we are going to continue to have.[206]

While the above were public remarks, in a private luncheon with the Secretary of State and other State Department officials immediately after the above ceremony, Nixon again underlined the hardline policy to these officials.

The President said if we come to a hard place again, the individual will know what we will do — the terrorists must know we have a hard-line and will provide no reward.[207]

It was a hardline approach that both Nixon and Kissinger had admired in Israel, which had a reputation of taking a hardline position toward terrorists. On May 17, 1973, in a meeting at the White House with Noel and Moore's widows, Nixon said he envied the "ruthlessness" of the Soviet and Israeli responses to terror, adding that "damned terrorism" was tearing other countries, like Lebanon,

---

[206]"Remarks at a Ceremony Honoring Slain Foreign Service Officers," March 6, 1973, at http://www. presidency.ucsb.edu/ws/index.php?pid=4132&st=Terrorism&st1=. Accessed June 6, 2016.

[207]U.S. Department of State, Office of the Historian. Foreign Relations of the United States, 1969–1976. Volume E-3, Documents on Global Issue, 1973–1976, Document 207. Memorandum for the President's Files by his Assistant to the President and Press Secretary (Ziegler), Washington, March 6, 1973, at https://history.state.gov/historicaldocuments/frus1969-76ve03/d207. Accessed September 23, 2017.

apart.[208] There was no major dissension among the public or media concerning this U.S. policy on hostage-taking. In September 1973, Nixon replaced Secretary of State William Rogers with Henry Kissinger. In October 1973, the administration contracted with the RAND Corporation to assess the no negotiations policy. The study's conclusions did not support the administration's hardline policy. The Interagency Working Group on Terrorism adopted some of the study's recommendations: U.S. officials should (1) remain silent during the incident, (2) screen information about the hostages to the media, (3) and include psychiatrists and police experts on the crisis task force.[209] On April 1, 1974, the State Department sent out an Airgram to all diplomatic posts stating that it was U.S. policy "not to pay ransom and to discourage other governments, companies, and individuals from making such payments." It also would not yield to international blackmail. According to the instruction, the administration sought three objectives in a hostage situation: release of the hostages, non-acquiescence to terrorist demands, and prosecution of the terrorists. As "a last resort," the administration accepted "the Bangkok Solution." [210]

The U.S. hostage-taking policy was tested again on March 22, 1974 when the U.S. Vice-Consul, John S. Patterson, was kidnapped in Hermosillo, Mexico by a mentally disturbed American. Initially, the U.S. thought that a gang was involved, and a previously unknown group called the People's Liberation Army of Mexico claimed responsibility. The kidnapper(s) demanded a ransom of $500,000. The U.S. government did not pay the ransom, but it decided that it could not prevent families of American citizens from taking action. On July 7, Patterson's body was found as he was apparently killed immediately after the kidnapping during a struggle. American Bobby Joe Keesee, a decorated military veteran, was later arrested for the kidnapping/murder. While it did not pay the ransom, the U.S. government did facilitate the paying of the ransom by Patterson's family by having U.S. diplomats in Mexico drive to Arizona and pick up the $500,000 ransom money and then illegally bring it across the Mexican border. In addition, it was using a U.S. government vehicle for these actions and three U.S. diplomats were involved in delivering the money.[211]

---

[208] Amir Oren, "For Yasir Arafat, Crime Certainly Paid," *Haaretz*, August 26, 2011, at http://www.haaretz.com/israel-news/for-yasser-arafat-crime-certainly-paid-1.380812. Accessed November 23, 2017.

[209] Judith Miller, "Bargain with Terrorists?" *New York Times Magazine*, July 18, 1987, pp. 38–39.

[210] *DS History*, p. 216.

[211] Association for Diplomatic Studies and Training, Moments in U.S. Diplomatic History: "Apparently I have been kidnapped" — The Death of a Vice Consul, at http://adst.org/2015/02/

In August 1974, Nixon resigned and was replaced by President Ford who retained Kissinger as Secretary of State. Knowing that Kissinger was a key author and proponent of the hardline policy on hostages, dissent soon surfaced from the mid and lower levels of the State Department's Foreign Service.[212] They saw the administration's policy as being too rigid and essentially condemning diplomats held hostage to death. The American Foreign Service Association even established a special "Working Group on Terrorism and Extraordinary Dangers" to examine the policy. However, the members of the association could not agree on a policy significantly different from the administration. It did, however, propose severe retaliation against states that helped the terrorists responsible for the hostage-taking or states that allowed them to go free.[213] Ultimately, the administration rejected any attempts by the American Foreign Service Association to water down the administration's policy. It stood as stated. The following are its key components:

- No concessions, no deals, and no negotiations with terrorists who held U.S. hostages.
- The terrorists could receive food, water, medicine, and safe passage with the release of the hostages.
- The U.S. reserved the right to talk with terrorists through a third party.
- The U.S. would use every appropriate influence to induce governments to adhere to the principle of arrest or extradition of terrorists. The full resources of the U.S. Government would be used to pursue such terrorists and to see that they were brought to appropriate justice.
- The U.S. would continue to publicly condemn states that aided or failed to punish terrorists, but policy interests would on occasion override other considerations.[214]

---

apparently-i-have-been-kidnapped-the-death-of-a-vice-consul. Accessed November 4, 2017; and Mickolus, *Transnational Terrorism: 1968–1979*, pp. 443–444.

[212] Scott W. Johnson, "How Arafat Got Away with Murder: The State Department covered up his responsibility for the 1973 slaughter of two American diplomats," The *Weekly Standard* Magazine, January 29, 2007, at http://www.weeklystandard.com/how-arafat-got-away-with-murder/article/ 14316. Accessed July 5, 2017. See also, Korn, *Assassination in Khartoum*, Chapter 21 "Dissent in the Ranks," pp. 222–231.

[213] Korn, *Assassination in Khartoum*, p. 229. Korn devotes an entire chapter to this conflict between the foreign service and the Nixon and Ford administrations — Chapter 21: "Dissent in the Ranks," pp. 222–231.

[214] *DS History*, p. 218; Korn, *Assassination in Khartoum*, pp. 229–230.

- The U.S. generally opposed but would not act to prevent foreign governments, private individuals, or companies from meeting terrorists' demands, including payment of ransom.[215]
- Because of effective FBI follow-through in recovering ransom and kidnappers in this country, the U.S. government could show more flexibility here than abroad in acquiescing to ransom payments.
- The safety of the U.S. hostages was primarily the responsibility of the host government with the U.S. having only an advisory role.

President Ford maintained this policy during his administration.

---

[215] U.S. Department of State, Office of the Historian, Foreign Relations of the United States, Nixon-Ford Administrations, Volume E-3, Documents on Global Issues. Document 218 — Memorandum from the Acting Secretary of State (Ingersoll) to Members of the Cabinet Committee to Combat Terrorism, November 6, 1974 at https://history.state.gov/historicaldocuments/frus1969-76ve03/d218 September 27, 2017. The memo also states that the U.S. would "advise other governments, companies, and other parties concerned of the disadvantages of payment of ransom in the long-range deterrent to terrorism. As a last resort and if the life of the hostage is clearly at stake, it would acquiesce to a non-US Government ransom." In fact, at the time, the U.S. government had no legal means to restrain such parties if they chose to pay ransom. See also, U.S. Department of State, Office of the Historian, Foreign Relations of the United States, 1969–1976, Nixon-Ford Administrations, Volume E-3, Documents on Global Issues, 1973–1976, document 220. Airgram A-775 from the Department of State to All Posts, Washington, February 5, 1975.

THE WHITE HOUSE

WASHINGTON

September 25, 1972

MEMORANDUM FOR

THE SECRETARY OF STATE

SUBJECT: Action to Combat Terrorism

Your report to me on the measures that are being taken to combat
terrorism indicates that we are moving effectively against the problem of thwarting acts of terrorism both here and abroad. The two
committees you have set up to cope with this major problem are
making commendable progress toward this end.

Because of the great importance and urgency I attach to dealing
with the worldwide problem of terrorism, which encompasses
diplomatic, intelligence, and law enforcement functions, I am
hereby establishing a Cabinet Committee to Combat Terrorism.

The Cabinet Committee will be chaired by the Secretary of State
and will comprise

> The Secretary of State
> The Secretary of Defense
> The Attorney General
> The Secretary of Transportation
> The United States Ambassador to
>   the United Nations
> The Director of Central Intelligence
> The Assistant to the President for
>   National Security Affairs
> The Assistant to the President for
>   Domestic Affairs
> The Acting Director of the Federal
>   Bureau of Investigation

and such others as the Chairman may consider necessary.

The Cabinet Committee will be supported by a Working Group comprised of personally designated senior representatives of the members
of the Committee, chaired by the designee of the Secretary of State.

Establishment of the Cabinet Committee to Combat Terrorism.

Source: CIA FOIA reading room.

Christians in Slavery in Algiers.

Source: Wikimedia Commons.

Fight between the USS Enterprise" and the Tripolitan Corsair "Polacca Tripoli" on August 1, 1801.

Source: U.S. Department of Navy.

Captain Stephen Decatur Jr. boarding the Tripolitan gunboat on August 3, 1804, painting by Dennis Malone Carter.

Source: U.S. department of Navy, Photographic Section, Naval History and Heritage Command, Photo # NH 44647-KN.

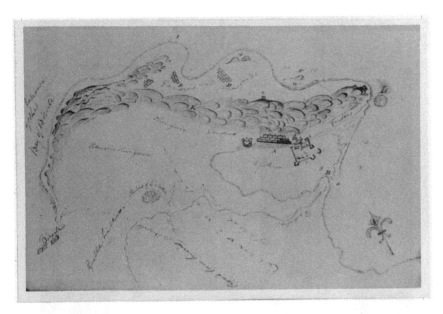

Drawing of Porta Farine, Tunisia, Oct 3, 1799 by William Eaton.

Source: U.S. Department of Navy.

Lt. Presley O' Bannon.

Source: Wikimedia.

Tripoli Monument at the U.S. Naval Academy. It honors heroes of the First Barbary War: Master Commandant Richard Somers, Lieutenant James Caldwell, James Decatur (brother of Stephen Decatur), Henry Wadsworth, Joseph Israel, and John Dorsey.

Source: U.S. Department of Navy.

The Evening World. (New York, N.Y.), October 7, 1901.

Source: Chronicling America: Historic American Newspapers. Library of Congress — public domain.

THE PERDICARIS INCIDENT.

The Sultan of Morocco being "persuaded" by Uncle Sam

1904 cartoon — U.S. threatening Morocco for release of Perdicaris.

Source: August 1904 edition of "Review of Reviews" — public domain.

The San Francisco Call, June 25, 1904.

Source: Chronicling America: Historic American Newspapers. Library of Congress — public domain.

March 2, 1970 — News conference where President Nixon, in referring to the seizure of two U.S. diplomats as hostages in Khartoum, Sudan by the Black September Organization, states that the U.S. would "not pay blackmail" to terrorists.

Source: Richard Nixon Presidential Library.

March 6, 1973 — President Nixon at the Department of State's memorial wall honoring U.S. diplomats killed overseas.

Source: Richard Nixon Presidential Library.

March 6, 1973 — President Nixon speaks at the Department of State on the murders of Ambassador Cleo Noel and Deputy Chief of Mission George C. Moore in Khartoum, Sudan.

Source: Richard Nixon Presidential Library.

Chapter 5

The Nixon and Ford Administrations (1969–1976): The Response — The Internal Threat

The Internal Terrorist Threat

Domestic Terrorist Threat

The presidential elections of 1968 were probably the most contentious and divisive in modern U.S. history. Senator Robert Kennedy and Reverend Martin Luther King, Jr., were assassinated that year. The Johnson administration, after proclaiming that the war was coming to an end, was hit with the January Tet Offensive in South Vietnam which shocked and dismayed the American public and further eroded support for the war and caused General Westmoreland to request more than 200,000 new troops in order to mount an effective counter-offensive.[1] President Johnson surprised the country by announcing that he would not run for re-election. Anti-Vietnam protests in the U.S. became more numerous, zealous, widespread, and violent. In late August, violent anti-war protests took place inside and outside the Democratic National Convention in Chicago where some 10,000 demonstrators were met by 23,000 police and National Guardsmen.[2] Crime rates for ordinary offenses were rising. Reported murders, rapes, aggravated assaults, robberies, and burglaries all increased rapidly, relative to population, from 1960 to 1970.[3] All the presidential candidates — Kennedy, Nixon,

---

[1] http://www.history.com/topics/vietnam-war/tet-offensive. Accessed June 3, 2017.

[2] https://en.wikipedia.org/wiki/1968_Democratic_National_Convention. Accessed November 16, 2017.

[3] William L. Anderson and Candice E. Jackson, "Law as a Weapon: How RICO Subverts Liberty and the True Purpose of Law," *The Independent Review: A Journal of Political Economy*, Summer 2004, at http://www.independent.org/publications/tir/article.asp?a=215. Accessed March 3, 2017.

Humphrey, and Wallace — were calling for "law and order." The historian Theodore White noted: "The two surest fire applause lines in any candidate's speech [during the 1968 election campaign] were always his calls for 'law-and-order' at home and 'peace' in Vietnam. This is what the American people — poor and rich, white and black — wanted to hear."[4]

In the end, the country elected Nixon as the president who made law and order a prominent component of his political platform. During the Johnson administration, there were racial riots and violence, campus protests and violence, and domestic terrorist organizations that were emerging. The Nixon administration faced the brunt of these issues. In addition, foreign spillover terrorism started to surface in the U.S. compounding the domestic security environment. A corollary concern of foreign spillover terrorism was the protection of foreign diplomats in the U.S. who were being targeted by these groups. If the U.S. demanded host countries to protect its diplomats, the U.S. had to act accordingly at home. The first domestic security priority for the Nixon administration was to address racial and campus protests and violence, and its alarming by-products — domestic terrorism.[5] For example, just in October 1970, President Nixon made the following public comments on these two issues:

- In remarks in the Ohio State House, Columbus, Ohio, on October 19, 1970, the president stated:

  All over this country today we see a rising tide of terrorism, of crime, and on the campuses of our universities we have seen those who instead of engaging — which is their right — in peaceful dissent, engage in violence, try to shout down speakers with obscene words. My friends, it is time to draw the line and to say we are not going to stand for that.

- In remarks on arrival at Grand Forks, North Dakota, on October 19, 1970, the president stated:

  And we also see a rising rate of terrorism and crime across this country. I have been trying to do something about it, but I need some help.

---

[4] As quoted in Ibid.

[5] All of Nixon's remarks are sourced to the American Presidency Project at the University of California at Santa Barbara which houses the Public Papers of the Presidents (president's public messages, statements, speeches, and news conference remarks), at http://www.presidency.ucsb.edu/ws/. Accessed August 4, 2017.

- In remarks in Kansas City, Missouri, on October 19, 1970, the president stated:

   I just got a report that in my home State of California, at the University of California campus at Irvine, only 10 miles from where I live, a bomb blew up a scientific laboratory, not one for defense in this case, but one that was used for the purpose of the environment, a senseless act, the kind of terrorism that we see over this country, sometimes in our universities, sometimes in our cities.

- In remarks at East Tennessee State University, on October 20, 1970, the president stated:

   Now, finally, on this great university campus, I do not want to miss the opportunity to speak briefly on another subject that concerns many Americans. You see it nightly, virtually nightly, on your television screens: the problems of what they call student protest. And usually what you see is violence or students shouting four-letter obscenities or students engaging in illegal protests, shouting down schools and the rest.

- In a statement about the disorders (anti-war protests) at San Jose, California, on October 29, 1970, the president stated:

   The stoning at San Jose is an example of the viciousness of the lawless elements in our society. This was no outburst by a single individual. This was the action of an unruly mob that represents the worst in America.... But the time has come to take the gloves off and speak to this kind of behavior in a forthright way. Freedom of speech and freedom of assembly cannot exist when people who peacefully attend rallies are attacked with flying rocks. Tomorrow night at Anaheim I will discuss what America must do to end the wave of violence and terrorism by the radical antidemocratic elements in our society.

The domestic security atmosphere at the time is also reflected in the following anecdotal points:

- Nixon was the first president who confronted angry protestors as his limousine rode from the Capitol to the White House on his inauguration. His motorcade took place "under a hail of garbage and curses, mocked by middle-finger salutes."[6]

- He had an attorney general (John Mitchell) who was inexperienced in law enforcement and "pushed for warrantless wiretaps, preventive detention, and other tactics associated with a police state."[7]
- In the summer of 1969, Nixon cancelled his commencement speech at the Ohio State University because of the ongoing campus unrest across the country.[8]
- The Department of Justice had established a new squad "aimed solely at campus radicals, which began compiling and cross-indexing files on nearly seven hundred fifty thousand potentially subversive American citizens and organizations."[9]
- The number two man in the Department of Justice testified to Congress on May 22, 1969 that the "government would round up radicals and revolutionaries and put them in detention camps if necessary."[10]
- "On May Day 1971, seven thousand protestors were arrested in the vicinity of the Justice Department headquarters and detained in Washington, D.C.'s football stadium, the largest mass arrest in the history of the United States."[11]
- In March 1970, California governor Ronald Reagan declared that "if it takes a bloodbath to silence the demonstrators, let's get it over with."[12]
- On May 8, 1970, the "Hard Hat Riot" occurred in Lower Manhattan when some 200 construction workers with crowbars and other tools attacked about 1,000 college and high school students and others peacefully protesting the Kent State shootings, the American invasion of Cambodia, and the Vietnam War near the intersection of Wall Street and Broad Street. Nearly all the construction workers carried American flags and signs that read "All the way, USA," and "America, Love it or Leave it." More than 70 students were injured. Financial district workers threw streams of ticker tape and data processing punch cards from their windows in celebration of the violence taking place below. Twenty-two of those construction workers were honored at the White House a few weeks later by President Nixon who thanked them for

---

[6]Weiner, *One Man Against the World*, p. 27.

[7]Ibid., p. 29.

[8]Ibid., p. 58.

[9]Ibid., p. 59.

[10]Ibid.

[11]Ibid.

[12]Betty Medsger, *The Burglary: The Discovery of J. Edgar Hoover's Secret FBI* (New York: Vintage Books, 2014), p. 25.

their patriotism. Vice President Agnew wrote a letter of thanks to the union official who organized the attacks on the students.[13]

- FBI Director J. Edgar Hoover stated in an article in the *Parent Teachers Association (PTA) Magazine* that the United States was confronted with:

> *a new style in conspiracy — conspiracy that is extremely subtle and devious and hence difficult to understand ... a conspiracy reflected by questionable moods and attitudes, by unrestrained individualism, by non-conformism in dress and speech, even by obscene language, rather than by formal membership in specific organizations.*[14]

Both the Johnson and Nixon administrations addressed the growing urban and campus disturbances by establishing national commissions to examine the problems and to provide recommendations for the future. In 1967, Johnson set up the "National Advisory Commission on Civil Disorders," also known as the Kerner Commission, to investigate the causes of race riots in the United States and to provide recommendations for the future. In 1970, Nixon created the "President's Commission on Campus Unrest," also known as the Scranton Commission to study the dissent, disorder, and violence breaking out on college and university campuses. These commissions did not stop the urban and campus violence, and their recommendations were general and long term. The Nixon administration determined that the most effective way to try and stem the urban and campus violence and the activities of domestic terrorist groups was to enhance criminal laws to empower the FBI and to essentially turn a blind eye to tactics the CIA, FBI, and NSA were using against anti-Vietnam War protestors, student radicals, and left-wing and black nationalist terrorist organizations. From the administration's perspective, it was necessary to allow the CIA, FBI, and NSA to do their jobs and provide them with the necessary resources and laws. It is important to note that at the time the administration as well as federal and local law enforcement and intelligence agencies felt that the U.S. was under attack by subversive elements that might be directed, supported, or influenced by foreign elements. This mindset partially explains the law

---

[13] Ibid., pp. 26–27; https://en.wikipedia.org/wiki/Hard_Hat_Riot September 12, 2016; and Homer Bigart, "War Foes Here Attacked By Construction Workers; City Hall Is Stormed," *New York Times*, May 9, 1970, at http://query.nytimes.com/gst/abstract.html?res=9906E1DF1439E63BBC4153DFB36 6838B669EDE. Accessed May 4, 2017.

[14] https://www2.fbi.gov/libref/historic/history/vietnam.htm. Accessed December 16, 2017.

enforcement and intelligence actions that were subsequently taken. Some of these actions were illegal and repressive. However, it is an axiom that the threat, perceived or real, drives the response.

Aside from providing political and moral support to the FBI, the Nixon administration promulgated several laws to target the growing political violence. On October 15, 1970, Congress passed the Organized Crime Control Act of 1970. Section 901(a) of this law enacted the "Racketeer Influenced and Corrupt Organizations Act," commonly referred to as the RICO Act or simply RICO.[15] This Act provided the FBI with new ways to attack organized criminal groups as a whole rather than as piecemeal as it had in the past. While it was originally constructed to target organized crime, the RICO Act was used against terrorist organizations. The statute was sufficiently broad to encompass illegal activities relating to any enterprise affecting interstate or foreign commerce and was later expanded and amended to apply to other organizations or enterprises, including terrorist organizations.[16] Consequently, the Nixon administration unintentionally provided a crime tool that when discovered by subsequent administrations could be used against terrorist organizations.[17] The most significant legal action the Nixon administration took against domestic terrorism was to seek an amendment to the 1970 Organized Crime Control that stiffened punishments and provided for the death sentence for those convicted of murder in arson or bombing cases. It also provided a section that authorized the involvement of federal law enforcement agencies in cases where there was a federal interest or federal support for an installation. Formerly, the FBI could only become involved in cases only when asked by the local law enforcement officials. This new amendment essentially authorized immediate federal intervention in cases of arson or bombing on any college or university campus receiving government funds. To enforce these new responsibilities, President Nixon also requested the hiring of 1,000 additional FBI agents to deal with campus outbreaks as well as aerial hijacking. The agents would supplement the FBI's force of 7,000 men and would cost an

---

[15] The idea for the acronym RICO came from the character Rico played by Edward G. Robinson in the 1930s gangster movie *Little Caesar*. Op. cit., Anderson and Jackson, "Law as a Weapon."

[16] https://www.justice.gov/usam/usam-9-110000-organized-crime-and-racketeering. Accessed December 14, 2017.

[17] See, for example, Zvi Joseph, "The Application of RICO to International Terrorism," *Fordham Law Review*, Vol. 58, Issue 5, 1990, at http://ir.lawnet.fordham.edu/cgi/viewcontent.cgi?article=2885&context=flr. Accessed July 4, 2017; and CRIMINAL RICO: 18 U.S.C. §§ 1961–1968, A Manual for Federal Prosecutors, 5th Revised Edition, October 2009, pp. 48–49, at https://www.justice.gov/sites/default/files/usam/legacy/2014/10/17/rico.pdf. Accessed March 21, 2017.

additional $23 million per year.[18] In signing the 1970 crime bill, the president noted:

> *This is a warning by signing this bill: We are going to give the tools to the men in the Justice Department and the men in the FBI and we shall see to it that those who engage in such terroristic acts are brought to justice.*[19]

What took place during the last years of the Johnson administration and Nixon's first term was an abuse of law enforcement and intelligence powers of primarily federal agencies and also some local police agencies. The trigger for this abuse was the assessment by these agencies and the White House that there were subversive elements in the country that were trying to undermine the security and stability of the United States. From the perspective of the U.S. government, these subversive elements included anti-war protestors and organizations, liberal political organizations, black civil rights organizations, progressive black political organizations, and left-wing student groups. The black, left-wing, and Puerto Rican terrorist organizations that emerged were simply extensions of these organizations. Compounding this internal security environment were terrorist attacks by the Jewish Defense League, Cuban exile groups, and Palestinians. The internal security environment in the United States during the Nixon and Ford administrations was the most severe and complex in U.S. history. The problem was that U.S. law enforcement and intelligence agencies had little experience in dealing with this type of broad-based threat and naturally used tools it was familiar with from its experience in dealing with criminal organizations, communist subversion, and foreign intelligence threats in the U.S. While acceptable when aimed at communist agents and facilities, they were controversial when directed at American citizens.

To address this extremist and terrorist threat in the U.S., the FBI, CIA, Army Intelligence, and NSA crossed many legal lines and occasionally operated at the edges of these lines. These actions in the late 1960s and early 1970s triggered a surge of presidential commissions and Congressional investigations that remain unmatched in their number, scope, and long-term impact. The U.S. Army domestic

---

[18] Bruce E. Johnson, "Nixon Asks for an FBI Role in Campus Bomb Probes," *The Harvard Crimson*, September 23, 1970, at https://www.thecrimson.com/article/1970/9/23/nixon-asks-an-fbi-role-in/. Accessed August 28, 2016.

[19] President Nixon. Remarks on Signing the Organized Crime Control Act of 1970. October 15, 1970, at http://www.presidency.ucsb.edu/ws/?pid=2720. Accessed November 23, 2017.

intelligence program was the first one to be publicly exposed. Christopher H. Pyle, a former Army Intelligence officer and instructor at the Army Intelligence School, in an article titled "CONUS Intelligence: The Army Watches Civilian Politics," in the January 1970 edition of *Washington Monthly* charged that "for the past four years, the U.S. Army has been closely watching civilian political activity within the United States." Pyle wrote that the U.S. Army most likely activated the system in 1965 in order to gather logistical information for the army's use during civil disturbances. But the increasing number of riots in the late 1960s and the military's insatiable desire for intelligence resulted in the army agents spying on all types of political activity.[20] "Today, the Army maintains files on the membership, ideology, programs, and practices of virtually every activist political group in the country," Pyle charged, "…including such nonviolent groups as the Southern Christian Leadership Conference, Clergy and Laymen United Against the War in Vietnam, the American Civil Liberties Union, Women Strike for Peace, and the National Association for the Advancement of Colored People."[21] In February 1971 and April 1974, Senate hearings were held on the issue of army domestic surveillance operations. A U.S. Senate committee charged the following:

- Surveillance files were also kept on many private citizens and public officials, on their financial affairs, sex lives, and psychiatric histories, as well as their connection with political organizations.
- Most of the information was acquired from public records, but information was also obtained from private institutions — sometimes through covert operations.
- In quantitative terms, the army in 1970 had reasonably current files on the political activities of 100,000 individuals unaffiliated with the armed forces.
- The army surveillance programs of the 1967–1970 period were apparently developed not only in the absence of legislative authorization but also without the knowledge or approval of senior civilian officials in the Department of Defense.[22]

---

[20] http://www.cmhpf.org/Random%20Files/senator%20sam%20ervin.htm. Accessed May 6, 2017. See also, Christopher H. Pyle, "CONUS Intelligence: The Army Watches Civilian Politics," *Washington Monthly*, January 1970, pp. 4–16 and Pyle's July 1970 article in the *Washington Monthly*: CONUS Revisited: The Army Covers Up, at http://jfk.hood.edu/Collection/White%20Materials/Surveillance/Surv%20053.pdf. Accessed October 22, 2018.

[21] Ibid.

[22] United States Senate. Committee on the Judiciary. Subcommittee on Constitutional Rights, "Military Surveillance." 93rd Congress, on S. 2318, April 9 and 10, 1974, p. 127, at https://archive.org/stream/militarysurveill00unit#page/2/mode/2up. Accessed May 4, 2017. See also, Lawrence M.

The FBI was next. It had the primary responsibility for dealing with the internal security environment. On March 8, 1971, eight amateur burglars associated with the ad hoc "Citizens' Commission to Investigate the FBI" broke into an FBI office in Media, Pennsylvania. The group stole over a thousand internal and classified files. The burglars/activists released some of these documents to media outlets. Some published them, many did not. Eventually, the issue received more attention and concern as many classified documents detailed the FBI's use of informants (postal workers, switchboard operators, school security guards, administrators, and even students and professors) to spy on black college students and non-violent black activist organizations. In one classified document, the acronym "COINTELPRO" appeared without any explanation as to what it stood for. In time, it was exposed as an FBI secret Counterintelligence Program aimed at political dissidents, anti-war activists, and others that involved intimidation, surveillance, infiltration, disinformation, snitch-jacketing, fabrication of correspondence and publications, false arrest and prosecution. Initially designed in 1956 to target the Communist Party in the United States, this program gradually expanded in the 1960s and the early 1970s to target a broad range of reported "subversive" elements that included militant black and Indian organizations, separatists, left-wing organizations, Cuban exiles, and white supremacist terrorist organizations in the United States. The techniques used

> *ranged from anonymously mailing reprints of newspaper and magazine articles (sometimes Bureau-authored or planted) to group members or supporters to convince them of the error of their ways, to mailing anonymous letters to a member's spouse accusing the target of infidelity; from using informants to raise controversial issues at meetings in order to cause dissent, to the 'snitch jacket' (falsely labeling a group member as an informant); from contacting members of a 'legitimate group' to expose alleged subversive background of a fellow member, to contacting an employer to get a target fired; from attempting to arrange for reporters to interview targets with planted questions, to trying to stop targets from speaking at all; from notifying state and local authorities of a target's criminal law violations, to using the IRS to audit a professor, not*

Baskir, Senate Committee on the Judiciary, "Reflections on the Senate Investigation of Army Surveillance," *Indiana Law Journal*, Volume 49, Issue 4, Summer 1974, pp. 618–653, for background information on the 1971 and 1974 hearings, at http://www.repository.law.indiana.edu/cgi/viewcontent. cgi?article=3019&context=ilj. Accessed December 27, 2018.

just to collect any taxes owing, but to distract him from his political activities.[23]

The above was in addition to wiretaps, planting bugs, black bag break-ins, forging documents, and opening mail. Over a 15-year period of the program, the FBI carried out over 2,370 plots to disrupt and harass American citizens and their organizations.[24] In 1974, a Justice Department Committee which examined COINTELPRO wrote that the program's activities "may" have violated the Civil Rights statute, the mail and wire fraud statutes, and the prohibition against divulging information gained from wiretaps; internal FBI documents indicate that bureau officials believed sending threats through the mail might violate federal extortion statutes.[25] The FBI's current (2019) historical site even notes that "although limited in scope (about two-tenths of 1% of the FBI's workload over a 15-year period), COINTELPRO was later rightfully criticized by Congress and the American people for abridging first amendment rights and for other reasons."[26]

If there was one unit within the FBI in the early 1970s that symbolized the FBI's attitude, tactics, and determination of dealing with the internal terrorist threat, it was probably "Squad 47" in the New York field office. It was a special internal counter-terrorism unit established in mid-1970. It was created just after the March 6, 1970 accidental explosion in a Weather Underground Organization safe house in Greenwich Village that killed three WUO terrorists. This incident and other terrorist bombings in early 1970 alarmed the White House and the FBI and caused the latter to conclude that "extraordinary measures were called for."[27] As Bryan Burrough notes in his seminal work on political violence in the 1970s, "the one thing everyone believed was that the Weatherman would never be brought down by traditional methods … that brought extraordinary

---

[23] U.S. Senate, 94th Congress, Final report of the Select Committee to Study Governmental Operations with Respect to Intelligence Activities, Supplementary Detailed Staff Reports on Intelligence Activities and the Rights of Americans, Book III, April 23, 1976, p. 8, at https://archive.org/stream/finalreportofsel03unit#page/2/mode/2up. Accessed October 22, 2017; see also, John T. Ellif, "Attorney General's Guidelines for FBI Investigations," *Cornell Law Review*, Volume 69, Issue 4, April 1984, pp. 785–815, at http://scholarship.law.cornell.edu/cgi/viewcontent.cgi?article=4351&context=clr. Accessed October 2, 2016.

[24] David Wise, "Intelligence Reforms: Less Than Half a Loaf," *Washington Post*, April 23, 1978, p. D3.

[25] Ibid.

[26] https://vault.fbi.gov/cointel-pro. Accessed December 2, 2018.

[27] Burrough, *Days of Rage*, p. 114.

pressure to bend the rules."[28] Squad 47 engaged in clandestine entries, intercepted mail, wiretapped phones, and carried out surveillance of Weathermen family members and friends — extraordinary measures that agents believed were necessary to deal with the nature of the terrorist threat at the time. The FBI lead case agent in charge of the Weather Underground terrorist group stated later that "we didn't know how to investigate terrorism ... we did not have enough intelligence on these people."[29] It is questionable how effective Squad 47 was as the unit never arrested a single Weatherman, but it certainly maintained a sustained level of counter-terrorism pressure on the Weatherman. Such pressure places psychological strain on the terrorists and can cause them to make operational mistakes and engender internal paranoia.

Foreign Spillover Terrorism

The terrorist focus on diplomatic targets emerged during the Nixon and Ford administrations. The following chart shows the number of terrorist incidents worldwide involving foreign diplomats:

1968: 80
1969: 80
1970: 213
1971: 153
1972: 210
1973: 187.[30]

Diplomats and diplomatic facilities were seen by terrorists as logical and attractive targets as they were the official representatives of a country. Attacking a diplomatic target was like attacking the country directly. The United States had the responsibility under international law to protect visiting foreign dignitaries and resident foreign diplomats in the U.S. According to article 22(2) of the 1961 Vienna Convention on Diplomatic Relations, "the receiving state is under special duty to take all appropriate steps to protect the premises of the mission against any intrusion or damage and to prevent any disturbance of the peace of the

---

[28] Ibid., p. 134.

[29] Tim Weiner. *Enemies: A History of the FBI* (New York: Random House, 2012), p. 285.

[30] U.S. Department of State. "Terrorist Attacks Against Diplomats: A Statistical Overview of International Terrorist Incidents on Diplomatic Personnel and Facilities from January 1968 to June 1981." December 1981, p. 4.

mission or impairment of its dignity."[31] Terrorist organizations targeting foreign interests in a host country caused embarrassment to the host government, created bilateral tensions, and strained the principle of reciprocity, that is, an agreement between two countries that each would protect the other's diplomatic interests. Given that the U.S. had the biggest diplomatic presence in the world, and its diplomats had been targets of domestic and international terrorists, the U.S. had more invested in this principle than most countries. An additional problem for the U.S. was that it was host to the United Nations' headquarters building in New York City with over 100 U.N. missions in the city. When the over 100 foreign consulates in the city are added, there were over 200 foreign diplomatic facilities that had to be protected — the largest foreign diplomatic footprint in the world.[32] This does not include the residences of foreign diplomats and foreign commercial buildings, or visits to the city by foreign dignitaries. The protection afforded to diplomatic missions is typically a function of local police forces, exemplified by post standing, uniformed presence, roving patrols, and marked police vehicles. The facility receives the protection, not individuals.

The two major security concerns in the U.S. were the assassination of diplomats and the seizure of diplomatic facilities with hostages. The latter was the most complicated incident as it tested U.S. hostage-taking policy in an internal incident. Embassy seizures worldswide were increasing during this period. According to a 1981 RAND study:

> *Seizing embassies became a common form of protest and coercion in the 1970s. Since 1971, terrorists and other militants have seized embassies on 43 occasions and attempted unsuccessfully to storm embassies on five occasions. And this does not include the numerous times mobs have sacked embassies or unarmed protestors have occupied them without taking hostages.*[33]

The protection of foreign diplomats is the responsibility of the host country. Therefore, in addition to the threat from domestic terrorist organizations and protests on campuses and in urban centers of major U.S. cities, federal law

---

[31] 1961 Vienna Convention on Diplomatic Relations, p. 7, at http://legal.un.org/ilc/texts/instruments/english/conventions/9_1_1961.pdf. Accessed February 3, 2016.

[32] https://www.embassypages.com/city/newyork. Accessed February 9, 2017.

[33] Brian M. Jenkins. *Embassies Under Siege: A Review of 48 Embassy Takeovers from 1971–1980.* R-2651-RC, January 1981, at http://www.dtic.mil/dtic/tr/fulltext/u2/a103326.pdf. Accessed May 6, 2016.

enforcement agencies had to address the foreign spillover terrorist threat. While this threat first surfaced under the Nixon administration, it was the Ford administration that faced the brunt of this threat. The four major terrorism actors behind this threat were: anti-Castro, Cuban exiles, anti-Turkish, Armenian terrorists, anti-Yugoslav, Croatian and Serbian terrorists, and anti-Soviet, Jewish terrorists. While these terrorists did not usually target U.S. interests on U.S. soil, their activities in the United States against foreign targets, including foreign officials, did pollute the security environment and create a problem concerning the protection of foreign officials in the United States. Negligence by the U.S. in carrying out this protective responsibility would have an impact on the U.S.'s relationship with other countries. An example of this concern can be found in a November 13, 1972 memo from the Secretary of State William Rogers to Attorney General Richard Kleindienst concerning Croatian terrorist activity directed at Yugoslav interests in the U.S. This memo was likely a response to an August 1972 aide memoire that the Yugoslav government presented to the U.S. that was entirely devoted to the problem of Croatian émigré groups. Very little space was devoted to Serbian groups.[34] Rogers' memo noted:

> *My purpose is to ask your views on how this Government can be most effective in combatting and preventing the promotion and practice of terrorist violence by Yugoslav émigré groups within the United States, to encourage your continued efforts to counter such activities, and to ask you to undertake a new investigation of these activities.*

> *We want to be sure that the United States is doing everything possible to prevent the use of our country as a staging ground for terrorism, ... to assure our continued good relations with Yugoslavia.... We have always been concerned about the dangers of terrorist activities by such émigré groups within the United States, but the recent escalation of émigré terrorism worldwide has heightened our concern. Yugoslav émigré groups have been responsible for the assassination of the Yugoslav ambassador in Stockholm in January 1971; for the bombing of a Yugoslav passenger aircraft on an international flight in January 1972, killing all but one of the passengers and crew; for the hijacking of a Swedish airliner to*

---

[34] CIA, Office of Official Estimates, "Memorandum — Yugoslavia: The Ustashi and Croatian Separatist Problem," September 27, 1972, p. 2, at https://www.cia.gov/library/readingroom/docs/CIA-RDP79R00967A000500020001-7.pdf. Accessed May 23, 2016.

Madrid in September, 1972; for the infiltration into Yugoslavia of an armed band of 19 men in June 1972 and for the ensuing deaths of 13 members of the Yugoslav police and army; and for numerous other acts of violence and killing, particularly in the Federal Republic of Germany and inside Yugoslavia.

As you know ... the Yugoslav Government is concerned that these attacks have been supported and sometimes instigated from within the United States. It has also expressed reservations about the adequacy of our efforts to prevent this. On August 21, the Yugoslav Government submitted a detailed memorandum expressing its particular concerns about specific individuals and groups within the United States whose activities it regards as threatening.

I would, therefore, appreciate your undertaking further investigation and study of such activities to determine if United States laws are being violated by Yugoslav émigrés, or whether additional legislation might be desirable. For example, if it appears that funds raised here are being channeled into terrorism abroad, we might wish to consider legislation to prohibit this.[35]

The JDL also created concerns and issues for the U.S. In a February 1975 memorandum from the Deputy Secretary of State to President Ford, it was pointed out that "the Jewish Defense League has resumed an aggressive nation-wide campaign against Soviet installations and others (French, Indians) with potentially serious diplomatic consequences."[36]

Whenever a foreign official or guest is killed in any country of the world by a terrorist organization, it is an embarrassment for the host country. One or two attacks do not generally stress diplomatic relations. However, a sustained terrorist campaign against a country's officials will lead the targeted country to question the host country's determination and effort and the level and effectiveness of its protective security measures. The U.S. has taken this attitude overseas when anti-American terrorist groups have attacked U.S. interests. The JDL carried out a

---

[35] http://2001-2009.state.gov/r/pa/ho/frus/nixon/e1/45558.htm. Accessed June 6, 2018.
[36] U.S. Department of State. Office of the Historian. Foreign Relations of the United States, 1969–1976, Volume E-3, Documents on Global Issues, 1973–1976, Document 221, Memorandum from the Acting Secretary of State (Ingersoll) to President Ford, Washington, February 18, 1975, at https://history.state.gov/historicaldocuments/frus1969-76ve03/d221. Accessed November 6, 2017.

sustained terrorist campaign against official and non-official targets of the Soviet Union and other countries under the Nixon, Ford, and Carter administrations. The response by the U.S. to provide protection for foreign diplomats in the U.S. was to: (1) advocate for international treaties to protect diplomats, official guests, and internationally protected persons, (2) promulgate U.S. laws to aid in this effort, and (3) provide increased protective security measures for high-risk foreign diplomatic facilities and personnel in the U.S.

The U.S. advocated and supported the 1971 OAS "Convention to Prevent and Punish Acts of Terrorism Taking the Form of Crimes Against Persons and Related Extortion that are of International Significance" and the 1973 U.N. Convention on the Prevention and Punishment of Crimes Against Internationally Protected Persons. On October 24, 1972, President Nixon signed P.L. 52–939 to amend Title 18 of the U.S. Criminal Code to provide for expanded protection of foreign officials. This act makes it a federal offense to: (1) harm or harass a foreign official or official guest, or member of his family; (2) destroy property belonging to, or used by, a foreign government, foreign official, or official guest; or (3) demonstrate within 100 feet of buildings belonging to, or used by, foreign officials. During the Ford administration, the U.S. wanted to ratify the 1971 OAS Convention and the 1973 U.N. Convention on the Prevention and Punishment of Crimes Against Internationally Protected Persons. The Senate gave its advice and consent to the ratification of both conventions, but it is the policy of the Department of State not to deposit an instrument of ratification for any treaty or convention unless it is assured that federal law will permit the United States to discharge its treaty obligations.[37] As a result, President Ford signed P.L. 94–467 (Act for the Prevention and Punishment of Crimes Against Internationally Protected Persons) on October 8, 1976 to conform current U.S. statutes in the federal criminal code which proscribe crimes against foreign officials and their families to the provisions of these conventions.

The signing of P.L. 94–467 allowed the U.S. to formally ratify on the same day the OAS and U.N. conventions. The new law amended Title 18 of the U.S. Criminal Code to conform to specific provisions in the OAS and U.N. conventions. The new law adds "internationally protected persons" to "foreign

---

[37] October 4, 1976 White House memorandum from Jim Cannon to President Ford titled "H.R. 15552 — Act for the Prevention and Punishment of Crimes Against Internationally Protected Persons," at https://www.fordlibrarymuseum.gov/library/document/0055/1669580.pdf. Accessed November 3, 2017.

officials," and "official guests" as being protected.[38] By adding "internationally protected persons" to the law, the U.S. acquired an extra jurisdictional basis for acting against persons who attack U.S. diplomats abroad and then are found in the United States. Under the OAS and U.N. conventions, signatory countries are required either to extradite or to prosecute offenders against internationally protected persons irrespective of whether the crimes occur within the territorial jurisdiction of a party State. The new U.S. law adds this provision. In addition, the U.N. Convention condemns attacks upon the premises or means of transportation of such persons and condemns threats and attempts as well. The OAS Convention also condemns extortion in connection with murder, kidnapping, and assault. All these modifications and additions were contained in the new law.

In a statement on the signing of P.L. 94–467, President Ford stated:

The Act for the Prevention and Punishment of Crimes Against Internationally Protected Persons will serve as a significant law enforcement tool for us to deal more effectively with the menace of terrorism and will assist us in discharging our important responsibilities under the two international conventions which I am today authorizing for ratification.[39]

---

[38] The law defines an internationally protected person (IPP) as a chief of state or the political equivalent, head of government, or foreign minister whenever such person is in a country other than his own and any member of his family accompanying him; or any other representative, officer, employee, or agent of a foreign government or international organization who at the time and place concerned is entitled pursuant to international law to special protection against attack upon his person, freedom, or dignity and any member of his family then forming part of his household. An IPP covers diplomats outside their own territory wherever they may be in the world. Foreign official is a chief of state or the political equivalent, president, vice president, prime minister, ambassador, foreign minister, or other officer of cabinet rank or above of a foreign government or the chief executive officer of an international organization, or any person who has previously served in such capacity, and any member of his family, while in the United States; and any person of a foreign nationality who is duly notified to the United States as an officer or employee of a foreign government or international organization, and who is in the United States on official business, and any member of his family whose presence in the United States is in connection with the presence of such officer or employee. A foreign official is essentially one who is foreign to the United States. An official guest means a citizen or national of a foreign country present in the United States as an official guest of the government of the United States pursuant to designation as such by the secretary of state, at https://www.gpo.gov/fdsys/pkg/STATUTE-90/pdf/STATUTE-90-Pg1997.pdf. Accessed August 4, 2017.

[39] Statement on Signing the International Terrorism Prevention Bill, October 10, 1976, at http://www.presidency.ucsb.edu/ws/index.php?pid=6438. Accessed September 3, 2017.

Increasing protective security measures around foreign diplomatic facilities and residences in the U.S. was also a major concern for the government. Decolonization, especially in Africa, in the 1960s led to more diplomats being assigned to New York City and Washington, D.C. There were many foreign missions in the United States, especially in New York City, where there were also U.N. missions, and in Washington, D.C. where all the embassies were located. In the early 1970s, there were some 32,000 members of diplomatic facilities in New York City — the largest in the world.[40] Smaller foreign consulates could also be found in other major U.S. cities. It was the acknowledged responsibility of the U.S. Government to provide adequate protection for these foreign officials and entities. However, this created a set of problems: (1) what agency (federal, state, or local) would provide the protection, (2) what was the legal basis for this protection, and (3) who and how would the state and local agencies be reimbursed for these protective duties? This issue was important to the U.S. government, particularly the State Department, as it could affect foreign relations and protective security reciprocity for U.S. diplomatic facilities and personnel overseas.

The Department of State relied solely on local police departments to provide protection to foreign diplomatic missions and establishments in the United States until March 19, 1970, when Congress passed P.L. 91–217 that established the Executive Protective Service (EPS) in the Treasury Department to protect buildings, in which presidential offices or members of his immediate family are located, and foreign missions in Washington, D.C. It also authorized the president to assign EPS officers to other areas of the country on a case-by-case basis to safeguard foreign missions. In conferring the latter authority upon the president, the Congress stated its intention that it be exercised in unique situations:

This authority extends only to situations of extraordinary gravity, where the local police force is totally incapable of providing a level of protection deemed essential to the international integrity of the U.S., or where the protection of the President himself, for example, would be involved. This additional authority is not, and may not be construed to be, a substitute for the responsibility of local police forces to provide protection for consulates, the United Nations, and similar foreign delegations within the U.S.[41]

---

[40] Kathleen Teltsch, "Diplomats to Get Tighter Security Under New Plan," *New York Times*, November 20, 1980, p. B1.

[41] U.S. Department of State, Office of the Historian, Foreign Relations of the United States, Nixon-Ford Administrations, Volume E-1, Documents on Global Issues, Document 37. Memorandum from

Congress' apparent opposition to the performance by federal authorities of protective functions traditionally provided by local police left little prospect for enactment of further legislation at the time.

In July 1970, the New York City Police Department (NYPD) announced it would no longer assign policemen inside a private building. However, it later manned inside posts in the most extreme circumstances when directed by the mayor. The police agreed to street coverage. (This was basically true of all police departments throughout the United States at this time.) As a result, the problem of providing coverage to the numerous U.N. missions and consulates located in private buildings in New York City was critical. The NYPD never refused to respond to a demonstration or a "hard threat" against a diplomatic mission. However, the NYPD faced a serious crime problem in New York City and a shortage of police officers at the time.

In June 1971, the U.S. Secret Service conducted a study of protective security costs in the New York City. The study determined it would cost $4,054,062 a year for EPS to provide the level of protection being afforded by the NYPD at that time. To reimburse the NYPD for such coverage would amount to $1,190.700. The study also noted that a private security organization could adequately protect the missions at a much lower cost than EPS. In the past, Congress attempted to reimburse New York City for extraordinary costs, but these bills died in the house, mostly never getting out of committee.[42] The use of a private security organization might have been more acceptable to the Congress than the regular use of EPS for this purpose. To do this, legislation authorizing the use of private guards by the federal government would be required in addition to an appropriation of funds. It was also felt that once the federal government received authority to provide this coverage, pressure would build up, not only in New York City but also in other major U.S. cities where foreign establishments were located, to have the federal government provide all protective services for these foreign diplomatic missions. The Department of State had taken the position in the past that it was neither appropriate nor consistent with the responsibilities of a host government to ask the foreign missions to provide their own protection.[43] In reality, no

the Acting Secretary of State (Rush) to President Nixon, Washington, April 30, 1974, at https://history. state.gov/historicaldocuments/frus1969-76ve03/d215. Accessed March 4, 2016.

[42] U.S. Department of State, Office of the Historian, Foreign Relations of the United States, 1969–1976, Volume E-3, Documents on Global Issues, 1973–1976, Document #205, "Memorandum from the Assistant Secretary of State for Administration (Donelan) to the Office of Management and Budget International Programs Division Chief (Frey), Washington," February 12, 1973, at https:// history.state.gov/historicaldocuments/frus1969-76ve03/d205. Accessed October 23, 2016.

[43] Ibid.

long-term solution to the problem of protecting foreign diplomatic facilities in New York City was found during the Nixon administration and it was simply passed on to subsequent administrations.

On October 11, 1972, Congress passed P.L. 92–539 (Act for the Protection of Foreign Officials and Official Guests of the United States). This law established three federal crimes of violence against official guests of the United States: 18 U.S.C. § 1116 covered murder, manslaughter, and attempted murder; 18 U.S.C. § 1201 covered kidnapping, abduction, and similar offenses; and 18 U.S.C. § 112 covered various forms of assault and the offering of violence. The law was designed to deter increasing harassment of and violence against foreign officials, particularly from the Soviet Union and Middle East nations.

By the mid-1970s, the two U.S. agencies that had the authority for the protection of visiting foreign dignitaries was the Department of State's Office of Security and the U.S. Secret Service and to a much lesser extent, other federal agencies (including the Central Intelligence Agency and the Department of Defense). Both the Secret Service and the Office of Security had legal authority for the protection of visiting foreign dignitaries. The legislation contained in 18 United States Code 3056 outlined the powers of the Secret Service and stated that subject to the direction of the Secretary of the Treasury, the Secret Service was authorized to protect the person of a visiting head of a foreign state or foreign government and, at the direction of the president, other distinguished foreign visitors to the United States and official representatives of the United States performing special missions abroad. Consequently, the Secret Service routinely provided protective services to every visiting chief of state or head of government unless that person declined the services in writing. The only other officials protected by the Secret Service were those whom the president specifically directed the Service to protect. Therefore, in the early 1970s when the Department of State began receiving protective requests from foreign governments for a number of officials such as presidents-elect, former presidents and prime ministers, cabinet-level ministers, opposition leaders, and other important dignitaries, the Secret Service pointed out its lack of authority for protecting these officials whom it was not presidentially directed to protect, and it refused to assume the additional responsibilities. Therefore, commencing in the mid-1970s, State's Office of Security again was tasked with providing protective security to all dignitaries other than current chiefs of state or heads of government.[44]

---

[44] Report of the Secretary of State's Advisory Panel on Overseas Security (1985), Section: Protection of Foreign Dignitaries and Missions in the United States, at https://fas.org/irp/threat/inman/part09. htm. Accessed September 23, 2017.

The State Department's Office of Security had applied its broad authority primarily to the protection of certain cabinet-level officials, primary family members of chiefs of state/heads of government, and persons of royalty. Often this protection was and is still today based on the principle of reciprocity and not solely on the presence of a specific threat. The role of local or state law enforcement agencies in the protection of visiting foreign officials (as opposed to resident diplomats) was generally that of a supportive nature to the federal agencies involved.[45] In July 1974, President Nixon tasked the Cabinet Committee to Combat Terrorism to develop a comprehensive study on the protection of foreign officials and establishments in the United States. The tasking stated that the study should define the goals of a program to protect foreign officials and establishments in the United States. Specifically, the study should consider the following:

- consider all foreign official personnel, the dependents of such personnel, and installations within U.S. territorial jurisdiction;
- identify levels of protection that should be afforded to various official personnel and installations, in view of such factors as status, location, purpose of visit, length of stay, etc., as appropriate;
- address the extent to which protection of the foreign official sector should exceed or differ from that afforded to people and property generally in the U.S.;
- assess the degree to which continuation of present federal, state, and local protection would meet program goals, noting particularly:
  - ○ any inadequacies in existing federal, state, and local laws,
  - ○ any problems of jurisdiction, and
  - ○ any shortcomings in federal, state, and local enforcement of present laws;
- identify and assess current federal, state, and local resources and capabilities and the extent of their availability for achieving program goals.

The tasking also asked for options that would specify assignment and coordination of responsibilities and jurisdiction among federal, state, and local authorities and organizations; implementing plan and schedule; sources of required human resources, equipment, and funds; any federal, state, and local legislative actions required; and a means for progress review and program revitalization.[46]

---

[45] Ibid.

[46] U.S. Department, Office of the Historian, *Foreign Relations of the United States, 1969–1976,* Volume E-3, Documents on Global Issues, 1973–1976, Document #216, "Memorandum From the

In general, from the Nixon administration on, the most pressing problems were who was going to provide the protection and who was going to pay for it. In most cases, the burden of protection fell on local police forces with some support from the federal government. As previously noted, New York City and Washington, D.C. were the locations of many foreign diplomatic interests. The New York police department (NYPD) lacked the manpower in the early 1970s to meet the demands for diplomatic protection in addition to its regular duties. New York City wanted to be reimbursed for these diplomatic protective duties. In 1974, the Nixon administration used funds from the Department of Justice's Law Enforcement Assistance Administration, which was created in 1965 to direct federal funds to assist state and local police forces. The U.S. Secret Service also delegated some funds to the New York City for local protection of U.N. missions. This issue carried over to the Ford administration.[47]

The following terrorist incidents aimed at foreign diplomatic targets in the U.S. from 1968 to 1974 are examples of the tactics, targets, and locations of foreign spillover terrorism:

- **1967**
  - New York City: The Cuban mission to the United Nations was bombed.
  - New York City: Bombs exploded at the Cuban, Yugoslav, and Finnish missions to the United Nations.
- **1968**
  - Washington, D.C.: A bomb damaged the Russian Embassy.
  - New York City: The Mexican mission to the U.S. was bombed.
  - Miami: The Mexican consul general's residence was damaged by a bomb.
  - Miami: The British Consulate was damaged by a bomb.
  - New York City: The Canadian Consulate and the tourist office, and the Australian National Tourist Office were bombed.
  - New York City: The Spanish National Tourist Office was bombed twice.

President's Assistant for National Security Affairs (Kissinger) to Treasury Secretary Simon, Attorney General Saxbe, and the Deputy Secretary of State (Ingersoll)," Washington, July 29, 1974 at https://history.state.gov/historicaldocuments/frus1969-76ve03/d216 November 13, 2017.

[47] *DS History*, pp. 285–286.

- o New York City: The Japanese National Tourist Office was bombed.
- o New York City: The Yugoslav and Cuban missions to the United States were bombed.
- o Chicago: The Mexican National Tourist Office was bombed.
- o New Jersey: A bomb was found and removed from the Mexican Consulate by police.
- o Los Angeles: The British Consulate was bombed twice
- o New York City: Police captured Cuban Power terrorists who attempted to assassinate the Cuban ambassador to the United Nations.

- **1970**
  - o New York City: The Jewish Defense League attempted to bomb the Soviet airline Aeroflot office.
- **1971**
  - o Washington, D.C.: The Jewish Defense League bombed the Soviet cultural offices.
  - o New York City: The Jewish Defense League strafed the Soviet mission to the United Nations.
  - o Washington, D.C.: Pipe bombs were found at the embassies of Vietnam, Cambodia, and Laos.
- **1972**
  - o New York City: The Jewish Defense League plotted to bomb the Long Island residence of the Soviet mission to the United Nations.
- **1973**
  - o Washington, D.C.: Suspected Palestinian terrorists shot and killed Yosef Alon, the Israeli Air Force attaché.
- **1974**
  - o New York City: A powerful bomb exploded shortly after midnight near the façade of the Yugoslav U.N. mission causing extensive damage.
- **1975**
  - o New York City: An unknown person fired .22 caliber rifle bullets through the fifth-floor windows of the Ukrainian mission to the United Nations.

The above wave of terrorist attacks on foreign diplomatic facilities in the U.S. during the Johnson, Nixon, and Ford administrations never occurred again.

INTERSTATE FLIGHT - MOB ACTION; RIOT; CONSPIRACY

WANTED BY FBI

The persons shown here are active members of the militant Weatherman faction of the Students for a Democratic Society - SDS.

Federal warrants have been issued at Chicago, Illinois, concerning these individuals, charging them with a variety of Federal violations including interstate flight to avoid prosecution, mob action, Antiriot Laws and conspiracy. Some of these individuals were also charged in an indictment returned 7/23/70, at Detroit, Michigan, with conspiracy to violate Federal Bombing and Gun Control Laws.

These individuals should be considered dangerous because of their known advocacy and use of explosives, reported acquisition of firearms and incendiary devices, and known propensity for violence.

If you have information concerning these persons please contact your local FBI Office.

William Charles Ayers
W/M, 25, 5-10, 170
brn hair, brn eyes

Kathie Boudin
W/F, 26, 5-4, 125
brn hair, blue eyes

Judith Alice Clark
W/F, 20, 5-3, 125
brn hair, brn eyes

Bernardine Rae Dohrn
W/F, 28, 5-5, 125
drk brn hair, brn eyes

FBI Wanted Poster on Bill Ayers, Kathie Boudin, Judith Clark, and Bernadine Dohrn, key members of the Weather Underground.

PRESIDENT'S COMMISSION ON CAMPUS UNREST
1337 H STREET, N.W.
WASHINGTON, D.C. 20006

LLIAM W. SCRANTON, *Chairman*
JAMES F. AHERN
ERWIN D. CANHAM
JAMES E. CHEEK
BENJAMIN O. DAVIS
MARTHA A. DERTHICK
BAYLESS MANNING
REVIUS O. ORTIQUE, JR.
JOSEPH RHODES, JR.

September 26, 1970

WM. MATTHEW BYRNE, JR.
Executive Director
JOHN J. KIRBY, JR
Deputy Director

The President
The White House
Washington, D.C.

Dear Mr. President:

With this letter, I transmit the report of your Commission on Campus Unrest.

The report is based on three months of work by the Commission and its staff. It explores the history and causes of campus unrest. It also contains recommendations to you, the Congress and state legislatures, university administrators and faculty members, students, the police, and the public at large.

Campus unrest is a fact of life. It is not peculiar to America. It is not new and it will go on. Exaggerations of its scope and seriousness and hysterical reactions to it will not make it disappear. They will only aggravate it.

When campus unrest takes the form of violent and disruptive protest, it must be met with firm and just responses. We make recommendations on what those responses should be.

Much campus unrest is neither violent nor disruptive. It is found on any lively college or university campus. It is an expression of intellectual restlessness, and intellectual restlessness prompts the search for truth. We should resist the efforts of some young people to achieve their goals through force and violence, but we should encourage all young people to seek the truth and participate responsibly in the democratic process.

Our colleges and universities cannot survive as combat zones, but they cannot thrive unless they are receptive to new ideas. They must be prepared to institute needed reforms in their administrative procedures and instructional programs.

Still, the essence of a college or university is not the details of this or that program; it is the school's commitment to teaching, learning, and scholarship. Even in this troubled and confusing time, and precisely because we need knowledge and wisdom in such a time, our colleges and universities must sustain their commitment to the life of the mind.

Respectfully,

William W. Scranton
Chairman

Report of President Nixon's 1970 President's Commission on Campus Unrest, aka: the Scranton Commission.

Source: Richard M. Nixon Presidential Library.

1971 break-in of FBI office in Media, Pennsylvania. The stolen document with the greatest impact as it identified the FBI code "COINTELPRO." From 2014 movie "1971" Press Kit.

NATIONAL SECURITY COUNCIL
WASHINGTON, D.C. 20506

~~SECRET/GDS~~   April 27, 1974

National Security Decision Memorandum   254

TO: The Chairman, Atomic Energy Commission

SUBJECT: Domestic Safeguards

The President has reviewed the report forwarded on February 15, 1974
on domestic safeguards, as directed by NSSM 120 and the subsequent
memorandum of May 4, 1971 for the Chairman of the U.S. Atomic
Energy Commission.

The President has noted the conclusions of the report, and particularly
those regarding the needs (1) to weigh the possibilities of sabotage,
plutonium contamination threats, and armed attacks (for example,
by terrorists) along with the nuclear device threat, (2) to have a
continuing process of threat assessment and establishment of appropriate countermeasures, and (3) to maintain fully adequate and
essentially equivalent, in terms of quality and extent, safeguards
systems in the licensed and license-exempt sectors.

Given the rapid growth of the nuclear power industry and especially
the increased availability of plutonium, the President has directed
that a priority effort be dedicated to ensuring the adequacy of safeguards systems and, in this regard, that:

-- Foreseeable improvements both in material control and
   accounting procedures and in physical protection measures,
   as mentioned in the report, be implemented on a timely basis
   in order to provide an improved overall safeguards system.

-- Full consideration be given the possibilities of utilizing specific
   measures now in effect for the license-exempt sector in the
   licensed sector.

In addition, the President has requested that the AEC, in coordination
with other agencies as appropriate, submit an annual report on the
effectiveness of the safeguards systems, program developments, and

~~SECRET/GDS~~

President Nixon's April 1974 NSDM #254 addressing threat to U.S. nuclear interests.

Source: Richard M. Nixon Presidential Library.

2002 Film documentary on the Weather Underground Organization — the primary domestic terrorist threat during the Nixon administration. From movie press kit.

May 10, 1970 — National Guardsmen pre-positioned in Executive Office Building (EOB) during "March on Washington" when over 100,000 protestors demonstrated against the U.S. incursion into Cambodia.

Source: Richard Nixon Presidential Library.

October 15, 1970 — President Nixon signs the Organized Crime Control Act which contained the RICO (Racketeer Influenced and Corrupt Organizations) Act.

Source: Richard Nixon Presidential Library.

Chapter 6

The Nixon and Ford Administrations (1969–1976): The Ford Administration

The Ford Administration (August 1974 to January 1977)

Overview

The Ford administration did not make any major changes to the Nixon administration's counter-terrorism organizational structure or policy. The fact that Kissinger served as Ford's national security advisor and secretary of state ensured that no significant alterations took place. However, there were tensions and disagreement within the administration over how important counter-terrorism should be and in evaluating the threat caused by terrorism — internal and overseas.[1] Statistically, there was no decline in international terrorist incidents and anti-American terrorist incidents during the Ford administration.[2] There was a decline

---

[1] See, for example, Timothy Naftali. *Blind Spot* (New York: Basic Books, 2005), pp. 78–98.

[2] In 1970, there were 300 international terrorist incidents, in 1971: 238; 1972: 529; 1973: 321, 1974: 416, 1975: 345, 1976: 456, and in 1977: 419. In terms of the number of Americans killed in overseas terrorist attacks, the following list shows two figures — the first is what the U.S. government reported at the time, the second in parentheses, are the author's as found in Appendix A. Over time, new information develops, and such statistics will change. The author has decided to show the statistics that government terrorism analysts and policymakers used to make assessments and decisions at the time, even though they may have turned out later to be inaccurate.

1970 — 12 (12)
1971 — 4 (2)
1972 — 24 (25)

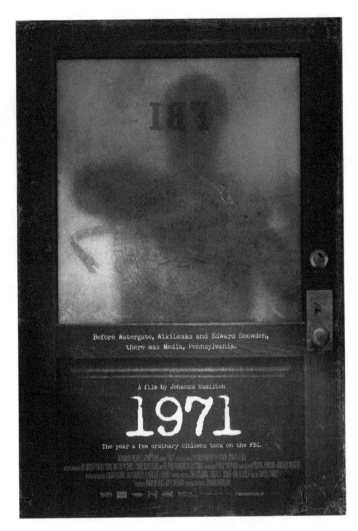

Poster from 2014 movie "1971" about the 1971 break-in of the FBI office in Media, Pennsylvania by eight amateur burglars associated with the ad hoc "Citizens' Commission to Investigate the FBI". From movie "1971" Press kit.

in secular Palestinian terrorist attacks as Yasir Arafat and the Palestine Liberation Organization (PLO) re-evaluated the political and public relations costs of engaging in terrorist attacks against Israeli and Western targets outside Israel. There was also a decline in the number of American fatalities due to overseas terrorist attacks.[3] However, this pullback from terrorism by the PLO caused a split within the Palestinian nationalist movement and led to the emergence of Palestinian "rejectionist" groups that opposed any negotiations with Israel and renunciation of terrorism outside Israel. The most prominent rejectionist group was Abu Nidal's Fatah Revolutionary Council (FRC)[4] which split from Arafat's Fatah in late 1974. The FRC became the most dangerous, lethal, and active secular Palestinian terrorist group in the 1980s. Therefore, while fedayeen attacks were on the decline during the Ford administration, developments in the Palestinian movement were ominous for the future. Left-wing terrorism continued to target U.S. interests overseas even though U.S. military involvement ended in Vietnam on August 15, 1973 as a result of the Case–Church Amendment passed by the U.S. Congress. The U.S. presence there essentially ended with the fall of Saigon on April 30, 1975.

The Ford administration maintained the Nixon administration's Cabinet Committee to Combat Terrorism (CCCT) and its more active working group as the primary government entity to coordinate and manage the government's response to terrorism at home and abroad. In a memorandum to President Ford in February 1975, Deputy Secretary of State Robert Ingersoll praised the Committee as a "bureaucratic innovation that over the past two and a half years has reduced

---

1973 — 25 (22)
1974 — 42 (21)
1975 — 18 (6)
1976 — 8 (6)
1977 — 5 (6)

In the 1970s, the U.S. government did not provide a public chronology of terrorist incidents overseas in which Americans were killed. It simply provided an annual total. In Appendix D, the author has provided a chronology of lethal terrorist incidents overseas involving Americans.

[3] In 1970, there were 21 fedayeen or Palestinian terrorist incidents, 1971: 10, 1972: 19, 1973: 46, 1974: 33, 1975: 17, and 1976: 17. Source: CIA, "International Terrorism in 1976," p. 19. In 1970, 12 Americans were killed in terrorist attacks overseas, 1971: 4, 1972: 24, 1973: 25, 1974: 42, 1975: 18, 1976: 8, and 1977: 5. Source: U.S. Department of State, Office for Combatting Terrorism, printed statistical chart, dated May 1998.

[4] FRC was the formal name of the organizations. The press and U.S. government used "Abu Nidal Organization" or ANO.

the risk to our people ... and is unique among governments as a mechanism for coping with terrorism."[5] Not all Ford administration officials agreed with this assessment. In January 1975, Ford's White House Counsel Philip W. Buchen and John O. Marsh, then his assistant for Congressional liaison, suggested that the Committee and its working group be abolished.[6] Some officials in the administration wanted to distance Ford from the Nixon administration whose political and counter-terrorism activities were under scrutiny. Abolishing the committee would break a key link. The committee however remained. There really was no pressing need to abolish this committee even though the terrorist threat was perceived by the Ford administration to be not as serious as under the Nixon administration. The overseas terrorist threat and internal terrorism did not disappear. It may have waned somewhat, but the grievances, groups, and states that used it remained.

Internal Terrorist Threat

Internally, Cuban exiles, Puerto Rican terrorists, the Weather Underground, the Jewish Defense League, the Black Liberation Army, Croatian terrorists, Armenian terrorists, the New World Liberation Front, and the United Freedom Front were all active during the Ford administration. It could even be argued that no administration faced such a large number of internal terrorism actors as the Ford administration. Nixon faced the most severe domestic terrorist threat in U.S. history due to the mixture of domestic terrorist organizations and violent protests on U.S. campuses and in urban areas. The latter component was not a major problem during the Ford administration. However, it did face an active internal terrorist threat environment. Twenty-five people were killed in terrorist attacks in the U.S. during the Ford administration. There were three major terrorist attacks that took place:

- On January 24, 1975, an Armed Forces of Puerto Rican National Liberation bomb exploded in the Fraunces Tavern of New York City, killing four people and injuring more than 50 others.

---

[5] U.S. Department of State. Office of the Historian. Foreign Relations of the United States, 1969–1976, Volume E-3, Documents on Global Issues, 1973–1976, Document 221, Memorandum from the Acting Secretary of State (Ingersoll) to President Ford, Washington, February 18, 1975, at https://history.state.gov/historicaldocuments/frus1969-76ve03/d221. Accessed June 6, 2017.

[6] Timothy Naftali, "Draft Section for Study of US Counterterrorism Strategy, 1968–1993," p. 4, at http://www.washingtondecoded.com/files/tngrf.pdf. Accessed October 13, 2017.

- On December 29, 1975, there was a bombing at a TWA baggage area in LaGuardia airport that killed 11 people and injured 75 others. This incident, remains unsolved. One theory is that the bombing was carried out by the UDBA in order to place blame on Croatian terrorists in the U.S. In addition, the bomb was not meant to kill anyone, but a faulty timer caused the bomb to explode leading to many casualties.[7]
- On September 10, 1976, five Croatian terrorists hijacked TWA Flight 355 out of New York with 85 passengers and crew. The terrorists also planted a bomb in a locker at the Grand Central Station in New York City that killed a New York policeman.

The issue of providing protection to foreign diplomatic interests in the U.S. continued to strain the relationship between the federal and city governments. On December 31, 1975, President Ford signed Public Law 94–126 that required the Executive Protection Service (EPS) to protect diplomatic missions in cities outside of Washington, D.C. that possessed 20 or more full-time missions, if the situation was an extraordinary protection need for which the city requested assistance and occurred at an international organization of which the U.S. was a member. The law was clearly designed to help New York City with the numerous U.N. missions there. The law also authorized the Treasury Department to reimburse states and cities that provided the protection. Federal reimbursement was limited to $3.5 million annually but allowed retroactive claims to July 1, 1974. This law appeared to have placated those New York City elements that had the massive responsibility to protect U.N. missions, the U.N. headquarters, and the influx of heads of state for the annual General Assembly meeting usually held in September. The issue of reimbursing New York City however did carry over into the Carter administration.[8]

Overseas Terrorist Threat

Overseas, the most serious anti-American terrorist incident took place on August 4, 1975 when five members of the Japanese Red Army (JRA) stormed the United States Embassy situated on the ninth floor of the AIA Insurance building in Kuala

---

[7] See John R. Schindler, "Why Hasn't Washington Explained the 1975 LaGuardia Airport Bombing?" *The Observer*, January 4, 2016, at http://observer.com/2016/01/why-hasnt-washington-explained-the-1975-laguardia-airport-bombing. Accessed 3, 2017.

[8] The section on PL 94-126 taken from *DS History*, p. 237.

Lumpur, Malaysia. The building housed other foreign embassies, including Sweden. The JRA gunman held 53 people as hostages, mostly Malaysians but also including U.S. Consul Robert Stebbins and six-seven other Americans and a Swedish diplomat, for four days. The Japanese deputy prime minister was visiting the U.S. at the time, and it was assumed the attack was timed to coincide with that visit. The JRA demanded that imprisoned JRA members in Japan be released. Since the JRA demands were aimed at Japan, the U.S. only adopted a monitoring role and its hostage-taking policy was not tested. The Malaysian government wanted to end the incident, so it favored giving in to the terrorists' demands. The Japanese government agreed to exchange four JRA prisoners whom they were holding for the hostages. However, one of the JRA prisoners wanted to stay in jail. The three terrorists were eventually given safe passage to Libya.[9] The Ford administration did not have to make any tough decisions on this incident. The incident however underlined the continuing anti-American terrorist threat overseas.

Counter-Terrorism Policy

In terms of counter-terrorism policy, the Ford administration adhered to the Nixon administration's policy on hostage-taking, emphasis on the criminality of terrorism, building international counter-terrorism cooperation, developing protective security measures at home and abroad, and not allowing terrorists to influence U.S. foreign policy. The Ford administration's views of the terrorist threat and the programs and policies needed to mitigate the threat can be found in three important documents.

In a November 6, 1974 memorandum from the Department of State to members of the CCCT titled "Subjects Guidelines for Dealing with Terrorism with International Connections or Implications," the following U.S. policies and positions were stated[10]:

---

[9] Association for Diplomatic Studies and Training, "More Moments in U.S. Diplomatic History: Terror on the 9th Floor — The Kuala Lumpur Hostage Crisis," ADST, May 1990 Interview with Robert Dillon, a foreign service officer in Kuala Lumpur at the time, at http://adst.org/2013/07/terror-on-the-9th-floor-the-kuala-lumpur-hostage-crisis/. Accessed March 23, 2017.

[10] U.S. Department of State. Office of the Historian. Foreign Relations of the United States, 1969–1976, Volume E-3, Documents on Global Issues, 1973–1976, Terrorism, Document 218, Memorandum from the Department of State to member of the CCCT, November 6, 1974, "Subjects Guidelines for Dealing with Terrorism with International Connections or Implications," at https://history.state.gov/historicaldocuments/frus1969-76ve03/d218. Accessed September 27, 2017.

- The host country is responsible for providing protection to foreign nationals within its territory, including securing their safe release from captors. U.S. officials will render all appropriate assistance to that country, particularly if U.S. citizens are held as hostages. Reciprocally, in an incident in the U.S. involving foreign nationals, the U.S. government will undertake negotiations to secure the release of hostages.

- The U.S. government has a policy not to pay ransom and to discourage other governments, companies, and individuals from making such payments. The U.S. will not release prisoners in response to terrorists' demands. Because of effective FBI follow-through in recovering ransom and kidnappers in this country, the U.S. government can show more flexibility here than abroad in acquiescing to ransom payments.

- For terrorist incidents within the U.S., the FBI has clear responsibilities, in collaboration with other law enforcement agencies. The Department of State exercises responsibilities in any aspects touching on relations with other governments.

- A terrorist should be prosecuted for criminally defined acts of terrorism within the country of commission or be appropriately extradited.

- The U.S. government will take measures at home against terrorism having international aspects and to do likewise abroad wherever international terrorists strike, bearing in mind that internal terrorism is within the jurisdiction of the country concerned.

- The U.S. government will establish effective communication with terrorists whose hostages are under U.S. protective responsibilities, avoiding hard-and-fast positions while seeking to reduce, or ideally to terminate, danger to hostages.

- The U.S. government recognizes the merit of elimination of causes of terrorism, including legitimate grievances which motivate potential terrorists. While political motivations such as the achievement of self-determination or independence are cited by some individuals or groups to justify terrorism, such issues should be addressed in the appropriate fora rather than by resorting to violence against innocent bystanders.

- The U.S. government is committed to pursuing legal remedies in dealing with terrorists and endeavors to influence other governments to do likewise.

- U.S. policy representations to other governments on essentially internal terrorism will be formulated in such a manner as to avoid interference in internal affairs, particularly if no U.S. citizens or interests are involved. At the same time, the U.S. government reserves the right to criticize other governments if they show irresponsibility in transferring international terrorists to the international community in cases which do not involve probable further bloodshed.

In a February 5, 1975 State Department Airgram A-775 titled "Revised Procedures for Responding to Acts of Terrorism Against Americans Abroad," guidance and policy was provided to all U.S. diplomatic and consular posts worldwide.[11] It was a revision of a July 3, 1973 Airgram on the same topic. The 1973 guidelines were refined and expanded with new emphasis placed on policy considerations, press guidance, possible stratagems, and possible psychological stress resulting from terrorism or the threat thereof. A special Airgram A-8515 titled "Terrorism: Advice to Businessmen" was also sent to posts to circulate to private Americans as to how to deal with "a terrorist-prone environment." The 1975 State Department Airgram to all posts on revised guidance reiterated most of the positions outlined in the November 1974 memorandum from State to the CCCT. However, it did provide some additional insights into U.S. government positions on the causes of terrorism and how to frame/paint the terrorists in the press:

- The U.S. government should continue to identify the causes of international terrorism and should seek to remove them. When such causes are within the domain of other governments, such influence as the U.S. Government may wish to exert naturally is restrained by the principle of non-interference in the internal affairs of another country and by other interests which the U.S. government may be obliged to protect in those countries. The U.S. example of an equitable system of justice, responsible government, and effective, legal counter-measures against terrorists should be not only a deterrent to violence at home but also an inspiration to other countries to follow similar patterns. The U.S. government wishes to share its counter-terrorism techniques with other governments but is even more eager to induce governments to see the merit, for anti-terrorist and other reasons, in the establishment of societies in which social-political-economic justice is ensured, thereby reducing legitimate grievances and the potential for terrorism to an absolute minimum.
- Press briefings might include the following philosophy, as appropriate: Terrorists are not heroes but rather criminals. Their threat to violate the right

---

[11] Ibid., Document 220. Airgram A-775 from the Department of State to All Posts, Washington, February 5, 1975, "Revised Procedures for Responding to Acts of Terrorism Against Americans Abroad," at https://history.state.gov/historicaldocuments/frus1969-76ve03/d220. Accessed February 23, 2016.

of life is intolerable in a modern, peace-loving society. Political passion, no matter how deeply held, cannot be a justification for violence against innocent persons. Until political terrorists accept such logic, they must be made to understand that it is unprofitable for them to kill innocents. Governments have a continuing obligation to protect their citizens from terrorist violence and can and should do so without violating other rights such as self-determination and individual liberty.

Lastly, in a February 18, 1975 memorandum to President Ford from the Deputy Secretary of State Robert Ingersoll some U.S. counter-terrorism programs, achievements, issues, and restated U.S. policies were outlined[12]:

- The Department of Transportation/Federal Aviation Administration has imposed mandatory screening of all passengers and their carry-on baggage, including foreign airports where permitted, and the U.S./Cuba bilateral agreement had effectively deterred hijacking of U.S. aircraft from the United States. However, the U.S. is still vulnerable to hijackers at many foreign airports where proper screening is not permitted. Another serious gap lies in the fact that many foreign carriers entering the United States do not regularly screen their passengers, thus leaving U.S. airports vulnerable to terrorist attacks. FAA is considering regulations which would impose on foreign airlines serving this country the same restrictions on security of hand baggage and persons boarding their incoming and outgoing aircraft as prevailing with the domestic U.S. airlines.
- The Department of State has created a new position of Security Coordinator, who will ensure that protection of foreign officials and installations is optimum. He will work closely with the Secret Service, the Executive Protective Service, and the Department of State as they provide supplemental protection to that which is furnished by the local authorities.
- Visa, immigration, and customs procedures remain tight. A deeper screening of visa applicants of Arab origin has shown some useful results. Japanese applicants have been given special attention following the seizure of hostages in the French Embassy in Holland by JRA terrorists.
- The Department of Treasury/Bureau of Alcohol, Tobacco, and Firearms, with the cooperation of the other departments and agencies, continues to search

---

[12] Ibid., Document 221, Memorandum from the Acting Secretary of State (Ingersoll) to President Ford, Washington, February 18, 1975, at https://history.state.gov/historicaldocuments/frus1969-76ve03/d221. Accessed March 23, 2107.

for cost-effective techniques to detect the presence of explosive materials and to "tag" explosives for identification.

- The FBI, the Secret Service, and the Department of State are training negotiators and other professionals for use in hostage situations.

- The Energy Research and Development Administration (ERDA) and Department of Defense (DOD) have tightened safeguards and security measures designed to forestall terrorist seizure of nuclear materials or attacks upon nuclear weapons storage, on the civilian and military sides, respectively. Defense has established a Physical Security Review Board responsible for policy and standards pertaining not only to the protection of nuclear weapons but also to DOD conventional arms, weapons, and explosives as well.

- The Postal Service operates a well-tested surveillance for letter bombs and has developed good international connections.

- NATO has been hesitant to engage in combatting terrorism, largely because of divergences over Middle East policies, but the U.S. has taken initiatives regularly to attempt to overcome this unrealistic reluctance.

- The Department of State engages in steady bilateral diplomacy to supplement multilateral efforts to convince governments that they should stand together, or they will hang separately. It also makes démarches to a wide variety of governments in cases where leniency toward terrorists can only foster new terrorism. The U.S. has been firm with the Sudanese and Egyptians in the matter of the terrorists who killed the U.S. Ambassador and his deputy in Khartoum in March 1973.

- The Department of Treasury and the U.S. Customs Service, in their daily working relationship, continue to exchange information and review Customs techniques on a one-to-one basis with their foreign counterparts.

- The Department of Transportation/FAA have offered a variety of technical assistance to foreign governments to help improve their airport and airline security. The FAA school at Oklahoma City is but one opportunity for foreigners in this program.

- Businessmen with overseas interests have been in mild panic in such areas as Latin America, where they are often terrorists' targets. State's coordinator for combatting terrorism has made a special effort to share with such Americans, techniques, intelligence, and counsel which can reduce the risk to these individuals.

- Following the murder of our diplomats in the Sudan, Congress was asked for special funds for additional personnel and materials to provide better security at our diplomatic and consular posts. A total of $19.6 million was appropriated and has been disbursed to the neediest posts.

- Terrorists benefit from improved technology, including communications and weaponry. The U.S. has attempted to restrain the Soviets and the Syrians from making a portable surface-to-air missile (SA-7) available to fedayeen groups who might allow this weapon to be diverted to use against civilian airliners as was the case in Rome in the winter of 1973.

- Research is given high priority. State and Defense have hired the RAND Corporation to prepare a confidential study to advice on the optimum management of hostage situations. Four or five agencies, including the Law Enforcement Alliance of America, are collaborating in a study to determine where municipal and international law may permit additional legal deterrents against terrorists. The U.S. is examining the possible utility of independent research to ensure that all possible gaps are being filled with counter-measures against terrorists who may wish to employ nuclear or biological-chemical weapons. ERDA is accelerating its research effort to develop more advanced physical security systems for the protection of nuclear materials in transit and in plants. Bilateral technical discussions on nuclear materials' protection have been held with France, the United Kingdom, and Israel. Defense has engaged a firm of consultants to analyze the political dynamics of Palestinian terrorist movements.

- The Working Group is giving increased priority attention to a more systematic utilization of behavioral science techniques.

- The U.S. remains gravely concerned over the gaps in the security screen surrounding foreign officials and installations in this country and has presented various recommendations to the White House calling for increased Federal resources to supplement, on a periodic basis, the traditional local protection accorded to the country's foreign guests. Of concern is New York City, where it is imperative that the U.S. does something more and soon to assist the good work of the New York City Police, who have done remarkably well in such situations as the Arafat visit. Other communities also periodically deserve additional limited Federal assistance.

By the end of the Ford administration, the following U.S. counter-terrorism objectives were put forth:

- To deter a terrorist from striking by placing legal, physical, or other barriers before him; should he strike, the U.S. would seek to apprehend him and ensure that he pays a sufficiently high penalty to discourage other potential terrorists.

- To demonstrate firmness with terrorists while at the same time compassion for the hostages.

- To find the broadest international consensus to counter the continuing threat and improvement of management and other techniques to outwit or to overcome the terrorist.
- To prevent or deter terrorists from striking at U.S. interests at home and abroad.
- To work with the international community to construct anti-terrorist treaties and conventions.
- To provide moral, financial, and logistical support to those countries who seek our counter-terrorism assistance.
- To arrest and try or extradite terrorists.
- To develop and share among U.S. agencies and allies, overseas terrorist-related intelligence, analysis, and research.

The major terrorist-related concerns were the following:

- Terrorist attacks on nuclear facilities and transport methods and the acquisition of nuclear materials.
- Terrorist acquisition and use of surface to air missiles.
- Rejectionist Palestinian terrorist groups.
- States engaging in support, sponsorship, or direction of terrorism.

The Ford Administration — The Response

As a result of the growing concern over terrorists possibly obtaining nuclear weapons and an uncoordinated and haphazard response by the U.S. Atomic Energy Commission to a 1974 hoax extortion threat that involved a nuclear bomb being planted in Boston, the Ford administration in November 1974 established a Nuclear Emergency Support Team (NEST) to deal with nuclear-related terrorist incidents. The mission of NEST was "to conduct, direct, and coordinate search and recovery operations for nuclear material, weapons or devices, and to assist in the identification and deactivation of Improvised Nuclear Devices (INDs) and Radiological Dispersal Devices (RDDs)."[13] On July 1, 1976, President Ford signed the "International Security Assistance and Arms Export Control Act of 1976" that created section 620A of the Foreign Assistance Act. Section 620A prohibits U.S. arms sales to nations which deny basic human rights; discriminate

---

[13] Cameron Reed, "The Nuclear Emergency Support Team (NEST)," *American Physics Society*, circa 2012, at https://www.aps.org/units/fps/newsletters/201301/reed.cfm. Accessed September 23, 2017.

against U.S. persons based on race, religion, sex, or national origin; grant sanctuary to international terrorists; or breach military assistance agreements with the United States. Section 620A was one of the first U.S. counter-terrorism laws aimed at State sponsors. This section stated that the U.S. would cut off foreign assistance to "any government which aids or abets, by providing sanctuary from prosecution to any group or individual that committed an act of international terrorism."[14] More significantly, it was also during the Ford administration that the executive and legislative branches initiated investigations into the internal surveillance activities of the intelligence agencies during the Johnson and the Nixon administrations. President Ford and Congress also implemented measures and procedures to prevent a recurrence of these internal surveillance abuses. In addition, the agencies themselves developed internal guidelines and oversight to ensure that they operate within the proscribed legal authorities.

While the media and congressional investigations of the Nixon administration were exposing illegal Army Intelligence and FBI activities, the CIA became caught in this investigative net during the Ford administration. The unmasking was triggered when the *New York Times* on December 22, 1974 published a lengthy article by Seymour Hersh detailing illegal CIA operations over the years (dubbed the "family jewels"). This article placed the spotlight on the CIA.[15] Hersh's article noted covert action programs involving assassination attempts against foreign leaders and covert attempts to subvert foreign governments. In addition, the article discussed efforts by intelligence agencies to collect information on the political activities of U.S. citizens, including the CIA.[16] Hersh reported that,

---

[14] Read more at the American Presidency Project: Gerald R. Ford: Statement on Signing the International Security Assistance and Arms Export Control Act of 1976, at http://www.presidency. ucsb.edu/ws/index.php?pid=6167#ixzz1M4xZ4OuA. Accessed March 26, 2017.

[15] The CIA's "family jewels" refers to the name given to a 693-page compilation of the recollections of CIA employees who had previously been directed by then DCI James Schlesinger to identify any past abuses or improprieties in which the CIA may have been involved over the span of decades, from the 1950s to the mid-1970s. See the entire report at http://nsarchive.gwu.edu/NSAEBB/NSAEBB222/ index.htm. Accessed September 23, 2017. See also, http://www.foia.cia.gov/collection/family-jewels October 23, 2016.

[16] Seymour M. Hersh, "Huge CIA Operation Reported in U.S. Against Antiwar Forces, and other Dissidents, *New York Times*, December 22, 1974, p. 1, at https://s3.amazonaws.com/s3.documentcloud. org/documents/238963/huge-c-i-a-operation-reported-in-u-s-against.pdf. Accessed September 25, 2017.

> *The Central Intelligence Agency directly violated its charter, conducted a massive illegal domestic intelligence operation during the Nixon administration against the anti-war movement and other dissident groups in the United States ... intelligence files on at least 10,000 American citizens were maintained by a special unit of the CIA ... the CIA authorized its agents to follow and photograph participants in anti-war and other demonstrations ... it also set up a network of informants who were ordered to penetrate anti-war groups.*[17]

The CIA activities, especially those aimed at U.S. citizens, triggered two government investigations. In 1975, President Ford established the "President's Commission on CIA Activities within the United States," also known as the Rockefeller Commission because it was chaired by Vice-President Nelson Rockefeller.[18] The Rockefeller Commission issued a single report in 1975, which delineated some CIA abuses:

- Spying on American citizens in the United States.
- Keeping dossiers on large numbers of American citizens; CIA's Operation CHAOS — the collection of substantial amounts of information on domestic dissidents from 1967 to 1973.[19]

---

[17] Ibid.

[18] The full report can be found at http://history-matters.com/archive/church/rockcomm/contents.htm. Accessed March 23, 2017.

[19] In a December 6, 1974 Memorandum for the Record, the CIA library provided a history of the creation of the "Terrorism / Dissidents File." It noted that in May 1968 the White House had tasked the Director of Central Intelligence to "provide a definitive study on student turmoil." This task was given as a special project to the Office of Current Intelligence which then tasked the CIA library to provide it with information on "the history of the movement, heroes and leaders, the movement in foreign countries, and dissident student organizations and demonstrations." The library provided this information to the office of current intelligence who wrote the required study. The CIA library was then "requested to collect material on this subject indefinitely." The materials used by the library were "articles from periodicals and newspapers that had been scanned for this subject, books, and reports." The library file was called the "Student Unrest File" and contained both domestic student and foreign student sections. The library was tasked with the foreign student section. Beginning in 1971, the maintenance and building of these files increased to encompass worldwide terrorism activities including internal terrorist activities. In November 1974, the assistant to the State Department's Director of the Counter-Terrorism Office and Chairman of the CCCT working group on terrorism visited the CIA library, reviewed the files and stated that "it was unique within the U.S. government and probably in the U.S." The assistant was keeping a similar file and he compared notes with the library. The memorandum further noted that the library's files were used my many agency components. (CIA, Memorandum for the Record, Subject: History of the Terrorism/Dissidents File, written by blacked

- Aiming these activities at Americans who expressed opposition to government policies.
- Intercepted and opened personal mail in the United States.
- Infiltrated domestic dissident groups and otherwise intervened in domestic politics.
- Engaged in illegal wiretaps and break-ins.[20]
- The HTLINGUAL Project, established in 1952 to intercept mails destined for the Soviet Union and China, was redirected to target domestic peace and civil rights activists.

The commission did note that the "great majority of CIA's domestic activities comply with its statutory authority ... and that the agency's actions in 1973–1974 have gone far to terminate the activities upon which this investigation has focused."[21] This commission also investigated allegations that the CIA was somehow involved in the assassination of President Kennedy. The evidence is clear however that the CIA did on occasion engage in illegal domestic activities against American citizens. The Rockefeller Commission was touted to be an independent investigation. However, on February 19, 2016, the George Washington University's "National Security Archive" released internal White House and Rockefeller Commission documents that indicated that the Ford White House significantly altered the final report of the 1975 Rockefeller Commission, over the objections of senior commission staff. The changes included removal of an entire 86-page section on CIA assassination plots abroad and numerous edits to the report by then-Deputy White House Chief of Staff Richard Cheney.[22] The Cheney editing undermines the alleged "independent" character of the Rockefeller Commission.[23] The Rockefeller Commission was seen by some as a whitewash and an attempt to fend off a

---

out name, CIA/LY/INFO section (someone in CIA library), dated December 6, 1974. (CIA FOIA document number RDP-80B01495R001400010003-3).

[20] Ibid., p. 9.

[21] Ibid., p. 10. See also, Timothy S. Hardy, "Intelligence Reform in the Mid-1970s," a declassified CIA historical document at https://www.cia.gov/library/center-for-the-study-of-intelligence/kent-csi/vol20no2/html/v20i2a01p_0001.htm. Accessed July 6, 2016.

[22] Read this 86-period section, at http://nsarchive.gwu.edu/dc.html?doc=2719480-Document-19. Accessed July 23, 2017.

[23] http://nsarchive.gwu.edu/NSAEBB/NSAEBB543-Ford-White-House-Altered-Rockefeller-Commission-Report/. Accessed November 20, 2017.

more thorough investigation of the CIA.[24] This second development failed as the 1975 Church Committee (see detailed description provided subsequently) carried out an extensive investigation of all the intelligence and law enforcement agencies.

The National Security Agency was not initially subjected to the intensive scrutiny of the media and Congress that was directed toward the CIA and FBI. To the chagrin of this historically low-profile agency, however, it eventually became a target. There were three key NSA programs that turned out to be, according to the Church Committee, "disreputable if not outright illegal." The first was a secret operation code-named "MINARET." It was set up by the NSA to monitor the overseas phone communications of Senators Frank Church and Howard Baker, as well as major civil rights leaders including Dr. Martin Luther King, Jr., and Whitney Young of the National Urban League, and prominent U.S. journalists, celebrities, and athletes who criticized the Vietnam War, like Jane Fonda, Dr. Benjamin Spock, and Muhammad Ali. In total, some 1,650 individuals were tracked by the NSA between 1967 and 1973, though the identities of most of those people remain unknown.[25] The second development was the construction of an NSA Watch List. The watch list concept was used previously by NSA for people who were suspected threats to the president, for drug dealers, and later for domestic terrorism. Given the anti-war protests and urban riots, President Johnson wanted to know if these developments were being instigated by outside forces and if leaders of domestic opposition organizations were in contact with hostile foreign powers. These presidential concerns by Johnson and later by Nixon initiated not only the CIA's Operation CHAOS but also the NSA's politicized Watch List. Both the CIA and NSA were adding domestic critics of the government and influential athletes, celebrities, politicians, civil rights leaders, and others who opposed the Vietnam War. It became more of a targeted political dissident list.[26]

---

[24] http://history-matters.com/archive/contents/church/contents_church_reports_rockcomm.htm. Accessed December 20, 2017; http://www.maryferrell.org/pages/Rockefeller_Commission.html. Accessed November 26, 2017.

[25] Ed Pilkington, "Declassified NSA files show the agency spied on Muhammad Ali and MLK," The *Guardian*, September 26, 2013, at http://www.theguardian.com/world/2013/sep/26/nsa-surveillance-anti-vietnam-muhammad-ali-mlk. Accessed March 23, 2017.

[26] Matthew M. Aid and William Burr, "'Disreputable if Not Outright Illegal': The National Security Agency versus Martin Luther King, Muhammad Ali, Art Buchwald, Frank Church, *et al*. Newly Declassified History Divulges Names of Prominent Americans Targeted by NSA during Vietnam Era," National Security Archive Electronic Briefing Book No. 441, September 25, 2013, at http://nsarchive.gwu.edu/NSAEBB/NSAEBB441. Accessed December 23, 2017; Nicholas Horrock,

The third development in the NSA was the use of a top-secret program code-named SHAMROCK. This program was in existence before the NSA was founded. It was created by President Truman in 1952 and was essentially a continuation of the military censorship program of World War II. Copies of foreign telegraph traffic had been turned over to military intelligence during the war, and when the war ended, the Army Security Agency (ASA) wanted this continued.[27] The NSA had access to most of the international telegrams leaving New York City for foreign destinations. Every day, NSA sent a courier to New York City on the train to visit the three major telegraph companies. He then returned to the NSA headquarters in Fort Meade with large reels of magnetic tape, which were copies of the international telegrams sent from New York the preceding day. The tapes were then processed for items of foreign intelligence interest, typically telegrams sent by foreign establishments in the United States or telegrams that appeared to be encrypted.[28] Even NSA's director in the mid-1970s, Lew Allen, stated that although not technically illegal, it did not pass the "smell test" very well.[29] It was a painful experience for NSA officials to appear before the various congressional committees and presidential commissions, given NSA's cultural penchant for anonymity.

The 1974 Hersh story in the *New York Times*, combined with the post-Watergate revelations concerning CIA and FBI activities, led to the establishment of the most significant congressional investigation ever conducted into U.S. law enforcement and intelligence methods and procedures — the 1975 "United States Senate Select Committee to Study Governmental Operations with Respect to Intelligence Activities" or the "Church Committee," named after Sen. Frank Church. The Church Committee examined the domestic intelligence methodology and landscape

---

"National Security Agency Reported Eavesdropping on Most Private Cables," *The New York Times*, August 8, 1975, p. 1.

[27]L. Britt Snider, "Recollections from the Church Committee's Investigation of NSA — Unlucky SHAMROCK," CIA Historical document, April 14, 2007, at https://www.cia.gov/library/center-for-the-study-of-intelligence/csi-publications/csi-studies/studies/winter99-00/art4.html. Accessed March 23, 2017.

[28]Ibid. For more on the SHAMROCK program, see U.S. Senate, 94th Congress, 2nd Session, Report #94-755, Final report of the Select Committee to Study Governmental Operations with Respect to Intelligence Activities, Supplementary Detailed Staff Reports on Intelligence Activities and the Rights of Americans, Book III, April 23, 1976, pp. 765–776, hereafter referred to as the "Church Committee," at https://archive.org/stream/finalreportofsel03unit#page/2/mode/2up. Accessed October 23, 2017.

[29]Thomas R. Johnson. *U.S. Cryptologic History: American Cryptology during the Cold War, 1945–1989 – Book III*, National Security Agency, Center for Cryptologic History, 1998, p. 84, at https://www.nsa.gov/Portals/70/documents/news-features/declassified-documents/cryptologic-histories/cold_war_iii.pdf. Accessed February 19, 2019.

in the United States from World War I to the early 1970s. The committee was looking for answers to the following questions:

- Which government agencies had engaged in domestic spying?
- How many U.S. citizens had been targets of government intelligence activity?
- What standards had governed the opening of intelligence investigations?
- What standards had governed the termination of intelligence investigations?
- Where had the targets fit on the spectrum of those who commit violent criminal acts and those who seek only to dissent peacefully from government policy?
- How much of the intelligence information included intimate details of the targets' personal lives or their political views, and had this information been disseminated to injure individuals?
- What actions beyond surveillance had the intelligence agencies taken?
- Had intelligence agencies been used to serve the political aims of presidents, other high officials, or the agencies themselves?
- How had the agencies responded either to proper orders or excessive pressure from their superiors?
- To what extent had the agencies disclosed or concealed activities from outside bodies charged with overseeing them?
- Had intelligence agencies acted outside the law?
- What had been the attitude of the intelligence community toward the rule of law?
- To what extent had the Executive branch and the Congress controlled intelligence agencies and held them accountable?
- How well had the Federal system of checks and balances between the branches worked to control the intelligence agencies?[30]

In its final report, the Church Committee answered these questions:

> *The answer to each of these questions is disturbing. Too many people have been spied upon by too many Government agencies and too much information has been collected. The Government has often undertaken the secret surveillance of citizens on the basis of their political beliefs, even when those beliefs posed no threat of violence or illegal acts on*

---

[30] Church Committee, "Book II: Intelligence Activities and the Rights of Americans," pp. 4–5.

behalf of a hostile foreign power. The Government, operating primarily through secret informants, but also using other intrusive techniques such as wiretaps, microphone "bugs", surreptitious mail opening, and break-ins, has swept in vast amounts of information about the personal lives, views, and associations of American citizens. Investigations of groups deemed potentially dangerous — and even of groups suspected of associating with potentially dangerous organizations — have continued for decades, despite the fact that those groups did not engage in unlawful activity. Groups and individuals have been harassed and disrupted because of their political views and their lifestyles. Investigations have been based upon vague standards whose breadth made excessive collection inevitable. Unsavory and vicious tactics have been employed — including anonymous attempts to break up marriages, disrupt meetings, ostracize persons from their professions, and provoke target groups into rivalries that might result in deaths. Intelligence agencies have served the political and personal objectives of presidents and other high officials. While the agencies often committed excesses in response to pressure from high officials in the Executive branch and Congress, they also occasionally initiated improper activities and then concealed them from officials whom they had a duty to inform.

Governmental officials, including those whose principal duty is to enforce the law, have violated or ignored the law over long periods of time and have advocated and defended their right to break the law. The Constitutional system of checks and balances has not adequately controlled intelligence activities. Until recently the Executive branch has neither delineated the scope of permissible activities nor established procedures for supervising intelligence agencies. Congress has failed to exercise sufficient oversight, seldom questioning the use to which its appropriations were being put. Most domestic intelligence issues have not reached the courts, and in those cases when they have reached the courts, the judiciary has been reluctant to grapple with them.[31]

The committee combed through more than 100,000 classified and unclassified documents to piece together a complicated history of past intelligence abuses. "Conducting much of its work behind closed doors, the panel interviewed 800 individuals including former CIA directors, FBI officials, and counterintelligence

---

[31] Ibid., pp. 5–6.

officers and agents, and conducted 250 executive and 21 public hearings."[32] To educate the public about the misdeeds of national intelligence agencies, the committee held televised hearings in the Senate Caucus Room. In 1975 and 1976, the Committee published 14 volumes of reports on a variety of intelligence activities from the 1950s through the early 1970s. These included the FBI's COINTELPRO program to infiltrate and disrupt domestic organizations, mail opening programs by the FBI and CIA, abuses by the Internal Revenue Service, and much more. Consequently, under public and congressional pressure, both the CIA and FBI imposed internal restrictions on their intelligence-gathering processes, techniques, and capabilities. This led to what some considered the "handcuffing" or "crippling" of these agencies to protect America from domestic and foreign terrorists. The Foreign Intelligence Surveillance Act (FISA) and Foreign Intelligence Surveillance Court (FISC) were by-products of the Church Committee.

While the final reports contained a plethora of conclusions and recommendations, the following warning in the report is both summative and prescient:

> *Our findings and the detailed reports which supplement this volume set forth a massive record of intelligence abuses over the years. Through a vast network of informants, and through the uncontrolled or illegal use of intrusive techniques — ranging from simple theft to sophisticated electronic surveillance — the Government has collected, and then used improperly, huge amounts of information about the private lives, political beliefs and associations of numerous Americans.*[33]

Senator Church later elaborated further on the electronic surveillance issue:

> *In the need to develop a capacity to know what potential enemies are doing, the United States government has perfected a technological capability that enables us to monitor the messages that go through the air. Now, that is necessary and important to the United States as we look abroad at enemies or potential enemies. We must know, at the same time,*

---

[32] http://www.senate.gov/artandhistory/history/minute/Church_Committee_Created.htm. Accessed February 23, 2016.

[33] Intelligence Activities and the Rights of Americans, Book II, Final Report of the Select Committee to Study Governmental Operations with Respect to Intelligence Activities, U.S. Senate, (Washington, D.C.: U.S. Government Printing Office, 1976), p. 290, at http://www.intelligence. senate.gov/pdfs94th/94755_II.pdf. Accessed December 13, 2017.

that capability at any time could be turned around on the American people, and no American would have any privacy left such is the capability to monitor everything — telephone conversations, telegrams, it doesn't matter. There would be no place to hide. If this government ever became a tyrant, if a dictator ever took charge in this country, the technological capacity that the intelligence community has given the government could enable it to impose total tyranny, and there would be no way to fight back because the most careful effort to combine together in resistance to the government, no matter how privately it was done, is within the reach of the government to know. Such is the capability of this technology.[34]

In addition to the 1975 Rockefeller Commission and 1975 Church Committee investigations of illegal domestic security activities, there was another investigation by the House of Representatives. In February 1975, the House of Representatives created a House Select Intelligence Committee (known as the Nedzi Committee after Democratic Congressman Lucien Norbert Nedzi of Michigan, which was replaced five months later by the Pike Committee, named after Democratic Congressman Otis G. Pike of New York). This committee was charged with investigating illegal activities by the CIA, FBI, and NSA.[35] The final report of the Pike Committee was never officially published, due to Congressional opposition. However, unauthorized versions of the (draft) final report were leaked to the press. Unlike the Church Committee, the Pike Committee was more interested in the structure, budget, and programs of the intelligence agencies. Pike's investigation initiated one of the first congressional oversight debates for the vast and secret collective of intelligence agencies. Pike focused his committee's investigations on the cost of U.S. intelligence, its effectiveness, and who controlled it.[36] His overriding question was whether all this money and programs were effective and were keeping America safer. This was information that heretofore the intelligence agencies were never asked to provide to Congress or the American public. Pike was able to elicit for the first time ever from CIA Director

---

[34] James Bamford, "Post-September 11, NSA 'enemies' include us," *Politico*, September 8, 2011, at http://www.politico.com/news/stories/0911/62999.html. Accessed December 14, 2017.

[35] U.S. House of Representatives. 94th Congress, 1st Session. Select Committee on Intelligence. "U.S. Intelligence Agencies and Activities: Domestic Intelligence Programs," October 9, November 13 and 18, and December 10, 1975, at http://www.scribd.com/doc/80651448/Pike-Committee-U-S-Intelligence-Agencies-and-Activities-In. Accessed December 21, 2017.

[36] https://www.cia.gov/library/center-for-the-study-of-intelligence/csi-publications/csi-studies/studies/winter98_99/art07.html. Accessed September 23, 2017.

William Colby that the NSA was routinely tapping American's phone calls and to persuade the head of the NSA, Lew Allen Jr., to testify in public for the first time.[37] From the perspective of U.S. intelligence agencies, the Pike Committee was far more intrusive and dangerous than the Church Committee. CIA historians have noted that the CIA Review Staff, who worked closely with both Committees and staff during these investigations, never developed the same cooperative relationship with the Pike Committee staff that it did with the Church Committee. The Review Staff pictured the Pike staff as "flower children, very young and irresponsible and naïve."[38]

However, as the CIA historian, Gerald K. Haines, concluded:

Despite its failures, the Pike Committee inquiry was a new and dramatic break with the past. It was the first significant House investigation of the IC since the creation of the CIA in 1947. In the final analysis, both the CIA and the committee were caught up in the greater power struggle between the legislative and executive branches in which the Congress in the late 1970s tried to regain control over US intelligence activities and foreign policy. The investigations were part of this overall struggle. And the inquiry foreshadowed, although it was not clear at the time, that Congress would become much more of a consumer of the intelligence product.[39]

The nature, level, and scope of the domestic security threat in the U.S. from the late 1960s through the mid-1970s was the most severe the U.S. government has ever faced. U.S. intelligence and law enforcement agencies were unsure as to how to address this threat. There were no historical templates or solutions for reference. In addition, there was little congressional oversight of the federal law enforcement and intelligence agencies during this period. These agencies did not know what tools or measures should be used to mitigate this threat. More importantly, these agencies were under pressure from the Nixon White House to do what was necessary, if not legal, to alleviate this threat. On June 5, 1970, President Nixon met with the heads of the FBI, CIA, NSA, and Defense

---

[37] Mark Ames, "The first Congressman to battle the NSA is dead. No one noticed, no one cares," *Pando Media*, February 4, 2014, at https://pando.com/2014/02/04/the-first-congressman-to-battle-the-nsa-is-dead-no-one-noticed-no-one-cares/. Accessed December 4, 2017.

[38] https://www.cia.gov/library/center-for-the-study-of-intelligence/csi-publications/csi-studies/studies/winter98_99/art07.html. Accessed December 23, 2018.

[39] Ibid.

Intelligence Agency (DIA). The NSA Director remembered: "The President chewed our butts."

> *The President said that 'revolutionary terrorism' was now the gravest threat to the United States. Thousands of Americans under the age of thirty were 'determined to destroy our society,' their homegrown ideology was 'as dangerous as anything they could import' from Cuba, China, or Russia. 'Good intelligence was the best way to stop terrorism.'*[40]

It is important to recognize that this is the same White House that constructed and then concealed a series of political dirty tricks and illegal operations like the Watergate break-in.[41] With top secret programs like COINTELPRO, HTLINGUAL, CHAOS, SHAMROCK, and MINARET, these agencies had already demonstrated their propensity for dealing with national security problems by periodically operating at the tipping point between legality and illegality. Given all of these developments and conditions during this period, it is not surprising that the government was overly aggressive in attempting to mitigate the rising domestic terrorist threat.[42] There is no question that agencies of the U.S.

---

[40] Tim Weiner. *Enemies: A History of the FBI* (New York: Random House, 2012), p. 290. The White House had proposed a program to enhance this collection of intelligence known as the Huston Plan, named after a White House aide, but the primary architect was William Sullivan, the FBI's head of intelligence. This plan directed the FBI "to keep on doing what it had been doing for decades, but to do more of it, do it better, and do it in concert with the CIA and the Pentagon" (Weiner, p. 291). While the Huston Plan was verbally approved by Nixon, it was never formally accepted by FBI Director Hoover, nor was any Nixon-signed paperwork initiated by the White House, but the thrust of its proposals was adopted and implemented. Then Attorney General John Mitchell discussed the formal authorization of the Huston plan, but both "agreed that it would be too dangerous" (Thomas R. Johnson. *American Cryptology during the Cold War, 1945–1989 — Book III, Retrenchment and Reform, 1972–1980*, National Security Agency, Center for Cryptologic History, 1999, p. 88, at https://www.nsa.gov/Portals/70/documents/news-features/declassified-documents/cryptologic-histories/cold_war_iii.pdf).

[41] For examples of these dirty tricks and other illegal operations by the Nixon White House, see Theodore Harold, *Breach of Faith: The Fall of Richard Nixon* (New York: Atheneum Publishers, 1975); Leon Friedman and William F. Levantrosser, eds. *Watergate and Afterward: The Legacy of Richard M. Nixon* (Santa Barbara, Calif.: Greenwood Publishing Group, 1992); and Tim Weiner. *One Man Against the World: The Tragedy of Richard Nixon* (New York: Henry Holt and Co., 2015).

[42] See, for example, "FBI Wiretaps, Bugs, and Break-Ins: The National Security Electronic Surveillance Card File and the Surreptitious Entries File," *University Publications of America* (1988), pp. V–VI, at http://www.lexisnexis.com/documents/academic/upa_cis/10755_FBIFileWiretapsBugs.pdf. Accessed September 23, 2017.

government engaged in operations "preventing the exercise of First Amendment rights of speech and association, on the theory that preventing the growth of dangerous groups and the propagation of dangerous ideas would protect the national security and deter violence."[43] However, were these actions necessary, were they effective, and what were the motivations behind them?

In the eyes of some federal law enforcement and intelligence agencies, some Attorneys General, and White House officials, including the president, the domestic surveillance operations were necessary. Some of these operations were illegal. Therefore, if one believes an illegal operation is necessary, it follows that the legal law enforcement and intelligence tools available at the time were insufficient or ineffective against an extraordinary domestic threat. William Dyson, the FBI agent in charge of the Weathermen cases at the time, later stated:

> *There were certain people in the FBI who made the decision: We've got to take a step — anything to get rid of these people. Anything! Not kill them, per se, but anything went. If we suspect somebody's involved in this, put a wiretap on them. Put a microphone in. Steal his mail. Do anything!*[44]

However, were these illegal measures effective? Given the scope of this threat, it is difficult to calculate how effective these measures were. What metrics would be applicable? Number of arrests? Number of convictions? Number of terrorist incidents? Number of plots discovered? Number of terrorist organizations? Number of demonstrations? Membership numbers in perceived subversive organizations? Number of informants? There is simply no quantitative way to measure the effectiveness of the illegal measures. It would be impossible to definitively link a particular result to a specific measure. For example, as previously noted, several black domestic terrorist organizations declined because of internal dissension and personality clashes. How much of that was attributable to FBI harassment, planting disinformation on leaders, and surveillance pressure on members of the organizations and their families?

While it is impossible to discern the individual and organizational motivations of the many agents, analysts, policymakers, and technicians who engaged

---

[43] U.S. Senate, 94th Congress, 2nd Session, Report #94-755, Final report of the Select Committee to Study Governmental Operations with Respect to Intelligence Activities, Supplementary Detailed Staff Reports on Intelligence Activities and the Rights of Americans, Book III, April 23, 1976, p. 3, at https://archive.org/stream/finalreportofsel03unit#page/2/mode/2up. Accessed December 21, 2017.

[44] As quoted in Burroughs, *Days of Rage*, p. 234.

in, supervised, or authorized domestic surveillance operations during the Nixon administration, the following anecdotes may reflect their belief that what they were doing was justified. On April 7, 1977, John J. Kearney, FBI Supervisory Special Agent of New York Squad 47 was indicted for "allegations that illegal investigative techniques were used by FBI Agents assigned to Squad 47." On the day of Kearney's arraignment, a group of around 300 FBI Agents gathered in New York's Foley Square outside the federal courthouse in a show of support — an unprecedented protest by FBI agents and one never matched to this day.[45] In addition, several defense funds were initiated, including the Citizen's Legal Defense Fund for the FBI and the Special Agent's Legal Defense Fund, sponsored by the Society of Former Special Agents of the FBI.[46] Would former and active FBI agents support a fellow agent who engaged in illegal activity for indefensible motives? Was there a collective belief within these agencies that the actions they were taking were necessary to protect the country and the people? There were certainly individuals like Army Intelligence Captain Christopher Pyle who felt the need to expose illegal domestic surveillance programs. It is difficult to recreate the mindset and political and security atmospheres during this period so that one can truly understand the contextual environment at the time. For most Americans, for most of the government and congressional officials, and for the majority of law enforcement and intelligence officials, America was under siege by a radical set of white and black militant youths. There was no Congressional oversight or guidelines as to how and what the law enforcement and intelligence agencies could do, but there was an administration that put pressure on them to mitigate this terrorist threat and it did not care how they did it.[47] A June 1976 top secret internal Justice Department report ultimately recommended against prosecution, concluding that "if the intelligence agencies possessed too much discretionary authority with too little accountability, that would seem to be a 35-year failing of Presidents and the Congress rather than the agencies." [48]

---

[45] Edith Evans Asbury, "300 Agents of F.B.I. Demonstrate in Support of Indicted Supervisor," *New York Times*, April 15, 1977, p. 42. One FBI agent conceded that he had never expected to be a participant in a demonstration, admitting that he had mingled among crowds of other people's demonstrations in the past. All the agents were at the courthouse on their own time — having taken annual leave or being scheduled to work later shifts.

[46] Society of Former Special Agents of the FBI. Susan Lloyd, "Edward S. Miller ..." *The Grapevine Magazine*, March 2014, p. 12, at http://c.ymcdn.com/sites/www.socxfbi.org/resource/resmgr/HIstory_Committee_Articles/Edward_S._Miller.pdf. Accessed July 3, 2017.

[47] Ibid., p. 11.

[48] Department of Justice, June 30, 1976 report, p. 171, at http://nsarchive.gwu.edu/NSAEBB/NSAEBB178/. Accessed November 23, 2017.

On April 10, 1978, former FBI Director L. Patrick Gray, Edward S. Miller, one-time head of Squad 47, and former FBI Assistant Director Mark Felt were indicted on felony charges for authorizing burglaries against relatives and friends of the Weather Underground Organization.

In an unprecedented action, former President Nixon and four former U.S. attorneys general testified for the defense that they would have given authorization at the time, if asked, for the surreptitious entries. Nixon testified that the authority to conduct warrantless break-ins was passed on from the office of the president directly to the FBI Director. He claimed that there was hard evidence that the Weathermen had connections to foreign powers and stated the group's intention was to overthrow the government. He testified that it was essential that the government strengthen its efforts to seek out persons responsible for bombings and other terrorist activities during the Vietnam War years. Referring to international terrorist attacks that had taken place during the Carter administration, Nixon stated "but all these concerns, I can assure you as one who went through it, were greatly magnified — I guess that's the proper word — by the fact that in 1969, 1970, 1971 we were at war." Nixon testified that in 1970 he had authorized a widespread domestic intelligence program (the Huston plan) involving illegal break-ins and surveillance aimed at the Black Panther Party and the Weathermen. He said that by approving this plan it "would remove the illegality as I understood it." Four days after he approved the plan, he withdrew his authorization following objections from the FBI Director. Of importance, however, is Nixon's trial statement that in withdrawing his approval he did not think he was prohibiting FBI Director Hoover from using these techniques.[49]

On November 6, 1980, Felt and Miller were convicted of having "conspired to injure and oppress the citizens of the United States" and sentenced to pay fines of $5,000 and $3,500, respectively. The indictment against Gray was later dropped. On April 15, 1981, President Reagan issued a full and unconditional pardon to both men. The pardon stated:

Their convictions in the U.S. District Court, on appeal at the time I signed the pardons, grew out of their good-faith belief that their actions were necessary to preserve the security interests of our country. The record demonstrates that they acted not with criminal intent, but in the

---

[49] Nixon testimony from Laura A. Kiernan, "Nixon Supports FBI On Break-In Authority," *Washington Post*, October 30, 1980, p. A1 and Laura A. Kiernan, "Nixon's Account: Final Chapter in FBI Aides' Trial, *Washington Post*, November 2, 1980, p. A14.

belief that they had grants of authority reaching to the highest levels of government.

America was at war in 1972, and Messrs. Felt and Miller followed procedures they believed essential to keep the Director of the FBI, the Attorney General, and the President of the United States advised of the activities of hostile foreign powers and their collaborators in this country...

Four years ago, thousands of draft evaders and others who violated the Selective Service Laws were unconditionally pardoned by my predecessor. America was generous to those who refused to serve their country in the Vietnam War. We can be no less generous to two men who acted on high principle to bring an end to the terrorism that was threatening our nation. [50]

After Miller was pardoned, former President Nixon sent him a bottle of champagne, accompanied by a personal note that read, "Justice ultimately prevailed. Congrats for sticking with it and thanks for your service to the nation."[51] Therefore, U.S. courts were indicting and convicting former FBI officials for illegal activity, while a former president, current president, and four attorneys general were condoning or forgiving this illegal activity. Of all the U.S. agencies involved in domestic surveillance operations during the Nixon administration, it was the FBI that suffered the most in terms of indictments and criminal charges against its agents and officials. Given that the FBI had the primary responsibility for addressing domestic security concerns, this is not surprising. As for an assessment of the motivations of the agents, analysts, and technicians involved in illegal domestic surveillance measures, two presidents held the view that they were honorable, if not justifiable in all cases.

After the Church Committee and Pike Committee had uncovered illegal activities in the U.S. Intelligence Community in the late 1960s and early 1970s, including the CIA's assassination operations, President Ford issued on February 18, 1976, Executive Order (EO) 11905. It was designed to end abuses by members of the intelligence community and clarify its legal authorities. It also banned political assassinations — "no employee of the United States Government shall

---

[50]"Statement on Granting Pardons to W. Mark Felt and Edward S. Miller, April 15, 1981, at http://www.reagan.utexas.edu/archives/speeches/1981/41581d.htm. Accessed February 4, 2016.

[51]Lloyd, "Edward S. Miller ...," pp. 12–13.

engage in, or conspire to engage in, political assassination." This point was a reaction to the Church Committee's hearings on the subject. The role of the director of Central Intelligence was enhanced, and the Intelligence Oversight Board was created. The Intelligence Oversight Board, which would have three presidential appointed expert members from outside the government, "would receive and consider reports by Inspectors General and General Counsels of the Intelligence Community concerning activities that raise questions of legality or propriety and periodically review the practices and procedures of the Inspectors General and General Counsels of the Intelligence Community designed to discover and report to the Oversight Board activities that raise questions of legality or propriety and review periodically with each member of the Intelligence Community their internal guidelines to ensure their adequacy."[52] Most important for the NSA, EO 11905 prohibited the intercept of communications from, or intended by, the sender to be received in, the United States, or directed against U.S. persons abroad, except "under lawful electronic surveillance under procedures approved by the Attorney General." EO 11905 also terminated several kinds of support NSA was then giving to the law enforcement community.[53] Ford also increased the membership of the Foreign Intelligence Advisory Board, established by President Eisenhower in 1956, "to meet the needs of effective oversight."[54]

NSA itself implemented stricter provisions in the process of signals intelligence to ensure compliance with all laws and to prevent abuses of power. While National Security Council Intelligence Directives and DoD Directives offered general guidance on the activities of NSA and the United States SIGINT System (USSS), more detailed guidance was provided by the director of NSA in the form of United States Signals Intelligence Directives (USSIDs).[55] USSID 18 was issued on May 26, 1976. USSIDs comprise the "constitution" of the cryptologic community, including not only NSA but also the Service Cryptologic Elements; USSIDs define all SIGINT activities and set out procedures by which they are to be conducted. USSID 18 not only defined and described the collection, processing, and storage of signals intelligence but also placed clear limits on these activities. The document clearly stated the rights of U.S. citizens and clearly

---

[52] https://www.fordlibrarymuseum.gov/library/speeches/760110e.asp#SEC5. Accessed March 3, 2017. See Sections 5 and 6.

[53] National Security Agency, *Center for Cryptologic History, United States Cryptologic History: Book III: Retrenchment and Reform, 1972–1980*, published 1999, p. 105, at https://www.nsa.gov/Portals/70/documents/news-features/declassified-documents/cryptologic-histories/cold_war_iii.pdf.

[54] https://www.fordlibrarymuseum.gov/library/document/factbook/intellig.htm. Accessed June 6, 2017.

[55] http://nsarchive.gwu.edu/NSAEBB/NSAEBB23/index.html#doc7. Accessed March 23, 2017.

prohibited any SIGINT actions that would violate those rights.[56] It is said that the NSA officials who had borne the brunt of the response to the congressional inquiries had a local trophy shop fashion a unique lapel pin for themselves — an Idaho potato with a pike through the middle. Senator Frank Church was from Idaho and the pike represented Congressman Otis G. Pike.[57]

Congress also acted to establish oversight on the intelligence community. Initially, it could not agree on a joint Senate-House committee on intelligence. However, the Senate established the Senate Select Committee on Intelligence in May 1976 and in July 1977, the House established the Permanent Select Committee on Intelligence.[58] No joint committee on intelligence was ever established. By the end of the Ford administration, it was reasonable to assume that all the illegal activities of the U.S. Intelligence Community had been exposed, safeguards introduced, and oversight established. Congressional committees, inspector generals and general councils of each intelligence agency, the Foreign Intelligence Advisory Board, Foreign Intelligence Surveillance Court, and the media were all on full alert for any breaches of legality. Given that some of the responsibility for the abuses of the intelligence agencies during the Nixon administration can be assigned to President Nixon and his staff, White House General Councils and the Attorney General's Office of Legal Council also became more vigilant, and by necessity, more innovative in their legal interpretations of executive power. More importantly, the American public became aware that top government officials and law enforcement and intelligence agencies abused their responsibilities and oaths of office. The tension between security and liberty in a democracy is a constant one that periodically tilts toward security, at the expense of liberty. This generally takes place during the emergence of domestic national security threats as a result of terrorism, civil wars, overseas wars, espionage, sabotage, subversion, and organized crime.

---

[56] Ibid.

[57] Cryptologic Almanac 50th Anniversary Series, "The Time of Investigations, Part 2 of 2," declassified by the NSA in January 2007, at https://www.nsa.gov/public_info/_files/crypto_almanac_50th/time_of_investigations_part_2.pdf. Accessed June 3, 2017.

[58] Ibid. Designating them as "select" committees meant that congressmen would not serve on them as a normal assignment but were chosen for the committee by the congressional leadership. The addition of the word "permanent" in the title of the House committee was needed, because otherwise, under House rules, select committees expire when the two-year term of the House ended. Special actions were taken to ensure that the committees would operate successfully in this sensitive area of government. First, strict rules were established for access to classified information by members and staff. Committee membership was carefully balanced among the shades of opinion about intelligence activities.

The New Field of Terrorism Analysis

Just as terrorism was a new political and security problem for governments, it was a new field of study for academics, think tanks, and government intelligence analysts. Prior to the Nixon administration, U.S. intelligence was monitoring and analyzing terrorism incidentally as part of its responsibility to follow overseas political developments, such as insurrectionary movements and their activities in places like Venezuela, Guatemala, Yemen, Algeria, and Israel. There were periodic reports like the Office of National Estimates 1968 special national intelligence estimate "Terrorism and Internal Security in Israel and Jordan" that looked at issues of terrorism in the Middle East, including state sponsorship.[59] Nevertheless, there was no substantial internal or external pressure to isolate overseas terrorism as a separate national security issue or concern. Domestically, terrorism was a foremost concern and a focus of the FBI which dedicated special units and agents to address the threat. The FBI was also monitoring Palestinian terrorism overseas for fear of spillover operations in the U.S. In June 1970, the FBI published a restricted seven-page monograph titled "The Fedayeen Terrorist — A Profile."[60] The FBI was the only government agency during the Johnson administration and early years of the Nixon administration that engaged in a focused approach to analyzing terrorists and terrorist organizations. This was carried out however by special agents and not dedicated intelligence analysts. The focus on terrorism overseas was also more tactical than strategic, more operational than analytical. This state of terrorism analysis in the government continued through Nixon's first two terms.

During the Nixon administration, there were no terrorism centers or institutes at universities, no academic courses on terrorism, no academic journals on terrorism, no government courses on terrorism for intelligence analysts, less than 50 books in English written on the subject, and only one think tank — RAND Corporation — that specifically addressed the issue for the first time in 1973.[61]

---

[59] "Terrorism Analysis in the CIA: The Gradual Awakening (1972–1980)," Declassified article, *Studies in Intelligence*, Volume 51, Issue 1, 2007, p. 20. Hereafter referred to as "Terrorism Analysis in the CIA," at http://nsarchive.gwu.edu/NSAEBB/NSAEBB431/docs/intell_ebb_017.PDF. Accessed June 23, 2017.

[60] https://www.documentcloud.org/documents/402497-doc-01-fbi-monograph-fedayeen-terrorist-june-1970.html. Accessed September 23, 2017.

[61] The first U.S. government-contracted research report on terrorism occurred in 1973 when the Department of State and the Defense Advanced Research Projects Agency (DARPA) tasked the RAND Corporation to write a study that would provide "government officials with a broad understanding of the origins, theory, strategy and tactics of modern terrorism, and identifying and exploring specific problem areas." Op. Cit., Jenkins, "RAND Research on Terrorism, p. 3.

As late as 1969, the *New York Times Index* did not include an entry for "terrorism."[62] No significant book on terrorism in English was written before 1969. As the U.S. was being targeted more often in the early 1970s and there were more high-profile terrorist attacks like the Munich Olympics, the issue attracted the attention of journalists, academics, think tanks, and government intelligence analysts. The pioneers in studying this field came primarily from the U.S. and Great Britain. They were initially reporters and counter-insurgency experts — Christopher Dobson, Brian Jenkins, Richard Clutterbuck, Walter Laqueur, David Tinnin, Edgar O'Balance, and Ovid DeMaris. There were few academics who were studying the subject. Those few were Martha Crenshaw, J. Bowyer Bell, Paul Wilkinson, and David Rapoport. The RAND Corporation was the first major think tank in the world to address the terrorism issue with Brian Jenkins, a counter-insurgency expert, as the lead researcher. Beginning in 1972, terrorism was developing into a distinct field of study as opposed to being considered a small part of the insurgency field.

During the early years of the Nixon administration, there were no government intelligence analysts who had a full-time terrorism portfolio. Country, regional, and topical analysts were writing on the subject as a corollary of their primary analytical portfolios. There were no special analytical units dedicated to monitor and analyze the terrorist threat overseas. Academically and analytically, terrorism was a disciplinary wilderness. After the attack on the Munich Olympics, the terrorism issue gradually acquired a higher priority in terms of collection and analysis in some governments around the world. There was also a more sustained interest by U.S. intelligence agencies, law enforcement agencies, and policymakers on the topic as opposed to the previous episodic concerns. The CCCT was tasked in late 1972 by Nixon to "coordinate, among the government agencies ... the collection of intelligence worldwide" on terrorism. When this responsibility devolved from the committee to its working group, that group became the driver for collection and analysis. The CIA was logically the agency that had to take the lead in this endeavor — both operationally and analytically.

In the 1960s, the Directorate of Intelligence (DI) in the CIA was collecting on and analyzing insurgencies around the world, especially those that had a direct or indirect impact on U.S. foreign policy and national security interests. What was called "terrorism" in the early 1970s was subsumed in this insurgency portfolio. The analytical insights and frameworks and skills acquired in analyzing

---

[62] Paul Wilkinson. *Terrorism and the Liberal State*, review by Thomas N. Thompson http://worldview. carnegiecouncil.org/archive/worldview/1978/10/3117.html/_res/id=sa_File1/v21_i010_a017.pdf. Accessed March 23, 2017.

these insurgencies were useful in addressing the problem of international terrorism that emerged in the late 1960s. In the early 1970s, terrorism was analytically addressed in the agency by country or regional analysts. In July 1972, the agency created a small "international terrorism group" (ITG) that was designated as "the focal point for information on terrorist groups and individuals." It received reinforced staff support from the various area divisions in the agency. As a result of the September 1972 terrorist attack on the Olympic Games in Munich and the subsequent Nixon establishment of the CCCT, the CIA, as well as other U.S. government agencies, raised the priority for the collection and analysis on terrorism.[63]

In September 1972, the Secretary of State sent a memo to the CIA director stating that the CIA "had a key role to play in providing 'accurate' and timely information about the terrorists ..." and that "we would find useful additional CIA analytical studies on terrorist organizations."[64]

In a September 20, 1972 set of briefing notes for the DCI from the DDI titled "CIA Role on Terrorism: DDI Activities," an assessment of CIA's current approach on terrorism was provided:

Regarding finished intelligence production, the Agency deals with the problem of terrorism on a regional geographic basis by analysts trained in covering a wide range of activities in the countries they specialize on. We will stick with this system and supplement it by adding a specialist on terrorism.

The careful scrutiny we have given to insurgencies all over the world during the last few years has given us insights and skills that have proven useful in analyzing problems of terrorism as well.

The recent increase in the use of terrorism has been reflected in our current reporting in daily intelligence production. We have also produced some specific studies over the last three months.

---

[63] CIA, Memorandum for the Record, Subject: Proposed Study on Terrorism, written by Dr. John R. Tietjen, Director of Medical Services, dated July 16, 1973. (CIA CREST system document number RDP78-05077A000100120020-8); CIA, Memorandum from Thomas H. Karamessines, Deputy Director for Plans to the Director, Subject: Cabinet Committee on Terrorism, dated September 28, 1976. (CIA CREST system document number RDP-80B01495R001400010005-1); CIA, Briefing Memorandum, Subject: CIA Role on Terrorism: DDI Activities, written by blacked out, dated September 30, 1972. (CIA CREST system document number RDP-80B01495R001400010004-2).

[64] "Terrorism Analysis in the CIA," p. 21.

a. *Following the Lod airport massacre in June, we produced an intelligence memorandum on the fedayeen and their ties with foreign terrorists...*

b. *In July we took a close look at Uruguay's Tupamaros movement...*

c. *Last week we surveyed the recent use of terror against U.S. business firms overseas...*

d. *Last week, we examined terrorist activities by the Ustashi or Croatian separatist terrorists, as reflecting a significant force within as well as outside Yugoslavia today.*

We plan to increase and intensify our attention to the terrorist problem in future intelligence production. We are surveying our own holdings of information on various terrorist groups around the world.... We are also taking stock of the adequacy of our analytical talent to meet the responsibility of a greater effort on terrorism, and we shall beef up our analytical capability wherever there might be a need to do so.[65]

In November 1972, the CIA's Directorate of Operations (DO) published a serial publication on terrorism titled "Weekly Situation Report on International Terrorism" (WSRIT). The WSRIT received input from the FBI and other agencies; listed terrorist events that intelligences sources say would or might occur; reviewed past terrorist events for lessons learned; and analyzed past terrorist activities as a means of predicting future operations. The WSRIT expanded its readership and analytical importance over time. It became the leading intelligence publication on terrorism-related events in the U.S. government. The WSRIT remained a DO product until October 1982 when it was transferred to the DI and changed its name to the "Terrorism Review." Within the CIA, the DO became the leading component in the agency's counter-terrorism program as the issue was perceived to be more of an operational and collection problem than an analytical issue. An example of the CIA's operational focus on terrorism was the Questioned Documents Laboratory and every other component of the Technical Support Directorate. The first Office of Technical Services (OTS) officer given a counter-terrorism portfolio was Pat Jameson, who was also the first OTS officer assigned to Vietnam and Laos. Jameson took what he learned from insurgent target analysis and planning paramilitary operations and applied it to terrorist operations and travel. Early OTS counter-terrorism operations involved "putting audio

---

[65]CIA FOIA document # RDP80B01495R001400010004-2.

devices into residences and offices of suspected terrorists," mostly in Western Europe.[66]

It was under the Ford administration that the academic, think tank, and government analysis of terrorism really began to advance as the terrorist attacks that took place under the Nixon administration convinced these communities that the overseas terrorist threat was not a short-term issue. Analytic resources and methods had to be deployed and developed to address and study it — both inside and outside the government. During the Nixon years, the U.S. government relied on the RAND Corporation for studies on terrorism. As previously noted, after the March 1973 Khartoum attack, the administration contracted with the RAND Corporation in October 1973 to assess the no negotiations policy of the U.S. The Working Group of the CCCT also relied on RAND for outside advice and research on terrorism issues. The U.S. government's analytical cadre on terrorism was small and inexperienced, and it took time to build up a larger and dedicated core of terrorism specialists. It is interesting to note that the government's first unclassified research study on terrorism, "International and Transnational Terrorism: Diagnosis and Prognosis," published in April 1976, sourced in the section "Establishing An Analytical Framework," included many of the reigning academic and think tank experts on terrorism: Ted Robert Gurr, Brian Jenkins, Paul Wilkinson, Martha Hutchinson (Crenshaw), Robert Moss, Brian Crozier, and Thomas Thornton. The USG analytical community had not yet established its own framework for assessing terrorism and the terrorism threat and logically built on those constructed in the academic and think tank communities.

It was also under the Ford administration that the first course for anti-terrorism/counter-terrorism for U.S. law enforcement was developed. This occurred in 1975 when Jim Stinson, wrote and ran the course at the California Specialized Training Institute (CSTI) while he was on leave from the California Department of Justice Directors Office. The course was 44-hours long, was federally funded, and had attendees from all the federal agencies. Stinson then designed and ran a specialized version for the USSS, NSA, and other federal agencies.[67] The next major terrorism training course was developed in the late 1970s by the U.S. Air Force at Hurlburt Field, Florida. It was called the "Dynamics of International Terrorism" course and was open to terrorism analysts from the federal government. Stinson helped develop this course based on his CSTI course which was modified to address "international terrorism."

---

[66]Robert Wallace and H. Keith Melton, *Spycraft: The Secret History of the CIA's Spytechs from Communism to al-Qaeda* (New York: Dutton, 2006), p. 323.

[67]February 6, 2018 email communication from Jim Stinson.

During the Ford administration, there were less than two dozen people in the U.S. government who were analytically and operationally focused full time on terrorism.[68] On August 18, 1976, the Director of Central Intelligence, George Bush appointed Cord Meyer Jr. to act as a CIA central point of contact for the State Department on intelligence relating to terrorism. Meyer managed and linked relevant CIA offices that could be involved in current or future research on terrorism: the Office of Political Research (OPR), the Office of Medical Services, the Office of Scientific Intelligence (OSI), the OTS, and the Office of Research and Development.[69] This was the agency's initial step in mobilizing house assets to focus on terrorism. Robert Kupperman was the chief scientist at the U.S. Arms Control and Disarmament Agency in 1975. In that role, he directed three top-secret studies at the end of that year and in early 1976. The studies examined the likely effects of a weapon of mass destruction terrorist attack on the United States. On May 21, 1975 the Working Group of the CCCT established an inter-agency Study Group, chaired by Kupperman, to examine possible terrorist threats or attacks involving nuclear, chemical, or biological weapons of mass destruction. The Study Group's report, submitted on September 17, 1975, effectively identified the issues involved in the USG's seeking to prevent, and if prevention failed, successfully dealing with such threats or attacks.[70] His third classified study was on "An Overview of Counter-Terrorism Technology."[71] Kupperman became a

---

[68] The author joined the State Department's Threat Analysis Group in January 1977 and spoke with many intelligence analysts in various government agencies at the time concerning tips on how to analyze terrorist threats and organizations. There were no USG courses on terrorism for intelligence analysts at the time. It was all on the job training.

[69] "Terrorism Analysis in the CIA," p. 24.

[70] Department of State, Office of the Historian. Foreign Relations of the United States, 1969–1976, Volume E-3, Documents on Global Issues, 1973–1976, Document 227, Briefing Memorandum from the Special Assistant to Secretary and Coordinator for Combatting Terrorism (Feary) to Secretary of State Kissinger Washington, June 1, 1976, at https://history.state.gov/historicaldocuments/frus1969-76ve03/d227. Accessed June 6, 2017. See also Department of State, Office of the Historian. Foreign Relations of the United States, 1969–1976, Volume E-3, Documents on Global Issues, 1973–1976, Document 223, Executive Summary, Mass Destruction Terrorism Study, Washington, September 17, 1975, at https://history.state.gov/historicaldocuments/frus1969-76ve03/d223. Accessed September 23, 2017; and https://www.cia.gov/library/readingroom/docs/LOC-HAK-74-2-17-9.pdf. Accessed May 16, 2016.

[71] Robert Kupperman testimony at Hearings Before the Committee on Governmental Affairs, U.S. Senate, 95th Congress, 2nd Session, on S. 2236 — An Act to Combat International Terrorism, Hearings held on January 23, 25, 27, 30 and February 22, and March 22, 23, 1978, pp. 129–144, at https://www.ncjrs.gov/pdffiles1/Digitization/54170NCJRS.pdf. Accessed June 3, 2017.

dedicated advocate for preparing the U.S. for such attacks and defending the key U.S. infrastructures from terrorist attacks.

As noted in chapter one, the CIA's OPR issued its first unclassified research study on international terrorism in April 1976 titled "International and Transnational Terrorism: Diagnosis and Prognosis." During the Nixon administration, the CIA also started to produce the WSRIT. The annual report and the WSRIT were the two most important analytical publications on terrorism in the U.S. government during the Nixon and Ford administrations.

Like the CIA, there was no dedicated terrorism analytical unit in the DIA during the Nixon and Ford administrations. The issue was subsumed in country and regional desk officer's portfolios at DIA. The agency had an interest in terrorism given the number of terrorist attacks on U.S. military personnel overseas. From 1968 to 1977, 14 U.S. military personnel were killed by terrorists in Guatemala, Brazil, Ethiopia, Philippines, Jordan, West Germany, and Iran. The terrorism issue however was marginal, given the agency's counter-insurgency concerns in South Vietnam.

NSA's initial involvement in collecting on terrorism intelligence began around 1967 when the CIA submitted requirements for "watch lists" dealing with acts of terrorism and the White House and FBI requirements for "watch lists" of foreign influence over domestic groups.[72] The National Security Agency did not respond organizationally to the terrorist threat as quickly as the CIA due to the nature of terrorist communications. Terrorist SIGINT was different than conventional SIGINT of governments, corporations, police, and the military. Terrorists lacked dedicated communications systems. In the first half of the 1970s, terrorist group communications were ad hoc and involved messengers, landline calls, and dead drops. The larger terrorist organizations and insurgent organizations like the PLO did have dedicated networks in command posts that used the same devices and frequencies. In addition, given the volume of SIGINT being swept and the subtlety of terrorist communications, the prospect of picking out the needles of terrorist transmissions in this haystack was daunting. In 1973, the NSA created a unit whose task was specifically international terrorism. Within the "G" Group, the NSA established a branch-level organization, G77, known as "Designated Topics." These included nuclear proliferation, arms trade, and international finance. In addition to terrorism, G77 was responsible for security for Secret

---

[72] Statement of Lt. General Lew Allen, Jr., Director of National Security Agency before the Senate Select Committee on Intelligence, October 29, 1975, pp. VI-2 and VI-6, at https://www.nsa.gov/news-features/declassified-documents/nsa-60th-timeline/assets/files/1970s/19751029_1970_Doc_3978970_LewAllen.pdf. Accessed June 6, 2017.

Service protectees, nuclear proliferation, alternate energy, advanced technology, and other issues. Within the division, a branch, G772, was organized to handle some special projects, one of which was international terrorism. In 1976, G77 was dissolved and replaced by a new organization, G11, the Synthesis Reporting Division, which started publishing a weekly Summary of International Terrorist Activity (SITA). This reporting vehicle culled all G Group reports for items dealing with terrorist activity. The SITA continued into the early 1990s.[73]

In the State Department, reporting on terrorism was carried out by desk officers and Bureau of Intelligence and Research analysts as part of their country/regional/topical portfolios. Overseas, the reporting came from the embassy and consulate political officers and occasional reports from the embassy regional security officers. In June 1976, State's Office of Security (SY) established a small four-person "Threat Analysis Group" (TAG) that had the responsibility to assess security threats to SY-protected foreign dignitaries, the Secretary of State, U.S. diplomatic facilities overseas, and U.S. business interests overseas. Given that the security threat to these components was primarily terrorism, TAG essentially developed into a terrorism analysis unit — one of the first in the government dedicated to monitoring and analyzing terrorism both at home and abroad. Given that SY had protective security responsibilities for all U.S. diplomatic facilities and personnel overseas, the increase in resources and responsibilities of SY paralleled the increase in the overseas terrorist threat. TAG was a logical extension of this growth as a unit was needed to assist SY in prioritizing the allocation of its protective security resources overseas and to identify terrorist threats to the Secretary of State and other department officials and to SY-protected foreign dignitaries visiting the U.S. TAG was unique in that it had legitimate analytical and threat assessment responsibilities to monitor terrorism at home and abroad. By the end of the Ford administration in January 1977, the major analytical players in terrorism were in CIA, FBI, State Department, and Air Force Office of Special Investigations (AFOSI). AFOSI special agents, at U.S. Air Force bases in

---

[73] Section on NSA from National Security Agency, Center for Cryptologic History, Cryptologic Almanac 50th Anniversary Series, "The First Round: NSA's Effort against International Terrorism in the 1970s," by Robert J. Hanyok at https://www.nsa.gov/news-features/declassified-documents/crypto-almanac-50th/assets/files/The_First_Round.pdf. Accessed June 3, 2017; and National Security Agency, Center for Cryptologic History, "United States Cryptologic History: Series VI — The NSA Period 1952–Present, Volume 5," by Thomas R. Johnson, published in 1999, Chapter 23 — The Rise of Terrorism and Unconventional Targets in the 1980s, at https://www.scrib.com/documents/344732541/170412-HIS-Cryptology. Accessed October 23, 2017.

Western Europe and in Asia, were excellent reporters of terrorist developments in their respective countries.[74]

The analysis of the domestic and overseas terrorist threat in the U.S. Secret Service was the responsibility of its Intelligence Division (ID). The ID began to follow terrorist developments overseas more closely when the Secret Service was given protective responsibility for National Security Council Director Kissinger in 1969. Kissinger made frequent trips to the Middle East at a time when Palestinian terrorism was increasing. Beginning in 1970, the Secret Service EPS, under Public Law 91-217, was assigned protective responsibility for diplomatic facilities in the Washington, D.C. area.[75] This law also authorized the president to assign EPS officers to other areas of the country on a case-by-case basis to safeguard foreign missions. This was mostly used with foreign missions in New York City. For example, after the September 1972 attack by Palestinian terrorists on Israeli athletes at the Munich Olympics, the Nixon administration asked the EPS to provide increased protection for Israeli, Arab, German, and Soviet diplomatic and consular establishments against attacks by the JDL or other groups. In response to Mayor Lindsay's request to the president for federal assistance, 40 Secret Service and EPS officers were made available to man 23 fixed posts in New York City.[76] Given these types of threat situations, the ID followed, along with the FBI, foreign spillover terrorism in the U.S. from Croatian, Serbian, Armenian, and Cuban exile terrorists. From 1973 to 1977, the Secret Service also assumed protective responsibility for Kissinger when he was Secretary of State. Kissinger is the only modern Secretary of State who was not protected by State's SY, now known as the Diplomatic Security Service. It was the Secret Service and SY that provided security details for all visiting foreign dignitaries and guests to the U.S. While the FBI had the primary responsibility for domestic terrorism, the USSS and SY were active monitors of that environment and were the primary authors of protective security "threat assessments."

---

[74] The author, who had responsibility for monitoring terrorism in Western Europe for the State Department from 1977 to the early 1990s, can testify to the excellent reporting on terrorism by OSI agents in Western Europe.

[75] The EPS was formerly known as the White House Police Force (WHPF). In 1977, the EPS was renamed the Secret Service Uniformed Division. The WHPF and EPS were under the U.S. Secret Service.

[76] Memorandum from the Secretary of State Rogers to President Nixon, Washington, September 18, 1972. Foreign Relations of the United States, 1969–1976, Volume E-1, Documents on Global Issues, 1969–1972, Document 102, at https://history.state.gov/historicaldocuments/frus1969-76ve01/d102. Accessed May 23, 2018.

Terrorist threat assessment became a prominent sub-category in the analysis of terrorism in the 1970s.

The problem in any new field of study is to determine how to approach it? Are there other fields that could help in understanding the new field, such as sociology, psychology, and political science? In terms of political terrorism, there was already scholarship on insurgencies and guerrilla movements. Terrorism was initially considered to be a sub-category of insurgency so there were already definitions, components, typologies, tactical menus, targeting patters, and analytical frameworks to apply. For large-scale insurgencies, terrorism was simply a tactic to be used in certain situations. The problem in the late 1960s and early 1970s was that smaller terrorist groups were emerging in which terrorism was a strategy, not just a tactic. These were the urban terrorist groups that were forming mostly in Western Europe and to a lesser extent in Latin America. It was easier to track larger, rural-based insurgencies that had several thousand members than the small, urban-based terrorist groups that had several hundred members or less. The latter had no training camps or controlled territory, had smaller organization units, were less centralized, had no dedicated communication systems, and refrained from direct contact with larger police or military units. Defining terrorism was and continues to be a problem, although that was and remains more of a concern to academics than governments. Were there different types of terrorist groups? How were they different in terms of goals, ideology, strategy, tactics, operational code, targeting patterns, propaganda, operational area, constituency, and organizational structure? What were the primary sources, methods, narratives of the group's announcements, and communiqués to its constituency, members, supporters, sympathizers, and the domestic and international publics? What content analysis techniques should be used on these communications?

Other questions to be considered were what was the group's gross operational product? This consisted of the group's operational tempo (frequency of attacks per quarter); quality of attacks (security level around target, tactics, manpower deployed, professionalism/skill level of operatives, political impact); sustainability (how long has the operational tempo been maintained — quarters/ years); operational area (geographic scope of operations); ability to attack in capitals; and ratio of plots to attacks (how many plots had been uncovered [due to internal vs. external factors] compared to attacks implemented [failed vs. successful]?). Did the group have any unique surveillance techniques or ruses and disguises? Did it carry out discriminate or indiscriminate attacks? What are the group's operational restraints? Does the group unintentionally telegraph its next attack target in its communiques? Did it adhere to certain operational patterns in terms of tactics, timing, target, and location of attacks? Did it maintain contact with other terrorist organizations at home or abroad? All the above questions had to be addressed by an intelligence analyst who was analyzing terrorism for the first time. The problem was that the above questions were not formally taught in any government intelligence analysis courses or in any academic course on terrorism.[77] A government intelligence analyst assigned to analyzing terrorism had to develop his/her own individual approach to the issue that was shaped by his/her educational background, previous analytical experience, specific agency responsibilities, and mentor training if available. There were no information technology aids for government intelligence analysts except for the rare database. This was the decade of the 3×5 card file, and hard copy intelligence reports, telegrams, Airgrams, and wire service reports. Analysts used typewriters and carbon paper, and hundreds of paper files for storage.

---

[77] The author developed these questions from 1977 to 1979 when he was given the terrorism portfolio for Western Europe in the State Department's Threat Analysis Group. Some of the questions were extracted from studies and books on terrorism by RAND Corporation and academics. Others were developed to complete specific analytical, protective security, and threat assessment responsibilities. Analytical exchanges with other agency analysts also produced new analytical approaches and metrics. U.S. government intelligence analysts with terrorism responsibilities during the late 1970s were not formally instructed on how to analyze terrorism.

94TH CONGRESS 2d Session	SENATE	REPORT No. 94-755

FOREIGN AND MILITARY INTELLIGENCE

BOOK I

FINAL REPORT

OF THE

SELECT COMMITTEE
TO STUDY GOVERNMENTAL OPERATIONS

WITH RESPECT TO

INTELLIGENCE ACTIVITIES
UNITED STATES SENATE

TOGETHER WITH

ADDITIONAL, SUPPLEMENTAL, AND SEPARATE
VIEWS

APRIL 26 (legislative day, APRIL 14), 1976

U.S. GOVERNMENT PRINTING OFFICE
69-983 O   WASHINGTON : 1976

For sale by the Superintendent of Documents, U.S. Government Printing Office
Washington, D.C. 20402 - Price $5.35

Stock No. 052-071-00470-0

Senate Committee investigation into domestic surveillance abuses by U.S. military intelligence.

Source: Wikimedia commons.

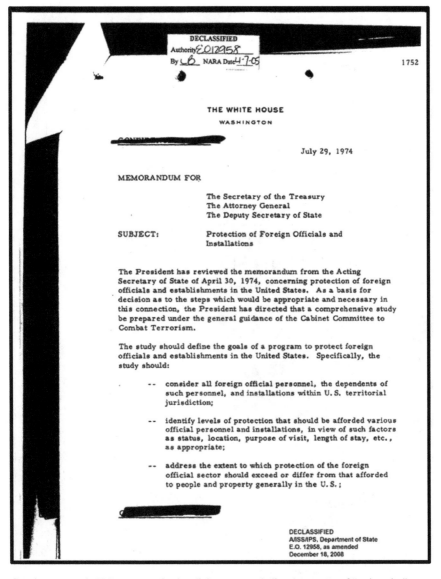

DECLASSIFIED
Authority *E O 12958*
By *L B* NARA Date *4-7-05*

1752

THE WHITE HOUSE
WASHINGTON

July 29, 1974

MEMORANDUM FOR

The Secretary of the Treasury
The Attorney General
The Deputy Secretary of State

SUBJECT: Protection of Foreign Officials and Installations

The President has reviewed the memorandum from the Acting Secretary of State of April 30, 1974, concerning protection of foreign officials and establishments in the United States. As a basis for decision as to the steps which would be appropriate and necessary in this connection, the President has directed that a comprehensive study be prepared under the general guidance of the Cabinet Committee to Combat Terrorism.

The study should define the goals of a program to protect foreign officials and establishments in the United States. Specifically, the study should:

-- consider all foreign official personnel, the dependents of such personnel, and installations within U.S. territorial jurisdiction;

-- identify levels of protection that should be afforded various official personnel and installations, in view of such factors as status, location, purpose of visit, length of stay, etc., as appropriate;

-- address the extent to which protection of the foreign official sector should exceed or differ from that afforded to people and property generally in the U.S.;

DECLASSIFIED
A/ISS/IPS, Department of State
E.O. 12958, as amended
December 18, 2008

Growing concern in U.S. to protect foreign diplomats to underline the concept of "reciprocity."

Source: CIA FOIA reading room.

June 1975

Report to the President
by the
COMMISSION ON CIA ACTIVITIES WITHIN THE UNITED STATES

President Ford's Commission on CIA Activities within the United States, also known as the Rockefeller Commission.

Source: CIA FOIA reading room.

First issue of the CIA's "Weekly Situation Report on International Terrorism."

Source: CIA FOIA reading room.

Research Study

International and Transnational Terrorism:
Diagnosis and Prognosis

PR 76 10030
April 1976

First unclassified publication of a major CIA study on international terrorism.

Source: CIA FOIA reading room.

September 23, 1976 — President Gerald Ford and Jimmy Carter meet at the Walnut Street Theater in Philadelphia to debate domestic policy during the first of the three Ford-Carter Debates.

Source: Gerald R. Ford Presidential Library.

On June 16, 1976, recently appointed Ambassador Frank Meloy (on left), along with Economic Counselor Robert Waring, were kidnapped by the Popular Front for the Liberation of Palestine. Both Meloy and Waring, along with the driver, were killed.

Source: U.S. Department of State.

Chapter 7

The Carter Administration (1977–1980) — The Overseas Threat

Overview

Terrorism was not a major issue during the 1976 presidential campaign between President Ford and Jimmy Carter. In his 2,932-worded address accepting the presidential nomination at the Democratic National Convention in New York City on July 15, 1976, Carter devoted one short sentence to terrorism — "Peace is action to stamp out international terrorism." What was an election issue, however, was government behavior toward its own citizens as Carter and the Democrats were tarring Ford and the Republicans with the government abuses under the Nixon administration. In his July 15 address, Carter stated:

"It is time for our government leaders to respect the law no less than the humblest citizen, so that we can end once and for all a double standard of justice."

"We can have an American government that does not oppress or spy on its own people but respects our dignity and our privacy and our right to be let alone."

"But in recent years our nation has seen a failure of leadership. We have been hurt, and we have been disillusioned. We have seen a wall go up that separates us from our own government."

> *"The embarrassment of the CIA revelations could have been avoided if our government had simply reflected the sound judgement and good common sense and the high moral character of the American people."*[1]

Having won the election, Carter also did not mention terrorism in his January 20, 1977 Inaugural Address. As with the Nixon and Ford administrations, the terrorism issue — at home and abroad, was not a major national security or foreign policy issue for Carter. According to National Security Council staff member William Odom, referring to Carter's National Security Advisor Zbigniew Brzezinski, "Brzezinski did not believe that terrorism was a strategic issue."[2] In addition, Admiral Stansfield Turner, the director of Central Intelligence at the time, noted that terrorism "was not a great deal of concern."[3] In an April 1977 memo to President Carter from Brzezinski in which he outlined "ten central objectives for the next four years," terrorism, directly or indirectly, was not mentioned.[4] It was a periodic irritant that at times had to be addressed. Carter's major

---

[1] All quotations from http://www.presidency.ucsb.edu/ws/index.php?pid=25953&st=Terrorism&st1=. Accessed September 21, 2017.

[2] As quoted in Naftali, *Blind Spot*, p. 101. In fact, in Brzezinski's 569-page memoir *Power and Principle: Memoirs of the National Security Adviser 1977–1981*, terrorism is mentioned once, on p. 84. Even when he mentions how the Carter administration was concerned about the possibility of the Italian Communist Party taking power in Italy — the infamous "Historic Compromise" — he does not mention the March 1978 kidnapping of Aldo Moro, a key leader of the Christian Democratic Party, by Red Brigade (RB) terrorists and their subsequent murder of Moro (pp. 312–313). The RB also opposed the "Historic Compromise" so the U.S. and Brigades had the same goal. The immediate consequence of the kidnapping was the exclusion of the communist party from any government cabinet in the following years.

[3] As quoted in Ibid., p. 102.

[4] U.S. Department of State, Office of the Historian, "Foreign Relations of the United States, 1977–1980, Volume I, Foundations of Foreign Policy, Document 36, Memorandum from the President's Assistant for National Security Affairs (Brzezinski) to President Carter, Washington, April 29, 1977, titled Four-Year Goals: Preliminary Statement. Brzezinski outlines "ten central objectives for the next four years," at https://history.state.gov/historicaldocuments/frus1977-80v01/d36. Accessed July 18, 2017. In addition, see U.S. Department of State, Office of the Historian, "Foreign Relations of the United States, 1977–1980, Volume I, Foundations of Foreign Policy, Document 24, Action Memorandum from the Director of the Policy Planning Staff (Lake) to Secretary of State Vance, February 24, 1977, Subject: Topics for Discussion at Cabinet Meetings. In response to the President asking cabinet members to "discuss interesting concepts or functions of their departments" during cabinet meetings, Anthony Lake proposed several topics for Vance to bring up. One was titled the "new global roster" in which he listed a "range of new and expanding concerns (energy, food, population, environment, science and technology, North-South dialogue) and upcoming events that will affect them (CIEC, LOS conference, UN Special Session) which demand the Department's attention." Terrorism was not listed. See also, media interviews and speeches, for example — Speech at an Organization of American States meeting on April 14, 1977; Address before U.N. General Assembly

problems were an economic crisis produced by rising energy prices and stagfla-
tion, the Panama Canal, the Middle East, the Soviet invasion of Afghanistan, the
1979 seizure of 52 American diplomats at the U.S. Embassy in Tehran, human
rights, and the 1979 oil crisis. Carter's national security team consisted of his
National Security Advisor Zbigniew Brzezinski, Secretary of State Cyrus Vance,
Secretary of Defense Harold Brown, and CIA Director Admiral Stansfield Turner.

In terms of the internal terrorist threat, the domestic terrorist groups that were
active under the Ford administration persisted under Carter, although several
faded away during the Carter administration. During the Carter administration,
19 people were killed in internal terrorist attacks. The most noteworthy domestic
terrorist attacks were the hostage-taking incident in Washington, D.C. in March
1977 by Hanafi Muslim gunmen; the bombing of a Department of Defense building in New York City in August 1977 by Puerto Rican terrorists that killed one
person; the murders of five African American workers in Greensboro, North
Carolina in November 1979 by members of the Ku Klux Klan and the American
Nazi Party; and the murder of three U.S. sailors in Puerto Rico in December 1979
by Puerto Rican terrorists. The foreign spillover terrorist threat also continued
under Carter with the assassination of Ali Akbar Tabatabai, an Iranian exile and
critic of Ayatollah Khomeini, in Bethesda, Maryland in July 1980 by an Iranian
hitman; and the assassination of Felix Garcia Rodriguez, a Cuban diplomat
assigned to the Cuban Mission to the U.N., in New York City in September 1980
by anti-Castro, Cuban exiles.

While the Nixon and Ford administrations were confronted with an overseas
terrorist threat emanating from secular Palestinian terrorists and left-wing terrorists, the Carter administration was faced with these two terrorist threats and two
new ones: state-sponsored terrorism and Islamic revolutionary terrorism. During
the Carter administration, 39 Americans died overseas in terrorist incidents. The
most noteworthy anti-American overseas terrorist attacks were the murder of the
niece of U.S. Senator Abraham Ribicoff in Israel in March 1978 by Palestinian
terrorists; the kidnapping/murder of the U.S. ambassador to Afghanistan in

---

on October 4, 1977; Interview with President Carter with Editors and Broadcasters on October 10,
1979; a March 25, 1979 News Conference; and Interview with Bill Moyers of the Public Broadcasting
Service on November 13, 1978. All can be found at http://www.presidency.ucsb.edu/ws/
index.php?pid=30161&st=Terrorism&st1. Accessed March 11, 2018. https://history.state.gov/
historicaldocuments/frus1977-80v01/d24. Accessed September 6, 2016; and U.S. Department of
State, Office of the Historian, "Foreign Relations of the United States, 1977–1980, Volume I,
Foundations of Foreign Policy, Document 29. Address by President Carter before the United Nations
General Assembly, New York, March 17, 1977. This was the first address by Carter to the U.N. — no
mention of terrorism, at https://history.state.gov/historicaldocuments/frus1977-80v01/d29. Accessed
June 17, 2016.

February 1979 by Islamic revolutionary terrorists; the murder of three Catholic nuns and a social worker in El Salvador in December 1980 by right-wing Salvadorian National Guard members; and the assassinations of four Americans in Istanbul, Turkey in December 1979 by Turkish left-wing terrorists.

As in the Nixon/Ford administrations, the most active terrorist regions for anti-American terrorism during the Carter administration were Western Europe and Latin America. The primary anti-American terrorism actors were left-wing terrorist groups and insurgent organizations in Western Europe and Latin America, and militant Palestinian organizations from the Middle East. Internally, the Carter administration was faced with domestic terrorism from Puerto Rican separatist terrorists, as well as left-wing terrorist organizations such as the United Freedom Front, the Weather Underground Organization, the New World Liberation Front, the George Jackson Brigade, and the May 19 Communist Organization; as well as foreign spillover terrorism from militant Cuban exiles, Croatian and Serbian militants, Armenian émigré groups, and the Jewish Defense League.

In response to this evolving terrorist threat at home and abroad, Carter modified some of the Nixon/Ford counter-terrorism policies, changed the government's counter-terrorism organizational structure, and added some counter-terrorism tools and measures. The Carter administration did advance the U.S. counter-terrorism program but only incrementally. The administration perceived the nature, level, and scope of the internal and external terrorist threat in a certain way and acted accordingly. Ironically, while international terrorism overseas was not a major security problem for the Carter administration, two international events in 1979 — the overthrow of the Shah of Iran by Islamic revolutionaries and the Soviet invasion of Afghanistan — created environments conducive for the emergence of a new strain of anti-American terrorism; Islamic revolutionary terrorism. The Shia version of this strain caused major security problems for the U.S. in the 1980s and the Sunni version produced al-Qaeda in the 1990s and the Islamic State in Iraq and Syria in the 2010s.

The Record

Overseas Terrorist Threat

Left-Wing Terrorist Threat

The left-wing terrorist threat against U.S. interests overseas continued during the Carter administration. Like the Nixon/Ford administrations, left-wing terrorism during the Carter administration was centered in Western Europe and Latin

America, where these groups attacked U.S. diplomatic, military, business targets and private U.S. citizens. The tactics employed were primarily bombings and assassinations and were generally discriminate in nature. U.S. military and business targets were attacked the most. During the Carter administration there were 41 major left-wing terrorist groups active in the world — 23 in Latin America, 16 in Western Europe, one in Asia, and one in the Middle East. Of the 39 Americans killed overseas in terrorist incidents from 1977 to 1980, 20 were killed by left-wing terrorists in Mexico (one), Argentina (one), Iran (two), Turkey (nine), Guatemala (one), El Salvador (four), and the Philippines (two). These 20 deaths consisted of five U.S. military personnel, four private U.S. citizens, three DOD contractors, and eight U.S. businesspersons. Five Americans were also killed by right-wing terrorist groups in El Salvador and Guatemala.

The primary triggers for these attacks were: (1) U.S. support for military or dictatorial regimes in Latin America, the Philippines, and Iran, and (2) the stationing of U.S. military personnel and bases in Western Europe, Latin America, Asia, and Iran. This U.S. military footprint in these countries was seen by militant leftists as "forces of occupation" and indicative of the imperialist agenda of the U.S. The governments of these countries were perceived to be "collaborators" with the U.S. in return for U.S. military and economic assistance. This was a major complaint of European left-wing terrorist groups.

Western Europe

During the Carter administration, Western Europe continued to have one of the most active terrorist environments in the world. In the decade of the 1970s, 38% of all international terrorist incidents and 39% of all anti-American terrorist incidents worldwide took place in Western Europe. Many of the left-wing terrorist groups that operated during the Nixon and Ford administrations continued their activities during the Carter administration. In addition to left-wing groups, ethnonational and Palestinian terrorist organizations were also active in the region. The following left-wing terrorist groups were active in Western Europe during the Carter administration:

- Red Army Faction (RAF) in West Germany;
- Movement 2 June in West Germany;
- Red Brigades (RB) in Italy;
- Angry Brigade in Great Britain;

- The Liberation Army of the Workers and Peasants of Turkey, the armed wing of the Communist Party of Turkey/Marxist–Leninist (TKP/ML) in Turkey;
- Turkish People's Liberation Army (TPLA);
- Revolutionary Cells (RZ) in Germany;
- Revolutionary Popular Struggle (ELA) in Greece;
- Revolutionary Organization 17 November (17N) in Greece;
- First of October/Anti-Fascist Resistance Groups (GRAPO) in Spain;
- Revolutionary Patriotic Anti-Fascist Front (FRAP) in Spain;
- Prima Linea in Italy;
- Revolutionary Left (Dev Sol) in Turkey, later renamed Revolutionary People's Liberation Party-Front;
- International Revolutionary Action Group in France, Spain, and Belgium;
- Direct Action in France;
- Marxist–Leninist Armed Propaganda Unit (MLAPU) in Turkey.

While there were anti-American terrorist groups operating in most Western European countries, the countries where the U.S. faced the most serious domestic terrorist threat were Germany, Spain, Turkey, and Greece.

Germany

Germany faced an acute domestic terrorist threat during the late 1970s.[5] This was due primarily to the activities of the RAF — the most active and dangerous left-wing terrorist organization in Germany. The RAF was a small group consisting of between 18 and 25 hardcore members with hundreds of supporters and sympathizers. For a small urban terrorist group, its tactics and targets were audacious. The primary objective for the RAF at the time was to force the release of its remaining imprisoned historical leadership — Andreas Baader, Gudrun Ensslin, and Jan-Carl Raspe. In April 1977, the RAF assassinated Siegfried Buback, the

---

[5] See, for example, Paul Hoffmann, "Europe Fears Holiday Terrorism," *New York Times*, December 14, 1977, p. 8; Paul Hoffman, "Germans Tighten Flight Security in Face of Threats to Lufthansa," *New York Times*, November 16, 1977, p. A3; and Paul Lewis, "Business Leaders in Germany Hiding," *New York Times*, September 18, 1977, p. 18. Lewis's article notes that "the corporate leaders of Europe's richest country have gone underground ... the politicians are hiding behind a vast deployment of barbed wire, armored cars, and policemen with machine guns ... a finance ministry high official lists terrorism as a factor contributing to what he termed German industry's lack of confidence in the future and its reluctance to invest ... there is no doubt that the terrorist wave has become a national obsession."

chief federal prosecutor of the imprisoned RAF leaders, in Karlsruhe. This was a pure punishment operation. The RAF code for the attack was "Operation Margarine."[6] In July 1977, the RAF attempted to kidnap Jurgen Ponto, the chairman of the Board of Directors of the Dresdner Bank, from his home in Oberursel. The kidnapping failed, and Ponto was killed in his home. Internally, the RAF referred to this operation as "Big Money." The apex of the RAF prisoner liberation campaign came in September 1977 when the group kidnapped Dr. Hanns-Martin Schleyer, the president of the German Employers Association and the Federation of Germany Industry, a board member of Daimler-Benz, and a personal friend of then West German Chancellor Helmut Schmidt, in Cologne by ambushing his two-car motorcade that included three bodyguards. It was, at the time, and remains, the most bold, important, and tactically complicated operation ever carried out by a German terrorist group. The RAF demanded the release of 11 imprisoned RAF leaders and members in exchange for Schleyer. To put additional pressure on Chancellor Schmidt and the German government, the RAF contacted the Popular Front for the Liberation of Palestine (PFLP)–Special Operations Group and requested the group to carry out a supporting hijacking of a German passenger plane. This was accomplished on October 13, 1977 when four Arab terrorists seized Lufthansa Flight 181 from Palma de Mallorca to Frankfurt.

The Lufthansa hijackers smuggled the weapons and grenades aboard using a false-bottom cosmetic case and a portable radio — a result of ineffective airport screening procedures at Palma de Mallorca Airport. There were 87 passengers and crew aboard, including two Americans. The terrorists demanded the release of imprisoned German and Palestinian terrorists. The hijacking was specifically designed to support the German terrorist group RAF and its kidnapping of Schleyer. This was the first time one terrorist group had hijacked an airplane to support another group. Despite the compounded pressure of the Schleyer kidnapping and the Lufthansa hijacking, the German government did not accede to the terrorists' demands. On the contrary, the German government went on the offensive and authorized a counter-terrorism raid on the hijacked German aircraft on the tarmac at the airport in Mogadishu, Somalia where the plane eventually ended up.

The raid was successfully carried out on October 18 by the GSG-9 special counter-terrorism unit resulting in three terrorists killed, one captured, and only

---

[6] Margarine was code for SB, a popular brand of margarine in Germany at the time and the initials for Siegfried Buback.

four hostages slightly injured.[7] Only one German citizen died during the hijacking — the Lufthansa pilot was shot in cold blood by the terrorists. This event triggered the decision to launch the raid. The news of the successful GSG-9 raid and rescue was picked up on concealed radios by the imprisoned RAF leaders. When the Schleyer kidnapping and Lufthansa hijacking were first carried out, the RAF prisoners were euphoric, believing that the government had to release them. Now despondent over the successful counter-terrorism raid, four RAF members, including Baader and Ensslin, committed or attempted to commit suicide in their prison cells on October 18. Baader and Raspe shot themselves, Ensslin hung herself, and RAF member Irmgard Moeller stabbed herself six times in the chest but lived. The guns, knife, and a small transistor radio used by the prisoners to listen to news reports were all smuggled into the prisons by RAF lawyers. At the time of the suicides, RAF supporters and sympathizers framed the suicides as executions by the government. To this day, imprisoned RAF members, and their sympathizers and supporters, believe that the RAF leaders were killed by the prison authorities.

According to a German government report on terrorism in Germany, as of October 1977, terrorists were responsible for 27 deaths, 102 attempted murders, 92 people injured in bombings and shootings, and 100 taken hostage; 14 terrorists died and 94 were in prison (30 serving life sentences and 64 awaiting trial); and 550 persons were under investigation for terrorism. While the RAF was responsible for most of the lethal terrorist attacks, other left-wing terrorism actors such as the Second of June Movement and RZ contributed to the above tolls.[8]

With the deaths of the historical leaders of the RAF and a clear message by the German government that it would not give in to hostage-taking operations and kidnappings, RAF prisoner liberation operations ceased — to the detriment of U.S. interests in West Germany. The RAF now shifted the focus of its operations away from German targets to U.S. and NATO targets. The opening salvo of this campaign took place on June 25, 1979, when the RAF attempted to assassinate NATO Commander in Chief, U.S. Army General Alexander Haig, just outside of Obourg, Belgium. It was a 14-minute trip from Haig's home in Obourg to his NATO office in Mons. He was traveling in an armored vehicle with lead and follow security cars when a bomb exploded in a culvert under the road on his way to Mons. The terrorist bomb was detonated by a dynamite hand plunger and the

---

[7] The GSG-9 was the elite counter-terrorism and special operations unit of the German Federal Police. It was formed in April 1973 and inspired the U.S. to develop a similar counter-terrorism rescue unit during the Carter administration.

[8] Paul Hoffman, "German Terror Stirs A Debate on Secrecy," *New York Times*, October 27, 1977, p. 5.

terrorist was off on his timing by about 1.5 seconds. The RAF later said that the "fuse was a 200-meter electrical cable, to be triggered at the moment when the front door of Haig's Mercedes was directly above the payload. We had determined that his car traveled two meters per tenth of a second. Our error was in thinking that we could manually trigger the explosion precisely enough with the target moving that quickly."[9] As a result of the RAF timing error, Haig was not injured and there were no serious injuries to others in the motorcade. In a written communiqué, the RAF stated that Haig was targeted because he "presents and executes with specific accuracy the 'new course' of American strategy."[10] The communiqué ended with the claim that "U.S. imperialism is still the mortal enemy of mankind" and called for the destruction of "U.S. imperialism and its bases everywhere in the world." The RAF continued its anti-American attacks in the 1980s and introduced a new auxiliary arm called "fighting units" that harassed U.S. interests in West Germany with bombings designed to cause solely property damage.

Spain

Spain was confronted by a domestic terrorist threat emanating from the Basque separatist terrorist group Basque Homeland and Liberty (ETA) and the left-wing groups, FRAP, and GRAPO. The terrorist threat level in Spain reached a point in 1977 that on January 29, Prime Minister Adolfo Suarez gave a televised speech appealing to Spaniards to remain calm in the face of an outburst of terrorism intended "to upset our march towards civilized coexistence."[11]

While ETA did not directly target U.S. interests in Spain, its tendency for mass casualty, indiscriminate attacks in Madrid posed an indirect threat to Americans visiting and living in the city. FRAP was a smaller urban terrorist

---

[9] RAF Communiqué on Haig Attack from J. Smith and Andre Moncourt, *The Red Army Faction: A Documentary History — Volume II: Dancing with Imperialism* (Quebec: Kersplebedeb Publishing, 2013), p. 116.

[10] RAF Communiqué on Haig from Pluchinsky, "An Organizational and Operational Analysis of the RAF," in *European Terrorism: Today and Tomorrow*, p. 63.

[11] James M. Markham, "Spanish Leader Asks Calm in Face of New Violence," *New York Times*, January 30, 1977, p. 3. See also, "Madrid Tells Press to Remain Silent in Terrorist Cases," *New York Times*, February 10, 1977, p. 11. This last article reported that on February 9, the Spanish government's Ministry of Interior ordered a news blackout on police investigations into terrorism. The government decree covered "acts, documents, and news and commentaries referring to the activities of the government and the police in the investigations and searches that are being undertaken regarding the terrorist activities that have taken place in recent days in Madrid." It did not apply to the foreign press based in Madrid.

group that had as one of its goals to expel the "Yankee Imperialists" from Spanish territory through an insurrection.[12] In August 1975, FRAP fired shots at a U.S. sailor in Valencia.[13] GRAPO, another small urban group, was a anti-U.S. terrorist group that sought the removal of all U.S. military forces from Spanish territory. It was active in the major cities of Madrid and Barcelona. During 1977–1980, GRAPO carried out the following major attacks in Madrid: in 1977, it kidnapped a Supreme Court judge and bombed the U.S. Cultural Center on the day Vice President Walter Mondale arrived in the capital for an official visit; in 1978, it assassinated the Director of Prisons in Madrid; in 1979, it assassinated a Supreme Court judge and an army general in the capital and bombed a café, killing eight people.[14]

On July 16, 1979, Spanish police raided a GRAPO safe house in Madrid and discovered plans by the group to kidnap or kill a high-ranking U.S. Air Force officer in the Royal Oaks military housing community. Royal Oaks is about five miles from Madrid and houses U.S. personnel assigned to the Torrejon Air Base. Police arrested two GRAPO members on the housing complex as they were finalizing plans for the attack. Another GRAPO cell had surveilled American officers and the housing community at least six times in the previous six months and had compiled a map of the housing area which the police found. The two arrested terrorists were at the point in the plot where they were trying to identify the different Air Force rank insignias and badges to determine which was the highest rank.[15] They had problems figuring out the U.S. Air Force rank system. In one surveillance note, they state, "they wear stars in this shape (with a drawing of what appears to be an oak leaf)."[16] The oak leaf was used to identify a major or lieutenant colonel. The terrorists were interpreting this oak leaf as a general's rank. In fact, the terrorists, on the day they were arrested, had been to the Madrid library where they looked at several publications on U.S. Air Force uniforms. The surveillance notes and hand-drawn maps were accurate and detailed. The Royal

---

[12]For information on FRAP, see Tomás Pellicer. *FRAP: Grupo Armado* (Bilbao: Gatazka Gunea, 2009), at http://www.frap.es/GRUPOARMADO.pdf. Accessed May 2, 2017; and a FRAP "blog", at http://www.frap.es/. Accessed March 23, 2017.

[13]Alejandro Munoz Alonso. *El Terrorismo en Espana* (Barcelona: Planeta Publishers, 1982), p. 62.

[14]For information on GRAPO, see http://www.signalfire.org/2012/04/05/a-brief-history-of-the-armed-struggle-of-grapo-in-spain. Accessed October 24, 2017; U.S. government, Department of Defense, Terrorist Group Profiles, (Washington, D.C.: GPO, 1988), pp. 45–47; and Alonso. *El Terrorismo en Espana*, Chapters 2–4.

[15]Mickolus, *A Chronology of Events, 1968–1979*, p. 862; and CIA, International Terrorism in 1979, p. 3.

[16]GRAPO surveillance document.

Oaks housing area was an open community, so surveillance was easy. The GRAPO surveillance note commented on the Americans living on the complex that "they live here very peacefully and complacently." An assassination or kidnapping of a U.S. Air Force officer was prevented by the Spanish authorities. The attack would have been significant as no U.S. military personnel were targeted up to that point. While the FRAP was neutralized in the late 1970s, GRAPO carried out more anti-American terrorist attacks in Spain during the Reagan administration.

Turkey

The terrorist threat to U.S. interests in Turkey during the Carter administration was high. The threat emanated from left-wing terrorist groups such as TKP/ML, TPLA, MLAPU, and Dev Sol, later renamed Turkish People's Liberation Party/ Front (DHKP/C). Right-wing terrorism, although not directed at U.S. interests, also contributed to the high terrorist threat level in Turkey.[17] Turkey had a history of domestic terrorism going back to the 1960s. In March 1971, the level of political violence reached a point where the Turkish military was compelled to intervene and force the country's Prime Minister to resign. The Turkish military told the people of Turkey at the time that the government had once again "pushed our country into anarchy, fratricide and social and economic unrest" and thus "the Turkish armed forces, fulfilling their legal duty to protect the republic, will take power." That technique, used successfully, came to be known as "coup by memorandum."[18] The military ruled the country for some two and a half years before it returned the government to civilian control after the military had reduced the level of terrorist activity in the country. In the late 1970s, however, a high level of domestic terrorist activity returned. In September 1980, it once again reached a point where the military ejected a democratically elected government. The military detained the nation's opposition leaders, announcing that they would control everything until it was possible for a working government to resume. The U.S. response was measured with no real criticism of the military action. It was "almost relieved" that the action came from the military and not communists or Islamist elements. Turkey was an important NATO ally and an important ally for the U.S. as it was used for U.S. listening stations on the Soviet

---

[17] See, for example, Steven V. Roberts, "Turkish Violence Increases the Pressure for Elections," *New York Times*, March 20, 1977, p. 8.

[18] http://time.com/4408850/turkey-coup-history/. Accessed May 7, 2017.

Union.[19] The military returned power to civilians in 1982 after the military believed it had again managed the terrorist threat.

In 1977, the *New York Times* noted that "everyday people are killed or wounded for political reasons ... school buses have been sprayed with machine gun fire, politicians shot down in their coffee houses, laborers shot on the way to work and young activists kidnapped off the street and 'taken for a ride,' gangland style."[20] In 1977, 248 people were killed in incidents of political violence.[21] In 1979, eight Americans were assassinated in Turkey by left-wing terrorist groups:

- On April 12, two U.S. Air Force noncommissioned officers were shot in Izmir, one fatally, by unidentified gunmen. The two were walking home when attacked. DHKP/C claimed responsibility for the attack.
- On May 11, as U.S. Army personnel in Istanbul waited for a bus in front of a transient hotel for U.S. military personnel, two gunmen opened fire on the soldiers. One U.S. soldier was killed and another wounded. The MLAPU claimed responsibility for the attack.
- On June 2, 1979, David Goodman, an American teacher at a private English-language school in Adana was shot and killed as he opened the door of his apartment in response to a knock by two unidentified gunmen. The DHKP/C claimed responsibility.
- On December 14, 1979, four Americans (one U.S. military and three Defense Department contractors from Boeing Services International) were shot and killed in Istanbul after returning from work. As a U.S. military minibus carrying the Americans stopped at their bus stop, terrorists who were prepositioned at the location ordered the Americans off the bus and opened fired on them when they attempted to flee. The MLAPU claimed responsibility.

In April 1980, a U.S. Navy Chief Petty Officer was shot and killed in Istanbul by MLAPU terrorists. In November 1980, two U.S. Air Force Senior Airmen were shot at in Adana by MLAPU terrorists. One of the airmen later died.

In addition to the above assassinations, there were dozens of bombings against American targets in Turkey, including the U.S. Cultural Center, U.S. military vehicles, the U.S. Information Agency office, American schools, the U.S.

---

[19] John M. Goshko, "From the Allies: Patience for Turkey, Understanding by the Allies," *Washington Post*, September 13, 1980, p. A1.

[20] Nicholas Gage, "Political Violence by Turkish Extremists Becoming a Fact of Daily Life," *New York Times*, December 18, 1977, p. 12.

[21] Ibid.

Consulate in Adana, Pan Am Airline offices, a military APO office, the U.S. Embassy in Ankara, the U.S. Communication Agency office, the Turkish-American Association office, the American Missionary Board office, a Wells Fargo office, a U.S. diplomatic residence, and a building that housed the offices of several U.S. multinationals.

Greece

The terrorist threat in Greece came from left-wing terrorist groups such as ELA and 17N. It was 17N that assassinated CIA chief of station (COS) Richard Welch in Athens in 1975. During the Carter administration, the group focused its attacks on Greek targets but shifted back to U.S. targets during the Reagan administration. Meanwhile, the ELA was active against U.S. targets in Greece during the Carter administration. In 1977, it detonated a bomb outside the U.S. Air Force Non-Commissioned Officer's Club in Athens. In 1978, the ELA bombed USIS and American Express offices in Athens to protest the official visit of U.S. Secretary of State Cyrus Vance. On February 16, 1980, Greek police arrested 11 Greek terrorists from a previously unknown group called the "Popular Frontal Initiative."[22] Subsequent investigation determined that the group had planned attacks against not only various Greek targets but also U.S. military installations and U.S. businesses in Greece. It also was planning to bomb various embassies including the U.S. Embassy. Maps and surveillance notes of the U.S. ambassador's residence in Athens were also found, including the daily hour that the ambassador would walk his dog. The leftist terrorist threat to U.S. interests in Greece would significantly increase during the Reagan administration.

Italy

The terrorist threat in Italy during the Carter administration was high. The 1970s were part of the "Years of Lead" in Italy. This was a period of social and political upheaval in Italy that lasted from the late 1960s until the early 1980s, marked by a wave of both left-wing and right-wing incidents of political terrorism. However, there were no serious terrorist incidents directed at U.S. targets in Italy. The Red Brigades was the most dangerous left-wing group in Italy at the time, but it focused its attacks on domestic targets. It should also be noted that right-wing terrorists in Italy carried out the most lethal right-wing terrorist attack in

---

[22] *Acropolis* (Athens), February 16, 1980.

European history during the Carter administration. On August 2, 1980, terrorists from the neo-fascist terrorist organization Armed Revolutionary Nuclei bombed the Central Station at Bologna, Italy, killing 85 people and injuring more than 200 others. At the time, it was the deadliest terrorist attack in post-World War II European history. With the September 26, 1980 bombing at the Munich Oktoberfest by a neo-Nazi terrorist that killed 11 people, there was a growing concern of right-wing terrorism in Western Europe. However, these two attacks turned out to be the high-water mark for the right-wing terrorist threat. Afterward, there were periodic attacks in Germany and Italy by right-wing elements, but they were episodic and generally limited to property damage attacks against immigrants and immigrant hostels.

Latin America

During the Carter administration, there were more left-wing terrorist groups and insurgent organizations operating in Latin America than all the other regions combined. Many of these groups also were active during the Nixon and Ford administrations. These 23 groups in Latin America operated in 11 countries and were responsible for the deaths of five Americans during the Carter administration — one each in Argentina, Guatemala, and Mexico; and two in El Salvador. Five Americans were also killed by right-wing terrorists in El Salvador and Guatemala. At the time, more anti-American terrorist attacks were carried out in Latin America than any other region. The major left-wing terrorist and insurgent groups active in Latin America during the Carter administration were:

- Revolutionary Left Movement (MIR) in Chile;
- People's Revolutionary Vanguard (VPR) in Brazil;
- Montoneros in Argentina;
- 19th of April Movement (M-19) in Colombia;
- Revolutionary Armed Forces of Colombia (FARC);
- National Liberation Army (ELN) in Colombia;
- Red Flag in Venezuela;
- 23rd of September Armed Communist League (LC-23) in Mexico;
- People's Revolutionary Army (ERP) in El Salvador;
- Popular Liberation Front (FPL) in El Salvador;
- Farabundo Martí National Liberation Front (FMLN) in El Salvador;
- Popular Revolutionary Bloc (BPR) in El Salvador;
- Armed Forces of National Resistance (FARN) in El Salvador;

- Revolutionary Party of the Central American Workers (PRTC) in El Salvador;
- Armed Forces of Liberation (FAL) in El Salvador;
- Revolutionary Vanguard in Peru;
- Sandinista National Liberation Front (FSLN) in Nicaragua;
- Revolutionary Organization of the People in Arms (ORPA) in Guatemala;
- Guerrilla Army of the Poor (EGP) in Guatemala;
- The Revolutionary Party of Central American Workers (PRTC-H) in Honduras;
- Manuel Rodríguez Patriotic Front (FPMR) in Chile;
- People's Liberation Movement-Chinchoneros (MPL-Cinchoneros) in Honduras;
- Shining Path in Peru.

The anti-American terrorist threat in Latin America during the Carter administration was highest in El Salvador, Colombia, and Guatemala.

El Salvador

The U.S. became involved militarily and economically in El Salvador from 1979 to 1992 to fend off the growing threat of communist expansion into Latin America. The fall of the Somoza regime in Nicaragua 1979 to the leftist FSLN, which was supported by Cuba, only reinforced that threat and led to a fear of a communist domino effect in the region. The Carter administration decided that the new Sandinista government posed a threat to the stability of Central America and to United States' interests in that region. Inspired by the success in Nicaragua, leftist terrorist activity in neighboring El Salvador increased in late 1979, triggered by the overthrow of the civilian government by a military junta. When the junta made promises to improve living standards in the country but failed to do so, discontent with the government prompted the five main guerrilla groups in the country at the time to unite into the FMLN. These five groups were the Popular Revolutionary Forces (ERP), the Farabundo Martí Liberation People's Forces (FPL), FAL, the FARN, and Revolutionary Forces of Central American Workers (ERTC). The FMLN was supported by the Nicaraguan, Cuban, and Soviet governments. The establishment of the FMLN coincided with increased U.S. involvement in the country as the U.S. backed the junta. The junta's ascension to power triggered a civil war in the country from 1980 to 1992 between the government and the FMLN. Both right-wing elements and leftist elements in the country opposed the junta and U.S. support for it. Significant tensions and violence had already existed, before the civil war's full outbreak, over the course of the 1970s. However, in 1979, U.S. targets started to be attacked at a higher rate than previously. El Salvador's Civil War became the third longest civil war in Latin America after the Guatemalan Civil War and the armed conflict in Peru. At the beginning of 1980, the U.S. Embassy in San Salvador estimated that there were between 3,000 and 5,000 terrorists in the ERP, FPL, and FARN.[23]

The following were the most significant anti-American attacks in late 1979:

(1) On September 21, Dennis McDonald, a U.S. engineer and general manager of Aplar, a subsidiary of Beckman Instruments of California, and Fausto Buchelli, a Puerto Rican, were kidnapped in San Salvador as they left the factory. Their driver/bodyguard was killed in the attack by two terrorist vehicles. The ERTC claimed responsibility. The Beckman Company ran ads in a dozen foreign newspapers to satisfy the kidnappers' demand. McDonald and Buchelli were released 45 days later.

(2) On September 23, an American was killed in San Salvador when he was caught up in a guerrilla attack against the Armed Forces Instruction Center located on the grounds of the president's residence.

(3) On October 28, the FMLN bombed the Bank of America office in San Salvador causing $120,000 in damage. The attack was carried out to support the demands of Popular Revolutionary Bloc members who had taken over government ministries.

(4) On October 30, an attack on the U.S. Embassy was carried out with gunfire and bombs. Two U.S. Marine Security Guards were injured. The ERP front group "Popular Leagues of 28 February" claimed credit.

(5) On December 11, Deborah Loff, a U.S. Peace Corps volunteer, was kidnapped by the "Popular Leagues of 28 February." She was eventually released unharmed.

(6) On December 17, the Bank of America office in San Salvador was bombed by the ERP. On the same day, a terrorist shot and killed Thomas Bracken, an American consultant to El Salvador's National Police, in San Salvador.

Left-wing attacks on U.S. targets continued into 1980. The U.S. Embassy in San Salvador was attacked over a dozen times in 1980, including being strafed, machine-gunned, firebombed, and hit with anti-tank rockets. U.S. Peace Corps offices were strafed, and U.S. multinationals were bombed.

---

[23] U.S. Embassy San Salvador, "Preliminary Assessment of Situation in El Salvador," March 18, 1980, at http://foia.state.gov/documents/elsalvad/738d.PDF. Accessed June 16, 2017.

Right-wing terrorists were also active in El Salvador and periodically targeted U.S. interests. On December 2, 1980, three American nuns and an American Catholic lay social worker were reported missing on their way home from the airport. Their bodies were later found in a grave, some 30 miles from the capital San Salvador. They had been raped and shot. The victims had been previously threatened by right-wing elements. A presidential mission sent by Carter to investigate the crime found complicity of the Salvadoran security forces either in the crime or in evading the investigation.[24] Five Salvadoran National Guard members were later found guilty for the murders. On January 3, 1981, the head of the El Salvador agrarian program and two American U.S. Agency for International Development (AID) contractors were shot and killed by two unidentified gunmen while eating dinner at the Sheraton Hotel. While no terrorist group claimed credit for the attack, the primary suspects were right-wing elements. Anti-American terrorist activity in El Salvador increased significantly during the Reagan administration.

Colombia

During the Carter administration, the three major left-wing anti-American terrorist groups in Colombia were the ELN, FARC, and M-19. The last two posed the most dangerous threat to U.S. interests in Colombia at the time. The most serious international terrorist incident in Colombia during the Carter administration was the February 27, 1980 siege of the embassy of the Dominican Republic in Bogota by 16 M-19 terrorists while a diplomatic reception was being held there. M-19 had infiltrated two M-19 couples into the reception. Outside, directly in front of the embassy, a dozen of the terrorists dressed in jogging suits were kicking a soccer ball on a grassy area about 120 feet from the embassy front door. Since there was a university nearby and the students were known to play soccer on any available open area, the terrorists attracted little attention. In addition, only one guard was posted in front of the embassy. The signal for the attack to begin was when one of the terrorist infiltrators in the reception fired some shots into the ceiling. The dozen M-19 terrorists outside quickly pulled out automatic weapons from their gym bags and stormed the embassy. Only one terrorist was killed during the assault. He was believed to have been killed by one of the U.S. ambassador's security officers. Inside, the terrorists held about 60 people, including 14 ambassadors (U.S. Ambassador Diego Asencio was one of them) and Colombian officials as hostages. The terrorists demanded the release of over 300 "political

---

[24] U.S. Department of State, Office of the Historian, *Central America, 1977–1980,* at https://history. state.gov/milestones/1977-1980/central-america-carter. Accessed December 16, 2016.

prisoners" and $50 million in ransom, and the publication of a M-19 communiqué in various international newspapers.

Over the next two months, the terrorists reduced their demands as various stages of negotiations took place with the government. In his memoirs, U.S. Ambassador Asencio noted that after their initial demands were rejected by the Colombian government, the terrorists were largely at a loss for what to do next. A small core of ambassadors, including Asencio, took the initiative and explained to their captors "how they could get out of their self-created mess with their dignity and their hides intact." This resulted in the emergence of a "hostage committee" which began to analyze "government negotiating documents for the M-19, suggesting new avenues of discussion, rewriting guerrilla manifestos to take out the more egregious ideological creeds and pointing out where the government had made perhaps not readily apparent concessions."[25] At the end, their demand for the release of dozens of prisoners was denied. The terrorists were given $2.5 million in ransom money and the government agreed to allow international human rights groups to monitor pending trials of imprisoned guerrillas for expeditiousness and justice. On April 27, the 16 terrorists left the embassy with the remaining 12 diplomatic hostages and boarded a Cubana Airlines flight to Cuba. When they landed in Havana, the hostage diplomats were released and returned to their home countries.

The M-19 was known for its spectacular, publicity-seeking operations. In 1974, the group stole the sword of the South American liberator, Simon Bolivar, from a Bogota museum. Simon Bolivar was the 19th-century liberator of what is now Colombia, Ecuador, Venezuela, Peru, and Bolivia. This sword was a worldwide symbol of liberation. M-19 used it as its own symbol until 1991 when it returned it to the government. This was the first time that a terrorist group seized a country's historical symbol. The M-19 used it to market the group as a legitimate successor of Bolivar's role as a liberator. On New Year's Eve in 1978, the group robbed a Colombian arsenal of more than 5,000 weapons which it removed through a tunnel it had taken months to dig. The FARC also engaged in kidnapping Americans in Colombia. At the beginning of the Carter administration, the FARC carried out its most prominent anti-American attack in Colombia when it

---

[25] Karen DeYoung, book review, *Our Man is Inside* by Diego and Nancy Asencio with Ron Tobias. *Washington Post Book World*, February 13, 1983, p. 5, at http://bailey83221.livejournal.com/72461. html. Accessed June 21, 2017; See also, Garry Clifford, "Hero Diplomat Diego Asencio Reflects on His 61 Perilous Days as a Hostage in Bogotá," *People Magazine*, June 20, 1980, at http://people.com/archive/hero-diplomat-diego-asencio-reflects-on-his-61-perilous-days-as-a-hostage-in-bogota-vol-13-no-26/. Accessed September 26, 2017.

kidnapped Richard Starr, a Peace Corps volunteer in February 1977. The group demanded a ransom payment. A private ransom of over $200,000 was eventually paid and he was released on February 12, 1980 after 1,093 days in captivity. In August 1980, the FARC kidnapped American citizen Ira Hubbard Jr. from his banana plantation in central Colombia. He was released three months later after a ransom of $125,000 was paid by his family. There was also a failed kidnapping in June 1980 by six FARC terrorists of Kenneth Reysen, an American executive of the Colgate-Palmolive Company, in Cali. Police and a watchman were able to fend off the attack.

In addition to the kidnappings discussed earlier, U.S. interests in Colombia were frequently bombed by left-wing groups. The U.S. Consulate in Cali was bombed several times during this period. Peace Corps and DEA offices were bombed in Bogota. There were several bombings near the U.S. Embassy in Bogota. In May 1980, the M-19 occupied the Colombian-American Center in Medillin. After giving anti-United States speeches, handing out literature, and painting the walls with slogans, the group left. No injuries were reported, and only a switchboard and a telephone were damaged. The terrorist threat to U.S. interests in Colombia significantly increased during the Reagan administration.

Guatemala

In 1954, the CIA supported a military coup in Guatemala led by Colonel Carlos Castillo Armas against the democratically elected President Jacobo Arbenz Guzmán. The U.S. considered Guzman a communist threat, especially after he legalized the communist party and moved to nationalize the plantations of the U.S.-owned United Fruit Company.[26] Col. Castillo was then elected president and was followed by successive military leaders or politicians supported by the military. The U.S. supported this series of military dictators, particularly after the victory of the Cuban revolution in 1959. In 1960, Guatemala's 36-year civil war began as left-wing terrorist and insurgent groups started battling government military forces. The Guatemalan Civil War ran from 1960 to 1996 and was fought between the government and various leftist terrorist and insurgent groups. The Guatemalan government was supported by the U.S. and engaged in severe human

---

[26]Talea Miller, Timeline: Guatemala's Brutal Civil War, *PBS News Hour*, March 7, 2011, at http://www.pbs.org/newshour/updates/latin_america-jan-june11-timeline_03-07/. Accessed March 11, 2016.

rights abuses and extra-judicial torture and assassinations of opponents.[27] In 1977, the Guatemalan government refused U.S. assistance after the Carter administration issued a report highly critical of the Guatemalans' performance on human rights. The U.S. Congress followed by imposing restrictions on military aid, citing the human rights situation. The Carter administration then announced a suspension of military aid to Guatemala, accusing the government of "gross and consistent human rights violations." It did note, however, that the situation was improving under the administration of the current president.

However, loopholes in Congressional restrictions on aid to Guatemala made it possible for the U.S. to continue to provide some military parts, instruction, and informal advice to the Guatemalan armed forces.[28] These restrictions were never meant to be more than partial and temporary. In addition, Guatemala also received weapons and military equipment from Israel, at least part of which was covertly underwritten by Washington.

While left-wing terrorism continued in Guatemala during the Carter administration, the terrorist threat to U.S. interests in the country was highest in 1980.[29] The two groups that caused the most concern were the EGP, and the Rebel Armed Forces (FAR). There were over a dozen assassinations and attempted assassinations of Guatemalan directors of Coca-Cola offices in Guatemala during this period. In June 1980, four people were killed who had connections with a Coca-Cola bottling plant in Guatemala City. Many of these attacks were claimed by or attributed to the FAR. In the same month, terrorists firebombed a Hardee's restaurant in Guatemala City. In August, unidentified gunmen shot and killed American George Frank Rials, an overseer for the Nell Teer Company, which was building roads in the jungles in El Zapote for petroleum exploitation. In September, terrorists strafed the United States Embassy in the capital. In December, suspected right-wing terrorists kidnapped Clifford Bevins, a U.S.

---

[27] See, for example the excellent study, Patrick Ball, Paul Kobrak, and Herbert F. Spirer, "State Violence in Guatemala, 1960–1996: A Quantitative Reflection," at https://web.archive.org/web/20130505225114/http://shr.aaas.org/guatemala/ciidh/qr/english/chap18.html. Accessed December 3, 2016.

[28] Richard J. Meislin, "U.S. Military Aid for Guatemala Continuing Despite Official Curbs", *New York Times*, December 19, 1982, at http://www.nytimes.com/library/world/americas/121982guatemala-us.html. Accessed February 13, 2017.

[29] For background on the leftist insurgency in Guatemala, see CIA, Directorate of Intelligence, "Intelligence Memorandum: The Communist Insurgency in Guatemala," No. 0624/68, September 20, 1968, at https://www.cia.gov/library/readingroom/docs/DOC_0000653094.pdf. Accessed July 5, 2017; and Alan Hiding, "Guatemala: State of Siege," *The New York Times Magazine*, August 24, 1980, p. 16N, at http://www.latinamericanstudies.org/guatemala/guatemala-siege.htm. Accessed March 23, 2016.

businessman, who was president of the Guatemalan subsidiary of Goodyear Tire and Rubber Company, from his home. The kidnappers demanded ransom and denounced the alleged U.S. government and U.S. business support of leftists. Bevin's body was found outside of Guatemala City in mid-August 1981. He had been shot in the head. On December 24, Laverle Osborne Cummings, an American who ran a health clinic in Santa Lucia, was kidnapped by the EGP. The terrorists demanded a $10 million ransom. Cummings was released on January 21, 1981 — the day after Reagan was sworn in as the 49th U.S. president.

Other Regions

As under the Nixon and Ford administrations, the left-wing terrorist threat to U.S. interests overseas during the Carter administration was primarily in Western Europe and Latin America. However, other regions also contained anti-American terrorist groups. Anti-American terrorist activity continued in Iran. The primary terrorist threat there was the Mujahideen E Khaq (MEK) or People's Struggle which had been active in Iran since the early 1970s. The group carried out mostly assassinations. In December 1978, Paul Grimm, a Texaco executive who was working for an Iranian oil company, was shot and killed by the MEK in Ahwaz as his car slowed down at an intersection. In January 1979, Martin Berkowitz, a former U.S. Air Force Colonel working for an American construction company, was stabbed to death in his home in Kerman. The words, "go back to your own country," were scrawled on the wall of his home. The attack was either carried out by the MEK or militant Islamists who were trying to overthrow the Shah at this time. In addition, over a dozen bombings of U.S. targets took place during this period: a U.S. contractor bus, a U.S. Air Force bus, a Lockheed bus, a Bell Helicopter bus, a Northrop motor pool, an English language center, and the residence of a U.S. military person. In August 1998, an Iranian restaurant was bombed in Tehran, injuring 10 Americans.

In the Philippines, left-wing groups such as the New People's Army and the April 6 Liberation Movement (A6LM) continued to target U.S. interests. In March 1979, an American missionary in Marawi City was kidnapped by another terrorist group, the Moro National Liberation Front. He was released two and a half weeks later after a private ransom was paid. In September 1980, six bombs exploded in various parts of Manila resulting in the death of an American, Annie Kuzmak. The "May 1 Sandigan" of A6LM claimed responsibility. In December 1979, an American businessman, Jeremy Ladd Cross, was shot and killed in Manila by two terrorists from a Sparrow Unit of the New People's Army, its urban terrorist cell. In October 1980, A6LM detonated a bomb in Manila at a meeting of the American Society of Travel Agents that injured seven Americans. The U.S. ambassador and the president of the Philippines were in attendance and only 50 feet from the explosion.

The Palestinian Terrorist Threat

Historically, secular Palestinian terrorist organizations have considered U.S. interests overseas a logical and attractive target given U.S. support for Israel and the U.S.'s role in facilitating the Egyptian peace treaty with Israel from 1978 to 1979. From 1968 to 1980, Palestinian terrorist groups carried out 104 terrorist attacks against Israeli interests. The U.S. was the second most preferred target with 44 attacks.[30] While the PLO in 1974 had renounced attacks on Israeli interests overseas, there were still Palestinian "rejectionist" groups that continued to attack Israeli and Jewish interests outside Israel. PLO elements limited their terrorist operations in most cases to inside Israel. During the Carter administration, there were only five Palestinian attacks aimed at U.S. interests, including two bombings in March 1979 by Saiqa terrorists at the U.S. embassies in Damascus, Syria and Ankara, Turkey. The most serious attack was the attempted assassination on August 27, 1980 of the U.S. Ambassador to Lebanon, John Gunther Dean. Unknown terrorists attacked U.S. Ambassador John Gunther Dean's motorcade in Beirut with a LAW (light anti-tank weapon) rocket and automatic weapons fire.

Around 7:40 p.m., Dean was riding in the middle car of a three-car motorcade from his residence outside Beirut to the residence of the president of the American University of Beirut in the city. His vehicle was fully armored while the other two were partially armored. As the motorcade came to the Beirut–Damascus highway, it made a right and then a quick U-turn between highway dividers to head west into Beirut. As the motorcade turned onto the road to Beirut, it encountered a parked red Mercedes on the right roadside with its emergency lights on. This caused the motorcade to slightly slow down. As it did, five or six terrorists in the dark on a small hill fired around 21 AK-47 tracer bullets and two U.S-made light anti-tank rockets at the motorcade. State Department Special Agent and Assistant Regional Security Officer Robert Morris, riding in the front right seat of the follow vehicle, fired more than 32 rounds from his M-16 at the terrorists.[31] The rocket and automatic weapon fire disabled the lead car. Under

[30] Ariel Merari and Shlomi Elad. *The International Dimensions of Palestinian Terrorism* (Colorado: Westview Press, 1986), pp. 111–113.

[31] Nora Boustany, "U.S. Ambassador Ambushed in Lebanon, Escapes Attack Unhurt," *Washington Post*, August 28, 1980, at https://www.washingtonpost.com/archive/politics/1980/08/28/

rifle fire, Dean's daughter and her fiancé, who were in the lead car, along with two Lebanese bodyguards fled from the lead car into the follow car. The ambassador's car had its tires hit and deflated.[32] The car continued however as it was fitted with "run flats," wheels made by bolting a doughnut-shaped portion of polycarbonate to the inside of the rim that enabled the car to keep rolling even after the tires had been deflated. The ambassador's vehicle and follow car left the scene. None of the ambassador's party or security guards were seriously wounded. Some shots struck the back, right seat window where Dean was sitting, but the bulletproof plastic windows saved his life.

Although there were never any credible claims of responsibility for the attack, Palestinian terrorists or Lebanese working on behalf of Palestinian groups were the logical suspects. However, Ambassador Dean publicly accused the Israeli government. After the attack, Lebanese security retrieved the two anti-tank canisters left at the attack site and eight that were found in a nearby safe house. They had made-in-America markings. After some stonewalling by the State Department, Ambassador Dean eventually learned that the anti-tank weapons were sold and shipped to Israel in 1974.[33] According to Dean, "I was seen by the Israeli Government and by some elements in the U.S. as a 'protector' of the Palestinians or, as some Israeli newspapers wrote at the time, a champion of Palestinian resistance against Israeli Zionist goals."[34] In official U.S. government documents noting this attack, possible Israeli involvement is not mentioned.

---

us-ambassador-dean-ambushed-in-lebanon-escapes-attack-unhurt/218130c3-6d7e-438f-8b0c-a42fc0e5eb57/?utm_term=.6f7d9c4c0997. Accessed March 23, 2017; see also, *Middle East Monitor*, at https://www.middleeastmonitor.com/20180824-israel-attempted-to-assassinate-us-ambassador-confirms-new-book. Accessed July 21, 2016; and author email communications with Robert Morris, January 10–13, 2017.

[32] Ambassador Andrew I. Killgore, "American Ambassador Recalls Israeli Assassination Attempt — With U.S. Weapons," *Washington Report on Middle East Affairs*, November 2002, p. 15, at http://www.ifamericansknew.org/us_ints/ambassador.html. Accessed September 23, 2016.

[33] Ibid; and Barbara Crossette, "US Envoy Writes of Israeli Threats," *The Nation*, March 31, 2009, at https://www.thenation.com/article/us-envoy-writes-israeli-threats. Accessed May 23, 2017; John Yemma, "Who attacked US envoy in Lebanon? Too many groups to be sure," *The Christian Science Monitor*, August 29, 1980, at http://www.csmonitor.com/1980/0829/082948.html. Accessed October 23, 2016. RSO Robert Morris has stated that "even though the LAW rockets were apparently part of a shipment from US to Israel, Lebanon was swarming with weapons of all kinds and many sources. It would be easy to steal such weapons to pin the attack on anyone else." January 6, 2017 email to author.

[34] Association for Diplomatic Studies and Training, Foreign Affairs Oral History Project, Interview with Ambassador John Gunther Dean on September 6, 2000, pp. 135–136, at http://oggo1.free.fr/oral%20history.pdf. Accessed May 7, 2017.

This attempted assassination of Ambassador Dean also underlined the importance of State Department Diplomatic Security special agents assigned overseas as regional security officers or temporary duty protective security agents. Given that U.S. interests overseas in the 1970s were under a high terrorist threat from left-wing and Palestinian terrorist groups and that U.S. diplomatic facilities and personnel were a frequent target, these special agents had an important and dangerous job overseas. Throughout their history, the State Department's diplomatic security agents have been relatively unknown to the public and media, unheralded by Congress, and unappreciated by other State Department personnel. No U.S. agency had more responsibility and deployed more security resources overseas to protect U.S. diplomatic interests, advise U.S. businesses and U.S. tourists overseas, and protect Congressmen traveling overseas than these agents. As a law enforcement special agent, it was one thing to operate inside the U.S. and quite another to function in an overseas environment that in many cases was a hostile one.[35]

There were also Palestinian terrorist attacks that killed American citizens living in or visiting Israel. On March 11, 1978, Gail Rubin, niece of U.S. Senator Abraham Ribicoff, was among 38 people shot to death by PLO terrorists on an Israeli beach in Tel Aviv. On June 3, 1978, a Fatah bomb exploded inside a city bus in Jerusalem, killing six people, one of whom was an American (Richard Fishman, a medical student from Maryland). On May 2, 1980, Eli Haze'ev, an American Israeli from Alexandria, Virginia, was killed in a PLO attack on Jewish worshippers walking home from a synagogue in Hebron. There is no information that these three Americans were directly targeted by these Palestinian groups. It is unlikely that Yasir Arafat would allow Americans to be directly targeted. It is more likely that these Americans were simply in the wrong place at the wrong time or assumed to be Israeli citizens. While Arafat restricted terrorist operations overseas, he continued to authorize attacks inside Israel. In subsequent years, many dual-citizen Israeli Americans were killed by terrorist attacks inside Israel. Few, if any, were directly targeted.

Palestinian terrorists killed an American businessman during the December 31, 1980 bombing in Nairobi, Kenya on New Year's Eve of the Norfolk hotel, a five-star hotel owned by Jack Block, an Israeli citizen. Sixteen people died,

---

[35]For additional information on the role of diplomatic security special agents, see Randall Bennett. *Taking Up the Sword: A Story of a Special Agent in the Diplomatic Security*; Nick Mariano. *For God and Country: Memories of A Diplomatic Security Service Special Agent*; U.S. Department of State, Office of Historian. *History of the Bureau of Diplomatic Security of the United States Department of State*; and Robert David Booth. *State Department Counterintelligence: Leaks, Spies, and Lies.*

including Kenneth Moyers, an American on a business trip for the Allied Signal Corporation. Over 100 were injured, including eight Americans. The damage was estimated at $3.4 million. The bomber was identified as a PFLP member. The bombing was in retaliation for the Kenyan government's aid to Israel in arresting two German members of the PFLP in 1976 who intended to fire a SA-7 missile at an El Al plane out of Nairobi Airport. This is another attack where Americans were not directly targeted.

Foreign Fighters in the Palestinian Cause

The major non-Arab, foreign fighters in the Palestinian cause were the Venezuelan "Carlos," German leftists, Latin American leftists, and members of the Japanese Red Army or JRA. Carlos did not carry out any attacks during the Carter administration but surfaced again in the Reagan administration. However, the Japanese Red Army was active during the Carter administration.

In September 1977, five JRA members hijacked Japan Airlines flight 472 out of Dacca, Bangladesh with 151 passengers and crew. The Japanese government gave in to the demands of the terrorists and released six imprisoned JRA terrorists and provided $6 million in ransom.[36] The plane ended up in Algeria where it was impounded by authorities and the remaining hostages were freed. The JRA members eventually ended up in Lebanon and gravitated toward the Palestinian cause. Three months later, on December 4, Malaysian Airline Flight 653, was hijacked in Kuala Lumpur 10 minutes after takeoff and then crashed while approaching to land in Singapore. Among the 93 passengers killed, one was an American (Donald O. Hoerr). The cockpit voice recorder indicates that the pilot and co-pilot were shot and killed by one or more hijackers. The circumstances in which the hijacking and subsequent crash occurred remain unsolved. However, the crew did report that the plane was hijacked. The cockpit voice recordings indicate noises suggestive of the cockpit door being broken in, along with screaming and cursing. Either the hijacker shot the pilot and co-pilot and then himself as the plane approached Singapore or the hijacker shot the crew and then attempted to fly the plane, causing the plane to crash.[37] The fact that the

---

[36] Andrew H. Malcolm, "Japanese Red Army's Hijacking and its Demands Said to Reflect Political and Financial Desperation," *New York Times*, September 30, 1977, p. 3.

[37] http://aviation-safety.net/database/record.php?id=19771204-0. Accessed October 26, 2017; and "All 100 Aboard Killed in Crash of Hijacked Malaysian Airliner," *The Toledo Blade* (Ohio), December 5, 1977, p. 1.

plane was hijacked is not disputed.[38] The JRA was and remains the primary suspect in this hijacking. However, the Japanese Red Army never claimed responsibility for this incident. If the objective was to hijack the plane and hold hostages, then the operation failed. The circumstances of this hijacking, why the plane crashed, and what group or person was behind this incident remain a mystery.

Ethno-National Terrorism

Ethno-national terrorist groups were responsible for the deaths of five Americans during the Carter administration. In all five cases, the Americans were directly targeted. In general, however, ethno-national terrorist groups did not directly target U.S. interests. Four of the five Americans were killed in Africa where ethno-national groups were more anti-colonial and more anti-foreign. In March 1977, Don McClure, an American missionary, was shot and killed in Ethiopia by the Ogaden National Liberation Front; another American missionary, Dr. Glen Eschtruth, was killed in April in Zaire by the National Liberation Front of the Congo; and George Pernicone, an American businessman working for Bechtel, was killed in November in Sumatra, Indonesia by the Front for the Liberation of Aceh, who left pamphlets warning Americans and other foreigners to leave the region. In June 1978, Archie Dunaway, an American evangelist, was bayoneted to death at the Sanyati Mission Hospital in Rhodesia by either the Zimbabwe African National Liberation Army (ZANLA) or the Zimbabwe People's Revolutionary Army (ZIPRA). In April 1979, Michael Lewy, an American working at a ranch in southwestern Rhodesia, was shot and killed by either the ZANLA or ZIPRA.

State-Sponsored Terrorism

During the Carter administration, the primary state sponsors of terrorism were Libya, the Soviet Union, and Cuba. The first two provided support to various Palestinian terrorist organizations which carried out periodic attacks on U.S. interests overseas. Cuba was a key supporter of left-wing terrorist and insurgent organizations in Latin America. All three states worked against U.S. international interests. However, it was Libya that presented a more direct threat to U.S.

---

[38] Captain Ganjoor radioed the control tower: "We have an emergency on board". Asked to clarify, he said, "We have a hijacker on board." "Hijacked airman's family still suffering 37 years after crash," *New Zealand Herald*, April 15, 2014, at http://www.nzherald.co.nz/nz/news/article.cfm?c_id=1&objectid=11238210. Accessed July 2, 2017.

interests. Because of a Libyan dispute with Egypt and the U.S. backing Egypt, Libya plotted an assassination attempt in late 1977 against the U.S. ambassador in Cairo. In April 1980, Libya demanded that all Libyan exiles return to Libya or else they would be "liquidated." In October, in Ft. Collins, Colorado, a Libyan-backed gunman attempted to assassinate Faisal Zagallai, a doctoral student at the University of Colorado. In September 1980, there were two instances where Libyan fighter aircraft confronted U.S. reconnaissance planes over the Gulf of Sidra, a body of water off the Libyan coast that was claimed by Libya. In December 1979, the Libyan government allowed a 2,000 strong Libyan mob to attack and burn the U.S. Embassy in Tripoli.[39]

Libya was also a major agitator against U.S. allies in North Africa and the Middle East. The following incidents attributed to Libya occurred just in the first half of 1980:

1. Tried to assassinate Egypt's Anwar Sadat.
2. Instigated unrest in Algeria.
3. Sponsored a raid into Tunisia.
4. Burned the French and British embassies (after burning the American Embassy).
5. Armed Polisario guerrillas fighting Morocco.
6. Enabled Muslim rebels to fight the Philippine government.
7. Dispatched tribesmen to resume the civil war in Chad.
8. Financed Ethiopia's Soviet arms.
9. Killed political dissidents on at least five continents.[40]

All these incidents involving Libya set the foundation for a more concerted anti-American terrorist campaign by Libya during the Reagan administration.

Islamic Revolutionary Terrorism

The Islamic revolutionary terrorism strain first emerged under the Carter administration. Indicators of this strain first surfaced in Egypt. On August 23, 1977, 54 members of an Islamic extremist group called "Takfir Wai Hijira" (Repentance from Sin and Retreat) were tried in a military tribunal in Cairo. They were charged with the kidnapping and murder in July of the former minister of

---

[39] Karen De Young, "Mob Invades U.S. Embassy in Tripoli." *Washington Post*, December 3, 1980, p. A1.

[40] "The Nastiest Regime Going," *Washington Post*, August 1, 1980, p. A12.

religious endowments, Dr. Mohammed Hussein al-Zahaoi, who had written articles against the group. At the trial, the leader of the group, Ahmed Mustapha Shukri, shouted "we will rule this society one day so that our religion will triumph."[41] The group's name, goals, mindset, and worldview signaled the development of a new destabilizing actor in the terrorist milieu — Islamic revolutionary terrorist organizations. Two years later, a series of events further underlined and propelled the new threat. In January 1979, the Shah of Iran was overthrown by Iranian Islamic revolutionaries led by Ayatollah Khomeini. In February, Islamic revolutionaries opposed to the then government in Afghanistan were responsible for the kidnapping and subsequent death of U.S. Ambassador Adolph Dubbs in Kabul. Dubbs was kidnapped to force the Afghanistan government to release some imprisoned comrades and to attract media attention to their cause.[42]

In November 1979, militant Iranian students loyal to Khomeini seized the U.S. Embassy in Tehran and held 52 U.S. diplomats hostage for 444 days. During that time, the student hostage-takers held news conferences where they lambasted the U.S. and President Carter. Outside the embassy, periodic anti-American protests took place where the American flag and an effigy of Uncle Sam were frequently burned. In that same month, the Grand Mosque in Mecca, Saudi Arabia was seized by about 500 heavily armed Islamic fundamentalists who were anti-Western and included in their demands broadcast from the mosque loudspeakers the cutoff of oil exports to the United States and expulsion of all foreign civilian and military experts from the Arabian Peninsula. Khomeini then publicly accused the U.S. of being behind this takeover of the mosque. This led to anti-American protests in front of U.S. embassies in the Middle East and Asia, including two mob attacks on U.S. embassies in Islamabad, Pakistan and Tripoli, Libya. On November 20, a 5,000-strong mob attacked the U.S. Embassy in Islamabad, set it afire, forced the Americans into the embassy safe haven, and killed two U.S. Embassy officials. On December 2, a government-backed Libyan mob stormed the U.S. Embassy in Tripoli in response to Khomeini's claim. The year ended with the Soviet invasion of Afghanistan, laying the groundwork for an international call for jihad in the country and creating conditions for the eventual formation of al-Qaeda. Taken together, these events signaled the launch of a new anti-American terrorism strain, one that intermittently plagued the U.S. over the next five decades. Its "grand opening" took place during the Reagan administration.

---

[41] "Militant Moslems on Trial in Cairo," *New York Times*, August 24, 1977, p. 2.

[42] John M. Goshko and Richard M. Weintraub, "U.S. Ambassador to Afghanistan is Kidnapped, Slain in Shootout," *Washington Post*, February 15, 1979, p. A1.

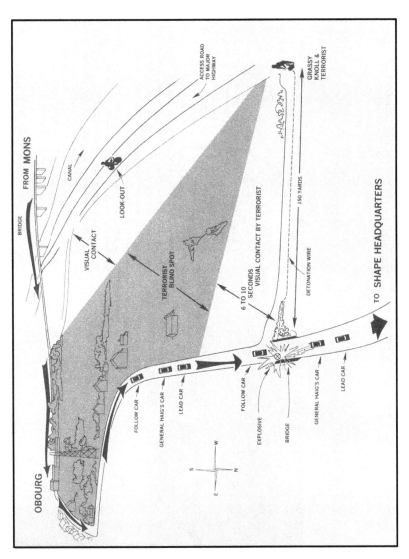

June 25, 1978: RAF attempted Assassination of NATO CINC General Alexander Haig near Mons, Belgium.

Source: U.S. Department of State.

Haig attack site. Photo shows culvert where bomb detonated.

Source: U.S. Department of State.

U.S. Ambassador to Afghanistan Adolph "Spike" Dubs kidnapped by Afghan militants then died during a botched rescue operation by Afghan police and Soviet advisors on February 14, 1979.

Source: U.S. Department of State.

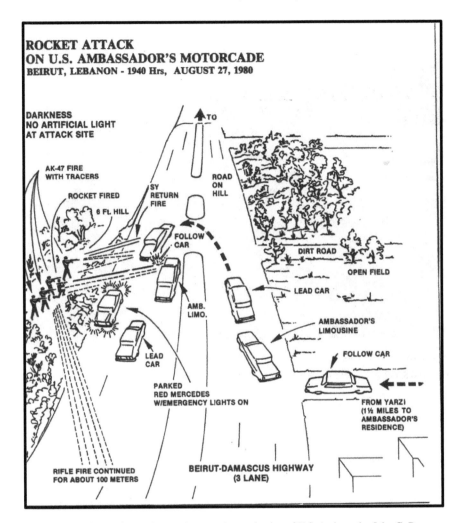

ROCKET ATTACK ON U.S. AMBASSADOR'S MOTORCADE
BEIRUT, LEBANON - 1940 Hrs, AUGUST 27, 1980

August 27, 1980 — Beirut, Lebanon: Attempted assassination of U.S. Ambassador John G. Dean.

Source: U.S. Department of State.

Site of attack on Ambassador Dean.

Source: U.S. Department of State.

December 1979 — Tripoli, Libya: Damage to U.S. Embassy from mob attack. Photo on right shows where embassy personnel threw oil down stairs to slow down protestors.

Source: U.S. Department of State.

November 21, 1979: 5,000 strong mob seizes U.S. Embassy in Islamabad. Two Embassy officials killed.

Source: U.S. Department of State.

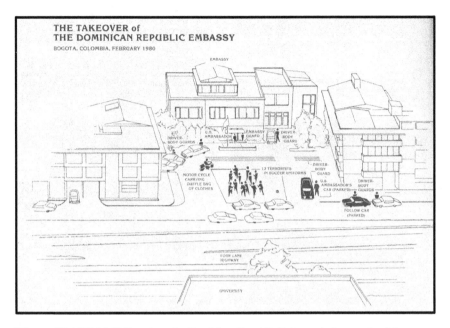

February 27, 1980: M-19 Terrorists seize Dominican Republic Embassy during a national day reception. U.S. Ambassador Diego Asencio was one of the hostages.

Source: U.S. Department of State.

Egyptian President Sadat, President Carter, and Israeli Prime Minister Begin at Camp David on September 6, 1978.

Source: Courtesy Jimmy Carter Library.

Chapter 8

The Carter Administration (1977–1980) — The Internal Threat

The Internal Terrorist Threat

The internal terrorist threat faced by the Carter administration was moderate. While the number of domestic and foreign spillover terrorism actors in the United States during the Carter administration can be accurately assessed, the number of attacks they carried out is problematic. The number of terrorist incidents carried out is one of several important metrics used to determine the level and scope of the internal terrorist threat. Frequency of operations is one measure of a group's operational capability. The type and target of the attack and the geographic distribution of the attacks are also key factors. The number of terrorist attacks carried out in the U.S. during the 1970s remains obscure. The FBI would be the logical agency to record such attacks. However, its statistics, or the media reporting on FBI statistics, can be confusing. For example, one report indicated that "according to the FBI, in the first four months (January–April 1977) of the Carter administration, there were 600 terrorist bombings that caused $3.8 million damage ... in 1976, there were 1,500 bombings ...."[1] However, another article stated that there were "65 terrorist related bombings in 1976."[2] In 1978, the FBI director stated that there were 116 terrorist bombings in 1976 and 111 in 1977.[3] In

---

[1] "600 Terrorist Bombings Reported in Four Months," *New York Times*, July 2, 1977, p. 6.

[2] Dena Kleiman, "The Potential for Urban Terror is Always There," *New York Times*, May 13, 1977, p. 155.

[3] Samuel T. and William T. Poole, "Terrorism in America: The Developing Internal Security Crisis," June 2, 1978, The Heritage Foundation, at http://www.heritage.org/research/reports/1978/06/terrorism-in-america-the-developing-internal-security-crisis. Accessed June 6, 2017.

December 1983, the FBI director stated that there were about 100 terrorist incidents (including bombings) in 1977.[4] Which figures are correct? A *Christian Science Monitor* article notes that "FBI figures show the total number of bombings attributed to terrorists dropped from 52 in 1979 to 17 in 1981."[5] According to the RAND terrorism database, there were 41 terrorist attacks in the U.S. in 1976, 26 in 1977, 20 in 1978, 24 in 1979, and 29 in 1980.[6]

The figures become even more inflated when the number of bombings in the early 1970s is reported. Bryan Burrough, author of *Days of Rage*, quoted the FBI as reporting that in 1971 and 1972, there were more than 2,500 bombings on U.S. soil.[7] However, the FBI's Counterterrorism Threat Assessment and Warning Group, in its "Terrorism in the U.S. — 1999" report noted that between January 1971 and June 1975, there were 641 terrorist incidents, 166 of which were bombings.[8] In June 1978, the Heritage Foundation quoted FBI figures indicating that in 1974, there were 2,044 bombing incidents that killed 24 people and 2,052 bombing incidents in 1975 that killed 69 people. In 1976, this same report stated that there were 1,564 bombings that killed 45 people. However, this report noted that the FBI director claimed that there were 45 terrorist bombings in 1974, 129 in 1975, 116 in 1976, and 11 in 1979.[9] It is clear then that two sets of figures were being used by the FBI and the media, one for bombings in general and one for terrorist bombings. Subtracting the terrorist bombings in 1974, 1975, and 1976 from the overall bombing totals for those years suggests that there were more bombings and bombing-related deaths in the U.S. by criminal elements, mentally unbalanced individuals, and business squabbles than by political terrorists. The differences in the above statistics could also be attributed to the definition of a terrorist incident, FBI retagging of past incidents, and terrorist bombings that were unclaimed. However, what is clear is that there were more terrorist bombings during the Nixon administration

---

[4]*Associated Press*, "FBI Head Says Terrorism in U.S. Down but Fear Rises, *New York Times*, December 15, 1983, at http://www.nytimes.com/1983/12/15/us/fbi-head-says-terrorism-in-us-is-down-but-fear-rises.html. Accessed July 17, 2016.

[5]Ward Morehouse III, "Puerto Rican terrorists, with low grass-roots support, change tactics," *The Christian Science Monitor*, January 7, 1983, at http://www.csmonitor.com/1983/0107/010749.html. Accessed October 4, 2016.

[6]Source: Max Roser and Mohamed Nagdy (2016) — 'Terrorism'. Published online at OurWorldInData. org. Retrieved from: https://ourworldindata.org/terrorism/. Accessed September 21, 2017.

[7]Burrough, *Days of Rage*, p. 3.

[8]FBI, Counterterrorism Threat Assessment and Warning Group, "Terrorism in the U.S. — 1999," FBI Publication #0308, p. 29.

[9]Samuel T. and William T. Poole, "Terrorism in America: The Developing Internal Security Crisis."

than the Ford and Carter administrations. It is also clear that during the Carter administration, the number of bombings had declined to less than 100 a year. What these statistics do not indicate is the prominence of the target or the political, economic, and diplomatic impact of an attack. The FBI also did not differentiate or keep separate statistics for domestic terrorist incidents and foreign spillover terrorist incidents. FBI statistics became more accurate beginning in the mid-1980s when it started to publish an annual report titled "Terrorism in the U.S."

One statistic that is somewhat easier to compile is the number of Americans killed in the U.S. as a result of internal terrorist activity. Nineteen people were killed in the U.S. in terrorist-related incidents during the Carter administration. Of these 19 people, 15 were civilians, one a police officer, and three were U.S. sailors. Thirteen were killed on the U.S. mainland and six on Puerto Rico. Of the 19 people killed in political terrorist attacks, six were killed by Puerto Rican separatists, five by right-wing terrorists, two by anti-Castro Cuban terrorists, two by Croatian terrorists, two by the Yugoslav secret service, one by an Iranian hitman, and one by Muslim terrorists.

The threat consisted of periodic terrorist attacks by domestic groups, Puerto Rican separatist groups, and foreign spillover terrorism conducted by Armenian, Anti-Cuban, and Croatian terrorist groups. Most of the domestic and foreign spillover terrorist groups that were active during the Ford administration continued into the Carter administration: Weather Underground Organization, Jewish Defense League, Anti-Castro Cuban exiles, the Justice Commandos of the Armenian Genocide, the Puerto Rican Armed Forces of National Liberation, Croatian and Serbian terrorists, the United Freedom Front, Anti-Abortion terrorists, and the New World Liberation Front (NWLF). New groups that emerged during the Carter administration were the Puerto Rican Macheteros, and the May 19 Communist Organization (M19CO). Many of these groups carried out sporadic attacks while a few engaged in a more sustained terrorist campaign in the U.S. Most of the attacks were carried out by foreign spillover terrorist organizations and not domestic terrorist groups.

Despite the number of groups and their activities, the internal terrorist threat was not a major concern for the Carter administration as it was under Nixon. However, three incidents stand out for their notoriety. On March 9–11, 1977, three buildings in Washington, D.C. were seized by American Muslim gunmen who took hostages. The gunmen demanded that the U.S. government hand over a group of men who had been convicted of killing seven relatives of the leader of the group and that the movie *Mohammad, Messenger of God* be destroyed because they considered it sacrilegious. The March 21 cover of *Newsweek* had a photo of the siege and proclaimed "Seizing Hostages: Scourge of the 1970s." This was the first major hostage-taking incident in the U.S. in the post-war period, and it attracted major media attention, amplified by its location in the nation's capital. In August 1978, another hostage-taking incident took place when two Croatian terrorists took six people as hostages in the West German Consulate in Chicago.[10] After 10 hours, the two terrorists surrendered. No hostages were harmed.[11]

The only terrorist hijacking in the United States during the Carter administration took place on June 20, 1979 when Nikola Kavaja, a Serbian nationalist and anti-communist, smuggled a homemade bomb aboard and seized American Airlines Flight 293 as it approached Chicago from New York City. There were 135 people on board. Kavaja was one of six Serbs convicted of the May 1979 bombing of a Yugoslav consul's home in Chicago and was a member of the Serbian Homeland Liberation Movement. The hijacker demanded the release of Stojilko Kajevich, a Serbian Orthodox priest and accomplice in the consul home bombing who remained in jail. The priest however refused the release and tried to talk the hijacker into giving up. After letting the passengers and most of the crew members go, Kavaja forced what was left of the crew to fly back to New York City, where he demanded and received a Boeing 707 to fly him eventually to Ireland after learning from his lawyer that Ireland did not have an extradition treaty with the United States. After arriving at Shannon Airport, he planned to take control of the airplane and fly it to Belgrade where he would crash it into the headquarters of the Yugoslav Communist Party. His lawyer persuaded him not to do this. Kavaja then surrendered to the Irish authorities, who then turned him over to the U.S. Kavaja was later sentenced to 67 years in an American prison but served only 20 years. Many nationalist Serbs considered Kavaja a hero and a patriot, while others thought of him as a ruthless terrorist.[12] Terrorist

---

[10] For additional information on terrorist targeting of diplomatic facilities in and outside the United States, see, Brian Jenkins, "Embassies Under Siege: A Review of 48 Embassy Takeovers from 1971–1980." RAND Corporation, #R-2651-RC, January 1981, at http://www.dtic.mil/dtic/tr/fulltext/u2/a103326.pdf. Accessed June 23, 2016.

[11] Chuck Sudo, "One For The Road: The 1978 West German Consulate Hostage Situation," *The Chicagoist*, August 17, 2012, at http://chicagoist.com/2012/08/17/one_for_the_road_the_west_german_co.php. Accessed September 4, 2016.

[12] "Serb Who Hijacked Plane in 1979 Dies," *The Associated Press*, November 11, 2008, at http://www.nbcnews.com/id/27665711/#.WHAFxFxF6Uk. Accessed October 5, 2017; and Bruce Weber, "Nikola Kavaja, Anti-Tito Hijacker of Jet, Dies at 75," *New York Times*, November 12, 2008, at http://www.

bombings, strafings, and assassinations also occurred in the U.S. during the Carter administration.

Domestic Terrorism

Weather Underground Organization

By the start of the Carter administration, the Weather Underground Organization was on the decline, confronted with internal problems. Some members left to form another group — the May 19th Communist Organization. The only action that can be attributed to the WUO took place in November 1977 when WUO members were arrested on conspiracy to bomb the office of California State Senator John Briggs. However, the WUO perished during the Carter administration.

The May 19 Communist Organization

M19CO was a small (less than 20) left-wing terrorist group that was active in the U.S. from 1978 to 1985. It advocated the overthrow of the U.S. government through armed struggle. The name of the group was based on the May 19th birthdays of North Vietnamese leader Ho Chi Minh and the black nationalist leader Malcolm X. It was founded by a faction of the Weather Underground that initially took the name The Prairie Fire Organizing Committee (PFOC). The east coast element of the PFOC then called themselves the M19CO. The M19CO was an alliance between various groups like the Weather Underground Organization, the Black

nytimes.com/2008/11/12/world/europe/12kavaja.html. Accessed May 4, 2017; Ronald Koziol and Sean Toolan, "Serb Switches Jets in N.Y. after Freeing 122 at O'Hare," *Chicago Tribune*, June 21, 1971, p. 1, at http://archives.chicagotribune.com/1979/06/21/page/1/article/hijacker-flying-to-ireland; David Funkhouser, "The Pilot and The Hijacker," *Hartford Courant*, February 3, 2002, at http://articles.courant.com/2002-02-03/news/0202030509_1_china-clipper-flight-school-national-guard/2; https://en.wikipedia.org/wiki/Nikola_Kavaja. Accessed July 14, 2017; and Christopher S. Stewart, 'Nikola Kavaja: Interview with an Assassin," *The Independent* (London), December 9, 2006, at http://www.independent.co.uk/news/people/profiles/nikola-kavaja-interview-with-an-assassin-427508.html. Accessed May 23, 2017.

Liberation Army, the Black Panthers, and the Republic of New Africa (RNA).[13] The M19CO had a significant lesbian leadership.[14] The stated objectives of all these groups were: (1) to free political prisoners held in American prisons, (2) to use appropriation of capitalist wealth to fund the third stage of revolution,[15] and (3) to initiate a series of bombings and terrorist attacks.[16] Although the M19CO emerged during the Carter administration, most of its attacks were carried out during the Reagan years. The few operations carried out during the Carter years were prison breaks.

On November 2, 1979, three M19CO terrorists, posing as prison visitors to the Clinton Correctional Facility in Clinton, New Jersey, freed Assata Shakur, a member of the Black Liberation Army, who was serving a sentence of life plus 26–33 years for the 1973 murder of Werner Foerster, a N.J. state trooper, and the wounding of another trooper, James M. Harper. Shakur had been called by associates "the soul of the Black Liberation Army." The Clinton facility where she was

---

[13] National Advisory Committee on Criminal Justice Standards and Goals, Task Force on Disorders and Terrorism. "Report of the Task Force on Disorders and Terrorism," December 1976, p. 518, at https://www.ncjrs.gov/pdffiles1/Digitization/39469NCJRS.pdf. Accessed May 23, 2017. The Revolutionary Action Movement (RAM) was organized in 1963 and advocated militant self-defense for blacks. In June 1967, police in New York City and Philadelphia detained 16 members of the group. Two were charged with plotting to assassinate black moderate civil rights leaders Roy Wilkins and Whitney Young. Four more were later arrested in Philadelphia on charges of conspiring to trigger a riot by poisoning the water supply. The arrest yielded 300 grams of potassium cyanide. By 1968, the group was inactive. RNA was founded in April 1968 by former RAM members. It had goals similar to that of RAM. In August 1970, 11 RNA members, including its leader, were charged with murder, assault, and waging war against the state of Mississippi. The RNA was resurrected by members of the Black Panthers and Black Liberation Army after the M19CO and black nationalist terrorists carried out the October 1981 robbery near Nyack, New York of a Brink's armored truck containing $1.6 million. Three security and police officers were killed in the attack. The goal of the resurrected RNA was to create a separate black nation that was to include the states of Alabama, Georgia, Louisiana, Mississippi, and South Carolina. The leader of the RNA in the 1980s was Randolph Simms, also known as Coltraine Chimurenga, a Harvard University doctoral student. See also, Maxwell C. Stanford, "Revolutionary Action Movement (RAM): A Case Study of an Urban Revolutionary Movement in Western Capitalist Society," M.A. Thesis submitted to Atlanta University, May 1986, at http://www.ulib.csuohio.edu/research/portals/blackpower/stanford.pdf. Accessed October 26, 2017.

[14] Adolfo Perez Esquivel. *Let Freedom Ring: A Collection of Documents from the Movements to Free U.S. Political Prisoners* (Oakland, CA: PM Press, 2008), p. 28.

[15] The third stage of revolution is direct physical confrontation with the powers that be, which involves a large number of citizens or all-out war.

[16] Karl A. Seger, "Left-Wing Extremism — The Current Threat," U.S. Department of Energy, Office of Safeguards and Security, Oak Ridge Institute for Science and Education: Center for Human Reliability Studies, April 2001, ORISE 01-0439. p. 1, at https://www.osti.gov/scitech/servlets/purl/780410. Accessed June 4, 2016.

being held was a minimum-security facility with one maximum-security building where Shakur was being held. The three visitors, using false documents, had their names checked but were not searched by guards. There was no metal detector at the registration building where visitors sign in before being taken by a van to see the inmates. The three terrorists were taken by a van to the maximum-security South Hall to see Shakur. They apparently commandeered the van during the trip, drew pistols, and seized two guards as hostages. They then freed Shakur and left the prison in the prison van with the two hostages and fled the correctional facility. The group later switched vehicles, released the two hostages, and escaped.[17] It is believed that Shakur lived as a fugitive in the U.S. and eventually fled to Cuba where she was granted asylum in 1984.[18]

On May 21, 1979, M19CO, BLA, and Armed Forces of Puerto Rican National Liberation (FALN) members engineered the escape of FALN member William Morales from Bellevue Hospital in New York City where he was recovering after a bomb he was building exploded in his hands. On February 28, 1979, Morales was convicted of possession of explosives and possession and transportation of explosives and a shotgun. Morales was believed to be the chief bomb

---

[17]Robert Hanley, "Miss Chesimard Flees Jersey Prison, Helped By 3 Armed 'Visitors'," *New York Times*, November 3, 1979, p. 1; Arnold H. Lubash, "Killer Says He Helped In Chesimard's Escape," *New York Times*, December 2, 1987, at http://www.nytimes.com/1987/12/02/nyregion/killer-says-he-helped-in-chesimard-s-escape.html. Accessed September 23, 2016; see also, "Assata Shakur: The Interview," *The Talking Drum*, 2001, at http://www.thetalkingdrum.com/bla4.html. Accessed May 23, 2016; and Mark Hemingway, "Behind the Controversy Over Rapper Common's Invitation to the White House," *The Weekly Standard*, May 11, 2011, at http://www.weeklystandard.com/behind-the-controversy-over-rapper-commons-invitation-to-the-white-house/article/560872. Accessed September 28, 2017.

[18]"Since May 2, 2005, the FBI has classified Shakur as a terrorist and offered a $1 million reward for assistance in her capture. On May 2, 2013, the FBI added her to the Most Wanted Terrorist List, the first woman to be listed. It is unlikely that Cuba will ever return Shakur to the U.S. The two countries do not have an extradition treaty and if the U.S. makes a serious request for Shakur, Cuba will likely counter with a request of its own for Luis Posada Carriles. Carriles, 86-year-old, is now living out his old age in Miami. Cuba wants him because he was convicted in Panama of the 1976 bombing of a Cuban airliner that killed 73 civilians and has been suspected of planting bombs in Havana in 1997 (including one that killed an Italian tourist). In addition, Cuba has long been a haven for African Americans who have committed what might be interpreted as political crimes. Black Panthers such as Eldridge Cleaver, Huey Newton, and Raymond Johnson spent time in Cuba in the 1960s (not always happily). At one time, it was speculated that as many as 90 African Americans were living in Cuba under asylum. It is likely that Shakur will die of natural causes in Cuba." See, Achy Obejas. "Why Cuba will never send Assata Shakur to the U.S.," *Chicago Tribune*, December 29, 2014, at http://www.chicagotribune.com/news/opinion/commentary/ct-cuba-assata-shakur-fbi-america-obama-perspec-1230-20141229-story.html. Accessed June 5, 2017.

maker for FALN and was implicated in 50 bombings between 1974 and 1978. Alan Berkman, a physician at Bellevue Hospital, was a member of M19CO. After Morales escaped from Bellevue Hospital, he fled to Mexico, where he was held by the authorities, before emigrating to Cuba in 1988.[19] As of December 2019, Morales remains on the FBI Most Wanted domestic terrorists list with a reward of $100,000 for information leading to his arrest.

Sam Melville/Jonathan Jackson Unit

The small, left-wing, northeastern-based Sam Melville/Jonathan Jackson Unit continued to operate during the Carter administration.[20] It still had only seven-eight members. The group carried out only four dynamite bombings from 1977 to 1980. The attacks were aimed at facilities of the W.R. Grace Company in Needham, Massachusetts; the Mobil Oil Corporation in Waltham and Wakefield, Massachusetts; and the Mobil Oil Corporation in Eastchester, New York. There were no injuries during these attacks. In Communique #7, the group stated that "we continue our attacks against the imperialist U.S. corporations in support of independence and justice" and claimed responsibility for the two October 27, 1978 attacks on Mobil Oil facilities.[21] It explained that it targeted Mobil Oil because "the oil and chemical companies are particularly entrenched in many Third World countries ... Mobil Oil — the world's 8th largest company — has extensive operations in Puerto Rico as does its subsidiary, the Container Corp. of America." The communiqué continued — "Mobil's foreign operations include Chile, Argentina, Brazil, Iran, Rhodesia, South Africa and others ... it has enabled Rhodesia to salvage its economy and oil its war machinery ... violating the United Nations sanctions against trade with Rhodesia and reaping huge profits ... their profits is blood money!" Mobil was also criticized for enabling South Africa's "fascist/racist government to continue its genocidal policies."

The group's communiqué also paid homage to the independence movement in Puerto Rico and called for the immediate release of the following people:

---

[19]Storer H. Rowley, "U.S. Angry At Mexico," *Chicago Tribune*, June 29, 1988, at http://articles. chicagotribune.com/1988-06-29/news/8801110512_1_bombings-william-morales-mexican-foreign-ministry. Accessed July 6, 2017.

[20]This east coast Melville–Jackson Unit should not be confused with the Jonathan Jackson–Sam Melville Unit of the NWLF which operated on the West Coast.

[21]All quotes in this communiqué come from a copy of this one-page typed communiqué in the author's possession.

- Oscar Collazo — the surviving member of the two-person Puerto Rican terrorist cell that attempted to assassinate President Harry S. Truman on November 1, 1950 while he was staying at the Blair House and
- Lolita Lebrón, Rafael Cancel Miranda, and Irving Flores Rodríguez — three of the four-person Puerto Rican terrorist cell that carried out the March 1, 1954 strafing of Congressmen from the visitor's gallery of the U.S. House of Representatives.[22]

The release of these Puerto Rican terrorists was also a frequent demand of several Puerto Rican separatist terrorist groups. The Melville/Jackson Unit communiqué dedicated the attacks on Mobil to two "revolutionaries," one of whom, Mariano Gonzalez, "was killed in action by N.Y.C. pigs on April 2, 1978." The other, Eric Thompson, was captured on the same day. The communiqué notes that the attacks on Mobil were timed to two upcoming anniversaries: October 30 — "the 28th anniversary of the armed uprising in Juyuya and other areas of Puerto Rico" and November 1 — the 20th anniversary of the Puerto Rican terrorist attack on the Blair House. The Melville/Jackson Unit underwent a metamorphosis from 1980 to 1981 and emerged in December 1982 during the Reagan administration as the "United Freedom Front."

Anti-Abortion Terrorism

In the 1973 Roe vs. Wade landmark decision, the U.S. Supreme Court ruled that abortion should be legal throughout the United States under certain conditions. In time, and in response to this decision, an anti-abortion movement [or the right-to-life movement or pro-life movement] emerged in the U.S. Adherents opposed elective abortion on both moral and sectarian grounds and supported its legal prohibition or restriction. Anti-abortion adherents argue that human life begins at conception and that the human embryo is a person and therefore has a right to life. Like most social movements, there was no central organization or leadership as the movement was composed of different organizations with different motives

---

[22] On October 6, 1977, President Carter granted clemency to the fourth terrorist involved in the attack on the House of Representatives, Andres Figueroa Cordero. Cordero had terminal cancer. The President commuted Cordero's sentence on humanitarian grounds because of his physical condition. The commutation order, which is not a pardon, was an act of clemency on the part of the President. See, Jimmy Carter: "Andres Figueroa Cordero Announcement of the Commutation of Mr. Figueroa Cordero's Prison Sentence," October 6, 1977. Online by Gerhard Peters and John T. Woolley, The American Presidency Project, at http://www.presidency.ucsb.edu/ws/?pid=6757. Accessed May 6, 2019.

and interpretations of abortion and under what circumstances it should be allowed. In addition, there were divisions within the movement in terms of the use of violence, against property and persons. Three years after Roe vs. Wade, in March 1976, during the Ford administration, concerted anti-abortion violence began in the U.S. when activists carried out an arson attack of Planned Parenthood in Eugene, Oregon which caused around $60,000 in damage. During the Carter administration, there were 14 arson and bomb attacks on abortion clinics in Minnesota, Texas, Nebraska, New York, Vermont, and Ohio which caused $2.4 million in damages.[23] All the attacks were carried out by lone-wolf terrorists — individuals acting alone — who wanted to instill fear in doctors, nurses, aides, and clinics performing abortion and in women seeking an abortion. Anti-abortion terrorism increased significantly during the Reagan, Bush, and Clinton administrations.

New World Liberation Front

NWLF, which emerged in 1974, is believed to have been involved in about 100 bombing attacks in its primary operational area, the San Francisco area and northern California, from 1974 to 1980 when it perished. It carried out around 20–22 bombings during the 1977–1980 Carter years. Most of the attacks took place in and around the San Francisco bay area and were aimed at mostly Pacific Gas and Electric (PG&E) transformers and substations. NWLF tended to focus on local grievances like conditions in area jails, slumlords, labor disputes, and rising electricity rates, and picked targets responsible for them: PG&E, the Federal Building, district attorneys, city supervisors, Coors beer distributors (worker's strike), and a Union 76 Refinery.[24] It also bombed the San Francisco War Memorial Opera House on September 9, 1977. Following its standard practice, a woman called the Associated Press and gave directions to a telephone booth which contained an NWLF communiqué. In this communiqué claiming responsibility for this attack, the group demanded that elderly tenants evicted in August from the International Hotel be allowed to return and the hotel "be

---

[23]Mireille Jacobson and Heather Royer, "Aftershocks: The Impact of Clinic Violence on Abortion Services," p. 5 and 37, at http://users.nber.org/~jacobson/JacobsonRoyer6.2.10.pdf. Accessed August 4, 2017.

[24]Les Ledbetter, "Terrorist Bombs in San Francisco Prompt Concern on Leader's Safety," *New York Times*, February 11, 1977, p. 14; "Bomb Found in San Francisco," *New York Times*, September 2, 1977, p. 30.

brought up to code."[25] It picked issues that the average person could sympathize with or support.

Estimates of the number of group members varied from 5 to 15 members. FBI Special Agent Stockton Buck, who tracked the group during this period, believed that it had six-seven members.[26] What confused the situation even more was the fact that different people and cells also used the NWLF name in attacks. It appeared that it was not a centralized, monolithic group but an umbrella term. It is also possible that only two people were behind it. The FBI was only later able to publicly identify two people as belonging to the group — Ronald Huffman and his girlfriend Maureen Minton. The FBI used fingerprint evidence found on communiqués and bombs to later build cases against them. They were linked forensically to 16 bombings and attempted bombings. Huffman and Minton had emerged from the radical scene in the San Francisco area where they had joined or supported various left-wing organizations there.[27] The demise of the "group" was baffling. It carried out a bombing on November 10, 1977 against a Union 76 Refinery, then went inactive for five months.

It resurfaced on March 14, 1978 to bomb a PG&E substation, expressing support for a coal miner's strike. It was the last attack and communiqué by the NWLF. There was no subsequent communiqué to explain what happened to the group. In 1978, its overt spokesperson declared that the group had suspended its bombings to assess their effectiveness. There was an implication that attacks on persons might be the next step.[28] There is evidence to suggest that Huffman and Minton were the founders and primary bombers for the NWLF. Moreover, the group stopped its bombing campaign due to the growing mental instability of Huffman. On September 23, 1979, he brutally killed Minton with a hatchet in their backyard. Escaping in a car, he took part of Minton's brain with him. He was quickly arrested by police. He was found guilty of murder and died in a California prison in 1999. An informant surfaced and provided more information to the FBI concerning Huffman and Minton's links to the NWLF. In addition, a new occupant of the house where the two had lived found a package buried in the backyard that contained NWLF literature, communiqués, codes, surveillance rules, cash, and a munitions manual. It was the end for one of the more enigmatic, most active domestic terrorist groups in U.S. history. One of the above ground

---

[25] "Bomb Explodes at Opera House," *New York Times*, September 10, 1977, p. 19.

[26] Burrough, *Days of Rage*, p. 356.

[27] This section dealing with Huffman and Minton comes from Burrough, *Days of Rage*, pp. 355–360.

[28] Jenkins, *Terrorism in the United States*, May 1980, p. 10.

spokespersons for the NWLF was a man named Jacques Rogiers who delivered its communiqués to the press. In January 1977, he was arrested. He was released from jail in July 1977. Friends and supporters held a getting out party for him. He never showed up and was never heard of again.[29]

George Jackson Brigade

The George Jackson Brigade (GJB) emerged during the Ford administration and perished during the Carter administration. In 1977, the GJB robbed four banks, a state liquor store, and carried out one failed bank robbery in Washington and Oregon. It bombed a Ranier National Bank, Puget Power Station, Two Dodge dealerships, one Buick dealership, one Mercedes dealership, the Diebold, Inc. company office, and a Power substation. As a result of the death of one member and the arrest of two others in 1976, the GJB was operating with three-four members in 1977. In November of that year, Rita Brown was arrested. On December 24, the group carried out its last attack when it bombed a new car sitting on a railroad car waiting for delivery to a dealership. Three months later, the group was neutralized by law enforcement.

On March 21, 1978, federal agents in Tacoma, Washington arrested three persons believed to be the only remaining members of the GJB terrorist group. The three were in a car eating hamburgers and drinking milkshakes at a drive-in restaurant just before they were about to rob the nearby J Street branch of the United Mutual Savings Bank. The three arrested were John William Sherman, Therese Ann Coupez, and Janine Bertram (at the time, the FBI did not know who she was, so they gave her the pseudonym of "Jori Uhuru," and her real name was found out later). All three were in disguise. The FBI said Sherman wore a priest's collar, Coupez a "painted-on mustache," and Uhuru wore a wig.[30] Law enforcement believed that all members of the GJB were now captured. The media did not believe the group was completely neutralized.[31] There must have been one or two

---

[29] Burrough, *Days of Rage*, pp. 346–349, 351–353, 357, 433.

[30] Daniel Burton-Rose. *Guerrilla USA: the George Jackson Brigade and the Anticapitalist Underground of the 1970s* (Berkeley: University of California Press, 2010), p. 273.

[31] Les Ledbetter, "Coast Bombing Expected to Go On Despite Arrests," *New York Times*, March 24, 1978, p. 7; "Suspect in Bombings In Northwest Arrested," *New York Times*, March 22, 1978, p. 18; Walter Wright, "Pages in the Life of Bruce Seidel: Two Sides of a Revolutionary," *Seattle Post-Intelligencer*, April 22, 1976; Walter Wright, "Slain Man's Document: Self-Implication in Three Bombings," *Seattle Post-Intelligencer*, April 21, 1976. In a subsequent interview, Rita Brown noted that "we hooked up with a guy at the Post-Intelligencer and he became our guy. Eventually, he was

other members who were still at large as a communiqué was issued on Easter Sunday 1978 from GJB signed by "the rest of us."

In this communiqué, the remaining members acknowledged that "our losses are heavy" with these arrests but vowed to "fight on."[32] These were hollow words. The GJB was never heard from again. In the end, this group was composed of Ed Mead, Bruce Seidel, Janine Bertram, John Sherman, Mark Cook, Rita Brown, and Therese Coupez. All were dead or captured.

Puerto Rican Separatism

Puerto Rican separatist terrorism continued during the Carter administration. As during the Ford administration, the Puerto Rican separatist groups were small and had little support from the Puerto Rican people. As during the Ford administration, the support for independence of Puerto Rico on the island was low during the Carter administration. In the general election in Puerto Rico in November 1976, the Puerto Rican Independence Party and the Puerto Rican Socialist Party received 6% of the vote between them.[33]

The Armed Forces of Puerto Rican National Liberation

In 1977, the FALN carried out 20 arsons and bombings on the U.S. mainland, 14 in 1978, and eight in 1979. The group also carried out a dozen bombings during this period on Puerto Rico.[34] Total bomb damage was estimated at $1.8 million. One person was killed and ten injured in these attacks. Most of the FALN attacks during this period took place in New York City, with some in Chicago and Washington, D.C. It was believed that the group in New York City had around 12 members.[35] Some of the FALN explanations for these bombings and other actions in 1977 are discussed below.

---

moved out of town by the company" (Daniel Burton-Rose, *Creating a Movement with Teeth*), pp. 260–261.

[32] Daniel Burton-Rose, *Creating a Movement with Teeth*, p. 140.

[33] Robert Reinhold, "Elusive FALN Terrorists, believed 12 in Number, Have Bombed Scores of Buildings in Recent Years," *New York Times*, August 4, 1971, p. B6.

[34] A chronology of FALN incidents from 1974 to 1983 can be found at the end of the "1983 Sentencing Memorandum," and Sater, "Puerto Rican Terrorists," pp. 21–29; at http://www.latinamericanstudies.org/faln.htm. Accessed May 5, 2016.

[35] Robert Reinhold, "Elusive FALN Terrorists, believed 12 in Number, Have Bombed Scores of Buildings in Recent Years," *New York Times*, August 4, 1971, p. B6.

On February 18, 1977, the FALN bombed the Merchandise Mart, which caused $1.3 million in damage, and the U.S. Gypsum building, which caused $23,000 in damage, in New York City.

> *Our actions are part of an offensive taken by us to further the cause of independence for Puerto Rico and the unconditional freedom of the five nationalist political prisoners, Irving Flores, Rafael Cancel Miranda, Lolita Lebrón, Oscar Callazo, and Andrea Figureoa Corder.... Furthermore, we want to demonstrate through our actions that the Yanki Imperialist's attempt at assimilating and annihilating the Puerto Rican Nation ... any attempt to suppress the Puerto Rican Liberation Movement by the Imperialist forces, the FBI, and the Carter administration shall be met with revolutionary violence ... we ask the Carter administration to grant the unconditional freedom to the five Puerto Rican nationalists, who are the longest incarcerated political prisoners in the Western Hemisphere.*[36]

On March 20, 1977, the FALN bombed the American Bank Note Company and the Whelan Drug Store (but aimed at the FBI office on the upper floor) in New York City, which caused $65,000 in damage and one injury.

> *We protest the use of the Federal Grand Jury against the Puerto Rican Independence Movement. We also protest the use of the Federal Grand Jury here in New York, Chicago, and its future use in the different parts of the United States.... The American Bank Note Company for being one of the chief administrators in the exploitation of the World's Working Class. For printing the stocks and bonds that decide which families will eat and live well and which ones will starve and die. This company is also the printer of the currency of several Latin American countries, Mexico and Guatemala being two of them.*[37]

On April 9, 1977, the FALN bombed a Macy's, Gimbel's, and Bloomingdale's Department stores in New York City, which caused over $60,000 in damages.

> *Today's actions mark our determined efforts to free our homeland from the control of Yanki Imperialists, and the attempted exploitation of our*

---

[36] FALN communiqué, typed, one page, dated 2/17/77, in author's possession.
[37] FALN communiqué, typed, one page, dated 3/20/77, signed by FALN Central Command, in author's possession.

*natural resources. At no time will we let any corporation or the colonial
government of Puerto Rico attempt to mine our natural resources. This
also includes any off-shore drilling for petroleum. These natural
resources belong to the Puerto Rican People and nobody else.*[38]

A rare FALN lethal attack took place on August 3, 1977 when it bombed a
Department of Defense office and Mobil Oil Building Employment Services
office in New York City. Damage was around $18,000 but the Mobil bombing
killed one person, Charles Steinberg, a 26-year-old newlywed lawyer, and injured
five others. A typed FALN communiqué was found at the Jose Julian Marti[39]
statue in Central Park that stated that the actions were just a warning to "multinational corporations" that "explore and exploit our natural resources" and are part
of "Yanki Imperialism." The communiqué also noted that the bombings were
timed to the fact that the status of Puerto Rico was to come up soon in the United
Nations.[40]

The downfall of the FALN was slow and gradual and caused both by mistakes by group members and the investigative will and capability of the FBI and
local police departments.[41] The first setback took place in December 1976 when
police located a FALN "bomb factory" in Chicago which led to the identification
of several FALN members, including Carlos Torres and Oscar Lopez-Rivera.
More importantly, the discovery of this FALN bomb factory led to the investigation
of Maria Cueto and the FALN's use of a legitimate charity as a quasi-front organization.[42] The second major setback took place in July 1978 when a bomb
accidentally exploded in a safe house in New York City. The bomb blew off the
hands of the FALN's key bomb maker, Willie Morales, but he survived.[43] The third

---

[38] FALN communiqué, typed, one page, dated 4/9/77, signed by FALN Central Command, in author's
possession.

[39] Jose Julian Marti campaigned for the liberation of Cuba from Spain and was imprisoned by Spanish
authorities in 1868. Fleeing to New York in 1880, he continued to advocate for Cuban freedom while
in exile and organized the Cuban Revolutionary Party in 1892. Marti returned to Cuba in 1895, at the
beginning of Cuba's successful fight for independence.

[40] Mary Breasted, "100,000 Leave New York Offices as Bomb Threats Disrupt City," *New York Times*,
August 4, 1977, p. B6.

[41] Mary Breasted, "3-Year Inquiry Threads Together Evidence on FALN Terrorism," *New York Times*,
April 17, 1977, p. 1. "One of the Federal Government's most difficult and extensive investigations,
reaching into New York, Chicago, Denver, New Mexico, Southern California, and Puerto Rico." See
also, "Woman Is Charged in F.A.L.N. Blast," *New York Times*, September 8, 1977, p. 1.

[42] Burrough, *Days of Rage*, pp. 382–386.

[43] Ibid., pp. 461–465. Morales later escaped from a prison hospital in May 1979 with the help of a
small left-wing terrorist group that called itself "The Family." See Burrough, *Days of Rage*, pp.

setback took place in April 4, 1980 when 11 members of the FALN were arrested, including Carlos Torres and Freddie Mendez. The latter turned on the FALN and provided information to the FBI — another blow to the FALN.[44] The last major setback occurred in May 1981 when Oscar Lopez was arrested in Chicago. The FALN was unable to recover from these setbacks. There was an attempt to resurrect the FALN in 1982–1983 but it was short-lived.

The Macheteros

The second most active and dangerous Puerto Rican separatist terrorist group was the Boricua Popular Army (EPB), also called Los Macheteros (The Machete Wielders). The machete is symbolic of the immediate past of most workers on Puerto Rico, who fed their families cutting sugarcane with machetes. It was the weapon of the poor and their work tool. It has been called the Caribbean hammer and sickle.[45] Puerto Rican separatist groups believed they were engaged in armed struggle on "two fronts, one in Puerto Rico and the other on the U.S. mainland." While the FALN focused its terrorist activities in the "second front," that is, on the U.S. mainland, the Macheteros emerged in the "first front" or Puerto Rico in 1976 to initiate a terrorist campaign there. The group was founded by Filiberto Ojeda Ríos, Juan Enrique Segarra-Palmer, and Orlando González Claudio. The group operated primarily during the Carter and Reagan administrations. Like most of the Puerto Rican separatist organizations the Macheteros embraced a Marxist–Leninist ideology and called for the independence of Puerto Rico. The group announced its operational birth as a terrorist organization in August 1978 by taking credit for killing a Puerto Rican police officer:

> *In the early morning of Thursday, August 24, 1978, a combat unit of the Ejercito Popular Boricua undertook to seize a police patrol in the neighborhood of Naguabo Beach. The objective of this operation was the seizure of uniforms, arms and the police vehicle. The surprise factor, our*

471–473 for information on this escape of a man with no fingers who pushed himself down a rope from a third-floor room.

[44] William B. Crawford, Jr., "Prosecutor Tells of FALN Bomb Factories," *Chicago Tribune*, July 9, 1985, at http://articles.chicagotribune.com/1985-07-09/news/8502140493_1_seditious-conspiracy-opening-statements-alejandrina-torres. Accessed June 7, 2017.

[45] Michael González-Cruz, "Puerto Rican Revolutionary Nationalism: Filiberto Ojeda Ríos and the Macheteros," *Latin American Perspectives*, Issue 163, Vol. 35 No. 6, November 2008, pp. 152–153, at http://citeseerx.ist.psu.edu/viewdoc/download?doi=10.1.1.943.4670&rep=rep1&type=pdf. Accessed July 5, 2018.

greater fire-power and our numerical superiority guaranteed our secu-
rity and the defeat of the enemy. Police officer Rodriguez did not heed our
order to surrender — and, drawing his gun, fired against our combatants,
who saw themselves obliged to respond. This was how police officer
Rodriguez fell in combat.[46]

The communiqué also contained six hand-drawn sketches of the attack to underline the group's warning to police "to pay attention to our orders to surrender....
If this is what they do, their lives will be respected.... Otherwise they assume
responsibility for that which could happen."

It has been speculated that the first Macheteros attacks may have been the
September 22, 1977 assassination of the American lawyer Allen A. Randall in
Santurce, Puerto Rico. The attack was claimed by a previously unknown group
calling itself the "Comandos Obreros" [Labor Commandos] in a short note left at
the scene. In a longer, follow-up communiqué, dated "Fall 1977," the group stated
that the "revolutionary execution of Allan H. Randall" was carried out because
"Randall was not an ordinary corporation lawyer.... His specific duties went
beyond those of that profession ... he planned and implemented anti-workers'
conspiracies developed at the highest levels of the intelligence service of the
United States, principally the Central Intelligence Agency (CIA)." There was
however widespread disapproval of this assassination by the Puerto Rican people
and criticism from Puerto Rican independence elements. It is for this reason that
the Macheteros most likely never claimed formal credit for this murder.[47] The fact
that this was the only terrorist attack claimed by the Commandos Obreros suggests that the parent terrorist group responsible for this attack was testing the
response to the attack before it would formally claim credit under the group's real
name, in this case, the Macheteros.

There are no credible sources in terms of the number of members in the
Macheteros. A September 29, 2005 article in *The Economist* states that at one
point the group had 1,100 members.[48] While the Wikipedia entry for the group
quotes a Puerto Rican academic as stating that the group "consists of approximately 5,700 members with an additional unknown number of supporters, sympathizers, collaborators and informants throughout the U.S. and other countries."[49]

---

[46] Movement for National Liberation Documents, pp. 89–90.

[47] Armando Andre, "Dawn of the Macheteros," *The Graphic Chronicle* (San Juan), 1987, at https://
groups.google.com/forum/#!topic/soc.culture.puerto-rico/e50CH7AMIGk. Accessed June 6, 2017.

[48] http://www.economist.com/node/4455267. Accessed July 7, 2018.

[49] https://en.wikipedia.org/wiki/Boricua_Popular_Army. Accessed October 5, 2017.

The operational or offensive strength of a terrorist group is generally determined primarily by the number of operatives or actual terrorists and not the number of supporters and sympathizers. The group's threat projection is partially based on how many terrorists it can use in offensive operations. An examination of the number of terrorist attacks claimed and attributed to the Macheteros, the number of terrorists involved in each attack, and the number of members arrested over time suggests that the above two figures are significantly inflated. A more practical estimate would be that the group had between 250 and 300 operatives in Puerto Rico and the U.S. mainland. Neither the FBI nor any other U.S. government agency ever provided a public figure for the group's membership.

During the Carter administration, the Macheteros generally carried out bombings designed to cause property damage. The group attempted to avoid civilian casualties. On two occasions it fired anti-armor rockets at government buildings. The group's lethal attacks were aimed mostly at U.S. military personnel and police in Puerto Rico.[50] On March 12, 1979, the Macheteros fired at three U.S. Army R.O.T.C. officers in Hato Rey, Puerto Rico, slightly injuring Lieutenant Colonel Robert Davenport. On July 14, three Federal Aviation Administration navigational stations and a Coast Guard navigation beacon were destroyed by bombs, disrupting air traffic between the United States and Latin America. Its most lethal attack, however, took place at the end of the year.

On December 3, 1979, four Machetero terrorists opened fire on a bus carrying 18 U.S. sailors to a Naval facility on Puerto Rico, killing CTO1 John R. Ball and RM3 Emil E. White, as well as wounding nine others. The group claimed joint responsibility for the attack along with two other separatist groups — the Armed Forces of Popular Resistance (FARP) and the Organization of Volunteers for the Puerto Rican Revolution (OVRP). In a communiqué dated December 3, the groups stated they carried out a "military action against the military forces of Yankee occupation." The communiqué accused the U.S. and Puerto Rican governments of "massacring two young patriots" in Cerro Maravilla[51] and killing Angel Rodriguez Cristobal. The latter was arrested in May for interrupting

---

[50] Jo Thomas, "Armed Puerto Rican Groups Focus on Military, *New York Times*, January 16, 1981, at http://www.nytimes.com/1981/01/16/us/armed-puerto-rican-groups-focus-attacks-on-military.html. Accessed June 6, 2018.

[51] The Cerro Maravilla massacre is the name given by the Puerto Rican public and media to describe the events that occurred on July 25, 1978, at Cerro Maravilla, a mountain in Puerto Rico. On that day, two young Puerto Rican pro-independence activists, Arnaldo Darío Rosado and Carlos Soto Arriví, were killed in a Puerto Rican police ambush. The event sparked a series of political controversies where, in the end, the police officers were found guilty of murder and several high-ranking local government officials were accused of planning and/or covering up the incident. The Macheteros

military exercises in Vieques[52] and then was "executed," according to Puerto Rican nationalists, in a federal prison in Tallahassee, Florida. Cristobal was found dead in his cell and prison officials alleged that he had committed suicide. The groups claimed that the killings of these patriots was carried out by "Yankee intelligence" and meant to "intimidate our people and their leaders, in a vain attempt to see that we cease our fight ... persisting in the imperialist perpetuation of control and exploitation of our people, they intend to paralyze the patriotic forces in this libertarian and revolutionary advance through a policy of terror and repression." It further noted that "we warned the imperialist Yankees who must respect the life and safety of our prisoners in agreement to the Geneva Convention on war ... we are willing to take this fight to the ultimate consequences."[53]

On January 12, 1981, 11 Machetero terrorists, disguised in military uniforms, cut a hole in a perimeter chain link fence, and attacked the Muñiz Air National Guard Base which was attached to the international airport in San Juan, Puerto Rico. The terrorists detonated 25 explosive devices that destroyed nine aircraft (several A-7 Corsair II light attack aircraft and a single F-104 Starfighter supersonic fighter-interceptor aircraft). Damage was estimated at $45 million. The entire operation took less than eight minutes. This was the first peacetime incident in which U.S. Air Force (USAF) aircraft were destroyed by a terrorist act and the first-time terrorists had attacked a USAF installation on U.S. soil. It was at the time the greatest material loss from any single act of terrorism perpetrated against the USAF anywhere in the world.[54] The attack was timed to coincide with the birthday of the Puerto Rican independence advocate Eugenio María de Hostos who was born on January 11, 1839. His anniversary is regularly marked by pro-independence protests against U.S. rule in Puerto Rico. In a communiqué, dated January 13, the Macheteros claimed responsibility for the attack on the air base,

---

believed that the Puerto Rican police were counseled by the FBI in this incident and that the students were "executed."

[52]Vieques is a small island off the mainland of Puerto Rico. The U.S. has used it since World War II as a U.S. Navy bombing range and weapons testing ground. Members of the local community and Puerto Rican nationalists have protested against the facility for among other issues the environmental impact of the weapons testing and the expropriation of their land by the Navy. The U.S. Navy eventually left the island in 2003 after a series of large protests that began in 1999.

[53]EPB, OVRP, FRAP one page, typed communiqué in Spanish, December 2, 1979, at http://www.cedema.org/uploads/FARP-OVRP-EPB-12-3-1979.pdf. Accessed October 23, 2017. See also, "Radicals Say Attack on Bus Is Retaliation for 3 Deaths; Involved in Vieques Protest", *New York Times*, December 4, 1979. p. A11, and Clyde Haberman, "Terrorists in Puerto Rico Ambush Navy Bus, killing 2 and Injuring 10", *New York Times*, December 4, 1979, p. A1, A10.

[54]From U.S. Air Force report on the incident at footnote 19, at https://en.wikipedia.org/wiki/Puerto_Rico_Air_National_Guard#1981_Terrorist_Attack. Accessed May 6, 2018.

citing the attack as "Operation Pitirre II." The communiqué notes that the attack was designed to express solidarity with the Farabundo Martí National Liberation Front in El Salvador which was "fighting the regime that oppresses and murders them." The attack was also a response to the "need of our people to continue the fight against the American colonial yoke — widely denounced by the international community in a resolution adopted by the General Assembly of the United Nations — to build a free, independent and neutral country without serving in a foreign killer army and Yankee military bases that expose our people to nuclear extermination." The phrase "serving in the foreign killer army" refers to the U.S. draft registration. The communiqué also denounced the "abusive regime of the colonial governor Romero Barceló that progressively becomes more repressive and dictatorial against vast sectors of our people."[55]

In a later internal assessment of the air base attack, the Macheteros' leadership praised the attack as it was "the most devastating blow given to the Yankees in 'North American territory' since Pearl Harbor and outside its territory since the TET offensive in Vietnam." The assessment continued, "our organization's prestige was greatly increased, and this has opened great organizational perspectives … the news agencies are attentive to our communiques and demonstrate a tendency to publish them, even though they might be edited … furthermore, it made us known all around the world, facilitating international work."[56]

The Macheteros attack on the air base triggered criticism of the base security measures. The National Guard Bureau was aware of the shortfalls in security at the Muniz air base and of the threat, yet corrective actions had not been implemented at the time. Immediately after the incident, the guard force at Muniz was doubled, and the force quickly grew from 10 to 60 on-duty guards. It was also recommended to increase the size of the day-to-day guard force, improve the fencing and lighting, use duress alarms, increase the number of training man-days, and install a closed-circuit television system. Security at the base was provided by both contracted civilian guards hired through operations and maintenance funds, uniformed military, and full-time and part-time Air National Guard Security Policemen.[57] Therefore, in addition to the $45 million in damage caused by the attack, tens of thousands of dollars were spent increasing security at U.S. bases on Puerto Rico

---

[55] EPB one page, typed communiqué in Spanish with group logo at top, dated January 13, 1981, at http://www.cedema.org/uploads/PRTP-EPB-1-13-1981.pdf. Accessed May 4, 2018.

[56] From a Macheteros document titled "Report of the Central Committee to the Congress," p. 22, at http://www.latinamericanstudies.org/puertorico/Macheteros-Central-Committee-Report.pdf. Accessed May 23, 2018.

[57] Op. cit., https://en.wikipedia.org/wiki/Puerto_Rico_Air_National_Guard#1981_Terrorist_Attack. Accessed August 4, 2017, footnote 19.

and in the U.S. as a result of the attack.[58] The Macheteros continued their terrorist attacks on Puerto Rico and occasional ones on the U.S. mainland during the Reagan administration.

The Unabomber — Ted Kaczynski

The parcel and pipe bombing campaign of Ted Kaczynski or the "Unabomber" began during the Carter administration. It continued through the Reagan and Clinton administrations. The first bomb attributed to Kaczynski was discovered on May 25, 1978. It was a mail parcel left on the campus of the University of Illinois–Chicago, wrapped in a brown paper bag. The return address on the parcel was of a professor at Northwestern University. School officials returned the package to Northwestern, where it exploded, causing minor damage. About a year later, on May 9, 1979, a pipe bomb was placed in a room at Northwestern University. A Northwestern graduate student picked up the bomb, and it exploded, injuring him. At this point, there were no indicators to suggest that these attacks were carried out by the same person, a potential serial bomber. Kaczynski escalated his attacks by targeting an airliner. On November 15, 1979, a parcel bomb concealed in a wooden box, with an altimeter, mailed from Chicago, partially exploded in the cargo compartment of American Airlines flight 444 from Chicago to Washington, D.C. Smoke quickly filled the passenger cabin, injuring 12 people through smoke inhalation. An emergency landing was made at Dulles Airport near Washington, D.C. The bomb did not ignite because instead of explosive powder, it contained barium nitrate, a powder often used to create green smoke in fireworks.[59] The explosion caused little damage to the plane other than blackening the inside roof of the cargo compartment. Officials said the aircraft's exterior was not pierced by the blast and that the plane's flight controls were unharmed.

Although this was not the first attack carried out by Kaczynski, it was the attack that brought the FBI in to investigate, as airliner bombing is a federal crime. Government officials knew of no previous incident in which a bomb sent

---

[58] See, Thomas C. Tompkins, Military Countermeasures to Terrorism in the 1980s," RAND Corporation, August 1984, N-2178-RC.

[59] "Unabomber Case and Trial," World of Forensic Science, 2005, at http://www.encyclopedia.com/people/social-sciences-and-law/crime-and-law-enforcement-biographies/unabomber. Accessed May 4, 2017. Chronology of Kaczynski's attacks from https://www.law.cornell.edu/background/unabom/history.html. Accessed October 3, 2017; and http://www.historycommons.org/timeline.jsp?timeline=us_domestic_terrorism_tmln&us_domestic_terrorism_tmln_specific_events=us_domestic_terrorism_tmln__unabomber__attacks. Accessed May 4, 2017.

through the mails was detonated aboard an aircraft.[60] Although there is disagreement as to whether the bomb if fully detonated would have brought the plane down, Kaczynski intended to kill the passengers on the plane.[61] In an April 1995 letter sent to various media outlets, Kaczynski threatened further violence and claimed that his bomb-making expertise was growing. In that letter, referring to the November 1979 bomb aboard the American Airlines plane, he wrote:

> *The idea was to kill a lot of business people who we assumed would constitute the majority of passengers. But of course, some passengers would likely have been innocent people — maybe kids or some working stiff going to see his sick grandmother. We're glad now that that attempt failed.*[62]

Given that his bomb was sent through the mails, he would have no way of knowing which flight it would be placed aboard. His broad assumption then was business people would be found on every flight, as would innocent people including women, babies, and children. Kaczynski used the term "we" instead of "I" to confuse investigators.

Kaczynski struck again on June 3, 1980, when Percy Wood, the President of United Airlines, received a letter in the mail. The letter informed him that he would soon be receiving a book of social significance. It was signed "Enoch W. Fisher." A week later, on June 10, Wood received a hollowed-out copy of "Ice Brothers," by Sloan Wilson. When he opened the book, it exploded, injuring him. U.S. postal inspectors responded to the Wood bomb but had little or no knowledge about Flight 444. They contacted the FBI to investigate the Wood bombing. A case file and task force were opened, and the case was called "UNABOM," according to the FBI's six-letter naming convention — "UNiversity and Airline BOMber." They linked the two university bombings in 78–79 with the 79–80 airline-related bombings. The press created the name Unabomber from that original task force designation. Some similarities noted among several of the four bombs were the homemade "initiator" used in each device; the "junkyard"

---

[60] Stephen J. Lynton, and Mike Sager, "Bomb Jolts Jet," *Washington Post*, November 16, 1979, at https://www.washingtonpost.com/archive/politics/1979/11/16/bomb-jolts-jet/f0cb8543-c2ab-44c5-bdd5-203c53efffe1/?utm_term=.289cd00df979. Accessed October 4, 2017.

[61] "Investigators found only a faulty timer prevented the bomb from obliterating the plane," at http://www.aerospaceweb.org/question/planes/q0283.shtml. Accessed June 17, 2018.

[62] George Lardner and Lorraine Adams, "Unabomb Victims, a Deeper Mystery," *Washington Post*, April 14, 1996, p. A1.

appearance of the devices; the soldering was clumsily done; and all the wood used in the devices was of low quality.

Hanafi Muslim Siege in Washington, D.C.

The only multiple terrorist barricade and hostage situation to take place in the United States occurred during the Carter administration. On March 9–11, 1977, three buildings (the city hall, B'nai B'rith headquarters, and the Islamic Center of Washington) in Washington, D.C. were seized by 12 American Muslim gunmen, led by Hamaas Abdul Khaalis, who left the Nation of Islam because he blamed them for the murder of his five children. The gunmen took 149 hostages and killed a journalist. The gunmen demanded that the movie *Muhammad: Messenger of God* be stopped from being shown in theaters, the dismissal of $750 in court costs from a 1973 court case, visits from Warith Deen Mohammed and champion boxer Muhammad Ali, and the turning over to him for punishment of seven Black Muslims on trial for the 1973 murder of four members of his family and the 1965 assassination of Malcom X. The hostage crisis lasted around 39 hours and ended as a result of the State Department-facilitated intervention of three Muslim ambassadors from Egypt, Pakistan, and Iran. There was no direct involvement from the White House or President Carter. All the hostages were released on March 11. In the final agreement, Khaalis and the others involved in the hostage-taking at the two sites where no one was killed were only charged and then freed on their own recognizance. They were all later tried and convicted.[63]

The Hanafi Muslim siege triggered the debate on the role of the press in a terrorist incident and how the authorities should negotiate for the lives of the hostages. There were very few such incidents in the U.S. prior to this incident so there were no templates or lessons learned for reference. Not surprisingly, these two issues — the role of the press and how to negotiate — became perennial concerns in future decades.

Foreign Spillover Terrorism

Anti-Castro, Cuban Exiles

Cuban exile terrorism continued during the Carter administration. The names used most often to claim these attacks were El Condor, Omega 7, the Pedro Luis

---

[63] Mickolus, *A Chronology of Events, 1968–1979*, pp. 679–688; Simon, *The Terrorist Trap*, pp. 124–125.

Boitel Commandos and Cesar Baez group. Of these, Omega 7 was the most active and violent. Omega 7 was responsible for 28 (ten in the Miami area) terrorist attacks during the Carter administration.[64] There appears to have been an operational shift by Omega 7 in 1976 from the Miami area to the New York/New Jersey area.[65] The New York area cell was led by Pedro Remon. This shift could have been dictated by the fact that Cuban diplomatic interests were concentrated in New York City. There were simply more "official" targets in New York City than in Miami. For example, in 1977, the group bombed the Venezuelan Mission to the United Nations to protest Venezuela's imprisonment of Cuban exile Orlando Bosch on charges of blowing up 73 passengers aboard a Cubana Airlines jet the previous year. In 1978, Omega 7 bombed the Cuban Mission to the U.N. for the third and fourth times, the Mexican Consulate in New York, and the Avery Fisher Hall in Lincoln Center, to protest a performance by a Cuban orchestra. In 1979, among other attacks, it bombed the Cuban Mission a fifth and sixth time (injuring two policemen), set off high explosives at the Soviet Mission to the U.N. (injuring four policemen and two mission employees), tried to assassinate Fidel Castro during his visit to the U.N. General Assembly in October, and tried to plant a suitcase bomb on a TWA flight from New York to Los Angeles, which exploded prematurely before being loaded.[66]

On March 25, 1979, a bomb in a suitcase exploded at the TWA Terminal at the Kennedy Airport in New York City, injuring four baggage workers, just as it was being loaded onto a non-stop flight to Los Angeles. About 157 passengers and crew members were on the flight. Minutes later, two bombs exploded in a building which housed a medical supply company owned by Cuban Americans in Union City, New Jersey which shipped household goods and medicines to

---

[64] http://www.eurekaencyclopedia.com/index.php/Category:Anti-Cuba_Terrorist_Campaign. Accessed May 9, 2017, and New York Times, March 3, 1980, p. B4; and information on Omega 7 founding and attacks, particularly the assassinations and attempted assassinations comes from http://www.latinamericanstudies.org/belligerence/Cuban-Militant-Organizations-AB-225.pdf. Accessed October 3, 2016.

[65] By early 1980, the Dade County Police anti-terrorist squad believed that anti-Castro violence in Dade County had disappeared." "Anti-Castro Units Trace Roots to Invasion Attempts of 1960s," *New York Times*, March 3, 1980, p. B4.

[66] Arnold H. Lubasch, "Cuban Exile Group Reportedly Planned to Kill Castro on his '79 U.N. Trip, *New York Times*, September 23, 1983, at http://www.nytimes.com/1983/09/22/nyregion/cuban-exile-group-reportedly-planned-to-kill-castro-on-his-79-un-trip.html. Accessed June 6, 2016; Robert Mcg. Thomas Jr., "Bomb Damages Russian Mission on East 67th St.," *New York Times*, December 12, 1979, p. 1.

Cuba and a travel agency that arranged flights between Cuba and the U.S. Another bomb exploded at the New Jersey Cuban Program, a refugee organization in Weehawken, New Jersey. There were no injuries. Omega 7 claimed responsibility via phone calls.[67] The caller claiming responsibility for the airport bombing said TWA was targeted because it had provided airplanes for tourist flights to Cuba. He also stated that the bomb was to explode when the plane was empty. "These actions were carried out in retaliation for the work presently performed by the agencies in enterprises in mutual agreement with the tyranny of Fidel Castro." However, TWA had stopped providing these planes several months ago. The caller continued: "Similar actions will continue until the source of revenue to Castro is cut off and as long as Castro's servants in the U.S. persist in trying to confuse the Cuban people with false promises of reunification, reunification without dignity and ignoring thousands of Cuban patriots killed or incarcerated by Castro."[68]

During the Carter administration, Omega 7 carried out two successful assassinations and several attempted assassinations. The two assassinations were carried out against a Cuban American and one against a Cuban diplomat. On November 25, 1979, Eulalio Jose Negrin, the Director of a Cuban Refugee Center whose moderate stance had triggered threats on his life, was shot and killed with an automatic weapon in Union City, New Jersey. He was a member of the Group of 75 who went to Cuba in 1978 to visit with Castro and negotiate the release of 5,000 political prisoners and extract an agreement from Cuba to allow Cuban Americans to visit friends and relatives in Cuba for the first time in two decades. He was a proponent of normalization of relations with Cuba. He knew that his time was running out and had prepared a will and bought a casket.[69] Omega 7 claimed responsibility for the Negrin assassination, stating that "we will continue with these executions until we have eliminated all the traitors living in this country." Negrin was the second member of the Committee of 75 to be killed in 1979. Carlos Munos, a travel agent, was killed in San Juan, Puerto Rico in May. In March 1980, the FBI declared Omega 7 the most dangerous terrorist organization in the country and said the government had assigned the highest priority to prosecuting its members. The FBI believed the group in

---

[67] Robert D. McFadden, "Kennedy Bomb Hurts 4 Workers in Baggage Area," *New York Times*, March 26, 1979, p. A1 and B6.

[68] "Omega 7 Used bombs for a Cause," *New York Times*, April 2, 1979, p. B4.

[69] Warren Hinckle and William Turner. *The Fish is Red: The Story of the Secret War Against Castro* (New York: Harper and Row, 1981), p. 328.

New York had no more than seven members — none of whom were known at the time.[70]

On September 11, 1980, Felix Garcia Rodriguez, a Cuban diplomat assigned to the Cuban Mission to the U.N. in New York City, was shot and killed with the same weapon as Negrin, a MAC10 machine gun. He was killed on the sixth anniversary of the founding of Omega 7. The group also planned to kill four Cuban officials on that day, but the plan was aborted when Omega seven members following the Cuban officials lost them in heavy traffic.[71] The assassination of Rodriguez was the first assassination of a U.N. diplomat in the United States. The FBI had investigative responsibility for the attack as it has jurisdiction over attacks on foreign officials with diplomatic immunity. There were also two attempted assassinations of Cuban diplomats in New York City and Washington, D.C. by Omega 7.

On March 25, 1980, an Omega 7 terrorist placed a bomb with a radio-controlled firing system on the gas tank of the car of Raul Roa-Kouri, the Cuban ambassador to the United Nations. The firing system for this bomb originally had been assembled for use in a bomb intended to assassinate Fidel Castro in October 1979 when he attended a session of the United Nations. However, that attempt was aborted because the terrorist was not able to place the bomb close enough to Castro. Omega 7 simply disassembled the bomb and retained it for future use.[72] In the attempt on Roa-Kouri, the bomb was attached to the gas tank of the car by magnets. However, the bomb fell off and was discovered after the ambassador's chauffeur accidentally backed into another vehicle while parking. The Omega 7 terrorist with the firing transmitter called off the attack after the bomb fell off the car because many school children were in the area. In late September 1980, Omega 7 attempted to assassinate Ramon Sanchez Parodi, Chief, Cuban Interests Section in Washington, D.C. The operation was cancelled when two Omega 7 terrorists were arrested in Belleville, New Jersey on September 24, 1980, while attempting to steal a car that was to be driven to Washington and used to kill Parodi in a likely car bombing.[73]

---

[70] Ken Szymkowiak, "Bomb Found at Office of Cuban-Charter Airline Here, *Miami News*, December 31, 1980, p. A7; Robin Herman, "Highest Priority Given by U.S. To Capture of Anti-Castro Group," *New York Times*, March 3, 1980, p. 1, B4.

[71] Jonathan Marshall, "The Earlier 9/11 Acts of Terror," September 10, 2014, at https://consortiumnews.com/2014/09/10/the-earlier-911-acts-of-terror/. Accessed June 5, 2016.

[72] Ibid.

[73] Information on Omega-7 founding and attacks, particularly the assassinations and attempted assassinations comes from http://www.latinamericanstudies.org/belligerence/Cuban-Militant-Organizations-AB-225.pdf. Accessed June 4, 2017.

The following factors contributed to the success of Omega 7 in the U.S. and hampered U.S. law enforcement's ability to neutralize the group for seven years:

- Omega 7 was a small, tightly knit group of dedicated anti-Castro fanatics, most of whom were unknown to law enforcement authorities.
- Omega 7 received financial support and some cooperation, at a minimum, silent approval which could be construed as tacit approval, from some elements of the Cuban exile community in the United States.
- The late 1980 split in the group and the creation of an entirely new group further hampered investigations.
- The government of Cuba identified Omega 7 as its number one enemy in the United States and in so doing enhanced the status of the group within the exile community in the U.S.
- When Cuban militants were arrested on various charges, they often refused, usually out of fear of retaliation, to provide information on the activities of the other militant exiles.
- Although the Cuban government was able to successfully penetrate most of the anti-Castro groups, they never penetrated Omega 7.

On December 11, 1979, Omega 7 bombed the Soviet Mission to the U.N. in New York City, injuring four policemen and two employees. This attack put pressure on the FBI to focus more on Omega 7. The next day, an FBI agent in New York City stated that the unit investigating Omega 7 is "starting to be beefed up."[74] One of the by-products of this pressure was the establishment in May 1980 of the first Joint Terrorism Task Force (JTTF) between the FBI and the N.Y. Police Department. More pressure was put on the FBI in September 1980 when Omega 7 assassinated the Cuban U.N. Diplomat in New York City. There was an outcry from the U.N., U.N. diplomats, and the U.S. State Department. Omega 7 now became the top terrorist concern for the FBI. Adding to the concern was the fact that the 1980 Olympic Winter Games were scheduled to be held in Lake Placid, New York. These were the first Olympic Games in the U.S. since the murder of Israeli athletes at the 1972 Summer Games at Munich that made security a top priority for Olympic events. There was concern that domestic terrorist groups might target the 1980 Olympic event. None did.

Law enforcement agencies got a break that led to the unraveling of Omega 7 in late December 1980. On December 22, 1980, two Omega 7 terrorists, Pedro

---

[74] Camille Kenny, "FBI Sets Sights on 'Hoods' of Omega 7," *The Hudson Dispatch*, December 13, 1979, p. 1, 10.

Remón and Ramon Saúl Sanchez Rizo, bombed the Cuban Consulate in Montreal. Several days later, while crossing the border to return to the United States, they were interrogated by American officials at the U.S. border. Their identities were confirmed, and they were released by U.S. Immigration and Naturalization Service (INS) officials. The information obtained by INS was forwarded to the FBI and the Omega 7 investigation began to focus on their activities and those of their associates Eduardo Arocena, Andres Garcia, and Eduardo Fernandez Losada. Investigation into Remon's background indicated that he was in frequent telephonic contact with Eduardo Arocena, with many of the telephone calls occurring around the times of Omega 7 crimes. Moreover, the JTTF record checks and interviews at car rental agencies disclosed that Arocena and Remon had rented cars at Newark International Airport shortly before several Omega 7 crimes. Comparison with NYPD records revealed that one of Arocena's rental cars received a parking ticket across the street from the Cuban Mission to the United Nations (CMUN) in New York on the day Omega 7 assassinated Cuban diplomat Felix Garcia Rodriquez in New York City. Subpoenaed records turned up a copy of Arocena's canceled check paying the parking ticket.[75] These investigations led to the grand jury proceedings on Arocena and other suspected Omega 7 members during the Reagan administration.

Jewish Defense League

Terrorist activity by militant Jews in the U.S. continued during the Carter administration. Although Soviet interests were their main targets, the JDL targeted anyone it considered a threat to the survival of radical Jewish nationalism. This included foreign diplomats, domestic radical-right organizations, Arab and Muslim activists, journalists and scholars, and Jewish community members who the JDL thought were not sufficiently supportive of their views.[76] At least seven attacks can be linked to Jewish terrorists. The name most frequently used to claim responsibility for these attacks was the Jewish Defense League. However, other names such "The Jewish Committee of Concern," "Jewish Armed Resistance," and "New Jewish Defense League" were also used. It is likely that these names were simply being used as cover names for the JDL to confuse law enforcement and to convey a broader Jewish militant base in the U.S. All the attacks were either bombings or arson attacks aimed at targets such as Iranian

---

[75] FBI Report on Omega-7, dated October 29, 1993 at http://cuban-exile.com/doc_001-025/doc0011.html, accessed June 24, 2018.

[76] https://www.splcenter.org/fighting-hate/extremist-files/group/jewish-defense-league. Accessed June 6, 2017.

banks, Egyptian diplomatic targets, a theater showing a pro-PLO movie, and the Democratic Party's Los Angeles headquarters. The attack on the Democratic Party office was to protest President Carter's "pressure on Israel." It is assumed this "pressure" had to do with President Carter's reported leaning on Israel during the Camp David accords meetings with Egypt in September 1978.

Several attacks on Egyptian diplomatic targets in 1978 clearly signaled opposition to these accords. On February 5, 1978, there was an arson attack on a New York home of an Egyptian employee at the United Nations. Then, on February 15, an arson attack was carried out on the home of an Egyptian official of the World Bank in Arlington, Virginia. A group calling itself "The Jewish Committee of Concern" claimed responsibility for both attacks, saying they were to protest President Carter's sale of military planes to Egypt. The group stated that "Egypt, which still seeks Israel's destruction, should not receive lethal U.S. Jet Fighters." U.S. law enforcement agencies saw similarities in both attacks.[77] In November, there was an attempted arson attack on the Egyptian Consulate in San Francisco claimed by the JDL. Terrorist attacks by the JDL were supplemented with periodic occupations or disruptions at various buildings or events: the West German Consulate offices in Miami, the New York offices of Hebrew University and American Friends of Hebrew University, the Temple Sinai synagogue in Washington, D.C., the New York office of the Soviet airline, Aeroflot, the offices of United Zionist Revisionists of America, and the Israeli Consulate and Mission to the U.N. in New York.

Anti-Yugoslav Terrorism

Croatian and Serbian terrorist activity continued worldwide during the late 1970s. The problem became so acute in West Germany that the West German government declared émigré Croatian separatism to be "the Number One problem with foreigners" in the country.[78] Yugoslav President Tito characterized the Croatian émigrés overseas as perhaps the greatest "threat to the [Yugoslav] regime and to

---

[77] Judith Valente and Eugene L. Meyer, "Egyptian's Md. Home Hit by Arson," *New York Times*, February 16, 1978, p. B4. Chronology of JDL attacks from Anti-Defamation League (ADL) website at http://archive.adl.org/extremism/jdl_chron.html. Accessed July 18, 2017.

[78] Mate Nikola Toki, "Diaspora Politics and Transnational Terrorism: An Historical Case Study," European University Institute Working Papers, Robert Schuman Centre for Advanced Studies, RSCAS 2009/42, p. 11, at http://cadmus.eui.eu/bitstream/handle/1814/12236/RSCAS_2009_42.pdf?sequence=1. Accessed October 23, 2017.

the survival of the federal state."[79] This issue remained a problem for the U.S. during the Carter administration. From 1977 to 1980, Croatian and Serbian terrorists carried out 12 attacks in the U.S. Eleven were linked to Croatian terrorists. Most were aimed at Yugoslav targets (bank, travel agency, and diplomatic facilities). Hitting such targets was a key part of the Croatian terrorist campaign against Yugoslavia. The Australia-based Croatian Revolutionary Brotherhood (HRB) instructed its members, "Destroy all Yugoslav embassies and consulates, kill Yugoslav diplomatic representatives because they are common criminals and Fascists. Prevent migrants from traveling on Yugoslav aircraft and destroy Yugoslav aircraft. Wreck the travel agencies."[80] Two of the Croatian terrorist attacks in the U.S. were also aimed at U.S. targets to call attention to their cause and one at a West German target to pressure the government not to extradite a Croatian terrorist to Yugoslavia. The attacks were carried out in New York City, Chicago, San Francisco, and Washington, D.C.

On June 14, 1977, less than a year after the hijacking of TWA 355 in New York City by Croatian terrorists, three armed Croatian nationalists coolly walking past a uniformed New York City policeman standing guard outside, and without arousing his suspicions, invaded the Yugoslav Mission to the United Nations, wounding one person. The terrorists went to the upper floor and pretended that they had seized a woman as a hostage, imitating her in a falsetto voice. They dropped leaflets from the upper floor calling for the independence of Croatia, hauled down a Yugoslav flag, and shouted to police that they wanted some of the leaflets delivered to the U.N. Secretary General Kurt Waldheim. After a few hours, the NYPD convinced the men to surrender, reminding them that the Yugoslavs could act with impunity against them in the consulate because they were technically not on U.S. soil. The three were sentenced in federal court to terms of between four and seven years.[81]

On August 17, 1978, two Croatian Americans from the Chicago area entered the West German Consulate there and demanded to talk to the Consul General. He was not in the building at the time. The terrorists then pulled out pistols and one claimed to have a bomb in his briefcase. They demanded the release of fellow Croatian terrorist, Stjepan Bilandzic, who was being held in West Germany.

---

[79]"Yugoslavia — The Ustashi and the Croatian Separatist Problem, 27 September 1972." In: From "National Communism" to National Collapse: U.S. Intelligence Community Estimative Products on Yugoslavia, 1948–1990, (Washington, D.C.: GPO, 2007), p. 470.

[80]Mate Nikola Toki, "Diaspora Politics and Transnational Terrorism," p. 10.

[81]William Claiborne, "Croat Terrorists Held in N.Y. Shooting," *The Washington Post*, June 14, 1977, p. A3.

Bilandzic, a leading Croatian nationalist, was serving a life sentence in West Germany for attempting to assassinate the Yugoslav Consul General in Dusseldorf. He was also the founder of a terrorist organization called the Croatian People's Resistance. A court ruling in West Germany in early August, opening the way for Bilandzic's extradition to Yugoslavia, apparently provoked the Croatians' seizure of the Chicago Consulate. The Yugoslav government had demanded Bilandzic's extradition and that of seven other Croatians held in West Germany in return for the extradition of four left-wing West German terrorists from the Red Army Faction (RAF) who were arrested and detained in Yugoslavia. The two Croatian terrorists in Chicago said they wanted to block Bilandzic's possible extradition to Yugoslavia because they feared he would be killed by Yugoslav authorities. They threatened to explode the bomb they carried if their demands were not met. Bilandzic's brother, McLaughlin Bilandzic, eventually convinced them that it was futile to hold out. After a 10-hour siege, the two Croatians released the hostages. The two terrorists were eventually sentenced to two and a half years in prison for "unarmed imprisonment of a foreign national."[82] On September 12, the West German government announced that it would refuse the Yugoslav request for the extradition of three Croatians wanted in Yugoslavia for terrorism.

On November 22, 1978, three Serbs were arrested in New York City for plotting to bomb a Yugoslav Consulate independence celebration in Chicago on November 29. Two men in Chicago were also charged with the same offense. U.S. law enforcement agencies had tapes of the defendants claiming involvement in seven bombings of Yugoslav diplomatic facilities and residences in 1977. Another said he was involved in the June 9, 1976 bombing of the Yugoslav Embassy in Washington, D.C., injuring three people; another said he was involved in the June 23, 1975 bombing of the Yugoslav mission to the U.N. in New York City. They were all charged with "conspiring to transport and receive in interstate commerce an explosive with knowledge and intent that it will be used to damage and destroy a building." These were the first U.S. government charges against Serbian terrorists in the U.S.[83]

---

[82]"Two Odpor Agents Convicted of Terrorism," *Associated Press*, December 1, 1978. The two Croatian terrorists were Bozo Kevala, 36, and Mile Kodzoman, 32. Prosecutors played a tape recording of a trans-Atlantic telephone call between the defendants and Stjepan Bilandzic during the siege. During the conversation, in Croatian, Kodzoman told Bilandzic: "But we still have six hostages on our hands.... If you want, we are ready, like Bozo said this morning, to throw them through the window."

[83]Peter Kihss, "5 Serbs Accused of Plot to Bomb Chicago Offices," *New York Times*, November 23, 1978, p. B4.

On June 20, 1979, Nikola Kavaja, a Serbian nationalist from New Jersey, claiming he had dynamite, hijacked American Airlines Flight #293 out of LaGuardia airport. There were 135 passengers and crew on the plane. He demanded the release of an imprisoned Serbian terrorist in a U.S. jail. Kavaja wanted to crash the plane into communist party headquarters in Belgrade, Yugoslavia, but needed the imprisoned Serbian's knowledge of the streets in Belgrade to fly into the building. However, once the imprisoned terrorist refused to be released, Kavaja had to abandon his plan for fear he would direct the plane into the wrong building. He soon surrendered, was convicted, and served 20 years in prison.[84] On December 4, 1979, the Jet and Cruise Travel Agency in New York City, owned by a native Yugoslav, was bombed. Three people were injured. The agency was apparently targeted because the terrorists felt that the owner's contact with Yugoslavia was detrimental to the Croatian cause. The terrorists called news agencies about an hour after the bombing and directed them to a locker in the Grand Central Station. A letter there identified the terrorists as the Croatian Liberation Fighters and warned of other bombs if their demands for an end to economic aid to Yugoslavia were not met.[85]

On June 3, 1980, a bomb exploded at the NW Washington home of the acting Yugoslav ambassador Vladimir Sindjelic. There were no injuries. In a two-page typewritten letter mailed to *The Washington Post* and other news media, the group, "Croatian Freedom Fighters," said it carried out the "action in Washington, D.C. as a sign of protest against the Yugoslav government" and its treatment of the Croatian movement's supporters. The letter, postmarked June 3, was in Croatian. The letter demanded, among other things, an "urgent investigation into the case of Miro Baresic" and that a Swedish doctor be allowed to visit Baresic in a Swedish prison.[86] "We are turning attention of the American and world

---

[84]Christopher S. Stewart, "Nikola Kavaja: Interview with an Assassin," *The Independent*, December 9, 2006, at http://www.independent.co.uk/news/people/profiles/nikola-kavaja-interview-with-an-assassin-427508.html. Accessed May 6, 2016. David Funkhouser, "The Pilot and The Hijacker," *Hartford Courant*, February 3, 2002, at http://articles.courant.com/2002-02-03/news/0202030509_1_china-clipper-flight-school-national-guard/2; and https://en.wikipedia.org/wiki/Nikola_Kavaja. Accessed June 3, 2016; and David Binder, "Serb and Croat Terrorism Laid to Tiny Exile Bands," New York Times, June 22, 1979, p. A3.

[85]The Associated Press, "Manager of Blast-Torn Shop Arrested on Weapons Charge," *New York Times*, December 5, 1979.

[86]Miro Baresic was a Croatian nationalist militant convicted for the April 7, 1971 murder of the Yugoslavian Ambassador to Sweden, Vladimir Rolovic, who was the former head of the Yugoslav Secret Service, the UDBA. On September 15, 1972, Croatian terrorists hijacked a Scandinavian Airlines domestic flight. They demanded the release of seven imprisoned Croatian terrorists, including Baresic. Sweden released all seven. Baresic was flown to Spain where he was held in Spanish

public and governments to the decision of the command of Croatian liberation forces that actions toward Croatian fighters and nationalists will no longer be tolerated," the letter said. The group said it would continue to make its demands "until the creation of a Croatian state." One State Department official theorized that the bombing of Sindjelic's home was "an attempt to throw a shadow" on President Carter's scheduled trip to Yugoslavia in July. President Carter was scheduled to visit the country to underscore continuing U.S. support for Yugoslav independence following the death of President Tito who died on May 4, 1980 after a long illness and was replaced by a new collective government.[87]

On the same day of the Washington, D.C. bombing, a time-delayed explosive device detonated in the Statue of Liberty's Story Room in New York City. As the bomb detonated after business hours, there were no injuries, but caused $18,000 in damage, destroying many of the exhibits. FBI investigators believed the perpetrators were Croatian terrorists seeking independence for Croatia from Yugoslavia, though no arrests were made.[88] Two letters from the Croatian freedom fighters claimed responsibility for the bombings. The letters were sent as a

custody for 19 months and then released. After his release, the Spanish and Paraguayan governments agreed that his life was in danger by the UDBA and arranged for Baresic to fly to Paraguay, where he was given a new identity, Toni Saric. Baresic/Saric became a lieutenant in the Paraguayan army and later worked for Paraguay's diplomatic service in 1977 and 1978 where he served as a bodyguard and interpreter for the Paraguayan ambassador to Washington. In July 1978, Baresic was turned over to American officials in Asuncion, Paraguay for prosecution on charges of fraudulently applying for a U.S. entry visa, which stemmed from his 1977 application in Paraguay for a U.S. entry visa. He was accused of using a false name and of filing false statements to obtain the visa. In 1980, the U.S. government extradited Baresic to Sweden. In 1985, his prison term in Sweden was reduced from life to 18 years. However, he was released from prison in December 1987 and returned to Paraguay. When the civil war started in Yugoslavia in 1991, Baresic returned to Croatia from Paraguay. He was killed in fighting with Serb forces in July the same year, aged 40. Information on Baresic condensed from Associated Press, December 28, 1979; Alan Riding, "Paraguay Accepts Terrorist and Stir Is Minor," *New York Times*, December 27, 1987; and Christopher Dickey, "Terrorist Worked as Ambassador's Bodyguard Here; Ambassador's Bodyguard Was Croatian Terrorist," *Washington Post*, July 25, 1979, p. A1. See also, The Associated Press, "U.S. Seeks To Extradite Terrorist To Sweden," December 28, 1979; and UNITED STATES OF AMERICA, Appellee, v. MILAN BAGARIC, MILE MARKICH, ANTE LJUBAS, VINKO LOGARUSIC, RANKO PRIMORAC, and DRAGO SUDAR, Defendants-Appellants Nos. 82-1247, 82-1249, 82-1251, 82-1253, 82-1255, 82-1257, Nos. 887, 932, 877, 876, 886 - August Term, 1982, at http://www.jasenovac-info.com/cd/biblioteka/pavelicpapers/baresic/mb0004.html. Accessed June 3, 2017.

[87] Timothy Robinson, "Croatian Group Says It Bombed Yugoslav Envoy's Home Here," *Washington Post*, June 5, 1980, p. A31.

[88] Paul L. Montgomery, "Statue of Liberty Is Site of a Blast in Exhibit Room," *New York Times*, June 4, 1980, p. B2.

call for "the world to notice the demands and rights and situation of the Croatian people"[89] In mid-September 1980, three Cleveland men were arrested in a Croatian terrorist plot to kill two people in Ohio and one in New York. The three men were identified as Vinko Logarusic, 34-year-old, also charged in the 1979 bombing of a Cleveland travel agency; Milan Butina, 32, a carpet layer, and his brother-in-law, Gaines Buttrey, 24, a welder. The three were charged with conspiracy to commit aggravated murder. Police confiscated $3,000 from Butina and Buttrey at the time of the arrests. The money was allegedly paid to the men to kill someone. No information was released about the three alleged targets for murder.[90]

Croatian terrorist activity also involved attacks on other Croatians. The terrorist organizations acquired money through worldwide extortion campaigns, especially in Western Europe, Australia, Canada, and the U.S. For those Croatian émigrés unqualified or unwilling to join such groups, blackmail and extortion were used to obtain at the very least their financial support. Restaurant and small business owners often were required to make "donations" to these militant groups, or, to paraphrase one owner of a fast food establishment, something should happen to either his enterprise or even physical well-being.[91] In the U.S., these extortion campaigns were aimed at Croatian Americans. In a 1983 indictment, the U.S. government charged Croatian terrorists with "acting through their criminal enterprise, they perpetrated an international extortion scheme against 'moderate Croatians' and persons they believed to be supporters of the government of Yugoslavia, resorting to multiple acts of violence against those not sufficiently sympathetic to their cause."[92] During the period 1978–1979, Croatian Americans received about 50 extortion letters mailed from Germany over a 12-month period, demanding that they send money to a Croatian exile organization in Paraguay.[93] The letters demanded that a specified sum of money, generally between $5,000 and $20,000, be mailed to a post office box in Asuncion, Paraguay, or "you will … compel us to set a horrible example by making you the

---

[89]"Croatians Are Suspected in Blast at Statue of Liberty," *New York Times*, June 6, 1980, p. 31.

[90]"3 Arrested in Cleveland In Alleged Terrorist Plot," *New York Times*, September 16, 1980, p. 16.

[91]Mate Nikola Toki, "Diaspora Politics and Transnational Terrorism," p. 8.

[92]"706 F2d 42 United States v. Bagaric," para. 2, at http://openjurist.org/706/f2d/42/united-states-v-bagaric. Accessed October 24, 2017.

[93]Dave Binder, "Serb and Croat Terrorism Laid to Tiny Exile Bands," *New York Times*, June 22, 1979, p. 3; and Nicholas M. Horrock, "FBI Is Studying Yugoslav Groups After a Murder and a Firebombing," *New York Times*, November 7, 1978, p. 22; and Nathaniel Sheppard, Jr., "Arrest of 9 in Terrorist Group Brings Uneasy Calm to Croatian-Americans," *New York Times*, July 23, 1981.

first object of the disciplinary rules."[94] There are several known instances of Croatians being killed when they failed to respond to these extortion letters. On September 28, 1978, Ante Cikoja, a Yugoslavian immigrant, was shot and killed by three bullets from a car waiting outside his home in Greenburgh, New York. Cikoja was on his way to his car when he was shot and collapsed on the front stoop. Croatian nationalists are suspected of being responsible for the incident because Cikoja had received a threat letter, three months prior to his murder, from a group calling itself the "Croatian Nationalist Army." The letter demanded that he pay $5,000 by August towards the group's cause for independence, or otherwise he would be killed. He refused to pay the money. At least 15 other Yugoslav immigrants in the metropolitan area had received similar letters."[95] In November 1978, Krizan Brkic, President of a Croatian group in southern California was shot and killed in Glendale, California after receiving one of the extortion letters.

There were numerous attempted assassinations of Croatian Americans who did not provide money to the terrorist organizations, opposed the violence of these groups, or were involved in business dealings with Communist Yugoslavia.[96] In April 1978, Croatian terrorists set fire to the Yugoslavian American Club in San Pedro, California. In November 1978, Chicago factory owner Danilo Nikolic, who had also received an extortion demand, narrowly missed becoming a victim when a bomb exploded near the section of his plant where flammable liquids were stored. On April 6, 1979, identical pipe bombs, constructed to explode upon impact and scatter metal shrapnel, caused property damage to the homes of two Croatian Americans. On May 23, 1979, two Croatians were killed in the process of arming a pipe bomb which detonated prematurely. At the time, the terrorists were sitting in an automobile parked 70 feet from the San Pedro, California home of the intended extortion victim. On May 25, 1980, in San Pedro, California, two improvised explosive devices exploded in the vicinity of two nearby businesses. Both stores were owned by Croatians and the suspects in these bombings were Croatian National Resistance (OTPOR) members, although no persons/groups claimed credit for the bombings. The IED utilized in the first bombing at Ante's Restaurant consisted of approximately three sticks of commercial dynamite. The IED was placed in a planter under the front window of the

---

[94] "706 F2d 42 United States v. Bagaric," para. 11.

[95] Nicholas M. Horrock, "Clashing Yugoslav-Americans Studied by Grand Jury," *New York Times*, June 21, 1979, p. 36.

[96] All of the following incidents of attacks on Croatian Americans are from "706 F2d 42 United States v. Bagaric," paragraphs 10–26, at http://openjurist.org/706/f2d/42/united-states-v-bagaric. Accessed May 4, 2017.

restaurant and caused extensive damage to the restaurant. The second IED, which exploded at Homeowner's Discount Plumbing, consisted of approximately six sticks of commercial dynamite. It was placed on the sidewalk in front of the store and caused extensive damage to the building and broke windows of numerous adjacent businesses. OTPOR had been attempting to infiltrate the American Croatian Club in San Pedro, and as a result, the club was expelling suspected OTPOR members. The two IED attacks were believed to have been in retaliation for these expulsions.

In 1979, a Federal Grand Jury in New York City opened an investigation of the violence and extortion among groups in the Yugoslav American community. The establishment of the Grand Jury was an indication of the growing concern in the federal government over the battle being raged in the U.S. by Yugoslav émigré groups.[97] There was another dimension to these attacks on Croatian Americans. Some of them could have been carried out by the Yugoslav Secret Services or UDBA, which had a known record of assassinating Croatians and Serbians outside Yugoslavia and of infiltrating Croatian and Serbian nationalist groups.[98] One of the most prominent incidents of possible UDBA murders during this period took place in July 1977. Dragisha Kasikovich, an editorial writer for the Serbian weekly *Liberty*, and nine-year-old Ivanka Milosevich, the daughter of Kasikovich's fiancé, were attacked in the Serbian National Defense office in Chicago. The attack was particularly brutal. Kasikovich was stabbed repeatedly in the face, nose and chest and his skull was crushed. The girl was stabbed nearly 60 times and her skull, too, was crushed.[99] The U.S. government rarely made any insinuations of possible UDBA involvement in murders of Croatian and Serbian émigrés in the U.S. However, on June 7, 1979, Herbert D. Clough Jr., the special agent in charge of the FBI Los Angeles field office, issued the first official statement in the U.S. that the FBI had not ruled out the possible involvement of the Yugoslav

---

[97] Horrock, "Clashing Yugoslav-Americans Studied by Grand Jury."

[98] Christopher Dolbea, "Croatia and the Malodorous UDBA Ghosts," *Occidental Observer*, August 12, 2013, at http://www.theoccidentalobserver.net/2013/08/croatia-and-the-malodorous-udba-ghosts. Accessed July 14, 2017; Terry Wilson and Henry Wood, "Croatian Radio Host Found Dead," *Chicago Tribune*, February 19, 1987, at http://articles.chicagotribune.com/1987-02-19/news/8701130486_1_croatian-body-found. Accessed September 23, 2017.

[99] Jack Lesar, "Serbian emigres: terrorists or victims of terror?" *United Press International*, November 5, 1981, at http://www.upi.com/Archives/1981/11/05/Serbian-emigres-terrorists-or-victims-of-terrorWhen-you-are-cornered-you-fight-you-lose-track-of-what-is-right-and-you-do-what-you-have-to-do-to-live-The-Rev-Stojilko-Kajevic/2493373784400. Accessed December 6, 2016.

Secret Services in the attacks on Croatian Americans in the Los Angeles area.[100] A classified CIA report in May 1980 noted that "Belgrade pursues an intensive anti-terrorist program at home and abroad that has included diplomatic pressure, propaganda to discredit émigré organizations,…". The rest of the sentence is blacked out because it most likely mentioned émigré assassinations by the Secret Service.[101]

A combination of factors in the 1970s contributed to gradual decline in Croatian and Serbian terrorist activity not only in the U.S. but also worldwide. One was Cold War détente, which severely limited the room to maneuver of all separatist and anti-Communist movements in Western Europe and weakened the motivation of Marxist-oriented members who, for example, like the German RAF, were opposed to NATO. A second was the dramatic increase in Western European left-wing terrorism, which led to increased government attention to countering all forms of political violence in Germany and elsewhere. The third was the effectiveness of the Yugoslav Secret Services both in infiltrating separatist groups and in liquidating leading separatist leaders. In just the first half of the 1970s, over 30 Croatian émigrés were murdered by the Yugoslav Secret Service in West Germany alone. The final factor was the ineffectiveness of the violence itself — inside and outside Croatia.[102] There was an uprising on June 20, 1972 when a 19-member HRB paramilitary formation (referred to as the "Bugojno group") infiltrated into Yugoslavia. They intended to initiate a rebellion in Croatia to establish an independent and democratic state of Croatia. They were detected by Yugoslav security forces and pursued and eventually neutralized by July 24.[103] Outside Yugoslavia, hijackings of

---

[100]Nicholas M. Horrock, "Clashing Yugoslav-Americans Studied by Grand Jury." *New York Times*, November 7, 1978, p. 36.

[101]CIA, National Foreign Assessment Center, Memorandum — Yugoslav Émigré Extremists, May 29, 1980, at https://www.cia.gov/library/readingroom/docs/CIA-RDP85T00287R000101220002-6.pdf. Accessed May 5, 2016; On page 10 of Director of Central Intelligence, National Intelligence Daily, CPAS NID 84-031 JX, February 7, 1984, at https://www.cia.gov/library/readingroom/docs/CIA-RDP87T00970R000100020023-5.pdf. Accessed July 6, 2017, the CIA stated " Yugoslav intelligence has for decades pursued an intensive anti-terrorism program at home and abroad, and it has *used a variety of techniques* to reduce the terrorist threat posed by emigres." Even in a Top Secret NID, the Agency did not state that these "techniques" included overseas assassinations of Croatian and Serbian émigrés.

[102]Mate Nikola Toki, "Diaspora Politics and Transnational Terrorism," p. 12, footnote 50.

[103]https://en.wikipedia.org/wiki/Bugojno_group May 5, 2016. They have been referred to as the "Bugojno" group because they were first spotted near the town of Bugojno, in central Bosnia and Herzegovina. The Yugoslav losses were 13 killed in action and 14 wounded. Of the 19 members of the group, 15 were killed, 10 in action, while five were summarily executed after having surrendered. The last four members of the group were captured, tried, and sentenced on December 21, 1972.

Yugoslav and Western aircraft, seizure of diplomatic facilities, bombings of Yugoslav buildings, and assassinations of Yugoslav diplomats were essentially being ignored by some European governments and these actions were unable to galvanize support against Tito and his successor governments. In the U.S., the ongoing FBI investigations into Croatian and Serbian terrorist activities during the Carter administration bore fruit during the Reagan years and eliminated the threat of Yugoslav émigré terrorism in the U.S.

Armenian Terrorism

Armenian terrorist activity aimed at Turkish interests in the U.S. continued during the Carter administration. The attacks were carried out by Armenian Americans who were members of the Justice Commandos Against the Armenian Genocide (JCAG). On October 6, 1980, Harut Sassounian attempted to kill the Turkish General Consul, Kemal Arikan by firebombing his home in Los Angeles. Harut's brother, Hampig or "Harry," assassinated Arikan in January 1982.

One week after the attempted assassination, on October 12, a bomb planted under a stolen car parked in front of the Turkish Center in the United Nations Plaza exploded at 4:50 p.m., minutes before hundreds of employees and tourists exited the United Nations building which closes at 5 p.m. The bomb, which had the force of nine sticks of dynamite, demolished the automobile, hurling parts of the vehicle in all directions. The flying pieces of metal and glass as well as flames from the blast injured five Americans. The explosion caused significant damage to the 11-story Turkish Center and blew out the windows of several nearby buildings. JCAG claimed responsibility for the attack.

State-Sponsored Terrorism

There were incidents of terrorism in the U.S. during the Carter administration that can be directly or indirectly linked to the intelligence services of three states — Iran, Libya, and Yugoslavia. There were three incidents aimed at anti-Khomeini Iranians living in the U.S. After the overthrow of the Shah of Iran's government in 1979, the new Islamic Republic of Iran initiated a policy of tracking down and killing former members of the Shah's regime and members of his family.[104]

Ludvig Pavlović, who was a minor, was sentenced to 20 years in prison, and the remaining three were executed by a firing squad on March 17, 1973.

[104]See, for example, Iranian Human Rights Documentation Center, *No Safe Haven: Iran's Global Assassination Campaign*, Appendix 1, at https://www.scribd.com/document/17774391/No-Safe-Haven-Iran-s-Global-Assassination-Campaign. Accessed May 5, 2017.

Several were killed or wounded in Western Europe. For example, on September 14, 1977, the twin sister of the Shah of Iran, Princess Ashraf Pahlavi, escaped an assassination attempt by two hooded gunmen who fired on her Rolls-Royce along the French Riviera coast. Her lady-in-waiting was killed instantly, and the driver was injured in the attack with semi-automatic pistols.[105] On December 7, 1979, Shahryar Shafiq, the son of Ashraf Pahlavi, the Shah's twin sister, was gunned down on a Paris street. An Iranian suspect was apprehended in Britain and extradited to France. This Iranian assassination campaign also extended into the U.S. On June 21, 1979, two men posing as delivery people entered the home of the Shah of Iran's nephew but fled after being confronted by a guard. The attackers were trying to kill the Shah's sister who had lived in the house until three months earlier. An Iranian group called "Red June" claimed credit. On July 22, 1980, Ali Akbar Tabatabai, who served as press attaché in the Iran Embassy in the United States during the Shah's regime and later joined the opposition after the Islamic Revolution in Iran, was shot and killed in his Bethesda, Maryland home by Dawud Salahuddin, a 29-year-old African American Muslim convert (aka: David Theodore Belfield). He was paid by the Iranian intelligence service to kill Tabatabai and eventually escaped to Iran where he reportedly still resides.[106]

Iranian agents also targeted Iranian dissidents who opposed the Khomeini regime. On July 31, 1980, an Iranian student was shot and wounded outside the Los Angeles home of Shah-Rais, a leader of an anti-Khomeini organization, and a friend of Ali Tabatabai. In an apparent response to the above attacks, on August 20, bombs exploded at a meeting of a pro-Khomeini student association in Berkeley, California. One person was injured. The previously unknown "Iran Liberation Army" claimed credit.

Libya was suspected of involvement in the October 14, 1980 attempted assassination of Faisal Zagalai in Ft. Collins, Colorado. Zagalai, a Colorado State University student and leader of the local Libyan dissident community, was shot and seriously wounded. The Jamahiriyya Arab News Agency, the official information bureau of the Libyan government, announced that the attack had been

---

[105] "Gunmen Try to Kill Shah's Sister," *Washington Post*, September 14, 1977, at https://www.washingtonpost.com/archive/politics/1977/09/14/gunmen-try-to-kill-shahs-sister/a7b4f15d-a720-434b-a86e-a1b0e361d945/?utm_term=.53e51b947aa0. Accessed October 23, 2017.

[106] Felicity Barringer and Donald P. Baker, "Anti-Khomeini Iranian Slain at Bethesda Home," *Washington Post*, July 23, 1980, p. A1. For an extensive and excellent report on Tabatabai's assassin and his connection to the Iranian intelligence services, see Ira Silverman, "An American Terrorist: He's an assassin who fled the country. Could he help Washington now?" *The New Yorker* Magazine, August 5, 2002.

carried out by one of Libya's revolutionary committees. The FBI traced the gun to a former U.S. Army Green Beret, Eugene Tafoya, who was recruited by the Libyan government to engage in a series of dissident assassinations in the United States. Tafoya was arrested on April 22, 1981 and had in his possession an address list of other Libyan dissidents living in the U.S.[107] This attack in Colorado was part of a Libyan campaign in the early 1980s to silence or intimidate dissident Libyan exiles.

The main task of the Yugoslav Department of State Security (UDBA), or secret police, was to monitor and wiretap people who were a threat to the regime, whether at home or abroad. One of the perceived main security threats to the country was Croatian and Serbian dissidents living abroad who agitated against Communist Yugoslavia and engaged in terrorist attacks on official Yugoslav targets. This 25-year counter-terrorist campaign by the Yugoslav secret police against Serbian and Croatian émigrés worldwide was one of the "great open secrets of the Cold War ... both the East and West knew about it but it was in neither of their interests to publicize it."[108] The Yugoslav secret police killed over 100 Serbian and Croatian émigrés in the West with "minimal repercussions to the Titoist regime."[109] The UDBA infiltrated émigré organizations and agitated inside them to foster intra-émigré conflicts. Most Western countries, including the U.S., attributed the deaths of Serbian and Croatian émigrés to intra-ethnic conflicts between various Croatian and Serbian militant groups —precisely as Belgrade wished. In the U.S., as noted in a previous section, the UDBA was believed responsible for the July 1977 brutal murders of a Serbian nationalist, Dragisha Kasikovich, and the nine-year-old Ivanka Milosevich, the daughter of Kasikovich's fiancé, in Chicago. They were also suspects in the August 17, 1977 murder of Bogdan Mamula, a prominent Serbian nationalist, in Gary, Indiana and the December 16, 1978 murder of Borislav Vasiljevich, a radio announcer and outspoken anti-Communist Serbian, in Gary.[110]

---

[107] Information on the Ft. Collins incident is summarized from Joseph T. Stanik. *El Dorado Canyon: Reagan's Undeclared War with Qaddafi* (Annapolis: U.S. Naval Institute Press, 2003), p. 43; *New York Times*, May 24, 1981; *Rocky Mountain News* (Denver), April 24, 1981; and *Denver Post*, April 23, 1981.

[108] John R. Schindler, "Defeating the Sixth Column: Intelligence and Strategy in the War on Islamist Terrorism," *Orbis*, Fall 2005, p. 704.

[109] Ibid., see also, Claus Bienfair, "Belgrade's Long Reach — Murder of Yugoslavs in the FRG," *Die Zeit* (Hamburg), May 7, 1982, pp. 33–35.

[110] Op. cit., Jack Lesar, "Serbian emigres: terrorists or victims of terror?" *United Press International*, November 5, 1981.

YUGOSLAV-RELATED TERRORIST ATTACKS
1962–1982 (JULY)

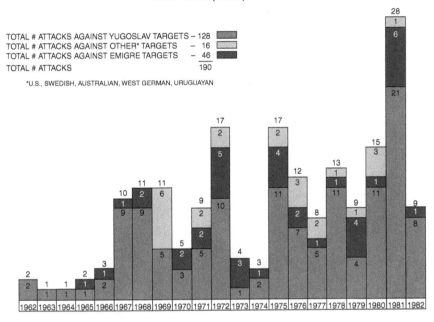

TOTAL # ATTACKS AGAINST YUGOSLAV TARGETS – 128
TOTAL # ATTACKS AGAINST OTHER* TARGETS – 16
TOTAL # ATTACKS AGAINST EMIGRE TARGETS – 46
TOTAL # ATTACKS 190

*U.S., SWEDISH, AUSTRALIAN, WEST GERMAN, URUGUAYAN

Terrorism involving Yugoslav-related targets (Yugoslav government, Croatian and Serbian emigres, and other countries) from the Kennedy through Reagan administrations.

Source: U.S. Department of State.

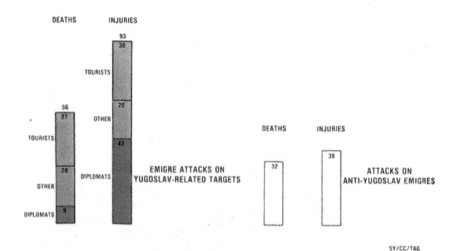

Deaths and injuries from Yugoslav-related terrorist attacks from 1962–1982.

Source: U.S. Department of State.

Aircraft of the Puerto Rico Air National Guard destroyed at Muñiz Air National Guard Base by Machetero terrorists on January 12, 1981.

Source: U.S. Department of Defense.

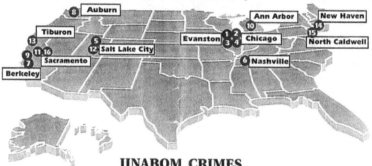

$1,000,000 REWARD

call
UNABOM Task Force
1-800-701-BOMB
(1-800-701-2662)

UNABOM CRIMES

1.	University of Illinois at Chicago, IL 5/25/78	(1 injured)	9. University of California, Berkeley, CA 5/15/85	(1 injured)
2.	Northwestern University, Evanston, IL 5/9/79	(1 injured)	10. University of Michigan, Ann Arbor, MI 11/15/85	(2 injured)
3.	American Airlines, Flight 444, Chicago, IL 11/15/79	(12 injured)	11. Rentech Company, Sacramento, CA 12/11/85	(1 death)
4.	President United Airlines, Chicago, IL 6/10/80	(1 injured)	12. CAAM's Inc., Salt Lake City, UT 2/20/87	(1 injured)
5.	University of Utah, Salt Lake City, UT 10/8/81		13. Physician/Researcher, Tiburon, CA 6/22/93	(1 injured)
6.	Vanderbilt University, Nashville, TN 5/5/82	(1 injured)	14. Professor, Yale University, New Haven, CT 6/24/93	(1 injured)
7.	University of California, Berkeley, CA 7/2/82	(1 injured)	15. Advertising Executive, North Caldwell, NJ 12/10/94	(1 death)
8.	Boeing Aircraft, Auburn, WA 5/8/85		16. President California Forestry Association, Sacramento, CA 4/24/95	(1 death)

Explosive devices have been either placed at or mailed to the above locations. This activity began in 1978, and has resulted in three deaths and 23 injuries. The last device was mailed in April of 1995 from Sacramento, California.

The **UNABOM** Task force will pay a reward of up to $1,000,000 for information leading to the identification, arrest and conviction of the person(s) responsible for placing or mailing explosive devices at the above locations.

Do you know the UNABOMBER?
Please contact the UNABOM Task Force at 1-800-701-BOMB/1-800-701-2662.

FBI reward poster for Unabomber.

Source: Federal Bureau of Investigation.

Chapter 9

The Carter Administration (1977–1980): The Response — Part I

The Response

The Carter administration's response to the terrorist threat at home and abroad was consistent with its evaluation from 1977 to 1981 that terrorism was not a major national security problem and therefore at most a tertiary concern. According to Zbigniew Brzezinski, his national security advisor, "Carter's personal philosophy was the point of departure for the foreign policy priorities of the new administration ... he came to the Presidency with a determination to make U.S. foreign policy more humane and moral ... and rejecting the 'Lone Ranger' style of the preceding administration ...."[1] The administration's pressing foreign policy objectives were seen as human rights, the Middle East, nuclear nonproliferation, the Strategic Arms Limitation Talks, Panama Canal Treaty, South Africa, Cyprus, North-South Strategy, Intelligence reform, arms sales policy, Korea, and the Philippines.[2] Terrorism was a security nuisance that had to be occasionally addressed. This view was similar to that of the Nixon and Ford administrations, as was the prevailing threat. Left-wing terrorism continued in Western Europe and Latin America and the international nature of Palestinian terrorism remained. While aware of and monitoring both overseas threats, the Carter administration did not believe that either would spillover into the U.S. The one terrorist threat that did occupy the most time and concern was state sponsorship of terrorism,

---

[1] Zbigniew Brzezinski. *Power and Principle: Memoirs of the National Security Advisor 1977–1981* (New York: Farar, Straus, Giroux, 1983), p. 48.
[2] Ibid., pp. 51–52. As noted in the topics of the first Presidential Review Memorandums of the Carter administration. See also, Jimmy Carter. *White House Diary* (New York: Picador, 2010), p. 45.

especially from Libya, and, in its nascent stage, from Iran. Internally, domestic and foreign spillover terrorism actors remained active but did not pose a major destabilizing threat as during the Nixon administration.

U.S. Government Counter-Terrorism Mechanisms and Policies

The Carter administration's first response to the issue of terrorism was to assess the current counter-terrorism structure and policies leftover from the Ford administration. This was accomplished with a National Security Council Presidential Review Memorandum (NSC/PRM). Only one of the 47 PRMs issued by the NSC during the administration was devoted to terrorism. This is not surprising as only one was required to assess the counter-terrorism program in place and whether alterations or upgrades were necessary. PRMs identified topics to be researched by the NSC, defined the problem to be analyzed, set a deadline for the completion of the study, and assigned responsibility for it to one of the two NSC committees.[3] It should also be noted that of the 63 Presidential Directives (PD) issued by President Carter, none dealt with terrorism.[4] The PD is a more accurate indicator of the administration's foreign policy concerns as they were generally triggered by the results of a PRM.[5] On June 2, 1977, roughly four months into the new administration, President Carter ordered a review of U.S. policy and procedures for dealing with terrorism. This demand for a review was contained in PRM-30, titled "Terrorism," and signed by NSC Director Brzezinski. This PRM tasked the NSC's Special Coordination Committee (SCC) to review the following six questions on policy and procedures:

---

[3] http://www.jimmycarterlibrary.gov/documents/prmemorandums/pres_memorandums.phtml. Accessed July 15, 2017.

[4] http://www.jimmycarterlibrary.gov/documents/pddirectives/pres_directive.phtml. Accessed August 23, 2016.

[5] Ibid. The results of a PRM were assigned to one of the two NSC committees — Policy Review or Special Coordination. A member was designated to serve as study chairman. The study chairman assigned an ad hoc working group to complete the study, which was ultimately reviewed by the responsible committee (either the Policy Review or SCC). When the committee was satisfied that the study had incorporated meaningful options and supporting arguments, the study's conclusions went to the president in a two- or three-page memorandum, which in turn formed the basis for a PD. An incoming presidential administration either maintained the previous administration's process and mechanisms or changed them. For the Carter administration, the PRM replaced the Ford administration's National Security Study Memorandum (NSSM), and the PD supplanted Ford's National Security Decision Memorandum (NSDM).

- Whether there should be an explicit policy for negotiating with terrorists and, if so, recommendations for alternative policies and the level at which the policy should be set.
- The adequacy of the current capabilities for dealing with a spectrum of terrorist threats.
- Recommendations on collection and dissemination of intelligence on terrorism activities.
- Further clarification of lines of authority and jurisdiction for handling terrorist incidents.
- Whether an interagency group like the Cabinet Committee to Combat Terrorism/Working Group should continue to exist.
- If an interagency group is to exist, the level of secretariat support that is required.

This review was to be no longer than 20 pages in length and completed by August 1, 1977.[6]

The task of writing the review was assigned to the NSC staffer William Odom, Brzezinski's military assistant. The PRM-30 review was carried out by a working group on terrorism under the supervision of the NSC and Odom in particular. To assist in this review, the working group was broken down into two committees with several subgroups to address the six questions on policy and procedures outlined in the PRM-30 memorandum. These interagency subgroups met around six times between June and August, 1977.[7] The three most contentious issues during these meetings were: (1) what the U.S. policy should be in dealing with terrorists (ranged from no policy, rigid policy, flexible policy, firm but flexible, one policy but multiple strategies), (2) who should coordinate intelligence activities on terrorism (basically the choice was between NSC elements and the Director of Central Intelligence's (DCI) interagency Critical Collection Problems Committee [CCPC]), and (3) who should chair the new interagency group on terrorism (Justice wanted a co-chairmanship with State while State believed there should be only one chairman — State). Departmental and agency

---

[6] http://www.jimmycarterlibrary.gov/documents/prmemorandums/prm30.pdf. Accessed May 16, 2017.

[7] See, for example, CIA Memorandum, dated June 21, 1977, titled "Progress Report on PRM 30 — Terrorism," CIA FOIA document CIA-RDP91M00696R000100030014-8; CIA Memorandum, dated June 29, 1977, titled "Progress Report on PRM 30 — Terrorism, CIA FOIA document CIA-RDP91M00696R000100030011-1; and CIA Memorandum, dated August 19, 1977, titled "Status Report on PRM 30 — Terrorism," CIA FOIA document RDP91M00696R00010003007-6.

turf protection shields went up during these meetings with Odom and the NSC essentially serving as ultimate arbiters.[8] Once these committees and subgroups of the working group finished their draft input into the "secret" PRM-30, it went to the NSC where Odom and Brzezinski reviewed it and then sent it to Carter who signed it on September 16.

The Carter administration's agreed upon counter-terrorism program was contained in the classified version of the PRM-30 and parts of it in an unclassified June 1979 publication issued by the NSC's SCC titled "The United States Government Antiterrorism Program: An Unclassified Summary Report of the Executive Committee on Terrorism."[9] This unclassified publication outlined the administration's mindset toward the terrorist threat and its approach to dealing with it. First, it was clear that the administration believed that the primary international terrorist threat was overseas and was unlikely to spillover into the U.S.[10] There were seven major U.S. counter-terrorism principles on international terrorism enunciated in PRM-30:

- The U.S. condemned all terrorist actions as criminal whatever their motivation.
- The U.S. would take all lawful measures to prevent terrorist acts and to bring to justice those who commit them.
- The U.S. would not accede to terrorist blackmail because to grant concessions only invites further demands.
- The U.S. would look to the host government when Americans are abducted overseas to exercise its responsibility under international law to protect all persons within its territories, and to ensure the safe release of hostages.
- The U.S. would maintain close and continuous contact with the host government during terrorist incidents, supporting the host government with all practical intelligence and technical services.
- The U.S. understands the extreme difficulty of the decisions governments are often called upon to make. For example, how as a practical operational matter to reconcile the objectives of saving the lives of the hostages and making sure that the terrorists can gain no benefit from their lawless action.

---

[8] CIA Memorandum, dated August 19, 1977, titled "Status Report on PRM 30 — Terrorism," CIA FOIA document RDP91M00696R00010003007-6, p. 1.

[9] National Security Council, *The United States Government Antiterrorism Program: An Unclassified Summary Report of the Executive Committee on Terrorism*, June 1979, 22 pages, (Washington, D.C.: U.S. Government Printing Office, 1979), hereafter "NSC June 1979 Report," at https://www.ncjrs. gov/pdffiles1/Digitization/62107NCJRS.pdf. Accessed September 16, 2016.

[10] Ibid., p. 1.

- International cooperation to combat terrorism is important. The U.S. intends to pursue all avenues to strengthen such cooperation.[11]

This unclassified publication referenced the June 1977 PRM-30 review and stated that "one result of that study was the recognition of a need in the United States for a responsive, but extremely flexible, anti-terrorism program at the federal level that would take into account both the contemporary nature of the terrorist threat and the wide range of federal resources that would have to be marshaled in any comprehensive anti-terrorism program."[12] The result was a "tri-level antiterrorism program" that envisaged at least four basic program components at the operational level:

- **Prevention:** International initiatives and diplomacy to discourage state support of terrorism and to build a broad consensus that terrorist acts are inadmissible under international law irrespective of the cause in which they are used.
- **Deterrence:** Protection and security efforts of the public and private sector to discourage terrorist acts — essentially target hardening.
- **Reaction:** Anti-terrorism operations in response to specific major acts of terrorism.
- **Prediction:** Intelligence and counterintelligence efforts in continuous support of the other three program components.[13]

In terms of the administration's counter-terrorism organizational structure, the final report of PRM-30 designated the NSC as the central coordinating counter-terrorism component by establishing an NSC SCC chaired by Brzezinski. This essentially replaced Nixon and Ford's CCCT. The SCC was the "focal point for oversight of the U.S. anti-terrorism program and support of the President should he wish to become involved in the management of specific terrorism incidents." In addition to terrorism, the SCC dealt with specific cross-cutting issues such as oversight of sensitive intelligence activities, arms control evaluation, and assistance to the president in crisis management.[14] The SCC delegated the management of U.S. counter-terrorism policy to a senior-level interagency Executive Committee on Terrorism (ECT) which was established on September 16, 1977

---

[11] Ibid., p. 2.
[12] Ibid.
[13] Ibid.
[14] Ibid., p. 7.

and consisted of representatives from state, justice, defense, energy, transportation, treasury, CIA, and the NSC staff. Representatives from the FBI and Joint Chiefs of Staff also participated regularly. The "ECT was responsible for government-wide policy formulation, operational coordination, responses to major terrorism incidents and related issues, periodic testing and evaluation of response capabilities, and long-range anti-terrorism program planning and analysis."[15]

Under the ECT was a Working Group on Terrorism (WGT) which was responsible for routine terrorist developments and incidents.[16] The WGT was chaired by the Director for Combatting Terrorism at the State Department with a representative from the Department of Justice as vice-chairman. The WGT membership was the same as under Nixon and Ford — representatives from some 29 different agencies and departments. The WGT "met as necessary to carry out the assigned responsibilities, which included information exchange, resolution of jurisdictional issues, and the coordination of the general antiterrorism activities of the various agencies."[17]

It served as a forum for the exchange of information, assessments, and for developing working relationships among the various agencies. WGT members were generally managers, planners, and coordinators of anti-terrorism activities for their respective agencies. WGT participants were assigned to special committees that dealt with specific problems and issues. Neither the ECT nor the WGT managed terrorist incidents. This was the responsibility of the lead agencies and the SCC. To complete the CT organizational structure, an Intelligence Coordination Committee similar to the one under Nixon and Ford continued under Carter, focusing attention on terrorism, improving the flow of intelligence, and handling any special intelligence issues from the WGT.[18]

In 1978, Anthony Quainton, the new Director of the Office for Combatting Terrorism in the State Department and new Chairman of the WGT, found the WGT "too cumbersome" with its representatives from 28 different government organizations.[19] He reorganized the WGT into seven standing committees that would convey information and relevant issues to the WGT.

---

[15] Ibid.

[16] Nixon and Ford's CCCT was abolished on September 16, 1977 by an NSC decision memorandum and the NSC/SCC working group on terrorism was formed to take its place. See, CIA FOIA document #RDP80M01048A001100030003-6, dated October 27, 1977.

[17] Ibid., p. 8.

[18] Tucker, *Skirmishes at the Edge of Empire*, pp. 14–15.

[19] *DS History*, p. 240.

- **Research and Development:** Coordinate the government's counter-terrorism research, respond to research proposals from private individuals and organizations, and carry out projects assigned by the Working Group and member agencies.
- **Domestic Security Policy Committee:** Manage border issues, the exchange of operational information among agencies involved in internal security, and vulnerability assessments of potential U.S. targets.
- **Foreign Security Policy:** Strengthen security at U.S. facilities overseas, provide assistance to U.S. businesses with an overseas footprint, and improve interagency cooperation in Washington and abroad.
- **Domestic Contingency Planning and Crisis Management:** Ensure all agencies had up-to-date contingency plans for incident management, train crisis managers, make available adequate intelligence for crisis management, and ensure that there was adequate data storage and retrieval.
- **Foreign Contingency Planning and Crisis Management:** Same as above with a foreign focus.
- **Public Information:** Review media guidelines for terrorist incidents, consider ways to prepare government officials to deal with media during an incident, and identify the most useful way to respond to media interest in terrorism.
- **International Initiatives:** Explore new ways to improve multilateral CT efforts, including new international conventions.[20]

Given the fact that the Carter administration did not place a high priority on terrorism, it was surprising that the administration constructed such a complicated organizational structure to deal with a back-burner issue. On June 25, 1979, the Carter administration enhanced Quainton's stature by nominating him for the rank of ambassador, which pertained when he was representing the United States at negotiations dealing with combatting terrorism.[21]

While it was a generally accepted arrangement during the Nixon administration that the State Department would take the lead in overseas terrorist incidents and the DOJ and FBI in internal terrorist incidents, Carter's PRM-30 formalized the concept of this "lead agency" rule. The State Department had the lead for overseas terrorism incidents, Justice for internal terrorist incidents, and the

---

[20] Tucker, *Skirmishes at the Edge of Empire*, pp. 14–15; NSC June 1979 Report, Figure 3.

[21] Negotiations on Combatting Terrorism Nomination of Anthony C. E. Quainton for the Rank of Ambassador While Representing the United States, June 25, 1979, at http://www.presidency.ucsb.edu/ws/index.php?pid=32543&st=Terrorism&st1=. Accessed June 3, 2016.

Federal Aviation Administration (FAA) for aircraft hijackings. While the Carter administration's organizational structure on terrorism was on paper impressive, it was not an accurate reflection of the low priority the issue had within the intelligence community. The then CIA Director Admiral Stansfield Turner has stated that "terrorism was not a great deal of concern" at the time.[22] Terrorism, however, was an issue that caught the eye of the media, the public, and Congress. This meant that the administration had to pay more attention to the terrorism issue and act accordingly.

Intelligence Reform

A successful and effective counter-terrorism program requires timely and accurate intelligence on terrorist groups and their activities. Like all new administrations, the Carter administration wanted to review the current intelligence structure. Given the intelligence abuses under the Nixon administration and the Congressional investigations of these abuses under the Ford administration, it was logical that Carter would address this issue early in his administration.[23]

On February 22, 1977, the administration issued PRM-11 "Intelligence Structure and Mission". PRM-11 was to "undertake a comprehensive review of major foreign intelligence activities and the organizational structure and functioning of the intelligence community." Key tasks of this review included the following: (1) evaluating the adequacy of existing laws, NSC intelligence directives and departmental directives concerning protecting sources and methods, privacy laws, the freedom of information act, and the balance between civil rights of U.S. persons and necessity for collection of foreign intelligence using electronic and physical surveillance, (2) reviewing the responsibilities and power of the DCI, and (3) assessing President Ford's Executive Order 11905 (reform the U.S. Intelligence Community [IC], improve oversight on foreign intelligence activities, and ban political assassination). PRM-11 was aimed at E.O. 11905, the DCI, and improving the intelligence community's performance. At the bottom of the PRM-11 memo, President Carter wrote "interrelationships among the various intelligence agencies will be assessed and recommendations made to me."[24]

---

[22] Naftali, *Blind Spot*, p. 102.

[23] See, Nicholas M. Horrock, "The Many Studies About the United States Intelligence Apparatus End the Same Way: Reform Is Needed," *New York Times*, August 7, 1977, p. E3.

[24] http://www.jimmycarterlibrary.gov/documents/prmemorandums/prm11.pdf. Accessed May 6, 2016.

The resultant review from the PRM-11 tasker was completed in early June and consisted of 65 pages.[25] This report consisted of four parts: (1) an examination of the objectives and principles for U.S. foreign intelligence, (2) identification of problem areas, (3) structural options, and (4) possible solutions in other areas, ranging from producer/consumer relations to counter-intelligence. The report's examination of structural options covered a wide variety of possibilities: increasing the DCI's authority; the creation of a Director of Foreign intelligence; increasing the Secretary of Defense's authority; and a radical restructuring of the intelligence community. The end result of the PRM-11 tasker and report was a three-page Presidential Directive (PD 17) on the "The Reorganization of the Intelligence Community," dated August 4, 1977.[26] While this directive did not accept the solution proposed in the CIA's April 22, 1977 paper of giving the DCI line authority over the NSA and National Reconnaissance Program (NRO), it did increase his budgetary authority over the National Foreign Intelligence Program which included the budgets for NRO and NSA as well as for the CIA. It also specified continuation of the DCI's intelligence-tasking authority in peacetime.[27]

There were six conclusions in PD 17, five concerning the DCI. All of them revalidated or strengthened his responsibilities and authority in the IC. It confirmed that the DCI "will continue to act as the primary advisor to the NSC and the president on substantive foreign intelligence and to have full responsibility for production of national intelligence in appropriate consultation with departmental analytics centers." Given that PD 17 underscores the DCI's responsibility for intelligence collection and analysis tasking, a "National Intelligence Tasking Center," directed by the DCI, was established.

On January 24, 1978, Carter signed Presidential Executive Order 12036 "U.S. Foreign Intelligence Activities" which was designed to change and strengthen President Ford's Executive Order 11905 signed on February 18, 1976 to reform and improve the intelligence community and ban assassinations of political leaders. Ford's E.O. 11905 was developed with significant CIA input.[28] Carter also intended the E.O. to be temporary until new

---

[25] For entire review, see http://nsarchive.gwu.edu/NSAEBB/NSAEBB144/document%2013.pdf. Accessed June 24, 2017. See also a CIA 15 page defense of the DCI's responsibilities in "CIA Views on the Future Management of the Intelligence Community," April 22, 1977, at http://nsarchive.gwu.edu/NSAEBB/NSAEBB144/document%2012.pdf. Accessed July 7, 2017.

[26] http://nsarchive.gwu.edu/NSAEBB/NSAEBB144/document%2014.pdf. Accessed May 3, 2017.

[27] http://nsarchive.gwu.edu/NSAEBB/NSAEBB144/. Accessed August 4, 2018.

[28] "CIA played a significant role in fashioning this Executive Order." CIA History Staff, 1993 (declassified August 10, 2011), p. 189, at http://nsarchive.gwu.edu/NSAEBB/NSAEBB362/chapters_11_through_13_and_appendices.pdf. Accessed June 6, 2017.

intelligence reform legislation could be put into law.[29] The new executive order retained much of the mechanism set up by Ford, including centralization of collection tasking within the DCI and retention of the Intelligence Oversight Board. The U.S. Intelligence Board was renamed the National Foreign Intelligence Board, but little was changed beyond the name. The DCI was authorized tighter control of the intelligence budget, and new mechanisms were set up to enforce this control. The tone of the executive order however was more punitive, and much of its language dealt with specific restrictions on the intelligence community.[30]

The restrictions were designed to ensure "full compliance with the laws of the United States." One of the main restrictions was that no intelligence operation was undertaken against a U.S. citizen "unless the President has authorized the type of activity involved and the Attorney General has both approved the particular activity and determined that there is probable cause to believe that the United States person is an agent of a foreign power." This included banning any Central Intelligence Agency electronic surveillance in the U.S. and leaving the Federal Bureau of Investigation as the only intelligence community member allowed to conduct physical searches within the U.S. The E.O. 12036 also expanded the U.S. ban on assassination by closing "loop-holes" and stating "No person employed by or acting on behalf of the United States Government shall engage in, or conspire to engage in, assassination." As for Carter's legislation for the intelligence community, which included a congressional charter for NSA, it never developed. In a Carter memo to a White House staffer at the time, he noted that "be sure not to approve Charter provisions which are excessively detailed, specific or an intrusion into my duties and responsibilities." A congressional charter for the NSA and other agencies would have certainly contained these limitations.[31]

Carter's E.O. 12036 is a more codified version of his PD 17. Both deal with restructuring of the intelligence community. There are two significant differences between an E.O. and a PD. First, for an E.O. to have legal effect, it must be published in the Federal Register (FR). This is a statutory requirement. A PD does not have to meet this publication requirement, which means it can more readily be "born classified." Second, there is a difference in circulation and

---

[29] https://en.wikipedia.org/wiki/Executive_Order_12036. Accessed June 3, 2016; For a full copy of E.O. 12036, see http://fas.org/irp/offdocs/eo/eo-12036.htm. Accessed May 6, 2017.

[30] Thomas R. Johnson, *American Cryptology during the Cold War, 1945–1989*, p. 199; David Wise, "Intelligence Reforms: Less Than Half a Loaf," *Washington Post*, April 23, 1978, p. D3.

[31] Johnson, *American Cryptology during the Cold War*, p. 199.

accountability. E.O.s are circulated to general counsels or similar agency attorneys, which can be readily accomplished by FR publication. A PD may be more selectively circulated, and this is done through developed routing procedures. Ultimately, EOs are captured not only in the FR but also in the annual volumes Code of Federal Regulations. PDs are maintained in the files of the NSC staff.[32]

The Carter administration was interested in improving intelligence collection and analysis on terrorism. In July 1977, the DCI's interagency CCPC undertook a baseline study of "intelligence activities directed against the terrorism problem." It found the intelligence community's effort against international terrorism to be "... a fragmented one, neither tightly organized nor closely coordinated in either its collection or analytical aspects." According to the CCPC study, a more coordinated IC approach would "provide much needed focus to departmental programs; promote better organization of Community resources involved; enable rationalization of the Community's work efforts; yield a better and more useful product at both departmental and national levels, and result in improved and more comprehensive support to U.S. Government efforts to combat international terrorism." Consequently, the CCPC recommended the establishment of a CCPC subcommittee on terrorism to deal with specific problem areas identified in the study. This study made 14 recommendations "intended to improve the overall intelligence effort concerned with international terrorism ... these relate to collection guidance, information management, and control practices, analysis and threat assessment, and legal problems and restrictions ... of special importance are those recommendations calling for the formulation of a community program for the production of finished intelligence on international terrorism.[33] However, the subcommittee's efforts to address the weaknesses noted in the CCPC study were curtailed with the 1978 establishment of the National Collection Planning Office (NCPO) under the newly reorganized Intelligence Community Staff. The NCPO charter was similar to the CCPC and thus the latter was perceived to be redundant and soon became moribund in December 1981. It was recommended at the time that the subcommittee on terrorism be maintained and report directly to the DCI.

---

[32] Steven Aftergood, "What's the Difference between an Executive Order and a Directive?," Federation of American Scientists, February 14, 2013, at http://fas.org/blogs/secrecy/2013/02/eo_pd/. Accessed October 24, 2017.

[33] CIA, "CCPC Study on Intelligence Activities Against International Terrorism," dated July 1, 1977, CIA FOIA document CIA-RDP80M00165A001600120027-6. See also, April 28, 1982 memo titled "Critical Intelligence Problems Committee Study on Terrorism," from the Director of the Intelligence Community Staff to the DCI and Deputy DCI, Attachment 4, p. 2, CIA FOIA document #CIA-RDP84M00395R00060012006-7.

However, the subcommittee simply became inactive and the NCPO provided no dedicated effort directed against the terrorism problem.

In 1982, the U.S. IC evaluated the U.S. government's intelligence efforts against terrorism during the Carter administration from 1977 to 1980 and concluded that:

> *There was during this period no effective, authoritative, central mechanism to give national direction to an overall counterterrorism program and bring the intelligence and non-intelligence elements of the government together to work out mutually supportive programs. With no one focusing on the management aspects of the problem at the national level, there was little impetus to focus on them at the Community level, particularly prior to 1980 when international terrorism was still a relatively low-priority item for the intelligence community.*[34]

The IC assessment continued its criticism:

> *In addition, there was during the period continued focusing of policymaker attention on the crisis management and foreign policy aspects of the terrorism problem almost to the exclusion of consideration of the need for the establishment and maintenance of a credible threat assessment capability. With policymaker attention thus riveted, there developed within the Intelligence Community a perception of a lack of national-level concern with, and policy for, a comprehensive U.S. counter-terrorism program. This perception, coupled with the low priority accorded the terrorism problem until 1979, resulted in limited resources being applied to the problem and the intelligence effort continued to be largely event-oriented and reactive in nature. As a result, in the absence of a Community focus on the threat assessment aspects of the terrorism problem, Intelligence Community organizations tended to go their individual ways in development of counterterrorism capabilities tailored to support for the most part departmental needs. The scope and nature of terrorism — the numbers and diversity of terrorist group activities, and the worldwide geographic dispersion of terrorist group operational areas — makes such an unfocused approach against an inherently difficult target less than efficient and effective.*[35]

---

[34] Ibid., April 1982 Memo, attachment 4, p. 3.
[35] Ibid.

The IC historical assessment also notes that since 1979, "international terrorism assumed a much more prominent place in the DCI's Directives priorities listing,[36] and since 1979 the priorities accorded the problem increased substantially." It seems likely that terrorism moved up on the administration and intelligence community's priority list due to several incidents in 1979:

- In February, the U.S. Ambassador to Afghanistan, Adolph Dubs, was kidnapped by Islamic revolutionary terrorists in Kabul and killed during a botched counter-terrorism raid.
- In June, the German left-wing terrorist group Red Army Faction attempted to assassinate NATO Commander in Chief, U.S. Army General Alexander Haig in Belgium by planting a bomb along his motorcade route.
- In late 1979, terrorist activity surfaced in El Salvador, triggered by the overthrow of the civilian government by a military junta. When the junta made promises to improve living standards in the country but failed to do so, discontent with the government provoked the five main guerrilla groups in the country at the time to unite into the Farabundo Martí National Liberation Front (FMLN). The FMLN carried out several anti-American terrorist attacks.
- In November, Islamic revolutionary students stormed the U.S. Embassy in Tehran and seized 52 U.S. hostages. Although not strictly a terrorist incident, the hostage seizure did signal a new, rising anti-American terrorism strain in the region, Islamic revolutionary terrorism, that haunted the U.S. throughout the 1980s.
- In November, hundreds of Islamic revolutionary militants from the Wahabi group "Ikhwan" seized the Grand Mosque, Islam's holiest site, in Mecca, Saudi Arabia, and demanded the overthrow of the House of Saud and institution of an Islamic state. The two-week siege, put down with the help of French forces, resulted in the deaths of about 250 people.
- In November, the U.S. Embassy in Islamabad was attacked and burned by an Islamic revolutionary-inspired mob that ended up destroying the embassy and killing two American diplomats because the mob was led to believe that the U.S. was behind the attack on the Grand Mosque in Mecca, Saudi Arabia, thanks in part to Soviet diplomats spreading this accusation.[37]

---

[36] Director of Central Intelligence Directive 1/2, effective February 17, 1977, which dealt with U.S. Foreign Intelligence Requirements, Categories, and Priorities, at https://www.cia.gov/library/reading-room/docs/CIA-RDP11T00973R000100070001-4.pdf. Accessed June 1, 2016.

[37] David C. Martin, "The Soviet's Dirty Tricks Squad," *Newsweek*, November 23, 1981, p. 52; and U.S. Department of State, Office of Public Affairs, Special Report No. 88, "Soviet Active Measures:

- In December, the U.S. Embassy in Tripoli was attacked and burned by a government-sanctioned mob that believed the U.S. was behind the attack on the Grand Mosque in Mecca, Saudi Arabia.

Candidate Carter was not enamored with the U.S. IC, especially the CIA. He signaled his distrust and skepticism of the intelligence community in his July 15, 1976 acceptance speech of the presidential nomination at the Democratic National Convention in New York City when he condemned the CIA as a "national disgrace."[38] DCI George H.W. Bush later commented on his transition briefings with the incoming president that "beneath his cool surface, he harbored a deep antipathy to the CIA." The consensus was summed up by intelligence historian John Ranelagh:

> *Carter had run against the CIA and Washington; he was an outsider, suspicious of Washington sophistication, and he stood fast against the corrupting compromises that informed people have to make.... He did not understand the need for secret intelligence — a failing that contributed to the Iranian crisis ... He saw no real use for the CIA. He had a view of intelligence as an order of battle — about detail.[39]*

In an October 15, 1977 memorandum from NSC staffer Paul Henze to the president's Assistant for National Security Affairs (Brzezinski), he noted that:

> *... the criticism and adverse publicity to which CIA has been subjected in the Western press for several years have taken a toll on morale and drive. New regulations and restrictions, more elaborate operational and administrative reporting procedures, concern in Langley about having everything documented, cross-checked, approved in advance to meet legal requirements, along with a tendency to play safe in the field, have not only discouraged initiative but have resulted in a situation where*

Forgery, Disinformation, Political Operations," October 1981, pp. 1,2, CIA FOIA document #RDP84B00049R001303150031-0.

[38] Tim Weiner, *Legacy of Ashes: The History of the CIA*, (New York: Anchor Books, 2008), p. 413.

[39] Thomas R. Johnson, *American Cryptology during the Cold War, 1945–1989*, Book III — Retrenchment and Reform, 1972–1980, Center for Cryptologic History, National Security Agency, 1998, Chapter 19 — The Rebirth of Intelligence during the Carter Administration, p. 193, at http://nsarchive.gwu.edu/NSAEBB/NSAEBB441/docs/doc%206%20%202008-021%20Burr%20Release%20Document%202%20-%20Part%20C.pdf. Accessed May 4, 2017.

even the most motivated field personnel put a great deal of time into unproductive tasks.[40]

Henze also noted the disillusionment in the CIA of Carter's approach to intelligence reform in the CIA.

> *CIA greeted the Carter Administration with a keen expectation that with new leadership it would leave behind a period of strain and controversy and be able to rebuild its own capabilities and redirect its energies to real USG priorities. No one in CIA expected to return to the free-wheeling days of earlier years and everyone respected the need for intelligent adjustment to new restrictions and legal requirements. But there was an enormous desire to take advantage of the opportunity to be creative and energetic in pursuit of agreed objectives and new challenges. Eight months later all this sense of excitement and optimism has dissipated. The prevailing mood of CIA, both on the operational and analytical sides of the agency is apprehension, depression, frustration.*[41]

While Carter may have been suspicious of the intelligence agencies because of what occurred during the Nixon administration, he still appreciated the capabilities of the CIA, especially its covert operations. Robert Gates, who worked in Carter's NSC and CIA, has stated that Carter "turned to covert action within weeks after his inauguration and increasingly frequently thereafter ... the most constant criticism of CIA ... was its lack of imagination and boldness in implementing the President's 'findings'."[42] Gates also notes that the U.S. "government's preoccupation with communist advances in Central America and the Caribbean, and Cuba's role in fostering these advances, did not begin with the Reagan administration ... nor did the use of covert action throughout the region as the preferred means of stopping Cuban-sponsored, violent revolutions aimed at installing Marxist governments."[43]

---

[40] Memorandum from Paul Henze of the National Security Council Staff to the President's Assistant for National Security Affairs (Brzezinski), Washington, October 15, 1977, document #63, p. 324, at https://s3.amazonaws.com/static.history.state.gov/frus/frus1977-80v28/pdf/frus1977-80v28.pdf. Accessed July 6, 2018.

[41] Ibid., pp. 327–328.

[42] Robert Gates. *From the Shadows: The Ultimate Insider's Story of Five Presidents and how They Won the Cold War* (New York: Simon and Shuster, 2006), p. 142.

[43] Ibid., p. 153.

Carter appeared to be more concerned about the intelligence community's processes, especially when they were directed at American citizens. He clearly valued the community's capabilities, especially technical intelligence like signal intelligence and photo intelligence. Carter, Brzezinski, and DCI Stansfield Turner all had an affinity for "technical intelligence."[44] Despite Carter's public chastisement of the intelligence community, especially the CIA and NSA, it appears that Carter's interest in intelligence was, like Lyndon Johnson's, "apparently insatiable and very much at odds with the public perception of an anti-establishment outsider determined to reduce the intelligence structure. He was definitely NSA's number one customer."[45] The intelligence agencies are the eyes and ears of the country. While presidents may have issues with the timeliness and quality of the intelligence, none can operate without an intelligence edifice. Each president will try to shape and manage these agencies.[46] However, the intelligence edifice is so large, complex, competitive, and embedded that instituting significant and enduring reforms is extremely difficult. In addition, whatever changes are made by one president could be changed by the next one.[47]

During the Carter administration, there were accusations that Congress's monitoring and control of CIA's covert activities overseas was weak.[48] The increased congressional monitoring was a by-product of the intelligence abuses under the Nixon administration. The first legislative response to the CIA abuses was the enactment in 1974 of the Hughes–Ryan Act that amended the Foreign

---

[44] Ibid., p. 194.

[45] Ibid., p. 196.

[46] Presidents can sometimes go too far and engage in the politicization of intelligence. For example, in 1978, some congressional and administration officials were "afraid that the Carter administration's drive to make analyses prepared by the intelligence community more relevant to the White House needs was raising questions over whether the CIA is able to exercise independence on sensitive policy issues." Richard Burt, "Closer CIA-White House Ties Raise Doubts on Agency's Independence," *New York Times*, April 30, 1978, p. 24.

[47] For example, President Carter's E.O. 12036 — U.S. Foreign Intelligence Activities, signed on January 24, 1978, was designed to change or strengthen President Ford's E.O. 11905 signed on February 14, 1976. President Reagan's Executive Order 12333 — United States Intelligence Activities signed on December 4, 1981 revoked Carter E.O. 12036. Reagan's E.O. 12333 was later amended by President George W. Bush's E.O. 13470, signed on July 30, 2008. All these Presidential Executive Orders dealt with the oversight of the intelligence community.

[48] Seymour Hersh, "Congress is Accused of Laxity on CIA's Covert Activity," *New York Times*, June 1, 1978, p. A2; James S. Van Wagenen, "A Review of Congressional Oversight: Critics and Defenders," CIA Center for the Study of Intelligence, at https://www.cia.gov/library/center-for-the-study-of-intelligence/csi-publications/csi-studies/studies/97unclass/wagenen.html. Accessed December 6, 2016.

Assistance Act of 1961. The Act was named for its co-authors, Senator Harold E. Hughes (D-Iowa) and Representative Leo Ryan (D-CA). This Act addressed the question of CIA covert actions and prohibited the use of appropriated funds for their conduct unless and until the president issues an official "Finding" that each such operation is important to the national security and submits this "Finding" to the appropriate Congressional committees. Some in Congress believed there was a loophole in this Act. In January 1975, President Ford issued a series of secret "worldwide findings" that determined "in advance" that any CIA covert operation dealing with narcotics, terrorism, or counterintelligence was prima facie important to national security. President Carter adopted Ford's interpretation shortly after taking office. Consequently, the CIA did not need formal approval to initiate overseas covert operations in those three categories of clandestine activity. CIA covert operations had to be approved by President Carter and his Cabinet-level Special Coordinating Committee headed by Brzezinski before they went to Congress. Some in Congress complained that the "worldwide findings" were vague and open-ended.[49] However, the passage of the Hughes–Ryan Act created both de facto and de jure Congressional veto power. This power could be used constitutionally, whereby the Congress could simply refuse to fund the covert action in question, either through withholding of funds or through leaking the issue to the press.[50]

Congressional response to the law enforcement and intelligence abuses during the Nixon administration started under the Ford administration and continued under Carter. On September 21, 1980, Congress enacted the Intelligence Oversight Act of 1980 which amended the Foreign Assistance Act of 1961 to repeal the reporting requirement of the Hughes–Ryan Amendment of 1974, which conditions expenditures for CIA covert operations on the timely reporting by the president to only two relevant congressional committees — the Senate and the House Select Committees on Intelligence. The Hughes–Ryan Act required that six to eight other committees also be informed. Key provisions of this Act were as follows:

- It retained the current requirement with respect to presidential findings.
- It deemed each covert operation a "significant anticipated intelligence activity" for the purposes of the new congressional oversight provisions established by this Act.

---

[49] Hersh, "Congress is Accused of Laxity on CIA's Covert Activity."
[50] https://en.wikipedia.org/wiki/Hughes%E2%80%93Ryan_Act. Accessed June 3, 2017.

- It amended the National Security Act of 1947 to add a new title V, "Accountability for Intelligence Activities."
- It required the DCI and the heads of all Federal entities involved in intelligence activities to keep the congressional intelligence committees fully and currently informed of all intelligence activities, including any significant anticipated intelligence activity. It stipulated that this notice did not mean prior approval of such committees was required for initiation of intelligence activity.
- It required the director and heads of federal entities to: (1) furnish information requested by the House and Senate Select Committees on Intelligence and (2) report in a timely fashion to such committees any illegal intelligence activity or significant intelligence failures.
- It directed the president to fully inform the Select Committees in a timely fashion of intelligence operations in foreign countries, other than those intended solely for obtaining intelligence, for which prior notice was not required.[51]

Concern over NSA's internal intelligence activities contributed to the promulgation of the Foreign Intelligence Surveillance Act (FISA) which was signed into law by President Carter on October 25, 1978. The passing of FISA was a bipartisan effort with the Senate voting 95–1 to pass it. FISA resulted from extensive investigations by Senate Committees into the legality of internal intelligence activities. It prescribes procedures for the physical and electronic surveillance (which at the time was almost exclusively landline telephone communications) and collection of "foreign intelligence information" between "foreign powers" and "agents of foreign powers" (which may include American citizens and permanent residents suspected of espionage or terrorism). The act was created to provide judicial and congressional oversight of the government's covert surveillance activities of foreign entities and individuals in the United States, while maintaining the secrecy needed to protect national security. It allowed surveillance, without court order, within the United States for up to one year unless the "surveillance will acquire the contents of any communication to which a United States person is a party." It does permit the electronic surveillance of American citizens and other U.S. persons only upon a judicial finding of probable cause to believe that the person is an agent of a foreign power. It does contain restrictions to prevent the resurgence of NSA "watch lists" concerning the international communications of listed Americans. FISA, however, does not deal with Americans

---

[51] https://www.congress.gov/bill/96th-congress/senate-bill/2284. Accessed December 5, 2017.

abroad and it still permitted the "vacuum cleaner" intercepts of electronic communications between the United States and other countries. The NSA was not prevented from intercepting the communications of Americans when the intercept was the result of targeting a non-U.S. person at a communications node outside of the United States. However, NSA had to operate under restrictions concerning how much information about the American participating in the intercepted conversation could be incorporated in intelligence reports or employed for law enforcement purposes. In many cases, the name or other identifying information would have to be removed and replaced by a term such as "U.S. person."[52]

FISA also established the three-judge United States Foreign Intelligence Surveillance Court (FISC) to oversee requests for surveillance warrants against foreign spies inside the United States by federal law enforcement and intelligence agencies, most often NSA and the FBI. Prior to FISA, surveillance activities had been conducted based upon a claim of constitutional authority of the president. According to Senator Birch Bayh (D-Indiana) at the time, "it establishes that the authority to conduct foreign intelligence surveillance in this country will be shared by all three branches of the government. It will no longer be the exclusive domain of the executive branch."[53] Since its establishment, FISA warrant requests have rarely been rejected by the FISC.[54] FISA was subsequently amended by ensuing administrations, especially after the 9/11 terrorist attacks. In a statement issued after the signing of FISA, President Carter noted:

> *...one of the most difficult tasks in a free society like our own is the correlation between adequate intelligence to guarantee our Nation's security on the one hand, and the preservation of basic human rights on the other. This is a difficult balance to strike, but the act I am signing today strikes it. It sacrifices neither our security nor our civil liberties. And it assures that those who serve this country in intelligence positions will have the affirmation of Congress that their activities are lawful... It will remove any doubt about the legality of those surveillances which are conducted to protect our country against espionage and international*

---

[52] http://nsarchive.gwu.edu/NSAEBB/NSAEBB178/. Accessed May 5, 2017. Such restrictions were first codified in the 1980 United States Signals Intelligence Directive "Limitations and Procedures in Signals Intelligence Operations of the USSS" (USSID 18), which was updated in 1993.

[53] George Larnder, Jr., "Carter Signs Bill Limiting Foreign Intelligence Surveillance," *Washington Post*, October 26, 1978, p. A2.

[54] For additional information on the FISC, see http://www.fisc.uscourts.gov/. Accessed December 6, 2017; and https://en.wikipedia.org/wiki/United_States_Foreign_Intelligence_Surveillance_Court. Accessed March 3, 2017.

terrorism. It will assure FBI field agents and others involved in intelligence collection that their acts are authorized by statute and, if a U.S. person's communications are concerned, by a court order. And it will protect the privacy of the American people...[55]

As the above actions by the Carter administration indicate, the administration did not rank terrorism as a major national security issue or problem, but it did modify and build on the counter-terrorism program that Nixon and Ford put in place. Carter was already predisposed to imposing restrictions on the intelligence agencies as a result of the revelations of intelligence abuse that surfaced during the 1975 Church committee. Congress was also examining ways to more effectively monitor the intelligence community, especially CIA's covert operations and NSA's electronic surveillance activities.[56]

Prior to the passing of FISA, it had been difficult for the executive and legislative branches to find that perfect balance between useful restrictions and timely and effective intelligence collection. For example, it was reported in June 1978 that the CIA reportedly refused or delayed a response to several recent foreign requests for help in dealing with terrorist actions, among them the 1978 Aldo Moro kidnapping by the left-wing Red Brigades and the 1977 hijacking of a German airliner to Somalia by Palestinian terrorists working on behalf of the German Red Army Faction. Also, in contrast to earlier practices, the CIA turned down a request by the Italian government for a psychiatrist trained in terrorism matters and sophisticated eavesdropping equipment. According to the *New York Times*:

Several officials said that the agency's attitude stemmed from what they described as an exceedingly cautious reading of prevailing legal curbs on conduct of covert operations and on the provision of aid to foreign police forces. These officials blamed the criticism the CIA received over its past activities and elsewhere. A high-ranking administration official: 'They're really gun-shy over there.' Current officials stated this situation is indicative of the new problems the Government is confronting

---

[55] http://www.presidency.ucsb.edu/ws/index.php?pid=30048&st=Terrorism&st1=. Accessed June 17, 2016.

[56] Nicholas M. Horrock, "Senate Panel Offers Legislation to Curb Intelligence Agents," *New York Times*, February 10, 1978, p. 18. "On February 9, 1978, after three years of investigation, the Senate Select Committee on Intelligence introduced legislation intended to prohibit political assassinations, limit the scope of covert operations abroad and protect the civil liberties of Americans against interference by the intelligence community."

*in attempting to enhance CIA effectiveness while restricting its ability to
intervene in the domestic affairs of other nations.*[57]

In fact, it was the 1974 Hughes–Ryan amendment requiring a presidential finding
to authorize a covert action that handcuffed the CIA, as Carter's E.O. 12036 only
permitted the CIA to respond to "international terrorism." Moro's kidnappers, the
Red Brigades, were initially perceived to be a domestic terrorist organization but
this was later reversed, and a finding was made and transmitted to Congress
allowing the agency to respond to further attacks by the Red Brigades. CIA legal
experts ruled when Moro was kidnapped that the agency was prohibited from
aiding the Italian police by a 1975 amendment to the Foreign Assistance Act,
forbidding the use of foreign aid funds to support foreign police activities.[58]

In the first two years of the Carter administration, there was an internal and
external debate over the seriousness of the terrorist threat, especially in the United
States.[59] The administration recognized that international terrorism overseas was
a continuing problem and that U.S. interests remained an attractive target for left-
wing and secular Palestinian terrorist organizations. For example, in October
1977, the CIA issued a report noting the increase of terrorist attacks on U.S. business interests overseas and predicting that such attacks would become more frequent. The report pointed out that in 1975 two out of every five attacks on
American interests were directed at U.S. business interests. The ratio was three
out of five in 1976.[60] In a report that analyzed international terrorism in 1978, the
CIA stated that "there was an increase in the number of international incidents
and their attendant casualties ... there were more attacks than the previous year,
both in relative and absolute terms on U.S. citizens and property."[61] There was
general agreement within and outside the administration that the overseas terrorist threat to U.S. interests was growing. However, disagreement surfaced over the
international terrorist threat inside the U.S. Within the administration, it was
reported that the State Department and Defense Department along with the FBI
believed that the "chance that the U.S. will suffer a major terrorist attack is

[57] Richard Burt, "CIA Refuses Foreign Bids for Anti-Terrorist Help," *New York Times*, June 25, 1978,
p. 3; see also Anthony Marro, "Intelligence Abuses Curbed: Panel Says," *New York Times*, May 19,
1977, p. 17.

[58] Richard Burt, "CIA Refuses Foreign Bids for Anti-Terrorist Help."

[59] Naftali, *Blind Spot*, 107; Tucker, *Skirmishes at the End of Empire*, p. 19.

[60] Drew Middleton, "CIA Sees a Danger to Americans Abroad: Major Increase in Terrorist Attacks on
Business Representatives and Concerns is Foreseen," *New York Times*, October 9, 1977, p. 11.

[61] CIA, "International Terrorism in 1978," March 1979, RP 79-10149, p.1, at https://www.cia.gov/
library/readingroom/docs/CIA-RDP80T00942A000800060003-8.pdf. Accessed June 5, 2016.

growing and that the U.S. is becoming a more tempting target." The CIA, in its April 1976 Research Study on International and Transnational Terrorism, warned that "…the odds are that the impact of transnational and international terror will be more sharply felt in the U.S. in the years just ahead."[62] However, Brzezinski, the NSC, and the Department of Justice did not believe that the overseas threat would spread to the United States and took the position that "the chance of a terrorist attack against the U.S. is actually decreasing."[63] President Carter apparently sided with the latter.[64]

It is not unusual in any administration to have differences of opinion over an issue. In terms of a counter-terrorism program, it is rare to find total agreement in an administration over counter-terrorism policy, structure, or actions. Officials and politicians have their own worldview, intellectual capability, political prejudices, and institutional turf they must protect, and they act accordingly. Given the terrorist environment overseas in 1977–1978 which was dominated by left-wing terrorist groups and secular Palestinian organizations, it was unlikely that either actor would have the inclination or capability to carry out an attack in the U.S. against a U.S. target. While there were domestic and foreign spillover terrorists operating in the U.S., it was questionable that international terrorists would strike American targets inside the U.S. In addition to this debate over whether there was a viable threat inside the U.S. from international terrorists, there was also disagreement by some members of Congress over whether the Carter administration had an effective and extensive counter-terrorism program in place to deal with the threat — at home and abroad.

The critics of the administration's counter-terrorism program pointed out that William E. Odom, who oversaw anti-terrorism planning overseas for the NSC, had no experience with terrorism. Neither did the chairman of the WGT, Ambassador Heyward Isham or his deputy, the DOJ representative Larry Gibson. It has been pointed out that few, if any, on the Carter WGT had any actual experience dealing with terrorism issues.[65] However, to be fair, few, if any, members of Nixon and Ford's WGT had any real experience dealing with terrorism. This is not surprising given that terrorism, as a national security phenomenon, was relatively new, albeit more so during the Nixon and Ford administrations than the

---

[62] CIA Research Study: International and Transnational Terrorism — Diagnosis and Prognosis, April 1976, p. 33, at http://www.higginsctc.org/patternsofglobalterrorism/1976PoGT-Research-Study.pdf. Accessed June 5, 2016.

[63] Arthur T. Hadley, "America's Vulnerability to Terrorism: Carter Sides with the Optimists in Government Dispute," *New York Times*, December 4, 1977, p. 4.

[64] Ibid.

[65] David Binder, "Antiterrorist Policy of U.S. Held Weak," *New York Times*, April 23, 1978, p. 1.

Carter administration. Still, whatever experience a Carter counter-terrorism official could have gained on the issue would have been sparse. Therefore, this is not a valid criticism of the Carter officials. While experience on an issue is clearly desirable, knowing how the government machinery works, who the key players are, and influence with the president, secretary of state, attorney general, or NSC Director Brzezinski would count more in attempting to enhance interagency cooperation on an issue. The more legitimate criticism of the Carter counter-terrorism program constructed in 1977 was that its organizational structure was flawed.

Congressional Counter-Terrorism Action

The two most vocal Congressional critics were Senators Jacob Javits (R-New York) and Abraham Ribicoff (D-Connecticut). Neither was impressed with Carter's restructuring of the counter-terrorism edifice. After PRM-30 on terrorism was signed by Carter in September 1977, Senator Javits, two months later, called Carter's restructuring "little more than a reshuffling of the already existing bureaucracy" and "functionally inadequate."[66] Others claimed that the U.S. "still lacks a clear-cut operational command structure for dealing with terrorist incidents at home and abroad."[67] It was pointed out that the U.S. lacked specially trained units to carry out rescue operations against hijacked planes and barricaded buildings, a crisis center with plans to manage the national and international aspects of a terrorist incident, enough trained negotiators, and had done little to prepare the media or to solve jurisdictional problems.[68] Critics of the DOJ, DOS, and FAA stated that in terms of terrorism, "the administration has not given the matter a high enough priority."[69] Senators Javits and Ribicoff drafted new legislation in an attempt to remedy what they believed were weaknesses in the Carter

---

[66]David Binder, "U.S. Revises Antiterrorist System, But Some Question Preparedness," *New York Times*, January 9, 1978, p. A14. See also, David Binder, "Javits Criticizes Administration Efforts on Terrorism," *New York Times*, November 14, 1977, p. 3.

[67]Binder, "Antiterrorist Policy of U.S. Held Weak," p. 1.

[68]Ibid., p. A14.

[69]Ibid. The author recognizes that unnamed sources in government may not be unimpeachable sources. However, it is generally recognized that dissent in government over issues, policy, and personalities surfaces first and foremost in the media. David Binder was known to have had good sources in the U.S. counter-terrorism community at the time of his articles. Therefore, one may challenge the motives behind these unnamed sources, but their comments clearly indicate some disagreement of the Carter administration's assessment of the terrorist threat and the approach and methods constructed to address it. Senators Javits and Ribicoff's criticism were more public.

counter-terrorism program. The new legislation was referred to as the "Omnibus Antiterrorism Act of 1977" and was constructed to "effect certain reorganization of the Federal Government to strengthen Federal programs and policies for combatting international and domestic terrorism."[70] Hearings were held on this bill on January 23, 25, 27, 30, February 22, and March 22, 23, 1978 before the Senate Committee on Governmental Affairs.

One of the triggers behind this bill was a personal one for Javits. On August 11, 1976, Popular Front for the Liberation of Palestine (PFLP) and Japanese Red Army (JRA) terrorists attempted to hijack an El Al airliner at Istanbul airport. Four civilians were killed, including American Hal Rosenthal, a 29-year-old Senate foreign policy legislative aide to Senator Javits (R-NY), a senior member of the Senate Foreign Relations Committee. A memorial service for Rosenthal was held in the Senate where Senator Walter Mondale of Minnesota, who previously employed Rosenthal, gave an emotional eulogy. Mondale challenged the attending senators and staffers at the service to "do something" about terrorism. "The result was the formation of a small bipartisan group of Senate Foreign policy staffers that helped develop a strong counter-terrorism bill that became part of the Omnibus Antiterrorism Act."[71] This bill contained the following significant federal counter-terrorism proposals:

- Upgrade the fight on terrorism to a national priority.
- Establish a Bureau of Counterterrorism in the State Department.
- Establish a comparable office in the Department of Justice.
- Move the interagency working group on terrorism to the executive office of the president.
- Identify and impose sanctions on countries that aid terrorists or terrorist organizations.
- The president must publicly list these countries.
- The president must develop and maintain a public list of dangerous foreign airports.

---

[70] S.2236 — Omnibus Antiterrorism Act of 1977, p.1. Complete text of bill found on pages 380–447 in Hearings Before the Committee on Governmental Affairs, U.S. Senate, 95th Congress, 2nd Session, on S. 2236 — An Act to Combat International Terrorism, Hearings held on January 23, 25, 27, 30 and February 22, and March 22, 23, 1978, at https://www.ncjrs.gov/pdffiles1/Digitization/54170NCJRS. pdf. Accessed March 4, 2017. Hereafter referred to as "Hearings — Omnibus Antiterrorism Act of 1977."

[71] Michael B. Kraft and Yonah Alexander, *Evolution of U.S. Counterterrorism Policy, Volume 1*, (Westport, CT: Prager Security International, 2008), p. 12. Mike Kraft was at this service and was one of the bipartisan staffers who laid the groundwork for the Act (email to author on June 17, 2016).

- Creation of a permanent international working group to combat terrorism.
- Make the taking of hostages a crime under international law.
- Explosives made or brought into the U.S. must have both identification and detection taggants.[72]

During Senate hearings on this bill from January through March 1978, executive branch officials and outside experts testified and evaluated the proposed bill. While all agreed with the spirit of the bill, many found fault with the reorganization proposed, the state sponsor list, and the foreign airport list. The opposition centered on Congressional interference in the president's ability to conduct foreign relations and the difficulty of constructing an accurate list of "dangerous" foreign airports. The Department of Transportation had some reservations about the United States unilaterally publishing a list of foreign airports due to the fact that "such a list could, by negative implication, suggest that all airports which are not on the list are safe ... because of ever-changing conditions and human factors, or because of sheer lack of U.S. resources to inspect all of the world's airports completely or regularly, the list might give inaccurate information."[73] Two outside experts — Brian Jenkins and Robert Kupperman — also believed that putting the word terrorism in the names of the counter-terrorism organizational entities, especially the one in the executive office of the president, elevated and might even exaggerate the problem since terrorists seek this type of attention. It was also suggested that small, permanent staffs be assigned to these entities.[74]

The Javits–Ribicoff draft Omnibus Antiterrorism Act of 1977 was opposed by the Carter administration which objected to the fact that that Congress would tell the president which states were state sponsors of terrorism and which ones should be punished.[75] In addition, the bill was an implied criticism of PRM-30 and the level of the Carter administration's attention to the terrorism issue. The administration planted a "definitional bomb" in the bill's discussion, the age-old terrorist vs. freedom fighter conundrum, and this eventually killed the bill in 1978.[76] For example, Senator Dick Clark (D-Iowa), the Chairman of the Senate Foreign Relations subcommittee on Africa, was concerned that the bill might affect the African National Council. The bill was brought up again in 1979 but

---

[72] Hearings — Omnibus Antiterrorism Act of 1977, pp. 409–411. This bill can also be found in the *Congressional Record*, Vol. 123, No. 172, October 15, 1977.

[73] Hearings — Omnibus Antiterrorism Act of 1977, p. 43.

[74] Ibid., Brian Jenkins, pp. 125, 127 and Robert Kupperman, p. 135.

[75] Naftali, *Blind Spot*, p. 112.

[76] Ibid., and Alexander and Kraft, *Evolution of U.S. Counterterrorism Policy*, Vol. I, p. 13.

died. Although the Omnibus Antiterrorism Act of 1977 failed to become law, it did propose measures that would eventually be implemented in subsequent administrations. For example, the U.S. Senate signed the Convention on the Marking of Plastic Explosives for the Purposes of Detection in 1991. The Senate consented to the measure in November 1993 and included it for implementation via the 1995 Omnibus Counterterrorism Bill. The Clinton administration's 1996 Antiterrorism and Effective Death Penalty Act contained a section that mandated the Secretary of the Treasury to conduct a study of the tagging of explosive materials which was called for in the 1977 Omnibus bill. Section 304 of the Omnibus Bill states that "No explosive may be imported, manufactured, or exported unless such explosive contains identification and detection taggants."[77] The Obama administration raised the State Department's Office for Combatting Terrorism to Bureau status in 2012 — as proposed in the 1977 Omnibus bill. In terms of the Omnibus bill's proposal of listing states who support terrorist organizations, Congresswoman Millicent Fenwick (R-New Jersey) later attached an amendment to the Export Administration Act (EAA) of 1979 bill that gave the State Department the responsibility to create a list of state sponsors of terrorism that were subject to export controls for equipment or services that could be used for military or terrorist purposes.

Overseas Terrorist Threat

The Carter administration correctly assessed that the primary terrorist threat against U.S. interests was overseas. While the Nixon and Ford administrations faced a more internal-oriented terrorist threat, Carter confronted one that was centered overseas. In July 1977, Secretary of State Cyrus Vance described the current threat as follows:

> *International airplane hijackings have increased in the past 2 years, after a brief pause in their frequency. Worldwide, the number of terrorist attacks, including bombings, assassinations, ambushes and arson, has been higher in the past 2 years than in any previous comparable period. There has been a shift away from attacks against U.S. Government officials and property to attacks on American businessmen and corporate facilities. The indications are that these threats on overseas facilities of*

---

[77] Hearings — Omnibus Antiterrorism Act of 1977, p. 415.

U.S. corporations and their employees could continue at least at their present level.[78]

The major terrorism actors overseas were left-wing and Palestinian terrorist organizations and state sponsors of terrorism. The bulk of the terrorist threat to U.S. interests remained overseas through the next four administrations — Reagan through George W. Bush. The primary overseas terrorist concern for the Carter administration was state sponsors of terrorism.

State Sponsors of Terrorism

Background

In general, the international community has opposed states that engage in or support terrorist activity against other states. The U.N. General Assembly declared in "The Declaration on Principle of International Law Concerning Friendly Relations," adopted on October 24, 1970, that:

> *Every state has the duty to refrain from organizing, instigating, assisting or participating in acts of civil strife or terrorist acts in another state or acquiescing in organized activities within its territory directed towards the commission of such acts, when the acts referred to ... involve a threat or use of force ... Also, no state shall organize, assist, foment, finance, incite or tolerate subversive, terrorist, or armed activities directed towards the violent overthrow of the regime of another state, or interfere in civil strife in another state.*[79]

It was clear even under the Nixon and Ford administrations that state support for terrorism was a key concern. Libya was the primary poster country for

---

[78] United States Congress. House Committee on International Relations. Subcommittee on International Operations: Protection of Americans abroad hearings before the Subcommittee on International Operations of the Committee on International Relations, House of Representatives, Ninety-fifth Congress, first session, July 12 and 14, 1977 (Washington, D.C.: U.S. Government Printing Office, 1977), p. 6, at https://babel.hathitrust.org/cgi/pt?id=purl.32754076915754;view=1up;seq=1. Accessed October 2, 2018.

[79] U.S. Department of State. Foreign Relations of the United States, 1969–1976, Volume E-1, Documents on Global Issues, 1969–1972, Document #100 — Telegram 167911 From the Department of State to the Mission at the United Nations, September 14, 1972, at https://history.state.gov/historicaldocuments/frus1969-76ve01/d100. Accessed May 5, 2016.

state-sponsored terrorism under both administrations.[80] Since 1972, the Libyan Government had actively assisted a number of terrorist groups and individuals.[81] On June 11, 1972, on the second anniversary of the evacuation of Wheelus Airfield,[82] Qaddafi in a speech urged Muslims to fight the United States and Great Britain and announced his support for black revolutionaries in the United States, revolutionaries in Ireland, and Arabs desiring to join the struggle to liberate Palestine. Both the U.S. and British Ambassadors in attendance walked out in protest.[83] The United States eventually withdrew its Ambassador from Tripoli on

---

[80]For excellent analyses of the evolution of U.S.–Libyan relations, see Brian L. Davis. *Qaddafi, Terrorism, and the Origins of the U.S. Attack on Libya* (New York: Praeger, 1990); Mattia Toaldo. *The Origins of the U.S. War on Terror: Lebanon, Libya, and the American Intervention in the Middle East* (New York: Routledge, 2012).

[81]Libya was a concern for the U.S. during the Nixon administration. "This was primarily a result of the importance of Libyan oil, primarily to Western Europe, the size of the American investment in the Libyan oil industry, the contribution which that investment makes to the U.S. balance of payments, the continued presence in Libya of approximately 2,800 American citizens and the political disruptive capability of Libya in Africa, the Middle East and elsewhere because of its vast financial reserves. The principal U.S. economic interest in Libya is the American-dominated oil industry which represents about 80% of Libya's production of 2.3 million barrels daily. The American investment in the industry has a net book value in excess of one billion dollars and a market value of well over four billion. The annual repatriated profits of the 11 American companies producing oil in Libya in recent years have averaged between $400 and $500 million, a significant positive element in the deteriorating American balance of payments. With respect to the Middle East, Libya pursues an extremist policy. Libya opposes the existence of Israel, argues for its liquidation by military means, and seeks to counter a negotiated settlement in any form. Its policy has been one of strong support of the Palestinian guerrillas and terrorists by arms, money and training." From Foreign Relations of the United States, 1969–1976, Volume E-9, Part I, Documents on North Africa, 1973–1976, Document #21. Study Prepared by the Ad Hoc Interdepartmental Group for Africa, Washington, July 6, 1973, Subject: U.S. Policy toward Libya. Study Pursuant to NSSM 185, at https://history.state.gov/historicaldocuments/frus1969-76ve09p1/d21. Accessed May 4, 2016.

[82]Wheelus was an American air base near Tripoli, Libya during King Idris' regime. When Idris was overthrown by a Qaddafi-led "Revolutionary Command Council" in September 1969, the Council demanded that the U.S. leave the base.

[83]For additional information on how the Nixon administration viewed Qaddafi and Libyan support for terrorism, see Foreign Relations of the United States, 1969–1976, Volume E-9, Part I, Documents on North Africa, 1973–1976, Document #15. Memorandum from Director of Central Intelligence Schlesinger to the President's Assistant for National Security Affairs (Kissinger), Washington, April 19, 1973. Subject: Libya and Qaddafi, at https://history.state.gov/historicaldocuments/frus1969-76ve09p1/d15. Accessed May 3, 2016; Foreign Relations of the United States, 1969–1976, Volume E-9, Part I, Documents on North Africa, 1973–1976, Document #19, National Security Study Memorandum 1851, Washington, June 5, 1973. Subject: Policy Towards Libya. "The President has directed that a study be made of U.S. policy toward Libya and of the options open to the United States in the light of Libyan attitudes toward the United States, international terrorism, the Arab-Israeli

November 7, 1972. In a December 13, 1972 memorandum from the Deputy Assistant Secretary of State (DASS) for African Affairs to Armin H. Meyer of the Office of the Secretary — Combatting Terrorism, the DASS stated:

> *I share your concern with the FBI report which indicates the Libyan Ambassador is connected with potential terrorist activities in the US. We believe Qaddafi was initially reluctant to support terrorism outside the Middle East, believing that Arabs should concentrate on guerilla activities aimed directly against Israel and the occupied territories. However, as you point out, there is growing evidence Qaddafi is willing to support terrorism outside the Middle East which, in his view, may have become a necessary if temporary expedient.*[84]

According to the State Department, it was also "a matter of public record that Libya had received and gave refuge to international terrorists involved in a long history of terrorist acts, including:

- The perpetrators of the October 1972 massacre at the Munich Olympics.
- The hijackers of the Lufthansa aircraft in October 1972.
- The hijackers of the Japanese Air Lines plane blown up in July 1973.
- The terrorists who attacked the TWA plane at Athens airport in August 1973.
- The terrorists who attempted to shoot down the El Al plane outside of Rome in September 1973.
- The terrorists who commandeered a train in Czechoslovakia bound for Austria in September 1973.

---

problem, subversion, international airspace, and the petroleum industry, at https://history.state.gov/historicaldocuments/frus1969-76ve09p1/d19. Accessed March 4, 2016; Foreign Relations of the United States, 1969–1976, Volume E-9, Part I, Documents on North Africa, 1973–1976, Document #21. Study Prepared by the Ad Hoc Interdepartmental Group for Africa, Washington, July 6, 1973, Subject: U.S. Policy toward Libya. Study Pursuant to NSSM 185, at https://history.state.gov/historicaldocuments/frus1969-76ve09p1/d21. Accessed April 23, 2016; Foreign Relations of the United States, 1969–1976, Volume E-9, Part I, Documents on North Africa, 1973–1976, Document #44. Memorandum from Robert B. Oakley of the National Security Council Staff to the President's Deputy Assistant for National Security Affairs (Scowcroft). Subject: The Libyan Threat, at https://history.state.gov/historicaldocuments/frus1969-76ve09p1/d44. Accessed March 6, 2017.

[84] U.S. Department of State, Foreign Relations of the United States, Nixon-Ford Administrations, Volume E-5, Part 2, Ch. 3. Libya, document #96 — December 13, 1972 memorandum from the Deputy Assistant Secretary of State for African Affairs (Ross) to Armin H. Meyer of the Office of the Secretary — Combatting Terrorism, at http://2001-2009.state.gov/r/pa/ho/frus/nixon/e5part2/89726.htm. Accessed June 4, 2017.

- The hijackers of the BOAC plane over Dubai of November 1974.
- The kidnappers of certain OPEC oil ministers in December 1975."[85]

The Libyan government under King Idris bought 16 U.S. C-130 military transport planes and eight were delivered. However, after the overthrow of Idris in 1969 and the emergence of Qaddafi as the country's leader, the U.S. in 1973, blocked delivery of the remaining pre-paid eight C-130s as a result of Libya's support for terrorism. The Nixon administration also decided not to sell Libya additional military weapons and related equipment that could enhance Libyan military capabilities. In January 1975, the U.S. also delayed the purchase of a $200 million air defense system and later refused entry of Libyan trainees for aircraft maintenance training.[86] The blocked C-130s became an obsessive issue for Qaddafi.

Libya also engaged in agitation and interventionist policies in neighboring countries. In June 1973, it invaded Chad and occupied the Aouzou Strip in a military/political conflict that ended by cease-fire in 1987. Libya and the U.S. also had a conflict over the Gulf of Sidra, which led to a minor incident on March 21, 1973, when two Libyan aircraft attacked a U.S. Air Force RC-130 reconnaissance plane that was 82 nautical miles off the Libyan coast. This incident planted the seeds for future U.S.–Libya air clashes over the Gulf of Sidra, which Qaddafi subsequently referred to its boundary as a "line of death." From that point on, anytime the U.S. wanted to send a message to Qaddafi and humble him, the U.S. authorized naval maneuvers in or near the Gulf of Sidra or fly reconnaissance planes along the line of death. The wisdom of such antics directed at a mercurial dictator like Qaddafi is suspect. However, Libya became the billboard for state sponsorship of terrorism for the U.S. and was the weakest and easiest to deal with compared to Iraq, Syria, the Soviet Union, Iran, and Cuba.

Aside from Libya, Syria and the Soviet Union were also providing weapons and other support to Palestinian terrorist organizations while Cuba was agitating in Latin America by supporting left-wing terrorist groups and serving as an occasional safe haven. In February 1976, the State Department's coordinator for counter-terrorism said that state support for terrorism was in its incipient stage.[87] In April 1976, the CIA published a research report that identified states' involvement in terrorist activities to various degrees as being a "key global

---

[85]Hearings — Omnibus Antiterrorism Act of 1977, p. 13, at https://www.ncjrs.gov/pdffiles1/Digitization/54170NCJRS.pdf. Accessed July 3, 2016.

[86]Ronald Bruce St John. *Libya and the United States, Two Centuries of Strife* (PA: University of Pennsylvania Press, 2002), p. 108.

[87]Tucker, *Skirmishes at the Edge of Empire*, p. 16.

environmental factor affecting the scope and nature of transnational terrorist activity."[88] The report goes on to discuss Libya, the Soviet Union, and Cuba as foremost examples of this problem. The direct or indirect involvement of a state in terrorist activity was clearly an escalation of the terrorist threat. If a state wanted to provide support to a subnational terrorist group, that support (finances, weapons, intelligence, false documents, access to new technology, use of diplomatic pouch, use of official documents) would enhance the capabilities and threat projection of that group. A state's decision to use its intelligence services to directly engage in terrorism would aggravate the threat environment as a state had more resources to employ in terrorist activities than a subnational group. State sponsorship of terrorism was and is the most dangerous manifestation of the international terrorist threat. There are multiple options a state can take against another state that engages in state-sponsored terrorist activity against it. A state can impose unilateral economic, diplomatic, travel, or aviation sanctions or engage in military action. A state can reduce or stop economic, security, or military assistance. It can also decide to seek multilateral actions against the state by lobbying other governments and regional and international organizations. The first step, however, is to recognize and assess the gravity of the problem in order to even consider these options.

While the Nixon and Ford administrations recognized that a state's involvement in terrorist activity was alarming, competing national security priorities and political and economic considerations limited the responses they were willing to take. Ford had two pieces of legislation he could have activated against Libya and other state sponsors of terrorism. The first was the Antihijacking Act of 1974 that: (1) revised the Federal Aviation Act by redefining "aircraft piracy" as commandeering or attempting to commandeer an aircraft by threat of force or violence, or by any other form of intimidation, and (2) authorized the president to suspend air service to any foreign nation which he determines is encouraging aircraft hijacking, or which he determines is used as a base of operations or training, or as a sanctuary for terrorist organizations using the illegal seizure of aircraft as an instrument of policy.[89] The second piece of legislation was the Assistance and Arms Export Control Act of 1976 that contained sections that prohibited U.S. arms sales to nations which, among other conditions, grant sanctuary to international terrorists and cut off foreign assistance to "any government which aids or abets, by providing sanctuary from prosecution to any group or individual that

---

[88] CIA Research Study: International and Transnational Terrorism — Diagnosis and Prognosis, April 1976, pp. 20–21.

[89] https://www.congress.gov/bill/93rd-congress/house-bill/3858. Accessed June 6, 2018.

committed an act of international terrorism."[90] The Ford administration, however, opted not to apply either of these acts against state sponsors. Like the Nixon administration, the Ford administration publicly associated Libya with support for terrorism. Yet, economic relations between the two countries continued as Libyan exports to the U.S. rose from $216 million in 1973 to $2,188 million in 1976, while American exports to Libya over the same period rose from $104 to $177 million. By 1977, the U.S. had become the single largest purchaser of Libyan oil, importing $3.8 billion worth of oil that year.[91] The U.S. remained the largest purchaser of Libyan oil until 1980.[92]

Carter Administration — State Sponsors of Terrorism

For the Carter administration, state sponsorship of terrorism became the most important and controversial terrorism-related concern. The issue of state support to terrorists crystallized during the Carter administration. Like Nixon and Ford, the Carter administration identified Libya as the exemplar state for this issue. It applied more punitive measures against Libya than the Nixon and Ford administrations, but their impact on changing Libya's behavior was minimal. In 1977, the Carter administration blocked the sale of Italian transport planes to Libya under the grounds that the engines for the planes were assembled under a license from an American company.[93] In May 1977, the State Department sent a letter to Senator Jacob Javits (R-New York) that named Libya, Somalia, Iraq, and South Yemen as states supporting terrorist groups. The Department also warned that "there is, unfortunately, every indication that international terrorism is on the increase and we will have to prepare ourselves to deal with further attacks on American citizens and installations abroad, including those of American companies."[94] In July 1977, Libya and Egypt were involved in military clashes over a four-day period. The two countries developed a strained relationship after the 1973 Arab–Israeli war, when Egypt moved closer to the U.S., ejected its Soviet advisors, and initiated steps for a peace treaty with Israel (which it signed in 1979). In addition, reunification (called the Federation of Arab Republics — FAR)

---

[90] http://digitalcommons.law.umaryland.edu/cgi/viewcontent.cgi?article=1029&context= mjil. Accessed October 24, 2017.

[91] Youssef M. Ibrahim, "U.S. Delays Sales Made to Libyans," *New York Times*, June 24. 1978, p. 25.

[92] Ronald Bruce St. John, *Libya and the United States*, p. 109.

[93] Ibid., p. 110.

[94] "U.S. Says Libya, Somalia, Iraq, and South Yemen Aid Terrorists." *New York Times*, May 9, 1977, p. 4.

talks between the two countries also ended in September 1973. The U.S. supported Egypt in these confrontations with Libya. In retaliation for this support and the growing relationship between Egypt and the U.S., Libya plotted an assassination attempt in late 1977 against the U.S. Ambassador in Cairo.[95]

On February 21, 1978, citing Libya's support for international terrorism, the U.S. Department of State recommended denying export licenses for two Boeing 727s ordered by Libyan Arab Airlines. Licenses were also denied for spare parts for Libyan C-130s, and Lockheed was denied permission to do on-site aircraft maintenance.[96] On May 9, the administration banned the export of all military equipment to Libya, including aircraft and selected agricultural and electronic equipment.[97] In September, the president's brother, Billy made a highly publicized trip to Libya with a group of Georgia legislators and businessmen eager to make deals, as C-130s were built in Marietta, Georgia. This was the start of Billy Carter's relationship with Libya that, although legal, became an embarrassment to the president and led to the "Billygate" scandal.[98] On October 4, Libya signed the Hague Convention on Hijacking — an action most likely taken to undermine its image in the West as a state that supports terrorist organizations. In the same month, it also agreed to provide written assurances to the U.S. that the two Boeing 727s ordered by Libyan Arab Airlines and denied transfer by the U.S. in February would not be used for military purposes. On November 2, after consultation with Congress, the Departments of State and Commerce approved the

---

[95] Ronald Bruce St. John, *Libya and the United States*, p. 110.

[96] https://politicalvelcraft.org/2011/03/07/libyas-gaddhafi-should-have-conveyed-that-its-time-for-obama-to-step-down/. Accessed May 4, 2016.

[97] The Commerce Department amended the Export Administration Regulations to require validated licenses for the export of certain off-highway transport vehicles to Libya. Until that time, such vehicles could be exported to Libya under a general license, that is, without prior notice to the Commerce Department. The statement accompanying publication of the amendment in the Federal Register did not explain the action. It did state that the proposed exports to Libya require "individual applications so that proposed transactions can be reviewed to determine whether they would be in the foreign policy interests of the United States." In a later statement, the Commerce Department claimed that such vehicles were capable of transporting tanks and other military vehicles. Furthermore, along with Iraq, South Yemen, and Syria, Libya was subjected to export controls for aircraft, helicopters, and certain crime control and detection equipment. Validated licenses were required for shipments of these goods, and applications for such licenses were considered on a case-by-case basis. Stanley J. Marcuss and D. Stephen Mathias, "U.S. Foreign Policy Export Controls: Do They Pass Muster under International Law," *Berkley Journal of International Law*, Vol. 2, Issue 1, Winter 1984, pp. 3–4, at http://scholarship.law.berkeley.edu/cgi/viewcontent.cgi?article=1010&context=bjil. Accessed May 4, 2017.

[98] http://historycommons.org/entity.jsp?entity=billy_carter_1. Accessed May 4, 2017; and http://www.pbs.org/wgbh/americanexperience/features/biography/billy-carter/. Accessed May 23, 2018.

export licenses. However, in early 1979 Libya used one of the aircraft to evacuate its troops from Uganda during the Uganda–Tanzania war (October 1978–April 1979).[99] Qaddafi had sent troops to aid Idi Amin when Amin tried to annex the northern Tanzanian province of Kagera. Amin lost the battle and later fled to exile in Libya, where he remained for almost a year before going to Saudi Arabia. He died there in 2003.

From 1977 to 1978, the U.S. had a strained but manageable relationship with Libya. Although it was recognized that Libya was supporting terrorist organizations and interfering in the internal affairs of neighboring countries, the Carter administration was hesitant to escalate the tensions. It still wanted to maintain an economic relationship, it was afraid of pushing Libya further toward the Soviet camp, and it did not need another crisis in the region. It was a delicate and hazardous approach to behavior modification of another state. The primary approach was export controls, public condemnation, diplomatic pressure, and support to some of Libya's adversaries. The emerging counter-terrorism policy of using sanctions against state sponsors, especially Libya, was causing concern within the Department of Commerce and in the U.S. business community. They believed that this negative reinforcement against foreign countries would worsen the American trade deficit, particularly with oil exporters.[100] They also argued that Libya would simply buy similar goods from other countries, particularly Western European countries. Like in all bilateral relationships there were probably missed opportunities for rapprochement by both sides. Of all the previous and subsequent administrations, the Carter administration was probably in the best position to develop an acceptable relationship with Libya. Unfortunately, the administration became preoccupied with two major ongoing crises: the Iran hostage crisis and the Soviet invasion of Afghanistan.

Beginning in 1979, the relationship between the U.S. and Libya started to degrade. Libya reneged on its promise not to use the Boeing 727s for military purposes as it used them in a military conflict in Uganda. The Carter administration was not particularly happy with Libya's intervention in the Uganda–Tanzania war. There was still some residue over Libya's military conflict with Egypt in late 1978. It was also in July 1979 that the Congress passed the Export Administration Act (EAA) that provided legal authority to the president to control U.S. exports

---

[99] Ronald Bruce St. John, *Libya and the United States*, p. 111.

[100] Youssef M. Ibrahim, "U.S. Delays Sales Made to Libyans," *New York Times*, June 24, 1978, p. 25; Tucker, *Skirmishes at the Edge of Empire*, p. 18.

for reasons of national security, foreign policy, and/or short supply. It became effective on September 29, 1979.[101] Section 3 (8) of that law stated that

> *It is the policy of the United States to use export controls to encourage other countries to take immediate steps to prevent the use of their territories or resources to aid, encourage, or give sanctuary to those persons involved in directing, supporting, or participating in acts of international terrorism. To achieve this objective, the President shall make reasonable and prompt efforts to secure the removal or reduction of such assistance to international terrorists through international cooperation and agreement before imposing export controls.*

The trigger for the bill was the discovery by House congressional staffers that mid-level Commerce and State Department regional officials were approving export licenses for U.S.-made equipment to Libya and Syria that could be used for military purposes (dual-use). Some in Congress believed that export of such dual-use equipment had important foreign policy implications and should only be approved by high-level officials in consultation with the Congress. New Jersey Congresswoman Millicent Fenwick, a junior Republican member of the House Foreign Affairs Mideast sub-committee, took the lead in crafting an amendment that added Section 6 (i) titled "Countries Supporting International Terrorism."[102] This section, which was supported by key Democrats, required the Secretary of Commerce and the Secretary of State to notify the Committee on Foreign Affairs of the House of Representatives and the Committee on Banking, Housing, and Urban Affairs of the Senate before any license was approved for the export of goods or technology valued at more than $7,000,000. This section applied to any country which the Secretary of State had determined met the following conditions: (1) such country had repeatedly provided support for acts of international terrorism, and (2) such exports made a significant contribution to the military

---

[101] Complete text of the 1979 EAA found https://www.gpo.gov/fdsys/pkg/STATUTE-93/pdf/STATUTE-93-Pg503.pdf. Accessed May 4, 2016. The 1979 Act took the place of the EAA of 1969 which expired on September 29, 1979. The original Act in 1949 was subsequently renewed in the following years without much change. The 1979 Act was the "most comprehensively rewritten" act. Ian F. Fergusson, "The Export Administration Act: Evolution, Provisions, and Debate," Congressional Research Service, July 15, 2009, p. 2, at https://www.fas.org/sgp/crs/secrecy/RL31832.pdf. Accessed September 26, 2017.

[102] Michael B. Kraft and Yonah Alexander, *Evolution of U.S. Counterterrorism Policy, Volume I,* pp. 13–14. Kraft was closely involved in the development of the Fenwick amendment which was a key modification to the Act in terms of punishing state sponsors of terrorism.

potential of such country, including its military logistics capability, or enhanced the ability of such country to support acts of international terrorism.

This section was essentially designed to ensure pre-notification of Congress that licensing decisions concerning dual-use equipment for state sponsors of terrorism were reviewed and approved by top levels of the State Department. Congress could then stop it and protest if it wished, or even pass a resolution or legislation to block the sales. The Fenwick Amendment also established what came to be known as the "state sponsor list" as it required the Secretary of State to designate which states sponsored terrorism. Historically, export controls have been used by the United States as a tool to further major policy goals and promote national security interests by denying the benefits of free trade to hostile governments. The export controls have been used to symbolically express U.S. disapproval of certain foreign conduct, with the intent of reversing the unfavorable foreign conduct.[103] The sanctions have become part of the "tool kit" to try to pressure governments to change their terrorism-related behavior. The Carter administration supported sanctions against state sponsors of terrorism named in the public list.[104] However, it opposed the concept of allowing Congress to be able to add states to this list and that Congress could mandate sanctions as improper restrictions on presidential authority to conduct foreign affairs.[105] In addition, the administration was concerned that sensitive intelligence information might be involved in properly making such decisions.

In terms of Libya, some members of the Carter administration wanted to send a stronger message to Qaddafi over his behavior. It was proposed in 1979 and 1980 that the U.S. carry out "freedom of navigation" (FON) exercises near the Gulf of Sidra off the Libyan coast to reinforce U.S. rights in the Gulf and to demonstrate that Qaddafi did not have the military force to back up his claim that

---

[103] Christopher J. Donovan. "The Export Administration Act of 1979: Refining United States Export Control Machinery," Boston College International and Comparative Law Review, Vol. 4, Issue 1, May 1, 1981, pp. 109–110, at http://lawdigitalcommons.bc.edu/cgi/viewcontent.cgi?article=1577&context=iclr. Accessed June 6, 2017.

[104] See Secretary of State Vance's testimony at the hearings for the Omnibus Antiterrorism Act of 1977, pp. 9–10. "The administration supports the concept of a public list of countries which aid or abet terrorist actions. Public exposure and condemnation can be effective in discouraging support for terrorist activities. Removal of a country from the list would signal a change toward greater responsibility and restraint ... we are prepared to support appropriate sanctions against countries appearing on such a list ..."

[105] Tucker, *Skirmishes at the Edge of Empire*, p. 17.

the Gulf was within Libyan territorial waters.[106] Carter rejected both proposals for the FONs. In September 1980, there were two instances where Libyan fighter aircraft confronted U.S. reconnaissance planes over the Gulf. In both cases, the administration did not publicly acknowledge the incidents and did not want to escalate tensions between the two countries.[107] Tensions however did escalate on December 2, 1979 when a mob of Libyan demonstrators chanting pro-Khomeini slogans stormed and burned the U.S. Embassy in Tripoli. No Americans were injured as they escaped through the back exit after pouring oil on the stairs to slow down the mob.[108]

The attack by militant demonstrators in Tripoli was part of a series of unco-ordinated mob attacks on U.S. diplomatic facilities in late 1979. On November 4, militant Iranian students seized the U.S. Embassy in Tehran. On November 20, around 500 well-armed Islamist revolutionaries seized the Grand Mosque in Mecca — the holiest site in Islam. The Mecca attackers called for a revolt against the Saudi monarchy claiming that it had betrayed Islamic principles and sold out to Western countries. When the Mecca siege started, Ayatollah Khomeini went on Tehran radio and commented: "It is not beyond guessing that this is the work of criminal American imperialism and international Zionism."[109] In response to Khomeini's insinuation of U.S. involvement in the Mecca attack, anti-American protests took place in the Philippines, Turkey, Bangladesh, India, the United Arab Emirates, and Kuwait. On November 21, a mob attacked the U.S. Embassy in Islamabad.[110] The Pakistani police and fire brigades were very slow in arriving. Two Americans were killed trying to defend the embassy. Then on December 2, a mob attacked the U.S. Embassy in Tripoli. On December 29, the U.S.

---

[106] Joseph T. Stanik. *El Dorado Canyon: Reagan's Undeclared War with Qaddafi* (Annapolis: Naval University Press, 2003), pp. 29–31.

[107] Ibid.

[108] Previously, on February 22, 1973, a Libyan mob burned a U.S. flag and broke the windows of the U.S. Embassy in Tripoli to protest the downing of a Libyan airliner by Israeli fighters over the Sinai Peninsula. A Libyan Boeing 727 was shot down by Israeli jets. A total of 102 passengers and eight crewmen were killed.

[109] Robin Wright. *Sacred Rage: The Wrath of Militant Islam* (New York: Simon and Schuster, 1986), p. 148.

[110] On the same day, a mob of perhaps 5,000 marched to the American Center in Lahore, Pakistan, burned it and then marched to the U.S. Consulate and attacked it. One of the U.S. diplomats in Lahore at the time, Jeffrey Lunstead, has stated — "… a dangerous rumor had been started. It was that a group that had attacked the Great Mosque in Mecca several days earlier had been identified as Israeli and American paratroopers." Jeffrey Lunstead, "Survivor of 1979 Consulate attack," Special to *CNN*, September 13, 2012, at http://www.cnn.com/2012/09/13/opinion/lunstead-1979-embassy-attack/. Accessed May 3, 2017.

government published the first official list of state sponsors of terrorism which named Libya, Syria, Iraq, and South Yemen. By the end of 1979, bilateral relations between the U.S. and Libya were at their lowest since Qaddafi assumed power in 1969.[111]

In 1980, tensions between the two countries continued. On February 4, Libyan demonstrators attacked and burned the French Embassy in Tripoli and the French Consulate in Benghazi over French support for Tunisia during a January 1980 clash between Libya and Tunisia. Three days later, the State Department withdrew six remaining staffers at the U.S. Embassy in Tripoli and left only an administrative officer and Charge d'affairs William Eagleton, Jr. to look after U.S. property and the needs of some 2,500 Americans working in Libya. The United States had already withdrawn the U.S. Ambassador to Libya in 1972. A Department of State spokesman said the February move was being taken to prevent an attack on the embassy after the United States increased military aid to Tunisia.[112] However, there was also concern that the Libyan government would not protect the embassy in the event of a mob attack. In addition to this concern over the protection of U.S. diplomatic interests in Libya, Qaddafi escalated his state sponsorship of terrorism on April 27. During an address to students at a military academy in Tripoli, he bluntly stated that, "all persons who have left Libya must return by this June 10 ... if the refugees do not obey this order they must be inevitably liquidated, wherever they are."[113] This policy was reinforced in early May, when a visiting member of the Libyan People's Committee told a Rome press conference that exiles working against the government of Colonel Qaddafi would be eliminated unless they came home under a general armistice."[114] On May 2, 1980, as a result of Qaddafi's April 27 statement, a series of attacks on Libyan dissident exiles, and harassment of Libyan students in the U.S. by

---

[111] For chronologies of significant events between the U.S. and Libya, at https://www.armscontrol.org/factsheets/LibyaChronology#1970. Accessed May 13, 2017; U.S. Department of State, Office of the Spokesman, Fact Sheet: Significant Events in U.S.-Libyan Relations, September 2, 2008, at http://2001-2009.state.gov/r/pa/prs/ps/2008/sept/109054.htm. Accessed May 5, 2016; and Corri Zoli, Sahar Azar, and Shani Ross, "Patterns of Conduct: Libyan Regime Support for and Involvement in Acts of Terrorism," Institute for National Security and Counter-Terrorism," Syracuse University, 2010. Prepared for M. Cherif Bassiouni, Chair, UNHRC Commission of Inquiry into Human Rights Violations in Libya, at http://insct.syr.edu/wp-content/uploads/2012/09/Libya-Report-27-April-2011-final-with-Cover.pdf. Accessed May 3, 2017.

[112] https://archive.org/stream/RonaldBruceStJohnHistoricalDictionaryOfLibya/Ronald-Bruce-St-John-Historical-Dictionary-of-Libya_djvu.txt. Accessed October 4, 2017.

[113] *United Press International*, May 10, 1980.

[114] *Reuters*, May 10, 1980.

members of the Libyan People's Bureau (LPB) in Washington, D.C., the United States declared four Libyan diplomats persona non grata and recalled its last two diplomats from Libya and closed the embassy.[115] The Carter administration did allow the LPB to continue to function and did not formally sever diplomatic relations with Libya.

The "liquidation" campaign against Libyan exiles initiated by Qaddafi in 1980 was an unprecedented and audacious flout of international law and the most brazen application of terrorism by a state in non-war conditions in modern history. By the end of 1980, ten Libyan exiles had been assassinated, four in Rome, two in London, and one each in Bonn, Milan, Manchester, and Athens. There were also attempted assassinations of Libyan exiles in Rome, Ft. Collins, Colorado, and Portsmouth, Great Britain.[116] The attack in the U.S. took place on October 14 when a gunman shot Faisal Zagallai, a doctoral student at the University of Colorado in Boulder. The bullets left Zagallai partially blinded.[117]

---

[115]U.S. Department of State at http://2001-2009.state.gov/r/pa/prs/ps/2008/sept/109054.htm. Accessed May 5, 2017; see also *New York Times*, May 7, 1981, p. A1.

[116]Dennis Pluchinsky, "Political Terrorism in Western Europe: Some Themes and Variations," in Yonah Alexander and Kenneth Myers, Editors. *Terrorism in Europe* (London: Croom Helm, 1982), p. 61.

[117]Police eventually arrested Eugene Aloys Tafoya, 48, a decorated Vietnam War hero who the authorities said was hired by Libyan officials to assassinate Zagallai. Federal officials said Zagallai was marked for elimination as a persistent critic of the regime of the Libyan leader, Muammar el-Qaddafi. However, a jury eventually found Tafoya guilty of two misdemeanors: third-degree assault and conspiracy to commit this assault. Maximum sentence: 24 months and a $5,000 fine. The complexity of the case apparently confused the jurors and they bought Tafoya's defense that he was only sent to rough up the student and he fired his gun only after a struggle during which Zagallai reached for a weapon of his own. See, William E. Schmidt, "Libya Case: 'Pretty Big' for Ft. Collins," *New York Times*, December 4, 1981, at http://www.nytimes.com/1981/12/04/us/libya-case-pretty-big-for-ft-collins.html. Accessed June 3, 2016. The jury did believe however that Tafoya was working for the Libyans. Prosecutors said Tafoya was hired by a former C.I.A. agent named Edwin P. Wilson, who was acting on behalf of the Libyan government. Wilson was believed to be living in Libya as a fugitive from a Federal grand jury indictment that accused him of smuggling explosives to Libya as part of a plot to train terrorists. Prosecutors said Tafoya fled the United States after the shooting of Zagallai and visited both London and Libya. In England, Tafoya was identified by neighbors as a visitor at a country estate owned by Wilson. See, William E. Schmidt, "Ex-Green Beret is Convicted of Assault on Libyan Student," *New York Times*, December 5, 1981, at http://www.nytimes.com/1981/12/05/us/ex-green-beret-is-convicted-of-assault-on-libyan-student.html. Accessed May 3, 2016, and Douglas L. Vaughan, "The Qaddafi Disconnection," *Washington Post*, November 22, 1981, at https://www.washingtonpost.com/archive/politics/1981/11/22/the-qaddafi-disconnection/1de84075-0068-46d7-925e-628dfcf63b41/. Accessed March 4, 2016.

The repercussions of the Fenwick amendment surfaced again in January 1980 when the Commerce Department approved a license for General Electric to export eight engine cores, valued at $11.4 million, to Italy, for use in the construction of four frigates destined for Iraq. Congresswoman Fenwick protested that the license violated the spirit of her amendment. The next month the Commerce Department, responding to congressional pressure, reversed itself and suspended the export license for the eight turbine engine cores.[118] In April, however, Secretary of State Cyrus Vance and National Security Adviser Zbigniew Brzezinski recommended allowing the sale of engine cores as a means of improving ties with Iraq. On April 7, the Arab Liberation Front, supported by Iraq, attacked an Israeli kibbutz, killing three. This caused Congressional criticism of the Iraqi frigate decision to escalate sharply and the deal was placed under review again.[119] In May, members of the House Subcommittee on Middle East accused the Carter administration of breaking the law by not notifying Congress of its decision in January to approve engine sales to Iraq via Italy. The State Department acknowledged the mistake but said the administration did not break the law because engines were not on the list of items restricted from sale to terrorist-supporting nations.[120] In July, the Carter administration announced that it was also considering the sale of five Boeing commercial jets to Iraq. In August, the State Department decided not to block the engine deal. However, in late August, the Department, responding to congressional pressure, reversed its decision on the commercial jets and disapproved the $208 million sale of commercial jets to Iraq.[121]

In September 1980, claiming the need to demonstrate neutrality in the Iran–Iraq war, the Carter administration suspended the export of six remaining turbine engine cores, two having been shipped already. A U.S. official stated that "In the middle of a conflict, when we proclaim our neutrality, we don't want stories saying that we are supplying either side, however indirectly." This decision came after Senator Richard Stone (D-FL), a Senate Foreign Relations Committee member, threatened to attach an amendment opposing the sale to an upcoming

---

[118]*New York Times*, February 7, 1980, p. D2 and the Peterson Institute for International Economics (PIIE). Case 80-2, US v. Iraq (1980–2003), at https://piie.com/publications/speeches-and-papers/case-80-2. Accessed October 25, 2017. "Hereafter PIIE, Case 80-2."

[119]Flores, David A., Export Controls and the US Effort to Combat International Terrorism. *Law and Policy in International Business*, Vol. 13, 1981, pp. 521–590; *New York Times*, April 10, 1980, p. A16, and PIIE, Case 80-2.

[120]*New York Times*, May 15, 1980, p. A16 and PIIE, Case 80-2.

[121]*New York Times*, August 6, 1980, p. A5; *New York Times*, August 30, 1980, p. A2; PIIE, Case 80-2; and Flores 1981, p. 575.

foreign aid bill "because of Iraq's support for international terrorism."[122] In December, Congressman Benjamin S. Rosenthal (D-NY) released a censored version of a General Accounting Office report that criticized the handling of the Iraqi frigate deal. The report blamed "bureaucratic bungling" for approval of the deal. Although the export license was technically still valid, the General Electric Company, which made the engines, voluntarily complied with a State Department request [made in September] not to ship them."[123]

Chile was another country that was affected by the Carter administration's policy to punish states that provide support to terrorists. On September 21, 1976, Orlando Letelier, a former Chilean ambassador to the U.S. and a leading opponent of Chilean dictator General Augusto Pinoche, was killed in a car bombing in Washington, D.C. The attack was carried out by agents of the Chilean secret police (the DINA). In 1978, a Washington grand jury indicted several of the agents for the assassination. A January 1979 trial in Washington, D.C. found several DINA agents guilty of the assassination. The U.S. asked Chile to extradite these agents but the Chilean Supreme Court rejected the United States' request on the grounds that the evidence against them had been obtained through plea bargaining, which is not acceptable under Chilean jurisprudence. The evidence came from Michael V. Townley, an American who worked for DINA and confessed to planting the bomb that killed Letelier. He further stated that the bomb was planted on orders from Colonel Espinoza and General Contreras of the DINA. There was an internal debate within the Carter administration as to what type of pressure should be applied to Chile. The State Department's Bureau of Human Rights and the Justice Department advocated a hardline approach while State's Bureau of Inter-American Affairs, and the Commerce and Treasury Departments opposed such an approach.[124] Some U.S. officials argued that punitive measures would not move the Chilean government toward extraditing the DINA officers because the government there stated it was a judicial matter nor would such measures improve human rights in Chile. Others believed that the measures would at least demonstrate to Chile and other countries that the U.S. would respond negatively to such issues. Ultimately, the U.S. announced a reduction in official diplomatic, economic, and military ties with Chile, accused the Chilean government of condoning international terrorism in the Letelier case, recalled the U.S. Ambassador to Chile for consultations, and in an unusual departure from diplomatic language,

---

[122]*New York Times*, September 26, 1980, p. A7 and PIIE, Case 80-2.

[123]*New York Times*, December 26, 1980, p. A23 and PIIE, Case 80-2.

[124]Graham Hovey, "Carter Said to Plan Cutbacks in Chile over Letelier Case," *New York Times*, November 30, 1979, p. A1.

the State Department called the DINA officers "terrorists."[125] The U.S. cut off $6 million in economic and military aid to Chile, reduced U.S. diplomatic and military staffs in Chile, and temporarily shut down the Export-Import Bank and the Overseas Private Investment Corporation, both U.S. government agencies, in Chile. The hardliners in the Carter administration wanted, but did not get, even more punitive measures — a break in diplomatic relations and moves to ban private U.S. loans and investments in Chile.[126] The diplomatic conflict with Chile over the Letelier assassination carried over into the Reagan administration.

Hostage-Taking

The Carter administration adhered to the stated policy and practice of previous administrations of no concessions/no ransom in hostage-taking incidents. A June 1979 NSC publication stated the policy as:

- We will not accede to terrorist blackmail because to grant concessions only invites further demands.
- We look to the host government when Americans are abducted overseas to exercise its responsibility under international law to protect all persons within its territories, and to ensure the safe release of hostages.
- We maintain close and continuous contact with the host government during terrorist incidents, supporting the host government with all practical intelligence and technical services.
- We understand the extreme difficulty of the decisions governments are often called upon to make. For example, how as a practical operational matter to reconcile the objectives of saving the lives of the hostages and making sure that the terrorists can gain no benefit from their lawless action.[127]

At no time during the administration's four years in office did it have to directly address and militarily respond to an overseas terrorist-related hostage situation.[128] Several hijackings of commercial aircraft with Americans onboard were dealt with by other countries. All these incidents were handled by the host countries

---

[125] Ibid., and "U.S. Cuts Chile Ties; Terrorism Cited," *Washington Post*, December 1, 1979, p. A14.

[126] Ibid.

[127] "NSC June 1979 Report," at https://www.ncjrs.gov/pdffiles1/Digitization/62107NCJRS.pdf. Accessed June 5, 2017.

[128] The author does not believe that the seizure of the U.S. Embassy in Tehran in November 1979 by a mob of militant Iranian students should be considered a "terrorist" incident.

and, in the case of the hijackings, countries whose aircraft were seized. The U.S. was an active observer in that it was in communication with host countries and was willing to share any relevant intelligence and operational knowledge.

Barricade and Hostage Incidents and Kidnappings

The first test of the Carter administration's policy on hostage-taking took place less than three weeks after taking office. On February 14, 1977, Richard Starr, a Peace Corps Volunteer botanist serving in Colombia, was kidnapped by the Revolutionary Armed Forces of Colombia (FARC) guerrilla group during an attack on a local police outpost. Latin American press at the time reported that Starr was a CIA agent and a Fellow of the "CIA-linked" Summer Linguistics Institute.[129] In May 1978, the FARC delivered two letters to the U.S. Embassy in Bogota. One was from Starr to U.S. Ambassador Diego Ascencio and the other was from the FARC demanding that another FARC guerrilla be released from prison in exchange for Starr. Colombian authorities ignored the FARC demand. FARC also rejected an offer of $140,000 ransom payment made by Starr's mother. The plea of Starr's mother to seek his release caught the attention of Washington columnist Jack Anderson. He published a plea to the terrorists, asking them to contact him for private negotiations that would bring Starr's release. After months of haggling, the FARC suddenly demanded a $250,000 ransom. Anderson borrowed the money from a business friend and sent his associate Jack Mitchell to Colombia for a rendezvous with the kidnappers.[130] The negotiations were successful and on February 12, 1980, Starr was released after 1,093 days in captivity. The U.S. government played a bystander role in this incident. The stated U.S. policy at the time was not to give in to terrorist's demands nor to negotiate with them. The U.S. did not pay any ransom for Starr's release. It kept in touch with the Colombian government through the U.S. Embassy and met with Starr's mother when she visited Colombia in 1977. The U.S. did however facilitate Jack Mitchell's access, who was bringing the Anderson ransom to Bogota and his contacts with the FARC.[131]

---

[129] Peace Corps Online — The Independent News Forum serving Returned Peace Corps Volunteers, at http://peacecorpsonline.org/messages/messages/467/2019711.html. Accessed March 3, 2017; David Vidal, "Colombia Abductions Create Climate of Insecurity," *New York Times*, June 26, 1978, p. A6.

[130] Ibid.

[131] The Association for Diplomatic Studies and Training Foreign Affairs Oral History Project, Interview with Anthony Quainton, interviewed by Charles Stuart Kennedy, interview date: November

The most serious terrorist hostage-taking incident that took place during the Carter administration occurred on February 27, 1980 when left-wing terrorists from the 19th of April Movement (M-19), Colombia's most active urban terrorist group, seized the embassy of the Dominican Republic in Bogotá, Colombia. The terrorists held nearly 60 people, including 15 ambassadors, hostage for 61 days. The U.S. Ambassador to Colombia, Diego Ascencio, was one of the hostages. The objectives of the operation were to seek the release of imprisoned M-19 members, embarrass the government just before the mid-term elections on March 9, and provoke the military to react with force.[132] The terrorists demanded the liberation of 311 imprisoned colleagues and $50 million. After 61 days, the hostages were released unharmed by their captors, who received no prisoners in exchange and a modest $1.2 million ransom. The incident, however, embarrassed the Colombian government and gained international attention for the group. The U.S. was not directly involved in the negotiations between the Colombian government and the hostage-takers. U.S. policy was to leave the negotiations to the host government with the expectation that it would do all it could to seek the safe release of the hostages.

Colombian authorities began negotiating with the guerrillas after they threatened to kill the hostages. Beginning on February 28 and continuing over the next two months, the government was able to convince the terrorists to release several groups of hostages at various times. On March 17, Cuba's Fidel Castro offered the terrorists asylum in Cuba. During these two months of negotiations, the terrorists reduced their demands as it became clear that the government would not accede to their demands, especially the release of imprisoned terrorists. The Colombian government did agree to allow international human rights groups to monitor pending trials of imprisoned guerrillas for expeditiousness and justice. On April 27, the 16 M-19 hostage-takers along with 12 hostage diplomats left on a plane for Cuba where the diplomats were released. U.S. Ambassador Diego Ascencio believed that the terrorists were overconfident in their demands and that once the Colombian government took a hardline approach to the demands, the terrorists did not have a Plan B. Several hostage diplomats, including Ascencio, formed a "hostage committee" to help with "analyzing government negotiating documents for the M-19, suggesting new avenues of discussion, rewriting guerrilla manifestos to take out

---

6, 1997, pp. 107–108, at https://www.adst.org/OH%20TOCs/Quainton,%20Anthony.toc.pdf?_ga=2.34482725.568066597.1557875620-92370665.1514835619. Accessed June 5, 2018.

[132]CIA, National Intelligence Daily, February 28, 1980, at https://www.cia.gov/library/readingroom/docs/DOC_0000651923.pdf. Accessed August 4, 2016.

the more egregious ideological parts and pointing out where the government had made perhaps not readily apparent concessions."[133]

Internally, two notable hostage incidents took place during the Carter administration. On March 7, 1977, Cory Moore, a black former U.S. Marine, took two white captives, a young woman and a police captain, in the Cleveland suburb of Warrensville Heights. Moore's demands ranged from all whites "to get off the earth" to burning all their money. He eventually released one hostage but did not release the other until he spoke with President Carter. During a televised press conference, President Carter announced he would talk to Moore if he first released the last hostage. Carter understood the precedent he was setting was dangerous. However, he weighed that against the life of the hostage and the fact that there was an ostensibly racial aspect to the incident.[134] On March 9, Moore released the last hostage and Carter talked to him for several minutes. In a rambling news conference after he surrendered, Moore complained that "white folks don't understand black America's needs ... there is a need for black America to come out of poverty and the hunger that exists all over the world," and that the television show "Roots" gave "white America a chance to see why I've taken the role I've taken."[135]

The second siege was the March 7, 1977 occupation of three buildings in Washington, D.C. by Hanafi Muslims. While Carter was talking to Moore on the phone, a dozen gunmen from the Hanafi Muslim sect initiated a coordinated hostage and barricade seizure of three buildings in Washington, D.C. in which 134 hostages were seized and one person killed. The Hanafi Muslim siege triggered the debate on the role of the press in a terrorist incident and how the authorities should negotiate for the lives of the hostages.[136] There were very few such incidents in the U.S. prior to this incident so there was no template or lessons learned for reference. Not surprisingly, these two issues — the role of the press and how to negotiate — became perennial concerns in future decades.

---

[133] Karen DeYoung, book review, *Our Man is Inside* by Diego and Nancy Asencio with Ron Tobias. *Washington Post* Book World, February 13, 1983, p. 5, at http://bailey83221.livejournal.com/72461. html. Accessed March 12, 2017.

[134] Simon, *The Terrorist Trap*, p. 123. See also, The President's News Conference, March 9, 1977, at http://www.presidency.ucsb.edu/ws/index.php?pid=7139&st=Terrorism&st1=. Accessed June 4, 2016.

[135] Peter P. Spudich Jr., "Carter Makes Promised Call to Surrendered Ohio Gunman," *Washington Post*, March 10, 1977, at https://www.washingtonpost.com/archive/politics/1977/03/10/carter-makes-promised-call-to-surrendered-ohio-gunman/3dfbc2b0-fbb4-4d3c-90c8-35346b5b1e10/. Accessed July 5, 2016.

[136] Carey Winfrey, "Hanafi Seizure Fans New Debate of Press Coverage of Terrorists," *New York Times*, May 19, 1977, p. 46; and Anthony Marro, "What Should be Given Up in Order to Save Hostages?," *New York Times*, March 20, 1977, p. 157.

Media Coverage of Terrorists and Terrorism

National and local TV coverage of the Washington, D.C hostage incident was extensive given that it occurred in the capital and involved multiple hostage-taking locations. NBC-TV assigned 18 mini-cam crews to the story; a total of about 100 NBC persons were assigned to the story and the story led off all three network evening news programs for three straight nights. Local WTOP-TV anchorman Max Robinson established contact with the leader Hamaas Abdul Khaalis' and transmitted his demands. The involvement of a reporter in this role became the subject of substantial debate.[137] U.S. and foreign media coverage of terrorist incidents, especially hostage-taking incidents, has always been a controversial issue. Psychologists, psychiatrists, law enforcement officials, government officials, broadcasting executives, and journalists themselves had different views of what the media's role should be in hostage-taking incidents whether they are carried out by criminals, crazies, or political terrorists. The following were the key questions: (1) How much media attention should be devoted to the event? (2) Should the reporting be censored by authorities, especially regarding information about possible rescue attempts or other counter measures? (3) Should reporters ever act as intermediaries? (4) Should the media report false information when requested by the police? (5) Should the media broadcast the demands of terrorists or publish demanded manifestos? (6) Should the event be covered live or delayed broadcast? (7) Did the coverage encourage further acts of terrorism? The ultimate question that has never really been conclusively answered was and remains, does the media coverage of the incident provide more of a service to its subscribers or the terrorists?

The U.S. television and newspaper media had covered terrorist hostage-taking incidents in the past, going back to the September 1970 Dawson Field hijackings and then the 1972 attack on Israeli athletes during the Summer Olympics in Munich. During the 1960s, the U.S. media also covered the numerous anti-war protests and the Vietnam War itself. Because the Vietnam War was the first war

---

[137] Herbert A. Terry, "Television and Terrorism: Professionalism Not Quite the Answer," *Indiana Law Journal*, Volume 53, Issue 4, Summer 1978, p. 754; and Carey Winfrey, "Hanafi Seizure Fans New Debate of Press Coverage of Terrorists," *New York Times*, May 19, 1977, p. 46, at http://www. repository.law.indiana.edu/cgi/viewcontent.cgi?article=3377&context=ilj. Accessed May 2, 2017. See also, M. Cherif Bassiouni, "Terrorism, Law Enforcement, and the Mass Media: Perspectives, Problems, Proposals," *Journal of Criminal Law and Criminology*, Vol. 72, Issue 1, Spring 1981, at http://scholarlycommons.law.northwestern.edu/cgi/viewcontent.cgi?article=6213&context=jclc. Accessed May 17, 2018.

where the media was subjected to minimal censorship by the U.S. government, the media was able to present images of death and destruction in the war that Americans did not see during World Wars I and II, except maybe in newsreels at movie theaters. With Americans now having access to their own TVs, the war was being brought straight into their living rooms. The Vietnam War has been tagged as the "television war" or "living room war." While opposition to the war was triggered by a plethora of moral, legal, political, religious, pragmatic, and personal arguments, it could also be argued, indeed, it is likely, that the visual images of the war shown on television contributed to the anti-war protests. The images crystalized the effects of the war on the Vietnamese and American military personnel and therefore provided moral and political certitude to the protestors. Similar arguments could be made for the media's reporting on terrorism in the late 1960s and early 1970s. It is one thing to read about a terrorist hijacking or a terrorist seizure of a building to hold hostages and another to watch it unfold on television, albeit, in most cases, on delayed tape. TV stations at this stage of technology were able to send remote vehicles out to cover news. However, a "remote" operation was a cumbersome and necessarily pre-planned process. "Equipment was bulky and costly to operate, so remotes were reserved mostly for events that could be anticipated in advance like political conventions and sports. It was not readily possible to do remote coverage for fast-breaking news. For that, film was more appropriate — but film took time to process and edit for television."[138] Also, film taken in Europe and other overseas places had to be flown back to the U.S. for processing and transmission.

Around 1973, three new pieces of TV equipment moved from the laboratory to production and revolutionized TV journalism technology. That revolution challenged existing TV ethics and practices. The equipment was simple: (1) small, light video cameras ("minicams"), (2) light, battery-powered video tape recorders, and (3) the real technological breakthrough — a device called the time-base corrector which converted the output of the light-weight video recorder into a picture with enough stability to be broadcast. With just these three pieces of equipment, news coverage could be speeded up substantially by eliminating the time for film processing. With one more piece of equipment — a portable microwave transmitter and receiver unit — images could be transmitted directly from field to studio and, if desired, broadcast live. With these electronic news gathering cameras and video recorders (ENG), TV news had at last become as

---

[138] Herbert A. Terry, "Television and Terrorism: Professionalism Not Quite the Answer," p. 749.

instantaneous with images as radio had long been with sound. The first known example of the media using ENG technology in a terrorist incident is likely the May 17, 1974 shootout between members of the Symbionese Liberation Army terrorist group and the Los Angeles police in Compton, California. Enhancing the news worthiness of this incident was the fact that at the time, police did not know if Patty Hearst was in the terrorist safe house. She was not, but millions of people watched live as CBS stations broadcast one of the largest police shootouts in history with a reported total of over 9,000 rounds fired. By the start of the Carter administration, over 75% of commercial TV stations had ENG cameras and video recorders, although some did not possess the microwave equipment needed for live transmission.[139]

As a result of the controversies that emerged from the media's coverage of terrorist incidents at home and abroad, CBS News issued on April 14, 1977, a set of guidelines for coverage of terrorist incidents. It contained guidelines that other major news organizations most likely followed to some degree. The following were the guidelines:

Coverage of Terrorists

Because the facts and circumstances of each case vary, there can be no specific self-executing rules for the handling of terrorist/hostage stories. CBS News will continue to apply the normal test of news judgment and if, as so often they are, these stories are newsworthy, we must continue to give them coverage despite the dangers of "contagion." The disadvantages of suppression are, among things, (1) adversely affecting our credibility ("What else are the news people keeping from us?"); (2) giving free rein to sensationalized and erroneous word of mouth rumors; and (3) distorting our news judgments for some extraneous judgmental purpose. These disadvantages compel us to continue to provide coverage. Nevertheless, in providing for such coverage there must be thoughtful, conscientious care and restraint. Obviously, the story should not be sensationalized beyond the actual fact of its being sensational. We should exercise particular care in how we treat the terrorist/kidnapper.

---

[139] All information in the paragraphs dealing with TV news technological developments was derived from the previously cited Herbert A. Terry's excellent article "Television and Terrorism: Professionalism Not Quite the Answer" in the *Indiana Law Journal*; at http://www.history.com/this-day-in-history/lapd-raid-leaves-six-sla-members-dead. Accessed May 6, 2018.

CBS policy stated:

(1) It would report the demands of the terrorists but avoid providing an excessive platform for the terrorists. Unless the demands are free of rhetoric and propaganda, it might be better to paraphrase the demands instead of presenting them directly from the terrorist.

(2) Only with the approval of the president or vice president of CBS News would there be live coverage of the terrorist as CBS did not want to give them an unedited platform.

(3) CBS reporters' phone lines to the terrorists should not interfere with the need by the authorities to communicate with them.

(4) CBS News would contact experts dealing with the hostage incident to determine whether they have any guidance on such questions as phraseology to be avoided, what kinds of questions or reports might tend to exacerbate the situation, etc.

(5) Names of CBS personnel should be given to the local authorities.

(6) CBS personnel should avoid the use of inflammatory catchwords or phrases, the reporting of rumors, etc., and obey all police instructions but report immediately to their superiors any such instructions that seem to be intended to manage or suppress the news.

(7) Coverage of this kind of story should be in such overall balance as to length that it does not unduly crowd out other important news of the hour/day.[140]

Aircraft Hijacking

After increased aviation security measures and international aviation conventions were implemented during the Nixon administration, aircraft hijackings in and outside the U.S. had declined, from 55 successful hijackings worldwide in 1970 to 11 in 1973, eight in 1974, and seven in both 1975 and 1976.[141] The majority

---

[140] Terry, "Television and Terrorism: Professionalism Not Quite the Answer," pp. 776–777.

[141] Hijacking statistics from Office of Civil Aviation Security, Federal Aviation Administration, "Aircraft Hijackings and Other Criminal Acts against Civil Aviation Statistical and Narrative Reports — Updated to January 1, 1986," Publication date: May 1986, pp. 2, 228, at http://oai.dtic.mil/oai/oai?v erb=getRecord&metadataPrefix=html&identifier=ADA192110. Accessed May 5, 2017. In the mid-1980s, the FAA classified a hijacking as either "successful" (hijacker controls flight and reaches destination or objective), "unsuccessful" (hijacker attempts to take control of flight but fails), or "incomplete" (hijacker is apprehended or killed during hijacking or as a result of "hot pursuit."). Not all of the hijackings in the FAA's above report were carried out by political terrorists. In fact, the majority were carried out by criminals, mentally unbalanced individuals, and asylum seekers. See also, R.P. Boyle,

of these hijackings were not terrorist-related. However, at the end of the Ford administration, two significant terrorist hijackings did occur. On June 27, 1976, Air France Flight 139 was hijacked by four German and Palestinian terrorists on behalf of the PFLP–External Operations. The hijackers demanded a ransom of $5 million and the release of imprisoned terrorists in five countries, including Israel. There were 257 passengers and crew aboard, including nine American citizens and 70 Israeli citizens. This incident ended on July 4 when Israeli commandos carried out a successful hostage rescue — "Operation Thunderbolt" — at Entebbe airport in Uganda where the hijacked plane landed. Afterward, it was determined that the terrorists were able to board the aircraft in Athens due to faulty security measures at the airport.[142] The successful hostage-rescue raid at Entebbe was the first of its kind in the international arena and triggered an internal discussion in the counter-terrorism and military communities in the United States about developing a similar capability. The second hijacking occurred during the Ford administration's last year in office, on September 10, 1976 when five Croatian terrorists seized TWA Flight 355 out of New York to publicize the cause of Croatian independence. They demanded that several major American newspapers publish the group's political manifesto. The hijackers eventually surrendered in France. The explosive devices used by the terrorists on the plane proved to be fake so there were no security flaws at the airport.

These two incidents in 1976 shaped the incoming Carter administration's attitude toward the aircraft hijacking problem. The problem was not as acute as in the early 1970s, but aviation security was still not invulnerable, especially overseas where security standards were still uneven. It was not a major concern however and would simply be addressed when and if the problem arose. In late 1977, the problem attracted more attention in the administration. On September 28, 1977, five members of the JRA hijacked Japan Airlines Flight 472 in Dacca, Bangladesh. The terrorists were armed with guns and grenades. The airport there had no metal detectors.[143] There were 156 passengers and crew aboard, including

---

"International Action to Combat Aircraft Hijacking," University of Miami *Inter-American Law Review*, October 1, 1972, pp. 460–473, at http://repository.law.miami.edu/cgi/viewcontent.cgi?article =2258&context=umialr. Accessed June 3, 2018; Robert T. Turi, Charles M. Friel, Robert B. Sheldon, John P. Matthews, "Descriptive Study of Aircraft Hijacking," Criminal Justice Monograph, Vol. III, Issue 5, 1972, Institute of Contemporary Corrections and the Behavioral Sciences, Sam Houston State University, at http://files.eric.ed.gov/fulltext/ED073315.pdf. Accessed June 4, 2017.

[142]Yossi Melman, "Setting the Record Straight: Entebbe Was Not Auschwitz," *Haaretz* (Israel), July 8, 2011, at http://www.haaretz.com/israel-news/setting-the-record-straight-entebbe-was-not-auschwitz-1.372131. Accessed August 4, 2017.

[143]Mickolus, *A Chronology of Events, 1968–1979*, p. 729.

12 Americans. The terrorists demanded $6 million and the release of nine impris-
oned JRA terrorists in Japan. The Japanese gave in to the demands and paid
ransom and released six of the prisoners. Ironically, the JRA hijackers did not
realize that there were diamonds worth almost $2 million in a case lying on an
aircraft seat throughout the whole six days of the hijacking.[144] As the Japanese
Prime Minister said at the time of his decision to agree to the hijackers' demands,
"the weight of a human life was heavier than the earth."[145] An editorial in the
Japan Times presented a cultural mindset of the Japanese behind the decision and
a view that some counter-terrorism specialists would support.

> *From our experience, it may be said that yielding to the seemingly
> unreasonably demand of a terrorist does not necessarily mean defeat. In
> the long run, the lawless turns out to be the loser. The handling of the
> Dacca case, too, is not to be viewed as a defeat for the law and reason.
> Rather, it should be regarded as reassurance of the importance of human
> life. And the turning over of the ransom and the requested prisoners to
> the terrorists is not the end of the affair. Efforts must be mounted imme-
> diately to hunt them down and retrieve the released prisoners.*[146]

The above policy was one where a government would accede to the demands of
the terrorists in order to free all the hostages unharmed and then engage in a massive, determined, and lengthy manhunt to track down all the terrorists. A variation
of this policy was to pay the ransom and publish manifestos but not to release any
imprisoned terrorists. In the Dacca incident, all passengers and crew were eventually released unharmed in Algeria, which granted the terrorists asylum and
allowed them to leave Algeria with the ransom money undetected. Algeria
defended its decision by saying that it had saved the lives of the passengers and
that the government was honor-bound to keep its word to the terrorists. The
Dacca incident however was another exemplar for those officials in the U.S. who
advocated international punishment for states who condone, support, and aid terrorists. Incidentally, no JAL plane was ever hijacked again. This undercuts somewhat the view that giving in to terrorists encouraged more hijackings. Terrorists
around the world would have known that the Japanese government caved in to the
terrorists and was ripe for the taking. In the 1970s and 1980s, no JAL plane, no
Japanese diplomatic facility, and no Japanese facility was seized by international

---

[144] Edgar O'Balance, *Language of Violence*, p. 280.
[145] Farrell, *Blood and Rage: The Story of the Japanese Red Army*, p. 190.
[146] Ibid., p. 191.

terrorists. It was not until 1996 that terrorists carried out a seizure of a Japanese facility. Peruvian terrorists seized the Japanese ambassador's residence in Lima. However, the incident was aimed at the Peruvian government and not the Japanese government.

Two weeks after the Dacca incident, on October 13, Lufthansa Flight 181 was hijacked by four members of the PFLP on a flight from Palma de Mallorca to Frankfurt. This incident ended when the German government carried out a hostage-rescue operation — Operation Fire Magic — by the GSG-9 (Border Protection Group 9 of the Federal Police), a special counter-terrorism unit, in Mogadishu, Somalia where the plane had landed. Three hijackers were killed, all the hostages were freed, and a pilot was killed by the terrorists before the raid.[147] This was the second successful international hostage-rescue operation in the past 16 months. Like the Israeli "Operation Thunderbolt" at Entebbe in June 1976, the German "Operation Fire Magic" at Mogadishu amplified the absence of a similar U.S. unit. The Carter administration would have to address this deficiency. Less than two months after the Lufthansa hijacking, on December 4, a lone suspected JRA terrorist hijacked Malaysian Airline System Flight 653 on its way to Singapore. There were 100 passengers and crew aboard, including one American. Something went wrong aboard the plane; the hijacker apparently shot the pilot and the plane crashed, killing all aboard.[148]

During 1977, the first year of the Carter administration, there were 32 airline hijackings worldwide (16 successful) — almost double the total for 1976 and more than any year since the 1968–1972 peak in worldwide hijackings. All but six of these hijackings were overseas. Of the six hijackings in the U.S., none was successful. At the time, the FAA security regulations covered 36 U.S. and 73

---

[147]The most accurate and detailed reconstruction of the hijacking and the various governments' response to it can be found in Stefan Aust, *Baader-Meinhof: The Inside Story of the RAF* (New York: Oxford University Press, 2009), pp.372–408. Aust also provides the linkage between the hijacking and the RAF kidnapping of the German industrialist Hanns-Martin Schleyer. Based on information from RAF terrorist Peter Jurgen Boock, who was in Baghdad at the time with the main group of the RAF during the hijacking, the hijacking plan was to have the plane land in Aden, have the hijackers depart, and replace them with a larger, better armed unit which would take over the hijacking. If the hijacking situation went on longer in Aden, this unit was to take the hostages off the plane and disappear into the Yemeni desert and thus out of reach of a rescue (Aust, p. 390). Either way, the hijacking was to end in Aden. However, to the chagrin of the PFLP representative in Aden, the Yemeni government, under pressure from its East German ally, forced the plane to take off.

[148]No definitive information has surfaced to date to prove or disprove the assumption that this was a failed JRA hijacking. For more information on suspected JRA involvement, at http://www.theinfolist.com/php/SummaryGet.php?FindGo=Malaysian%20Airline%20System%20Flight%20653. Accessed May 4, 2018.

foreign airlines operating some 15,000 scheduled passenger flights each day to and from 620 U.S. and foreign airports and boarding some 585,000 passengers and 800,000 pieces of carry-on baggage daily. No other mode of travel at the time had such wide-ranging security measures to protect its passengers.[149] In a speech to the International Civil Aviation Organization in late 1977, U.S. Transportation Secretary Brock Adams noted that 20 of the 28 hijackings carried out from January to October 1977 were due to "failures in passenger screening procedures." He also pointed out that since 1973, when the U.S. strengthened U.S. airport screening, "not a single hijacking incident has occurred attributable to failure to detect guns and weapons in the screening process."[150] In 1978, there were 31 hijackings worldwide (10 successful) of which 13 took place in the U.S. Only two of the 13 were successful. In 1979, there were 27 hijackings worldwide (14 successful) of which 13 took place in the U.S. Six of those 13 were successful. In 1980, the last year of the Carter administration, there were 41 hijackings worldwide (22 successful) of which 22 took place in the U.S. Thirteen of those 22 were successful.

There were Americans on board the hijacked September 28, 1977 Japanese and October 13, 1977 German commercial planes. The hijackers on both planes diverted them to several different countries. The Japanese plane ended up in Algeria while the Lufthansa plane landed in Somalia. There were over 45 different nationalities aboard these two aircraft. The U.S. had little control over the actions of all the countries directly or indirectly involved. It could influence and provide intelligence and operational advice if needed, but it could not dictate actions. The responsibility for these hijacked planes rested first with the parent nation of the planes and then with the countries where the planes eventually landed. Many countries refused the planes permission to land on their territory — 20 countries alone refused to allow the JAL plane to land on their territory. Given that Japan did not have a hostage-rescue capability or the willingness to carry out such an operation, the Japanese government quickly gave in to the terrorists' demands.[151] The U.S. may not have agreed with this decision, but it accepted it. There was one last opportunity to capture and punish the Japanese hijackers and that was when the plane with the hijackers and released imprisoned terrorists

[149] Op. cit., July 1977 House Committee on International Relations. Subcommittee on International Operations: Protection of Americans abroad hearings…, pp. 40–41.

[150] Richard Witkin, "U.S. Calls for Better Screening to Avert Air Piracy," *New York Times*, November 5, 1977, p. 3, and "Safe Airlines and Unsafe Airports," *New York Times*, November 1, 1977, p. 34.

[151] Shortly after the incident, Japan's National Police Agency established a Special Assault Team to deal with future acts of terrorism.

landed in Algeria. Algeria could have arrested all the terrorists and seized the ransom. It did not. Both Japan and Algeria agreed to the demands of the terrorists for a humanitarian reason — to save as many lives as possible. Both countries were criticized for their actions. Their approach was opposite to what countries like the U.S. and Israel would have taken.

In the Lufthansa hijacking, the German government did have a hostage-rescue capability and was willing to deploy it when necessary. The trigger for the decision was the cold-blooded execution in front of the passengers of the plane's captain and the threat of more executions. Consider also that at this time the German government was confronted with a unique situation — a terrorist pincer movement — with German leftist terrorists holding a kidnapped German industrialist and Palestinian terrorists holding hostages aboard a hijacked German commercial plane. No government has ever confronted a similar terrorist dilemma. To its credit, the German government did not accede to the terrorists' demands and authorized the GSG-9 raid. The German government essentially bribed the Somalian government with promises of future aid to allow the GSG-9 raid. The German government informed the U.S. of the decision and the U.S. did not oppose the raid. Therefore, in both hijackings the U.S. played an interested observer role and was never confronted with making a major policy or operational decision. The Carter administration never had to face an overseas terrorist hostage situation where it had to implement its stated hostage-taking policy. In two years, however, it faced a unique and momentous hostage situation overseas when American diplomats were seized and held captive in Tehran.

UNCLASSIFIED

THE WHITE HOUSE

WASHINGTON

CONFIDENTIAL/GDS
UNCLASSIFIED

June 2, 1977

Presidential Review Memorandum/NSC-30

TO: The Vice President
        The Secretary of State
        The Secretary of Defense

        ALSO: The Secretary of the Treasury
                The Attorney General
                The Secretary of Transportation
                The Chairman, Joint Chiefs of Staff
                The Director of Central Intelligence
                The Administrator, Energy Research
                and Development Administration

SUBJECT: Terrorism (C)

The President has directed that the Special Coordination Committee review our policy and procedures for dealing with terrorist incidents. The review -- which should be no more than 20 pages in length -- should be completed by August 1, 1977, and should:

1.   Review current U. S. policy on terrorism, considering specifically:

    a.   Whether there should be an explicit policy for negotiating with terrorists and, if so, recommendations for alternative policies and the level at which the policy should be set.

    b.   The adequacy of current capabilities for dealing with a spectrum of terrorist threats.

    c.   Recommendations on collection and dissemination of intelligence on terrorist activities.

CONFIDENTIAL/GDS
UNCLASSIFIED

Declassified/Released on 12/4/91
under provisions of E.O. 12356
by S. Tilley, National Security Council

(FFF-264)

UNCLASSIFIED

PRM-30 — a standard presidential practice for an incoming administration — establish a tasker to review the previous administration's policy and procedures on an issue to see what to keep or change.

Source: U.S. Government.

**THE UNITED STATES GOVERNMENT
ANTITERRORISM PROGRAM**

AN UNCLASSIFIED SUMMARY REPORT

June

1979

Prepared by the

EXECUTIVE COMMITTEE ON TERRORISM

For the

SPECIAL COORDINATION COMMITTEE

NATIONAL SECURITY COUNCIL

The unclassified version of the finished PRM-30.

Source: U.S. Government.

Libyan leader Colonel Muammar Qaddafi.

Source: Wikimedia Commons.

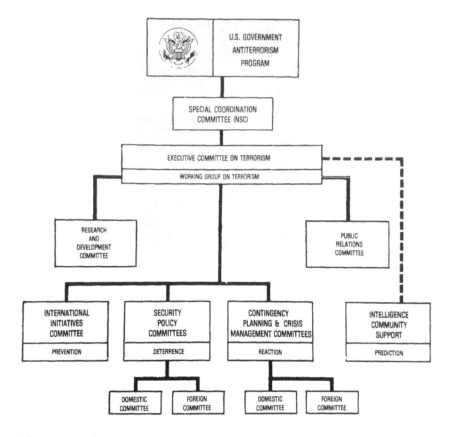

U.S. government's counter-terrorism program structure during the Carter administration.

Source: U.S. Government.

Congresswoman Millicent Fenwick (D-NJ) — In office January 3, 1975 — January 3, 1982. Her 1979 amendment ("the Fenwick amendment") to the Export Administration Act laid the foundation for the government's "state sponsors list."

Source: U.S. government.

Chapter 10

The Carter Administration (1977–1980): The Response — Part II

The Iranian Seizure of the U.S. Embassy in Tehran

Beginning in the post-World War II period, Iran became a key U.S. foreign policy interest. Until 1953, the U.S. took a hands-off approach to oil-rich Iran and supported an independent, monarchy-ruled Iran. In 1953, however, Iranian Prime Minister Mohammed Mossadegh was developing into a threat against the monarchy and intended to develop better relations with the Soviet Union. Both developments were contrary to the U.S. foreign policy objectives in the region. Iran was valuable to the U.S. because it provided oil to the West and it acted as a buffer between the Soviet Union and the Persian Gulf and the oil states. Consequently, in August 1953, the CIA, authorized by President Eisenhower and Secretary of State John Foster Dulles, initiated a coup against Mossadegh to restore power in Iran back to the Shah. From 1952 to 1978, the U.S. and Great Britain provided political and military support to the government of Shah Mohammad Rezi Pahlavi as Iran was a valuable Cold War ally in the Middle East. The revenues from Iranian oil allowed the Shah to lead the country into a period of increased wealth in the 1960s. This prosperity was tempered, however, by the Shah's use of the SAVAK, the Iranian secret police, which "has long been Iran's most hated and feared institution ... with virtually unlimited powers to arrest and interrogate, to torture and murder thousands of the Shah's opponents."[1] In addition, there was a growing resentment against an uneven distribution of the oil wealth and the

---

[1] "World: SAVAK: Like the CIA," *Time*, February 19, 1979, at http://content.time.com/time/magazine/article/0,9171,912364,00.htm. Accessed May 1, 2016.

465

political, economic, and cultural influence of the United States. These factors and others led to a clash with Islamic clergy in Iran in 1963. The Shah's forces suppressed the uprising, sending its clerical leader, Ayatollah Ruhollah Khomeini, into exile in Iraq in 1964 where he remained until October 1978 when he left for France.

The DST, the French secret service, opposed his entry, but the French President overruled them and granted Khomeini political asylum.[2] It was a critical boost for the Islamic revolutionary forces in Iran. With superior French telephone and postal connections (compared to Iraqi ones), Khomeini was able to produce audio cassettes which were sent to his supporters who then flooded Iran with tapes and recordings of his sermons and speeches for clandestine broadcast. In addition, the Western media discovered him and sought numerous interviews with him. Khomeini reportedly gave 132 radio, television, and print interviews over the four months of his stay in France.[3] While Khomeini's house in Neauphle-le-Château, just outside Paris, was not "the" command center for the revolution taking place in Iran since different secular and religious elements were also involved in the uprising,[4] it was "the" command center for the Islamic revolutionaries who wanted an Islamic state in Iran.[5] Khomeini understood that illiteracy in Iran was a problem so he integrated audio cassette tapes of his speeches and sermons into the distribution of his propaganda into Iran. He also used telephones, fax machines, media interviews, video cassettes, and Xerox machines to communicate, propagate, mobilize, and recruit. Khomeini was likely the first person in the post-World War II period to use technology to facilitate a

---

[2] https://www.brusselsjournal.com/node/1857. Accessed June 3, 2018.

[3] Ibid.

[4] See, for example, Ervand Abrahamian, "The Guerrilla Movement in Iran, 1963–1977," *Middle Eastern Review of International Politics*, #86, (March–April 1980), pp. 3–15, at https://mideast-rica. tau.ac.il/sites/humanities.tau.ac.il/files/media_server/mideast_africa/untitled%20folder/7.1.1.%20 Guerilla%20Movement%20%5BAbrahamian%5D%20-%203-15.pdf. Accessed June 6, 2017.

[5] Richard Falk, who visited Khomeini in France on his last day there before leaving for Iran, offered the following observations: "My impression of Khomeini was of a highly intelligent, uncompromising, strong-willed, and severe individual, himself somewhat unnerved by the unexpected happenings in a country he had not entered for almost 20 years. Khomeini insisted on portraying what had happened in Iran as an 'Islamic Revolution'; he corrected us if we made any reference to an 'Iranian Revolution'." Richard Falk, "Was it Wrong to Support the Iranian Revolution in 1978 (because it turned out badly)?" *Foreign Policy Journal*, October 12, 2012, at http://www.foreignpolicyjournal. com/2012/10/12/was-it-wrong-to-support-the-iranian-revolution-in-1978-because-it-turned-out-badly/.

revolution.[6] It was a victory for the revolutionary use of "small media" over the Iranian government's efforts to control the "big" media.

> *The scope of the traditional oppositional network was extended through a highly innovative use of modern communication media and telecommunications technologies to create the world's most successful example to date of alternate media mobilizing for revolution. The complex interplay and cultural resonances of traditional and modern, religious and secular, oral and printed, was what worked so well, not simply that small media were put to audacious new uses. Two main forms of "small media" were used in the Iranian movement: first, cassette tapes, which acted like an electronic pulpit (minbar), and second, photocopied statements, known as elamieh.[7]*

On January 16, 1979, Iranian revolutionary forces forced the Shah of Iran to flee Iran for exile to Egypt. On February 1, the key leader of this revolution, Ayatollah Khomeini returned to Iran from his exile in France. On his return, Khomeini immediately called for the expulsion of all foreigners — "I beg God to cut off the hands of all evil foreigners and their helpers." Given the growing hostility to the U.S., the U.S. Embassy in Tehran feared and anticipated an attack on the embassy. The U.S. Ambassador had reduced the number of U.S. personnel at the embassy and shipped most of the classified files back to Washington. On the day Khomeini returned to Iran, the State Department evacuated 1,350 Americans from Iran. On February 12, the Iranian military unit protecting the U.S. Embassy was ordered back to its barracks, leaving only the U.S. Marine Security Guard (MSG) detachment to protect the embassy. Two days later, 75 Iranian left-wing militants climbed over the embassy wall and opened fire on the chancery. Ambassador William Sullivan ordered embassy personnel to seek shelter in the designated embassy safe haven, the communications vault on the second floor. The embassy's regional security officer and the MSGs fired tear gas at the militants to slow

---

[6]Bernard Lewis. *The Middle East; a Brief History of the Last 2000 Years* (New York: Simon and Shuster, 1995), p. 13.

[7]Annabelle Sreberny-Mohammadi and Ali Mohammadi, "The 'Heavy Artillery': Small Media for a Big Revolution," in *Small Media Big Revolution: Communication, Culture and the Iranian Revolution*, (Minnesota: University of Minnesota Press, 1994), pp. 119–136, at http://www.jstor.org/stable/10.5749/j.ctttbf8.13. Accessed June 6, 2018. See also in this book, Chapter 2, Small Media and Revolutionary Change: A New Model (pp. 19–40); Chapter 9, A Communication-based Narrative of the Revolution (pp. 139–162); and Conclusion: The Importance of the Iran Experience (pp. 189–194).

them down as embassy personnel escaped into the vault. While the ambassador sought assistance from the interim Iranian government, embassy staff shredded the classified documents and destroyed about $500,000 in cryptographic equipment.[8] Two hours later, forces loyal to Ayatollah Khomeini arrived at the embassy to expel the militants. Khomeini had even dispatched a delegation of mullahs to the embassy to convey his apologies for actions "contrary to his wishes" and his belief that no Americans had been killed.[9] Property damage was moderate but there were no injuries. This incident has been referred to as the "Valentine Day Open House" by some U.S. officials.[10] As a result of this incident, the State Department moved quickly to increase physical security at the embassy. State's Office of Security modified the chancery entrance, added electronic surveillance cameras, set up remote-controlled tear gas devices, and added heavy steel doors with automatic alarm systems. However, over the summer, several U.S. agencies returned many boxes of classified files back to the embassy, creating what one official described as a "paper albatross around the embassy's neck."[11]

In exile, the Shah of Iran wanted to come to the U.S. for evaluation and treatment of his cancer. Some U.S. officials in Washington and Tehran understood that this was a volatile issue for the current Iranian government. Iran was demanding that countries where the Shah fled should return him to Iran for trial. Initially, Carter rejected the Shah's request. However, citing humanitarian reasons but also reacting to pressure put on him by some influential political figures like Henry Kissinger, President Carter changed his mind on October 22, 1979 and gave permission for the Shah to come to the U.S. for treatment of his cancer. Iran at this time was in a state of some turmoil as the composition of the new government, the nature of the new state, and the type of constitution were still unsettled. In addition, there were tensions between secular and religious revolutionary elements. The attitude of the new government toward the U.S. was also unresolved. The Iranian political environment was in a state of flux.

The Carter administration faced one of the most unique hostage-taking incidents in modern history on November 4, 1979 when militant Iranian students led the takeover of the U.S. Embassy in Tehran and forcibly held 52 U.S. diplomats for 444 days. All but three of these hostages were held at the embassy for the

---

[8] Mickolus, Chronology of Events: 1969–1979, p. 828.

[9] Robin Wright, *In the Name of God — The Khomeini Decade* (New York: Simon and Shuster, 1989), p. 64. This is an excellent and recommended book for understanding the key events in Iran in the 1980s.

[10] William Daugherty. *In the Shadow of the Ayatollah: A CIA Hostage in Iran* (Annapolis: Naval Institute Press, 2001), p. 10.

[11] Information on the February 14 attack comes from *DS History*, pp. 252–256.

duration of their captivity. Three U.S. diplomats, who were visiting the Iranian Foreign Ministry at the time of the takeover, were subsequently detained at the ministry until 17 days before the ultimate release of all the hostages in January 1981. This incident remains a singular traumatic event in the relations between the Islamic Republic of Iran and the United States. It was an affront that the U.S. had never suffered before or since. Although President Carter initially referred to the takeover as a "terrorist incident," it was not. It was more of a mob assault with subsequent government culpability. The incident did however telegraph the development of a new anti-American terrorism strain — Islamic revolutionary terrorism — that haunted the U.S. into the 2020s.

The date November 4, 1979 was picked by the students because it marked two notable anniversaries for Islamic revolutionaries in Iran who advocated for a more anti-American policy. On November 4, 1963, during a bloody clash between the Shah's security forces and young protestors at Tehran University, several protestors were killed by American-trained Iranian soldiers.[12] On November 4, 1964, Ayatollah Khomeini was sent into exile from Iran for protesting the Shah's government policy of giving diplomatic immunity to American military personnel. In response to the U.S. allowing the Shah to enter the U.S. and for other domestic political objectives,[13] pro-Khomeini students on October 26 1979 conducted a meeting to plan a sit-in at the U.S. Embassy that they hoped could last for several days. The students had printed maps of the embassy and developed special armbands and identity cards for the protestors. They also received some inside information identifying vulnerable entrance points to the chancery.[14] On November 4, several hundred militant Iranian students, calling themselves "students of the Imam's line," stormed the U.S. Embassy in Tehran. The security modifications instituted after the February 14 attack provided some time for the embassy staff, but these measures were primarily designed for a situation where the host government would quickly send forces to rescue the embassy staff. According to international law, it was the responsibility of the Iranian

---

[12] Wright, *In the Name of God*, p. 76.

[13] It has been argued that the primary reason for seizing the U.S. Embassy was not an act of anti-American hatred or the U.S. allowing the Shah to enter the U.S. but to seize the momentum in the volatile Iranian domestic political environment against moderates and leftist elements. See, for example, "The Real Roots of Arab Anti-Americanism," *Foreign Affairs*, November/December 2002, at http://www.cfr.org/polls-and-opinion-analysis/real-roots-arab-anti-americanism/p5260. Accessed June 3, 2018; and Patrick Clawson, "The Paradox of Anti-Americanism in Iran," *Middle Eastern Review of International Affairs*, Vol. 8, No. 1 (March 2004), pp. 16–24, at https://www.washingtoninstitute.org/uploads/Documents/opeds/4224d6e335288.pdf. Accessed June 6, 2017.

[14] Ibid., p. 77.

government to take actions to secure the safe release of the U.S. hostages. The students may have been surprised by how easily they were able to take over the embassy and seize hostages. For the Americans, it was wiser not to put up any resistance and simply wait for a rescue from the host government, similar to what happened on February 14. The protestors demanded that the U.S. turn over the Shah to Iran to stand trial before a revolutionary court. What started out as a temporary sit-in began to gradually and accidentally escalate into a unique opportunity to humiliate the "Great Satan"[15] — a derogatory name for the U.S. — and energize and solidify the Islamic revolutionary forces in Iran.

At this point, Iranian government officials or even Khomeini himself could have intervened and allowed the students one or two days of protests inside the embassy to vent their frustrations. The incident could have been contained and managed. However, as more and more students began to show up at the embassy, the situation magnified. Government officials were paralyzed due to the current political uncertainty in the country. To interfere entailed a risk. While Khomeini did not order the takeover, he quickly recognized the political benefits of allowing the students to continue. On November 6, Tehran radio announced that "Khomeini had given his blessing to the seizure of the den of spies."[16] Consequently, two key members of the provisional government then resigned, including the Prime Minister, effectively conceding control to the pro-Khomeini Revolutionary Council. The Islamic revolutionaries' secular opponents were now on the defensive and the Iranian people subsequently voted for an "Islamic" constitution in October. In December, Khomeini assumed the title of Supreme Leader. As Supreme Leader, he had either direct or indirect control over the executive, legislative, and judicial branches of government, as well as the military and media.[17] Khomeini succeeded in establishing an anti-Western Islamic theocracy in place of the pro-U.S./Western monarchy of the Shah. Khomeini and the Revolutionary Council were now steering Iran. Once Khomeini gave his blessing to the takeover on November 6, the incident assumed a unique historical perspective — leaders of a host government allowed its citizens to seize a diplomatic facility, hold

---

[15]Khomeini first used this term to describe the U.S. on November 5, 1979. Christopher Buck. *Religious Myths and Visions of America: How minority faiths redefined America's World role* (New York: Praeger Publishers, 2009), p. 136. "It is a term used for domestic consumption. The Iranian revolution expelled the 'Great Satan' from Iran and must not allow it to come back. Iran has kicked the 'Great Satan' out of the front door and it should not allow it back in through a window, that is Iranians, and some of its leaders should not be seduced by the Great Satan".

[16]Wright, *In the Name of God*, pp. 79–80.

[17]U.S. Institute for Peace. "Iran Primer: The Supreme Leader," at http://iranprimer.usip.org/resource/supreme-leader. Accessed May 6, 2018.

diplomats as hostages, and engage in mental and physical torture of those diplomats. As the hostage situation was prolonged, the militant students, while jubilant, were also astonished that "a single small failure could put a superpower on the defensive for a very long time ... and that the U.S. was prepared to sacrifice its national interests to secure the release of its citizens held hostage."[18]

In addition to humiliating the U.S. government with the takeover and creating a conundrum as to how it should be handled, the militants were also able to embarrass the U.S. by exposing classified U.S. documents — some intact and others shredded but patiently pieced back together by Iranian "volunteers." The students published these documents in a series of books, some 70 volumes, called "Documents from the US Espionage Den," which included telegrams, correspondence, and reports from the U.S. Department of State and Central Intelligence Agency, some of which remain classified to this day.[19] Most of the shredded materials were CIA cables that related to clandestine contacts with Iranians.[20] The cables supported the Islamic revolutionaries' view of the CIA and the U.S. and reinforced what many Iranians already assumed about the U.S. involvement in Iranian affairs. The embassy documents were also used to undermine moderate Iranian politicians who did not fully support Khomeini. The militant students used carefully selected cables to imply that these politicians were working for the CIA. The embassy documents, which contained cables from the embassy to Washington reporting on the meetings with these officials, recorded the desire of the officials for better relations with the U.S. and dissatisfaction with clerical rule.[21] Based on these embassy documents, the deputy to the Prime Minister and

---

[18] Amir Taheri, *Holy Terror: Inside the World of Islamic Terrorism* (Maryland: Adler and Adler, 1987), pp. 208–209. Taheri quotes a Muslim sociologist who opined that this was due to "the fact that the two sides did not attach the same importance to the lives of individuals." (p. 209) The Iranian Islamic revolutionaries would never dream of offering the slightest concession to secure the release of its own members being held hostage or prisoner by its enemies.

[19] Federation of American Scientists, Secrecy & Government Bulletin, Issue Number 70, September 1997, at https://fas.org/sgp/bulletin/sec70.html. Accessed May 4, 2017.

[20] "20 Years after the Hostages: Declassified Documents on Iran and the United States," National Security Archive Electronic Briefing Book No. 21, Published — November 5, 1999, Document 4, at http://nsarchive.gwu.edu/NSAEBB/NSAEBB21/. Accessed May 3, 2018.

[21] Shaul Bakhash. *The Reign of the Ayatollahs: Iran and the Islamic Revolution* (New York: Basic Books, 1990), p. 115; and Mohammad Ayatollahi Tabaar, "Strategic anti-Americanism in Iran from the hostage crisis to nuclear talks," *Washington Post*, November 4, 2014, at https://www.washingtonpost.com/blogs/monkey-cage/wp/2014/11/04/strategic-anti-americanism-in-iran-from-the-hostage-crisis-to-nuclear-talks/. Accessed January 4, 2017. Tabaar argues that "Contrary to conventional wisdom, the U.S. Embassy was not seized in response to the admission of the deposed shah to the United States. To be sure, the reluctant decision of the Carter administration to allow the dying dictator in brought

the Minister of Information, among others, were arrested. As one American hostage remembered:

> *They would hold a press conference, and they would call it 'a press conference with revelations' and they would publish a series of Embassy documents. They were going through Embassy documents and there were a lot of them. And they were hunting for Iranians they didn't like. Not royalists. They were after nationalists, secularists, liberals, people who had been part of their own coalition and selectively releasing documents about them. And they were holding press conferences and presumably they had enough allies in the system that they had access to radio and TV. And their targets, as I said, were not former royal officials or Americans, but people associated with the old National Front, people associated with the social democratic movement, people they called 'the liberals.'[22]*

The documents were also used to influence the January 1980 Presidential elections in Iran and to prevent certain politicians from taking their seats in the parliament.[23] The fact that the U.S. Embassy failed to destroy the classified documents contributed to the Islamic revolutionaries' purge of secular and moderate officials and enhanced their rise to eventual power in Iran. If the U.S. government did not want a repetition of this problem in other countries, it would have to develop a solution for document destruction.

It has been argued that the following were the three key precipitants of the hostage-taking incident in Tehran: (1) the interference of the U.S. in the internal affairs of Iran since 1953, (2) the outreach of the Carter administration to members of the more secular Provisional Government of the Islamic Republic of Iran, and (3) the admission of the exiled Shah to the U.S.[24] It is clear, however, based

---

back memories of the 1953 CIA-backed coup and did not help reduce growing anti-American sentiment in Iran. But the ideological challenge posed by the anti-imperialist leftists was perceived as far more dangerous than the potential U.S. threat." He also argues that the taking of the U.S. Embassy was designed to show who was more "anti-American," the Iranian Marxists or the Islamic revolutionaries.

[22] Former hostage John Limbert, Association for Diplomatic Studies and Training, "Moments in U.S. Diplomatic History: 444 Days: Memoirs of an Iran Hostage," at http://adst.org/2013/10/444-days-memoirs-of-an-iranian-hostage/. Accessed June 6, 2018.

[23] Ibid.

[24] Roham Alvandi, "The Precipitants of the Tehran Hostage Crisis," The Online Journal *Al Nakhlah*, Fall 2003, p. 1, The Fletcher School, Tufts University, at http://fletcher.tufts.edu/~/media/Fletcher/Microsites/al%20Nakhlah/archives/pdfs/alvandi.pdf. Accessed May 28, 2017.

on interviews with Khomeini at the time that admitting the Shah into the U.S. was the most grievous action that triggered the hostage incident.[25] Khomeini considered Carter allowing the Shah to enter the U.S. an insult to the Iranian people who demanded that the Shah return or be returned to Iran to disclose where he had hidden all his money and to stand trial. Initially, the U.S. government felt that the hostage situation would in time defuse as it did in February 1979. However, the incident was combustible and spread quickly to the general population and, it could be argued, developed into a political wildfire where initial objectives were subsumed by shifting domestic political objectives. What was at first a student-planned mob assault on the embassy evolved into an unplanned state hostage-taking act.[26] While the U.S. had a policy for dealing with terrorist hostage-taking incidents, it did not, nor did other countries at the time, have a blueprint for addressing this hostage-taking aberration. There were no previous examples in the 20th century of an internationally recognized state, during non-war conditions, intentionally holding the diplomats of another country as hostages for domestic and foreign policy objectives. The Iranian hostage incident was and remains an unprecedented international criminal act by a recognized state. As President Carter stated in his news conference on November 28, 1979:

> *The actions of Iran have shocked the civilized world. For a government to applaud mob violence and terrorism, for a government actually to support and, in effect, participate in the taking and the holding of hostages is unprecedented in human history. This violates not only the most fundamental precepts of international law but the common ethical and religious heritage of humanity.*[27]

---

[25] See, for example, CBS Reporter Mike Wallace interview with Khomeini around November 18, 1979, at https://www.youtube.com/watch?v=ArW8BGv1RyM. Accessed June 6, 2016.

[26] In a November 4, 2018 interview, on the 39th anniversary of the U.S. Embassy seizure, the Iranian Revolutionary Guard Commander-in-Chief Mohammad Ali Jafari stated that "Iranian officials knew about the decision to storm the embassy." He also noted that "a limited number of students attacked the U.S. embassy based on a spontaneous decision." However, in an apparent contradiction, he said "this was how the embassy was attacked, in order to pretend that it was the mob that made the decision." *Radio Farda*, "IRGC Commander Defends 1979 Seizure of U.S. Embassy, Says 'Officials Were Aware,'" November 4, 2018. "Radio Farda" is the Persian language broadcaster at Radio Free Europe/ Radio Liberty, at https://en.radiofarda.com/a/iran-irgc-commander-jafari-seizure-us-embassy-tehran/29582065.html. Accessed November 6, 2018.

[27] The President's News Conference, November 28, 1979, at http://www.presidency.ucsb.edu/ws/index.php?pid=31752&st=Terrorism&st1=. Accessed June 3, 2017.

The Carter administration initially referred to this incident as terrorism and Ambassador Anthony Quainton, head of the Working Group on Terrorism and Director of the Office for Combatting Terrorism at the State Department, quickly established a crisis working group at State. As the hostage-taking incident did not end itself in a few days or a week, and as Khomeini began to provide political backing to the takeover, the incident evolved into a serious foreign policy crisis. Quainton's counter-terrorism working group was now obsolete. Ambassador Quainton later noted that "the hostage-takers were no longer considered terrorists; this had become an international and political issue."[28] The crisis was managed by the National Security Council (NSC) and the White House. As the incident became drawn out, U.S. and foreign media paid more attention to it. This in turn fueled the incident's extension as the student militants in the U.S. Embassy and Khomeini and his gang realized that the media attention worked to their benefit. The world was now witnessing the extended humiliation of a super power by a small band of Islamic revolutionary students. In addition, Khomeini's reputation and notoriety was increasing as the international media sought interviews with him in Tehran. Khomeini used technology to facilitate the Islamic revolution in Iran and was now using the media to embellish and strengthen it. Ultimately, the hostage-taking incident led to the ascension of Khomeini and his brand of Islamic revolutionary doctrine to power in Iran and the promulgation of an Islamic constitution.

Although the Shah of Iran left the U.S. for Panama on December 15, 1979, the hostage crisis continued. Even when he died in Egypt on July 27, 1980, the hostage situation continued. From November 1979 to April 1980, the Carter administration implemented a standard set of responses to this extraordinary situation. It imposed economic sanctions and applied diplomatic pressure to compel Iran to negotiate for the release of the hostages. The United Nations Security

---

[28] Segment on Quainton from Naftali, *Blind Spot*, pp. 113–114. Quainton quote also from Naftali. See also, Library of Congress, The Association for Diplomatic Studies and Training Foreign Affairs Oral History Project, Interview with Anthony Quainton, interviewed by: Charles Stuart Kennedy, interview date: November 6, 1997. Section on Quainton's counter-terrorism career, pp. 101–126, at https://cdn. loc.gov/service/mss/mfdip/2004/2004qua01/2004qua01.pdf. Accessed June 16, 2017. Although the hostage-takers may not have been considered "terrorists," the Carter administration continued to state that Iran was supporting an "act of international terrorism." For example, on April 17, 1980, President Carter stated at a news conference that "Earlier this month, April the 7th, I announced a series of economic and political actions designed to impose additional burdens on Iran because their Government was now directly involved in continuing this act of international terrorism." The President's News Conference, April 17, 1980, at http://www.presidency.ucsb.edu/ws/index.php?pid= 33288&st=Terrorism&st1=. Accessed June 4, 2106.

Council passed a resolution calling for Iran to release the hostages. The Carter administration suspended oil imports from Iran. It cut diplomatic ties with Iran and ordered all Iranian diplomats to leave the United States. It froze about $8 billion of Iranian gold and bank assets in the U.S. It engaged in back channel secret negotiations using third parties. It prohibited all financial transactions and imports from Iran and travel to and from Iran. It also impounded all military materiel previously under order from Iran. The Carter administration applied every known political and economic bilateral and multilateral pressure point on Iran. Most states would have caved in at some point. However, Iran was being led by a religious-oriented regime that fed on the crisis. Given the current conditions in Iran, the domestic political benefits of continuing to hold the American hostages outweighed the negative political and economic impact of the sanctions.

President Carter "was committed to the safe return of the hostages while protecting America's interests and prestige ... he pursued a policy of restraint that put a higher value on the lives of the hostages than on American retaliatory power or protecting his own political future."[29] However, with the Iranian government showing no signs of releasing the hostages, Carter decided to take an acknowledged risk and use force. On April 11, 1980, he approved a high-risk rescue operation called "Eagle Claw" that the military had been scripting for three months. At the time, many Americans had been calling for military action to free the hostages.[30]

Counter-terrorism Unit Established/Operation Eagle Claw

Prior to the Carter administration, the U.S. had no dedicated, specialized counter-terrorism rescue force for overseas operations. Since 1973, the U.S. Army had trained at least two Ranger battalions as anti-terrorist units who were reportedly capable of dealing with terrorist incidents involving Americans abroad. They were based at Ft. Stewart, Georgia, and Ft. Lewis, Washington. Information of these units was published in the May 1977 issue of *Army* — a magazine published by the Association of the U.S. Army.[31] However, these Ranger battalions were "only part-timers" in the counter-terrorism field and it "takes full-time

---

[29] The Jimmy Carter Presidential Library, "The Hostage Crisis in Iran," at https://www.jimmycarterlibrary. gov/documents/hostages.phtml. Accessed June 6, 2017.

[30] See, for example, PBS, American Experience, "Reactions to the Hostage Crisis," at http://www.pbs. org/wgbh/americanexperience/features/general-article/carter-444-text. Accessed June 3, 2017; and Rose McDermott. *Risk-Taking in International Politics: Prospect Theory in American Foreign Policy* (University of Michigan Press, 1998), Chapter 3: The Iranian Hostage Rescue Mission, p. 47.

[31] October 20, 1977 — Bernard Weinraub, "U.S. is Training Units to Fight Terrorists," *New York Times*, October 20, 1977, p. 17.

professionals who spend as much time on the subject as the enemy does."[32] Impressed by the July 1976 Israeli counter-terrorism raid at Entebbe airport in Uganda to free hostages in an Air France hijacking and the October 1977 German raid at Mogadishu airport in Somalia to free hostages in an Lufthansa hijacking, the Carter administration encouraged the military to develop a similar full-time professional unit. Other countries were also to use force to deal with hostage incidents.[33] On November 21, 1977, Carter authorized "Project Blue Light," the formation of a special unit from the U.S. Army Special Forces for counter-terrorism purposes until a more permanent unit could be constructed and trained. This new unit was called Special Forces Operational Detachment — Delta or Delta Force and it existed outside the Special Forces chain of command. This led to initial competition between the Blue Light unit and Delta.[34] In July 1978, Delta became the sole, permanent, top secret U.S. counter-terrorism unit.[35]

The first actual counter-terrorism deployment of Delta took place in response to the November 4, 1979 seizure of the U.S. Embassy in Iran by militant Iranian students. Carter had tried to apply political, economic, and diplomatic sanctions against Iran but when they failed, he used his last option — the use of military force — deploying Delta in a rescue mission codenamed "Operation Eagle Claw." The planning and deployment of this mission was a well-kept secret and caught Iran, and the American public, by surprise. It was initiated on April 25, 1980. The plan was as follows:

> It called for three USAF MC-130s to carry a 118-man assault force from
> Masirah Island near Oman in the Persian Gulf to a remote spot 200 miles
> southeast of Tehran, code-named Desert One. Accompanying the MC-130s
> were three USAF EC-130s which served as fuel transports. The MC-130s
> planned to rendezvous with eight RH-53D helicopters from the aircraft
> carrier USS Nimitz. After refueling and loading the assault team, the heli-
> copters would fly to a location 65 miles from Tehran, where the assault

---

[32] Quote from Col. Charlie Beckwith in his book *Delta Force: The U.S. Counter-Terrorist Unit and the Iran Hostage Rescue Mission*, (New York: Harcourt, Brace, Jovanovich, 1983), pp. 103–104.

[33] In February 1978, Egyptian commandos attempted a counter-terrorism rescue on Cyprus on a hijacked Egyptian Airliner, but Cypriot national guardsmen fired on the commandos and drove them away from the plane, killing 15 of the commandos. In March 1978, Dutch marines carried out a rescue raid on South Moluccan terrorists holding children and others hostages in a train and school house in the Netherlands. See also, Phil McCombs, "Nations Turn to Force to Combat Terror," *Washington Post*, March 15, 1978, p. A22.

[34] Beckwith, *Delta Force*, pp. 133–134.

[35] "Carter Orders Commando Unit," *Washington Post*, March 3, 1978, p. A5.

team would go into hiding. The next night, the team, dependent upon trusted agents, drivers, and translators, would be picked up and driven the rest of the way to the Embassy compound. After storming the Embassy, the team and the freed hostages would rally at either the Embassy compound or a nearby soccer stadium to be picked up by the helicopter force. The helicopters would then transport them to Manzariyeh, 35 miles to the south, by that time secured by a team of U.S. Army Rangers. Once at Manzariyeh USAF C-141 transports would fly the assault team and hostages out of Iran while the Rangers destroyed the remaining equipment (including the helicopters) and prepared for their own aerial departure.[36]

What occurred was an operation that began to unravel as soon as it began. A series of unforeseen incidents and developments took place that doomed the mission to failure.

The mission began when the first MC-130, carrying the mission commander and USAF combat controllers, arrived at the landing site. The combat controllers were tasked with establishing the airstrips and marshalling the aircraft once they had landed. Soon after the first MC-130 arrived, the plan began to fall apart. First, a passenger bus approached on a highway bisecting the landing zone. The advance party was forced to stop the vehicle and detain its 45 passengers. Soon, a fuel truck came down the highway. When it failed to stop, the Americans fired a light anti-tank weapon which set the tanker on fire and lit the surrounding area. Finally, a pickup truck approached but turned around and departed the area. The assault team commanders, however, decided to continue with the mission. Soon the other five MC-130s aircraft arrived at Desert One to wait for the helicopters. The RH-53 helicopters departed the Nimitz and were en route to Desert One. During the flight, two helicopters aborted because of flight instrument and mechanical problems while the pilot of a third helicopter decided to continue on to Desert One despite hydraulic problems. Soon the remaining six helicopters

---

[36] http://www.afhso.af.mil/topics/factsheets/factsheet.asp?id=19809. Accessed June 4, 2018; see also Edward T. Russell, Crisis in Iran: Operation Eagle Claw, at http://www.afhso.af.mil/shared/media/document/AFD-120823-014.pdf. Accessed May 2, 2018; Mark Bowden, "The Desert One Debacle," *The Atlantic Monthly*, May 2006 issue, at http://www.theatlantic.com/magazine/archive/2006/05/the-desert-one-debacle/304803/. Accessed May 3, 2017.

encountered an unexpected severe dust storm and proceeded individually to Desert One, arriving nearly an hour behind schedule.

Once at Desert One, the RH-53 with hydraulic problems could not be repaired, which left the team with one less helicopter than was required to carry the assault team and hostages. With just five helicopters available, the on-scene commander aborted the mission. The plan then shifted to getting the assault team back on the MC-130s while the helicopters refueled and returned to the Nimitz. At that point, tragedy struck. One of the helicopter's rotor blades inadvertently collided with a fuel-laden EC-130. Both aircraft exploded, killing five airmen on the EC-130 and three marines on the RH-53. The team commanders ordered the remaining helicopters abandoned and everyone to board the EC-130s, which soon departed for Masirah Island. With that, Operation Eagle Claw came to an end. President Carter was notified of the mission's failure, and the wreckage at Desert One was broadcast to the world by the Iranian government.[37]

This failed rescue mission is probably the most analyzed and written about U.S. military special operation mission of the post-World War II era. Iran commemorates the event every year as a symbol of the failure of U.S. plots against the Islamic Republic. While the Iran hostage rescue mission was a military failure, it did announce to the world that the U.S. had developed a counter-terrorism unit and even a liberal American president was willing to deploy it. The decision did cost Carter his Secretary of State, Cyrus Vance, as Vance opposed the operation and resigned — effective when the operation was concluded. Vance also saw "what he regarded as a drift on the part of the United States toward more militant reactions to world events."[38] There was also the issue of his influence with the President declining while Carter's national security adviser, Zbigniew Brzezinski's, was increasing.

---

[37] http://www.afhso.af.mil/topics/factsheets/factsheet.asp?id=19809. Accessed May 4, 2017, Fact Sheet for "Operation Desert Claw."

[38] Daniel Southerland, "What Vance resignation means," *Christian Science Monitor*, April 29, 1980. Vance was only the second Secretary of State in U.S. history to resign. The first was William Jennings Bryan, a known pacifist, who resigned in 1915 over President Wilson's policies that Jennings believed were leading the U.S. into war.

In support of Carter's decision to launch the rescue mission, the Holloway Commission report,[39] contained several reinforcing conclusions:

1.   The concept of a small clandestine operation was valid and consistent with national security objectives. It offered the best chance of getting the hostages out alive and the least danger of starting a war with Iran.
2.   The operation was feasible and the decision to execute was justified.
3.   The rescue mission was a high-risk operation.
4.   Command and control were excellent at the upper echelons.[40]

The remaining conclusions of the report dealt primarily with the planning, operational security, resource support, and command and control at the lower levels.

One can question whether Carter made the right decision to deploy Delta. It is useless to debate the pros and cons as these were all known to Carter when he made the decision. The decision was made by the President only. Presidents, like all people, are mentally wired differently and have different levels of intelligence, experience, and critical thinking skills. As a trained engineer, the President would have analyzed all costs and benefits of such a risky decision. If the operation had succeeded and the hostages were rescued, it most likely would have been seen by the American public as a courageous and great decision. Certainly, some governments would still have criticized it, Republicans would have found some fault in it, some media commentators would have questioned it, and some scholars and retired military officers would have pointed out short- and long-term negative repercussions of the operation. There is ultimately no way to assess whether the President's decision to authorize a rescue operation was the correct choice. What is clear is that bad luck and flaws in mission planning, command and control, and inter-service operability of the operation all contributed to its failure.[41]

---

[39] In 1980, the Department of Defense established the "Special Operations Review Group" to investigate Operation Eagle Claw. It was chaired by Admiral James L. Holloway III and the investigative report is popularly known as the Holloway Commission Report.

[40] Holloway Commission Report, p. v.

[41] See, Holloway Commission Report, at http://nsarchive.gwu.edu/NSAEBB/NSAEBB63/doc8.pdf. Accessed June 2, 2017; and John E. Valliere, "Disaster at Desert One: Catalyst for Change," *Parameters*, Autumn 1992, U.S. Army Strategic Studies Institute, pp. 69–81, at http://strategicstudiesinstitute.army. mil/pubs/parameters/Articles/1992/1992%20valliere.pdf. Accessed July 3, 2017. Other excellent sources are Charles Beckwith and Donald Knox, *Delta Force* (New York: Avon, 2000); Mark Bowden, *Guests of the Ayatollah* (Boston: Atlantic Monthly Press, 2006); James Kyle and John Eidson, *The*

Two and half months after the failed hostage rescue mission, the Shah of Iran died in Cairo in July 1980. In September, Khomeini issued some modified demands: (1) expression of remorse or an apology for the United States' historical role in Iran, (2) unlocking of Iranian assets in America, (3) withdraw any legal claims against Iran arising from the embassy seizure, and (4) promise not to interfere in Iran in the future.[42] The denouement of the hostage crisis began on September 22, 1980 when Iraq invaded Iran igniting an eight-year war between the two countries. By this time, the value of the American hostages had eroded as U.S. economic and military sanctions on Iran were hurting the Iranian economy and its military readiness and one of the primary generators of the takeover — the Shah — was dead. Having squeezed all the necessary enthusiasm from the Iranian people against the "Great Satan," Khomeini now needed to motivate the Iranian people even more for the approaching war against Iraq. Besides, the initial enthusiasm triggered by the embassy takeover was waning as the event was entering its 11th month. Khomeini also did not want to fight two enemies at once. Strategically, it made sense to wind down the hostage incident and mobilize for the war against Iraq. From November 1980 to January 1981, Deputy Secretary of State Warren Christopher led the negotiations with Iran through mediators in Algeria to negotiate the release of the hostages. On January 19, 1981, the United States and Iran signed an agreement to release the hostages and unfreeze Iranian assets. The hostages left Iran on January 21, 1981 hours after Ronald Reagan was sworn in as the new President. It is generally agreed that the Iranian government purposely delayed the takeoff of the plane with the hostages aboard until Reagan was sworn in — a final insult aimed at former President Carter. The hostages had been held in captivity for 444 days.

Indictment and Implications

The Iranian hostage crisis had an impact on the 1980 elections. The perceived weakness of the Carter administration's approach to the crisis contributed to the election of Republican presidential candidate Ronald Reagan, who during the campaign claimed he would be more proactive and forceful in dealing with

---

Guts to Try (New York: Ballantine Books, 2002); and Paul Ryan, *The Iranian Rescue Mission* (Annapolis: Naval Institute Press, 1985).

[42]CNN Library, "Iran Hostage Crisis Fast Facts," updated October 29, 2016, at http://www.cnn.com/2013/09/15/world/meast/iran-hostage-crisis-fast-facts/index.html. Accessed June 4, 2018; and Mark Bowden, *Guests of the Ayatollah: The Iran Hostage Crisis — The First Battle in America's War with Militant* Islam (Boston: Atlantic Monthly Press, 2006), p. 549.

enemies of the U.S. Given that the Iran hostage crisis was an extraordinary international event with no historical templates, blueprints, or lessons learned for the Carter administration to refer to, it is understandable that there was domestic and international criticism. How would the Carter administration know which was the correct approach to take? It addressed the crisis by applying a standard set of economic, political, diplomatic, and military pressure points.[43] Five days after the hostages were seized, Carter cut off all oil imports from Iran which damaged the American economy as gas prices quickly spiked since the U.S. relied on Iran for nearly 4% of its daily consumption.[44] Polls at the time indicated that economic issues like inflation, rising gas prices, high cost of living, taxes, energy, and fuel shortages were foremost on the minds of the electorate.[45] The Iranian hostage crisis damaged America's economy, and this played a role in Carter's defeat in the 1980 election. This role was indirect, not direct. In his memoirs, Carter's National Security Advisor Zbigniew Brzezinski admitted that "Iran was the Carter Administration's greatest setback."[46] The failed rescue attempt certainly did not help Carter.

The key problem was that the administration did not understand the "enemy." The mercurial and dogmatic Khomeini had established a unique politico-religious

---

[43] The U.S. applied diplomatic pressure on Iran. The U.S. twice obtained United Nations (U.N.) Security Council resolutions (on December 4 and 31, 1979) against Iran's actions, and on November 29, 1979, the U.S. filed suit against the Iranian government in the International Court of Justice (which ruled in favor of the United States in May 1980). The U.S. expelled Iranian diplomats from the U.S. and broke diplomatic relations with Iran in April 1980. In addition to diplomatic pressure, there were three key Iranian-related executive orders issued by President Carter: Executive Order 12170 (November 14, 1979) — which froze all Iranian assets held in the U.S., held by the government of Iran and the Central Bank of Iran; Executive Order 12205 (April 7, 1980) — which prohibited commercial trade with Iran with the exception of food, medical supplies, and donations of clothing; and Executive Order 12211 (April 17, 1980) — which prohibited the import of Iranian goods or services into the United States and financial transactions supporting travel to Iran. See more at http://www.defenddemocracy.org/united-states-sanctions/#sthash.oiYJsJIM.dpuf. Accessed June 4, 2018.

[44] Pierre Salinger, *America Held Hostage: The Secret Negotiations* (New York: Doubleday and Company, 1981), p. 50.

[45] M.K. Collins, "The Effect of the Iranian Hostage Crisis on the 1980 Presidential Election," *Tenor of Our Times*, Volume II, Article 6, Spring 2013, pp. 31–32, at https://scholarworks.harding.edu/cgi/viewcontent.cgi?referer=&httpsredir=1&article=1017&context=tenor. Accessed May 3, 2018; see also, Tyler Q. Houlton, "The Impact of the 1979 Hostage Crisis in Iran on the U.S. Presidential Election of 1980," Master's Thesis, Georgetown University, April 12, 2011, at https://repository.library.georgetown.edu/bitstream/handle/10822/553335/houltonTyler.pdf?sequence=1&isAllowed=y. Accessed June 4, 2018.

[46] Zbigniew Brzezinski, *Power and Principle: Memoirs of the National Security Adviser, 1977–1981* (New York, Farrar, Straus, Giroux, 1983), p. 354.

situation in Iran that was not susceptible, at first, to these standard pressure points. The domestic political environment in Iran was also in a state of flux. Khomeini was playing off shifting domestic political events and developments that the U.S. had problems "reading." On the other side, Khomeini and his Islamic revolutionary students did not understand the U.S. They interpreted the U.S. reliance on non-violent pressure points as a sign of weakness rather than an indicator of a rational foreign policy.

President Carter was criticized for not using immediate force to rescue the hostages or to engage in more provocative retaliation measures against Iran, but such force could have led to the deaths of some or all the hostages and/or triggered an international jihad against the U.S. The final record showed that no Americans were killed in the takeover of the U.S. Embassy and that all the hostages were eventually released unharmed. The absence of force in the initial stages of the crisis and then the failure of a hostage rescue operation was perceived by the American public as tarnishing our national honor. However, national honor is a concept that cannot be measured, and therefore, it is difficult to know how much honor was tarnished and whether the safe release of all the hostages was an acceptable price to pay for that lost honor. The Carter administration did not manage the crisis perfectly, but, upon consideration, it did not handle it badly. The Iran hostage crisis has been called a "hinge event" — "a rare event that changes the way people think and governments act, therefore altering the course of history."[47] However, it could be argued that the "hinge event" was not the hostage crisis but the Islamic Revolution in Iran.

The most significant terrorism ramification for the U.S. to emerge from the Carter administration was the introduction of a new and powerful source of anti-American sentiment and terrorism. Prior to the Islamic Revolution in Iran, there were two major anti-American terrorist strains that confronted U.S. interests overseas — the left-wing, especially in Europe and Latin America, and secular Palestinian terrorism strains. The Islamic Revolution in Iran created the conditions for the development of a new strain — Islamic revolutionary terrorism — that would haunt the U.S. for the next three and a half decades.[48] Before the

---

[47] Don Oberdorfer, "Iran: Rare Hinge Event," *Washington Post*, November 25, 1979, p. A1.

[48] To the Carter administration's credit, it did recognize that the developments in Iran were a precursor to more long-term problems in the region. On December 11, 1979, the NSC's Special Coordination Committee approved a plan to authorize $1 million to expand Voice of America (VOA) broadcasts in Persian, which at the time occupied only two hours a day. The VOA had resumed broadcasting in Persian to Iran in the spring of 1979 after a hiatus of more than 20 years. Two million dollars was also allocated for broadcasts to be carried out in seven languages of Moslems in the Soviet Union. The U.S. also bought time on Saudi, Egyptian, and Israeli transmitters for broadcasting into the Soviet

revolution in Iran, there was little Islamic revolutionary terrorist activity in the world. The most salient example was the spate of hijackings carried out by supporters of Imam Musa Sadr, an Iranian cleric who was sent to Lebanon by Khomeini to politically mobilize the Shia. He then founded a Shia political organization called Amal (hope) and became the spiritual leader of the Lebanese Shia. In August 1978, Sadr visited Libya to meet with Qaddafi and mysteriously disappeared. His supporters, believing that Qaddafi had either killed or kidnapped Sadr, engaged in a series of eight hijackings to call attention to Sadr's disappearance. From January 1979 to February 1982, Sadr's followers hijacked eight flights involving Libyan Arab Airlines, Middle Eastern Airlines, Kuwait Airlines, and Al-Italia. All the hijackings were carried out to secure the release of Sadr from Libyan hands (on the assumption that he was not dead). Sadr's disappearance created a vacuum in Amal which eventually led to a split in the group. One faction was more moderate, pro-Western, willing to work with the U.S., and sought to work for increased Shia influence in Lebanon using non-violent methods. The other faction called itself Islamic Amal and was aligned with Iran and Khomeini thereby providing Iran with an access point into the growing unstable Lebanese political environment. This access allowed Iran through its "foreign fighters," the Islamic Revolutionary Guards, to train, coach, and support the Shia terrorist group, the Lebanese Hezbollah (Party of God) which initiated a series of anti-American terrorist attacks in and outside Lebanon in the 1980s.

It was also clear that the Islamic Revolution in Iran was not going to be contained inside Iran. Khomeini wanted to export his model of revolution to Shia communities in neighboring countries. This would involve engaging in agitation and propaganda in those countries and fostering the creation of Shia militant groups or providing aid to those already present. Iraq, Saudi Arabia, Kuwait, Jordan, and Pakistan were primary targets of Iranian agitators. Iran was intent upon undermining the political stability of some key U.S. allies in the region. Khomeini's revolution in Iran acted as a beacon for Islamic revolutionaries — Shia or Sunni — in other countries. It laid the foundation for the later emergence of al-Qaeda and the Islamic State. In terms of the anti-American terrorist threat, the Islamic Revolution in Iran contributed more to that threat

---

Union to some 50 million Moslems there. The expansion of the broadcasting services to the Islamic world was largely pushed for by Paul B. Henze, the NSC specialist on U.S. propaganda. He believed that the entire Islamic world was undergoing a revival of spirit and identity that was destined to continue for years and should be addressed in American propaganda undertakings. See, David Binder, "U.S., Wary of Islamic Upheaval, to Increase Broadcasts to Moslems," *New York Times*, December 17, 1979, p. A16.

after 1979 than any other international event or development. Only the Vietnam War comes close to having had a similar impact on the level and scope of the anti-American terrorist threat as it fueled anti-American terrorist attacks by left-wing terrorist groups in and outside the U.S. Khomeini had politicized Islam and gave it an anti-American orientation, having identified the U.S. as the "Great Satan," not only for past U.S. interference in Iranian affairs but also due to the political, economic, and social DNA of the U.S. Playing the anti-American card in Iran at that time was the popular, logical, and most effective policy for Khomeini to pursue. It is the old strategy of using an external enemy to mobilize the population and to undermine domestic adversaries by linking them to the enemy. Khomeini disliked what the U.S. stood for and did not trust it, but his initial bout of anti-American fervor in 1979–1980 had a more pragmatic domestic political foundation. Still, the fact that he identified the U.S. as a primary enemy of Islam, if not *the* primary enemy, and broadcast it to the Muslim world, only aggravated that sentiment in other Shia militant groups. These groups translated that in their respective countries into anti-American attacks. There is no doubt that the terrorist threat to U.S. interests overseas significantly increased after the Islamic Revolution in Iran. Whether this revolution initiated or awakened an anti-American sentiment in Islamic revolutionaries around the world, the result was the same — the emergence of an anti-American terrorism strain that exploded in the decade of the 1980s and laid the foundation for the development of a global jihadist terrorist threat in subsequent decades.

It was no coincidence that after Khomeini returned to Iran to manage the Islamic revolution there, and students loyal to him seized the U.S. Embassy in Tehran, a series of violent events took place later that year that were aimed directly at the U.S. or involved the U.S. On November 20, 1979, a little more than two weeks after the U.S. Embassy in Tehran was seized, several hundred Sunni Islamic revolutionaries seized the Grand Mosque in Mecca, Saudi Arabia. The attack shocked the Islamic world as the Grand Mosque is the largest mosque in the world and surrounds Islam's holiest place, the Kaaba, a stone cube structure which is considered by Muslims to be the first House of Worship built or re-built by Ibrahim and Ishmael on God's instructions.[49] The terrorists seized hundreds of hostages and they were scattered in both the above-ground structures of the Grand Mosque and the labyrinth that is underneath which contained about a thousand rooms connected with corridors in the basement. The objective of the terrorists was to trigger a revolt against the Saudi monarchy, which they accused of having

---

[49] https://www.al-islam.org/story-of-the-holy-kaaba-and-its-people-shabbar/kaaba-house-allah. Accessed June 4, 2017.

betrayed Islamic principles and selling out to Western countries. They claimed that the ruling Saud dynasty had lost its legitimacy because it was corrupt, ostentatious, and had destroyed Saudi culture by an aggressive policy of Westernization. It took two weeks for the Saudi authorities to re-establish control of the Grand Mosque on December 4. The total number of casualties is unknown as the Saudis attempted to downplay the figures. There were most likely hundreds, maybe more than a thousand casualties.

When the siege began, the State Department pointed the finger at Ayatollah Khomeini. However, Khomeini went on the radio and accused the U.S. and Israel of being behind the attack. Khomeini's indictment triggered dozens of anti-American protests, some violent, in Muslim countries.[50] On November 21, Pakistani students, enraged and emboldened by Khomeini's radio report, stormed the U.S. Embassy in Islamabad, and burned it to the ground, killing U.S. MSG Corporal Steven Crowley and Army Warrant Officer Bryan Ellis. In December, the U.S. Embassy in Tripoli, Libya, was burned during protests triggered by Khomeini's allegations. Anti-American demonstrations also took place in the Philippines, Turkey, Bangladesh, eastern Saudi Arabia, and the United Arab Emirates. On December 9, *Time* magazine had a front-page cover titled "Attacking America: Fury in Iran, Rescue in Pakistan." This was religious-induced political violence aimed at the U.S. This was another indicator that a developing political Islam was being manipulated by Islamic revolutionaries with the goals of restoring the lost glory of Islam, establishing Islamic states, and expelling Western cultural, economic, and political influences from Muslim populated states. The terrorist manifestation of this phenomenon fully emerged during the Reagan administration.

The Iranian hostage crisis also had an impact on the collective impression of Islam and Iran by the American people. Many Americans knew little about Islam, the religion of the Iranian people. What they knew they picked up in general and brief references in Western civilization textbooks used in courses taught at middle and high schools. The technological advancements in commercial broadcast television news in the 1970s now made it possible for ABC, CBS, and NBC, using telecommunication satellites, to show remote broadcasts live instead of having to record remote stories on tape and then transport them across country, oceans, or continents. These news organizations were now bringing the developments in

---

[50]National Public Radio. "1979: Remembering The Siege of Mecca," Interview with Yaroslav Trofimov, a reporter with The *Wall Street Journal* and the author of *The Siege of Mecca: The 1979 Uprising at Islam's Holiest Shrine* (New York: Anchor Press, 2008), August 20, 2009, at http://www.npr.org/templates/story/story.php?storyId=112051155. Accessed August 4, 2017.

Iran live and directly to the American people. The images Americans saw were of an Iran and Islam that was anti-American, fanatical, and violent. They saw Iranian students chanting "Death to America," and "Death to Carter," and the burning of the U.S. flag and effigies of Uncle Sam. They saw a laconic, serious, bearded old cleric insulting the President of the U.S. and referring the U.S. as the "Great Satan." These were powerful images that shaped the collective impression of Islam by the American people.

> *The Iran hostage crisis was quintessentially visual in nature. It evokes visual memories of angry crowds outside the U.S. embassy in Tehran, armed "students" who overran the embassy and seized hostages, the bearded Ayatollah Khomeini surrounded by followers, clergy visits to the hostages at Easter and Christmas, and charred bodies of U.S. servicemen left in the desert after an abortive rescue mission. Additional imagery emanated from the United States: repeated briefings by State Department press spokesman Hodding Carter, comments from the White House by President Carter's press secretary, Jody Powell, the statements and activities of hostage wives and families, ABC's creation and promotion of an evening news special called "America Held hostage" and, not least, Walter Cronkite's weeknight newscast reminders of the duration of the hostages' captivity.[51]*

Compared to the sterile, silent images seen in the newspaper and magazines, the TV images were animated, vocal, and induced anger and confusion in the American people. An early 1980 Roper survey indicated that 77% of the respondents indicated they had been getting most of their news about the Iran hostage crisis from television, compared with only 26% who cited newspapers as the major source.[52]

No international story, other than war, dominated television news as long as the Iranian hostage crisis.[53] ABC News' "The Iran Crisis — America Held

---

[51] James F. Larson, "Television and U.S. Foreign Policy: The Case of the Iran Hostage Crisis." *Journal of Communication*, Vol. 36, Issue 4, Autumn 1986, p. 109, at https://www.researchgate.net/publication/228039839_Television_and_US_Foreign_Policy_The_Case_of_the_Iran_Hostage_Crisis. Accessed May 4, 2018.

[52] Ibid., p. 109.

[53] "Television — The Iranian hostage crisis," at https://www.americanforeignrelations.com/O-W/Television-The-iranian-hostage-crisis.html. Accessed May 4, 2018. See also, Milan D. Meeske and Mohammad Javeheri Hamidi, "Network Television Coverage of the Iranian Hostage

Hostage — Day xxx" debuted on November 8, 1979. The name of the program was changed to "Nightline" on December 1, 1979 with Ted Koppel as host with the daily introduction of "This is an ABC News Special: The Iran Crisis: America Held Hostage: Day xx."[54] Ted Koppel, in his book *Nightline: History in the Making and the Making of Television*, stated that the "the effect the show ultimately had on the American public notably changed the public discourse on the presidential election of 1980.... The nightly reminder of how long the hostages remained in captivity surely impacted the American electorate."[55] Over on CBS, Walter Cronkite, television's most respected news anchor, added to his famous sign-off — "and that's the way it is" — then a reference to the number of days Americans were held hostage.[56] This drumbeat of daily reminders of how long the hostage crisis was going on not only shaped the collective image of Islam for most Americans but also underlined the failure of the Carter administration to solve the crisis. It gave the impression that the administration was weak and ineffective. No President before or since has been publicly reminded for such an extended period of a foreign policy failure as Carter was during the Iranian hostage crisis.[57]

Crisis," *Journalism Quarterly*, Vol. 59, Issue 4, Winter 1982, p. 641; and https://www.whitehouse-history.org/teacher-resources/jimmy-carter-and-the-iranian-hostage-crisis. Accessed June 4, 2018.

[54] https://en.wikipedia.org/wiki/Nightline; at http://abcnews.go.com/Nightline/video/1980-nightline-debuts-29879145; http://adst.org/2013/10/444-days-memoirs-of-an-iranian-hostage/. Accessed July 7, 2018.

[55] M.K. Collins, "The Effect of the Iranian Hostage Crisis on the 1980 Presidential Election," p. 34.

[56] Op. cit., Television: The Iranian hostage crisis.

[57] See, for example, William Safire, "Essay: Mistakes in Iran," *New York Times*, March 3, 1980, p. A19. Safire posits six mistakes by Carter:

1. *When the U.S. Embassy in Tehran was seized, Carter failed to make clear that we would resist future violations of our territorial integrity.*

2. *When the U.S. diplomats in Tehran warned that the admission of the Shah to the U.S. for medical treatment might provoke attacks, the Carter administration failed to reduce the Embassy staff or direct the securing of our records.*

3. *When the interim Iranian Prime Minster assured us that our embassy would be protected, the Carter administration mis-assessed the political realities in Iran.*

4. *When the U.S. Embassy was seized, Defense Secretary Harold Brown rejected a plan to land two plane loads of U.S. commandos in Qum to counter-kidnap the Ayatollah Khomeini — then lightly guarded — so as to arrange a trade.*

5. *When urged by U.S. hawks to embargo food to Iran, which would have caused scarcities and raised prices in Iran and shown that kidnapping Americans was not without cost, Carter administration officials said it was "ridiculous" to use food as a weapon.*

In Iran today, the U.S. Embassy remains closed, but it serves as an Islamic Cultural Center and museum. The main embassy building has been used by the Iranian Revolutionary Guards Corps as a training facility and was later used by the Basij militia, a civilian auxiliary force.[58] For Iran, this "den of spies" is a monument to the pinnacle of the Iranian Revolution when militant Islamic revolutionary students held America and President Carter as political hostages for 15 months, influenced an American election, solidified Khomeini's control of Iran, and painted a picture of a weak America to parts of the world. Every year, on the anniversary of the student takeover of the embassy, Iran hold rallies at the U.S. Embassy where crowds burn the U.S. flag and shout, "Death to America."[59] On one of the embassy walls is a quote from Khomeini that reads — "The United States is regarded as the most hated government in the world." The Iranian hostage crisis was a precursor of a strained U.S.–Iranian relationship that continues to the present. It was a traumatic international event for Americans and a unique pivotal political opportunity for Khomeini to galvanize his supporters and undermine his opponents and enemies in order to pave the way for the establishment of an Islamic state in Iran.

The first extended hostile seizure of a U.S. diplomatic facility in U.S. history triggered a series of increased security proposals at the U.S. diplomatic facilities worldwide. The U.S. had one of the largest diplomatic footprints overseas. By 1977, there were 250 U.S. diplomatic facilities in 118 countries.[60] In December

---

6. *When the Shah was admitted to the U.S. — an ally once embossed by President Carter — and he became an embarrassment to the U.S, he was secretly hustled out of the country to Panama — which Iranian FM Ghotbzadeh called America's acquiescence to Iranian pressure "a great victory."*

[58] Thomas Erdbrink, "A Symbol for Iran of the 1979 Revolution Attracts Pride and Dust," *New York Times*, November 1, 2013, p. A13; Jennifer Rizzo, "Former U.S. Embassy in Iran: mistrust endures where hostages held," *CNN*, January 30, 2014, at http://www.cnn.com/2014/01/30/politics/iran-embassy-mistrust/. Accessed June 4, 2018; and *Time* Magazine, "The Great Satan's Old Den: Visiting Tehran's U.S. Embassy," July 14, 2009, at http://content.time.com/time/world/article/0,8599,1910361,00.html. Accessed September 23, 2018.

[59] Associated Press, "Iranians mark anniversary of US Embassy takeover in Tehran," November 3, 2016, at https://www.washingtonpost.com/world/middle_east/iranians-mark-anniversary-of-us-embassy-takeover-in-tehran/2016/11/03/1343f1be-a1b0-11e6-8864-6f892cad0865_story.html. Accessed May 4, 2017. The Basij or The Organization for Mobilization of the Oppressed is a para-military volunteer militia established by Khomeini in Iran in 1979 and consists of civilian volunteers who serve as an auxiliary force engaged in activities such as internal security, law enforcement auxiliary, providing social services, organizing public religious ceremonies, policing morals, and suppressing of dissident gatherings, at https://web.archive.org/web/20040803084837/http://bso.ir/BSO/Index.htm. Accessed October 23, 2018.

[60] United States Congress House Committee on International Relations. Subcommittee on International Operations: Protection of Americans abroad hearings before the Subcommittee on International

1979, less than a month after the seizure of the U.S. Embassy in Tehran, the State Department ordered all diplomatic facilities to take three actions to improve security: (1) review and update its contingency planning, (2) reduce non-essential classified file holdings to an absolute operational minimum, and (3) contact host country and discuss protection of U.S. Embassy and personnel during crisis situations. The Department also centralized responsibility for post security with the Chief of Mission and granted more authority to the Regional Security Officer. In addition, Congress gave the Department a supplemental appropriation for an "extensive security enhancement program" (SEP) of $6.1 million in Fiscal Year 1980 and $35.8 million in 1981. The SEP had four objectives: (1) harden embassies against mob attacks, (2) provide security in case the host country fell short of its protective responsibilities, (3) ensure U.S. personnel were not killed or taken hostage, and (4) prevent national security information from being compromised. The total amount for all appropriations and supplementals to harden U.S. embassies at the time was $200 million. In comparison, in 1965, the House Appropriations Committee complained when the State Department's Chief Security Officer obtained a $1 million appropriation for increased security. The attack on U.S. Embassies in Iran, Pakistan, and Libya compelled the U.S. to adopt a "total approach" to security, an attitude that was non-existent prior to 1979.[61] The above measures were designed for a seizure of a U.S. diplomatic facility in a country where the host government would likely protect the embassy and its personnel. However, at that time, there were no embassies anywhere in the world that could long withstand the attack of a mob, if the mob had the support of the host government itself.

The Iran–Iraq War

In addition to being a major factor in the decision of the Iranian government to release the U.S. hostages, the Iran–Iraq War also demonstrated the willingness of Iran to engage in state-sponsored terrorism in and outside the Middle East. Iran initiated three terrorist campaigns in 1980–1981: (1) against Iraq as a prelude to the war, (2) against European countries that were aiding Iraq's development of nuclear energy, and (3) against France for its supply of French Mirage fighter planes to Iraq. These Iranian-backed terrorist campaigns in 1980–1981 were and remain unprecedented terrorist acts from a modern state. In early 1980, there were

---

Operations of the Committee on International Relations, House of Representatives, Ninety-fifth Congress, first session, July 12 and 14, 1977 (Washington: U.S. Govt. Print. Off., 1977), p. 78, at https://babel.hathitrust.org/cgi/pt?id=pur1.32754076915754;view=1up;seq=1. Accessed March 23, 2018.

[61] *DS History*, pp. 259–260.

increasing political and military tensions between Iran's Shia theocratic government and Iraq's Sunni secular government headed by Saddam Hussein. Iran needed money and materials to prepare itself for war with Iraq and realized that releasing the U.S. hostages would give them access to unfrozen assets. No country was more endangered by the rise of a Shia Islamic fundamentalist government in Iran than neighboring Iraq which was concerned about Iranian agitation to its delicate Sunni–Shia balance. This concern crystalized in April 1980 when the Iranian-supported Islamic Dawa Party in Iraq attempted to assassinate both the Iraqi Foreign Minister and the Iraqi Minister of Culture and Information. The Iraqi government responded with a crackdown on Dawa members and sympathizers and the torture and brutal execution of a Dawa leader, Muhammad Baqir Al-Sadr and his sister. These incidents underlined the perceived threat that Iran posed to Iraq and signaled the beginning of a terrorist war between the two countries as a prelude to the outbreak of full war between the two countries.

On April 29, there was an attempted assassination of the Iranian Foreign Minister during an official visit to Kuwait. The next day, six Iraqi-backed terrorists seized the Iranian embassy in London and held 26 people hostage for six days before a British counter-terrorism assault freed the hostages and killed five of the terrorists. On May 26, the Iranian airline office was bombed in Kuwait City. On June 4, the Iraqi embassy in Rome was attacked by Iranian gunmen. On the same day, an anti-armor rocket was fired at the Iranian embassy in Kuwait City. On June 28, Greek police defused two bombs at the Iranian embassy in Athens. On July 27, the Iraqi second secretary in Abu Dhabi was killed, and two other Iraqis were injured when a bomb exploded near the Iranian embassy in Vienna. Two Iraqi diplomats were expelled from Austria on the next day. These terrorist attacks between the two countries were supplemented with cross-border sabotage incidents. The terrorist phase of the Iran–Iraq conflict dissipated in September when Iraq invaded Iran. Periodic terrorist attacks took place against each country's embassy in Beirut but the attacks in Western Europe subsided. Iraq's reason for invading Iran was to settle a border dispute involving the Shatt al-Arab Waterway which runs into the Persian Gulf and helped delineate the border between Iraq and Iran. The area is a strategic bottleneck, surrounded by significant oil resources and close to important shipping lanes.

There was a second terrorism phase for Iran as a result of the war. Iran wanted to intimidate French and Italian firms that were exporting nuclear equipment and technology to Iraq. Iran also desired to prevent Iraq from developing a nuclear capability. It was obviously in Iran's interest (as well as Israel's and Syria's) to prevent Iraq's development of nuclear energy. In November 1975, France signed a formal agreement with Iraq to equip it with a nuclear research center and was criticized by Iran and Israel. Israel may have gone beyond just words. In April

1979, a French factory near Toulon, which was constructing two nuclear research reactors for Iraq, was heavily damaged when five explosive charges were set off by unknown saboteurs. It was estimated at the time that the damage caused by the bombs would set back by at least 18 months the delivery of the reactors to Iraq. A French environmental group initially claimed responsibility for the attack but French authorities "doubted that environmental protestors had the knowledge, sabotage skills, and technical atomic information that was needed for the highly professional and successful operation."[62] The speculation at the time centered on Israeli commandos. There were certainly precedents for Israeli pre-emptive and retaliatory commando strikes. On December 24, 1969, Israel expropriated five missile-launching patrol boats from a port in Cherbourg, France that it previously purchased. However, France blocked their delivery due to its 1969 arms embargo on Israel.[63] In the 1970s, there were Israeli retaliatory strikes against Palestinian terrorists involved in the Munich Olympics attack in 1972. Israel was also suspected of carrying out a June 1980 assassination in Paris of an Egyptian nuclear scientist who was assisting the Iraqis with their nuclear program.

On August 7, 1980, a previously unknown terrorist group calling itself the "Committee for Safeguarding the Islamic Revolution" claimed responsibility for planting a bomb which exploded outside the home of a bookshop owner in Paris. The man had the same last name as a French nuclear scientist with ties to Iraqi nuclear projects. In claiming responsibility for the bombing against the wrong target, the group stated that the nuclear scientist "had been decorated for helping Iraq make nuclear weapons."[64] On the same day, the same group bombed the offices of the Italian firm SNIA-Techint in Rome and also attempted to bomb the home of the firm's director. In a statement, the group stated that it had bombed the firm's offices because of the support it was giving to the "oppressive Iraqi regime."[65] On August 11, five French companies participating in the construction

---

[62] This section on Iranian use of terrorism during the Iran–Iraq War and the following section on Israeli and Iranian terrorist operations aimed at preventing Iraq from developing nuclear energy are from Dennis Pluchinsky, "Political Terrorism in Western Europe," in Yonah Alexander and Kenneth Myers, editors, *Terrorism in Europe* (London: Croom Helm, 1982), pp. 65–68.

[63] The Cherbourg incident was an Israeli military operation codenamed "Operation Noa." See Abraham Rabinovich, "Israel Military Intelligence: The Boats of Cherbourg, Jewish Virtual Library, at https://www.jewishvirtuallibrary.org/jsource/History/Cherbourg.html. Accessed June 4, 2018; and Abraham Rabinovich, *The Boats of Cherbourg* (Annapolis: Naval Institute Press/Bluejacket Books, 1997).

[64] Pluchinsky, "Political Terrorism in Western Europe," p. 66.

[65] Pluchinsky, "Political Terrorism in Western Europe," p. 66; The *Economist Foreign Report*, February 4, 1981, p. 4; and Uri Sadot, "Osirak and the Counter-Proliferation Puzzle," *Journal of Security Studies*, Vol. 25, Issue 4, 2016, pp. 646–676.

of a nuclear research reactor in Iraq received threatening letters from the above group.[66] Then, on August 25, this same group sent a letter to the Reuters News Agency in which it threatened six French and five Italian firms allegedly helping Iraq develop nuclear energy. The letter stated that the "governments of Italy and France have taken a very dangerous course in taking the decision to arm the dictatorial regime of Iraq with atomic bombs." The letter went on to state that the "goal of the Islamic revolution is to put an end to the interference of imperialism in the internal affairs of Iran."[67] There were no further attacks or threats against French or Italian firms for their involvement in Iraqi nuclear development after August 1980.[68] It is likely that the September invasion of Iran by Iraq diverted Iran's attention from Europe to the Iran–Iraq border. On June 7, 1981, Israel carried out an air strike on the Osirak nuclear reactor outside of Baghdad that destroyed the facility, and this may have temporarily eased Iran's anxiety of an Iraqi nuclear capability.

In the war, France had a contract to supply Iraq with French Mirage fighter planes. The delivery of these planes was scheduled around the start of the Iran–Iraq War. Iran wanted France to cancel this delivery. On December 26, 1980, an anti-tank rocket was fired at the French embassy in Beirut and a French embassy vehicle was bombed. The next day, a group calling itself the "Forces of Struggling Ranks" claimed responsibility for the attacks. An alleged spokesperson for the group stated that it "would continue to strike at French interests if Paris supported Iraq in the war" and that the group would attack again "if France went ahead with the planned sale of Mirage fighter planes to Iraq." Lastly, the group demanded that France no longer allow Shapour Bakhtiar, the Iranian Prime Minster under the former Shah of Iran, to live in Paris.[69] France refused to stop delivery of the Mirage planes, and in February 1981, it started the delivery of the planes to Iraq.[70]

---

[66] *The Times*, August 13, 1980; Edward Mickolus. *International Terrorism in the 1980s: A Chronology of Events, Volume I, 1980–1983* (Iowa: Iowa State University, 1989), p. 75.

[67] Pluchinsky, "Political Terrorism in Western Europe," p. 66. The last two quotes are from a copy of the written communiqué.

[68] Ibid., 67. In April and October 1980, bombs were discovered near the nuclear equipment factory Framatome near Chalon-sur-Soane, France.

[69] Pluchinsky, "Political Terrorism in Western Europe," p. 67.

[70] On February 1, the Iranian embassy in Paris stated that the "Iranian people will never forget this act by the French government." It should be noted that since the start of the Iran–Iraq War, France had not delivered any military equipment to Iraq. France saw the Mirage plane delivery as "special" since they were ordered and presumably paid for before the start of the war. Iraq, at the time, was France's second largest oil supplier and also one of its best customers for arms (*The Times*, February 2, 1981). Ironically, the Shah of Iran had ordered and paid for 12 naval vessels, including three high-speed, missile-launching patrol boats (called "Tabarzin"), from France. All but the three patrol boats were

In April, 1981, the French embassy in Beirut received threat letters from a "pro-Iranian Palestinian group."[71]

In summation, the Iranian Revolution in 1979 triggered a series of developments that ultimately produced a new "enemy" for the U.S. and one that did not hesitate to engage in using terrorism as an instrument of its foreign policy. The major state sponsors of terrorism at the time were Libya and Syria. After the revolution, Iran and later Iraq (after its invasion of Kuwait) were added to that list. The November 1979 takeover of the U.S. Embassy in Tehran and the seizure of U.S. hostages, while not traditionally or technically a terrorist act, did signal the Islamic regime's inclination to ignore international norms to further the progress of the revolution. Using terrorism as Iran did in 1980–1981 to further its foreign policy objectives was simply another dimension of this disregard for generally accepted practices in international relations. Iran was perceived as a rogue state. By the end of the Carter administration, it was clear that Iran was hostile to the U.S. and a state sponsor of terrorism. These two developments merged and reached their apex during the Reagan administration when Iran sponsored terrorist attacks on U.S. targets in the Middle East. The foundation for these attacks were laid during the Carter administration. The Iranian Revolution in 1979 also triggered a rise in Islamic militancy around the world — a development that would later contribute to the formation of global jihadist terrorist groups such as al-Qaeda and the Islamic State.

Soviet Invasion of Afghanistan

It has been argued that the weak response by the Carter administration to the Iranian hostage crisis projected a weak America to its adversaries.[72] Although the

---

delivered to Iran. After the Iranian Revolution, the French government impounded the three patrol boats not yet delivered. When Francois Mitterand became President, he ordered the release of the three patrol boats which left France on August 2, 1981. However, on August 13, as the three patrol boats were on their way to Iran, one of them was hijacked off the Spanish coast by about 20 members of a monarchist group called Azadegan, or Born Free, who were dedicated to overthrowing the Islamic government of Iran. The hijackers took the boat to Marseille. In Tehran, the Foreign Minister claimed that the hijackers "were mercenaries paid by the United States, headed by a major of the army of the deposed Shah" who was in turn "helped by former U.S. Secretary of State Cyrus Vance" (Frank J. Prial, "Iranian Hijackers Sail to Marseilles," *New York Times*, August 19, 1981. http://www.nytimes.com/1981/08/19/world/iranian-hijackers-sail-to-marseilles.html June 6, 2018).

[71] *Le Point*, April 13, 1981, p. 73.

[72] U.S. Department of State, Office of the Historian, "The Iranian Hostage Crisis," at https://history.state.gov/departmenthistory/short-history/iraniancrises. Accessed March 23, 2018; and The National Security Archive, Steve Galster, "Afghanistan: The Making of U.S. Policy, 1973–1990," October 9, 2001, at http://nsarchive.gwu.edu/NSAEBB/NSAEBB57/essay.html. Accessed May 4, 2017.

Soviet Union was considering its options in Afghanistan before the Iranian hostage crisis, this perceived weakness may have been a contributing factor to the final decision to intervene in Afghanistan some seven weeks after the takeover of the U.S. Embassy in Tehran. On December 24, 1979, the Soviet Union sent 30,000 troops (later to grow into 100,000) to Afghanistan with the objective of shoring up a pro-Soviet socialist regime that was under threat from internal fighting in the government, and Islamic rebels opposed to the land and social reforms and communist nature of the government. It was also an implementation of the "Brezhnev Doctrine," named after Leonid Brezhnev, the leader of the Soviet Union at the time, which held that once a country became socialist, Moscow would never permit it to return to the capitalist camp. Moscow was interested in Afghanistan as it would be "a major step toward overland access to the Indian Ocean and to domination of the Asian subcontinent."[73] Whatever the tactical and strategic objectives of the intervention, it was a "watershed event in the Cold War, marking the only time the Soviet Union invaded a country outside the Eastern Bloc."[74] This intervention must be considered within the context of a series of communist bloc successes in the mid-1970s. Soviet-supported Marxist rebels made strong gains in Angola and Mozambique in 1975, Ethiopia in 1977, and Nicaragua in 1979. The Soviet-backed Socialist Republic of Vietnam fought a successful border war with China and took over Cambodia from the Chinese-backed Khmer Rouge in a chessboard move in the ongoing Sino–Soviet conflict.

In his State of the Union Address on January 23, 1980, President Carter cautioned:

> *The region which is now threatened by Soviet troops in Afghanistan is of great strategic importance: It contains more than two-thirds of the world's exportable oil. The Soviet effort to dominate Afghanistan has brought Soviet military forces to within 300 miles of the Indian Ocean and close to the Straits of Hormuz, a waterway through which most of the world's oil must flow. The Soviet Union is now attempting to consolidate a strategic position, therefore, that poses a grave threat to the free movement of Middle East oil.*[75]

---

[73] From a Defense Intelligence Agency report issued several days after the Soviet intervention, as quoted in Steve Galster, "Afghanistan: The Making of U.S. Policy, 1973–1990."

[74] U.S. Department of State, Office of the Historian. "The Soviet Invasion of Afghanistan and the U.S. Response, 1978–1980," at https://history.state.gov/milestones/1977-1980/soviet-invasion-afghanistan. Accessed 24, 2016.

[75] The American Presidency Project. "The State of the Union Address Delivered Before a Joint Session of the Congress, January 23, 1980," at http://www.presidency.ucsb.edu/ws/?pid=33079. Accessed May 4, 2016.

As a result of this strategic concern that the Soviet Union was seeking domination in the Persian Gulf region, Carter warned in this address that the U.S. would use military force, if necessary, to defend its national interests in the Persian Gulf. It became known as the "Carter Doctrine." The geopolitical ramifications of the Soviet intervention in Afghanistan and the U.S. responses to that event are not within the scope of this book. However, the most significant development that emerged from the Soviet intervention in Afghanistan that affected the anti-American terrorist threat was that it created the conditions for the birth of al-Qaeda and the development of a global jihadist terrorist movement.

The Soviet invasion of a Muslim country triggered a religious call by Islamic militants and moderate Muslim clerics in official religious establishments, and prominent Islamic scholars, for a jihad or armed Islamic struggle to expel the Soviet invaders. This appeal prompted Muslim males from dozens of countries to come to Afghanistan and participate in this jihad. These calls for jihad by mainstream Islamic clerics supported by the state and Islamic scholars "gave the Afghan struggle a strong religious legitimacy and an internationalist flavor that enabled it to touch a chord with Muslims wherever they may be."[76] Moreover, many secular Muslim countries "turned a blind eye to the fact that so many of their nationals were streaming into Afghanistan to join the jihad" and Egypt even released Islamic militants from prison "on the condition that they continued their jihad in Afghanistan rather than home."[77] The Afghan jihad was the first post-World War II conflict in a Muslim country where jihad was sanctioned by both Islamic militants and moderates and unofficially approved by Muslim countries.

These Afghan Arabs or "foreign fighters" were compelled to come by a myriad of motivations and possessed an array of skills, some even relevant to combat. The Afghan Arab contingent in the country was never a monolithic entity but a complex network that was subjected to infighting and competition among its prominent personalities. However, the significance of the Afghan jihad for the Afghan Arabs was that it created the conditions for concentration, interaction, indoctrination, training, combat experience, and the formation of comradeship. It created a jihadist experience where they earned a "combat badge" and became

---

[76] Alison Pargeter. *The New Frontiers of Jihad: Radical Islam in Europe* (Philadelphia: University of Pennsylvania Press, 2008), p. 11; see also, Fawaz A. Gerges. *The Far Enemy: Why Jihad Went Global* (New York: Cambridge University Press, 2005), p. 82 — "Never before in modern times had so many Muslims from so many lands who spoke different tongues separately journeyed to a Muslim country, to fight together against a common enemy."

[77] Pargeter, *New Frontiers of Jihad*, p. 11.

part of a jihadist fraternity. The "most powerful effect of the war, however, was to make the Arab Afghans believe that they were truly invincible."[78] The defeat of the Soviet military was "a military victory for Islam, the first in several hundred years, and it undermined the pervasive defeatism that had haunted many in the Muslim world for more than a century."[79] After the Soviet Union withdrew from Afghanistan in 1989, some of these newly minted jihadists stayed in Afghanistan, some went back to their respective countries to initiate armed struggle there, some went to other conflict areas like Bosnia, Algeria, Tajikistan, and Chechnya, and some gravitated to entities like al-Qaeda that sought conflict with another superpower — the United States. In turn, al-Qaeda facilitated the emergence of a global jihadist movement that later produced global jihadist flagship terrorist organizations such as al-Qaeda in Iraq and the Islamic State in Syria and Iraq.[80] The Soviet invasion of Afghanistan in 1979 essentially initiated a series of historical drivers that significantly contributed to the expansion and intensification of the anti-American terrorist threat in the Clinton, Bush, and Obama administrations.

The Stinger Missile Program and Blowback

Until the Soviet invasion, U.S. covert aid to Afghanistan was limited to less than a million dollars of nonlethal support over six weeks in 1979.[81] The Carter administration decided to support Afghan rebels or "mujahedeen" in their fight against the Soviet military in order to bleed and tie down the Soviet Union and demonstrate the costs of staying in Afghanistan. This support would involve training, finances, logistics, advice, and weapons. The primary U.S. agency charged with this task was the CIA. The operation was called "Cyclone" and it

---

[78] Ibid., p. 13.

[79] Michael Scheuer. *Osama bin Laden* (Oxford University Press, 2011), p. 49.

[80] For assessments of the importance of the Afghan jihad in the development of the global jihadist terrorist threat, see Gerges, *The Far Enemy*, pp. 12, 13, and 84. On p. 85, Gerges sums it up as follows: "It is doubtful that transnational jihadi would have materialized without the prolonged Afghan war and its socializing and mobilizational effects on the Arab jihadis"; Peter Bergen. *Holy War, Inc. — Inside the Secret World of Osama bin Laden* (New York: Free Press, 2001), p. 56 — "The Afghan jihad plays a central role in the evolution of the Islamist movement around the world." Gilles Kepel, as quoted in Bergen; and Scheuer, *Osama bin Laden*, p. 48 — "Decades hence, even historians may begin to recognize the size and significance of the transformation in the Muslim world that began with the Afghan jihad's victory over the Soviet Union."

[81] Robert Gates. *From the Shadows: The Ultimate Insider's Story of Five Presidents and How They Won the Cold War* (New York: Simon & Schuster, 1996), pp. 142–149.

was initiated just before the Soviet Union intervened in Afghanistan, as a communist regime took over in the country in April 1978 and that regime signed a Treaty of Friendship with the Soviet Union in December. Operation Cyclone was one of the longest and most expensive covert CIA operations ever undertaken. The budget was $20–$30 million per year in 1980, increased to $122 million in 1984, and rose to $630 million per year in 1987. By the end of the 1980s, about $3 billion was funneled to the Afghan rebels.[82] The U.S. funding for the rebels continued even after the Soviet military withdrew as the Soviet Union continued to aid the socialist People's Democratic Party of Afghanistan (PDPA) until 1991 when the Soviet Union dissolved. The PDPA collapsed one year later. The problem for the CIA was that it used the Pakistani Intelligence Services as the conduit for the aid and gave it complete control over how to use the money and to what rebel groups to distribute the money. There were two primary reasons for this: (1) the U.S. wanted a cutout so that it could argue that it was not directly involved in confronting the Soviets in Afghanistan, and (2) it was assumed that the Pakistanis had more knowledge and a better "read" on the rebel groups.

While there is a myriad of reasons of why the Soviets were forced to withdraw from Afghanistan in 1989, there is general agreement that the CIA distribution of the Stinger anti-aircraft weapon was a contributing factor, but not necessarily a determining factor.[83] The Stinger, made by General Dynamics, was

---

[82] Peter Bergen. *Holy War, Inc. — Inside the Secret World of Osama bin Laden* (New York: Free Press, 2001), p. 68; Alan J. Kuperman, "The Stinger missile and U.S. intervention in Afghanistan," *Political Science Quarterly*, Vol. 114, Issue 2, Summer 1999, at www.dtic.mil/dtic/tr/fulltext/u2/a413880.pdf. Accessed December 23, 2018.

[83] There is no accurate, generally accepted percentage of the success rate of Stinger attacks on Soviet aircraft. It ranges from 20% to 70%. The following articles tout the impact of the Stinger on the Soviet withdrawal: Bergen, *Holy War,* p. 73; Ken Silverstein, "Stingers, Stingers, Who's Got the Stingers?" *Slate*, October 3, 2001, at http://www.slate.com/articles/news_and_politics/the_gist/2001/10/stingers_stingers_whos_got_the_stingers.html. Accessed June 23, 2107; David B. Ottaway, "U.S. Missiles Alter War in Afghanistan," *Washington Post*, July 19, 1987; Bernard E. Trainor, "Military Analysis: Afghan Air War: U.S. Missile Scores on Russians," *New York Times*, July 7, 1987; *United Press International*, "Afghans Have U.S. Stinger Missiles, Soviet Confirms," December 19, 1986, at http://articles.latimes.com/1986-12-19/news/mn-3705_1_u-s-stinger-missiles. Accessed June 4, 2018; Michael M. Phillips, "Launching the Missile That Made History: Three former mujahedeen recall the day when they started to beat the Soviets," *Wall Street Journal*, October 1, 2011, at http://www.wsj.com/articles/SB10001424052970204138204576598851109446780. Accessed March 23, 2018; Matthew Schroeder, "Stop Panicking About the Stingers," *Foreign Policy*, July 28, 2010, at https://web.archive.org/web/20100731223411/http://www.foreignpolicy.com/articles/2010/07/28/The_Taliban_Doesn%E2%80%99t_Have_Stingers. Accessed August 23, 2017; https://www.washingtonpost.com/archive/politics/1987/07/19/us-missiles-alter-war-in-afghanistan/

relatively simple to fire, had a vertical range of about 10,000 feet, and employed a heat-seeking sensor to home in on an aircraft's engine. The Stinger could be fired from as far away as five miles and was capable of bringing down military helicopters, air-fueling tankers, and low-flying military aircraft. In the fall of 1986, the CIA shipped a load of 300 Stingers to the rebels and 700 more the following year. "We were handing them out like lollipops," an American intelligence official later told the *Washington Post*.[84] After the Soviet military withdrew from Afghanistan, the Afghan rebels dispensed Stingers to their Islamic allies — rebel groups in places like Tajikistan, Chechnya, and Algeria. This weapon transfer problem forced the CIA in 1993 to initiate a buyback program for unaccounted Afghan Stingers with the aid of the Pakistani intelligence services. The CIA reportedly allocated $65 million for the program — twice the cost of the original 1,000 sent to the Afghan rebels. The CIA offered so much for the missing Stingers, reportedly at least $100,000 per weapon and possibly as much as $200,000, that the program drove up the price of Stingers on the international black market.[85] All of the missing Stingers were never accounted for. Some found their way into the hands of al-Qaeda and appeared in the group's first major propaganda and training video released in June 2001 titled "The

---

d865174f-bae0-4615-8925-8fe690b6fc14/. Accessed June 4, 2018; and Richard Norton-Taylor, "Taliban trust in the Stinger may be misplaced," *The Guardian*, October 16, 2001, at https://www.theguardian.com/world/2001/oct/17/afghanistan.terrorism5. Accessed September 3, 2017. The case for the Stinger impact being minimal to moderate is as follows: "The Stingers certainly forced a shift in Soviet tactics. Helicopter crews switched their operations to night raids since the mujahideen had no night-vision equipment. Pilots made bombing runs at greater height, thereby diminishing the accuracy of the attacks, but the rate of Soviet and Afghan aircraft losses did not change significantly from what it was in the first six years of the war. The Soviet decision to withdraw from Afghanistan was made in October 1985, several months before Stinger missiles entered Afghanistan in significant quantities in the autumn of 1986. None of the secret Politburo discussions that have since been declassified mentioned the Stingers or any other shift in mujahideen equipment as the reason for the policy change from indefinite occupation to preparations for retreat." From Jonathan Steele, "10 myths about Afghanistan," *The Guardian*, September 27, 2011, at https://www.theguardian.com/world/2011/sep/27/10-myths-about-afghanistan. Accessed June 23, 2017.

[84] As quoted in Ken Silverstein, "Stingers, Stingers, Who's Got the Stingers?" "In late 2001, Pentagon officials acknowledged that some of the 2,000 missiles sent to Afghan fighters during the 1980s might have fallen into the hands of Taliban or Al-Qaeda fighters … military historians say the Stinger missiles were critical to the success of mujahedeen fighters against Soviet forces … it is now impossible to confirm how many of the 2,000 Stingers actually made it to Afghan fighters, or how many are still operational." Ron Synovitz, "Afghanistan: Kabul Confirms New Effort to Buy Back U.S.-Built Stinger Missiles," Radio Free Europe / Radio Liberty, January 31, 2005, at http://www.rferl.org/a/1057196.html. Accessed June 23, 2017.

[85] Silverstein, "Stingers, Stingers, Who's Got the Stingers?"

Destruction of the American Destroyer USS Cole."[86] However, the only attack to date carried out by al-Qaeda using surface-to-air missiles took place on November 28, 2002 when al-Qaeda operatives fired two Soviet Strela 2 (aka: SA-7 Grail) missiles at an Arkia Airlines charter flight (Israeli owned) in Mombasa, Kenya. Both missiles missed the plane. There have been no reported instances of an Afghan Stinger being fired at a U.S. target outside a declared conflict country.[87]

The Middle East Peace Process

President Carter played an active and effective role in engineering the peace agreement between Egypt and Israel, referred to as the Camp David Accords, which was signed on September 17, 1978. It is considered one of Carter's most important accomplishments as President. This agreement paved the way for a

---

[86] Al-Qaeda's first major propaganda video titled "The Destruction of the American Destroyer USS Cole," a 100-minute, two-DVD production by the "Assahab Foundation" was distributed in June 2001. The author has an original set of these DVDs in their original packaging that were sold in Pakistan. The second part of the video shows jihadist training in Afghanistan which includes firing a Stinger.

[87] Given that there are probably several hundred Afghan Stingers not accounted for and that the shelf life of a Stinger is about 20 years depending on how and where they were stored and maintained, it is likely that the threat of terrorists using an Afghan Stinger against an American target is low. However, more advanced and newer Stingers were provided to the Iraqi military in the post-Saddam era. In the summer of 2014, Islamic State forces captured territory in Iraq where they accumulated some Stinger missiles from captured Iraqi military depots (Fox News, "US-made Stinger missiles have likely fallen into ISIS hands, officials say," June 16, 2014, at http://www.foxnews.com/world/2014/06/16/us-made-stinger-missiles-have-likely-fallen-into-isis-hands-officials-say.html. Accessed July 23, 2017. A 2013 report by the Arms Control Association estimates that 47 non-state groups worldwide now possess man-portable air-defense systems (MANPADS), which have already been used in 50 attacks against civilian aircraft that have killed nearly 1,000 civilians (Arms Control Association, "Facts and Briefs: MANPADS at a Glance," March 2013, at https://www.armscontrol.org/factsheets/manpads. Accessed June 4, 2017). Meanwhile, a State Department study reports that since 1975, at least 40 civilian aircraft have been hit by different types of MANPADS, causing about 28 crashes and more than 800 deaths around the world, at http://www.telegraph.co.uk/news/worldnews/al-qaeda/10115887/Al-Qaedas-how-to-guide-for-using-surface-to-air-missiles-found-in-Mali.html. Accessed July 23, 2017. All of these attacks have taken place primarily in known conflict areas in Africa, Asia, and the Middle East. No surface-to-air missile has been fired to date at a commercial airliner taking off or landing at a European, North American, or Latin American airport. With the exception of the Al-Qaeda fired missiles in November 2002 in Mombasa, Kenya, the MANPAD attacks to date have taken place in civil war conflict zones. The primary concern of the MANPAD threat is having one fired at a commercial airliner landing at a major European, Canadian, or American airport. The impact of such an attack would produce millions of dollars in aviation protected security measures and severely damage the airline industry.

permanent peace treaty between the two countries which was signed on March 26, 1979 in Washington, D.C. This treaty laid the foundation for new progress in the Middle East, and it ended the long-running hostilities between the two countries.[88] A state of war had existed between Egypt and the State of Israel since Egypt and other Arab countries invaded the newly declared Israeli state in 1948 and they had fought wars in 1956, 1967, and 1973. Egyptian President Sadat and Israeli Prime Minister Begin received the Nobel Peace Prize in 1978 for their courage in participating in the Camp David negotiations and working toward this peace treaty. Of the two, Sadat risked the most. The reaction to this proposal in the Arab world was very negative. In 1979, Egypt was expelled from the Arab League, and internal opposition to Sadat's policies led to a rise in domestic political tensions. On October 6, 1981, Sadat was assassinated by Muslim extremists in Cairo while viewing a military parade commemorating the 1973 Yom Kippur War.[89]

The Camp David Accords set in motion a series of events, including Sadat's assassination, that created a fertile environment in Egypt for the emergence of a domestic jihadist terrorist threat that simmered in the 1980s, emerged and reached its high-water mark in the 1990s, and flared up again in the 2000s and 2010s. The jihadists wanted a government run according to the Koran while Sadat had created a secular, pro-Western regime with correct, if not friendly relations with Israel. Prior to the Sadat assassination, jihadist terrorist attacks in Egypt were episodic and directed at Egyptian targets. After his assassination, there was an increase in jihadist terrorist attacks that culminated in the 1990s with a sustained terrorist campaign that included foreign targets, including the U.S. The pinnacle of anti-American terrorist activity in the post-World War II period was reached during the Reagan administration as state sponsors, secular Palestinian terrorist groups, and Islamic revolutionary groups would target U.S. interests in Asia, the Middle East, and Western Europe. The involvement of the U.S. in bringing Egypt and Israel together and breaking the Arab front against Israel was simply another grievance that the three major threat actors had against the U.S.

---

[88] https://history.state.gov/departmenthistory/short-history/carter. Accessed June 23, 2016. Carter invited Israeli Prime Minister Menachem Begin and Anwar El Sadat to Camp David for negotiations which he mediated.

[89] Association for Diplomatic Studies and Training. Interview with U.S. Ambassador Alfred Leroy Atherton, Jr. who was in the reviewing stands with Sadat during the attack, at http://adst.org/2013/09/the-assassination-of-anwar-sadat-part-i/. Accessed June 23, 2017.

Ayatollah Khomeini of Iran.

Source: Wikimedia Commons — public domain.

Shredding embassy documents.

Source: U.S. Department of State.

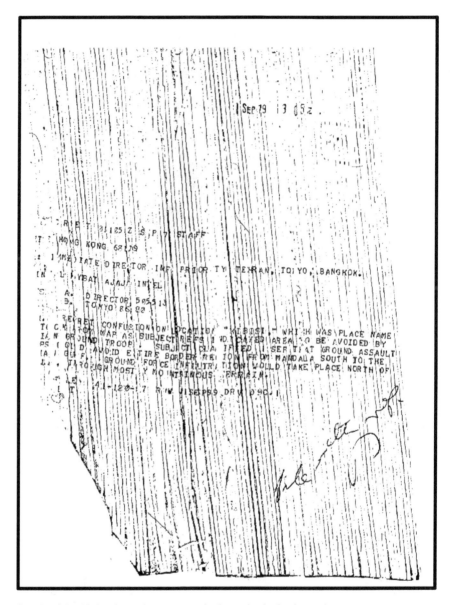

Sample of shredded embassy documents put back together by Iranian students.

Source: Wikimedia Commons.

Iranian students on steps of U.S. Embassy in Tehran.

Source: Wikimedia Commons.

Operation Eagle Claw — Tehran Hostage rescue mission.

Source: Wikimedia Commons.

Memorial in Arlington National Cemetery to the men who died during Operation Eagle Claw.

Source: Wikimedia Commons.

The 52 released American hostages in a hospital in Germany.

Source: U.S. Department of Defense.

January 27, 1981 — U.S. hostages return to U.S. at Andrews Air Force Base.

Source: Department of Defense — "The appearance of U.S. Department of Defense visual information does not imply or constitute DOD endorsement".

Chapter 11

The Carter Administration (1977–1980): The Response — Part III

Internal Terrorist Threat

A response to the internal terrorist threat was directly and indirectly addressed by the Carter administration in a set of measures constructed during the first two years of the administration: the 1977 Presidential Directive #17 on The Reorganization of the Intelligence Community, the 1977 Presidential Review Memorandum #30 on Terrorism, the 1978 Executive Order 12306 U.S. Foreign Intelligence Activities, and the 1978 Foreign Intelligence Surveillance Act. All had a direct and indirect impact on how U.S. intelligence agencies, especially the FBI and NSA dealt with domestic and foreign spillover terrorism in the U.S. Aside from these measures, no new specific counter-terrorism legislation was passed during the Carter administration. What had passed during the Nixon and Ford administrations and the above measures were enough for dealing with the internal terrorist threat. The level of this threat was internally and externally debated. The Carter administration did not perceive the internal threat as being high nor did it believe that the international terrorist activity taking place overseas would spread to the U.S. Some members of Congress, the media, and outside terrorism experts disagreed. Consequently, there was an ongoing debate in and outside the government as to the nature, level, and response to this internal terrorist threat. The March 1977 Hanafi Muslim seizure of three buildings in Washington, D.C., the Puerto Rican and Croatian terrorist bombings in New York City, the assassination of a Cuban diplomat in New York City, the assassination of a former Iranian diplomat in the Washington, D.C. area, bombings in the San Francisco area by the New World Liberation Front, and the emergence of the

"Unabomber" and anti-abortion terrorism, all underlined the growing internal terrorist threat.

The U.S. intelligence agencies recognized the growing terrorist threat overseas and dedicated increased intelligence resources to the problem. Internally, U.S. law enforcement agencies were apprehensive over the persistent terrorist activity in the U.S. One of the responses to this growing threat was the establishment in 1980 of the U.S.'s first Joint Terrorism Task Force (JTTF). In May 1980, to address the frequent bombings in New York City by a plethora of terrorism actors like the Jewish Defense League (JDL), Armed Forces of National Liberation (FALN), and Omega 7, the New York City Police Commissioner and the FBI Special Agent in Charge (SAIC) of the New York field office, Joseph MacFarlane, signed a memorandum of understanding creating the JTTF. The JTTF was created in response to this pressing law enforcement crisis. It was founded on the belief that interagency cooperation and the timely sharing of intelligence was essential to effectively tackle terrorism because the complex crime of terrorism cuts across agency lines and must transcend agency rivalries. Over the years, there had been a traditional rivalry, as well as outright resentment, between the FBI and many local police agencies.[1] This was the first JTTF between local police and federal agents. It was modeled after a successful joint task force between the New York City Police Department (NYPD) and FBI set up in August 1979 to investigate bank robberies, the first time that such a joint force was established for bank robberies.[2] According to the FBI, the NYPD in 1979 experienced a substantial increase in the number of bank robberies. Records indicate the City of New York had 928 robberies, of which 319 were armed robberies. However, immediately after a task force was formed, the robberies dropped to 687, including 251 armed.[3]

The New York JTTF was composed of ten NYPD officers and ten FBI agents. By agreement, JTTF investigations would comply with federal rules of criminal procedure and would be prosecuted in federal court. It was funded by the federal government and housed within the FBI's New York City office. The NYPD

---

[1] Joe Valiquette and J. Peter Donald, "The History of the First Joint Terrorism Task Force that Began in NY," at http://ticklethewire.com/2010/12/09/the-history-of-the-first-joint-terrorism-task-force-that-began-in-ny/. Accessed June 3, 2016. Joe Valiquette was a retired FBI supervisory special agent and J. Peter Donald was a public affairs specialist for the FBI in New York; and Leonard Buder, "FBI and City Police Plan Anti-Terrorist Squad," *New York Times*, May 15, 1980, p. B1.

[2] Executive Forum — "FBI: 100 Years of Cooperation," January 2008, p. 9, at https://www.iletsbeiforumjournal.com/images/Issues/FreeIssues/ILEEF%202008-8.1.pdf. Accessed June 3, 2016.

[3] Michael Savasta, "The FBI Joint Terrorism Task Force," *Law and Order*, at http://www.hendonpub.com/law_and_order/articles/2015/09/the_fbi_joint_terrorism_task_force. Accessed May 23, 2018.

detectives selected for the JTTF received security clearances giving them access to the FBI's classified files. Additionally, they were designated as Deputy U.S. Marshals, which allowed them to carry out operations with their FBI partners outside of their New York City jurisdiction.[4] The first cases that the JTTF investigated involved the unraveling of FALN safe houses in New York City after the arrest in April 1980 of FALN leaders, including Carlos Alberto Torres and his wife by local police in Evanston, Illinois. The Torres arrest triggered the decline of the FALN. The JTTF also investigated the assassination of Cuban diplomat Felix Garcia by Omega 7 in New York City on September 11, 1980. The most extensive JTTF investigation during its early years was the 1981 Brinks' armored truck robbery in Nanuet, New York by the Weather Underground and Black Liberation Army. One Brinks guard and two Nyack Police Officers were killed. All but one of the terrorists were identified, located, and convicted.[5] The JTTF model expanded to other cities in the 1980s and became the primary organizational structure by which U.S. police investigated terrorist activity in the U.S.[6]

Domestic Terrorist Threat

The FBI, in cooperation with state and local police, had the primary responsibility for addressing the internal terrorist threat. After the latitude it enjoyed under the Nixon administration and the investigations it endured under the Ford administration, the FBI faced many uncertainties during the Carter administration. Given that President Carter had clearly and consistently stated that he would initiate intelligence reform and adamantly protect the rights of American citizens, the FBI understood that it would face changes and restrictions in how it conducted terrorism investigations. In mid-1977, the FBI put together a six-person training team at its training center in Quantico, Virginia to train new agents on how to deal with terrorists.[7] The instruction most likely included what agents could and could not do in terms of conducting terrorism investigations. The FBI was also frequently reminded in the press of its past abuses. In April 1978, a federal grand jury in Washington indicted L. Patrick Gray III, the former acting director of the bureau, and two of his former top executives, Deputy Director Mark Felt and

---

[4] Valiquette and Donald, "The History of the First Joint Terrorism Task Force."
[5] Ibid.
[6] Mathieu Deflem, "Joint Terrorism Task Forces," in Frank G. Shanty, editor. *Counterterrorism: From the Cold War to the War on Terror, Volume 1* (Santa Barbara, CA: Praeger, 2012), pp. 423–426.
[7] Dena Kleiman, "The Potential for Urban Terror is Always There," *New York Times*, May 13, 1977, p. 155.

Assistant Director Edward Miller, on charges of depriving United States' citizens of their rights.

In April 1978, President Carter submitted his 1979 budget request for the FBI which called for a cut of $2.6 million or, 30%, in the FBI's internal security and terrorism investigation program. However, on April 26, the House Appropriations subcommittee voted to raise Carter's request by $6.7 million, specifically approving reinstatement of the $2.6 million for the internal security and terror investigation program. There was some disagreement between legislators who wanted to revive the FBI's internal intelligence operation targeted against alleged terrorists and those who feared the revival could cause new abuses as in the past.[8] Senator Birch Bayh (D-Ind.) was reported to be concerned that the FBI was trying to get its internal intelligence operation back on track by waving the terrorism threat in front of Congress. Former FBI assistant director Thomas Fuentes was quoted at the time as stating:

> *If you're submitting budget proposals for a law enforcement agency, for an intelligence agency, you're not going to submit the proposal that "We won the war on terror and everything's great," cuz the first thing that's gonna happen is your budget's gonna be cut in half. You know, it's my opposite of Jesse Jackson's 'Keep Hope Alive'—it's 'Keep Fear Alive'.*[9]

In January 1979, a retired FBI agent, M. Wesley Swearingen, who claimed to have spent "20 percent of my career" conducting illegal burglaries for the bureau, provided the Justice Department with detailed information about some of the most sensitive of the bureau's operations. He alleged that in the early 1970s he and other FBI agents assigned to track down fugitive members of the Weather Underground broke into private residences in Los Angeles on at least four occasions without search warrants and that one of the agents involved in the break-ins later denied under oath before the federal grand jury that the burglaries had taken place. He also claimed that subsequent efforts by FBI officials to justify the break-ins based on suggested links between the Weathermen and hostile foreign governments or by asserting that they were countenanced by presidential authority were without foundation.[10]

---

[8]Walter Pincus, "FBI Terrorism Funds Split Lawmakers," *Washington Post*, May 16, 1978, p. A3.

[9]Ibid.

[10]John Crewdson, "Details on F.B.I.'s Illegal Break-Ins Given to Justice Dept.," *New York Times*, January 27, 1979, p. 9. See also M. Wesley Swearingen. *FBI Secrets: An Agent's Expose* (Boston, MA: South End Press, 1995).

In another remedial act to prevent U.S. law enforcement and intelligence abuses under his watch, President Carter sent to Congress on July 31, 1979 a proposed legislation, the FBI Charter Act of 1979, which provided the first comprehensive Charter for the functioning of the FBI and governed all its investigative and law enforcement functions. The foreign intelligence and counter intelligence functions of the Bureau were governed by a separate charter for the entire foreign intelligence community. Carter's charter was intended to bring together in one statute the authorities and responsibilities that the FBI now exercises as a matter of custom and practice.

Although most departments and agencies operate under detailed statutory schemes, the FBI had up to that point lacked a statutory framework, although it is one of the most important and sensitive of all Executive Branch agencies. A one-paragraph 1908 law creating the Bureau was all that existed at the time. Nonetheless, the act proposed by Carter was never passed, and the FBI even to this day does not operate under a general statutory charter but under Attorney General Guidelines that have been revised from time to time.[11]

There was anecdotal evidence at the time that some FBI agents felt that Carter's intelligence reform measures did hamper their ability to effectively address the internal terrorist threat. In February 1978, Nick Stames, SAIC of the FBI's Washington Field Office (WFO), stated that FBI efforts at monitoring terrorist groups had been hampered by the new regulations that barred the agency from infiltrating such groups.[12] The *New York Times* reported in April 1978 that "United States security officials consistently argue that they must work with greater handicaps than their counterparts in even such democratic nations as Great Britain, and that as a result this country has weaker defenses against espionage or terrorism."[13] Even though the FBI Director claimed to have raised the priority level of terrorism within the bureau, there was criticism that the bureau's intelligence collection was not sufficient.[14] The FBI was being handcuffed in terms of its investigative tools and then criticized for being handcuffed.

---

[11] Carter's message to Congress concerning the proposed FBI Charter Act of 1979 can be found at http://www.presidency.ucsb.edu/ws/index.php?pid=32676&st=Terrorism&st1=. Accessed June 3, 2016. Historical Background of the Attorney General's Investigative Guidelines for the FBI can be found at https://oig.justice.gov/special/0509/chapter2.htm. Accessed May 23, 2018.

[12] Judith Valente and Eugene L. Meyer, "Egyptian's Md. Home Hit by Arson," *New York Times*, February 16, 1978, p. B4.

[13] Nicholas M. Horrock, "What Exactly Is the F.B.I. Doing Now?" *New York Times*, April 16, 1978, p. 162.

[14] David Binder, "Antiterrorist Policy of U.S. Held Weak," *New York Times*, April 23, 1978, pp. 1, 14.

The record indicates that U.S. law enforcement, led by the FBI, significantly reduced the internal terrorist threat in the U.S. during the Carter administration. Compared to the number of internal terrorist incidents that occurred during the Nixon and Ford administrations, internal terrorist incidents during the Carter administration had declined. During the Carter administration, two domestic terrorist groups expired — the New World Liberation Front (NWLF) and the George Jackson Brigade (GJB), the first due to internal problems, the second to FBI and local law enforcement investigative successes. While the Weather Underground Organization, and its holding organization the Prairie Fire Organizing Committee (PFOC), started to unravel in 1976 due to internal ideological conflicts, the FBI and the Carter administration could take some credit in neutralizing it completely in 1977–1980.[15] On November 20, 1977, five Weather Underground members were arrested in Los Angeles and Houston on conspiracy charges to bomb a California State Senator's office. The FBI and the California Criminal Intelligence Division had infiltrated the Weather Organization and uncovered the plot. The arrests were front-page news in the *Los Angeles Times* with the article continuing on page 2 and placed next to one titled "FBI Took Credit for Black Panther Split, Files Show." The irony was that some felt that the FBI infiltrators had engineered the ideological dissension and resulting split in the Weather Underground/PFOC in 1976.[16] For some, the November 1977 arrests seemed to be the death blow for the Weather Underground.[17]

On President Carter's second day in office, January 21, 1977, he issued a pardon to those who had failed to register for the draft or left the country to avoid service during the Vietnam War. Carter's pardon stated that only civilians who were convicted of violating the Military Selective Service Act by draft-evasion acts or omissions committed between August 4, 1964 and March 28, 1973 were eligible. The pardon was unconditional and wiped criminal records clean, but it only applied to civilians, not the estimated 500,000 to 1 million active-duty personnel who went absent without leave or deserted during the war.[18] Taking advantage of this new atmosphere from the Carter administration, in 1978, Weather

---

[15] Ron Jacobs, *The Way the Wind Blew: A History of the Weather Underground* (New York: Verso, 1997), pp. 83–85, at https://libcom.org/files/32709343-Way-the-Wind-Blew-A-History-Of-The-Weather-Underground.pdf. Accessed January 23, 2017.

[16] Ibid., pp. 86–87.

[17] David Gilbert, *Students for a Democratic Society and the Weather Underground Organization* (Abraham Guillen Press: Canada, 2002), p. 39; and Jacobs, *The Way the Wind Blew*, p. 88.

[18] Lee Lacaze, "President Pardons Viet Draft Dodgers," *Washington Post*, January 22, 1977, at https://www.washingtonpost.com/archive/politics/1977/01/22/president-pardons-viet-draft-evaders/dfa064a5-83fc-4efb-a904-d72b390a909e/?utm_term=.ee5ad7e8aa63. Accessed June 6, 2017.

Underground founding member Mark Rudd turned himself in. In 1980, Cathy Wilkerson, Bernadine Dohrn, and Bill Ayers, other founding members, also turned themselves in. Other Weather Underground members surrendered or were arrested. The FBI's COINTELPRO's abuses became widely known during this period; Carter's pardon signaled a certain lenient attitude by the government. The U.S. government was also concerned that allowing Weather Underground defense attorneys the process of "discovery" (pre-trial questioning of witnesses) could have endangered "national security." All these factors combined to ensure that many Weather Underground members were never prosecuted while others had their convictions overturned.[19]

The FBI dealt a significant blow to the Puerto Rican terrorist group, FALN, on April 9, 1980 when a counter-terrorism raid in Chicago resulted in the arrest of 11 members of the group. This led to the discovery of FALN safe houses in Milwaukee and Jersey City, N.J. Authorities found ammunition, dynamite, home-made bombs, detonating devices, rifles, and boxes full of communiqués purportedly outlining FALN plans to kidnap prominent Americans and bomb public buildings as part of an effort to gain independence for Puerto Rico. The charges included seditious conspiracy for plotting to oppose the government through illegal means, automobile theft, and illegal use and possession of weapons. The seditious conspiracy charge was rarely used in United States courts. However, in two previous cases involving Puerto Rican nationalists, it resulted in convictions.[20] While the FALN carried out some attacks in the 1980s, it was never able to fully recover from the April 1980 arrests.

President Carter also addressed one of the grievances of the Puerto Rican separatists by releasing from prison Puerto Rican terrorists arrested for two attacks in the 1950s against the House of Representatives and President Truman. The release of the prisoners was a frequent demand from both the FALN and the Macheteros, as well as some domestic left-wing groups. On October 6, 1977, President Carter granted clemency to the fourth terrorist involved in the attack on the House of Representatives, Andres Figueroa Cordero. The president commuted his sentence to time served. Cordero had terminal cancer. Carter commuted Cordero's sentence on humanitarian grounds because of his physical condition. The commutation order, which is not a pardon, was an act of clemency

---

[19]Leonard Lehrman, "Visiting David Gilbert in Prison," *Jewish Currents*, January 28, 2014, at http://jewishcurrents.org/visiting-david-gilbert-prison/. Accessed May 23, 2017.

[20]"10 Convicted in Chicago FALN Trial," *New York Times*, February 12, 1981, at http://www.nytimes.com/1981/02/12/us/10-convicted-in-chicago-faln-trial.htm. Accessed May 14, 2017.

on the part of the president.[21] On September 6, 1979, Carter commuted the sentence of Oscar Collazo, the terrorist convicted of the 1950 attempted assassination of President Truman at the Blair House. His original death sentence was commuted by Truman himself. In prison, Collazo was asked why he had targeted Truman, who was in favor of self-determination for Puerto Rico and who had appointed the first native-born Puerto Rican governor. Collazo replied that he had nothing against Truman, saying that Truman was "a symbol of the system. You don't attack the man, you attack the system."[22]

On September 10, 1979, Carter granted clemency to Irving Flores, Rafael Cancel Miranda, and Lolita Lebrón, the last of the four terrorists who had been imprisoned for the 1954 attack on the U.S. House of Representatives. They had served 25 years in prison. The Governor of Puerto Rico, Carlos Romero Barceló, publicly opposed the pardons granted by Carter, stating that it would encourage terrorism and undermine public safety.[23] The terrorists were received in Puerto Rico with a heroes' welcome from roughly 5,000 people at the San Juan International Airport. As reported by *Time* magazine at the time,

> *For a brief moment last week San Juan's international airport took on the atmosphere of a revolutionary carnival, as some 5,000 Puerto Ricans gathered to welcome an American Airlines jet. Young couples swayed to the rhythm of revolutionary songs, vendors did a brisk business selling tiny Puerto Rican flags, and young leftists passed out leaflets calling for armed struggle.*[24]

In releasing the four terrorists involved in the attack on Truman, Carter gave the following reasons:

- A favorable recommendation was made by the Attorney General to commute the sentences of these individuals to time served.

---

[21] See, Jimmy Carter: "Andres Figueroa Cordero Announcement of the Commutation of Mr. Figueroa Cordero's Prison Sentence.," October 6, 1977. Online by Gerhard Peters and John T. Woolley, The American Presidency Project, at http://www.presidency.ucsb.edu/ws/?pid=6757. Accessed June 4, 2106.

[22] "Jimmy Carter Commutes the Sentences of Puerto Rican Nationalists," at http://potus-geeks.livejournal.com/261609.html. Accessed June 23, 2017.

[23] http://potus-geeks.livejournal.com/261609.html. Accessed June 23, 2017.

[24] "We Have Nothing to Repent," *Time*, September 24, 1979, at http://content.time.com/time/magazine/article/0,9171,947395,00.html. Accessed January 24, 2016.

- Each of the four had served an unusually long time in prison, and the Attorney General believed that no legitimate deterrent or correctional purpose was served by continuing their incarceration.
- The consensus of the law enforcement officials consulted was that commutation would be appropriate and would pose little substantial risk of the defendants' engaging in further criminal activity or becoming the rallying point for terrorist groups.
- The Secretary of State was of the belief that the release of these four prisoners would be a significant humanitarian gesture and would be viewed as such by much of the international community.[25]

When Oscar Collazo arrived on Puerto Rico, he told the crowd at the airport: "First we will have to see how far American terrorism has gone in Puerto Rico and then we will decide whether terrorism by our side is necessary." Lebrón and Collazo blamed "American aggression and repression" in Puerto Rico for prompting their attacks in the 1950s.[26]

FBI investigations into Croatian and Serbian terrorist activities in the U.S. during the Carter administration bore fruit during the Reagan years and eliminated the threat of Yugoslav émigré terrorism in the U.S. The FBI and local police in the state of Washington also dealt a death blow to the GJB in March 1978 when they arrested three persons believed to be the only remaining members of the terrorist group. FBI investigations and pressure on domestic and foreign spillover terrorist groups during the Carter administration reduced the internal terrorist threat that the incoming Reagan administration faced. This was accomplished with more guidelines, oversight, media scrutiny, and legal restrictions on the agency than at any other time in the bureau's history.

The Threat of Nuclear Terrorism

The threat of terrorist attacks on nuclear facilities, terrorist theft of nuclear materials, and developing nuclear bombs first emerged as a serious security concern under the Nixon administration. This concern continued during the Ford and Carter administrations. One month into the Carter administration, the Nuclear Regulatory Commission (NRC), replaced the Atomic Energy Commission,

---

[25] "Puerto Rican Nationalists Announcement of the President's Commutation of Sentences," September 6, 1979, at http://www.presidency.ucsb.edu/ws/?pid=32827. Accessed June 4, 2016.

[26] Joanne Omang, "Puerto Rican Nationalists Don't Rule Out Violence," *Washington Post*, September 12, 1979, p. A3.

concluded a year-long study on the threat of nuclear terrorism and concluded that "the possible threat of terrorist actions against the nation's 74 civilian-operated nuclear facilities requires an immediate and significant increase in security."[27] There were also concerns that terrorists might be able to seize plutonium or highly enriched uranium from the 14 facilities then licensed to handle such materials, which could be used to build a bomb, or that they might sabotage one of the nation's 60 nuclear power reactors. The study noted that the changed assessment of danger was not based "upon a perception of imminence of threat to the nuclear fuel industry; rather it is based upon the judgment of the task force as to what constitutes a prudent level of protection."[28]

The primary tactical concern was over terrorists hijacking nuclear materials while they were being transported or hijacking a commercial airliner and flying it into a nuclear power plant. While an attack on a nuclear power plant was possible, it was unlikely given the complexity of such an operation and the protective security measures in place at the time. However, security was always a concern and issue. The NRC study proposed extensive background and security investigations on selected employees, increased firepower for security guards, and the hiring of more guards and providing them with better training. The cost for these measures and others was estimated to be \$20 million for construction and equipment and \$10–15 million more annually for guards.[29] Then, in August 1977, the NRC revealed "that more than four tons of bomb-grade uranium and plutonium could not be accounted for in the country's nuclear research and development facilities."[30] There were no signs that the material was stolen, but the fact that the government had problems with its inventory of these materials only caused more concern over the threat.

In late 1977, the Department of Defense's Studies, Analysis, and Gaming Agency ran a secret exercise that simulated a hypothetical situation of a theft of an American nuclear weapon by terrorists.[31] This was reportedly the first major "war game" against terrorism. The *New York Times* reported that Carter officials were "particularly worried over the possibility that criminal or political extremists might acquire advanced conventional bombs, nuclear bombs, or toxic chemicals

---

[27] Front-page article by David Burnham, "74 Nuclear Plants Told to Strengthen Antiterrorist Guard: Regulatory Agency Concerned over a Possible Theft of Plutonium or Sabotage of Reactors," *New York Times*, February 19, 1977, p. 1.

[28] Ibid.

[29] Ibid.

[30] Naftali, *Blind Spot*, p. 103.

[31] Richard Burt, "Pentagon Game Simulates a Nuclear Blackmail Case," *New York Times*, November 15, 1977, p. 10.

to further their claims."[32] In early 1978, three college students from Harvard, Princeton, and MIT developed plans for a nuclear weapon which further amplified the concern over the threat of nuclear terrorism. One, a 22-year-old Harvard student had only one year of college-level physics. On March 22, he appeared before the Senate Governmental Affairs Committee's Subcommittee on Nuclear Proliferation.[33] The committee was considering ways to significantly tighten security controls surrounding special nuclear materials that could be turned into homemade weapons.

These Carter administration concerns on nuclear terrorism ran counter to the primary conclusion issued in a January 8, 1976 classified CIA Research Study on "Potential Terrorist Use of Nuclear Weapons." This study examined the near-term (next year or two) possibility of such an act. It concluded that: "the inherent constraints against a foreign terrorist attempt to acquire and use nuclear explosives against the U.S., taken in conjunction with the difficulties entailed, are sufficiently great that we judge such an attempt to be unlikely in the next year or two."[34] The study did note that "the judgments we make here are of necessity generalizations based on patterns of terrorist behavior which are subject to change ... we have excluded consideration of domestic U.S. terrorist groups as being outside our area of responsibility." More importantly, the study warned that "in view of the increase in the tempo of terrorist attacks and in their daring and efficiency, however, we cannot have complete assurance that an attempt will not occur.... Over the longer term, if the current trend of increasing terrorist violence continues, we would expect a corresponding erosion of the constraints against terrorist use of nuclear explosives." The following additional points were made in the study:

- Terrorists are and will continue to be greatly sensitive to the quantity and quality of security systems protecting nuclear weapons and the materials from which nuclear explosives might be made.
- None of the individual steps involved would be beyond the capabilities of a sophisticated, well-funded group, but the probability of successfully completing all the steps is low.

---

[32] Ibid.

[33] David Burnham, "A Student's Bomb Design Prompts Call for More Nuclear Safeguards," *New York Times*, March 23, 1978, p. A18.

[34] The study was NIO IIM 76-002 8, dated January 1976. It can be found at Foreign Relations of the United States, 1969–1976, Volume E-3, Documents on Global Issues, 1973–1976, Document 225 — CIA Research Study on Potential Terrorist use of Nuclear Weapons, Washington, January 8, 1976, at https://history.state.gov/historicaldocuments/frus1969-76ve03/d225. Accessed June 26, 2016.

- If an attempt at seizure of a weapon was made, the one targeted would probably be a U.S. weapon deployed abroad. This is true not only because of the wide deployment of such weapons but, more importantly, because of the great political importance assigned by terrorists to targets involving the U.S. presence abroad. A foreign terrorist group which had achieved possession of a nuclear explosive abroad would probably use it against the U.S. presence or against U.S. allies and interests rather than against targets in the continental U.S.

- Because foreign terrorist groups have had little success and have shown little inclination to operate within the continental U.S., an attempt to seize a nuclear weapon there, though possible, is less likely.

- By the nature of terrorist behavior patterns, we believe that some form of indirect use of nuclear explosives is more probable than direct use. Specifically, a major motivation for terrorist seizure of a nuclear weapon would be to acquire a credible threat for blackmail and/or publicity. It is judged that most terrorist groups attempting to seize a weapon would do so without the specific intention of detonating it. The subsequent threat that a workable nuclear device had been fabricated would have to be taken seriously. In an extreme situation, however, some might attempt a detonation.

- Of the many terrorist groups operating in the world today, the most competent to attempt seizure of a nuclear weapon would be one of the Palestinian groups such as the Popular Front for the Liberation of Palestine or the present-day version of the Black September Organization. West European groups, because they operate in areas where U.S. weapons are widely deployed, need to be carefully watched but have not yet demonstrated the sort of capabilities which would make a successful attempt very likely. One factor which could significantly increase the danger to U.S. weapons in Europe would be joint operations between or among a Palestinian group, a West European group, and, possibly, the Japanese Red Army.

The concern over the possible use of nuclear materials or weapons by terrorists has paralleled the tactical and targeting evolution of political terrorism going back to even before the Nixon administration. The level of concern over the issue, the attention paid to it, and the resources devoted to mitigating the threat evolves concurrent with the terrorist threat in general. The ability to accurately assess the viability and probability of a terrorist tactic is enhanced, the longer the historical record of that tactic. The longer that tactic has been used, the more refined and accurate the counter-terrorism responses. At the beginning of the Carter administration, the record of nuclear-related terrorist incidents was short and spotty. Most of the nuclear facilities in the world at the time were in the U.S., the Soviet Union, or Western Europe. By one account, from 1966 to 1977, there were 10 terrorist incidents directed against European nuclear installations.[35] However, it was the increase in the incidents over the years that triggered a greater concern of the threat under the Carter administration.

While there were no serious terrorist attacks on nuclear facilities during the Nixon, Ford, and Carter administrations, the following attacks helped shape the concern over the threat:

November 1971, New York: An arsonist struck the Indian Point 2 nuclear power plant at Buchanan, New York, causing an estimated $10 million in damage.

March 25, 1973, Argentina: Fifteen members of the People's Revolutionary Army (ERP) attacked the Atucha Atomic Power Station 60 miles north of Buenos Aires. The group overpowered the plant's five guards, seized firearms from security posts, and began to break into the power plant itself. The police were able to confront the terrorists and drive them off. The attack was part of a campaign of terrorism by the ERP in Argentina which later included several other unsuccessful attacks on nuclear power facilities.

May 1975, France: Two bombs detonated at a partially constructed Fessenheim power station causing a fire but no casualties. The anarchist group Meinhof-Puig Antich claimed responsibility.

August 15, 1975, France: Two bombs planted by Breton separatists exploded at the Mt. d'Arree Nuclear Power Station in Brittany. The

---

[35] Jerimiah Denton, "International Terrorism–The Nuclear Dimension," in Paul Leventhal and Yonah Alexander, editors, *Nuclear Terrorism: Defining the Threat* (Washington, D.C.: Pergamon-Brassey's, 1986), p. 152. Denton was a Republican U.S. senator from Alabama. According to Senator Denton's article, there were 32 acts of intentional damage or suspected sabotage at U.S. domestic nuclear facilities from 1974 to 1986.

damage was minor, and the reactor was shut down temporarily for inspection.

May 12, 1976, Maine: Two bombs exploded in the headquarters of the Central Maine Power Company in Augusta. The Fred Hampton Unit of the People's Forces claimed responsibility and demanded an end to the expansion of nuclear power plants.

October 10, 1977, Oregon: A bomb exploded next to the visitor center at the Portland General Electric Trojan Nuclear Power Station near Ranier. The Environmental Assault Unit of the New World Liberation Front claimed responsibility.

February 1979, Switzerland: A bomb blast wrecked a building at the Kaiser Augat Plant causing $528,000 damage. There were no injuries.

April 6, 1979, France: Suspected Israeli agents sabotaged the Osirak reactor awaiting shipment to Iraq at La Seyne-sur-Mer.

September 1979, New York: The Puerto Rican terrorist group, the FALN, active in the U.S., threatened that it would blow up the Indian Point nuclear plant in New York.[36]

November 5, 1979, Switzerland: A bomb exploded at the Goesgen reactor, the country's newest and biggest nuclear power station. The explosion wrecked an electrical pylon, disrupting power to the surrounding area.[37]

---

[36]William Sater, "Puerto Rican Terrorists: Possible Threat to U.S. Energy Installations?" RAND Note, N-1764-SL, October 1981, p. 1, at https://www.rand.org/content/dam/rand/pubs/notes/2005/N1764.pdf. Accessed June 5, 2017.

[37]Chronology of attacks from Denton's article, and Anthony Kimery, "Rightwing Extremist 'Hit List:' Worrisome? Overblown? Or are Jihadis the Greater Threat?," April 20, 2015, *Homeland Security Today*, at http://www.hstoday.us/columns/the-kimery-report/blog/rightwing-extremist-hit-list-worrisome-overblown-or-are-jihadis-the-greater-threat/ab5f323163f03bfeeafbc5fd51555215.html. Accessed July 4, 2017, and Konrad Kellen, "Appendix: Nuclear Related Terrorist Activities by Political Terrorists," in Paul Leventhal and Yonah Alexander. *Preventing Nuclear Terrorism: The Report and Papers of the International Task Force on Prevention of Nuclear Terrorism* (New York: Lexington Books, 1987), pp. 123–130.

In March 1980, the FALN threatened the United States: "you must remember … you have never experienced war in your vitals and that you have many nuclear reactors."[38]

The most extensive anti-nuclear terrorist campaign ever carried out by a terrorist group took place from 1977 to 1982 when the Basque separatist terrorist group Basque Homeland and Liberty (ETA) opposed the construction of the Lemoniz nuclear power plant, 10 miles outside of Bilbao, the capital of the Basque region in Spain. There was an active anti-nuclear movement in the Basque region that also opposed the plant's construction. ETA engaged in attacks on the plant's construction site and its employees and engaged in an economic sabotage campaign against Iberduero, Spain's largest private utility that was constructing the plant. Five plant workers were killed by ETA including the chief engineer of the power station, José María Ryan and Ángel Pascual, his successor. ETA also bled the finances of Iberduero by carrying out over 100 attacks on the company's electrical pylons and transformers in the Basque region, causing numerous blackouts and $30 million in repair costs.[39] The bombing attacks on the power plant caused an additional $25 million in damages. The terrorist campaign also intimidated workers at the power plant. The Lemoniz power plant was shut down and remains so. While not the determining factor in the stoppage of the power plant (a new Socialist government elected in 1984 initiated a moratorium on new nuclear power plants in Spain), ETA's terrorist campaign was a major contributing factor.

These attacks on nuclear-related targets demonstrated that terrorists were aware of the high impact and psychological effect of these attacks. Even the threat of such attacks produced impact for the terrorists. In the 1970s, political terrorism was a nascent development. Its tactical and targeting restraints were unknown. How far would a terrorist group go in trying to accomplish its goal? Would the acquisition of nuclear materials or the development of a nuclear weapon be enough for the group? If a group acquired a nuclear device, would it be necessary to use such a device? What would be the blowback from the group's supporters, sympathizers, constituency, and the international community? Both governments and terrorist organizations faced a myriad of questions whose answers were unknown. A RAND Corporation report in January 1986 titled "The Threat of

---

[38] William Sater, "Puerto Rican Terrorists," p. 2.

[39] Ana Martinez-Soler, "Spanish nuclear power plant short-circuited by Basque terrorists," *Christian Science Monitor*, May 7, 1982, at http://www.csmonitor.com/1982/0507/050747.html. Accessed June 4, 2017.

Nuclear Terrorism: A Reexamination," concluded that "to date there has been no serious incident of nuclear terrorism. The constraints, both self-imposed and external, against terrorists' 'going nuclear' have apparently been stronger than the attractions toward such involvement ... we would not ascribe a high likelihood to major acts of nuclear terrorism. Given the technical difficulties, risks, and possible negative repercussions for them and their state sponsors few terrorists would be willing to try such a daring tactical innovation."[40] This report essentially supported the January 1976 CIA Report on the same issue. While the terrorist nuclear threat may not have been probable, there were enough security vulnerabilities around nuclear power plants and the transportation of nuclear materials that a prudent government had to take some remedial security steps.[41] The threat of nuclear terrorism was passed on to each subsequent administration which allocated the necessary attention and resources based on the nature and perception of the terrorist threat at the time.

Domestic Terrorism and Civil Disorders

The U.S. faced the most serious domestic terrorist threat and civil disorders under the Nixon administration. The response to these threats was excessive and recalibrated under the Ford administration as various congressional committees examined these abuses and proposed more oversight solutions. President Carter's attitude toward dealing with domestic civil disorders surfaced during a March 9, 1977 press conference. The president was asked to comment on the recently released 600-page report of the Law Enforcement Assistance Administration (LEAA) task force on terrorism and violence which recommended the use of mass arrests and the use of preventive detentions should such disorders occur as they did in the 1960s.[42] President Carter replied that "I would be opposed to mass

---

[40] Peter deLeon, Bruce Hoffman, with Konrad Kellen, and Brian Jenkins, "The Threat of Nuclear Terrorism: A Reexamination," RAND Corporation Note, N-2706, January 1986, p. 15, at http://www.dtic.mil/dtic/tr/fulltext/u2/a220305.pdf. Accessed January 24, 2017.

[41] The 1968 nuclear Non-Proliferation Treaty (NPT) requires non-nuclear-weapon states to accept safeguards administered by the International Atomic Energy Agency on all their nuclear activities. But, when the NPT was drafted, nuclear terrorism was not perceived as a significant threat, and the safeguards consisted of monitoring and accounting measures designed to prevent non-nuclear-weapon states from diverting nuclear material from peaceful nuclear activities to weapons programs. The safeguards were not intended to prevent theft of nuclear material by outsiders or the bombing of reactors and spent fuel by terrorists.

[42] This report can be found at, LEAA's National Advisory Committee on Criminal Justice Standards and Goals, "Report of the Task Force on Disorders and Terrorism," March 2, 1977, at https://babel.hathitrust.org/cgi/pt?id=umn.31951p008901837;view=1up;seq=542. Accessed June 3, 2017.

arrests, and I would be opposed to preventive detention as a general policy and even as a specific policy, unless it was an extreme case." The president clarified that he had not read the report nor was he familiar with it, "but I think the abuses in the past have in many cases exacerbated the disharmonies that brought about demonstrations, and I think the arrest of large numbers of people without warrant or preventive detention is contrary to our own best system of government."[43] While domestic terrorism occurred during the Carter administration, there were no major civil disorders from the urban areas or campuses like those that took place during the Nixon years.

Foreign Spillover Terrorism

Foreign spillover terrorism is an ancillary problem for any country. The U.S. had a problem in that New York City is host to the U.N. headquarters buildings. At the start of the Carter administration, there were 149 member states in the U.N.[44] There were over 200 U.N. missions and foreign consulates in New York City. Many of these diplomatic facilities were co-located in buildings with other countries' diplomatic facilities or in buildings with non-diplomatic entities. This meant that a bombing against one country's diplomatic facility could also cause damage or injuries to others. If there was no claim, then which country was being targeted? Many of these foreign diplomatic facilities were under various degrees of a terrorist threat either in the U.S. or abroad. U.S. domestic terrorist groups rarely attacked foreign diplomatic interests in the U.S., so this was a foreign spillover terrorist problem, and, to a lesser extent, possibly a state-sponsored dilemma.

Like Nixon and Ford, the Carter administration had to address the issue of protecting foreign diplomatic interests in the U.S. The problem had three parts: (1) Which federal agency would provide this protection? (2) How would U.S. law enforcement agencies neutralize the terrorist groups posing this threat? (3) Who would pay for this protection? Protection of foreign diplomats in the U.S. was not a new problem as it surfaced during both the Nixon and Ford administrations. The problem was more acute under Carter as a Cuban diplomat was assassinated in New York City, terrorists shot their way into the Yugoslav U.N. mission in New York City, an Indian diplomat was stabbed in Washington, D.C., and dozens of

---

[43] The President's News Conference, March 9, 1977, at http://www.presidency.ucsb.edu/ws/index. php?pid=7139&st=Terrorism&st1=. Accessed December 5, 2016.

[44] http://www.un.org/en/sections/member-states/growth-united-nations-membership-1945-present/ index.html. Accessed May 4, 2017.

bombings were carried out against foreign diplomatic facilities and personnel in New York City, Washington, D.C., San Francisco, and Los Angeles. After the assassination of the Cuban diplomat, the U.S. Ambassador to the U.N., Donald McHenry, called the assassination "a stain on the United States" and warned:

> *It will be very bad for the U.S. if they don't find the killer and bring him to justice. The U.S. has received the active support of the whole world on their plea that Iran release the hostages and respect the time-honored code of diplomatic immunity. They cannot expect to do less than they expect others to do for them.*[45]

Other U.N. diplomats expressed outrage over the killing and demanded more protective measures from the U.S.

Under the Nixon and Ford administrations, it was determined that the U.S. Secret Service would protect all heads of state and its executive protection service (EPS) would protect foreign diplomatic missions in New York City and Washington, D.C. However, deploying EPS protection required a presidential directive and the deployment was only for 60- and 90-day increments. The Carter administration at first questioned the expenses of the EPS for guarding U.N. missions. The Secret Service questioned whether the EPS should even be protecting U.N. missions. The Secret Service noted that the EPS was supposed to be tasked to New York for a short time; the EPS officers did not have any authority to challenge visitors to the mission; and it had no police function except to be present in the event of an emergency. The Secret Service proposed a more permanent solution by suggesting that either the government reimburse the NYPD for its protective security functions or create a permanent U.N. security detail manned by Department of State security agents. The State Department opposed these proposals arguing that even though the EPS provided minimal protection, it did satisfy protective and reciprocity demands.

Another issue was reimbursing local and state law enforcement agencies for the costs they incurred when protecting foreign diplomatic interests. The NYPD had the biggest burden as it had U.N. missions and foreign consulates in New York City to protect. No other city had such a protective security workload. During the Nixon administration, beginning in 1974, the funding for NYPD protection duties came from the Department of Justice LEAA which was created in

---

[45]Bernard D. Nossiter, "McHenry Terms Slaying a 'Stain on United States,'" *New York Times*, September 13, 1980, p. 24.

1965 to direct federal funds to state and local police forces. On December 31, 1975, President Ford signed a bill for the protection of U.N. diplomats — Public Law 94-196. It stated that the U.S. would protect diplomatic missions in cities outside of Washington that possessed 20 or more full-time missions. This bill was clearly aimed at New York City. It also required the Treasury Department to reimburse state and local entities that provided such protection to foreign diplomatic interests. Federal reimbursement was limited to $3.5 million annually. This law appeared to have settled the reimbursement issue and the debate over the protection of U.N. interests.

However, during the Carter administration the issues of protective security duties and reimbursement continued to surface. A December 1979 *New York Times* editorial titled "Share the Bomb Burden in New York City," complained that an "unfair financial burden was put on New York City by requiring it to assume national duty for the protection of U.N. diplomats." It noted that "Washington consistently refused to pay fairly for this service ... no federal money was available to pay city policemen assigned to fixed posts ... and only part of the extraordinary costs arising from official visits are met by the federal government."[46] The reimbursement issue was partially resolved during the Carter administration in 1980. In the spring, the Treasury Department revised its regulations and authorized reimbursement to New York City for costs incurred during fixed post assignments and extraordinary protective operations (for example, the annual meeting of the U.N. General Assembly). New York City received about $9 million from the federal government for reimbursement of expenses for safeguarding visiting foreign leaders and administrative costs to host the U.N. delegations.[47] The Treasury Department regulation, however, only reimbursed costs connected with protecting U.N. missions and foreign dignitaries. It did not include costs related to protecting diplomatic residences of foreign commercial offices nor did it cover costs associated with maintaining order during demonstrations outside the U.N. headquarters building. Such demonstrations proliferated during the annual General Assembly meeting which also stretched NYPD, USSS, and State Department security protective resources.[48] By November 1980, federal officials and NYPD officials were discussing establishing a permanent security

---

[46]"Share the Bomb Burden in New York City," Editorial, *New York Times*, December 16, 1979, p. 18

[47]Kathleen Teltsch, "Diplomats to Get Tighter Security Under New Plan," *New York Times*, November 20, 1980, p. B1.

[48]This section on the issues of reimbursement and protective security responsibilities for U.N. missions in New York City is derived from *DS History*, pp. 234–238.

unit for U.N. missions and consular facilities. There was concern over the "growing problem of European-style terrorism being exported to New York."[49]

NYPD officers who were assigned to protective security duties for foreign diplomatic facilities in New York City, especially to fixed posts outside the facilities, were never happy with these additional security responsibilities. In 1970, NYPD officers from the 19th Precinct staged a protest against the fixed posts near the Soviet mission. They claimed that foreign missions in the U.S. received better protection than the nation's cities.[50] In March 1980, some 100 NYPD officers, charging that their safety had been endangered, went to court to challenge the NYPD's authority to assign them to foot posts outside the Cuban Mission to the U.N. They also challenged foot patrols outside the U.S. Mission to the U.N. The police officers stated that the Cuban mission was a "bomb-prone location." The Omega 7 terrorist group had bombed the mission over a half dozen times. The officers asked that they be allowed to sit in police cars outside the location so they could view the premises from a safer location. They claimed that foot patrols gave them no protection or opportunity to escape harm should a bomb go off. They also complained that they had received no proper training on what action to take during a bombing.[51]

An example of how this issue of U.S. responsibility for protecting foreign diplomats and facilities in the U.S. can create bilateral tensions took place in early March 1978 when Communist Yugoslav President Josip Tito visited the U.S. Tito's visits to the United States usually avoided most of the Northeast due to large minorities of Albanian, Serbian, and Croatian emigrants bitter about communism in Yugoslavia. Security for his state visits was usually high to keep him away from protesters, who would frequently burn the Yugoslav flag. During this March visit, when Tito visited the U.N., emigrants shouted "Tito murderer" outside his New York hotel. About 60,000 Croatians lived in a tight-knit, patriotic community in New York. Tito protested to the United States' authorities about these demonstrators.[52] Before coming to the U.S. for this visit, Tito gave an interview in which he complained that on his previous two visits to this country, U.S. authorities had done little to curb émigré demonstrators who had harassed him. During this March visit, Tito met with President Carter who pledged to "take firm

[49]Kathleen Teltsch, "Diplomats to Get Tighter Security Under New Plan."

[50]*DS History*, p. 235.

[51]Leonard Buder, "Police Officers, Charging a Risk, Challenge Duty at Cuban Mission," *New York Times*, March 18, 1980, p. B4. See also, Kathleen Teltsch (Security Review for U.N. Diplomats), *New York Times*, December 27, 1979, p. A1.

[52]Associated Press, "Anti-Tito Protest Planned," *Herald-Journal*, March 5, 1978, p. A8.

measures to prevent and to prosecute" criminal terrorist activities by anti-Tito Yugoslav émigré groups in this country. This went further than any previous American policy statements on Yugoslavia and, according to Yugoslav officials, was particularly gratifying to President Tito.[53] This issue of protecting foreign diplomats and facilities in the U.S. continued during the Reagan administration.

Another U.S. response to the foreign spillover terrorist threat in the U.S. was to exchange terrorist information with those countries being targeted. The countries whose diplomatic interests in the U.S. were targeted the most were the Soviet Union, Cuba, Turkey, Israel, and Yugoslavia. There were no major issues in exchanging such information with Turkey and Israel. However, the other three presented political and intelligence problems. All three were communist countries. Of the three, the Cuban and Yugoslav intelligence services were the most aggressive in presenting indiscriminate "lists of terrorists" to the U.S. government. The Yugoslavs were particularly aggressive before visits of President Tito. Despite not having diplomatic relations with Communist Cuba, the U.S. exchanged information with Cuba on Cuban exile activities in the U.S. The explanation was that this was done "in our common efforts to control the threat of international terrorism."[54] On March 15, 1977, President Carter issued Presidential Directive #6, Subject: Cuba, which called for the achievement of normalization of U.S. relations with Cuba and to begin direct and confidential talks with Cuba. This directive also stated that the "Attorney General should take all necessary steps permitted by the law to prevent terrorism or illegal actions launched from within the United States against Cuba and against U.S. citizens and to apprehend and prosecute perpetrators of such actions."[55] It was a basic responsibility for the U.S. to ensure that Cuban, as well as other countries' interests were protected in the U.S. The question was whether to provide information on U.S. citizens to communist countries whose definition of a terrorist was anyone who opposed their regimes.

These foreign spillover terrorism attacks on foreign diplomatic interests in the U.S. also produced U.N. pressure on the U.S. government and New York Police Department to take the necessary protective security actions. There were dozens of bombings of U.N. missions and foreign consulates in New York City in

---

[53] David Binder, "U.S. Affirms Backing for Yugoslav Unity, *New York Times*, March 10, 1978, p. 3. See also, "Visit of President Tito of Yugoslavia Joint Statement, March 9, 1978," at http://www.presidency.ucsb.edu/ws/index.php?pid=30471&st=Terrorism&st1=. Accessed January 24, 2016.

[54] "U.S. has Exchanged Data on Political Dissidents," *New York Times*, August 11, 1977, p. 18. This was acknowledged by the USG on August 3, 1977, at https://www.nytimes.com/1977/08/11/archives/us-has-exchanged-data-on-political-dissidents.html.

[55] http://nsarchive.gwu.edu/news/20020515/cartercuba.pdf. Accessed August 24, 2017.

the 1970s. However, the three incidents that had the most impact were the June 1977 assault and temporary takeover of the Yugoslav U.N. mission, the December 1970 bombing of the Soviet U.N. mission that injured seven people, and the September 1980 assassination of the Cuban U.N. Diplomat Felix Garcia Rodriguez. Of the three, the assassination produced the most outrage. This was the first time that a diplomat from a U.N. country was assassinated in the U.S. The attack made the front page of the *New York Times*. Three times on the day after the assassination, U.N. Secretary General Kurt Waldheim expressed his horror at the crime. He communicated with the U.S. representative at the United Nations, demanding that full measures be taken to guarantee the safety of all the Cuban personnel in New York and insisted that the tragic event be thoroughly investigated. U.S. Secretary of State Ed Muskie called it a reprehensible act and asked for all the relevant federal agencies as well as the New York Police Department to cooperate in the investigation.[56] Nevertheless, Muskie refrained from specifically condemning the anti-Cuban terrorism.

The problem of foreign spillover terrorism that began under the Nixon administration reached its zenith during the Carter administration and then dissipated during the first term of the Reagan administration. Under the Nixon administration, the domestic terrorism component of the internal terrorist threat was the most problematic. However, under Ford and Carter, foreign spillover terrorism was the most pressing concern in terms of the internal terrorist threat. Such activity polluted the security environment in cities like New York, Chicago, San Francisco, Miami, and Washington, D.C. Although aimed at foreign targets, the tactics and location of the attack carried the potential of causing casualties to innocent bystanders. More importantly, such attacks embarrassed the U.S. government, strained bilateral relations, created tension and rancor between local police agencies and the federal government, and threatened the principle of reciprocity for U.S. diplomatic interests overseas. No other country in the world faced the level and scope of foreign spillover terrorism as the U.S. There were more foreign diplomatic facilities and personnel in the U.S. than any other country.

---

[56]Robert McFadden, "Cuban Attache at U.N. Is Slain from Ambush on Queens Road," *New York Times*, September 12, 1980, p. 1, 27.

The Field of Terrorism Analysis

As the international terrorist threat overseas matured and the internal terrorist threat in the U.S. continued to cause problems, terrorism as a distinct field of study continued to grow during the Carter administration. Policy, operational, analytical, protective security, intelligence, technological, and cooperation (internal and international) issues on political terrorism that surfaced during the 1970s re-emerged during subsequent administrations. Many of the typologies, principles, theories, analytical frameworks, definitions, and concepts on terrorism in the 1970s have generally stood the test of time over subsequent decades.

In the private sector, as the terrorist threat increased, one of the first responses was the emergence of companies that provided electronic security systems, bodyguards, armored vehicles, and crisis negotiators for a fee. "Risk analysis" became the illustrative term of the decade. The British firm Control Risks, Ltd., founded in 1975, was one of the first to see this opportunity. It quickly became a $2 million a year operation. It became one of the first companies to provide advice to clients involved in kidnapping situations. It analyzed a company's risk, set up or advised on security systems, and when the need arose, masterminded the negotiation of ransoms.[57] While governments can adopt a no-negotiating, no-ransom policy, this was an unrealistic approach for companies and families of the victims. Companies face legal problems if they refuse to bargain. They cannot say there are issues of national security.[58]

There was also a growing business for armoring vehicles in the 1970s. For example, one U.S. company, Custom Armor Manufacturing, made $1.7 million in 1977, $3.2 million in 1978, and $6.4 million in 1979. Armor industry analysts at the time expected that there would be 3,500 armored cars worldwide by the end of 1981. Statistics at the time indicated that 90% of assassination attempts took place while the victim was riding in a car.[59] Depending on the country, the terrorist threat compelled businessmen, government officials, and diplomats to travel in bullet-proof Cherokee Chiefs, Jeep Wagoneers, Chevrolet Suburbans, or International Scouts. These vehicles could be fitted with an entire passenger compartment armored, curved windshield and side glass, floor armor, protected batteries and fuel tanks, gun ports, ramming bumpers, run-flat tires, and tear-gas outlets behind fenders that produced a 50-foot toxic cloud. Most of these growing

---

[57] Robert D. Hershey, Jr., "Where Kidnapping is Business: London Firm Takes on Risk and Ransom," *New York Times*, December 29, 1979, p. 27.
[58] Ibid.
[59] "New Growth Business — Arming Cars," *New York Times*, June 9, 1981, p. D1, D17.

protective security revenues came from armored vehicles, protective security guards, training and hardware, rather than from information or risk assessments.

To support these protective security operations and to more efficiently allocate these resources, threat analysts were needed to determine the nature and level of the threat in a country. Consequently, the emergence of private sector threat/terrorism analysts took place in the late 1970s. To better collect, store, and retrieve relevant threat information, databases were created.

In June 1978, Risks International Inc. was founded by Dr. Charles A. Russell, former chief of the acquisition and analysis section of the Office of Special Investigations (OSI), and Roy Tucker, the former commander of OSI. In 1979, they developed the first private sector computerized database on terrorist activities with the capacity to extrapolate information on any terrorist organization or on such activities in any major city or country in the world. Clients could use the database for an annual fee of $960. The database at the time had 5,000 significant incidents of terrorism since 1970. RAND Corporation senior terrorism analyst, Brian Jenkins was quoted at the time as stating that Russell's database was one of the best inside or outside the U.S. government. In 1979, Risks provided a monthly eight-page summary of patterns and trends in terrorism. The founding of Risks reflected a growing terrorism industry that had been developing since the early 1970s. In 1975, the industry was believed to be doing $2–3 billion worth of business in the United States alone, with a 12% annual growth rate.[60] During the Carter administration, the terrorism field in the private sector security firms expanded to now include intelligence analysts, threat analysts, country analysts, or regional analysts and the establishment of terrorism databases. They were all designed to primarily support the hardware side of the company.

However, what Risk International began was more of an information service for clients. Travel agencies, airlines, and multinational businesses were now interested in the security environment of countries where they had interests, directly or indirectly. U.S. airlines and multinationals had an in-house security department that was responsible for the protection of the company's assets, including facilities and personnel. They also had a large footprint overseas where domestic and international terrorism was growing. Subscribing to these information services allowed companies to make their own decisions as to what protective security measures to implement. At this time, the U.S. government had no specific office that catered to the security concerns of U.S. companies. Government information on security conditions in a country were usually delivered to visiting corporate

---

[60] A.O. Sultzberger Jr., "Data on Terrorism is New Venture's Product," *New York Times*, January 15, 1979, p. D1, D6.

security officers by relevant U.S. Embassy personnel, in particular the regional security officer. Keep in mind that U.S. businesses were the primary target of terrorists overseas throughout the 1970s. From 1968 through 1979, there were over 1,300 anti-American terrorist attacks overseas. Of the attacks, 36%, or 487 attacks, were aimed at U.S. businesses. U.S. diplomatic targets came in second with 20%.[61] The increase in security firms in the 1970s was a clear byproduct of U.S. and foreign businesses becoming preferred targets for both domestic and international terrorist groups. The nascent business of political risk assessment had grown to the point where in 1980, a new trade group was formed in the U.S. — the Association of Political Risk Analysts.

In academia, more attention was being directed at the terrorism issue during the Carter administration. New institutes and centers dedicated to studying terrorism were created. New journals on terrorism were founded and conflict-centered journals started to address this issue. The first institute in the U.S. dedicated to terrorism was the Institute for Studies in International Terrorism at the State University of New York (Oneonta) established in 1977 by Dr. Yonah Alexander, an early specialist on terrorism. Institutes and centers on conflict and strategic studies also started to pay more attention to terrorism by setting up small research groups on the issue, bringing in terrorism specialists, and holding conferences or seminars on the issue. The following were some of these: the Institute for the Study of Conflict started in 1970 in London; the Jaffe Center for Strategic Studies founded in 1977 at Tel Aviv University; the Institute for Conflict and Policy Studies started in 1977 in Washington, D.C.; the Jonathan Institute founded in 1979 in Tel Aviv; and the Center for Conflict Studies started in 1980 at the University of New Brunswick in Canada. The Jaffe Center and the Jonathan Institute held two of the most significant conferences on terrorism in 1979 in Tel Aviv. The Jaffe Center's international conference on terrorism in Tel Aviv was attended by authorities on terrorism like Brian Jenkins, J. Bowyer Bell, Yonah Alexander, Robert Kupperman, Robert Moss, Paul Wilkinson, and Hans-Joseph Horchem. Of the 46 attendees, 21 were government officials. The Jonathan Institute's conference in June had participants like George H.W. Bush, Ray Cline, Claire Sterling, George Will, and U.S. Senators John Danforth and Henry Jackson. Such conferences were designed to enhance the reputation of these entities, influence government policy on the issue, network, and attract money. However, some of these institutes and centers adopted a certain view on terrorism and counter-terrorism and thus attracted or invited like-minded individuals. Some

---

[61] CIA, National Foreign Assessment Center, "International Terrorism in 1979: A Research Paper," Document number PA80-10072U, April 1980, p. 14.

of these entities became, in effect, lobbies for their governments and their policies on terrorism.

The first English-language international journal dedicated to terrorism was established in 1977 by Yonah Alexander. It was called *Terrorism: An International Journal.* The purpose of the journal was to "offer dialogue on definitional, histori-cal, biological, sociological, psychological, philosophical, political, strategic, legal, economic and future perspectives on the subject for the purpose of advanc-ing the cause of peace and justice." The journal's board of editors contained such authorities on terrorism as J. Bowyer Bell, Ted Gurr, Brian Jenkins, Robert Kilmarx, David Rapoport, Paul Wilkinson, and Frank Ochberg, who was a mem-ber of the 1976 Justice Department Task Force on Terrorism and Disorder. The journal's international advisory board listed terrorism specialists such as Walter Laqueur and Bernard Lewis. In 1978, George K. Tanham, a counter-insurgency expert at the RAND Corporation, founded *Conflict: An International Journal.* In the summer of 1980, the Canadian journal *Conflict Quarterly* was founded by David Charters and Maurice Tugwell at the Centre for Conflict Studies at the University of New Brunswick. These three journals were the first significant English-language international journals that focused on the issue of terrorism. By the end of the Carter administration, academia had in place resident terrorism experts, special centers or institutes on terrorism, and journals dedicated to the issue. More books on terrorism were also being authored during the Carter administration. However, there were few university courses on terrorism in the United States. The first was taught by Steve Sloan in 1975 at the University of Oklahoma. In the next decade, academia's attention to terrorism surged as the anti-American terrorist threat escalated. U.S. government research grants to uni-versities to study terrorism also increased.

In the government, more intelligence analysts were being assigned a terror-ism-related analytical portfolio.[62] However, the number of analysts was still small

---

[62]Based on the author's experience as an intelligence analyst in the State Department's Threat Analysis Group (TAG) which he joined in January 1977. The number of USG intelligence analysts solely dedicated to terrorism increased as terrorism in Europe and the Middle East increased in the later 1970s. Within DIA, FBI, CIA, NSA, State, and AFOSI, there were probably fewer than 60 dedi-cated "terrorism analysts" in Washington. The group was so small that we were able to set up informal networks to exchange information and hold informal meetings on certain groups. I distinctly remem-ber in early 1978 holding a meeting at the State Department with government terrorism analysts who had responsibility for following the German Red Army Faction terrorist group. The invite was sent out to all the above agencies and we had nine analysts who attended. The key agencies, except NSA, were represented. The point is that all key analysts in Washington responsible for the RAF were in a single conference room sitting around a small conference table and we all knew each other by first

fewer than 60 in all of Washington, D.C. This made it easier to establish informal networks and relationships with other analysts working a similar problem, threat, group, or issue. As during the Ford administration, in general, terrorism-related problems were farmed out to other departments or desks to address. At the State Department, terrorism continued to be addressed by the counter-terrorism office, regional bureaus, country desk officers, and Bureau of Intelligence and Research (INR) regional analysts. Sometime in 1979–1980, INR assigned the terrorism portfolio to one person: John Bedrosian. State's Office of Security TAG grew from four to six terrorism analysts during the Carter administration. TAG had a terrorism responsibility as it analyzed the terrorist threat to U.S. diplomatic facilities and personnel overseas and produced threat assessments for foreign dignitaries visiting the U.S. and for overseas travel by the Secretary of State. It also provided threat assessment to U.S. corporate security officers when necessary, had responsibility for monitoring the crime threat overseas, and assessed threat letters sent by mentally unbalanced individuals to department officials. Similar terrorism-related assignments occurred in the U.S. Secret Service, the CIA, DIA, and NSA.

In general, there were few significant terrorism-specific analytical units established in the U.S. government during the Carter administration. For U.S. government intelligence analysts, terrorism was not a career field but simply a supplementary analytical responsibility. Terrorism was a concern, but not a mission. While the U.S. Intelligence Community started to dedicate collection assets to the terrorism issue after the 1972 attack on Olympic athletes in Munich, the issue was still not a top-tier issue that required the establishment of special terrorism analytical units. Terrorism was subsumed in the "global issues" box. While there continued to be episodic terrorist attacks on U.S. interests overseas, there was no detectable sustained terrorist threat. The proliferation of U.S. intelligence analytical, operational, and technical efforts on terrorism took place during the Reagan administration. During the Carter administration, there were also few, if any, government-run intelligence analysis courses on terrorism. In March 1977, the FBI assembled a staff of six people to solely train agents to deal with terrorism.[63] Given the FBI's responsibility for the domestic terrorist threat and the rise in the threat under the Nixon administration, it was logical for the FBI to set up such a course for its agents, albeit a little late.

---

name. One can only imagine how big a room would have to be to hold a similar meeting in 2019 of all al-Qaeda or Islamic State analysts in the government.

[63] Kleiman, "The Potential for Urban Terror is Always There," *New York Times*, March 13, 1977, p. 155.

In 1980, the FBI addressed the analytical and research dimensions of the terrorist threat by establishing the Terrorist Research and Analytical Center (TRAC). TRAC was situated at the FBI's headquarters building. Its functions were to: (1) automate and analyze information collected on known terrorists and terrorist groups, (2) make assessments of the information, and (3) publish various reports and forecasts of potential terrorist threats. TRAC's most important publication was its annual "FBI Analysis of Terrorist Incidents in the United States" which contained a chronology, statistical charts, and research profiles on terrorist groups and key terrorism issues and threats in the United States. The report addressed domestic terrorist groups and international terrorist incidents in the U.S. The first issue was published in 1981 and was called "Analysis of Claimed Terrorist Incidents in the United States."[64] This report was distributed to FBI personnel, appropriate U.S. government agencies, and occasionally to foreign or domestic law enforcement agencies, depending upon the subject of the investigations and the intended targets — for example, a head of state. This annual FBI Report became the premier, unclassified annual government assessment of domestic and international terrorist activity in the United States.

It is also important to point out that during this period, intelligence analysts did not have the technological aids that are used today. The capability of an intelligence analyst is not only based on their intellectual ability but also on the information processing tools available to them. How is the information received, recorded, stored, and retrieved? What is the speed and storage capability of these tools? The digital age had not yet started in the U.S. government. Compared to intelligence analysts in the 21st century, the analysts of the late 1970s were equivalent to primordial analysts. Consider that information from other agencies and from overseas arrived at an analyst's desk in hard copy. After being read, the report had to be tagged with key words and then placed in a usually numbered file folder which was kept in a central filing system. If there were any key points in the report that had to be recorded, the analyst would write them in a rudimentary "analyst's notebook," usually a brown, spiraled, Federal Supply Service notebook, classified accordingly. The files and notebooks were stored in cabinets and safes. Retrieval? Gray matter retrieval — the analyst's memory. First, you had to remember that a specific report had come in, and then remember what file folder you put it in. Once you put all the relevant information together, you typed your

---

[64]The name of this publication was changed to "FBI Analysis of Terrorist Incidents in the United States" and then to "Terrorism in the United States" in 1987. U.S. General Accounting Office, "International Terrorism: FBI Investigates Domestic Activities to Identify Terrorists," GAO / GGD-90-112, September 1990, p. 45.

report on an IBM Selectric typewriter with carbon paper for duplicates. Wang word processors had just started to appear in the late 1970s and photocopy machines were around since the 1960s. However, not every U.S. government office had a Wang 1977 OIS (Office Information System) word processor or a Xerox machine.[65] These machines did not appear in abundance until the early 1980s. Just as the understanding of the terrorism problem was narrow, rudimentary, and nascent, so were the analytical tools available to "terrorism analysts" at the time.

The second rendition of the CIA's annual publication on terrorism appeared in August 1978 and was called "International Terrorism in 1977" or document #RP-79-10255U. This rendition also added for the first time the subheading "a research paper." It was 12 pages long and now published by the CIA's National Foreign Assessment Center (NFAC). No author is identified. This report notes that its goal was to "identify significant trends over the past year in terrorist activities, government support to terrorists, and in international efforts to curb terrorism, and examines the implications of these trends for the remainder of 1978." The report now added to its goals not only to look backward and forward but also to evaluate state support to terrorists and international counter-terrorism efforts. The August 1978 report contained an appendix that noted how the statistics were compiled and what and why certain incidents were included or excluded. Concerning the statistical data, it noted that: (1) the data are "based solely on unclassified material published during the last decade" and (2) "the criteria used in the present study are unavoidably arbitrary." It also emphasized that "readers of the previous studies will note differences between statistics presented in the present study and its predecessors ... improved data have led to a considerable expansion of the listing of incidents as well as a number of deletions." The third rendition was published in March 1979 under the title "International Terrorism in 1978" or document #RP-79-10149. It was still published by NFAC, was 11 pages long, and had no identifiable author. The only major change was that the stated goals at the front of previous reports were now gone. The fourth rendition of this publication was released in 1980 and added two

---

[65]Richard Moose has stated that he ordered the State Department's Wang system in the late 1970s when he was the Deputy Under-Secretary for Management under President Jimmy Carter. At that time, he recalled, Pentagon officials who visited the State Department salivated at its leading-edge equipment. Steven Greenhouse, "The State Department: A Snail in Age of E-Mail," *New York Times,* March 6, 1995, at http://www.nytimes.com/1995/03/06/world/the-state-department-a-snail-in-age-of-e-mail.html. Accessed June 24, 2016.

new appendices: "Interpreting Statistics on International Terrorism" and "List of Group Names and Acronyms."

CIA's Office of Technical Services (OTS) also contributed to the new field of terrorism analysis. Many of its projects remain classified. However, in the late 1970s, OTS compiled a handbook identifying false passports used by terrorists. It was so popular that other countries and agencies also used this book.[66] Dr. Jerrold M. Post, a noted political psychologist, founded the CIA Center for the Analysis of Personality and Political Behavior in the late 1970s. The center was an interdisciplinary behavioral science unit which provided assessments of foreign leadership and decision-making for the president and other senior officials to prepare for summit meetings and other high-level negotiations and for use in crisis situations. He also initiated a U.S. government program in understanding the psychology of terrorism in the late 1970s. As it was during the Nixon and Ford administrations, the CIA, given its functions, resources, and overseas assets, remained the primary analytical and operational agency addressing the terrorist threat overseas during the Carter administration. It was in the CIA that the U.S. government's early terrorism experts emerged. Few were publicly named. In addition to David Milbank and Ed Mickolus, there was also Eloise Page, and Hildegard Durieux.[67] A growing relationship between the government and the private sector also emerged as many former FBI, CIA, DIA, Secret Service, and other government agents left the government to establish or join private sector security firms with their "special" background and experience skills. Control Risks in London was formed with the help of three former Special Air Services operatives.[68] Risks International in the U.S. was founded by two U.S. Air Force OSI personnel.

In 1977, the U.S. Army established the Intelligence and Security Command (INSCOM). In January 1978, the Army created the Intelligence and Threat

---

[66] Benjamin B. Fisher, Center for the Study of Intelligence, CIA History Staff, The Central Intelligence Agency's Office of Technical Services, 1951-2001 (no date, likely 2001), p. 25, at http://www.foia. cia.gov/sites/default/files/document_conversions/89801/DOC_0001225679.pdf. Accessed June 23, 2016.

[67] Bart Barnes, "Eloise Page Dies at 82," *Washington Post*, October 19, 2002, at https://www. washingtonpost.com/archive/local/2002/10/19/eloise-page-dies-at-82/37b7e41a-e08e-4c25-a13a-2dfab1ae835e/?utm_term=.6f38f2832ee3. Accessed May 3, 2018; http://www.foia.cia.gov/sites/default/files/document_conversions/1820853/2009-05-05.pdf. Accessed June 4, 2016; and http://www.foia.cia.gov/sites/default/files/document_conversions/1820853/1977-05-27b.pdf. Accessed December 23, 2017.

[68] https://wikispooks.com/wiki/Control_Risks. Accessed June 3, 2017. See also, Tony Geraghty. *Guns for Hire: The Inside Story of Freelance Soldiering* (London: Piatkus Publishing, 2008).

Analysis Center (ITAC) as a subordinate element of INSCOM. Within ITAC, there was a Counterintelligence Analysis Division which in the early 1980s was changed to the Counterintelligence and Terrorism Division. The Army was one of the first services to address the terrorism problem by setting up a dedicated unit.

By the end of the Carter administration the U.S. Intelligence Community's interest in terrorism had grown but the issue was handled by assets already in place — intelligence analysts, operatives, and collectors. Some government officials realized that the terrorist threat overseas was unique, increasing, and durable and required the establishment of a specialized set of intelligence assets — analytical, operational, and technical. This view grew in the government and translated into resources and manpower during the Reagan administration as a new anti-American terrorist strain emerged — Islamic revolutionary terrorism. The private sector and academia also recognized the staying power of the terrorist threat and acted accordingly by setting up institutes, centers, journals, and protective security hardware and information firms that addressed the terrorist threat. Academic, think tank, and media authorities on terrorism surfaced. All these elements combined to create an emerging terrorism industry that first materialized during the Carter administration. It continued to grow during each subsequent administration and surged after the 9/11 attacks.

November 21, 1979: 5,000 strong mob seizes U.S. Embassy in Islamabad. Two Embassy officials killed.

Source: U.S. Department of State.

Joint Terrorist Task Force established in New York City in May 1980.

Source: Federal Bureau of Investigation.

NCE COPY 022-1090   (EHC)

THE WHITE HOUSE   7707356 · A
WASHINGTON
UNCLASSIFIED   March 15, 1977

Jimmy Carter

Presidential Directive/NSC-6

TO: The Vice President
           The Secretary of State
           The Secretary of Defense

           ALSO: The Secretary of the Treasury
                    The Attorney General
                    The Secretary of Commerce
                    The United States Representative to
                       the United Nations
                    The Director of Central Intelligence

SUBJECT: Cuba

After reviewing the results of the meeting of the Policy Review
Committee held on Wednesday, March 9, 1977, to discuss U.S. policy
to Cuba, I have concluded that we should attempt to achieve normalization of our relations with Cuba.

To this end, we should begin direct and confidential talks in a
measured and careful fashion with representatives of the Government of Cuba. Our objective is to set in motion a process which
will lead to the reestablishment of diplomatic relations between the
United States and Cuba and which will advance the interests of the
United States with respect to:

--   Combating terrorism;

--   Human rights;

--   Cuba's foreign intervention;

--   Compensation for American expropriated property; and

--   Reduction of the Cuban relationship (political and military) with
     the Soviet Union.

Declassified Release JUV 20   16/98
under provisions of E.O. 12958
by R. Soubers, National Security Council

DF

UNCLASSIFIED

President Carter's 1977 Presidential Directive #6 on Cuba. It tasked the Attorney General to prevent
terrorist attacks from U.S. soil against Cuba and U.S. citizens.

Source: https://nsarchive2.gwu.edu/news/20020515/cartercuba.pdf.

National
Foreign
Assessment
Center

International Terrorism
in 1978

A Research Paper

*Information as of 14 January 1979 has been used
in preparing this report.*

Comments and queries on this unclassified report
are welcomed and may be directed to:
Director for Public Affairs
Central Intelligence Agency
Washington, D.C., 20505
(703) 351-7676

For information on obtaining additional copies,
see the inside of front cover.

RP 79-10149
March 1979

This is the 3rd unclassified CIA research paper on international terrorism. Previous research papers were published in 1976 and 1977.

Source: CIA FOIA reading room.

Approved For Release 2003/09/02 : CIA-RDP80T00942A000800060003-8

Table 4

Geographic Distribution of International Terrorist Incidents, 1968-78, by Category of Attack

	North America	Latin America	Western Europe	USSR/ Eastern Europe	Sub-Saharan Africa	Middle East/North Africa	Asia	Oceania	Trans-regional	Total
Kidnaping	2	133	23	0	39	33	11	2	0	243
Barricade-hostage	6	11	23	0	2	15	3	0	0	60
Letter bombing	14	9	78	0	14	6	37	0	4	162
Incendiary bombing	29	69	249	2	4	52	28	4	0	437
Explosive bombing	198	388	575	7	10	237	46	12	0	1,437
Armed attack	2	33	34	1	21	58	13	0	0	162
Hijacking [1]	5	22	19	0	7	24	15	0	0	92
Assassination	15	56	69	0	15	31	12	1	0	199
Theft, break-in	3	44	13	0	0	14	2	0	0	76
Sniping	11	28	8	1	1	11	3	0	0	63
Other actions [2]	8	15	39	1	1	11	1	0	0	76
Total	293	808	1,130	12	114	492	171	19	4	3,043

[1] Includes hijackings by means of air, sea, or land transport, but excludes numerous nonterrorist hijackings.
[2] Includes occupation of facilities without hostage seizure, shootouts with police, and sabotage.

Table 5

International Terrorist Attacks on US Citizens or Property 1968-78, by Category of Attack

	1968	1969	1970	1971	1972	1973	1974	1975	1976	1977	1978	Total [1]
Kidnaping	1	2	17	9	2	20	8	20	7	4	5	95 (7.5)
Barricade-hostage	0	0	3	0	1	2	2	1	1	3	0	13 (1.0)
Letter bombing	2	1	2	0	3	0	1	0	2	1	0	12 (1.0)
Incendiary bombing	12	18	40	26	13	19	25	4	36	24	49	266 (20.9)
Explosive bombing	30	58	77	93	73	52	90	63	44	35	40	655 (51.5)
Armed attack	1	4	3	4	6	6	5	3	8	3	11	54 (4.2)
Hijacking [2]	0	4	12	3	4	0	0	2	5	4	0	34 (2.8)
Assassination	3	2	9	2	2	3	2	7	13	5	6	54 (4.2)
Theft, break-in	0	3	15	8	0	0	3	3	1	0	8	41 (3.2)
Sniping	2	1	5	2	2	0	3	1	5	4	3	28 (2.2)
Other actions [3]	0	0	5	6	3	0	0	0	3	1	1	19 (1.5)
Total	51	93	188	153	109	102	139	104	125	84	123	1,271

[1] Figures in parentheses are percentages of the total accounted for by each category of attack.
[2] Includes hijackings of means of air, sea, or land transport, but excludes numerous nonterrorist hijackings, many of which involved US aircraft.
[3] Includes occupation of facilities without hostage seizure, shootouts with police, and sabotage.

9

Approved For Release 2003/09/02 : CIA-RDP80T00942A000800060003-8

Samples of CIA terrorism statistics from March 1979 CIA Research paper "International Terrorism in 1978".

Source: CIA FOIA reading room.

Chapter 12

Summation and Prognosis

Summation

The Eisenhower, Kennedy, and Johnson administrations initiated or continued U.S. foreign policies that created events and developments that sparked and fueled an emerging anti-American sentiment in the 1960s. This translated, during subsequent administrations, into anti-American terrorism in Western Europe, Latin America, and the Middle East carried out by left-wing and secular Palestinian terrorist groups and insurgent organizations.

The Nixon Administration (January 1969–August 1974)

The Nixon administration was the first administration to recognize, confront, and respond to this developing international terrorist threat. It encountered the first phase of this threat that created national security, political, economic, and diplomatic difficulties and occasional crises for the U.S. over the next 40 years. In phase one, the international terrorist threat was generated by left-wing and secular Palestinian terrorist groups and insurgent organizations. The threat had reached a level where the U.S. and the international community saw it as a long-term problem that required more enduring responses — such as treaties, domestic legislation, counter-terrorism units, international cooperation and assistance. The terrorist tactics that appeared in phase one were assassinations, bombings, kidnappings, hijackings of aircraft, mid-air bombings of aircraft, letter bombs, and barricade and hostage incidents. Terrorists recognized the value of international publicity in an age of global communications and worldwide television coverage. The targets of anti-American terrorist groups overseas were not only business and government targets but also military and diplomatic targets. In general, the tactics were more discriminate than indiscriminate. State sponsorship of terrorism, while a concern, was not a pressing problem.

The 1970s was a decade in which the U.S. and the world were introduced to a phenomenon that, while not new, had become more appealing and dangerous by new technologies, worldwide communications, global travel, and the Cold War — the internationalization of political terrorism. Given the terrorist developments taking place in the late 1960s, it was only a matter of time before a terrorist incident attracted the attention of the Nixon administration and compelled it to act.

On September 5, 1972, eight Palestinian terrorists from the Black September Organization stormed the Olympic Village in Munich, West Germany, and shot and killed two Israeli athletes and seized nine others as hostages. This was the first terrorist attack on an international sporting event, one that is arguably the most iconic in history. The hostage-takers demanded the release of 234 Palestinians and non-Arabs jailed in Israel, and two imprisoned German terrorists from the Red Army Faction terrorist group. The incident ended the next day when miscalculations took place among German authorities as the terrorists and their hostages were about to board an aircraft at a nearby airfield. A shootout ensued, the terrorists killed all the Israeli hostages and all the terrorists were killed by the police. Although there were previous terrorist incidents that involved U.S. targets and fatalities, it was this event that generated a significant U.S. government reaction. On September 25, 1972, 19 days after the attack on the Munich Olympics, President Nixon established the Cabinet Committee to Combat Terrorism (CCCT) — the first organizational response by a U.S. administration to the international terrorist threat. From this point on, the government's counter-terrorism edifice gradually grew, rarely constricting, into the most extensive, expensive, experienced, and controversial counter-terrorism system in the world.

It is important to note that the generally recognized beginning of the modern age of international terrorism started around 1968 when the Popular Front for the Liberation of Palestine (PFLP) on July 22 hijacked El Al flight 426 departing from Rome and headed for Tel Aviv. While not the first hijacking of an airliner, it was the first that targeted a high-value symbolic target — Israel — and used civilians as bargaining chips against a government. It was also the longest political hijacking (40 days) of a commercial aircraft at the time. Therefore, from 1968 to 1972, the level of counter-terrorism experience addressing international terrorism for the U.S. and most other countries was only four years. When Nixon established the CCCT in 1972, there was no proven set of counter-terrorism tools developed by Nixon's predecessors or an internationally developed counter-terrorism blueprint. Establishing an organizational structure dedicated to dealing with the problem was a logical first step. This structure could then propose counter-terrorism policy and programs and establish additional organizational elements as needed. As a result of this inexperience, it is understandable that the Nixon administration would make some errors in dealing with the terrorist threat overseas.

The Nixon administration addressed this embryonic but growing international terrorist threat overseas by: (1) working for the construction, passage, and ratification of several anti-terrorism treaties and conventions, (2) establishing a central coordinating body to develop, coordinate, evaluate, and fix U.S. counter-terrorism policies, programs, and activities, (3) developing a coherent, if somewhat flawed, policy in hostage-taking incidents, (4) setting up mechanisms to share intelligence and analysis with other countries, (5) framing terrorism as a criminal endeavor and not a political act, (6) understanding the danger of states becoming directly or indirectly involved in sponsoring, supporting, or directing terrorist activity, (7) recognizing the possibility that terrorists could acquire nuclear, radiological, chemical, and biological agents, (8) not allowing terrorists to use violence to alter U.S. foreign policy, and (9) being the first administration to break out the term "terrorism" from the larger category of "insurgency" and give it a separate identity. Under Nixon, a basic counter-terrorism package was put in place, rudimentary policies were established, and a satisfactory organizational structure was created. Considering the era and given the administration's priorities, it was an acceptable, if flawed, attempt to deal with this problem. There were still sharing and coordination problems within the intelligence community and not all government agencies viewed the terrorist threat as a pressing priority.

Internally, the Nixon administration faced the most serious domestic civil disorder in the post-World War II era. There were multiple causes for this disorder, but opposition to the Vietnam War, rising black discontentment in urban areas which led to urban ghetto riots and black militancy, and a generational clash of culture, values, goals, priorities, and social mores were the most powerful forces to ignite this disorder. Domestic terrorist groups emerged from this turbulence. Like the problems it faced in addressing the overseas terrorist threat, the U.S. faced difficulties in dealing with not only domestic but also foreign spillover terrorism with the available intelligence and law enforcement tools. Foreign spillover terrorism in the U.S. consisted of terrorist activities by Cuban American, Armenian American, Croatian and Serbian American, and Jewish American militants who were using the U.S. as a battleground to settle overseas grievances. The United States had never confronted, nor has it ever confronted since that time, such a quantity and mix of domestic terrorism actors. In addition to U.S. law enforcement and intelligence agencies using the wrong methods to deal with the domestic terrorist threat, President Nixon and key administration officials flagrantly utilized the FBI and government intelligence agencies for political purposes. These executive office abuses, illegal FBI counter-intelligence methods, and illicit surveillance activities by the U.S. intelligence agencies triggered a strong and adverse reaction by the Congress and the media. After President Nixon resigned in August 1974 over the Watergate scandal, it fell to the Ford administration to deal with these criticisms and the resultant increased restrictions and oversight on "the collection, retention, dissemination, and use of intelligence information at all levels of government."[1] The Ford administration was the first one to operate under these larger legal restrictions and congressional and media oversight.

What was important, however, was that the Nixon administration assessed the overseas terrorist threat correctly, that it was not transient but durable, and it took certain actions to address and mitigate this threat. It established a counter-terrorism foundation that subsequent administrations could build on or modify depending on the nature and scope of the terrorist threat that each confronted. It is difficult to deal with any new security phenomenon and the Nixon administration, while not constructing the perfect counter-terrorism framework in government, at least provided an adequate and malleable foundation.

The Ford Administration (August 1974–December 1976)

The two-year Ford administration essentially kept most of the Nixon administration's counter-terrorism organization and adhered to most of its policies on hostage-taking, emphasis on the criminality of terrorism, building international counter-terrorism cooperation, developing protective security measures at home and abroad, and not allowing terrorists to influence U.S. foreign policy.

Internally, domestic terrorist groups such as the New World Liberation Front, the United Freedom Front, the Puerto Rican terrorist groups FALN and Macheteros, the Weather Underground, and the Black Liberation Army were active during the Ford administration. The foreign spillover terrorist threat came from the Jewish Defense League, Croatian terrorists, Armenian terrorists, and Cuban exiles. It could be argued that no administration before or since was confronted with the number of internal terrorism actors as the Ford administration. Three serious internal terrorist attacks took place during the

---

[1] Sorrel Wildhorn, Brian Michael Jenkins, and Marvin M. Lavin, "Intelligence Constraints of the 1970s and Domestic Terrorism: Volume I — Effects on the Incidence, Investigation, and Prosecution of Terrorist Activity," RAND Corporation Note, Document #N-1901-DOJ, December 1981, p. v, at https://www.rand.org/pubs/notes/N1902.html. Accessed June 3, 2017.

administration: (1) the 1975 bombing of the Fraunces Tavern in New York City by the Puerto Rican Armed Forces of National Liberation that killed four people, (2) the 1975 bombing of the TWA baggage area in LaGuardia airport by unknown terrorists (primary suspects: Croatian terrorists or the Yugoslav secret police — UDBA) that killed 11 people, and (3) the 1976 hijacking of TWA Flight 355 out of New York by Croatian terrorists, ending with the death of one New York policeman.

Overseas, the secular Palestinian threat declined during the Ford administration — from 79 fedayeen[2] incidents during 1973–1974 to 34 in 1975–1976.[3] In 1974, the Palestine Liberation Organization (PLO) issued a declaration in Cairo that was interpreted by more militant Palestinian nationalists as PLO acquiescence to the existence of Israel, and a commitment to establishing a state alongside of Israel (two-state solution). Moreover, the PLO renounced the use of terrorism outside Israel and the Occupied Territories. These policies triggered a split between PLO-aligned groups and moderate Arab states and a new "rejectionist" front of radical Palestinian groups and radical Arab states. After 1974, Arafat and the PLO shifted its strategy from one based purely on terrorism to one that would include the diplomatic and political elements necessary for significant discussion. In November 1974, the world was exposed to the spectacle of Yasir Arafat, the leader of a Palestinian terrorist organization, a revolver showing at his hip, addressing the U.N. Assembly amid noisy acclaim from Arab countries. In 1974, Palestinian militant Abu Nidal broke from Arafat's Fatah party over his 1974 shift and formed a new rejectionist terrorist organization called Fatah–Revolutionary Council (FRC). The name was designed to imply that Abu Nidal's FRC was the authentic Fatah. The FRC, using several different operational names, became one of the most dangerous international terrorist groups in the 1980s. Therefore, while fedayeen attacks declined during the Ford administration, developments in the Palestinian nationalist movement and the West were ominous for the future.

Left-wing terrorism continued to target U.S. interests overseas during the Ford administration even though the U.S. military involvement in South Vietnam ended on August 15, 1973 as a result of the Case-Church Amendment passed by

---

[2] Palestinians used the term "fedayeen" to describe their "guerrillas." The word is from an Arabic word that means "those who sacrifice themselves." This is the term the CIA used in its first publicly released assessment of international terrorism in 1976 ("International Terrorism in 1976," Document # RP 77-10034U, July 1977).

[3] Ibid., p. 19.

the U.S. Congress.[4] The U.S. presence essentially ended in the country with the fall of Saigon on April 30, 1975. The Vietnam War, however, was only one element in the grievance package left-wing terrorists and insurgent organizations had with the U.S. What changed for the Ford administration was the absence of major civil disorders that Nixon had to face from 1969 to 1972.

The historical ledger of terrorist attacks during the Nixon and Ford administration was 2,789 international terrorist attacks, of which 1,204, or 43%, were directed at U.S. targets, resulting in the deaths of 95 Americans overseas. Internally, it is estimated that there were around 1,000 terrorist attacks that killed 76 people.

Under the Nixon and Ford administrations, the field of terrorism analysis was in its infancy both inside and outside the government. In the next decade, it became an academic and think tank industry and a resource magnet for government intelligence and law enforcement agencies.

The Carter Administration (January 1977–December 1980)

There were no significant changes to the international terrorist threat overseas for U.S. interests during the Carter administration. Left-wing and secular Palestinian terrorist groups were still the main actors, to varying degrees of activity. Of the two, left-wing terrorist groups and insurgent organizations in Western Europe and Latin America were the most active, responsible for 22 of the 39 Americans killed in overseas attacks. While secular Palestinian terrorist attacks during the Carter administration had decreased, the administration participated in developments that would spark an increase during the Reagan administration. The primary trigger was President Carter's active participation in negotiating a peace treaty between Egypt and Israel, via the Camp David Accords. This development antagonized radical Middle Eastern states, rejectionist Palestinian terrorist groups, and Egyptian jihadist terrorist groups. It led to the assassination of Egyptian President Sadat in October 1981 by Egyptian jihadist terrorists.

The singular event that triggered the most severe political crisis for the Carter administration was the November 1979 seizure of the U.S. Embassy in Tehran by Iranian students with the acquiescence of the Iranian government. This was a complicated foreign policy problem that objectively speaking would have

---

[4]Named after Senators Clifford P. Case (R-NJ) and Frank Church (D-ID). See also, Richard L. Madden, "Sweeping Cutoff of Funds for War is Voted in Senate," *New York Times*, June 15, 1973, at https://www.nytimes.com/1973/06/15/archives/sweeping-cutoff-of-funds-for-war-is-voted-in-senate-casechurch.html. Accessed June 17, 2017.

confounded any U.S. administration. This was hostage-taking by a foreign government that was based on Islamic tenets and ruled by a cadre of religious fanatics who had just overthrown one of the U.S. government's key allies in the Middle East. The December 3, 1979 front-page cover of *Time* Magazine captured the prevailing anti-American threat at the time. It was a photo of Muslim militants holding an American flag that was on fire superimposed over the slogan "Kill the American Dogs!" Above the cover photo were the headlines: "Attacking America: Fury in Iran, Rescue in Pakistan." Not only was the U.S. Embassy in Tehran seized by a mob, but U.S. embassies in Islamabad and Tripoli, Libya were also seized by Muslim mobs in December 1979.

This confluence of conditions would have stumped most administrations. The confusion of the Carter administration in dealing with the crisis was perceived by the American public, the media, and Republican Presidential candidate Ronald Reagan, to be weakness, indecision, and a hesitancy to project American power. The Iranian hostage crisis was perceived to be a terrorist event. When President Reagan received the freed hostages in the White House Rose Garden on January 27, 1981, he put the hostage seizure in the context of a terrorist act: "Let terrorists be aware that when the rules of international behavior are violated, our policy will be one of swift and effective retribution. We hear it said that we live in an era of limit to our powers. Well, let it also be understood, there are limits to our patience."[5] While Carter's handling of the hostage crisis was a contributing factor to his defeat in the 1980 election, it was not the determining factor. Polls at the time indicated that the American public was more concerned with the economic situation in the country. However, the hostage crisis did take a toll on the economy as gas prices shot up when the oil imports from Iran suddenly stopped.

In response to the politicizing and abuses of U.S. law enforcement and intelligence abuses during the six-year Nixon administration, the Carter administration began in 1977 with a publicly stated desire to reform the intelligence agencies and a distrust of the CIA.[6] However, President Carter eventually recognized the value of CIA covert operations and used such operations, particularly against the Soviet Union.[7] He also developed an affection for photo and signal intelligence from the NSA.

---

[5] https://www.reaganlibrary.gov/research/speeches/12781b. Accessed July 17, 2016.
[6] Gates, *From the Shadows*, p. 136. Gates notes that Vice-President Mondale was a member of the Church Committee that was investigating the abuses of the intelligence agencies and that several members of Carter's National Security Council staff were staff members of the Church Committee.
[7] Ibid., p. 142.

The Carter administration faced an internal terrorist threat that was composed of periodic bombings by left-wing domestic groups and bombings and assassinations by foreign spillover groups. The latter caused the administration diplomatic problems and created issues between various federal and local authorities over protective security responsibilities and reimbursement of expenses. During a period when U.S. diplomats overseas were being targeted by terrorist groups, the issue of host country responsibility for protecting foreign diplomats became a serious one and triggered concern over reciprocity.

Despite the above terrorist developments, all available evidence indicates that terrorism was not a top-tier or mid-level-tier domestic or foreign policy concern for the administration. However, the record does not indicate a "reduced risk of terrorist attacks against the United States" during the Carter administration.[8] The historical ledger of terrorist attacks during the Carter administration was 1,882 international terrorist attacks, of which 648, or 34%, were directed at U.S. targets, resulting in the deaths of 39 Americans overseas. Internally, it is estimated that there were 260 terrorist attacks that killed 19 people. There were over 50 anti-American terrorist groups operating worldwide at the time.

For the Carter administration, terrorism was simply one of many "global issues" that it had to periodically address. The administration reviewed the counter-terrorism organizations and policy of the previous administrations and made some cosmetic and minor modifications. The Carter administration did however make positive contributions to U.S. counter-terrorism efforts. It established the first dedicated U.S. counter-terrorism rescue force; it recognized the danger of state-sponsored terrorism; it supported the use of tabletop training exercises to manage terrorist incidents, especially weapons of mass destruction attacks; and it increased security around U.S. nuclear facilities and provided more support for the Nuclear Emergency Support Team (NEST).

Could the Carter administration have done more to strengthen and expand the U.S. counter-terrorism program? Given the administration's perception of the threat, probably not. An objective analysis of: (1) the Carter administration's domestic and foreign policy goals, (2) the domestic and foreign policy crises that took place during the administration, (3) the nature, level, and scope of the anti-American terrorist threat during the administration, and (4) the mindset, worldview, and temperament of President Carter, his National Security Director, and national security team, would conclude that the Carter administration acted appropriately in its assessment of the terrorist threat and development of the U.S. counter-terrorism program. It moved that program forward, albeit incrementally.

---

[8] Quote from former President Carter in his book *White House Diary* (2010), p. 121.

As it was during the Nixon and Ford administrations, the issue of terrorism was not politicized by the two political parties during the Carter administration. In general, it received bipartisan support. Over the next decade, the overseas terrorist threat to U.S. interests would reach its historical high water mark and the U.S. would develop a counter terrorism program that would progress for decades. Terrorism would no longer be a skirmish or back burner issue but a "war" and would become a substantial national security issue for subsequent administrations.

In phase one of the international terrorist threat that confronted the U.S., there were 4,671 international terrorist attacks, of which 1,852, or 47%, were directed at U.S. targets, resulting in the deaths of 134 Americans overseas. Over this 12-year period of phase one, the above statistics averaged out to 389 international terrorist attacks, 154 anti-American terrorist attacks, and 11 Americans killed overseas annually. During the Nixon, Ford, and Carter administrations, over 140 new terrorist groups had emerged in nearly 50 nations or disputed territories.[9] It should also be noted that while there were foreign spillover terrorist attacks in the U.S. during all three administrations, there was little or no foreign incursion terrorism.

Prognosis

Terrorist-related events and developments took place in the first phase of the international terrorist threat during the Nixon, Ford, and Carter administrations that spilled over and grew during the Reagan and subsequent administrations:

- In 1974, the PLO shifted its goals and strategy. This led to the rise of the Abu Nidal terrorist group that became one of the most dangerous international terrorist groups in the 1980s and early 1990s.
- In 1975, the Lebanese Civil War began between leftist Palestinian-backed Muslims and rightist Christians thereby creating conditions for the later chaos in the country in the 1980s that significantly contributed to the unprecedented rise in the international and anti-American terrorist threat in the decade. The Lebanese Army split along sectarian lines. Syrian troops intervened in Lebanon in 1976 and Israel intervened in 1977. Lebanon became a battleground for competing intelligence services of Western and Arab countries, a fertile

---

[9] David Burnham, "A Student's Bomb Design Prompts Call for More Nuclear Safeguards," *New York Times*, March 23, 1978, p. A18. Senator John Glenn's statement, quoting an unclassified CIA study, at https://www.nytimes.com/1978/03/23/archives/a-students-bomb-design-prompts-call-for-more-nuclear-safeguards.html. Accessed August 23, 2017.

environment for the training of international terrorist groups, and a magnet for contending foreign policy objectives of the U.S., Israel, Jordan, Iran, and Syria.

• In 1979, two major events took place that expanded in the 1980s and created circumstances that contributed to the emergence and advancement of two new anti-American terrorist strains — Islamic revolutionary terrorism and state-sponsored terrorism:

(a) The Islamic revolution in Iran and

(b) The Soviet invasion of Afghanistan.

Along with the Lebanese Civil War, these developments would combine to make the 1980s the high-water mark of the international and anti-American terrorist threats in the post-World War II era.

It should also be noted that while Libya was considered a state-sponsor concern during the Ford and Carter administrations, it would only develop into a state-sponsor threat during the Reagan administration, when two strong-willed personalities would clash — President Reagan and Muammar Gaddafi.

Another carryover development from the Nixon, Ford, and Carter administrations to subsequent administrations was the issue of intelligence "reform." As a result of the politicization and abuses by law enforcement and intelligence agencies during the Nixon administration, Congress imposed restrictions on and oversight of the intelligence community during the Ford administration. President Carter accepted them. President Reagan would remove the restrictions and, in a sense, unleash the Intelligence Community. This clash of contraction and expansion of intelligence capabilities and processes contributed to the recurring debate of "security" vs. "civil liberties" and the quest for a balance that few states have achieved.

The threat of terrorist use of chemical, biological, radiological, and nuclear (CBRN) weapons emerged during the Nixon administration and continued under Ford and Carter. With the emergence of state sponsorship of terrorism and a rising Islamic revolutionary terrorism in the 1980s, the issue would attract more concern and resources as there would be more terrorism actors with the capability (states) and will (religion) who might carry out a CBRN attack.

Few in government or academia during the Carter administration could have predicted the level and scope of the international and anti-American terrorist activity that would emerge in the 1980s — the start of phase two of the international terrorist threat.

Appendix

A. Statistical Snapshots

		Nixon Administration (1969–August 1974)			
Year	International Incidents	Anti-U.S./% of International	U.S. Killed Overseas	Internal Incidents	Fatalities in the U.S.
1969	184	109 (59%)	1	?	8
1970	300	194 (65%)	12	?	9
1971	238	165 (69%)	2	244	11
1972	529	158 (30%)	25	195	12
1973	321	142 (44%)	22	124	9
1974	416	160 (38%)	21	72	3

		Ford Administration (August 1974–1977)			
1975	345	121 (35%)	6	129	21
1976	456	155 (34%)	6	116	3

		Carter Administration (1977–1980)			
1977	419	148 (35%)	6	110	5
1978	530	201 (38%)	5	69	3
1979	441	147 (34%)	14	52	10
1980	499	152 (30%)	14	29	1

B. Statistical Snapshots — Regional Breakdown
of International and Anti-American Terrorist Incidents — Top Two
Regions Only

	Nixon Administration (1969–August 1974)				
Year	Total International Incidents	Latin America	Western Europe	Middle East	Asia
1968	142	47	24		
1969	184	72	32		
1970	300	123	86		
1971	238	74	68		
1972	529	206			175
1973	321	159	145		
1974	416				

Year	Total Anti-American Incidents	Latin America	Western Europe	Middle East	Asia
1968	54	38	8		
1969	109	59	20		
1970	194	85	51		
1971	165	58	51		
1972	158	43	50		
1973	142	50	63		
1974	160	72	53		

	Ford Administration (August 1974–1977)				
Year	Total International Incidents	Latin America	Western Europe	Middle East	Asia
1975	345		131	64	
1976	456	115	228		

Year	Total Anti-American Incidents	Latin America	Western Europe	Middle East	Asia
1975	121	27	35		
1976	155	48	80		

Carter Administration (1977–1980)				
Year	Total International Incidents	Latin America	Western Europe	Middle East	Asia
1977	419	63	241		
1978	530		230	121	
1979	441		176	109	
1980	499	123	178		

Year	Total Anti-American Incidents	Latin America	Western Europe	Middle East	Asia
1977	148	31	88		
1978	201	67	69		
1979	147	49	49		
1980	152	58	51		

Note: The above statistics were the ones used by U.S. government terrorism analysts and policymakers to assess the prevailing terrorist threat.

C. Anti-American Terrorist Incidents Overseas from 1950 to 1969

1950

- **April 27, Indonesia:** Militants kidnapped and killed two Americans —Yale Sociology Professor Raymond Kennedy, 43 and Robert James Doyle, 31, *TIME-LIFE* Far Eastern correspondent in Tomo, on Java Island in Indonesia.

1951

- **July 8, Argentina:** The USIS library in Buenos Aires was bombed.

1954

- **July 14, Egypt:** Incendiary devices ignited in the U.S. Information Service (USIS) Libraries in Cairo and Alexandria. Egyptian authorities blamed the fires on the Israeli intelligence service.
- **July 15, Chile:** A bomb exploded in the Binational Center in Santiago causing minor damage. Binational Centers are autonomous, foreign institutions dedicated to the promotion of mutual understanding between the host country and the United States. English teaching is usually a major component of their cultural, educational, and information activities. Binational Centers often work in close cooperation with USIS posts overseas but are independent in their financial and administrative management.
- **December 23, Ecuador:** A bullet was fired through the bedroom door of a local employee of the USIS press section in Quito.

1955

- **June 28, Tunisia:** A powerful bomb exploded at the entrance of the USIS building in Tunis causing moderate damage.

1956

- **March 22, Cyprus:** A U.S.-owned car was firebombed in Kyrenia.
- **June 16, Cyprus:** A bomb intended for a British citizen detonated in a restaurant in the Greek section of Nicosia, killing U.S. Vice Consul William P. Boteler, and injuring three other American diplomats. Colonel Grivas, head of EOKA, immediately issued a statement denying a deliberate attempt to target American citizens. He further warned American officials, for their own safety, to avoid the establishments patronized by "our British enemy."

1957

- **July 30, Lebanon:** Bombs exploded at two USIS Libraries and the Voice of America studio in Beirut.
- **September 2, Jordan:** A bomb exploded outside the USIS building in Amman.
- **October 22, Vietnam:** A bomb exploded in the USIS Library in Saigon causing major property damage.
- **October 22, Vietnam:** Bombs exploded in front of a U.S. officer's quarters and under a bus filled with U.S. enlisted men. Both bombings injured 13 U.S. servicemen. Media reports indicated that the bombings were to protest the Colombo conference being held in Saigon.
- **December 13, Greece:** Three bombs severely damaged the USIS Library in Athens. Motive: Leftists targeting the U.S. and/or NATO or protesting the Cyprus debate taking place at the United Nations.

1958

- **January 27, Turkey:** A bomb was thrown at a book store in Ankara that was mistaken for the USIS library a block away.
- **June 26, Cuba:** Cuban rebels attacked a subsidiary of the Freeport Sulphur Company of New Orleans located in the northern province of Oriente. Ten Americans were kidnapped. The rebels put several demands on the U.S. government including stop military support for the Cuban government, forbidding Cuban planes to take on arms at GITMO, and recognition of rebel-held territory on Cuba. The U.S. announced that it would not give in to blackmail. By July 11, all the Americans had been released by the rebels without any ransom payments.
- **October 20, Cuba:** Cuban rebels kidnapped two Americans employed at the Texaco refinery in Santiago de Cuba. The U.S. ambassador informed the kidnappers that if the Americans were not released, the U.S. would renew shipments of arms to the Batista government. The Americans were released on October 23.

1959

- **January 18, Argentina:** A powerful bomb exploded in front of the USIS office in La Plata causing moderate damage. Motive: Peronist disapproval of President Frondizi's visit to the United States.
- **July, Vietnam:** Two U.S. advisors were the first Americans killed in a guerrilla attack 20 miles north of Saigon.

1960

- **December 25, Bolivia:** A bomb exploded at the residence of the U.S. Ambassador, Carl W. Strom.

1961

- **January 5, Bolivia:** Dynamite was thrown from a passing truck at the car of the U.S. Ambassador, which was parked outside the university in La Paz.
- **January 20, Algeria:** A small bomb detonated in front of the U.S. Consulate. An anonymous caller claimed the attack was in honor of President Kennedy who favored autonomy.

1962

- **October 27, Venezuela:** Four U.S.-owned electric power stations were bombed in the vicinity of Lake Maracaibo. Primary suspect was Army of Venezuelan Liberation.
- **November 2, Venezuela:** Bombs exploded at four pipes of the U.S.-operated pipeline installations in Puerto La Cruz causing moderate damage. Army of Venezuelan Liberation.

1963

- **November 27, Venezuela:** The U.S. Army Attache and Deputy Chief of the U.S. Military Mission in Caracas, Colonel James K. Chenault, was kidnapped by four members of the Armed Forces of National Liberation (FALN) outside his home. The group demanded the release of 70 political prisoners. The government gave into the demands and Col. Chenault was released six days later. The Armed Forces of National Liberation (FALN) was a pro-Castro terrorist group active in Venezuela in the 1960s.
- **December 7, Bolivia:** Bolivian tin miners kidnapped two U.S. Information Service officials and Peace Corps volunteer Robert Ferestrom during a strike. They were held hostage for 10 days. The hostages were held at a miners' union center in Catavi in retaliation for the government's arrest of two leftist union leaders.

1964

- **September 9, Uruguay:** The government broke diplomatic relations with Cuba on this day. The Tupamaros bombed the Montevideo offices of the

First National City bank, Moore-McCormick lines, and two U.S. diplomatic cars parked in front of the U.S. embassy.

- **October 3, Venezuela:** Lt. Col. Michael Smolen, Deputy U.S. Air Force Attache in Caracas, was kidnapped by two FALN terrorists in front of his home. The group claimed the attack was in protest of U.S. interference in Venezuelan affairs. A police dragnet found Smolen on October 12 and freed him. His kidnappers tried unsuccessfully to swap him for the life of a young Vietnamese man, Nguyen Van Troi, who was executed in Saigon — today Ho Chi Minh City — the capital of South Vietnam at the time, for attempting to assassinate the U.S. defense secretary.
- **November 3, Venezuela:** The FALN dynamited seven U.S. subsidiary-owned pumping stations and an oil pipeline in El Tigre.

1965

- **January 29, Canada:** Two U.S. jets (F-84s) being overhauled by Northwest Industries in Edmonton, Alberta were destroyed and a third was damaged when a left-wing group protesting the Vietnam War dynamited the planes; a security guard was killed during the incident.
- **February 9, Guatemala:** The Revolutionary Movement of the Thirteenth attempted to assassinate the chief of the U.S. military mission to Guatemala, Col. Harold Hauser.
- **May 6, Uruguay:** The Tupamaros bombed the offices of the All-American Cable and Western Telegraph.
- **May 18, Brazil:** A bomb was discovered in the U.S. Embassy.
- **June, Argentina:** U.S. Consul Temple Wanamaker was shot and seriously injured.
- **July 30, Brazil:** A small bomb exploded in front of the Bela Horizonte Binational Center.
- **July 31, Malaysia:** A bomb was found in front of the U.S. Consulate General–USIS building in Singapore.
- **August 27, Ecuador:** A bomb failed to explode in front of the Guayaquil Binational Center.
- **September 30, Brazil:** A small bomb exploded in the corridor outside the USIS and the American Consulate on the 12th floor of an office building in Belo Horizonte, causing minor damage. Another unexploded bomb was found nearby.
- **November 11, Peru:** A small bomb exploded in front of the Miraflores Binational Center causing minor damage. Protest was against the upcoming visit of Senator Robert F. Kennedy.

1966

- **March 26, Argentina:** Molotov cocktails were thrown at the Mendoza Binational Center causing minor damage. Leaflets found in the street protested the U.S. position on Vietnam.
- **May 16, Peru:** Molotov cocktails were thrown at the front entrance of the Miraflores Binational Center.
- **May 21, Turkey:** Two incendiary devices and a small bomb were detonated in front of the USIS office in Istanbul causing minor damage.
- **June 8, Brazil:** An unexploded incendiary device was found outside the Sao Paulo Binational Center.
- **June 12, Brazil:** A failed arson attack was directed at the Belo Horizonte Binational Center.
- **June 29, Brazil:** A small bomb exploded in front of the Brasilia USIS information center causing minor damage.
- **July 25, Brazil:** A bomb exploded inside an U.S. Agency for International Development (AID) building in Recife causing minor damage.
- **September 20, Italy:** A powerful bomb exploded outside the USIS Cultural Center in Rome causing minor damage.

1967

- **January 23, Uruguay:** Tupamaros bombed the U.S. Consulate in Montevideo.
- **January 26, South Vietnam:** A bomb was discovered in a USIS Cultural Center in Can Tho.
- **May 27, Lebanon:** A bomb exploded near the American Embassy in Beirut causing minor damage.
- **June 7, West Germany:** A small incendiary device was thrown at the Amerika Haus in Hamburg causing minor damage.
- **June 9, Dominican Republic:** A bomb was found inside the USIS library in Santo Domingo.
- **June 9, France:** An attempted assassination was carried out against the U.S. Ambassador Charles E. Bohlen.
- **June 10, Sudan:** Two bombs were thrown at the rear gate of the USIS building in Khartoum causing minor damage.
- **August 1, Brazil:** The U.S. Peace Corps office in Rio de Janeiro was bombed.
- **September 13, Hong Kong:** A small bomb was found outside the USIS Library.

- **September 27, Brazil:** A bomb exploded at the U.S. Embassy Air Attaché's home.
- **September 29, Israel:** An eight-pound bomb was found inside a briefcase left in the U.S. Cultural Center in Tel Aviv.
- **October 12, Dominican Republic:** A small bomb was found in the USIS Library in Santo Domingo.
- **December 13, Peru:** A Molotov cocktail was thrown through the window of the Trujillo Binational Center during a student protest against suspension of classes.
- **December 26, Peru:** A Molotov cocktail was found inside the entrance to the Lima Binational Center.

1968

- **February 9, Argentina:** Terrorists strafed the second floor of the U.S. Embassy residence with 15 rifle bullets from a passing vehicle.
- **February 12, Dominican Republic:** A small bomb was found in the USIS Lincoln Library in Santo Domingo.
- **February 13, Uruguay:** A Molotov cocktail was thrown outside the U.S. Labor Exhibit in Montevideo causing minor damage.
- **February 15, Dominican Republic:** A Molotov cocktail was thrown at the Santiago de Los Caballeros Binational Center.
- **February 16, Columbia:** A powerful bomb exploded on the U.S. Embassy grounds causing minor damage. Leaflets found near the attack site were pro-Viet Cong.
- **February 20, Chile:** A bomb exploded on the patio of the Santiago Binational Center causing moderate damage.
- **February 22, Ecuador:** A bomb exploded in the Quito Binational Center causing extensive damage.
- **March 8, Argentina:** The USIS Office in Rosario was strafed with machine-gun fire in the early morning house. A note left at the attack site was signed by the "Frente de Liberacion National del Vietnam del Sur."
- **March 12, Chile:** A small bomb exploded in the woman's restroom on the second floor of the U.S. Consulate outside the USIS offices in Santiago causing extensive property damage.
- **March 12, Guatemala:** A bomb was thrown over the wall surrounding the U.S. Marine Security Guards house in Guatemala City.
- **March 16, Chile:** A bomb exploded inside the U.S. Cultural Center in Santiago causing minor damage.

- **March 19, Brazil:** A bomb exploded in the USIS library in Sao Paulo causing moderate damage and injuring three Brazilians.
- **March 25, Spain:** A bomb exploded inside the Madrid Casa Americana (American House) causing extensive damage. One person was injured.
- **March 25, Spain:** A bomb exploded in the U.S. Embassy in Madrid causing moderate damage.
- **April 29, Brazil:** Molotov cocktail was thrown at the U.S. Consulate General in Recife causing minor damage.
- **April 29, Dominican Republic:** A small bomb was found in a bathroom at the Binational Center in Santiago de Los Cabelleros.
- **May 2, Uruguay:** An unexploded Molotov cocktail was found on the steps of the Binational Center in Montevideo.
- **May 24, Canada:** A small bomb damaged the entrance door of the U.S. Embassy in Quebec.
- **May 24, Belgium:** A Molotov cocktail was thrown against the wall of the USIS Library in Brussels causing minor damage.
- **July 20, Ecuador:** A small bomb exploded at the Quito home of the U.S. Public Affairs officer causing minor damage.
- **August 10, Turkey:** Two firebombs were thrown at the USIS office in Izmir causing minor damage.
- **August 18, Israel:** Fatah threw hand grenades in Jerusalem's Jewish section, injuring eight Israelis and two Americans.
- **August 21, Israel:** A Palestinian terrorist bomb exploded in the garden of the U.S. Consulate in East Jerusalem causing minor damage.
- **October 1, Argentina:** Two Molotov cocktails exploded outside of the U.S. Embassy in Buenos Aires. Pamphlets found nearby were signed by the "Movemento Peronista."
- **October 3, Argentina:** A bomb exploded next to the Binational Center building in Cordoba causing minor damage.
- **October 3, Argentina:** A bomb attempt took place at a USIA exhibit in Buenos Aires.
- **October 9, Argentina:** A bomb exploded at the Binational Center in Cordova causing minor damage.
- **October 9, Bolivia:** A bomb exploded at the entrance of the USIS building in La Paz.
- **October 14, Brazil:** A large bomb was discovered inside the gate of the Fortaleza Binational Center.
- **October 16, Argentina:** A bomb exploded inside the USIS Library in Buenos Aires causing minor damage.

- **October 27, Brazil:** A Sears store was bombed.
- **October 31, Ecuador:** A bomb was discovered at the Quito Binational center.
- **December 11, Ecuador**: A bomb was discovered at the Quito Binational center.

1969

- **January 8, West Germany:** An arson attack was carried out on the Amerika Haus Library in Frankfurt causing minor damage.
- **January 9, Thailand:** Shots were fired at a U.S. Bangkok Relay station vehicle.
- **January 11, Bolivia:** A bomb was thrown at the U.S. Consulate in Cochabamba causing minor damage.
- **February 17, Spain:** A USIS-supported facility in Valencia (North American Study Center) was bombed causing minor damage.
- **March 2, Australia:** Molotov cocktails were thrown at U.S. Consulate in Melbourne causing minor damage.
- **March 3, Ecuador:** Molotov cocktails were thrown at the U.S. Consulate General's office in Guayaquil causing minor damage.
- **March 9, West Germany:** Molotov cocktails were thrown at the American Memorial Library in Berlin causing minor damage.
- **March 12, West Germany:** A Molotov cocktail was thrown at the Amerika Haus in Munich causing minor damage.
- **April 8, Peru:** Two Molotov cocktails were thrown at the front door of the USIS Building in Lima causing minor damage.
- **May 30, Bolivia:** A small bomb was thrown from a passing car at the wall of the Bolivian-American Center causing moderate to extensive damage.
- **June 11, Brazil:** A powerful bomb was discovered inside the USIS building in Fortaleza. It could have destroyed the two-story building.
- **June 19, Argentina:** A bomb was thrown at the USIS building in Rosario as students burned the U.S. flag.
- **June 20, Uruguay:** Tupamaros dressed in police uniforms attacked a General Motors plant in Montevideo, and as a result of the fire, damage was estimated at $1 million. The attack took place just after New York Governor Nelson Rockefeller's visit.
- **June 26, Argentina:** Fourteen Rockefeller-owned Minimax supermarkets were bombed shortly after New York Governor Nelson Rockefeller arrived in Buenos Aires. Seven stores were destroyed. Damage was estimated at $3 million.

- **June 27, Uruguay:** Tupamaros attacked a General Motors plant in Penarol and stole some money.
- **July 17, India:** Small bombs exploded in the USIS reading room in the U.S. Consulate in Calcutta. Two minor injuries occurred.
- **July 19, Sudan:** A bomb exploded at the USIS library in Khartoum causing minor damage.
- **July 22, Philippines:** Two grenades were thrown at the USIS Library and Consulate building in Manila, killing a Filipino.
- **July 23, Greece:** A small bomb was discovered in the USIS library in Athens.
- **July 30, Japan:** A Japanese youth attempted to assassinate the U.S. Ambassador Armin H. Meyer as he accompanied the Secretary of State William Rogers at Tokyo International Airport. The youth was armed with a knife.
- **August 9, Greece:** A bomb exploded at an Olympic Airlines office in Athens, injuring 2 American tourists.
- **August 11, India:** Two small bombs were thrown at the USIS office in Calcutta during a student demonstration causing minor damage.
- **August 29, Italy:** TWA Flight 840 was hijacked by PFLP terrorists out of Rome. The hijackers said they were the "Che Guevara Commando Unit of the PFLP." They read a statement: "We have kidnapped this American plane because Israel is a colony of America and the Americans are giving the Israelis Phantom jets." Passengers were eventually taken off the plane in Syria; the plane was then damaged with explosives, but not completely destroyed. Most of the passengers and crew members were Americans. They were all eventually released unharmed.
- **September 3, Japan:** Two Molotov cocktails were thrown at the U.S. Embassy in Tokyo causing minor damage.
- **September 4, Brazil:** The U.S. Ambassador, Charles B. Elbrick, was kidnapped from his vehicle in Rio de Janeiro by the Revolutionary Movement October 8 (MR-8) and the National Liberation Action. The demands were the release of 15 imprisoned comrades and the publication of a three-page communiqué. A captured terrorist later told the police that the group had placed a female spy in the military intelligence agency to collect information about the Ambassador's travel habits. The Ambassador was eventually released unharmed. Fernando Gabeira, one of the MR-8 leaders who planned the kidnapping, later wrote a book about the kidnapping entitled "O que é isso, companheiro?" (What is this, comrade?) in 1979. This book was used as the basis for the movie on the kidnapping *Four Days in September*.

- **September 9, Argentina:** Several bombs and Molotov cocktails were thrown at the USIS building in Rosario during a student demonstration causing minor to moderate damage.
- **September 9, Ethiopia:** The U.S. Consul General in Asmara, Murray E. Jackson, was kidnapped from his car along with his driver by the Eritrean Liberation Front (ELF). He and a British businessman were held for two hours and then released. There were no ransom demands. The Consul had to sign a paper stating that he listened to the group's grievances.
- **September 12, Jordan:** A bomb exploded on the porch of the home of the U.S. Assistant Army Attache in Amman causing minor damage.
- **September 13, Italy:** Two Molotov cocktails were thrown at the entrance of the U.S. Consul General in Palermo causing minor damage.
- **September 27, Bolivia:** A bomb was thrown in front of the U.S. Consul General's home in La Paz.
- **September 29, Brazil:** Three terrorists robbed an American store. They then set fire to the store causing about $22,000 in damage.
- **October 1, Canada:** A Molotov cocktail was thrown at the entrance of the U.S. Consulate in Vancouver.
- **October 6, Argentina:** Bombs damaged offices of the First National City Bank, Pepsi-Cola, Squibb, and Dunlop tires in Cordova.
- **October 6, Argentina:** The San Miguel de Tucuman offices of IBM and General Electric were damaged by bombs.
- **October 7, Colombia:** Bombs exploded on the porch of the Bucaramanga Binational Center causing minor damage.
- **October 7, Argentina:** A Molotov cocktail was thrown at the USIS Library in Buenos Aires.
- **October 8, Argentina:** Bombs damaged a branch of the Bank of Boston in Buenos Aires and the Santa Fe office of Remington RAND.
- **October 10, Peru:** A bomb exploded in the Arequipa Binational Center causing extensive damage.
- **October 23, Peru:** Five Molotov cocktails were thrown at the U.S. Embassy in Lima.
- **October 25, Bolivia:** A bomb exploded in front of the U.S. Peace Corps headquarters in La Paz causing minor damage.
- **October 26, Lebanon:** A bomb exploded under the car of the U.S. Embassy Regional Communications officer in Beirut.
- **November 1, Japan:** A bomb was discovered near the reception desk of the U.S. Cultural Center in Tokyo.

- **November 9, Bolivia:** A bomb was thrown at the La Paz Binational Center causing no damage.
- **November 17, Japan:** A bomb was found near the guard box of the U.S. Consulate in Yokohama.
- **November 19, Ecuador:** Molotov cocktails were thrown at the Binational Center in Quito during a student demonstration.
- **November 20, Argentina:** Bombs were detonated at the office of 9 American companies in Buenos Aires by Peronist Armed Forces.
- **November 27, Greece:** Terrorists threw hand grenades into the Athens office of El Al, killing a Greek child and injuring three Americans.
- **December 5, Argentina:** A large bomb exploded in the restroom of the Binational Center in Rosario.
- **December 5, West Germany:** Two Molotov cocktails were thrown at the Amerika Haus in Frankfurt.
- **December 12, West Germany:** An incendiary device was discovered in the Amerika Haus in West Berlin.
- **December 13, West Germany:** A bomb exploded outside a U.S. Officer's club causing minor damage.
- **December 20, Turkey:** A small bomb exploded outside the USIS office in Ankara.
- **December 21, Greece:** PFLP terrorists were arrested while trying to board a TWA plane flying from Tel Aviv to Athens to New York. They were planning to hijack the aircraft.
- **December 29, Philippines:** Philippine nationalists attempted to assassinate Vice-President Spiro Agnew by throwing a bomb at his car.

D. Lethal Terrorist Attacks Against Americans Overseas from 1960 to 1980

1960

- **February 17, South Vietnam:** USN Lt. Commander George Wood Alexander of the MAAG was killed when his fixed wing aircraft was shot down. In addition, USN Lt. Commander Roger Hugh Mullins and USN Chief Aviation Electronics Technician William Wallace Newton were also killed. (4)

Note: Bracketed numbers indicate the number of Americans killed in the attacks.

1961

- **December 22, South Vietnam:** U.S. Army SP/4 James Thomas Davis was shot and killed in Cau Xang by small-arms fire. Davis was the first battlefield fatality of the Vietnam War. He was killed on a road near the old French Garrison of Cau Xang. He had been assigned to the 3rd Radio Research Unit at Tan Son Nhut Air Base near Saigon, along with 92 other members of his unit. Davis Station in Saigon was named after him. President Lyndon Johnson later termed Davis "the first American to fall in the defense of our freedom in Vietnam."

1964

- **November, Stanleyville, Republic of the Congo:** Maoist-inspired militants calling themselves "Simbas" rounded up the remaining white population of Stanleyville and its environs. The whites were held hostage in the Victoria Hotel in the city and were to be used as bargaining tools with Patrice Lumumba's Armée Nationale Congolaise (ANC). The United States and Belgium tried to negotiate with the rebels. However, in order to recover the hostages, Belgian parachute troops were flown to the Congo in an American aircraft to intervene. On November 24, as part of Operation Dragon Rouge, Belgian paratroopers landed in Stanleyville and quickly secured the hostages. In total, around 70 hostages and 1,000 Congolese civilians were killed but the majority were evacuated. Two American missionaries were among the slain: Dr. Paul Carlson and Phyliss Rine. Operation Dragon Rouge was the most ambitious peacetime military operation ever performed by the government of the United States up to that time. (2)

1965

- **March 30, South Vietnam:** The Viet Cong detonated a car-bomb outside the U.S. Embassy, killing one female embassy employee (Barbara A. Robbins), U.S. Navy enlisted man SK2 Manolito W. Castillo, 19 Vietnamese, and injuring 183 others. (2)

1966

- **August 4, Columbia:** A powerful bomb exploded in a ground floor ladies' room of the Bogota Binational Center, killing an American citizen (Robert Raymond Smetek) and two Columbians. Two other Americans (Thomas and Carolyn Withers) were injured. The attack was linked to the President's inauguration. The pro-Chinese Communist Party of Columbia, Marxist–Leninist claimed responsibility for the act. (1)

1967

- **Dominican Republic:** An American teacher was killed by a Dominican terrorist. Subsequent events led to the deployment of U.S. Marines in the country. (1)

U.S. Government Terrorism Database Starts

1968

- **January 16, Guatemala:** The Commander of the U.S. Military Advisory Group (MAAG) in Guatemala (Col. John D. Webber) and the Head of the Naval Section in the MAAG (Lt. Cdr. Ernest A. Munro) were assassinated when terrorists strafed their vehicle as they were returning from lunch. Two U.S. military personnel were also wounded in the attack. The Rebel Armed Forces claimed responsibility for the attack, citing U.S. creation of Guatemalan Army assassination squads and revenge for the January 12 killing of Rogelia Cruz Martinez, Miss Guatemala of 1950, by the right-wing group "La Mano Blanco." (2)
- **August 28, Guatemala:** The U.S. Ambassador, John Gordon Main, was killed when a kidnapping attempt by the Rebel Armed Forces (FAR) failed. Main's car was blocked by two terrorist vehicles in downtown Guatemala City and the ambassador tried to run away. FAR claimed that it wanted to kidnap the ambassador and demand the release of a FAR leader. (1)
- **October 12, Brazil:** U.S. Army Captain Charles R. Chandler was shot and killed outside his home in Sao Paolo by the Popular Revolutionary Vanguard. Pamphlets left at the scene claimed that Captain Chandler was a Vietnam war criminal who had been sent to Brazil to train war criminals. (1)

1969

- **December 27, West Bank:** Leon Holtz, 48, a tourist from Brooklyn, New York, was killed when PLO terrorists fired shots at a tourist bus near Hebron. (1)

1970

- **January 11, Ethiopia:** An American soldier serving in Ethiopia was shot and killed in a tavern in Asmara. The Eritrean Liberation Front (ELF) was suspected. (1)
- **February 21, Switzerland:** Fifteen minutes after Swissair Flight 330 left Zurich airport, a bomb exploded on board the plane forcing it to crash, killing

everyone on the plane. The passenger list included six Americans and 14 Israelis. In Beirut, Lebanon, a spokesman for Ahmed Jabril's Popular Front for the Liberation of Palestine–General Command (PFPL-GC) claimed responsibility. Worldwide condemnation of the attack forced the group to withdraw its claim of responsibility. The Americans killed were Melvin Meyerson, Thomas Lingafelter, S. Silvershots and his wife, Dr. and Mrs. Ware, and Dr. and Mrs. Weinermann. (6)

- **February 23, West Bank:** Terrorists fired on a tourist bus in Halhul, killing one American, Barbara Ertle, wife of Reverend Theodore Ertle, of Michigan and wounding two other Americans. Secular Palestinian terrorists were the primary suspect. (1)
- **April 2, Philippines:** Two American servicemen at Clark Air Force base were kidnapped by elements of the New People's Army (NPA) outside the air base. On April 14, 1970, the bodies of the two Americans were found in a shallow grave. (2)
- **May 10, Jordan:** Major Bob Perry, U.S. Military Attache, was assassinated in his home in Amman in front of his wife and kids. On June 10, the PFLP claimed responsibility for murdering Major Perry. (1)
- **July 31, Uruguay:** Daniel A. Mitrione, a Public Safety Advisor with the U.S. Agency for International Development (USAID) was kidnapped in Montevideo by the Tupamaros guerrilla group. Mitrione was killed on August 10, 1970 when a demand to release 115 imprisoned Tupamaros was not met. (1)

1971

- **September 26, Phnom Penh, Cambodia:** Two U.S. Embassy personnel were killed — Marine Security Guard Charles W. Tuberville, and a U.S. Army master sergeant when a bomb was thrown onto a softball field where a game was being played. No claim of responsibility was made. (2)

1972

- **January 16, Gaza Strip, Occupied Territories:** An American nurse was killed, and several people were injured when terrorists opened fire on their car. Secular Palestinian terrorists were the primary suspect. (1)
- **May 8, Austria:** Five terrorists from the Black September Organization (BSO) hijacked a Sabena flight from Vienna–Athens–Tel Aviv route and forced the plane to land at the Lod Airport in Israel. The terrorists demanded the release of 317 fedayeen prisoners, or they would blow up the plane and all aboard. Israeli security forces stormed the plane killing three of the

terrorists. Five passengers were injured, one of them an American was fatally wounded. The two other hijackers received life sentences. (1)

- **May 11, West Germany:** Three homemade pipe bombs exploded at the headquarters of the 5th U.S. Army Corps in Frankfurt, killing one American army officer and injuring 13 other Americans. The Red Army Faction claimed responsibility. 1st Lt. Paul A. Bloomquist was killed. (1)
- **May 24, West Germany:** Two car bombs with stolen U.S. military license plates exploded outside the mess hall and computer center of the European headquarters of the U.S. Army in Heidelberg. Three American servicemen, U.S. Army Captain Clyde R. Bonner, U.S. Army Specialist Ronald A. Woodward, and U.S. Army Specialist Charles Peck were killed, and five Americans were injured. The Red Army Faction claimed responsibility. (3)
- **May 30, Israel:** Three members of the Japanese Red Army (JRA) fired machine guns and threw grenades at passengers arriving from an Air France flight at Lod Airport. Among the 28 killed were two terrorists and 17 Puerto Rican Catholic pilgrims — Reverend Angel Berganzo, Carmela Cintrón, Carmen E. Crespo, Vírgen Flores, Esther González, Blanca González de Pérez, Carmen Guzmán, Eugenia López, Enrique Martínez Rivera, Vasthy Zila Morales de Vega, José M. Otero Adorno, Antonio Pacheco, Juan Padilla, Consorcia Rodríguez, José A. Rodríguez, Antonio Rodríguez Morales, Carmelo Calderón Molina. (17)
- **September 5, Germany:** During the Olympic Games in Munich, Black September, a front for Fatah, took hostage 11 members of the Israeli Olympic team. Nine athletes were killed including the weightlifter David Berger, an American Israeli from Cleveland, Ohio. (1)
- **December 8, Australia:** An American businessman was killed when a bomb exploded in an automobile parked outside a Serbian Orthodox church in Brisbane. The primary suspect was UDBA, the Yugoslav secret police. (1)

1973

- **March 1, Sudan:** Eight terrorists from the Black September Organization (BSO) seized the Saudi Arabian Embassy in Khartoum during a diplomatic reception. The terrorists demanded the release of 60 Palestinians held in Jordan, all Arab women detained in Israel, Sirhan B. Sirhan (assassin of Senator Robert F. Kennedy), and imprisoned members of the Red Army Faction terrorist group in Germany. On March 2, after negotiations failed, the BSO terrorists executed U.S. Ambassador Cleo Noel, U.S. Deputy Chief of Mission George C. Moore, and the Belgian charge who were among the hostages. The terrorists surrendered the next day. They were sentenced by the Khartoum government to life sentences, but the Sudanese President Numaryi later reduced the sentence to seven years and had the terrorists deported to Egypt. President Sadat reportedly released them to the PLO. (2)

- **June 2, Iran:** Two gunmen shot and killed a U.S. military advisor, Lt. Col. Lewis Hawkins, working for the U.S. Army Military Aid and Assistance Group in Tehran. The assailants were believed to members of the People's Mujahedeen of Iran or the Mojahedin-e-Khalq (MEK). (1)

- **August 5, Greece:** Two terrorists claiming to be from the "Seventh Suicide Squad," but belonging to the Ahman Abd-Al Ghaffur's group of Fatah dissidents opened fire with machine guns and hand grenades on passengers waiting to board a TWA flight in Athens. (It was later learned that they were ordered to attack the TWA flight to Tel Aviv, but the passengers were already on board the plane.) Among the five people killed were three Americans: Elbert Kersing, Jeanne Salandri, and Laura Haack. A total of 55 other people were wounded, and 35 people were seized as hostages. The two terrorists eventually surrendered to the Greek police and were expelled to Libya on May 5, 1974. (3)

- **October 18, Lebanon:** Five members of the Lebanese Socialist Revolutionary Organization stormed the Bank of America in Beirut and took 39 hostages. The group made several demands including that the bank pay them $10 million dollars to help "finance the Arab war effort against Israel" and the Lebanese government release all fedayeen guerrillas. When the government refused their demands, the terrorists killed one of the hostages, a Lebanese American citizen (John Crawford Maxwell). Two of the terrorists were killed when police stormed the bank, the other two were arrested. (1)

- **November 22, Argentina:** John Swint, a U.S. citizen who was the general manager of Transax (a transmission and axle plant owned by the Ford Motor Company) and two of his bodyguards were shot and killed in Cordoba in an ambush by a group of 15 men. The People's Revolutionary Army was responsible. (1)

- **December 17, Italy:** After police discovered weapons in the luggage of an Arab traveler at Rome's Fiumicino airport, four other Arabs opened fire in the crowded transit lounge. The gunmen said that they belonged to the Arab Nationalist Youth Organization for the Liberation of Palestine. The terrorists took several hostages and with the police in tow, came upon Pan American flight 110 that was loading passengers for a flight to Beirut. The terrorists threw hand grenades into the plane killing 29 passengers, including 14 American employees of the Arab–American Oil Company ARAMCO:

W. Stoelzel, Margaret Echmann, R. E. Ghormley, C. P. Heywood, Mrs. Alex Szostek, Clarence Hilderbrand, Mrs. Robert Oertley, J. Leadbeater, D. R. Kirby, Julia Hunt, W. B. Turner, Mr. Wamp, Al Dowell, and Dr. C. B. Haggard. The Pan Am captain's wife, Bonnie Erbeck, and a Pan Am purser Diane Perez were also killed in the attack. The terrorists, with their hostages, then hijacked a Lufthansa aircraft to Athens and eventually flew to Kuwait where they surrendered to Kuwaiti authorities and released their hostages after receiving a safe conduct guarantee. On March 2, 1974, the terrorists were flown from Kuwait to Cairo, where they were to be tried by the Palestine Liberation Organization, but Egyptian authorities did not release them. The five terrorists were flown to Tunis in response to the demands of four terrorists who hijacked a British plane on November 22, 1974. They went to Libya in December with the second group of hijackers and two terrorists released by the Netherlands. Libya reportedly imprisoned all 11, but they later appeared to have been freed. (14)

1974

- **April 13, Philippines:** Three U.S. Navy officers (Capt. Thomas J. Mitchell, Cmdr. Leland R. Dobler, and Lt. Charles H. Jeffries) were shot and killed near the Subic Bay by the New People's Army (NPA). (3)
- **August 19, Cyprus:** U.S. Ambassador Rodger P. Davies and a female Foreign Service National (FSN) embassy secretary were shot and killed in Nicosia by a Greek Cypriot militant sniper during an anti-American protest at the embassy. The sniper fired at the ambassador's office. Greek Cypriot demonstrators were protesting what they believed was a pro-Turkish policy of the U.S. in the Greek–Turkish dispute. They were angry that the U.S. did not stop the July invasion of Cyprus by Turkish forces. The right-wing paramilitary EOKA-B was responsible. (1)
- **September 8, Greece:** The pilot of TWA flight from Tel Aviv to New York radioed that he was having trouble with one engine. The plane went into a deep-nose dive and crashed into the Ionian Sea. All 88 passengers, including 17 Americans were killed. On January 11, 1975, investigators from the U.S. and Britain announced that tests of some debris from the aircraft conclusively showed that a high explosive had gone off in the rear cargo compartment of the plane. The Organization of Arab Nationalist Youth for the Liberation of Palestine issued a press statement in Beirut stating that a member of their organization exploded a bomb he was carrying around his waist. First suicide attack? Among the Americans killed were Katherine Hadley Michel and son Jeremiah Michel, Frederick and Margaret Hare, Seldon Bard and son Eitan

Bard, Dr. and Mrs. Stohlman, Don H. Holliday, Jon L. Cheshire and Ralph H. Bosh. (17)

1975

- **February 26, Argentina:** U.S. Consular Agent John P. Egan, was kidnapped by the Montoneros guerrilla group in Cordoba. He was killed 48 hours later when the government refused the terrorists' demand for the release of four of its imprisoned comrades. (1)
- **May 21, Iran:** U.S. Air Force officers Col. Paul Shaffer and Lt. Col. Jack Turner were shot and killed in Tehran on their way to work. The People's Mujahedeen of Iran or the Mojahedin-e-Khalq (MEK) claimed responsibility for the attack. (2)
- **June 25, Honduras — Los Horcones Ranch:** Several religious leaders and students were killed in what is known as the Los Horcones Massacre. They were killed by the U.S.-trained and -funded Honduran military. Among those killed was Father Michael Jerome Cypher (Padre Casimiro), a 35-year-old priest visiting from Medford, Wisconsin, United States who was tortured to death during an interrogation. (1)
- **November 21, Israel:** Michael Nadler, an American Israeli from Miami Beach, Florida, was killed when axe-wielding terrorists from the Democrat Front for the Liberation of Palestine, a PLO faction, attacked students in the Golan Heights. (1)
- **December 23, Greece:** CIA station chief Richard Welch was shot and killed outside his home in Athens. A previously unknown group called the Revolutionary Organization 17 November claimed credit for the attack. (1)

1976

- **June 16, Lebanon:** U.S. Ambassador to Lebanon Francis E. Meloy, Jr., and U.S. Embassy Economic Counselor Robert O. Waring, and their Lebanese driver were shot and killed at a roadblock in Beirut by unidentified gunmen. PFLP was responsible. (2)
- **August 11, Turkey:** Two terrorists from the Popular Front for the Liberation of Palestine (PFLP) attacked the passengers preparing to board an El Al aircraft at Yesilkoy airport (now Ataturk airport) in Istanbul. Four persons, including one American (Harold Rosenthal, an aide to U.S. Senator Jacob Javits) were killed in the attack. The terrorists were caught and sentenced to life imprisonment. (1)
- **August 28, Iran:** Three American officials of Rockwell International (William C. Cottrell, Robert R. Krongard, and Donald G. Smith) were

assassinated in Tehran as they were being driven to work at an Iranian Air Force installation. The Iranian People's Struggle (Mojahedin-e-Khalq) claimed responsibility. (3)

1977

- **January 20, Mexico:** Mitchel Andreski, President of the Duraflex Corporation was shot and killed in Mexico City by members of the 23rd of September Armed Communist League (LC-23). (1)
- **March 27, Ethiopia:** American missionary Don McClure was shot and killed outside his home in Gode by suspected Ogaden National Liberation Front (ONLF) rebels. (1)
- **April, Zaire:** American missionary Dr. Glen Eschtruth was killed by suspected Front for the National Liberation of the Congo (FNLC) rebels. (1)
- **November 29, Indonesia:** George Pernicone, an American businessman from Bechtel Corporation, was shot and killed in Sumatra by suspected Front for the Liberation of Aceh rebels who then left pamphlets warning Americans and other foreigners to leave the country. (1)
- **December 2, Argentina:** A U.S. businessman from Chrysler and his two bodyguards were shot and killed in Buenos Aires while driving in his car. The primary suspect was the Montoneros. (1)
- **December 4, Malaysia:** Malaysian Airline System Flight 653 which was hijacked in Kuala Lumpur 10 minutes after takeoff crashed while approaching to land in Singapore. Among the 93 passengers killed, one was an American (Donald O. Hoerr). It was the first fatal air crash for Malaysia Airlines. The cockpit voice recorder indicates that the pilot and co-pilot were shot and killed by one or more hijackers. The circumstances in which the hijacking and subsequent crash occurred remains unsolved. The primary suspect was the Japanese Red Army. (1)

1978

- **March 11, Israel:** Gail Rubin, niece of U.S. Senator Abraham Ribicoff, was among 38 people shot to death by PLO terrorists on an Israeli beach in Tel Aviv. (1)
- **June 3, Jerusalem, occupied territory:** A bomb exploded inside a city bus in Jerusalem, killing six people, including American Richard Fishman, a medical student from Maryland. Fatah was responsible. (1)
- **June 15, Rhodesia (now Zimbabwe):** American evangelist Archie Dunaway was bayoneted to death at the Sanyati Mission Hospital in Sanyati by nationalist guerrillas. The primary suspects were the Zimbabwe African National Liberation Army and the Zimbabwe People's Revolutionary Army. (1)

- **September 5, Jerusalem:** Stephen Michael Hilmes, a U.S. bomb expert, died from injuries when a bomb exploded in the city. (1)
- **December 23, Iran:** Texaco executive Paul Grimm, who was working for an Iranian oil company, was shot and killed in Ahwaz as his car slowed down at an intersection. The Mojahedin-e-Khalq claimed responsibility. (1)

1979

- **January 14, Iran:** Martin Berkowitz, a former U.S. Air Force officer working for an American construction company, was stabbed to death in his home in Kerman. The words "go back to your own country" were scrawled on the wall of his home. The primary suspect was the Iranian Mojahedin-e-Khalq. (1)
- **February 14, Afghanistan:** U.S. Ambassador Adolph Dubs, was kidnapped by jihadist terrorists in Kabul, who were opposed to the current government. The ambassador was killed after the Afghan police stormed the hotel room where the ambassador was being held by his captives. The identity and aims of the militants who kidnapped Dubs remain unknown. Soviet involvement has been speculated. Forensic and other evidence concerning this incident was not shared with the U.S. (1)
- **April 12, Turkey:** U.S. Air Force noncommissioned officer Master Sergeant Edward A. Claypool was shot and killed in Izmir by the Turkish People's Liberation Party/Front (DHKP/C). (1)
- **April 30, Rhodesia (now Zimbabwe):** Michael Lewy, an American volunteer working at a ranch in the Southwestern Bikita district was shot and killed in a guerrilla ambush. Primary suspects: Zimbabwe African National Liberation Army or the Zimbabwe People's Revolutionary Army. (1)
- **May 11, Turkey:** As U.S. Army personnel were waiting for a bus in front of a transient hotel in Istanbul for U.S. military personnel, two gunmen opened fire on the soldiers. One soldier was killed (Cpl. Thomas Mosley) and another wounded. The Marxist–Leninist Armed Propaganda Unit (MLAPU) claimed responsibility for the attack. (1)
- **June 2, Turkey:** David Goodman, an American teacher at a private English-language school in Adana, was shot and killed as he opened the door of his apartment in response to a knock by two unidentified gunmen. The Turkish People's Liberation Party/Front (DHKP/C) claimed responsibility. (1)
- **September 23, El Salvador:** Three Americans — William Kong, Edwin Mendoza, and Moises Magana — were killed in San Salvador when they was caught-up in a guerrilla attack against the Armed Forces Instruction Center located on the grounds of the President's residence. (3)

- **November 21, Pakistan:** A mob, enraged by a radio report claiming that the United States had bombed the Masjid al-Haram, Islam's holy site at Mecca, stormed the U.S. Embassy in Islamabad and burned it to the ground. The U.S. diplomats survived by hiding in a reinforced area, although Marine Security Guard Corporal Steven Crowley, 20, Army Warrant Officer Bryan Ellis, 30, and two Pakistan staff members were killed in the attack. These deaths are not counted in the chronology as the deaths were caused by a mob and not terrorists.
- **December 14, Turkey:** Four Americans (Sgt. James Smith and three Defense Department contractors from Boeing Services International -Jim Clark, Elmer Cooper, and Robert Frantz) were shot and killed in Istanbul after returning from work. As a U.S. military minibus carrying the Americans stopped at their bus stop, terrorists ordered them off the bus and opened fire on them when they attempted to flee. The Marxist–Leninist Armed Propaganda Unit (MLAPU) claimed responsibility. (4)
- **December 17, Philippines:** An American businessman, Jeremy Ladd Cross, was shot and killed by two unidentified men on motorcycles as he and his Filipino wife were leaving their offices in Manila. The primary suspect was a Sparrow Unit of the New People's Army. (1)

1980

- **March 3, San Salvador, El Salvador:** American citizen Rogelio J. Alvarez was found strangled near the University of Central America. Political violence was suspected, but perpetrators were unknown. (1)
- **April 10, Rome, Italy:** A double bombing damaged the Turkish Airlines and Tourist Office. Two men, one an American (Dante Sena), were killed in the explosion. The Armenian Secret Army for the Liberation of Armenia claimed responsibility. (1)
- **April 16, Istanbul, Turkey:** Sam Novello, a U.S. Navy Chief Petty Officer, and a Turkish friend were shot and killed by two gunmen as they left Novello's home and were about to enter his truck. The Marxist–Leninist Armed Propaganda Unit (MLAPU) claimed responsibility for the attack. (1)
- **May 2, Hebron:** West Bank. Eli Haze'ev, an American Israeli from Alexandria, Virginia, was killed in a PLO attack on Jewish worshippers walking home from a synagogue in Hebron. (1)
- **August 7, Guatemala:** A group of unidentified gunmen shot and killed American George Frank Rials, an overseer for the U.S. Nello L Teer Company, which was building roads in the jungles for Petroleum exploitation. (1)

- **September 12, Manila, Philippines:** Six bombs exploded in various parts of the city resulting in the death of an American (Annie Kuzmak). A group called the May 1 Sandigan of the April 6 Liberation Movement claimed responsibility. (1)
- **November 15, Adana, Turkey:** As two U.S. Air Force Senior Airmen were backing out of the driveway on their way to work, two unidentified gunmen approached the front of the car. One of the men pulled out a gun and shot and killed the driver (Sgt. William C. Herrington). The other airman got out of the car on the passenger's side and escaped unharmed. The Marxist–Leninist Armed Propaganda Unit (MLAPU) claimed responsibility for the attack. (1)
- **December 2, El Salvador:** Three nuns and a Catholic lay social worker, all U.S. citizens, were reported missing on their way home from the airport. Their bodies were later found in a grave, some 30 miles from the capital San Salvador. They had been shot. The victims had been previously threatened by right-wing elements. Five Salvadorian National Guard members were later found guilty for the murders. The dead Americans were Ita Ford, Maura Clarke, Dorothy Kazel, and Jean Donovan. (4)
- **December 7, Guatemala City, Guatemala:** Clifford Bevins, a U.S. businessman, president of the Guatemalan subsidiary of Goodyear Tire and Rubber Company was kidnapped from his home. The kidnappers demanded ransom and denounced the U.S. government and U.S. business support of leftists. The businessman's body was found outside of Guatemala City in mid-August 1981. He had been shot in the head. Right wing elements were responsible. (1)
- **December 17, San Salvador, El Salvador:** A terrorist shot and killed Thomas Bracken, an American consultant to El Salvador's National Police, in San Salvador. The primary suspects were left-wing terrorists. (1)
- **December 31, Nairobi, Kenya:** A bomb exploded during a New Year Eve's celebration at the Norfolk hotel, a five-star hotel owned by Jack Block, an Israeli citizen. Sixteen people died, including Kenneth Moyers, an American who was on a business trip for the Allied Signal Corporation. Eight Americans were injured. Damage was estimated at $3.4 million. The bomber was identified as Qaddura Muhammad abd-al-Hamid, a Moroccan and PFLP member. The bombing was in retaliation for the Kenyan government's aid to Israel in arresting two German members of the PFLP in 1976 who intended to fire a SA-7 missile at an El Al plane out of Nairobi airport. (1)

E. Chronology of Lethal Terrorist Attacks in the United States from the Johnson to the Carter Administrations — 1963–1980

JOHNSON (16 — 1 law enforcement officer)

- **June 12, 1963:** Jackson, Mississippi: NAACP organizer Medgar Evers was killed in front of his Mississippi home by a member of the Ku Klux Klan. (1)
- **September 16, 1963:** Birmingham, Alabama: 16th Street Baptist Church bombing. A member of the Ku Klux Klan bombed a Church in Birmingham, Alabama, killing four girls. (4)
- **June 21, 1964:** Philadelphia, Mississippi: Three civil rights workers were murdered in Philadelphia, Mississippi by the Ku Klux Klan. (3)
- **February 21, 1965:** New York City, New York: Malcolm X fatally shot. (1)
- **March 25, 1965:** Montgomery, Alabama: The Ku Klux Klan murdered Viola Liuzzo, a Southern raised white mother of five who was visiting Alabama from her home in Detroit to attend a civil rights march. At the time of her murder, Liuzzo was transporting Civil Rights Marchers. (1)
- **January 10, 1966:** Hattiesburg, Mississippi: Vernon Dahmer died in the firebombing of his own home in Mississippi at the hands of the Ku Klux Klan. (1)
- **October 17, 1967:** Oakland, California: Police officer John Frey was shot to death in an altercation with Huey P. Newton during a traffic stop. In the stop, Newton and backup officer Herbert Heanes also suffered gunshot wounds. Newton was convicted of voluntary manslaughter at trial. This incident gained the Black Panther party even wider recognition by the radical American left, and a "Free Huey" campaign ensued. (1)
- **April 4, 1968:** Memphis, Tennessee: Martin Luther King Jr. was shot and killed by James Earl Ray. (1)
- **June 5, 1968:** Los Angeles, California: Senator Robert F. Kennedy, while campaigning during the 1968 United States Presidential election, was shot to death by Palestinian Sirhan B. Sirhan in the kitchen of the Ambassador Hotel in Los Angeles. (1)
- **January 14, 1969:** Los Angeles, California: The Black Panther Los Angeles chapter gets into a shootout with members of a competing organization, and two Panthers were killed. (2)

NIXON (47 — 28 law enforcement officers)

- **May 1969:** Los Angeles, California: Two more southern California Panthers were killed in violent disputes with competing organization members. (2)

- **May 21, 1969:** Middlefield, Connecticut: Three members of the Black Panthers New Haven chapter tortured and murdered Alex Rackley, a 19-year-old member of the New York chapter, because they suspected him of being a police informant. (1)
- **November 14, 1969:** Chicago, Illinois: Officer John J. Gilhooly and Officer Frank G. Rappaport were ambushed by a member of the Black Panthers on a false call of a "man with a gun." The suspect was later shot and killed by other officers. (2)
- **March 29, 1969:** Detroit, Michigan: A gun battle occurred in a church following a meeting of a black separatist group, the Republic of New Africa; one policeman was killed, one was wounded; four blacks were wounded. (1)
- **February 18, 1970:** San Francisco, California: Sergeant Brian McDonnell succumbed to wounds sustained two days earlier when a bomb exploded in the Park Police Station. Although Sergeant McDonnell's murder was never solved, it is believed the bomb was set by members of the domestic terrorist group Weather Underground. (1)
- **March 5, 1970:** Puerto Rico: The Commandos of Armed Liberation killed one U.S. Marine in retaliation for the murder of Antonia Martinez. (1)
- **April 24, 1970:** Baltimore, Maryland: Baltimore City Police Department Officer Donald Sager was shot and killed and his partner was seriously wounded as they sat in their patrol car writing a report. Three men, members of the Black Panthers, walked up behind the patrol car and opened fire with automatic handguns. (1)
- **August 7, 1970:** San Rafael, California: Jonathan Jackson brought guns into Superior Court Judge Haley's courtroom, where San Quentin inmate James McClain was on trial. McClain was freed along with two other San Quentin inmates, Black Panther members Ruchell Magee and William Christmas, who were present at the trial as witnesses. Jackson and the prisoners took Haley and three female jurors as hostage and attempted to escape. Haley, Jackson, McClain, and Christmas were killed as the abductors attempted to drive away from the courthouse. This was an attempt to negotiate the freedom of the Soledad Brothers (including his older brother George) through the kidnapping. (1)
- **August 17, 1970:** Omaha, Nebraska: Officer Larry D. Minard, Officer John Tess, and six other officers responded to an anonymous 911 report of a woman screaming. As they searched the vacant structure for the alleged victim, a booby-trapped suitcase exploded in Minard's face, killing him instantly. The ensuing investigation revealed that the 911 call was part of an elaborate plot to lure the officers into an ambush with the handmade bomb.

The incident was one of the several bombings throughout the Midwest, including Nebraska, Iowa, Minnesota, and Wisconsin. Two men, Edward Poindexter and Mondo we Langa (born David Rice) were convicted for their involvement in the August 17 incident and sentenced to life in prison. The attack was attributed to the Black Panthers. (1)

- **August 24, 1970:** Madison, Wisconsin: Sterling Hall was bombed at the University of Wisconsin–Madison in protest against the Army Mathematics Research Center at UWM and the Vietnam War, killing one. Bombers Karleton Armstrong, Dwight Armstrong, David Fine, and Leo Burt claimed the death of physicist Robert Fassnacht was unintentional but acknowledged that they knew the building was occupied when they planted the bomb. (1)

- **September 18, 1970:** Toledo, Ohio: Patrolman William A. Miscannon was shot and killed while sitting in his marked patrol car at the intersection of Dorr and Junction Avenues, outside the headquarters building for the Black Panthers, during race riots. A vehicle pulled up behind Miscannon's patrol car and one of the occupants walked up and shot him at point-blank range. (1)

- **September 24, 1970:** Brighton, Massachusetts: Three terrorists held up a Brighton branch of the State Street Bank shortly after it opened for business and shot a Boston patrolman, Walter Schroeder, 42, in the back while making their getaway. The four people involved in the robbery were the following: William "Lefty" Gilday, 41, Stanley R. Bond, 26, Kathy Power, 21, and Susan Saxe, 21. All four were involved in left-wing radical organizations. In November 1970, Power and Saxe became the 16th and 17th persons on the FBI's Most Wanted Fugitives list. (1)

- **October 22, 1970:** San Francisco, California: Officer Harold Hamilton was shot and killed after responding to a bank robbery at a Wells Fargo Bank. At the officer's funeral, members of the Black Liberation Army planted a time bomb outside of the church. The bomb exploded but did not injure any mourners. (1)

- **Spring 1971:** Oakland, California: The Huey Newton and Eldridge Cleaver factions of the Black Panthers engaged in retaliatory assassinations of each other's members, resulting in the deaths of four people. (4)

- **May 21, 1971:** New York City, New York: As many as five BLA members participated in the shootings of two New York City police officers, Joseph Piagentini and Waverly Jones. Those arrested and brought to trial for the shootings include Anthony Bottom (aka Jalil Muntaqim), Albert Washington, Francisco Torres, Gabriel Torres, and Herman Bell. (2)

- **June 5, 1971:** New York City, New York: Four men associated with the Black Liberation Army attempted to hold-up a night club called the Triple O. One cab driver was killed. (1)
- **August 1971:** Philadelphia, Pennsylvania: Militants associated with the Black Panther Party and the New African Liberation Army attacked a Park police outpost and killed Sgt. Frank Von Colln. (1)
- **August 29, 1971:** San Francisco, California: Three armed men murdered San Francisco police sergeant John Victor Young while he was working at a desk in his police station. Two days later, the San Francisco Chronicle received a letter signed by the Black Liberation Army (BLA) claiming responsibility for the attack. (1)
- **November 3, 1971:** Atlanta, Georgia: Officer James R. Greene of the Atlanta Police Department was shot and killed in his patrol van at a gas station. His wallet, badge, and weapon were taken, and the evidence at the scene pointed to two suspects. The first was Twymon Meyers, who was killed in a police shootout in 1973, and the second was Freddie Hilton (aka Kamau Sadiki), who evaded capture until 2002, when he was arrested in New York on a separate charge and was recognized as one of the men wanted in the Greene murder. Apparently, the two men had attacked the officer to gain standing with their compatriots within Black Liberation Army. (1)
- **November 8, 1971:** Albuquerque, New Mexico: Charles Hill, Ralph Lawrence, and Albert Finney were driving a carload of weapons to Louisiana for the Republic of New Afrika militant group. They murdered New Mexico State Police officer Robert Rosenbloom during a traffic stop and escaped to Albuquerque where at gunpoint they hijacked a TWA 727 to Cuba on November 27. (1)
- **January 22, 1972:** Saint Louis, Missouri: Two police officers were killed. This was a suspected terrorist incident. (2)
- **January 26, 1972:** New York City, New York: Jewish Defense League firebombed two Sol Hurok offices killing two persons and injuring 13 others. (2)
- **January 27, 1972:** New York City, New York: The "George Jackson Squad" of the Black Liberation Army assassinated police officers Gregory Foster and Rocco Laurie outside a Lower East Side restaurant. After the killings, a note sent to authorities portrayed the murders as a retaliation for the prisoner deaths during 1971 Attica prison riot. (2)
- **October 6, 1972:** Chino, California: Four people — Andrea Holman-Burt, Jean Hobson, Bob Seabock, and Benton Douglas Burt — helped Chino Penitentiary prisoner Ronald Wayne Beaty escape. These four were from the

Palo Alto/Hayward, California area, and were part of the radical Maoist organization Venceremos, which was headed by Stanford Professor H. Bruce Franklin. The ambush and subsequent escape occurred at night when Beaty was being transported to a hearing in San Bernardino County. The two guards transporting Beaty were unarmed and one, Jesus Sanchez, was killed in the ambush while the other, George Fitzgerald, was critically injured. (1)

- **December 31, 1972 and January 7, 1973:** New Orleans, Louisiana: Mark James Robert Essex was an American mass murderer and former Black Panthers member who killed nine people, including five policemen (Alfred Harrell, Edwin Hosli Sr., Phillip Coleman, Paul Persigo, and Louis Sirgo), and wounded 13 others in New Orleans. Before the attack, the television station WWL received a handwritten note from Essex. It read:

Africa greets you. On December 31, 1972, aprx. 11 p.m., the downtown New Orleans Police Department will be attacked. Reason — many, but the death of two innocent brothers will be avenged. And many others.

P.S. Tell pig Giarrusso the felony action squad ain't shit.
Mata

Essex also dropped a Pan African flag on the bodies of two of his civilian victims. In addition, police searched Essex's apartment and found it completely covered from floor to ceiling with anti-white graffiti. (9)

- **May 2, 1973:** East Brunswick, New Jersey: Members of the BLA were arrested after a shootout; one State patrolman, Trooper Werner Foerster, was killed, one was wounded; one BLA member died, the driver escaped, but was subsequently captured in East Brunswick, N.J. (1)
- **June 1, 1973:** Chevy Chase, Maryland: Yosef Alon, the Israeli Air Force attaché in Washington, D.C., was shot and killed outside his home in Chevy Chase, Maryland. The Palestinian militant group Black September was suspected, though the case remains unsolved. (1)
- **January 2, 1973:** Brooklyn, New York: During the robbery of a social club, BLA members shot and killed a victim. (1)
- **June 5, 1973:** New York City, New York: Police Officer Sidney L. Thompson, a transit detective, was killed when he stopped two BLA members from entering without paying. Before he died, he shot both; one was captured, and the other escaped. (1)
- **November 6, 1973:** Oakland, California: Symbionese Liberation Army killed Marcus Foster, a black school superintendent. (1)

FORD (27 — 3 law enforcement officers)

- **August 27, 1974:** Berkeley, California: Thomas Jackson, a doorman at the Brass Rail, was killed in Berkeley, California by the Squad, a secret bodyguard unit in the Black Panthers linked to Huey P. Newton. (1)
- **August 1974:** Oakland, California: Huey Newton shot and killed a 17-year-old prostitute Kathleen Smith for calling him "Baby," a moniker he hated. He also pistol-whipped his tailor, Preston Callins, for making the same mistake. Arrested and charged with the murder and the assault, he managed to post $80,000 bond and flee to Cuba with a girlfriend. He remained there until 1977. (1)
- **December 13, 1974:** Berkeley, California: Accountant Betty van Patter was murdered, after threatening to disclose irregularities in the Party's finances. (1)
- **January 24, 1975:** New York City, New York: A bomb exploded in the Fraunces Tavern of New York City, killing four people and injuring more than 50 others. The Puerto Rican nationalist group the Armed Forces of Puerto Rican National Liberation, carried out other bomb incidents in New York in the 1970s, claimed responsibility. No one was ever prosecuted for the bombing. (4)
- **January 25, 1975:** Berkeley, California: Willy Ralph Duke and Billy Carr were killed outside the Brass Rail in Berkeley, California, by Black Panther gunmen from the Squad. (2)
- **April 26, 1975:** Oakland, California: Vernon McInnis was shot and killed by suspected Black Panther gunmen from the Squad (Robert Heard and George Robinson). (1)
- **April 28, 1975:** Carmichael, California: The remaining four members of the SLA robbed the Crocker National Bank. Myrna Opsahl, a bank customer, was killed. (1)
- **June 25, 1975:** Pine Ridge Indian Reservation, South Dakota: During an armed confrontation between American Indian Movement (AIM) activists and the FBI and their allies, which became known as the "Pine Ridge Shootout," two FBI agents, Jack R. Coler and Ronald A. Williams, and an AIM activist Joe Stuntz were killed. (2)
- **December 29, 1975:** New York City, New York: LaGuardia Airport was bombed, resulting in the deaths of 11 people and injuring 75 others. Croatian terrorists and the Yugoslav intelligence service were the primary suspects. The bombing remains unsolved. (11)
- **September 11, 1976:** New York City, New York: Croatian terrorists hijacked a TWA airliner and diverted it to Newfoundland and then Paris, demanding

a manifesto be printed. One police officer was killed and three injured during an attempt to defuse a bomb that contained their communiqués in a New York City train station locker. (1)

- **September 21, 1976:** Washington, D.C.: Orlando Letelier, a former member of the Chilean government, was killed by a car bomb in Washington, D.C. along with his assistant Ronni Moffitt. The killing was carried out by members of the Chilean Intelligence Agency, DINA. (2)

CARTER (19 — 1 law enforcement officer)

- **March 9–11, 1977:** Washington, D.C.: Three buildings (the city hall, B'nai B'rith headquarters, and the Islamic Center of Washington) in Washington, D.C. were seized by 12 Muslim gunmen, led by Hamaas Abdul Khaalis, who left the Nation of Islam because he blamed them for the murders of five of his children. The gunmen took 149 hostages and killed a journalist. The gunmen demanded that the U.S. government hand over a group of men who had been convicted of killing seven relatives of Khaalis and that the movie Mohammad, Messenger of God be destroyed because they considered it sacrilegious. The hostage crisis lasted around 39 hours and ended as a result of the intervention of three Muslim ambassadors from Egypt, Pakistan, and Iran. (1)
- **July 18, 1977:** Chicago, Illinois: Dragisa Kasikovich, an editorial writer for the Serbian weekly Liberty, and 9-year-old Ivanka Milosevich, the daughter of Kasikovich's fiancé, were attacked in the Serbian National Defense office in Chicago. The attack was particularly brutal. Kasikovich was stabbed repeatedly in the face, nose, and chest and his skull was crushed. The girl was stabbed nearly 60 times and her skull, too, was crushed. Primary suspects were the UDBA–Yugoslav secret police. (2)
- **August 4, 1977:** New York City, New York: FALN bombs exploded in a building in New York City, which housed United States Department of Defense security personnel, and the Mobil Building at 150 East Forty-Second Street, killing one, Charles Steinberg. (1)
- **September 23, 1977:** San Juan, Puerto Rico: New York Lawyer Allan Randall who was involved in labor negotiations was shot and killed by two men. A written note left nearby stated he was "executed today" by the Comandos Obreros. The subsequent communiqué claimed Randall was working with the CIA. (1)
- **August 24, 1978:** San Juan, Puerto Rico: The Macheteros accepted responsibility for the murder of San Juan police officer Julio Rodríguez Rivera while attempting to steal his police car. (1)

- **September 28, 1978:** Greenburgh, New York: Ante Cikoja, a Yugoslavian immigrant, was shot and killed from a car waiting outside his home. The primary suspects were Croatian terrorists engaged in an extortion campaign against Croatian-Americans. (1)
- **November 1978:** Glendale, California: Krizan Brkic, president of a Croatian group in southern California, who received extortion letters from a Croatian terrorist organization was shot and killed. (1)
- **May 1979:** San Juan, Puerto Rico: Carlos Munos, a travel agent, was killed in San Juan, Puerto Rico by suspected Omega 7 terrorists. Munos was a member of the Group of 75 who went to Cuba in 1978 to visit with Castro. (1)
- **November 3, 1979:** Greensboro, North Carolina: Members of the Ku Klux Klan and the American Nazi Party fired on a meeting of members of a Communist group who were trying to organize local African American workers in Greensboro, North Carolina, killing five. (5)
- **November 25, 1979:** Union City, New Jersey: Eulalio Jose Negrin, a pro-Castro Cuban activist was shot and killed. Negrin was a member of the Group of 75 who went to Cuba in 1978 to visit with Castro. Omega 7 was suspected. (1)
- **December 3, 1979:** Sabanca Seca, Puerto Rico: Macheteros opened fire on a bus carrying sailors to Naval Security Group Activity Sabana Seca, killing CTO1 John R. Ball and RM3 Emil E. White. A second attack, on off-duty sailors returning from liberty, killed one and wounded three. (3)
- **July 22, 1980:** Bethesda, Maryland: Ali Akbar Tabatabai, an Iranian exile and critic of Ayatollah Khomeni, was shot in his Bethesda, Maryland, home. Dawud Salahuddin, an American Muslim convert, was apparently paid by Iranians to kill Tabatabai. (1)

Index

CPSIA information can be obtained
at www.ICGtesting.com
Printed in the USA
LVHW051640170921
698105LV00022B/2156